D1465484

WARSHIPS

The Encyclopedia of the World's
WARSHIPS

**A technical directory
of major fighting ships from 1900
to the present day**

**Author Hugh Lyon
Consultant Captain J. E. Moore R.N.**

a Salamander book
Published by Salamander Books Limited
LONDON

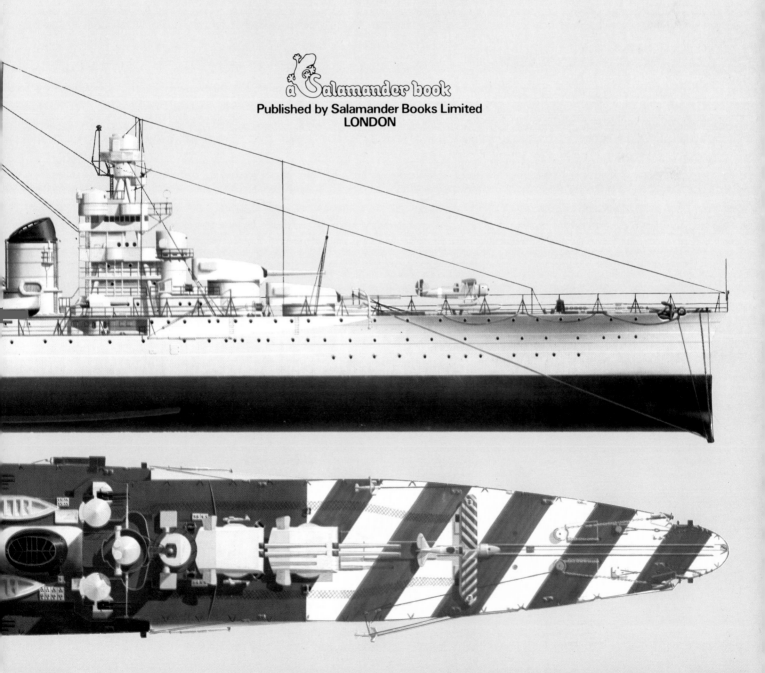

A Salamander Book

Published 1978 by Salamander Books Ltd,
27 Old Gloucester Street,
London WC1
United Kingdom
© Salamander Books Ltd 1978

ISBN O–86101–007–8

Second Impression 1978

Distributed in Australia/New Zealand
by Summit Books, a division of Paul
Hamlyn Pty Ltd, Sydney, Australia.

All rights reserved. Except for use in a
review, no part of this book may be
reproduced, stored in a retrieval system,
or transmitted, in any form or by any
means, electronic, mechanical,
photocopying, recording or otherwise,
without the prior permission of
Salamander Books Limited.

All correspondence concerning the
content of this volume should be
addressed to Salamander Books Limited.

Credits

Editorial consultant:
Captain J. E. Moore, RN
Editor: Philip de Ste. Croix
Designer: Chris Steer

Colour drawings of warships:
© Profile Publications Limited

Line drawings of warships:
© Siegfried Breyer and Salamander
Books Ltd

Picture Research: Jonathan Moore

Filmset by SX Composing, Leigh-on-Sea,
Essex, England

Colour reproduction by Paramount
Litho, Basildon, Essex, England, and
Autographic Lithoplates Limited, Bromley,
Kent

Printed in Belgium by Henri Proost,
Turnhout, Belgium

Introduction

Man's use of the sea over the last two thousand years has varied with the ambitions of those involved. The pragmatic Chinese were content to see it as a means for peaceful trade and not until the more aggressive European nations, aided by increasing technical advances, found it a means for looting other countries, for conquest and for religious advance did there become a need for navies. Over the years, improvements in ships' designs allowed them greater range and improved capacity. Exploration opened up new areas for the garnering of raw materials hitherto unknown in Europe. As these were brought to their home ports and as armies were transported to conquer other countries so the fighting fleets were evolved and the tactics they employed depended on the capabilities of their ships. From the Elizabethan era onwards these fleets were to change but slowly, and the emblem of naval power became the line of battle. In this there was a steady improvement in the size and armament of the ships involved. Rigid adherence to doctrine was mandatory and it was not until the late eighteenth century that individual thought began to engender variations from this attitude. Despite such changes the line-of-battleship was the hub of naval power and so it remained throughout the nineteenth century. At this time Great Britain, successful in all maritime aspects of the wars with France despite the superior design of the French ships, was content to rely on the lessons of the past. Naval thought has always been conservative in accepting wholesale changes resulting from technical advances. The Industrial Revolution had provided the means for such improvements and the inventiveness of many men had capitalised on this new richness. Nevertheless, in 1900, it was still possible for a distinguished British naval writer to state, 'The chief advantage of a submarine boat is to travel on the surface partially submerged.' By this time Marconi had established wireless communication from England to France, Parsons' turbine had been at sea for two years, new gunnery systems had been

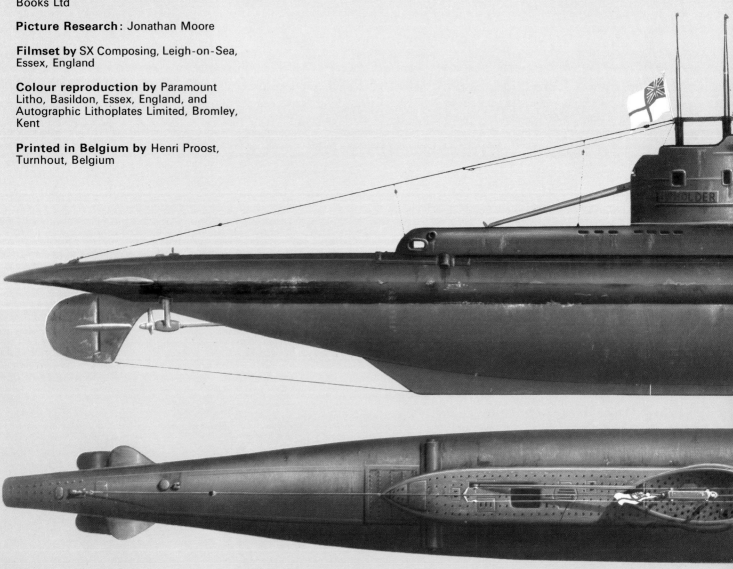

developed, Mr Whitehead's torpedo was an acknowledged instrument and improved shipbuilding methods had speeded up production.

What is most important, however, is that the tradition of the line of battle had endured. The concept of great fleets battling it out at sea was a primary tenet of naval belief. The battleship was, therefore, the summit of all naval construction. On this, it was believed, depended the whole principle of naval power. While this may have been true for the next few years, the requirement did not exist for the smaller navies. Many moved into a building race based on the majesty of these great ships. There was scant appreciation of the true role of navies and this was to be reflected over the next forty years.

Before ten years had passed submarines had proved their ability to wound the battle fleet. In 1909 Clément Ader had foreshadowed the modern aircraft carrier and in 1910 the first flight from a naval ship was carried out from the USS *Birmingham*. From then on it was the Royal Navy which led the way in the development of the aircraft carrier, closely followed by the US Navy and that of Japan. These first attempts at embarking what later became known as 'organic air' made little impression on the majority of the politicians and naval officers who were involved in the series of naval treaties begun in 1921.

In the years between the wars the astonishing successes of the German submarine force in 1914–18, the successes of British submarines in several theatres and the rapid advance of naval air forces made little impression on the overall scene. In 1939 the battleship was still the core of the world's navies. This situation was very rapidly destroyed. The loss of battleships to both air and submarine attack, the range and lethality of the aircraft of the carriers of the three major naval powers and the fact that Great Britain managed to survive by only a hair's breadth during the main assault of the German U-boats had totally altered the balance of naval thinking. In the immediate post-war years there was considerable confusion of thought in the aftermath of the nuclear assaults on Japan. Nuclear fission provided further problems for the planners with the introduction of nuclear propulsion. This, combined with the new concept of missile assault, meant a totally new attitude to maritime affairs. Sinkings by medium range missiles were an indication of the future. With the introduction of the helicopter and, later, of the V/STOL aircraft, the main thrust of naval construction was to be focused on those ships which could carry aircraft and missiles in addition to the nuclear submarine armed with ballistic missiles or cruise missiles or long-range torpedoes. In addition changes in the propulsion of ships, which included primarily the gas turbine, were to alter the whole balance of ships' designs. The navies of 1977 are a more radical departure from those of forty years ago than were those of 1900 from their predecessors of two centuries.

John Moore

Contents

Author's Foreword

So many warships have been built this century that no single volume can cover more than a small fraction in adequate detail. This book is intended to describe a representative sample of the most famous and significant warships that have been built in this century. Particular attention has been paid to vessels that served during World War II, but World War I and present day warships have not been neglected. Space has been allocated to navies in proportion to their size and importance, and minor navies have only been included where the significance of individual designs has justified it. Inevitably, many interesting warships have had to be excluded, in particular the smaller ships of the Austro-Hungarian Navy, which was disbanded in 1918. Within each national entry, ships have been arranged chronologically under the following categories: aircraft carrier, battleship, cruiser, destroyer, submarine, escort, light craft. Occasionally, however, design requirements or the mechanics of tipping in gatefolds have demanded that this pattern be slightly modified.

In the case of major warships, vessels nominally of the same class often differ considerably from each other and have very different careers, so one ship from each of these classes has been singled out and described in greater detail, though data is given for the entire class. However, in the case of the British *County* type and US *Baltimore* class heavy cruisers, the size of the classes makes such treatment impossible, and as with the minor warships each class or type is considered as a whole.

A standard layout has been adopted for the data to enable comparisons to be made between the various classes. Data is given in both Imperial and metric units, except in the case of some light AA guns which are always referred to by their metric sizes, and in the case of miles and nautical miles. Most navies use nautical miles rather than kilometres as units of distance. A ? indicates that it has been impossible to obtain reliable data. Some information for older vessels no longer exists, and accurate details of modern warships are often unobtainable because of problems of security. A — indicates that the item is not applicable to that ship or class.

Because ships can be in service for 20 years or more, they are sometimes rebuilt to cope with a new threat or to fit them for another role, and almost all warships built since 1914 have at least had their AA armament altered during their careers. Some ships are rebuilt more than once, and may have completely different roles, displacements, dimensions, armament and machinery from when they were first built. Therefore the data in the various columns in each entry only refers to the specific named ship or class at the specific date given.

Warship data, particularly data concerning displacement and range, can often be misleading because it is often only approximate, and it is not readily comparable because it depends very greatly on the system used by the individual navy to calculate it. Also, nominally identical ships usually differ slightly in displacement and dimensions. Because the apparent accuracy of the original data is often misleading, the metric conversions have been rounded out, except where the original figures are totally accurate. Speeds attained on trials can be misleading, too, because of the differing conditions under which they have been run. British and American warship trials have normally been conducted with the ships equipped and ready for sea, whereas up to 1945 Italian and Russian trials in particular were often made before most of the armament and equipment was on board, and with very small amounts of fuel. This gave very high trials speeds which could not be attained in service.

In some cases two or three classes of similar type have been described in one entry to show that type's development more clearly. Some warships have served in a number of roles during their career, and the ship type given at the head of each entry is that of their final period of service.

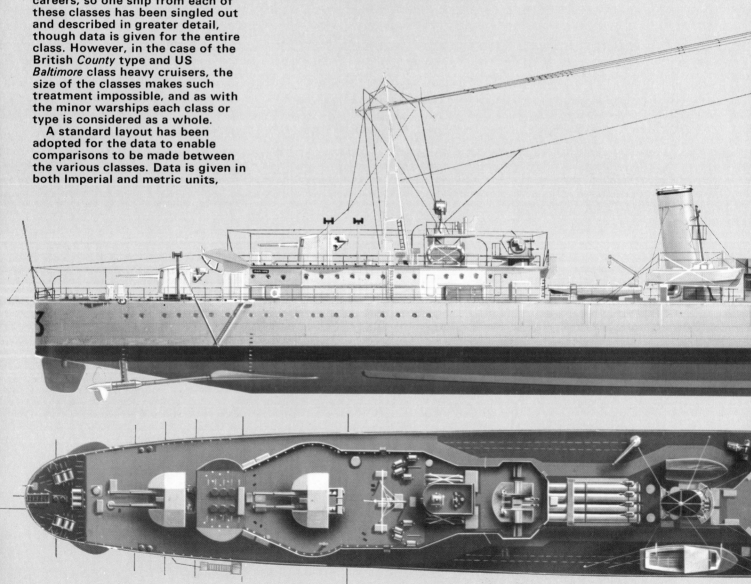

CLASS: The number of ships in each class is the number that have entered service. Where space has permitted, the names of each ship to have entered service are listed, otherwise only the names of the most famous ships are given.

DISPLACEMENT: The standard displacement is calculated in the same way for all ships, but different navies have different methods of computing normal and full load displacement, so these figures are only approximately comparable between the various navies.

DIMENSIONS: The wl length (where given) is usually that at normal displacement, as is the draught, but both vary considerably with displacement. The beam is at the water line, but the flight deck width is also given where applicable.

ARMAMENT: This is accurate only for the specified dates. The figure for aircraft is the maximum design capacity, but most carriers cannot operate that many at one time.

ARMOUR: Where possible minimum and maximum figures are given. Most armour schemes were very complicated, and only the most important thicknesses are given in this book. The maximum thickness of the belt and decks normally only extended over the magazines and engines, and the main belt usually covered only a few feet above and below the water line. Most protective decks did not extend the full length of the ship.

MACHINERY: Only the main machinery is listed.

POWER: The HP given is the total for all the main engines. The trials figure (where given) is the maximum attained on the full power trial.

PERFORMANCE: The designed speed is the designed full speed, the cruising speed would be very considerably lower. The trials speed (where given) is the maximum sustained speed attained. The range is the maximum range at the given speed (normally the most economical cruising speed), but these figures are only approximately comparable between different countries.

FUEL CAPACITY: Maximum where not otherwise stated. The normal capacity is that at normal displacement.

CREW: This figure is only approximately comparable because it can be affected by a number of factors including whether the ship is at peacetime or wartime establishment and whether it is serving as a flagship.

CAREER: Where space permits, ships are individually listed, and include all projected members of the class, whether completed or not. Larger classes are dealt with together. The date of authorization is when permission was given to construct the ship. In some navies the completion date is the commissioning date, others distinguish between them.

TEXT: Within the limitations imposed by the size of the book, the text is designed not only to describe each class, but to show how it fits into the development of that country's navy and why it was given its particular characteristics, to bring out the good and bad points in its design and how it performed in service, and finally to enable it to be compared with similar designs in foreign navies.

Hugh Lyon

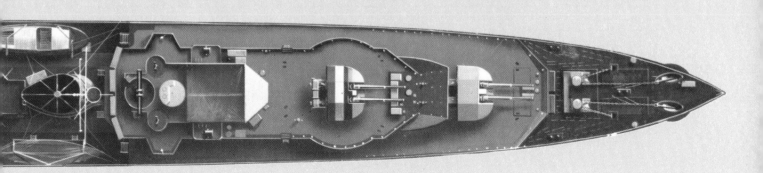

Viribus Unitis

BATTLESHIP
CLASS: *Viribus Unitis* class (4 ships)
Viribus Unitis · Tegetthoff · Prinz Eugen · Svent Istvan

Service career VIRIBUS UNITIS
1914–1918 Flagship, Austro-Hungarian fleet.
1915 (24 May) Bombarded Ancona.
1915 Six 2·6in (66mm) guns replaced by two 2·6in (66mm) 45cal anti-aircraft guns.
1917 2·6in (66mm) 45cal anti-aircraft guns replaced by four 2·6in (66mm) 50cal anti-aircraft guns.
1918 (31 Oct) Transferred to Yugoslavia as flagship of Yugoslav Navy; to be renamed *Frankopan*.
1918 (1 Nov) Sunk in Pola harbour by Italian swimmers with limpet mines.
1930 Scrapping of wreck completed.

From 1907 the Austro-Hungarian Navy was built up in an attempt to equal the strength of the Italian Navy. In that year the three pre-dreadnought *Radetzky* class were laid down, but they were completely outclassed by foreign

Above: The Viribus Unitis *class battleship* Tegetthoff, *completed in 1913. The compactness of the design is evident*

dreadnoughts. The *Viribus Unitis* class was an enlarged version of their design, but adopted a single calibre main armament. To reduce the length of the hull and the weight of armour needed to protect it, the main armament was arranged in four triple turrets, designed and built in the Austro-Hungarian Skoda armament works. To appease the Hungarians, *Svent Istvan* was built at the only Hungarian shipyard capable of building a battleship. Even so, it had to be considerably enlarged, and *Svent Istvan* took longer to build than the other three. They were impressive ships, and although slightly slower and having one less 12in gun than their Italian counterparts, were much better arranged. Like most Mediterranean warships they had a short range, but possessed a reasonable freeboard. Their worst feature was their vulnerability to underwater attack. The torpedo bulkhead covered only the machinery and the compartmentation was not particularly thorough. While they were completing the main turret and conning tower armour was increased, which added weight high up in the ships and diminished stability. Although they took part in several offensive patrols and bombardments, they did not take part in any major surface action. However, they tied up most of the French and Italian battle fleets for the entire war and as a 'fleet in being' were an excellent investment. Four enlarged versions with 13·8in (350mm) guns, the *Ersatz Monarchs,* were projected but not built in 1914. *Svent Istvan* was sunk in the southern Adriatic near Premuda Island by two torpedoes from the Italian motor torpedo boat *MAS 15*. *Tegetthoff* was scrapped by the Italians after they had considered incorporating her in their navy. *Prinz Eugen* was used for bombing and firing experiments by the French before being sunk as a target by the French battleships *France* and *Bretagne.*

Displacement:

normal tons (tonnes)	20,224 (20,548)
full load tons (tonnes)	21,255 (21,595)

Dimensions:

length (pp)	468·3ft (143m)
(wl)	495·8ft (151·4m)
(oa)	498·5ft (152·2m)
beam	89·4ft (27·3m)
draught	26·9ft (8·2m)

Armament	in 1914	in 1918
guns		
12in (305mm) 45cal	12	12
5·9in (150mm) 50cal	12	12
2·6in (66mm) 45cal	18	16
torpedo tubes		
21in (530mm)	4	4

Armour:

side (belt)	5·9–11in (150–280mm)
deck (upper)	1·9in (48mm)
(lower)	1·9in (48mm)
main turrets	11in (280mm)
barbettes	11in (280mm)
battery	7·1in (180mm)

Machinery:

boilers (type)	Yarrow
(number)	12
engines (type)	Parsons turbines
shafts	4

Total SHP:

designed	25,000
trial	25,638

Fuel capacity:

coal normal tons (tonnes)	900 (914)
max tons (tonnes)	2,000 (2,032)

Performance:

designed speed	20kts
trial speed	20·98kts
range	5,000 miles (4,200nm) @ 10kts
Crew:	1,046

Ship:	**VIRIBUS UNITIS**	**TEGETTHOFF**	**PRINZ EUGEN**	**SVENT ISTVAN**
Where built:	Stabilimento Tecnico, Trieste	Stabilimento Tecnico, Trieste	Stabilimento Tecnico, Trieste	Ganz & Danubius, Fiume
Authorised:	1911	1911	1911	1911
Laid down:	24 July 1910	24 Sept 1910	16 Jan 1912	21 Jan 1912
Launched:	20 June 1911	31 March 1912	30 Nov 1912	17 Jan 1914
Completed:	6 Oct 1912	14 July 1913	8 July 1914	17 Nov 1915
Fate:	Sunk 1 Nov 1918	Scrapped 1924–1925	Sunk 28 June 1922	Sunk 10 June 1918

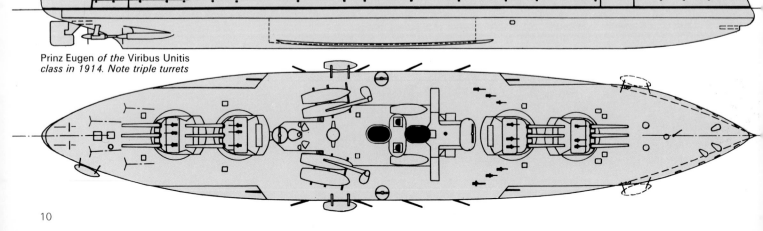

Prinz Eugen of the Viribus Unitis *class in 1914. Note triple turrets*

Minas Geraes

BATTLESHIP

CLASS: *Minas Geraes* class
(2 ships) *Minas Geraes · Sao Paulo*

Service career MINAS GERAES
1910 Mutiny at Lisbon on delivery voyage.
1917-1918 Central area patrol.
1923 Refit in USA.
1934-1937 Modernised at Rio de Janeiro: new boilers, new bridge and superstructure with only one funnel added; secondary armament altered.
1952 Stricken.
1954 Scrapped in Italy.

These two ships were designed by Armstrong Whitworth, and were intended to counter the Chilean pre-dreadnoughts *Constitucion* and *Libertad* (later HMS *Triumph* and *Swiftsure*) that had also been designed by Armstrong

Above: The British-built battleship Minas Geraes before reconstruction. The use of wing turrets restricted the broadside to 10 guns

Whitworth. Originally intended to be pre-dreadnoughts, the *Minas Geraes'* design was altered before they were laid down to incorporate the all big-gun armament adopted by HMS *Dreadnought*. An expanded version of the *Constitucion's* design was adopted, and the result was a cramped and unsatisfactory compromise. Superimposed turrets were used to reduce hull length, but the freeboard was much lower than that of *Dreadnought* and the 4·7in (120mm) guns were unworkable even in moderate seas. Reciprocating engines were adopted because the Brazilians lacked the facilities to maintain turbines. Both ships spent most of their lives in harbour. *Sao Paulo* was not modernised. She disappeared without trace in the Atlantic after the tow was slipped in bad weather on her way to Italy to be scrapped.

Displacement:

normal tons (tonnes)	19,280 (19,588)	
full load tons (tonnes)	21,200 (21,540)	

Dimensions:

length (pp)	500ft (152·7m)	
(wl)	530ft (161·8m)	
(oa)	543ft (165·8m)	
beam	83ft (25·3m)	
draught (max)	28ft (8·5m)	

Armament:

	as built	Minas Geraes in 1937
12in (305mm) 45cal	12	12
4·7in (120mm)	22	14
3in (76mm)	—	4
3pdr (47mm)	8	—
40mm	—	4

Armour:

side (belt)	4–9in (102–229mm)	
(ends)	4in (102mm)	
deck (upper)	1·25in (32mm)	
(main)	2in (51mm)	
(lower)	1in (25mm)	
main turrets	8–12in (203–305mm)	
barbettes	9in (229mm)	

Machinery:

boilers (type)	Babcock (coal)	Thornycroft (oil)
(number)	18	6
engines (type)	vertical triple expansion	
shafts	2	

Total IHP:

designed	23,500	30,000

Fuel capacity:

coal normal tons (tonnes)	800 (813)	
max tons (tonnes)	2,360 (2,398)	—
oil tons (tonnes)	—	2,200 (2,235)

Performance:

designed speed	21kts	22kts
range	10,000 miles (8,400nm) @ 10kts	?
Crew:	900	1,087

Ship:	MINAS GERAES	SAO PAULO
Where built:	Armstrong Whitworth, Elswick	Vickers, Barrow
Ordered:	1907	1907
Laid down:	1907	1907
Launched:	10 Sept 1908	19 Apr 1909
Completed:	Jan 1910	July 1910
Fate:	Scrapped 1954	Lost 4 Nov 1951

Above: Sao Paulo of the Minas Geraes class. Note bearing clock below control top on tripod mast and low mounted 4·7in (120mm) casemates and wing turrets

Sao Paulo of the Minas Geraes class in 1917 before refit in USA

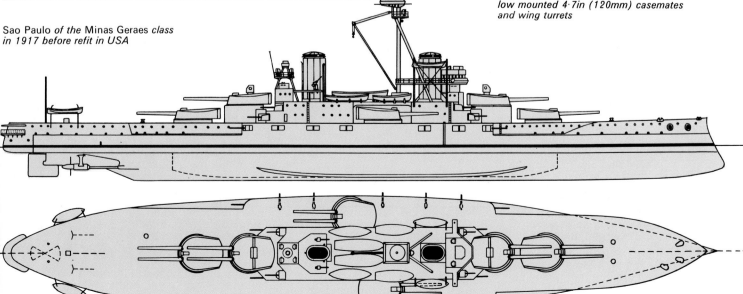

BRITAIN

THERE is nothing worse for a heavyweight boxer than to be incomparably better than his possible opponents. Training suffers as well as the fighter's attitude of mind. This was the situation in which the Royal Navy, had it chosen to think of the matter, found itself towards the end of the nineteenth century.

When Sir John Fisher became First Sea Lord in 1904 the self-satisfied were in for a sudden awakening; although in the previous three years the efforts of Beresford and himself in command of the Channel and Mediterranean Fleets had begun to force improvement upon the Royal Navy. On 10 February 1906 HMS *Dreadnought* was launched, the end of an era and the recognition of the need for the concentration of power which this new battleship could bring to bear. From now on the Admiralty was continually frustrated in its plans by the inability of so many politicians to read the lesson of history and realise the vital place seapower occupied in Britain's safety and prosperity. Frustration to many came also from Fisher's insistence on being a one-man-band.

He accepted no opposition to his views, detested the thought of a Naval Staff and, while appreciating the need for modern thinking, would accommodate no alternatives to his stated preferences.

In October 1911, a year and a half after Fisher had retired, another gale blew through the Admiralty — Winston Churchill had arrived as First Lord. It was the combination of the impacts of these two men which provided a fleet in readiness when the war, so long expected, began in August 1914. In July, after a test mobilisation preceding the Review of the Fleet, both active and reserve, at Spithead Prince Louis of Battenberg, then First Sea Lord, delayed demobilisation after news of the assassination of the Archduke at Sarajevo.

Thus on 4 August the whole of the Royal Navy was ready for war, with a strength of 20 dreadnoughts, 35 pre-dreadnoughts, 7 battlecruisers, 25 armoured cruisers, 57 light cruisers, 156 destroyers and 74 submarines. This was an immensely powerful fleet, despite the problems placed in the Admiralty's path over the previous ten years.

With the prevailing insistence upon the line of battle, the Grand Fleet refused to be drawn into close blockade off the German coast but nearly lost the war by the Admiralty's refusal to appreciate the menace of the submarine. By the end of 1918 the war had been won but it is doubtful, at this range, if the true lessons had been learned. The battleship was still considered the hub of naval affairs, the submarine was not fully appreciated and the aircraft was very much the arena of the enthusiast.

These were views which were reflected in the agreements of the various naval conferences of the inter-war years. The main restrictions were placed upon the capital ships, submarines were not limited and a measure of appreciation was given to aircraft carriers. The Royal Navy was confident of its capability to hunt submarines but its numbers of escorts were restricted not only by treaties but by Treasury requirements. Blindly, in 1935, the British Government came to a naval agreement with Germany restricting the latter's naval forces to 35 per cent of British tonnage although they might build submarines to equality with the Royal Navy. But by 1938 the need for more escorts was foreseen and in July 1939 the first of 135 *Flower* class corvettes was ordered, four months after the lead ships of the *Hunt* class destroyers were signed for. Had it not been for this forward-thinking and the transfer of 50 US *Four-Stackers*, the United Kingdom could well have been defeated at sea. Command of the sea was sustained, but only just — if the U-boats had received more support the result might have been very different.

The balance of the naval war of 1939–45 hung in the North Atlantic — great ships were sunk, fleets kept at a disadvantage but while the home base remained intact, the fight was sustained. Today the perimeter of naval defence has been drawn in as Treasury restrictions take their toll but for the first time in nearly 300 years the Royal Navy no longer has control over the sources of raw materials which sustain Britain's industry and economy —sources far beyond the much-vaunted boundaries of NATO.

HMS Tiger *(C20) off Portsmouth in
1975 with the Fast Training Boat,* Scimitar *(P271)*

Furious

AIRCRAFT-CARRIER
CLASS: *Furious* class (1 ship)
Furious

Service career FURIOUS
1917 (15 Mar–26 June) Forward barbettes removed; hangar and flight deck fitted on fo'c's'le.
1917 (26 June–4 July) Trials.
1917 (2–5 Aug) Deck landing trials.
1917 (Oct–Nov) Patrols in North Sea.
1917 (17 Nov–15 Mar 1918) Reconstruction at Elswick: aft turret and barbette removed; 5·5in (140mm) guns rearranged; landing deck and hangar added aft.
1918 (Mar–June) Experiments.
1918 (18 June) Aircraft shoots down German seaplane.
1918 (17 July) Tondern raid: Zeppelins *L54* and *L60* destroyed.
1919 In Baltic.
1919 (21 Nov) In reserve.
1922 (June–1 Sept 1925) Converted at Devonport to flush deck carrier with retractable navigating position.
1926 (6 May) First night deck landing.
1930 (1 July–May 1931) Refit at Devonport: three 3in (76mm) AA guns added.
1931–1934 Home Fleet.
1934 Mediterranean Fleet.
1934–1939 Home Fleet.
1938 (Nov–May 1939) Refit: 5·5in (140mm) guns removed; twelve 4in (102mm) and sixteen 2pdr (40mm) added; island bridge fitted.
1939 (Sept–April 1940) Patrols in North Sea and Atlantic.
1940 (Apr) Norwegian campaign.
1940 (June–Oct 1941) Patrols in North Sea and Atlantic.
1941 (7 Oct–April 1942) Refit at Philadelphia, USA.
1942 (Apr–Jan 1943) In Mediterranean.

1942 (Aug–Oct) Ferrying Spitfires to Malta.
1942 (Nov) Covered North African landings.
1943 (Jan–Sept 1944) Home Fleet: operations against Norway.
1944 (Apr–June) Four attacks on *Tirpitz* in Kaa fjord.
1944 (15 Sept) In reserve.
1945 (26 May–1948) Explosives target ship.
1948–1954 Scrapped.

Continued on page 16▶

Above: HMS Furious *after the aft 18in (457mm) gun had been replaced by a landing deck in 1918. She was originally built as a large light cruiser*

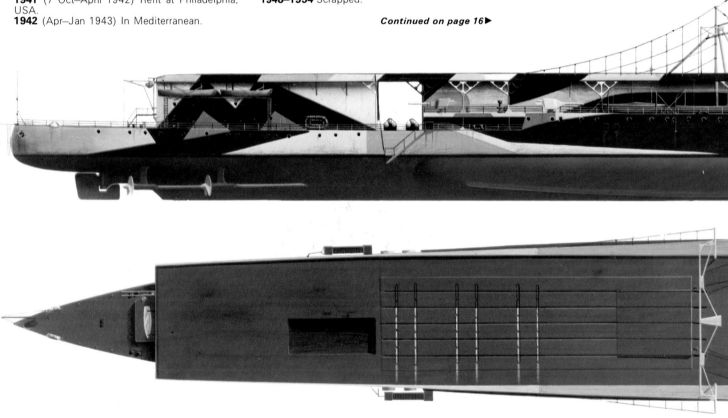

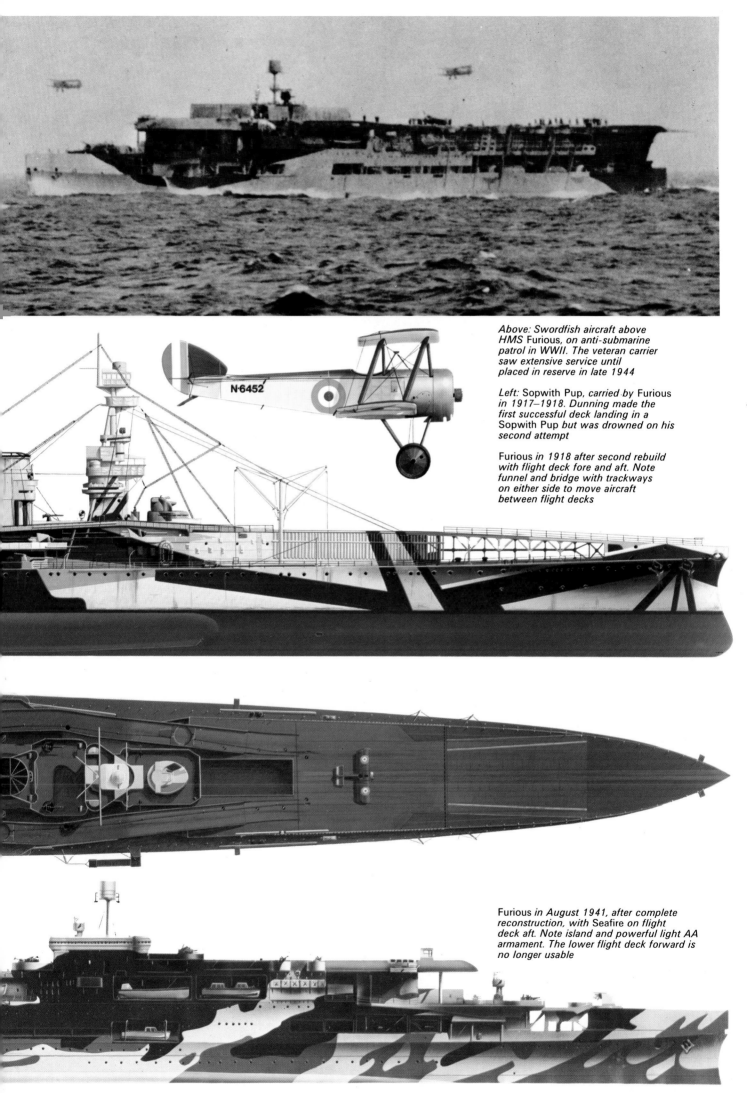

Above: Swordfish aircraft above HMS Furious, on anti-submarine patrol in WWII. The veteran carrier saw extensive service until placed in reserve in late 1944

Left: Sopwith Pup, carried by Furious in 1917–1918. Dunning made the first successful deck landing in a Sopwith Pup but was drowned on his second attempt

N·6452

Furious in 1918 after second rebuild with flight deck fore and aft. Note funnel and bridge with trackways on either side to move aircraft between flight decks

Furious in August 1941, after complete reconstruction, with Seafire on flight deck aft. Note island and powerful light AA armament. The lower flight deck forward is no longer usable

Above: HMS Furious *at speed in 1944. Note the island and the 4in (102mm) mounts on the fo'c's'le below the round down. Flying is not in progress and the wireless aerials are raised*

► *Furious*

Displacement:	as designed (large light cruiser)	in 1944 (as an aircraft-carrier)
standard tons (tonnes)	—	22,450 (22,810)
normal tons (tonnes)	19,100 (19,400)	—
full load tons (tonnes)	22,405 (22,764)	28,500 (28,960)
Dimensions:		
length (pp)	735·25ft (224·5m)	735·25ft (224·5m)
(oa)	786·25ft (240m)	786·25ft (240m)
beam (hull)	88ft (26·9m)	90ft (27·4m)
(ext)	—	107·8ft (32·7m)
draught (mean)	21·5ft (6·6m)	24ft (7·3m)
(max)	25ft (7·6m)	27·75ft (8·5m)
Armament:		
guns		
18in (457mm) 40cal	2	—
5·5in (140mm) 50cal	11	—
4in (102mm)	—	12
3in (76mm)	4	—
3pdr (47mm)	4	—
2pdr (40mm)	—	32
20mm	—	22
torpedo tubes		
21in (533mm)	18	—
aircraft	—	33
Armour:		
side (belt)	3in (76mm)	
(ends)	2in (51mm)	
deck (fo'c's'le)	1in (25mm)	
(upper)	1in (25mm)	
(main)	0·75–1·75in (19–44mm)	
(lower)	1–3in (25–76mm)	
main turrets	5–9in (127–229mm)	
barbettes	6–7in (152–178mm)	
Machinery:		
boilers (type)	Yarrow small tube	
(number)	18	
engines (type)	Brown-Curtis single reduction geared turbines	
(shafts)	4	
Total SHP:		
designed	90,000	
trial	90,820	
Fuel capacity:		
oil tons (tonnes)	3,393 (3,447)	4,010 (4,074)
Performance:		
designed speed	31·5kts	—
trial speed	30kts	—
service speed	—	29·5kts
range	7,140 miles (6,000nm) @ 20kts	?
Crew:	745	approx 1,200

Ship:	**FURIOUS**
Where built:	Armstrong Whitworth, Elswick
Ordered:	May 1915
Laid down:	8 June 1915
Launched:	15 Aug 1916
First conversion:	15 Mar–26 June 1917
Completed:	26 June 1917
Fate:	Converted to flush deck carrier June 1922–1 Sept 1925; scrapped 1948–1954

Nothing better illustrates the need for a naval staff to study requirements for new ships than the design of the large light cruisers *Courageous, Glorious* and *Furious*. As with the *Renowns, Courageous* and *Glorious* were intended to take advantage of the spare 15in (381mm) turrets made available by the cancellation of the last three *Revenge* class battleships. They were intended to provide high speed fire support for 'Jackie' Fisher's proposed landings in Pomerania, and with their high speed, two twin 15in (381mm) turrets and shallow draught they admirably fulfilled Fisher's requirements. Unfortunately, the Pomeranian landings were never a practicable operation of war, and *Courageous* and *Glorious* were totally unfitted for any other role. Unlike the monitors, they were too large to be expendable, but they were very lightly armoured, and before radar gunnery sets were introduced in World War II, four heavy guns were inadequate to guarantee hits at long range. *Furious*, with two single guns, was even worse in this respect. She had a modified hull form, and was intended as a trials ship for the new 18in (457mm) 42cal and 5·5in (140mm) guns. The latter replaced the unsuccessful triple 4in (102mm) mountings tried in the *Renown* and *Courageous* classes. To guard against failure of the 18in (457mm) gun, the barbette was the same size as that used by the twin 15in (381mm) turret, so that the latter could be fitted if necessary. *Furious* was really too small and too lightly built to carry such a heavy gun, and all three light cruisers used valuable shipyard capacity that could have been better used in other ways. A large number of men had to be employed on them because they were built in very short times, and their construction was hastened in a number of ways, including the use of two sets of light cruiser machinery to achieve the required power. They were the first large British warships to have small-tube boilers. The Battle of Jutland revealed the need for a carrier with a sufficient margin of speed over the battlefleet to be able to keep pace and operate and recover aircraft, so *Furious* was altered before completion to have a take-off deck and hangar in place of the forward heavy turret, which was never fitted. Trials revealed the advantage of having a landing-on deck aft, so one was fitted with a hangar beneath, and lifts were fitted fore and aft. Unfortunately, eddies from the funnel and superstructure prevented the landing-on deck being used by anything except airships. Meanwhile, the Italian liner *Conte Rosso*, building at Beardmores, Dalmuir, purchased in August 1916 and renamed *Argus*, had been completed in September 1918 with a flush-deck. After trials had shown this to be a success, and it had been realised that it would be cheaper to convert *Furious* than build a new ship, *Furious* was modified to have a flush upper flight deck over two hangars. This enabled her to carry more aircraft than *Hermes* or *Eagle*, which it had already been realised were too small. Aircraft could take off from the upper hangar using the old take-off deck forward, and the upper flight deck was raised up at the forward end to give sufficient height in the forward upper hangar. There was originally a retractable navigating position in the centre of the upper flight deck forward, with a small starboard navigating position for use during flying operations, but this was later replaced by a small fixed island. *Furious* saw considerable service during World War II, but was worn out by 1944

Hermes

AIRCRAFT-CARRIER
CLASS: *Hermes* class (1 ship)
Hermes

Service career HERMES
1920 (Jan–July 1923) Completed at Devonport.
1924–1926 Experiments.
1926–1932 Home and Mediterranean fleets.
1932–1933 Refit: second lift and a catapult fitted; Aircraft capacity reduced to 15.
1934–1936 China Station.
1937–1940 Home Fleet.
1940 (8 July) Aircraft from *Hermes* hit French battleship *Richelieu* with a torpedo at Dakar.
1940–1942 East Indies Station: four 2pdr (40mm) and five 20mm guns added.
1942 Eastern Fleet.
1942 (9 Apr) Sunk by aircraft from *Akagi*, *Hiryu* and *Soryu* off Ceylon.

Eagle

AIRCRAFT-CARRIER
CLASS: *Eagle* class (1 ship)
Eagle, ex-*Almirante Cochrane*

Service career EAGLE
1920 (Apr) Sailed to Portsmouth Dockyard: two boilers operational; only one funnel fitted.
1920 (10 May–27 Oct) Flying trials.
1921 (21 Feb–24 Mar 1923) Completed at Portsmouth Dockyard: bulge fitted, flight deck extended.
1924–1926 Mediterranean Fleet.
1926: Refit: longitudinal arrester wires removed.
1926–1928 Mediterranean Fleet.
1931 (Apr–Nov 1932) Refit.
1933–1934 China Station.
1935 Mediterranean Fleet.
1936 (Feb 1937) Refit: AA armament strengthened.
1937–1939 China Station.
1939 (Sept–Apr 1940) Indian Ocean.
1940 (May–Apr 1941) In Mediterranean: convoy escort and offensive strikes against Italy and Italian North Africa.
1940 (9 July) Action off Calabria.

Continued on page 18 ▶

Below: Bombed by aircraft from the Japanese carriers Akagi, Hiryu *and* Soryu, *HMS* Hermes *sinks in the Bay of Bengal, south of Trincomalee, 9 April 1942*

Displacement:	Hermes as built	Almirante Cochrane as designed	Eagle in 1942
standard tons (tonnes)	10,850 (11,020)	—	22,600 (22,960)
normal tons (tonnes)	—	28,600 (29,060)	—
full load tons (tonnes)	13,000 (13,210)	32,120 (32,630)	27,500 (27,940)
Dimensions:			
length (pp)	548ft (167m)	627·1ft (191·4m)	627·1ft (191·4m)
(oa)	600ft (182·9m)	661ft (201·5m)	667·5ft (203·5m)
beam (hull)	70·25ft (21·4m)	103ft (31·4m)	105ft (32m)
draught	21·5ft (6·6m)	28ft (8·5m)	26·6ft (8·1m)
Armament:			
guns			
14in (356mm) 45cal	—	10	—
6in (152mm) 50cal	—	16	9
5·5in (140mm) 50cal	6	—	—
4in (102mm)	4	—	4
3pdr (47mm)	—	4	—
2pdr (40mm)	—	—	16
20mm	—	—	12
0·303in (7·7mm)	—	—	4
torpedo tubes			
21in (533mm) submerged	—	4	—
aircraft	20	—	21
Armour:			
side (belt)	3in (76mm)	7–9in (178–229mm)	1–4·5in (25–114mm)
(ends)	1·5–2in (38–51mm)	4in (102mm)	—
deck (flight)	—	—	1in (25mm)
(fo'c's'le)	—	1in (25mm)	—
(upper)	1in (25mm)	1·5in (38mm)	1·5in (38mm)
(main)	1in (25mm)	1in (25mm)	1·5in (38mm)
(lower)	—	2–4in (51–102mm)	—
main turrets	—	9–10·5in (229–267mm)	—
barbettes	—	10in (254mm)	—
casemates	—	6in (152mm)	—
Machinery:			
boilers (type)	Yarrow small tube	Yarrow	Yarrow
(number)	6	21	32
engines (type)	Parsons	Parsons single	Parsons single
shafts	2	4	4
Total SHP:			
designed	40,000	37,000	50,000
trials	?	—	52,102
Fuel capacity:			
coal tons (tonnes)	—	3,300 (3,350)	—
oil tons (tonnes)	?	520 (540)	2,810 (2,860)
Performance:			
designed speed	25kts	22·75kts	24kts
trial speed	?	—	24·37kts
range	?	4,400 miles (3,700nm) @ 10kts	3,570 miles (3,000nm) @ 17·4kts
Crew:	approx 850	1,167	950

Ship:	HERMES	EAGLE
Ordered:	July 1917	1911
Laid down:	15 Jan 1918	22 Jan 1913
Suspended:	—	Aug 1914–June 1917
Launched:	11 Sept 1919	8 June 1918
Converted to carrier:	—	Feb 1918–Nov 1919
Completed:	July 1923	Sept 1923
Fate:	Sunk 9 Apr 1942	Sunk 11 Aug 1942

▶Hermes/Eagle

1940 (12 Oct) Near-missed by 12 bombs: damaged.
1940 (Nov) Repairs.
1941 (Apr–Oct) Anti-raider patrols in Indian Ocean and South Atlantic.
1941 (30 Oct–9 Jan 1942) Refit in UK: AA armament strengthened; radar fitted.
1942 (Feb–Aug) In Mediterranean: escorted nine operations ferrying aircraft to Malta.
1942 (11 Aug) Hit by four torpedoes from *U-73* off Tunisia: sank in four minutes; 161 crew killed.

Although the Japanese *Hosho* was the first to be completed, *Hermes* was the first ship to be designed as an aircraft-carrier. She embodied several features incorporated in most subsequent carriers, including a starboard island and a flight deck extending the length of the ship. She had a large amount of flare forward, and the shell plating was extended up to the flight deck, a feature adopted in all British purpose-built carriers until *Invincible* (CAH-1). The hangar was under the aft part of the flight deck, with a single lift at the stern. This proved inadequate, and a second lift was later added. The island was developed with the aid of wind tunnel experiments after the inadequacy of the 'goal-post' arrangement intended for all the early British carriers had been realised – fortunately before any ship had been completed with it. There was a single funnel and a massive control top on a tripod mast. *Hermes* was based on light cruiser practice, and had light cruiser machinery, scantlings and gun armament, though on a somewhat larger hull. *Eagle*, on the other hand, was converted from the unfinished hull of the Chilean battleship *Almirante Cochrane*

(ex-*Santiago*). Her sister *Almirante Latorre* (ex-*Valparaiso*), which was much nearer completion, was purchased by Britain in September 1914 and renamed *Canada*. She was completed in September 1915 virtually to the original design. They were designed by the British firm of Armstrong Whitworth and were longer, faster versions of the British super-dreadnoughts, with thinner armour, less range, and 14in (356mm) guns. When it was decided to complete *Eagle* as a carrier, the main armour belt was removed (the upper strake was fitted in the battle-cruiser *Renown*) and replaced by thinner armour. Like *Hermes*, her flight deck extended the length of the ship, but she had two lifts, and the starboard island had two funnels. She ran trials in 1920 in an incomplete condition, with only one funnel and two boilers, to prove the concept of a starboard island, and it was not until these were successfully concluded that *Eagle* and *Hermes* were finally completed. *Hermes* was in many respects the better ship, but the number of aircraft that both could carry was inadequate, and they were too slow. After her 1922–1925 conversion the faster *Furious*, which could operate 33 aircraft, was a much more useful ship. *Courageous* and *Glorious*, which were converted into aircraft-carriers between 1924 and 1930 with an island and flight deck, and which could operate 48 aircraft, were better still. There was a proposal to scrap *Hermes* and *Eagle* in 1924 so that improved ships could be built within the tonnage permitted by the Washington Treaty, but this was rejected on the grounds of cost. By 1939 they were both totally obsolete. *Canada* was sold back to Chile in 1920 and renamed *Almirante Latorre*. She was not finally scrapped until 1959.

Above: HMS Eagle, *a battleship conversion completed in 1923, at sea in company with* Queen Elizabeth *class battleship* Malaya *in 1942*

Left: Hermes *had several features that were incorporated in later aircraft carriers, notably the fixed island and a flight deck extending the ship's length*

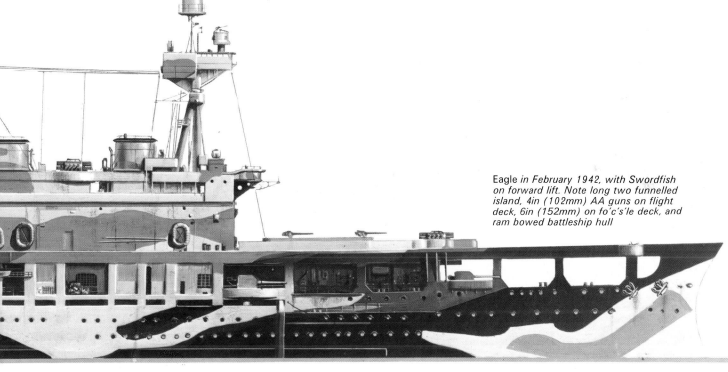

Eagle *in February 1942, with Swordfish on forward lift. Note long two funnelled island, 4in (102mm) AA guns on flight deck, 6in (152mm) on fo'c's'le deck, and ram bowed battleship hull*

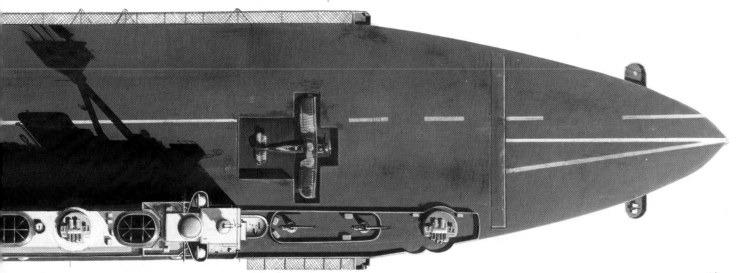

Ark Royal

AIRCRAFT-CARRIER
CLASS: *Ark Royal* class (1 ship)
Ark Royal

Service career ARK ROYAL
1939 (Jan–March) Shakedown cruise to Mediterranean.
1939 (March–Oct) Home Fleet.
1939 (Sept) A/S patrols off Northern Ireland.
1939 (14 Sept) Missed by two torpedoes from German submarine *U-39*.
1939 (26 Sept) Near miss by bomb from German aircraft: Germans announce *Ark Royal* sunk for first time.
1939 (Oct–Feb 1940) In South Atlantic with British battle-cruiser *Renown* searching for German pocket battleship *Graf Spee* and German supply ships.
1940 (23 Apr–June) Norwegian campaign.
1940 (12 June) Aircraft strike Trondheim.
1940 (June–Oct) Force H in Mediterranean.
1940 (3–6 July) Mers-el-Kebir.
1940 (3 July) Aircraft lay minefields and unsuccessfully attack French battle-cruiser *Strasbourg*.
1940 (6 July) Aircraft torpedo French battle-cruiser *Dunkerque*.
1940 (July) Refit and repairs at Gibraltar.
1940 (2 Aug) Strike on Cagliari harbour.
1940 (23–25 Sept) Dakar.
1940 (8 Oct–6 Nov) To UK for refit.
1940 (27 Nov) Unsuccessful action with Italian fleet off Cape Spartivento.
1941 (Feb–Apr) Search for German cruiser *Hipper* and battle-cruisers *Scharnhorst* and *Gneisenau* in Atlantic.
1941 (May) Ferried Hurricanes to Malta.
1941 (26 May) In Atlantic: aircraft torpedo German battleship *Bismarck*; one hit amidships and another aft which jammed *Bismarck*'s rudder.
1941 (June–Nov) Ferried Hurricanes to Malta.
1941 (24 Aug) Strike against Sardinia.
1941 (9 Sept) Bombardment of Genoa: aircraft attack Leghorn and La Spezia.
1941 (13 Nov) Hit by one torpedo from *U-81* near Gibraltar.
1941 (14 Nov) Sank near Gibraltar.

Between 1924 and 1930 Britain converted the two light battle-cruisers *Courageous* and *Glorious* into aircraft-carriers. Each had two hangars and could operate 48 aircraft, and they

Displacement:	
standard tons (tonnes)	22,000 (22,350)
full load tons (tonnes)	27,720 (28,160)
Dimensions:	
length (pp)	685ft (209·2m)
(wl)	721·5ft (220·3m)
(oa)	800ft (244·3m)
beam (wl)	94·75ft (28·9m)
(flight deck)	96ft (29·3m)
draught (max)	28ft (8·5m)
Armament:	
guns	
4·5in (114mm)	16
2pdr (40mm)	48
0·5in (12·7mm)	32
aircraft	72
Armour	
side (belt)	4·5in (114mm)
deck (lower hangar)	2·5in (64mm)
(upper)	2·5in (64mm)
(lower)	3·5in (89mm)
Machinery:	
boilers (type)	Admiralty 3-drum
(number)	6
engines (type)	Parsons single reduction geared turbines
shafts	3
Total SHP:	
designed	102,000
trial	103,000
Fuel capacity:	
oil tons (tonnes)	4,620 (4,690)
Performance:	
designed speed	30·75kts
trial speed	31·75kts
range	8,775 miles (7,620nm) @ 20kts
Crew:	1,636 (including aircrew)

Ship:	**ARK ROYAL**
Where built:	Cammell Laird, Birkenhead
Authorised:	1934
Laid down:	16 Sept 1935
Launched:	13 Apr 1937
Completed:	16 Nov 1938
Fate:	Sunk 14 Nov 1941

Above: HMS Ark Royal *under way, photographed from one of her own Swordfish torpedo bombers*

had what was for the time an extremely powerful AA armament controlled by four directors. They were the best of the early British conversions and it was unfortunate that both ships were lost early in World War II. Based on experience gained with these ships and her other early carriers, Britain planned after the 1930 London Naval Treaty to build a force of five new carriers capable of operating a total of 360 aircraft. The first, *Ark Royal*, was not ordered until 1935 because of financial restraints. Although the treaty permitted carriers of up to

27,000 tons (27,432 tonnes) standard displacement, *Ark Royal*'s was restricted to 22,000 tons (22,352 tonnes), 500 tons (510 tonnes) less than *Courageous* and *Glorious*. This was because Britain was pressing for the lower figure to be adopted as the upper limit for all carrier construction. The Second London Treaty of 1935 actually adopted an upper limit of 23,000 tons (23,368 tonnes) but *Ark Royal*'s design was too far advanced to take advantage of this. Her hull dimensions were determined by the size of drydocks at the Royal Dockyards, and in practice

Ark Royal in 1939. Note high silhouette, bow catapults and massive stern overhang

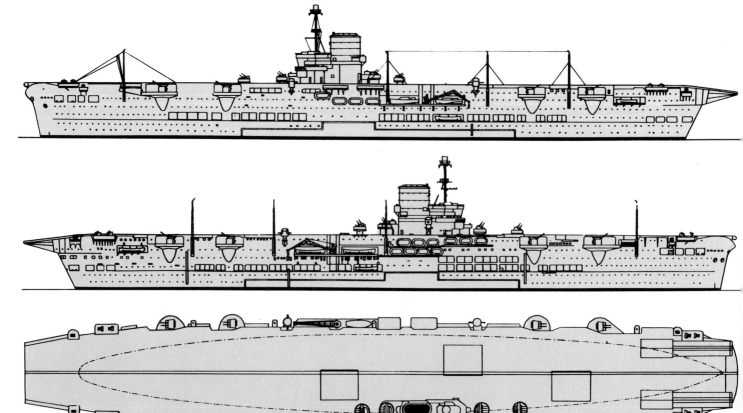

this restricted her hangar capacity to 60 aircraft, but in order to have as large a flight deck as possible she was given a massive stern overhang. Her speed was fixed by the need to be able to operate with cruisers, and extensive tank tests ensured that this was possible despite her short, beamy hull. A three-shaft arrangement was adopted for the first time on a major British warship to save weight and ensure sufficient power. Although the two-level hangars and flight deck were not armoured, she had a main belt and armour deck at lower hangar level capable of defeating 6in (152mm) shells and 500lb (227kg) bombs. She relied on her aircraft and surface escorts for defence against major surface threats, but had an extremely powerful and well arranged AA armament, consisting of eight twin 4·5in (114mm) DP mounts, six multiple 2pdr (40mm) pom-poms and eight multiple 0·5in (12·7mm) machine-guns controlled by four directors. In *Courageous* and *Glorious* the AA guns were carried low down, where they were affected by heavy seas, and their arcs of fire were restricted. In *Ark Royal* they were mounted on sponsons just below the flight deck, an arrangement repeated in future

British carriers. Her aircraft handling arrangements were well thought out. A moveable barrier was provided to enable aircraft to be launched and recovered simultaneously, and there were two catapults. Three lifts were provided, each of which served both hangars. Unfortunately they were very narrow because unlike contemporary American or Japanese carriers the flight deck was the main strength deck, which made large openings undesirable. She was also fitted with a comprehensive system for operating aircraft at night. However, this required specially trained pilots, and so it was not used very extensively during wartime operations. The forward and after 'round-down' were adopted after extensive wind-tunnel tests, as were the shape of the funnel and island. Unfortunately trials revealed that funnel smoke was sucked down over the deck, and so the funnel had to be raised by 8ft (2·4m). *Ark Royal* was very seaworthy and manoeuvrable, and she could operate her aircraft in rough weather. She was not much modified in service, mainly because for most of her brief life she was Britain's only modern fleet carrier. It was intended to fit radar, but this was not done before she was sunk. Although

considerable thought had been given to damage control during her design, she was sunk by only one torpedo, which hit on the starboard side abreast the bridge. This revealed an unexpected weakness, because as she listed, water was eventually able to cover the boiler uptakes. This deprived the pumps of power and ensured her loss. Had the torpedo hit anywhere else it is most unlikely that she would have been sunk. Apart from this one weakness she was an excellent and well-thought-out design, many of whose features were adopted as standard for future construction. In all respects except maximum speed she was superior to her American and Japanese contemporaries *Yorktown* and *Hiryu*, though Britain's hasty rearmament meant that she carried inferior aircraft because aircraft firms were forced to concentrate on planes for the RAF.

Below: Struck on the starboard side abreast the bridge by a single torpedo from U-81, *off Gibraltar on 13 November 1941,* Ark Royal *lists to starboard*

Illustrious
AIRCRAFT-CARRIER

CLASS: *Illustrious* class (6 ships)
Group 1 (3 ships) *Illustrious ·
Formidable · Victorious*
Group 2 (1 ship) *Indomitable*
Group 3 (2 ships) *Implacable ·
Indefatigable*

Service career ILLUSTRIOUS
1940–1941 In Mediterranean.
1940 (16–17 Sept) Aircraft attacked Benghasi.
1940 (Sept–Oct) Escorted Malta convoys.
1940 (11–12 Nov) Aircraft attacked Taranto.
1940 (Nov–Jan 1941) Escorted Malta convoys.
1941 (10 Jan) Hit by 6 bombs: badly damaged.
1941 (10–23 Jan) Temporary repairs at Malta under constant air attack.
1941 (Jan–May) To USA for repairs.
1941 (12 May–2 Nov) Repairs at Norfolk Navy Yard USA.

1941 (Dec) Returned to UK.
1942 (March–Apr) To Madagascar.
1942 (May) Covered Madagascar landings.
1942 (May–Jan 1943) In Indian Ocean.
1943 (Feb–June) Refit in UK.
1943 (July) Sweep to Norwegian coast.
1943 (Aug) To Mediterranean.
1943 (Sept) Covered Salerno landings.
1943 (Oct) Returned to UK.
1944 (Jan) To Indian Ocean.
1944 (Apr–Aug) Air strikes on Dutch East Indies.
1944 (Aug–Oct) Refit at Durban.
1944 (Nov) Rejoined Eastern Fleet.
1944 (Dec–Jan 1945) Air strikes against Palembang.
1945 (Feb) Centre propeller removed.
1945 (March) Rejoined Eastern Fleet.
1945 (March–Apr) Covered Okinawa landing.
1945 (6 Apr) Damaged by *kamikaze:* speed reduced to 19kts.
1945 (May–June) Returned to UK.
1945 (June–June 1946) Refit as trials carrier: catapult modernised.
1948–1954 Trials and training carrier.
1954 (Dec) In reserve.
1956 Scrapped.

	Illustrious as built	Indomitable as built	Implacable as built	Victorious in 1958
Displacement:				
standard tons (tonnes)	23,207 (23,579)	24,680 (25,075)	27,000 (27,432)	30,530 (31,018)
full load tons (tonnes)	28,619 (29,078)	29,730 (30,206)	32,110 (32,624)	35,500 (36,068)
Dimensions:				
length (pp)	673ft (205·5m)	673ft (205·5m)	673ft (205·5m)	?
(oa)	743·75ft (234m)	754ft (230·2m)	766·5ft (233·9m)	781ft (238·5m)
beam (ext)	?	?	131·25ft (40m)	146·75ft (44·8m)
beam (hull)	95·75ft (29·2m)	95·75ft (29·2m)	95·75ft (29·2m)	103·3ft (31·5m)
draught (mean)	24ft (7·3m)	25ft (7·6m)	26ft (7·9m)	31ft (9·5m)
Armament:				
guns				
4·5in (114mm)	16	16	16	—
3in (76mm)	—	—	—	12
2pdr (40mm)	48	48	48	—
40mm	8	8	37	6
20mm	8	8	37	—
0·303in (7·7mm)	—	17	—	—
aircraft	36	48	54	54
Machinery:				
boilers (type)	Admiralty 3-drum	Admiralty 3-drum	Admiralty 3-drum	Foster Wheeler
(number)	6	6	8	6
engines (type)	Parsons single reduction geared turbines			
shafts	3	3	4	3
Total SHP:				
designed	110,000	110,000	148,000	110,000
Fuel capacity:				
oil tons (tonnes)	4,854 (4,932)	4,854 (4,932)	4,850 (4,928)	?
Performance:				
designed speed	30·5kts	30·5kts	31·5kts	31kts
range	11,000 miles (9,250nm) @ 14kts	11,000 miles (9,250nm) @ 14kts	?	?
Crew:	1,500	1,592	2,200	2,200

Unlike contemporary American and Japanese aircraft carriers, which were designed to operate in the Pacific where the threat from land-based aircraft was small, the *Illustrious* class were intended mainly for the restricted waters of the North Sea and Mediterranean, where the threat from land-based aircraft was increasing and the danger of surface attack considerable. They were therefore fitted with an armoured box around the hangar that gave protection against 550lb (250kg) SAP bombs dropped from 7,000ft (2,000m) and 6in (152mm) shells. Treaty limitations restricted the standard displacement to about 23,000 tons (23,370 tonnes), and in order to carry the extra weight on only a slightly enlarged displacement, they had only one hangar deck compared with *Ark Royal*'s two, halving the number of aircraft that could be carried. Although radar later

Continued on page 24 ▶

Right: Albacore torpedo-bombers flying from HMS Illustrious. *Tonnage limitations and the need for armour protection limited the first* Illustrious *group to 36 planes*

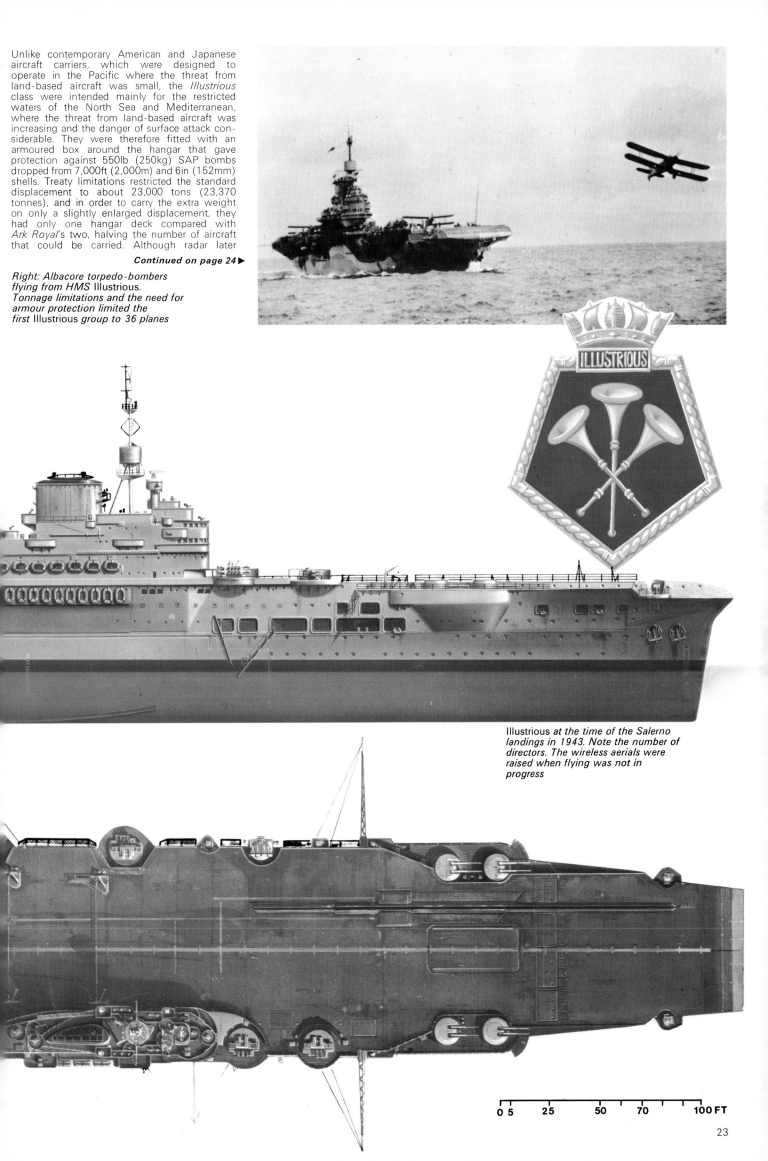

Illustrious *at the time of the Salerno landings in 1943. Note the number of directors. The wireless aerials were raised when flying was not in progress*

0 5   25   50   70   100 FT

▶Illustrious

made carriers less vulnerable to air attack, this decision was justified at the time, given the standard of protection required and the limited displacement available. They were intended to rely mainly on their anti-aircraft guns for defence against air attack, and they carried the same powerful anti-aircraft armament as *Ark Royal*. However, the 4·5in (114mm) guns were mounted higher up in power-operated turrets which had limited arcs of fire across the flight deck. This tended to damage the carrier's own aircraft and was little used. As with *Ark Royal*, four directors were carried for the 4·5in (114mm) guns, giving an excellent anti-aircraft defence. The same three-shaft arrangement was used, but slightly more powerful machinery was fitted. Of the two ships of the 1937 programme, *Formidable* was completed as designed, but on *Indomitable* the treaty limits were abandoned and her aircraft capacity increased. Her hangar side armour was reduced in thickness, allowing

an extra half hangar to be fitted under the main hangar aft, but hangar height had to be reduced by 2ft (0·6m) to achieve this. The design of the last two ships was partially recast. More powerful four-shaft machinery was fitted, the hull was slightly lengthened, the bow form was altered, and it was originally planned to fit two full length hangars. However, the personnel required for the more powerful machinery and extra aircraft had to be housed in the fore-part of the lower hangar. An extra director was fitted for the 4·5in (114mm) guns, and radar direction was provided for the 2pdr (40mm) guns — the latter being retrofitted to the earlier ships. Completion of the *Implacable* and *Indefatigable* was delayed by the need to concentrate on escorts. The anti-aircraft armament of all units was strengthened before they went to the Pacific, and by 1945 the earlier ships could operate 54 aircraft and the last two 81 by using permanent deck parks and outriggers. The value of the armoured box was clearly demonstrated in the

Mediterranean in the first years of the war. All six were hit by *kamikaze* aircraft in the Pacific, but were able to operate aircraft again after a short time, whereas the American carriers with wooden flight decks were often much more extensively damaged. *Victorious*, *Formidable* and *Indomitable* all saw a great deal of action during World War II but *Implacable* and *Indefatigable* were only completed in time to serve in the Pacific. *Victorious* was comprehensively rebuilt in the 1950s to enable her to operate modern aircraft. She was lengthened and fitted with a strengthened, angled, flight deck, a new armament and Type 984 3-dimensional radar on an enlarged island. Because this conversion took so long and was very expensive, none of the others was converted.

Below: HMS Indomitable *had her hangar capacity increased to 48 aircraft. An Albacore flies over a Fulmar fighter*

Ship:	ILLUSTRIOUS	FORMIDABLE	VICTORIOUS	INDOMITABLE	INDEFATIGABLE	IMPLACABLE
Where built:	Vickers-Armstrong, Barrow	Harland & Wolff, Belfast	Vickers-Armstrong, Tyne	Vickers-Armstrong, Barrow	John Brown, Clydebank	Fairfield, Govan
Ordered:	13 Jan 1937	9 March 1937	13 Jan 1937	6 July 1937	19 June 1939	11 Oct 1938
Laid down:	27 Apr 1937	17 June 1937	4 May 1937	10 Nov 1937	3 Nov 1939	21 Feb 1939
Launched:	5 Apr 1939	17 Aug 1939	14 Sept 1939	26 May 1940	3 Dec 1942	10 Dec 1942
Completed:	21 May 1940	24 Nov 1940	15 May 1941	1 Oct 1941	3 May 1944	24 Aug 1944
Fate:	Scrapped 1956	Scrapped 1955	Rebuilt 1950–1958; scrapped 1969	Scrapped 1953	Scrapped 1956	Scrapped 1957

Ark Royal R-09

AIRCRAFT-CARRIER
CLASS: *Audacious* class (2 ships)
Eagle (R-05) · *Ark Royal* (R-09)

Service career ARK ROYAL (R-09)
1945–1948 Suspended: design recast.
1955 (Feb) Completed work: partially angled deck (5·5°) and deck edge lift.
1956 Forward port 4·5in (114mm) turrets removed.
1959 Deck edge lift and starboard forward 4·5in (114mm) turrets removed.
1961 Steam catapult, Hilo guidance system and deck landing sight fitted.
1964 4·5in (114mm) turrets in port and starboard aft sponsons removed.
1967 (Mar–Feb 1970) Fully angled deck (8·5°) and new steam catapult and arrester gear fitted; island increased in size; in service.

Japan's entry into World War II meant that more British fleet carriers would be needed, and the first designs for them were produced early in 1942. These were for enlarged *Implacables*, with two complete hangars and thicker deck armour to withstand larger bombs. The design was later further enlarged to accept the larger American carrier-borne aircraft. Two lifts and two catapults were provided, and the armament was similar to that fitted to the *Implacables* except that the light anti-aircraft battery was composed entirely of 40mm guns. The machinery was arranged in a similar fashion to that of the *Implacables* but was slightly more powerful. A modified transom stern was also fitted. Four *Ark Royals* were laid down, but only *Audacious* (later renamed *Eagle*) was near launching at the end of the war. Three larger *Malta* class carriers were also projected. These were to have had a standard displacement of 46,900 tons (47,650 tonnes) and would have been very similar in size to the American *Midways*. Only *Malta* had been laid down by the end of the war, and all three were cancelled. To fill the gap before the new fleet carriers became available, several light fleet carriers were built. Ten *Colossus* and five of the improved

Above: Ark Royal *in the background passing* Eagle *at Devonport.* Eagle *(in the foreground) has already been laid up, though she retains the Type 984 3-D radar at the fore end of the island.* Ark Royal *has been refitted with the improved steam catapults for operating Phantoms, and* Eagle *has been cannibalized to allow her half sister to remain in service. A* Lyness *class storeship is in the background*

Majestic class were completed, and one *Majestic, Leviathan,* was scrapped incomplete. They had a standard displacement of between 13,190 and 15,700 tons (13,400–15,950 tonnes), and by accepting mercantile scantlings and sub-division, a light anti-aircraft armament and destroyer machinery giving a speed of only about 25kts, they were completed much more quickly than the larger carriers. They proved very economical ships for peacetime navies, and examples were transferred or sold postwar to Argentina, Australia, Brazil, Canada, France, India and the Netherlands. Several remain in service. After World War II those carriers on which little work had been done were scrapped, and the remainder suspended. *Eagle* (R-05, ex-*Audacious*) was eventually finished to virtually the original design, but *Ark Royal* was completed with the new British-developed angled deck and steam catapults, as well as the American form of deck-edge lift. Both ships were progressively modified. *Eagle* was last refitted between April 1966 and September 1967, but although she was fitted with Type 984 three-dimensional radar which *Ark Royal* did not receive because of financial economies, she was not fitted with the very powerful steam catapults that *Ark Royal* received in her 1967–1970 refit. Since being discarded, *Eagle* (R-05) has been cannibalized to keep her sister operational. It was originally intended to replace these carriers with new 50,000 ton (50,800 tonne) carriers, but the first, CVA-01, was cancelled in 1965 when the programme was abandoned. It is planned to discard *Ark Royal* in 1978.

Displacement:	Ark Royal as built	Ark Royal in 1977
standard tons (tonnes)	43,340 (44,030)	43,060 (43,750)
full load tons	53,340 (54,190)	50,786 (51,600)
Dimensions:		
length (pp)	720ft (219·5m)	720ft (219·5m)
(oa)	808·25ft (246·8m)	845ft (257·6m)
beam (wl)	112·8ft (34·4m)	112·8ft (34·4m)
(ext)	158ft (48·2m)	165·7ft (50·6m)
draught	36ft (11m)	36ft (11m)
Armament:		
guns		
4·5in (114mm)	16	—
40mm	34	—
aircraft	80 (approx)	39
Armour:		
side (belt)	4·5in (114mm)	
(hangar)	1·5in (38mm)	
deck (flight)	1·5–4in (38–102mm)	
(lower hangar)	1–2·5in (25–63mm)	
Machinery:		
boilers (type)	Admiralty 3-drum	
(number)	8	
engines (type)	Parsons single reduction geared turbines	
shafts	4	
Total SHP:		
designed	152,000	
Fuel capacity:		
oil tons (tonnes)	5,500 (5,590)	
Performance:		
designed speed	31·5kts	
range	?	
Crew plus aircrew:	2,345	

Ship:	EAGLE, ex-AUDACIOUS (R-05)	ARK ROYAL (R-09)	AFRICA	EAGLE
Where built:	Harland & Wolff, Belfast	Cammell Laird, Birkenhead	Fairfield, Govan	Vickers-Armstrong, Tyne
Ordered:	1942	1942	1942	1942
Laid down:	24 Oct 1942	3 May 1943	1943	1943
Cancelled:	—	—	1945	1945
Launched:	19 Mar 1946	3 May 1950	—	—
Completed:	1 Oct 1951	25 Feb 1955	—	—
Major rebuild:	(1) 1959–1964 (2) 1966–1967	(1) 1959 (2) 1961 (3) 1967–1970	—	—
Fate:	Stricken 1972	In service	Cancelled	Cancelled

Invincible

THROUGH-DECK CRUISER

CLASS: *Invincible* class (2 ships)
Invincible (CAH-1) · *Illustrious*
(CAH-2) with one more forecast

The British withdrawal from the Mediterranean and from east of Suez, the cancellation of the large carrier *CVA-01* and the associated transfer of responsibility for maritime air roles to the (land-based) Royal Air Force in the mid-1960s left British naval planning in some disarray. However, a definite requirement still existed for vessels capable of operating and maintaining a number of ASW helicopters to counter the ever increasing threat from Russian submarines. As an interim measure two of the three *Tiger* class cruisers were converted between 1965 and 1972. They had been laid down as conventional *Swiftsure* class cruisers in 1941–1942, but were suspended at the end of World War II and not finally completed until 1959–1961. They were armed with the complex and unreliable automatic 6in (152mm) and 3in (76mm) mounts. *Tiger* (C-20) and *Blake* (C-99) had their aft twin 6in (152mm) turret replaced by a hangar and flight deck capable of operating four Sea King ASW helicopters. These conversions were very costly for the limited results achieved, so *Lion* (C-34) was scrapped without being converted. The definitive ASW design was *Invincible* (CAH-1). Political and financial considerations delayed her order, but this was finally confirmed on 17 April 1973. Even after this date she has been delayed by financial stringency, and as an economy measure will probably not mount the MM-38 Exocet SSM quadruple-launcher with which she was originally intended to be fitted. She is much the same size as the *Majestic* class light fleet carriers, and is the largest warship laid down in Britain since World War II. She mounts a Sea Dart SAM twin-launcher on the fo'c's'le just forward of the flight deck in a position giving clear arcs of fire in most directions. There is a long island with two masts and funnels, and she has a clear flight deck angled slightly to port of the centrally mounted Sea Dart SAM launcher. There are two lifts, but she has no catapults or arrester-wires. She is the first large Western warship to be powered by gas turbines — the Tynes are for cruising and the Olympus engines provide full power. The clear flight deck was designed to enable the *Invincibles* to operate V/STOL aircraft as well as ASW helicopters. For several years this was not considered possible for political reasons, because of the decision to transfer maritime air roles to the Royal Air Force, and this capability was thinly disguised by the designation 'through-deck cruiser'. However, the advantages of carrier-borne aircraft, including the much quicker reaction times possible, eventually proved unanswerable, and when *Invincible* (CAH-1) enters service she will operate a mixed complement of Sea King ASW helicopters and Sea Harrier V/STOL aircraft. Although the *Invincibles* are roughly similar in size to the Russian *Moskvas*, their aircraft are much more versatile despite the ships' smaller armament. The projected French nuclear-powered PA-75 type helicopter carriers will be very similar in all respects except for the type of machinery. In the gap between *Ark Royal* (R-09) being phased out in 1978 and *Invincible* (CAH-1) entering service in 1980 her place will be taken by *Hermes* (R-12). The original light fleet carriers were excellent ships within their limitations, but more speed was needed for fleet operations, and eight *Hermes* class with a designed standard displacement of 18,300 tons (18,590 tonnes) and a speed of 29·5kts were laid down in 1944–1945. Four were cancelled at the end of World War II. One, *Centaur* (R-06), was completed in 1953 to the original design. Two, *Albion* (R-07) and *Bulwark* (R-08) were completed in 1954 with a partially angled deck, and one, *Hermes* (R-12), was completed in 1959 with a fully angled deck, steam catapults, a deck-edge lift and Type 984 3-dimensional radar. *Bulwark* (R-08) became the prototype commando carrier in 1960, and *Albion* (R-07) was converted to a slightly improved standard in 1962. *Centaur* (R-06) was not converted and was deleted in 1971, and *Albion* (R-07) and *Bulwark* (R-08) were deleted in 1972 and 1976 respectively, although *Bulwark* is now refitting. *Hermes* (R-12) was too small to operate modern aircraft and

was converted into a commando carrier to replace *Albion* (R-07) in 1971. Her Type 984 radar was removed and the steam catapults and arrester gear were also landed. In 1976–1977 she was refitted to operate Sea King ASW helicopters, and she will receive Sea Harrier V/STOL aircraft in 1979.

Above: The launch of the through-deck cruiser HMS Invincible *(CAH-1), at Vickers, Barrow, 3 May 1977*

Below: Invincible *will operate 10 Sea King helicopters and 5 Sea Harrier V/STOL aircraft*

Displacement:			
standard tons (tonnes)	16,000 (16,256)		
full load tons (tonnes)	19,500 (19,810)		
Dimensions:			
length (pp)	632ft (192·9m)		
(oa)	677ft (206·6m)		
beam (wl)	90ft (27·5m)		
(flight deck)	104·6ft (31·9m)		
draught	24ft (7·3m)		
Armament:			
missiles			
Sea Dart SAM twin-launcher	1		
aircraft	15		
Machinery:			
gas turbine (type)	Rolls Royce Olympus and Rolls Royce Tyne		
(number)	4+2		
shafts	2		
Total SHP:			
designed	110,000		
Fuel capacity:			
oil tons (tonnes)	?		
Performance:			
designed speed	approx 28kts		
range	5,000 miles (4,342nm) @ 18kts		
Crew:	900 excluding aircrew		

Ship:	INVINCIBLE (CAH-1)	ILLUSTRIOUS (CAH-2)	? (CAH-3)
Where built:	Vickers, Barrow	Swan Hunter, Wallsend	—
Authorised:	?		?
Laid down:	20 July 1973	?	—
Launched:	3 May 1977	?	—
Completed:	—	—	—
Fate:	Under construction	Ordered 14 May 1976	Projected

King Edward VII

BATTLESHIP
CLASS: *King Edward VII* class
(8 ships) including *King Edward VII · Commonwealth*

Service career KING EDWARD VII
1905 (7 Feb) Commissioned.
1905 (Feb–March 1907) Flagship, Atlantic Fleet.
1907 (March–March 1909) Flagship, Channel Fleet.
1909 (March–June 1911) Flagship, 2nd Division, Home Fleet.
1911 (Aug–May 1912) Flagship, 3rd and 4th Division, Home Fleet.
1912 (May–Aug 1914) Flagship, 3rd Battle Squadron, Home Fleet.
1915 (Aug and Sept 1915–Jan 1916) Flagship, 3rd Battle Squadron, Grand Fleet.
1916 (6 Jan) Mined and sunk.

The development of Harvey's and then Krupp's improved methods of manufacturing armour meant that thinner armour belts could provide the same protection as before, and the weight saved was used to keep the size of battleships virtually constant throughout the 1890s despite improvements in armament, machinery and protection. From the *Majestics*, built between 1893 and 1898, British battleships had standardised on a main armament of two twin 12in (305mm) turrets and a secondary armament of twelve 6in (152mm) guns. However, by 1900 the improved protection made possible by fitting Krupp armour meant that the 6in (152mm) guns became less effective against the armoured parts of foreign battleships, and the *King Edward VII* class therefore mounted 9·2in (234mm) guns which were capable of penetrating battleship armour at the short ranges then current. At the same time the *King Edward VII*s were the first British battleships to have fire control positions for longer range fire in place of the previous fighting tops. Improved gunnery and manufacturing techniques meant that it was becoming both practical and necessary to fight at the extended ranges that long-barrelled guns with slow burning powder had made possible since the 1880s. The restrictions of existing drydocks meant that the *King Edward VII*s were no bigger than the much less heavily armed *Formidable*, *London* and *Queen* classes built between 1898 and 1904, so their freeboard had to be reduced somewhat. Combined with the high metacentric height caused by the beam turrets, this made them wet ships, and they rolled very quickly. Because of this they were nicknamed the '*Wobbly Eight*'. However, they were still much more seaworthy than most foreign contemporaries, and they were very handy ships. It was originally intended that the last three should be completed to a much larger design, with four 12in (305mm) and twelve 9·2in (234mm) guns, but this would have been too large for the existing docks. A smaller modified version of this design with only ten 9·2in (234mm) guns was used for the *Lord Nelson* and *Agamemnon*. These were excellent ships, if a little cramped, and in all respects except for speed and freeboard were at least an equal match, when first built, to *Dreadnought*. Indeed their armour protection was superior. However, with the improvements in fire control and concentration on firing at extreme ranges, the problems caused by a mixed main armament outweighed the benefits of having the lighter guns. *King Edward VII* was mined off Cape Wrath and *Britannia* was torpedoed by *UB-50* off the West African coast. Both ships took several hours to sink, a tribute to the original design. *Commonwealth* and *Zealandia* were altered for use as coast bombardment ships in 1918.

Above, left: HMS King Edward VII, *name-ship of the 'Wobbly Eight'*

Above: HMS Hibernia, *1905. The* King Edward VII *class were the first British battleships with fire control positions*

Displacement:
normal tons (tonnes)	16,350 (16,610)
full load tons (tonnes)	17,500 (17,780)

Dimensions:
length (pp)	425ft (129·8m)
(wl)	439ft (134m)
(oa)	453·75ft (138·5m)
beam	78ft (23·8m)
draught (normal)	24·5ft (7·5m)

Armament
guns	King Edward VII as built	Commonwealth in 1918
12in (305mm) 40cal	4	4
9·2in (234mm) 45cal	4	4
6in (152mm) 50cal	10	—
12pdr (76mm)	14	—
3pdr (47mm)	14	—
torpedo tubes		
18in (457mm)	4	4

Armour:
side (belt)	4–9in (102–229mm)
(ends)	1·5–2·5in (38–63mm)
deck (main)	1·5–2in (38–51mm)
(middle)	1–2in (25–51mm)
(lower)	2·5in (63mm)
main turrets	8–12in (203–305mm)
barbettes	6–12in (152–305mm)
secondary turrets	4in (102mm)
battery	7in (178mm)

Machinery:
boilers (type)	Babcock & Wilcox, or Babcock & Wilcox and Cylindrical, or Niclausse and Cylindrical
(number)	15–16
engines (type)	vertical triple expansion
shafts	2

Total IHP:
designed	18,000
trial	18,112–18,624

Fuel capacity:
coal normal tons (tonnes)	950 (965)
max tons (tonnes)	2,150 (2,180)
oil tons (tonnes)	380 (390)

Performance:
designed speed	18·5kts
trial speed	18·12–19·35kts
range	7,000 miles (5,880nm) @ 10kts

Crew:
777

Class:	**KING EDWARD VII class**
Where built:	various yards
Authorised:	1901–1903
Laid down:	1902–1904
Launched:	1903–1905
Completed:	1905–1906
Fate:	*King Edward VII* sunk 6 Jan 1916 *Britannia* sunk 9 Nov 1918 remainder paid off 1921

King Edward VII as built. Note control tops and 9·2in (234mm) turrets

Dreadnought

BATTLESHIP
CLASS: *Dreadnought* class (1 ship)
Dreadnought

Service career DREADNOUGHT
1907 (5 Jan–23 March) Home Fleet: Trials cruise to Mediterranean and Trinidad.
1907 (Apr–March 1909) Flagship Nore.
1909 (March–March 1911) Flagship 1st Division, Home Fleet.
1911 Refit at Portsmouth.
1912 (May–Dec) 1st Division, Home Fleet.
1912 (Dec–Aug 1914) Flagship 4th Battle Squadron, Home Fleet.
1913 Main topmast removed.
1914 (Aug–May 1916) Flagship 4th Battle Squadron, Grand Fleet.
1915 (18 March) Rammed

Displacement:	
normal tons (tonnes)	17,900 (18,185)
full load tons (tonnes)	21,845 (22,190)
Dimensions:	
length (pp)	490ft (149·3m)
(wl)	520ft (158·4m)
(oa)	527ft (160·6m)
beam	82·1ft (25m)
draught (mean)	26·5ft (8m)
Armament:	
guns	
12in (305mm) 45cal	10
12pdr (76mm)	27
torpedo tubes	
18in (457mm)	5
Armour:	
side (belt)	8–11in (203–279mm)
(ends)	4–6in (102–152mm)
deck (upper)	0·75in (19mm)
(lower)	3in (76mm)
main turrets	3–11in (76–279mm)
barbettes	4–11in (102–279mm)
Machinery:	
boilers (type)	Babcock & Wilcox
(number)	18
engines (type)	Parsons turbines
shafts	4
Total SHP:	
designed	23,000
trials	26,350
Fuel capacity:	
coal normal tons (tonnes)	900 (910)
max tons (tonnes)	2,900 (2,950)
oil tons (tonnes)	1,120 (1,140)
Performance:	
designed speed	21kts
trials speed	21·6kts
range	7,870 miles (6,620nm) @ 10kts
Crew:	773

Dreadnought *in 1914. Note the wing turrets and the foremast abaft the fore funnel. Yards are turned through 90° to show rigging*

and sank German submarine *U-29.*
1915 Refit: director added, fore topmast reduced, 12pdr (76mm) armament altered and re-arranged.
1916 (Spring) Minor refit.
1916 (May–March 1918) Flagship 3rd Battle Squadron, Sheerness.

1916–1917 Magazine protection improved.
1918 (March–July) 4th Battle Squadron, Grand Fleet.
1918 (July–March 1920) In reserve.
1920 (31 March) Deleted.
1921 (May) Sold for scrap.
1923 (Feb) Scrapped.

Dreadnought was an immense propaganda success. Built in 366 days, a record not equalled by any major warship since, she was the first battleship in recent times to have an all-big-gun armament, and the first to have turbine propulsion. She was considerably larger than any

Continued on page 30▶

Ship:	**DREADNOUGHT**
Where built:	Portsmouth Dockyard
Authorised:	1905
Laid down:	21 Oct 1905
Launched:	10 Feb 1906
Completed:	1 Oct 1906
Fate:	scrapped 1923

Above: The launching of
HMS Dreadnought *on 10 February 1906.*
She was the first modern all
big-gun battleship and the
first to have turbine propulsion.
Note the 'ram' bow, insisted on by Fisher,
and the height of the fo'c's'le above water

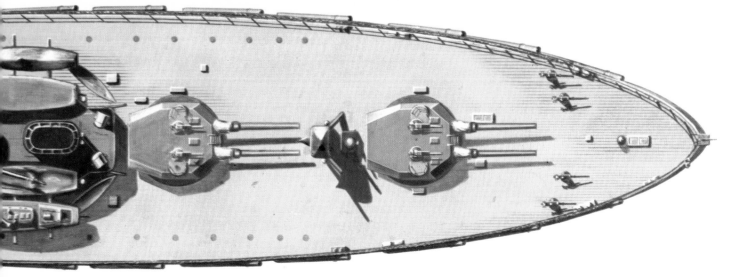

▶ Dreadnought

previous British warship, benefiting from the relaxation of limitations on maximum dimensions caused by the small size of some British docks — limitations that had hamstrung the design of the *Lord Nelsons* and *King Edward VIIs*. *Dreadnought* was very seaworthy, carrying her foremost turret on a raised fo'c's'le one deck higher than any British pre-dreadnought. The idea of a large fast ship with a heavy armament was current in several navies in the early 1900s. The Japanese *Kuramas* and Italian *Vittorio Emanueles* were fast, though they were lightly armoured and carried a mixed main armament, and the first battleships designed with an all-big-gun main armament were the American *South Carolinas*, though they were not laid down until *Dreadnought* was nearly complete. It was the use of turbines, the aggressive appearance, and above all the sheer speed of construction that caused *Dreadnought* to stand out from her contemporaries. The reason for the remarkably short time she took to build lay partly in excellent organisation at Portsmouth Dockyard, but was mainly due to the fact that part of her materials, most of her auxiliaries and all of her turrets were already being manufactured for the two *Lord Nelsons*. Both were seriously delayed as a result of these being used in *Dreadnought*. The turrets were particularly vital. If they had had to be ordered new, *Dreadnought* could not have been completed on time, because each took over two years to construct. The credit for *Dreadnought* — and the blame for her many defects — rests almost entirely with 'Jackie' Fisher. He had long advocated a powerful and

very large capital ship, and soon after he became First Sea Lord on 21 October 1904 he appointed a Committee on Designs mainly to consider this question. The committee consisted of a number of naval and civilian experts, but it was controlled by Fisher. Very little consideration was given to what kind of ships were needed — Fisher himself decided the types he required — and his personal obsession with high speed and powerful end-on fire dominated the battleship design. This meant that less weight was available for protection, and her armour was inferior to the *Lord Nelsons*. Ten 12in (305mm) guns gave her much more striking power than the mixed-calibre main armament of the two preceding classes of British battleships, but the great improvements in accuracy attainable at long ranges were not fully reaped until after the introduction of director firing after 1910. *Dreadnought* herself was not fitted with a director until 1915. Experiments showed that the 12pdr (76mm) gun was too light to repel torpedo boats, and the otherwise very similar *Bellerophons* of 1907 were fitted with 4in (102mm) guns. The Committee on Designs looked at a number of different arrangements for the main armament, and also considered using the Armstrong 10in (254mm) gun. This was thought to fire too light a shell, and the eventual layout of 12in (305mm) guns was determined by Fisher's insistence on six-gun end-on fire both fore and aft. This was achieved to some extent to the detriment of broadside fire, which he considered less important. Superimposed turrets were considered, but were not adopted until the *Neptune* of 1909 because of

blast problems. The use of turbines was a complete success. They were already known to be reliable, and though no comparative trials in the cruiser *Amethyst* had been carried out when *Dreadnought* was designed, the turbine designer Charles Parsons — who was a member of the Committee on Designs — was able to guarantee their performance from that attained in merchant ships. Unlike reciprocating engines, early turbines used a lot of fuel at cruising speeds, but could run at full speed for long periods and were much less prone to vibration. Also, because the weight was concentrated low down in the ship, the main armament could be carried higher. In contrast, fitting the tripod foremast behind the forefunnel was disastrous — the control top was perpetually filled with smoke, and the *Bellerophons* had their foremast mounted in front of the forefunnel. By 1914 *Dreadnought* was already obsolete, and she was withdrawn from the Grand Fleet before the Battle of Jutland. Her speed had dropped and her underwater protection in particular was inadequate for modern warfare. She became the flagship for the squadron of *King Edward VII* class battleships based at Sheerness to counter any German attack on the Thames. So great was British naval superiority by mid-1918 that *Dreadnought* was put into reserve before the end of the war. She never fired her guns in anger at a surface target.

Below: With a main armament of ten 12in/305mm guns, Dreadnought *was the product of Fisher's insistence on high speed and powerful end-on fire*

Iron Duke

BATTLESHIP
CLASS: *Iron Duke* class (4 ships)
*Iron Duke · Marlborough · Benbow ·
Emperor of India* (ex-*Delhi*)

Serice career IRON DUKE
1914 (Aug–Nov 1916) Flagship, Grand Fleet.
1915 Aft two 6in (152mm) guns remounted fo'c's'le deck.
1916 (31 May) Battle of Jutland.
1916 (Nov–1919) 2nd Battle Squadron, Grand Fleet.
1919-1926 Mediterranean Fleet.
1926-1929 Atlantic Fleet.
1931 Demilitarised under London Naval Treaty: B and Y 13·5in (343mm) turrets, conning tower, main belt, torpedo tubes and some boilers removed; speed reduced to 18kts.
1932-1939 Gunnery training ship.
1939-1945 Depot ship. Scapa Flow.
1939 (17 Oct) Hit by bombs from German aircraft: beached and disarmed.
1946 Scrapped.

The first increase in main armament over *Dreadnought* came with the *St Vincents*. Triple 12in (305mm) turret designs were prepared in 1906, but the simpler twin turret was preferred with the more powerful 12in (305mm) 50cal gun. Unfortunately this suffered increased barrel wear because of higher muzzle velocities than the 12in (305mm) 45cal gun, and was less accurate at long range. It was also fitted in *Neptune, Colossus* and *Hercules,* but the *Orions* mounted ten 13·5in (343mm) guns. This fired a heavier shell at a lower muzzle velocity, and was an extremely effective and accurate weapon. For the first time in a British dreadnought, all main armament was mounted on the centreline, with superimposed turrets fore and aft and with Q turret abaft the funnels. The first 'superdreadnoughts', they were large powerful ships marred only by having the tripod mast mounted behind the forefunnel, as in *Dreadnought,* and the control top was frequently obscured by smoke and fumes. The next class, the *King George Vs,* were similar but had their 4in (102mm) secondary armament redistributed and were completed with a pole foremast in front of the forefunnel. The *Iron Dukes* were improved *King George Vs,* with a 6in (152mm) secondary armament mounted in a slightly longer hull. They compared favourably with the contemporary German *König* class battleships, having a more powerful main armament but thinner, though still adequate, armour. Despite their narrower beam (restricted by the size of British docks) the *Iron Dukes'* underwater protection proved to be quite effective. *Marlborough* was hit amidships by a torpedo during the Battle of Jutland, but kept her place in the line until the end of the main fleet action. The worst feature of the design was the arrangement of the 6in (152mm) guns, which had to be placed low down to offset the extra weight compared with the 4in (102mm) guns carried on preceding superdreadnoughts. The fore and aft guns in particular were useless in heavy weather, and the latter were soon repositioned. *Marlborough, Benbow* and *Emperor of India* had similar careers to *Iron Duke,* but were discarded under the terms of the London Naval Treaty of 1930.

Iron Duke in 1916. Note position of 6in (152mm) casemates and Q turret

Displacement:		
normal tons (tonnes)	25,820 (26,230)	
full load tons (tonnes)	30,380 (30,870)	
Dimensions:		
length (pp)	580ft (177m)	
(wl)	614ft (187·5m)	
(oa)	623ft (190·2m)	
beam	90ft (27·5m)	
draught	29·5ft (9m)	

Armament:	as built	Iron Duke in 1939
guns		
13·5in (343mm) 45cal	10	6
6in (152mm) 50cal	12	12
3in (76mm)	2	—
3pdr (47mm)	4	—
torpedo tubes		
21in (533mm)	4	—

Armour:	
side (belt)	8–12in (203–305mm)
(ends)	2·5–6in (63–152mm)
deck (upper)	1·25–2in (32–51mm)
(middle)	1·5in (38mm)
(lower)	1–2·5in (25–63mm)
main turrets	4–11in (102–279mm)
barbettes	7–10in (178–254mm)
battery	2–6in (51–152mm)

Machinery:	
boilers (type)	Babcock & Wilcox, Yarrow
(number)	18
engines (type)	Parsons turbines
shafts	4
Total SHP:	
designed	29,000
trial	30,040
Performance:	
designed speed	21kts
trial speed	21·6kts
range	7,780 miles (6,540nm) @ 10kts
Fuel capacity:	
coal normal tons (tonnes)	1,000 (1,020)
max tons (tonnes)	3,250 (3,300)
oil normal tons (tonnes)	1,050 (1,070)
max tons (tonnes)	1,600 (1,630)
Crew:	925 (up to 1,022 in wartime)

Ship:	IRON DUKE	MARL-BOROUGH	BENBOW	EMPEROR OF INDIA
Where built:	Portsmouth Dockyard	Devonport Dockyard	Beardmore, Dalmuir	Vickers, Barrow
Authorised:	1911	1911	1911	1911
Laid down:	12 Jan 1912	25 Jan 1912	30 May 1912	31 May 1912
Launched:	12 Oct 1912	14 Oct 1912	12 Nov 1913	27 Nov 1913
Completed:	10 March 1914	2 June 1914	7 Oct 1914	12 Oct 1914
Fate:	demilitarised 1931–1932; scrapped 1946	scrapped 1931	scrapped 1931	scrapped 1931

Right: HMS Iron Duke *fires her 13·5in/343mm main armament against Bolshevik forces in Kaffa Bay (Feodosiya Gulf), in the Black Sea, in 1919*

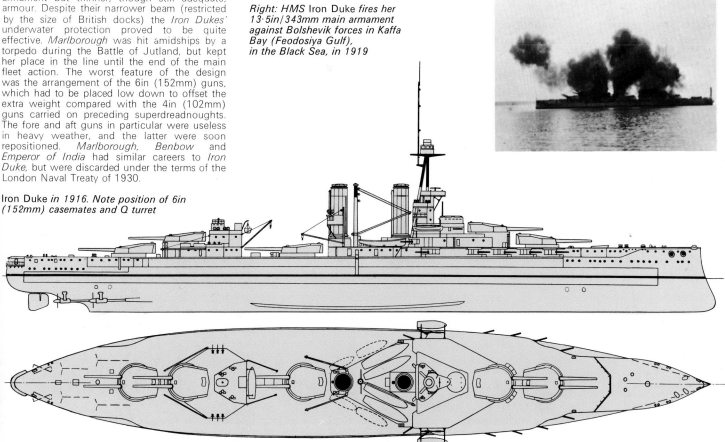

Queen Elizabeth

BATTLESHIP
CLASS: *Queen Elizabeth* class
(5 ships) *Queen Elizabeth · Valiant ·*
Warspite · Barham · Malaya

Service career QUEEN ELIZABETH
1915 (Feb–May) At Dardanelles.
1915 (26 May–11 July 1916) 5th Battle Squadron, Grand Fleet.
1915 Four aft 6in (152mm) removed.

1916 (22 May–4 June) Refit.
1917 (8 Jan–1 Feb) Refit as fleet flagship.
1917 (Feb–July 1919) Flagship Grand Fleet.
1919 (July–1924) Flagship Atlantic Fleet.
1924 (June–1926) Flagship Mediterranean Fleet.
1926 (June–Oct 1927) First reconstruction: bulges added; funnels trunked; four 4in (102mm) guns added; superstructure modified; new fore-top fitted.
1927–1929 Mediterranean Fleet.
1929 Atlantic Fleet.
1929–1937 Mediterranean Fleet.
1937 (Aug–Jan 1941) Second reconstruction: engines and boilers replaced; superstructure and funnel rebuilt; tower bridge fitted; 15in (381mm) guns' elevation increased to 30°; 6in (152mm) guns and casemates removed; 4·5in (114mm) DP battery fitted; 4in (102mm) armour added to middle deck over magazines; 2·5in (63mm) armour added over machinery; 1·5–2in (38–51mm) armour added to main deck forward 2in (51mm) armour fitted round 4·5in (114mm) guns; catapult and two hangars fitted.
1941 (Jan–May) Home Fleet.
1941 (May–Dec) Mediterranean Fleet.
1941 (June) Covered evacuation of Crete.
1941 (19 Dec) Severely damaged by Italian human torpedoes in Alexandria harbour.
1941 (Dec–May 1942) Temporary repairs at Alexandria.
1942 (6 Sept–1 June 1943) Repairing at Norfolk Navy Yard, USA.
1943 (July–Dec) Home Fleet.
1944 (Jan–July 1945) Eastern Fleet.
1945 (Aug) In reserve.
1948 (June) Deleted.
1948 (July) Scrapped.

The *Queen Elizabeths* were developed from the *Iron Dukes*, but carried a 15in (381mm) main armament to counter the 14in (356mm) guns being fitted to foreign battleships. Adopting the 15in (381mm) gun for these ships was a calculated risk, because although it had been

Displacement:	Queen Elizabeth as built	Queen Elizabeth in 1945
standard tons (tonnes)	—	32,190 (32,710)
normal tons (tonnes)	27,500 (27,940)	
full load tons (tonnes)	33,020 (33,550)	37,400 (38,000)
Dimensions:		
length (pp)	601·4ft (183·3in)	601·4ft (183·3m)
(oa)	646·1ft (196·9m)	640·9ft (195·3m)
beam	90·5ft (27·6m)	104ft (31·7m)
draught (max)	30ft (9·1m)	34·75ft (10·6m)
Armament:		
guns		
15in (381mm) 42 cal	8	8
6in (152mm) 50cal	16	—
4·5in (114mm) 45cal	—	20
3in (76mm)	1	—
3pdr (47mm)	1	—
2pdr (40mm)	—	32
20mm		54
torpedo tubes		
21in (533mm) submerged	4	—
Armour:		
side (belt)	6–13in (152–330mm)	
(ends)	4–6in (102–152mm)	
deck (fo'c's'le)	1in (25mm)	
(upper)	1·25–2in (32–51mm)	
(main)	1·25in (32mm)	
(middle)	1in (25mm)	
(lower)	1–3in (25–76mm)	
main turrets	5–13in (127–330mm)	
barbettes	4–10in (102–254mm)	
casemates	4–6in (102–152mm)	
Machinery:		
boilers (type)	Babcock and Wilcox	Admiralty 3-drum
(number)	24	8
engines (type)	Parsons turbines	Parsons single reduction geared turbines
shafts	4	4
Total SHP:		
designed	74,000	80,000
Fuel capacity		
oil tons (tonnes)	3,300 (3,350)	3,570 (3,630)
Performance:		
designed speed	25kts	24kts
service speed	23kts	23·5kts
range	8,600 miles (7,230nm) @ 12·5kts	13,500 miles (11,350nm) @ 10kts
Crew:	925	1,124

Ship:	QUEEN ELIZABETH	VALIANT	WARSPITE	BARHAM	MALAYA	AGIN-COURT
Where built:	Portsmouth Dockyard	Fairfield, Govan	Devonport Dockyard	John Brown, Clydebank	Armstrong Whitworth, High Walker	Devonport Dockyard
Authorised:	1912	1912	1912	1912	1913	1913
Cancelled:	—	—	—	—	—	Aug 1914
Laid down:	21 Oct 1912	1 Jan 1913	31 Oct 1912	24 Feb 1913	20 Oct 1913	
Launched:	16 Oct 1913	4 Nov 1914	26 Nov 1913	31 Dec 1914	18 Mar 1915	—
Completed:	Jan 1915	Feb 1915	Mar 1915	Oct 1915	Feb 1916	
First reconstruction:	1926–1927	1929–1930	1924–1926	1927–1928	1927–1929	—
Second reconstruction:	1937–1941	1937–1939	1934–1937			
Fate:	Scrapped 1948	Scrapped 1948	Total loss 23 Apr 1947; Scrapped 1950–1956	Sunk 25 Nov 1941	Scrapped 1948	

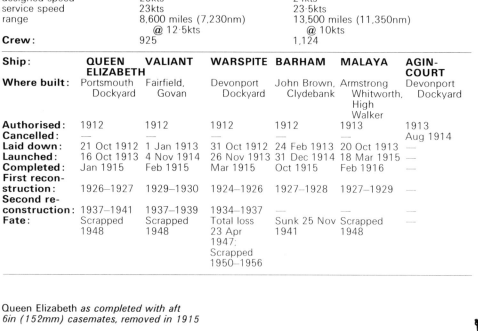

Queen Elizabeth *as completed with aft*
6in (152mm) casemates, removed in 1915

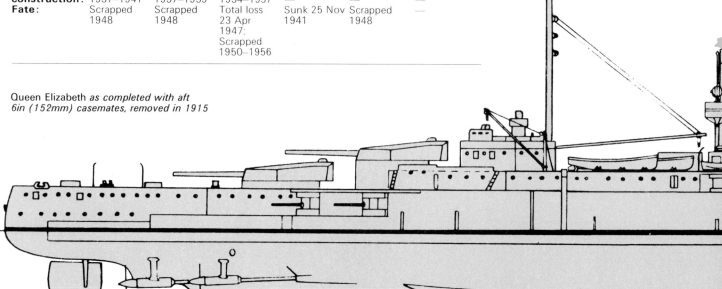

designed it had not yet been tested. In the event, the British 15in (381mm) 42cal gun proved to be one of the most successful heavy guns ever built. The first design for the new battleships had five twin turrets arranged as in the *Iron Dukes*, but it was realised that by dropping one turret, sufficient machinery could be fitted to produce a fast battleship squadron, with all its attendant tactical advantages. Britain now had sufficient tankers and oil storage facilities to enable the *Queen Elizabeths* to be totally oil-fired, but most of the weight saved by not using coal had to be used to provide better armour protection to make up for the loss of the coal bunkers that had previously provided part of the protection. The main advantages of using oil were in making refuelling easier and in reducing the engine room complement. The *Queen Elizabeths* were adequately armoured by the standards of the day, but like all contemporary battleships other than the American ones, a large part of the armour was too thin to withstand heavy shells. *Queen Elizabeth* was completed with four 6in (152mm) guns in casemates aft, but these proved impossible to work in most weathers and were soon removed. The remainder of the class were completed without them. The fifth ship, *Malaya*, was an extra vessel paid for by the Federated Malay States, and a sixth, to have been named *Agincourt*, was cancelled when two battleships building in British yards for Turkey were taken over at the start of World War I, forming a useful heavy support for the battlecruisers. *Warspite* and *Barham* in particular survived heavy damage at the Battle of Jutland, 31 May 1916, when their 15in (381mm) shells caused considerable damage to the German High Seas Fleet. The entire class were reconstructed during the late 1920s, when extra protection was worked in and the funnels trunked. *Warspite* was thoroughly reconstructed in the mid-1930s, receiving new machinery and superstructure but retaining her 6in (152mm) guns. *Queen Elizabeth* and *Valiant* benefited

from experience gained with her, and had a new second battery fitted as well. Unfortunately there was not time to rebuild *Barham* and *Malaya*. During World War II the class saw extensive service, and was used in most theatres. *Barham* was sunk by three torpedoes from the German submarine *U-331* off Sollum. *Warspite* was very badly damaged by a German glider bomb at Salerno in 1943, and was used only as a bombardment ship after that. She ran aground in Prussia Cove whilst being towed to be scrapped, and was dismantled *in situ*. *Malaya* was disarmed and used as an accommodation ship after 1944. *Valiant* was damaged by Italian human torpedoes at the same time as *Queen Elizabeth* in Alexandria harbour. She was also repaired and returned to service. The last British pre-World War I battleship design was the *Royal Sovereign* class, which were 15in (381mm) gunned versions of the *Iron Duke*

Above: Queen Elizabeth *bombarding Turkish positions at the Dardanelles in 1915. Although her 15in (381mm) guns were very effective, she was too valuable to risk and was soon recalled*

Below: HMS Queen Elizabeth *with another ship of her class behind and three* Royal Sovereign *class astern at an early 1920s Fleet Review*

class, with four twin turrets. They were originally to have been coal-fired, but were altered to oil-firing before completion. With a speed of only 22kts, they were not radically rebuilt in the inter-war years, and spent much of World War II on convoy escort duty.

Rodney

BATTLESHIP
CLASS: *Nelson* class (2 ships)
Nelson · Rodney

Service career RODNEY
1927–1939 Atlantic and Home Fleet.
1931 (Sept) Invergordon Mutiny.
1934 Refit: fitted with catapult on C turret.
1939 Fitted with radar.
1939 (Sept–Dec) Patrols in North Sea and Atlantic.
1939 (Dec) Repairs to steering gear.
1940 (Apr) Norwegian campaign.
1940 (9 Apr) Hit by dud bomb.
1940 (June–Sept) Flagship.
1941 (15–16 Mar) Sighted German battle-cruisers *Scharnhorst* and *Gneisenau*, but no action took place.
1941 (24–27 May) Searched for German battle-ship *Bismarck*.
1941 (27 May) With *King George V* destroyed *Bismarck*.
1941 (May–Aug) Refit at Boston, USA.
1941 (Sept–Nov) Mediterranean: escorted operation 'Pedestal'.
1941 (Dec–May 1942) Refit.
1942 (Nov–Oct 1943) Mediterranean: covered North Africa, Sicily and Salerno landings.
1943 (Oct–May 1945) Home Fleet.
1944 (June–Aug) Covered Normandy landings.
1945–1948 In reserve.
1948 Scrapped.

Although the British fleet was the largest and most powerful in the world at the end of World War I, both the US and Japan had laid down capital ships that outclassed anything in the Royal Navy. Britain therefore ordered four battle-cruisers on 21 October 1921 and intended to order four battleships during 1923. In designing these ships, Britain had the inestimable advantage of not only having conducted intensive tests on her own and German vessels, but also of having four years experience of battle damage and operational requirements. Neither the US nor Japan could match this, and it is not surprising that the British designs were superior to anything contemplated abroad. The battle-cruisers would have been armed with three triple 16·5in/420mm (later 16in/406mm) turrets, and would have had a speed of 33kts on a standard displacement of 46,500 tons (47,240 tonnes). They were intended to have had a 12–14in (305–356mm) armour belt inclined at 25° and an 8–9in (203–229mm) armour deck over the magazines. The battleships were to have had a speed of 23·5kts, an armament of three triple 18in (457mm) 45cal turrets and an armour belt of 15in (381mm) on a standard displacement of 48,000 tons (48,770 tonnes). Both designs were to have had their main armament concentrated forward and their machinery aft to shorten the armour belt and save weight. The bridge was to have been between the second and third turrets. However, both types were cancelled by the Washington Naval Treaty. This left Britain without any modern 16in (406mm) gunned battleships to counter the American *Colorado* class and Japanese *Nagato* class. Britain was therefore allowed to build two 16in (406mm) gunned battleships, but their maximum standard displacement was fixed at 35,000 tons (35,360 tonnes). The best features from the cancelled ships were worked into the design. The three triple 16in (406mm) turrets were mounted forward, and the bridge moved aft to shorten the hull, armour belt and deck still farther. The beam was restricted to 106ft (32·4m) by the dimensions of existing drydocks. For the first time on a British battleship an all-or-nothing protection system was adopted and the inclined armour belt was fitted about 25ft (7·6m) inboard, above the torpedo bulkhead. The outer part of the hull could be filled with water to improve the shock loading, and restrict damage. The secondary armament was concentrated aft, and consisted of six twin 6in (152mm) turrets. For the period a powerful AA armament was mounted. To save weight a twin-screw arrangement was adopted, and although *Nelson* and *Rodney* had a small turning circle, the use of twin screws, the long fo'c's'le and the tall tower bridge (adopted for the first time in a battleship) made them very unhandy ships. Also the triple 16in (406mm) turrets proved troublesome, and the 16in (406mm) gun itself was something of a disappointment when compared with the excellent British 15in (381mm) gun. However, *Nelson* and *Rodney* were very powerful ships. They were better protected than most subsequent battleships, and were superior in most respects to their foreign contemporaries. *Nelson* had a similar active career to *Rodney*, and also survived World War II.

Displacement:		
standard tons (tonnes)	33,900 (34,440)	
full load tons (tonnes)	38,000 (38,610)	
Dimensions:		
length (pp)	660ft (201·5m)	
(oa)	710ft (216·8m)	
beam	106ft (32·4m)	
draught (max)	31·5ft (9·6m)	
Armament:	**as built**	**in 1945**
guns		
16in (406mm) 45cal	9	9
6in (152mm) 50cal	12	12
4·7in (120mm) 40cal	6	—
4in (102mm)	—	8
2pdr (40mm)	—	16
40mm	—	16
20mm	—	61
torpedo tubes		
24in (610mm)	2	2
Armour:		
side (belt)	14in (356mm)	
deck (middle)	3–6·25in (76–159mm)	
(lower)	6·25in (159mm)	
main turrets	7–16in (178–406mm)	
barbettes	14–15in (356–381mm)	
secondary turrets	1–1·5in (25–38mm)	
Machinery:		
boilers (type)	Yarrow small tube	
(number)	8	
engines (type)	Brown-Curtis single reduction geared turbines	
shafts	2	
Total SHP:		
designed	45,000	
trials	46,000	
Fuel capacity:		
oil tons (tonnes)	3,755 (3,815)	
Performance:		
designed speed	23kts	
trial speed	23·8kts	
range	16,500 miles (13,870nm) @ 12kts	
Crew:	1,314	

Ship:	**RODNEY**
Where built:	Cammell Laird, Birkenhead
Ordered:	1922
Laid down:	28 Dec 1922
Launched:	17 Dec 1925
Completed:	10 Nov 1927
Fate:	Scrapped 1948

Above: Nelson *class battleship leading the Atlantic fleet in the 1930s. She is followed by* Royal Sovereign *and* Queen Elizabeth *class battleships. Note the paravane amidships.*

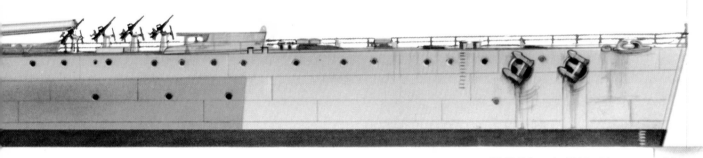

HMS Nelson *in 1945 with augmented AA armament and late war paint scheme. This class was unmistakable with three main turrets forward and the superstructure aft.*

Above: HMS Hood *in Scapa Flow in 1940 after the 5·5in (140mm) secondary armament had been removed. The battlecruiser* Renown *lies immediately astern with* Repulse *behind*

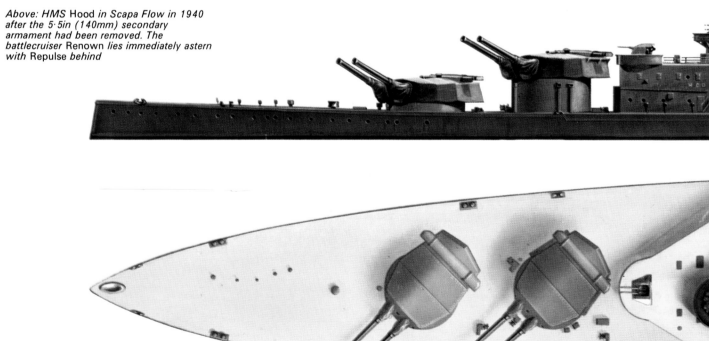

Right: Nelson *near the end of World War II. Note the 20mm forward and on C turret and the 40mm at the base of the tower bridge. She has been fitted with radar*

Right, middle: Nelson *firing a six guns broadside early in World War II. Note the camouflage scheme on the hull, turret and bridge sides. This was intended to break up her silhouette*

Above: A photo taken from Prinz Eugen *of the German battleship* Bismarck *engaging HMS* Hood *off Greenland on 24 May 1941.* Bismarck *has just fired a four gun salvo*

HOOD

VENTIS SECUNDIS

HMS Hood *in 1941. Note the UP (Unrotated Projectile) launcher on B turret. The Vice-Admiral's flag was flown during the* Bismarck *action because Vice-Admiral Whitworth was aboard*

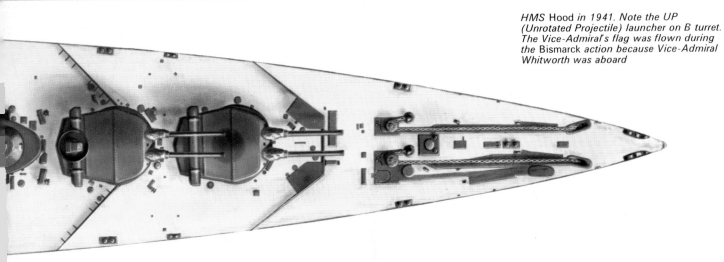

Hood

BATTLE-CRUISER
CLASS: *Hood* class (1 ship) *Hood*

Service career HOOD

1920-1929 Atlantic and Home Fleets.
1923 World Tour with 'Special Service Squadron'.
1929 (May–May 1931) Refit at Portsmouth: two octuple 2pdr (40mm) fitted and catapult mounted at stern.
1931-1936 In Home waters.
1931 (Sept) Involved in Invergordon Mutiny.
1933 Catapult removed.
1936-1939 In Mediterranean: served on Spanish neutrality patrol.
1938 Four single 4in (102mm) and octuple 2pdr (40mm) mount fitted; two 5·5in (140mm) removed.
1939 (Feb–Aug) Refit at Portsmouth: single 4in (102mm) removed and replaced by four twin mounts.
1939 (Aug–March 1940) Home Fleet: patrols in North Sea and Atlantic.
1939 (26 Sept) Hit by bomb from German aircraft: no damage.
1939 (Nov–Dec) Temporarily attached to French anti-raider squadron.
1940 (March–May) Refit at Devonport: three twin 4in (102mm) mounts added and all remaining 5·5in (140mm) removed.
1940 (June–Aug) With Force H in Mediterranean.
1940 (3 July) Bombardment of French fleet at Mers-el-Kebir: fired fifty-six 15in (381mm) shells; French battleship *Provence* and battle-cruiser *Dunkerque* badly damaged, battleship *Bretagne* sunk; stripped turbine chasing battle-cruiser *Strasbourg*.
1940 (Aug–Jan 1941) Home Fleet: patrols in North Sea and Atlantic.
1941 (Spring) Refit at Rosyth: radar fitted.
1941 (21 May) Sailed with *Prince of Wales* from Scapa Flow to intercept German battleship *Bismarck*.
1941 (24 May) Action with *Bismarck*: *Hood* sunk.

In 1914 the restrictions in the size of British capital ships imposed by the dimensions of existing drydocks were relaxed, and it became possible to plan for really large vessels. A number of different combinations of armament, armour and speed were considered, but by late 1915 the Admiralty had decided on a design with the same main armament as the *Queen Elizabeths* – eight 15in (381mm) guns – but with a speed of 33kts and comparatively light armour protection. Four ships were ordered to this design, but even before the Battle of Jutland it was realised that the protection was inadequate. Over 5,000 tons (5,100 tonnes) more armour was worked into the final design ordered in September 1916. When she was built *Hood* was the largest and most powerful capital ship in the Royal Navy. In all but name she was a fast battleship rather than a battle-cruiser, being fitted with an inclined main belt which gave equal protection to the thicker vertical armour on contemporary British battleships, and superior horizontal and underwater protection. Although the same weight of thicker armour over a small area would have given even better protection, *Hood* was well armoured by the standards of her day. Using small-tube boilers meant that she developed nearly 30 per cent more power from the same weight of machinery as the preceding large-tube boilered *Renown* class battle-cruisers. By 1917 it was obvious that Germany was concentrating on submarines at the expense of the *Mackensen* class, and so *Anson*, *Howe* and *Rodney* were suspended and then cancelled. It was recognised that better designs could be prepared in the light of wartime experience, but it was decided to complete *Hood* mainly to gain experience with a very large fast ship and to try out an inclined belt and the new system of underwater protection, which used tubes inside the bulges to absorb torpedo damage. She would also be a counter to the German battle-cruiser *Mackensen* (which was never completed) and provide continuity of work for the British armour manufacturers. If *Anson*, *Howe* and *Rodney* had been completed they would have differed significantly from *Hood*, with revised armour incorporating improved horizontal protection, modified hull and superstructure, and funnels

Displacement:	in 1920	in 1941
standard tons (tonnes)	41,200 (41,860)	42,100 (42,770)
full load tons (tonnes)	44,600 (45,310)	46,200 (46,940)
Dimensions:		
length (pp)	810ft (246·8m)	810ft (246·8m)
(oa)	860·6ft (262·8m)	860·6ft (262·8m)
beam (wl)	95ft (29m)	95ft (29m)
(ext)	105·2ft (34·5m)	105·2ft (34·5m)
draught (max)	31·5ft (9·6m)	33·3ft (10·2m)
Armament:		
guns		
15in (381mm) 42cal	8	8
5·5in (140mm) 50cal	12	—
4in (102mm)	4	14
2pdr (40mm)	—	24
0·5in (12·7mm)	—	8
torpedo tubes		
21in (533mm)	6	4
Armour		
side (belt)	5–12in (127–305mm)	
(ends)	5–6in (127–152mm)	
deck (fo'c's'le)	1·5in (38mm)	
(upper)	0·75–1in (19–25mm)	
(main)	1·5–3in (38–76mm)	
(lower)	1–2in (25–51mm)	
Machinery:		
boilers (type)	Yarrow small tube	
(number)	24	
engines (type)	Brown-Curtis single geared turbines	
shafts	4	
Total SHP:		
designed	144,000	144,000
trials	151,280	?
Fuel capacity:		
oil normal tons (tonnes)	1,200 (1,220)	
max tons (tonnes)	4,000 (4,060)	
Performance:		
designed speed	31kts	—
trial speed	32·07kts	28·8kts
range	5,950 miles	?
	(5,170nm) @ 18kts	?
Crew:	1,169	1,421

Ship:	HOOD	ANSON	HOWE	RODNEY
Where built:	John Brown, Clydebank	Armstrong Walker	Cammell Laird, Birkenhead	Fairfield, Govan
Ordered (original design):	17 Apr 1916	July 1916	April 1916	April 1916
(final design):	1 Sept 1916	1 Sept 1916	1 Sept 1916	1 Sept 1916
Laid down:	1 Sept 1916	1 Sept 1916	1 Sept 1916	1 Sept 1916
Cancelled:	—	Oct 1918	Oct 1918	Oct 1918
Launched:	22 Aug 1918	—	—	—
Completed:	5 March 1920	—	—	—
Fate:	Sunk 24 May 1941	Scrapped incomplete	Scrapped incomplete	Scrapped incomplete

Above: Hood *running trials in 1920. She is in light condition and the quarterdeck (unusually) is well clear of the water. She has not yet been handed over to the Navy*

set much closer together. When cancelled they were only from 3 to 4 per cent complete. *Hood* had an impressive appearance and was extensively used for 'showing the flag' between the wars. She was a good seaboat, but the extra armour made her ride deep, and the quarter deck was frequently awash, especially in shallow water. Her plans were shown to the Americans near the end of World War I, and had a great influence on their subsequent designs. It had been intended to reconstruct her completely in 1939 in a similar fashion to *Queen Elizabeth* and *Renown*, because her anti-aircraft armament and horizontal protection were no longer adequate. Her 5·5in (140mm) and 4in (102mm) guns were to be replaced by eight twin 5·25in (133mm) dual-purpose mounts, and her horizontal protection was to have been increased. Her armoured control tower and forward superstructure were to have been replaced by a tower bridge, and the remaining superstructure remodelled. New machinery was to be installed, and the vertical armour and underwater protection strengthened. However, this would have taken at least two years, and the threat of war was too great to allow a major unit to be out of action for so long. Her armour was still adequate at short and medium ranges, but she was hit by *Bismarck*'s fifth salvo before she had closed the range sufficiently. This may have penetrated a magazine, but it is more likely that they set off *Hood*'s upper deck torpedoes, and she was blown in two. Only three of the crew survived.

Duke of York

BATTLESHIP

CLASS: *King George V* class
(5 ships) *King George V · Prince of Wales · Duke of York* (ex-*Anson*) · *Anson* (ex-*Jellicoe*) · *Howe* (ex-*Beatty*)

Service career DUKE OF YORK

1941 (10–22 Dec) Takes Mr Churchill to USA.
1942 (3–17 Jan) Work-up cruise to Bermuda.
1942 (30 Jan) To Scapa Flow.
1942 (2–10 March) Search for German battleship *Tirpitz*.
1942 (March-Sept) Covers Russian convoys.
1942 (May 6–July 8) Flagship of Home Fleet.
1942 (Oct) Refit.
1942 (Oct 30–Nov 15) Flagship of Force H: covers North African landings.
1942 (Nov 26) Returns to Scapa Flow.
1942 (Dec–March 1943) Refit.
1943 (8 May–18 Sept 1944) Flagship of Home Fleet: covers Russian convoys and air strikes against German battleship *Tirpitz*..
1944 (23 Dec–1 Jan) Covers convoy JW55B.
1943 (26 Dec) Battle of North Cape: destroys German battle-cruiser *Scharnhorst*.
1943 (27 Dec) Arrives at Kola Inlet, USSR.
1944 (1 Jan) Returns to Scapa Flow.
1944 (Sept–March 1945) Refit: anti-aircraft armament improved; bridge modified.
1945 (April–July) Sails to Far East.
1945 (July–June 1946) Flagship of British Pacific Fleet.
1945 (2 Sept) In Tokyo Bay for Japanese surrender.
1946 (June–July) Returns to UK.
1946 (July–April 1949) Flagship of Home Fleet.
1949 (July–Sept 1951) Flagship of Home Fleet.
1951 (Nov) In reserve.
1957 (May) Deleted.
1958 Scrapped.

Although a number of battleship designs were prepared in the late 1920s and early 1930s, these were mostly intended to show whether various suggested limitations in size and armament were practical. Under the terms of the Washington Treaty, the standard displacement of battleships was limited to 35,000 tons (35,560 tonnes), and the maximum calibre of the main armament to 16in (406mm). The first designs for the *King George Vs* were prepared in 1934, and were for relatively slow ships with a main armament of nine 15in (381mm) guns in triple turrets, and a secondary armament of 6in (152mm) guns. This was almost immediately altered to twin 4·7in (120mm) mounts, and the final design had *Dido* light cruiser type

5·25in (133mm) DP twin turrets. The 1935 designs were for faster ships, but the Naval Limitation Treaty of that year laid down a maximum calibre of 14in (356mm) unless a Washington Treaty signatory failed to ratify this. Great Britain had already placed orders for 14in (356mm) guns in the early 1930s, and their use was decided upon by the Admiralty on a practical rather than a treaty viewpoint. Japan failed to ratify this provision, and so 16in (406mm) guns were permitted after April 1937. By this time two of the *King George V* class were already being built. However, partly as a safeguard against the provision not being ratified, and partly as a counter to existing foreign

Above: The King George V *class battleship HMS* Duke of York *steaming at high speed, ready to open fire with her main armament*

ships, the *King George Vs* were armoured against 16in (406mm) shells, and were much better protected than any foreign contemporaries. The original armament was to have been twelve 14in (356mm) guns in three triple turrets, but to ensure that the horizontal protection was adequate B turret was reduced to a twin mount and the weight saved was used for extra armour. Like the *Nelsons*, this class had all-or-nothing armour protection, but the sloping

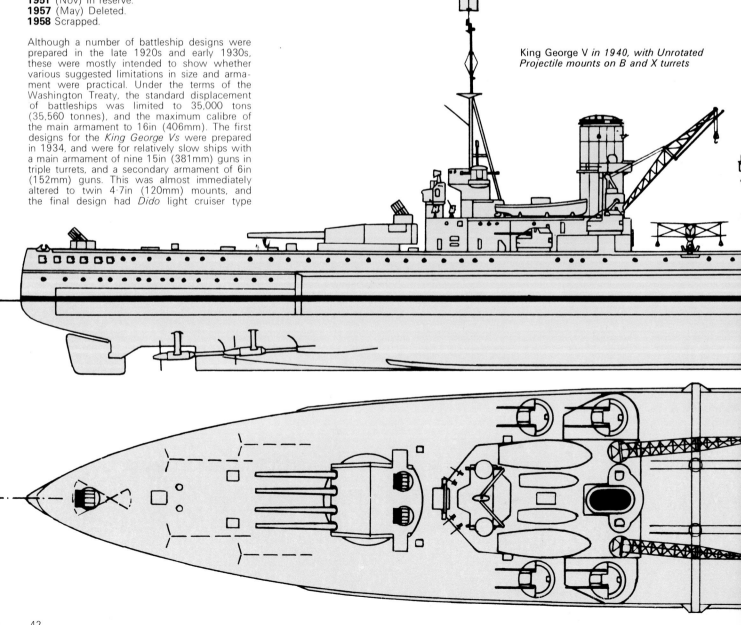

King George V in 1940, with Unrotated Projectile mounts on B and X turrets

internal belt was abandoned: it was too difficult to repair when damaged and an external belt provided a greater armoured reserve of buoyancy. They also had improved horizontal armour and protection for the ends of the ship. The main armour deck rested on top of the deep belt with all the ship's communications arranged beneath it. The adoption of a smaller gun than their foreign equivalents was not particularly important. The 14in (356mm) shell was quite adequate to pierce most battleship armour at most battle ranges. The problem with sinking the German battleship *Bismarck* was that *King George V* and *Rodney* were forced to close the range too much to ensure hits before their fuel ran out. The *Bismarck* action and later operations in the Pacific highlighted the *King George Vs'* short range. This was a deliberate choice to ensure that the ships had sufficient offensive and defensive qualities on the limited displacement. Although they were not as manoeuvrable as the American *Washington* class battleships, they were a considerable improvement on the *Nelsons*. Their worst feature was the limited freeboard at the bow, caused by a staff requirement for point-blank fire dead ahead from A turret. Although the quadruple turrets had some teething troubles (most notably on *Prince of Wales* during the action with *Bismarck*), those were inevitable on any complex turret, and were soon overcome. *Prince of Wales*, though hit by several shells from *Bismarck* (most of which failed to explode), was very little damaged. Her loss seven months later was primarily due to the lack of recent experience with shock damage. Attacked by Japanese bombers and torpedo aircraft off Malaya, her auxiliary motor mountings were broken by blast from near misses, and this deprived the AA armament and

pumps of power. The remaining ships of the class were later modified to prevent this problem recurring. *King George V* was flagship of the Home Fleet for some time, took part in the sinking of *Bismarck*, and later went to the Pacific, as did *Howe* and *Anson*. The later ships incorporated a number of improvements suggested by early war experience. All surviving ships were fitted with radar and a much improved light AA armament in the later part of World War II, and had their aircraft removed in 1943–1944. Four modified versions with nine 16in (406mm) guns were laid down as the *Lion* class, but were cancelled in 1940. A final battleship, *Vanguard*, was built in the later part of World War II. She incorporated four old twin 15in (381mm) turrets to speed production, and was a larger and more seaworthy ship.

Displacement:	Duke of York as designed	Duke of York in 1945
standard tons (tonnes)	35,990 (36,566)	39,460 (40,090)
full load tons (tonnes)	40,990 (41,646)	44,780 (45,496)
Dimensions:		
length (pp)	700ft (213·7m)	
(oa)	745ft (227·5m)	
beam	103ft (31·5m)	
draught	34·5ft (10·5m)	
Armament:	**in 1941**	**in 1945**
guns		
14in (356mm) 45cal	10	10
5·25in (133mm)	16	16
2pdr (40mm)	48	88
40mm	—	8
20mm	—	55
0·5in (12·7mm)	16	—
aircraft	3	3
Armour:		
side (belt)	4·5–15in (114–381mm)	
deck (main)	5–6in (127–152mm)	
(lower)	2·5–5in (63–127mm)	
main turrets	6–13in (152–330mm)	
barbettes	11–13in (280–330mm)	
secondary turrets	1–1·5in (25–38mm)	
Machinery:		
boilers (type)	Admiralty 3-drum	
(number)	8	
engines (type)	Parsons single reduction geared turbines	
shafts	4	
Total SHP:		
designed	125,000	
Fuel capacity:		
oil tons (tonnes)	3,700 (3,760)	
Performance:		
designed speed	29·5kts	
range	14,000 miles (11,770nm) @ 10kts	
Crew:	1,644	

Ship:	KING GEORGE V	PRINCE OF WALES	DUKE OF YORK (ex-ANSON)	ANSON (ex-JELLICOE)	HOWE (ex-BEATTY)
Where built:	Vickers- Armstrong, Tyne	Cammell Laird, Birkenhead	John Brown, Clydebank	Swan Hunter, Wallsend	Fairfield,
Authorised:	?	?	?	?	?
Laid down:	1 Jan 1937	1 Jan 1937	5 May 1937	20 July 1937	1 June 1937
Launched:	21 Feb 1939	21 Feb 1939	28 Feb 1940	24 Feb 1940	9 Apr 1940
Completed:	1 Oct 1940	31 Mar 1941	4 Nov 1941	22 June 1942	29 Aug 1942
Fate	Scrapped 1957	Sunk 10 Dec 1941	Scrapped 1958	Scrapped 1957	Scrapped 1958

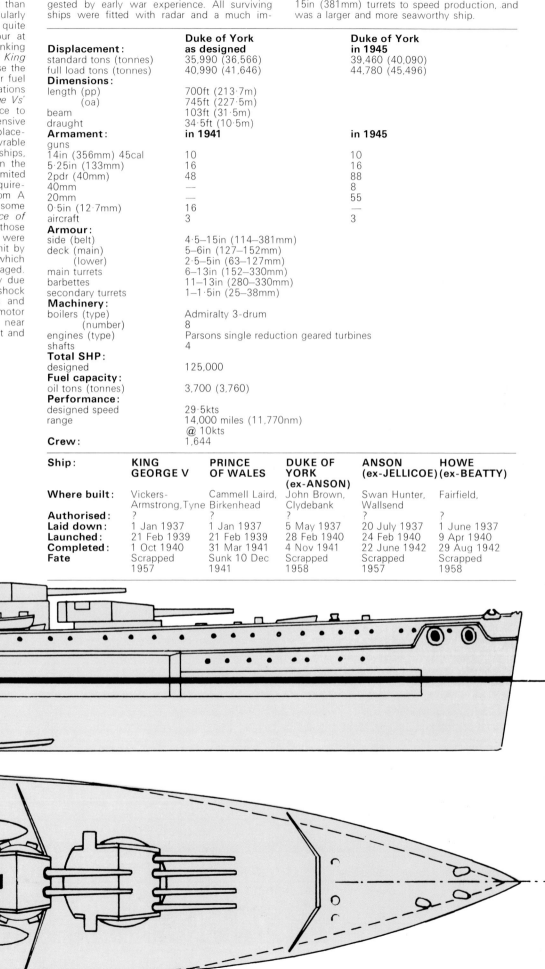

Agincourt

BATTLESHIP

CLASS: *Agincourt* class (1 ship)
Agincourt (ex-*Sultan Osman I*,
ex- *Rio de Janeiro*)

Displacement:	
normal tons (tonnes)	27,500 (27,940)
full load tons (tonnes)	30,250 (30,734)
Dimensions:	
length (pp)	632ft (193m)
(oa)	668ft (204m)
beam	89ft (27·2m)
draught	27ft (8·2m)
Armament:	
guns	
12in (305mm) 45cal	14
6in (152mm)	20
3in (76mm)	10
torpedo tubes	
21in (533mm)	3
Armour:	
side (belt)	6–9in (152–229mm)
(ends)	4–6in (102–152mm)
deck (fo'c's'le)	1·5in (38mm)
(upper)	1·5in (38mm)
(main)	1–2·5in (25–63mm)
(lower)	1–1·5in (25–38mm)
main turrets	8–12in (203–305mm)
barbettes	9in (229mm)
casemates	6in (152mm)
Machinery:	
boilers (type)	Babcock & Wilcox
(number)	22
engines (type)	Parsons turbines
shafts	4
Total SHP:	
designed	32,000
trial	40,279
Fuel capacity:	
coal normal tons (tonnes)	1,500 (1,524)
max tons (tonnes)	3,200 (3,250)
oil tons (tonnes)	620 (630)
Performance:	
designed speed	22kts
trial speed	22·42kts
range	4,500 miles
	(3,780nm) @ 10kts
Crew:	1,115

Ship:	AGINCOURT, ex-SULTAN OSMAN I, ex-RIO DE JANEIRO
Where built:	Armstrong Whitworth, Elswick
Authorised:	Oct 1910
Laid down:	14 Sept 1911
Launched:	22 Jan 1913
Completed:	20 Aug 1914
Fate:	Scrapped 1924

Service career AGINCOURT

1911–1914 Built for Brazil as *Rio de Janeiro.*
1914 (9 Jan) Sold to Turkey: renamed *Sultan Osman I.*
1914 (July) Ran trials without two 12in (305mm) guns.
1914 (3 Aug) Seized by UK and renamed *Agincourt.*
1914 (30 Aug) Completed: boat decks removed.
1916 (31 May) Battle of Jutland.
1918 Two 3in (76mm) added; bridge enlarged.
1919 For disposal.
1922 Started conversion to training ship.
1922 (Dec) Sold to Rosyth Shipbreaking Co.
1924 Scrapped.

After studying designs with 14in (356mm) and 16in (406mm) guns, the Brazilians adopted the same twin 12in (305mm) turret as that fitted to *Minas Geraes* for *Rio de Janeiro* in order to simplify ammunition and spares supply and maintenance. Although this meant a long hull in order to carry the seven turrets necessary to outgun the Argentinian *Morenos*, she was little longer than the Chilean *Almirante Latorres*, and was almost as well protected as the Argentinian and Chilean ships. Moreover, the large number of twin turrets permitted large salvos, an important point for a South American navy. She was sold to Turkey during a financial crisis because of doubts about the value of the design, and was seized by the Royal Navy to increase its superiority over the German High Seas Fleet, and to ensure that *Sultan Osman I*, as she had been renamed, was not used against the British in the Mediterranean.

Above: Originally built for Brazil and seized from Turkey in 1914, HMS Agincourt *leads the 4th Battle Squadron into Scapa Flow in April 1915*

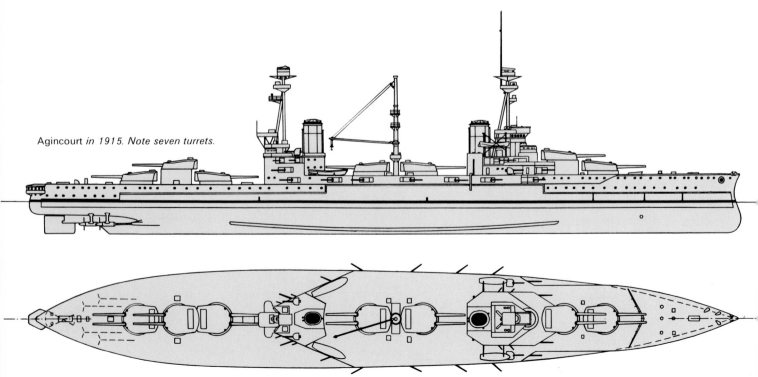

Agincourt *in 1915. Note seven turrets.*

Warrior
ARMOURED CRUISER
CLASS: *Warrior* class (4 ships)
Cochrane · Achilles · Natal · Warrior

Service career WARRIOR
1908–1914 In Mediterranean.
1914 1st Cruiser Squadron in Mediterranean.
1914–1916 1st Cruiser Squadron, Grand Fleet: flagship of Rear-Admiral Arbuthnot.
1916 (31 May) Battle of Jutland: hit by about 15 heavy shells; disabled and towed by *Engadine*.
1916 (1 June) Foundered.

The *Warriors* were half sisters of the preceding *Duke of Edinburghs*, which were the first British armoured cruisers for ten years to mount 9·2in (234mm) guns. They carried six such guns, one on a raised fo'c's'le, two on either broadside and one at the stern. Ten 6in (152mm) guns were mounted in casemates beneath the broadside guns. These were unworkable in most seas, and were replaced on the *Warriors* by four 7·5in (190mm) guns, mounted two on each broadside between the 9·2in (234mm) guns in single turrets. They were succeeded by the less successful *Minotaurs*, which mounted four 9·2in (230mm) and ten 7·5in (190mm) guns, but both were completely outclassed by the *Invincible* class battle-cruisers, completed at the same time as the *Minotaurs*. Nevertheless, the *Warriors* compared very well with foreign armoured cruisers, and would have been more than a match for the German *Scharnhorsts*. *Cochrane* was stranded in the Mersey, *Achilles* survived World War I, and *Natal* suffered an internal explosion in Cromarty Firth and blew up.

Below: HMS Warrior, *name-ship of a class of four armoured cruisers completed in 1907, early in 1915. The fifth funnel belongs to a merchant vessel alongside*

Displacement:	
normal tons (tonnes)	13,550 (13,767)
full load tons (tonnes)	15,230 (15,474)
Dimensions:	
length (pp)	480ft (146·6m)
(oa)	505·5ft (154·4m)
beam	73·5ft (22·4m)
draught (max)	27·5ft (8·4m)
Armament:	
guns	
9·2in (234mm) 45cal	6
7·5in (190mm) 50cal	4
3pdr (47mm)	24
0·303in (7·7m)	4
torpedo tubes	
18in (457mm)	3
Armour:	
side (belt)	6in (152mm)
(ends)	3–4in (76–102mm)
deck	0·75–1·5in (19–38mm)
main turrets	6–8in (152–203mm)
barbettes	7in (178mm)
Machinery:	
boilers (type)	Yarrow large tubes and cylindrical
(number)	19 and 6
engines (type)	vertical triple expansion
shafts	2
Total IHP:	
designed	23,500
Fuel capacity:	
coal normal tons (tonnes)	1,000 (1,020)
max tons (tonnes)	2,050 (2,080)
oil tons (tonnes)	600 (610)
Performance:	
designed speed	22·33kts
range	?
Crew:	704

Ship:	COCHRANE	ACHILLES	NATAL	WARRIOR
Where built:	Fairfield, Govan	Armstrong, Elswick	Vickers, Barrow	Pembroke Dockyard
Authorised:	?	?	?	?
Laid down:	24 March 1904	22 Feb 1904	6 Jan 1904	5 Nov 1903
Launched:	20 May 1905	17 June 1905	30 Sept 1905	1 Nov 1905
Completed:	1907	1907	1907	1907
Fate:	Total loss 14 Nov 1918	Sold for scrap 9 May 1921	Blew up 30 Dec 1915	Foundered 1 June 1916

Warrior as built. Note two 7·5in (190mm) turrets amidships between 9·2in (234mm)

Lion

BATTLE-CRUISER

CLASS: *Lion* class (3 ships) *Lion ·
Princess Royal · Queen Mary*

Service career LION
1914 (Aug–1915) Flagship 1st Battle-Cruiser
Squadron.
1914 (28 Aug) Battle of Heligoland Bight.
1915 (24 Jan) Battle of Dogger Bank: hit by 18
heavy shells; damaged and feedwater con-
taminated; towed by battle-cruiser *Indomitable.*
1915–1918 Flagship Battle-Cruiser Force.
1916 (31 May) Battle of Jutland: hit by 12
heavy shells; Q turret burned out.
1916 (June–July) Repaired: Q turret temporarily
removed.
1917 (17 Nov) Battle of the Heligoland Bight.
1922 (Dec) Deleted.
1924 Scrapped.

From the *Cressys* onward, most British armoured
cruisers had been designed as larger, faster and
lighter armed and armoured versions of contemporary battleships. Many had 9·2in (234mm)
guns which were capable of penetrating contemporary battleship armour at close range, and
they were sufficiently well protected to be used
in the line in an emergency. The 17,250 ton
(17,530 tonne) normal displacement *Invincible*
class battle-cruisers built between 1906 and
1908 were similarly designed as larger, faster
and more lightly armoured versions of *Dreadnought*, and (unlike earlier armoured cruisers)
they had the same calibre main armament. This
was on the insistence of 'Jackie' Fisher, who
visualised them overwhelming hostile armoured
cruisers, and being able to cut off and destroy
portions of a slower hostile battlefleet. When
they were designed in 1904–5 the maximum
battle-range envisaged was 9,000 yards
(8,240m), and they were armoured against
individual 12in (305mm) shell hits at this range.
Indeed it is doubtful whether *Invincible*'s loss
at Jutland on 31 May 1916 was due to her
armour being pierced, even though the range
was greater. Most probably she exploded and
sank because of the sensitive cordite and faulty
flash arrangements fitted in British heavy gun
turrets. However, though their armour protection was better than most critics make out, they
were not suited to the role of fast battleship
as envisaged by Fisher, and they were larger and
heavier armed than was necessary for reconnaissance and running down hostile armoured
cruisers. Nonetheless, again at Fisher's insistence, three very similar ships of the *Indefatigable* class were built between 1909 and
1913. These differed mainly from the *Invincibles*
in having a larger hull to permit the two amidships echelon turrets to fire over large arcs on
each broadside. Whereas the design of the
Invincibles could be justified by the lack of any
foreign equivalents, the first true German battle-
cruiser, *Von der Tann*, was already under construction when the *Indefatigables* were designed,
and sufficient details were known in Britain for
it to be certain that they were outclassed before
they were laid down. Fisher, who dominated
British warship design during this period, was
obsessed by speed and gunpower, and failed to
realise the necessity for producing better
balanced designs which would not be so
speedily outclassed by later construction.
Without his influence, it would have been
possible to produce a much better ship with a
similar performance and armament, but with
much better protection, on a similar displacement. The *Lions*, which were designed when

Displacement:	Lion		Queen Mary	
normal tons (tonnes)	26,270 (26,990)		26,500 (26,924)	
full load tons (tonnes)	29,680 (30,155)		29,680 (30,155)	
Dimensions:				
length (pp)	660ft (201·2m)		660ft (201·2m)	
(oa)	700ft (213·4m)		704ft (214·6m)	
beam	88·5ft (27m)		88·5ft (27m)	
draught	28·8ft (8·8m)		28·8ft (8·8m)	
Armament:	**Lion as built**		**Lion in 1918**	
guns				
13·5in (343mm) 45cal	8		8	
4in (102mm)	16		15	
3in (76mm)	—		1	
torpedo tubes				
21in (533mm)	2		2	
Armour:				
side (belt)	4–9in (102–229mm)			
deck (upper)	1in (25mm)			
(main)	1–2·5in (25–63mm)			
main turrets	4–9in (102–229mm)			
barbettes	9in (229mm)			
Machinery:				
boilers (type)	Yarrow			
(number)	42			
engines (type)	Parsons turbines			
shafts	4			
Total SHP:	**Lion**		**Queen Mary**	
designed	70,000		75,000	
trials	73,800		78,700	
Fuel capacity:				
coal normal tons (tonnes)	1,000 (1,016)		1,000 (1,016)	
max tons (tonnes)	3,500 (3,556)		3,700 (3,760)	
oil tons (tonnes)	1,135 (1,153)		1,130 (1,148)	
Performance:				
designed speed	27kts		27kts	
trial speed	27kts		28kts	
range	5,610 miles (4,720nm) @ 10kts			
Crew:	997			

Ship:	LION	PRINCESS ROYAL	QUEEN MARY
Where built:	Devonport Dockyard	Vickers, Barrow	Palmers, Jarrow
Authorised:	1909	1909	1910
Laid down:	29 Nov 1909	2 May 1910	26 Mar 1911
Launched:	6 Aug 1910	29 Apr 1911	20 Mar 1912
Completed:	May 1912	Nov 1912	Sept 1913
Fate:	Scrapped 1924	Scrapped 1926	Sunk 31 May 1916

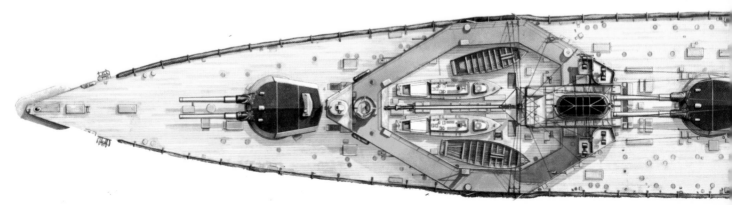

Fisher was still First Sea Lord, were much better ships, but this was not because they were better balanced but because they were much larger and more powerful. They were laid down almost simultaneously with the *Indefatigables,* but were battle-cruiser versions of the *Orion* class superdreadnoughts. They were 95ft (29m) longer overall and 7,770 tons (7,890 tonnes) larger than the *Indefatigables.* There were four twin centreline 13·5in (343mm) turrets, with a superfiring pair forward, Q turret at fo'c's'le deck level amidships, and X turret on the quarterdeck aft. The position of Q turret was the worst feature of this design. Although it permitted a lighter hull by not concentrating the weight at the ends of the ship, it inconveniently separated the boiler rooms, and severely restricted Q turret's arcs of fire. Despite much criticism the armour (albeit thin) was adequate, though in this respect the *Lions* compared

badly with contemporary German battle-cruisers. *Lion* and *Princess Royal* when first completed had the tripod foremast and main fire control behind the forefunnel. Winston Churchill, when he became First Lord of the Admiralty, rightly insisted that this should be altered to prevent the fire control being made uninhabitable by smoke. The tripod mast was therefore repositioned in front of the forefunnel. *Queen Mary* was completed in this form, and she also incorporated other modifications gained from experience with the first two ships. Faulty flash arrangements in British heavy gun turrets caused her loss at Jutland, when a hit on the roof of Q turret set off its magazine. After Jutland the other two ships were modified along with the rest of the Grand Fleet to eliminate this fault. Both ships were discarded under the terms of the Washington Treaty. *Tiger* was to have been completed to a similar design as *Queen Mary,*

Above: HMS Lion *in*
1914 after the foremast had been
moved in front of the forefunnel

but incorporated modifications fitted in the Japanese battle-cruiser *Kongo,* which was based on the *Lions.* Although the third and fourth turrets were still separated by the engines, the third turret was sited aft of the funnels and boiler rooms, and had clear arcs of fire aft. Like the contemporary *Iron Duke* class battleships she had a 6in (152mm) secondary armament. Because of the extra weight over the *Lions'* 4in (102mm) guns, they were carried a deck lower. A reason for the relatively poor performance of this excellent ship during World War I may have been because a large part of her crew was made up of deserters and defaulters. She was discarded under the terms of the 1930 London Naval Treaty.

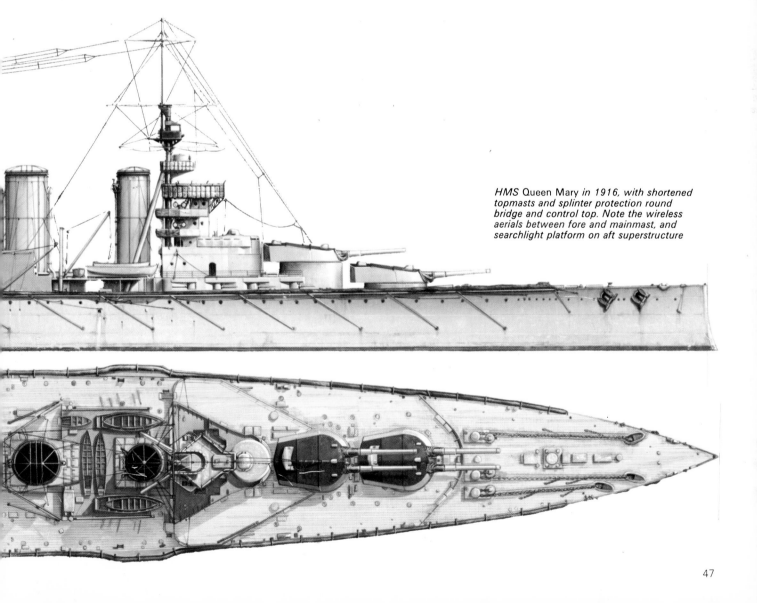

HMS Queen Mary *in 1916, with shortened topmasts and splinter protection round bridge and control top. Note the wireless aerials between fore and mainmast, and searchlight platform on aft superstructure*

County Class

CRUISER
CLASS: *Kent* class (7 ships)
Britain 5 ships *Kent · Berwick ·*
Cornwall · Cumberland · Suffolk ·
Australia 2 ships *Australia · Canberra*

CRUISER
CLASS: *London* class (4 ships)
London · Devonshire · Shropshire ·
Sussex

CRUISER
CLASS: *Norfolk* class (2 ships)
Norfolk · Dorsetshire

During the early part of World War I Britain concentrated on building *Arethusa* and C class cruisers, which were suitable for operations in the North Sea but were too small and too short ranged for use overseas. A new design for a large light cruiser was prepared and five were built during the later part of the war by yards with surplus capacity for building large warships. These were the *Vindictive* class. They had a standard displacement of between 9,550–9,800 tons (9,700–9,960 tonnes). Four were built with an armament of seven 7·5in (191mm) guns and one, *Vindictive*, was completed as an aircraft-carrier, though she was rebuilt as a cruiser between 1923 and 1925. The existence of these recent ships caused the Washington Treaty cruiser limits to be set at 10,000 tons (10,160 tonnes) standard displacement with a maximum calibre of 8in (203mm) guns. However, the *Vindictives* did

not serve as the basis for future British cruiser development because they were designed too soon to incorporate the lessons learned during World War I. Immediately after the end of the war Britain, like the other major powers, considered building very large long ranged cruisers with a heavy armament, but after the Washington Treaty limits had been set a new design was prepared to comply with them. The *Counties* were designed for Pacific operations (this being considered the most likely area of conflict in the 1920s) and they had an excellent range and high freeboard as well as a strong and durable hull. Although the number of guns was less than those mounted in most foreign contemporaries, the higher rate of fire of the *Counties'* power-worked twin turrets more than compensated for this. The 8in (203mm) guns were given 70° elevation to enable them to be used for AA defence. This made the mounting very complicated, and it was some years before all the problems were ironed out. However, the result was an excellent turret and the 8in (203mm) gun performed very well during World War II, penetrating German heavy armour with ease. Much ill-informed criticism was levelled at these excellent ships, but although some foreign contemporaries made less attempt to comply with the treaty limitations, none could compare with the *Counties'* strength, seaworthiness, habitability or weight of fire. The *Kents* had external bulges, and were originally completed with short funnels which were raised almost immediately. The *Londons* had better distributed armour and were fitted with internal bulges. They were completed with the taller funnels, and the bridge was 15ft (4·6m) farther aft than on the *Kents*. The *Norfolks* could be distinguished from the *Londons* by their lower bridge. Two further ships, *Northumberland* and *Surrey*, were cancelled in 1930 in favour of 6in (152mm) cruisers, numbers being considered more important than size. They would have differed considerably from the earlier ships, with much greater armour protection to match developments abroad. The *Counties* were designed to have multiple 2pdr (40mm) mountings, but these were not available until the early 1930s, when they were fitted along with catapults and aircraft. The British *Kents* were reconstructed between 1935 and 1938, when twin 4in (102mm) mounts replaced some of the single mounts and a large hangar and extra armour were fitted. *Kent*, *Cumberland* and *Suffolk* were cut down aft, but this proved to be unnecessary and *Berwick* and *Cornwall* retained the flush deck. *Suffolk* was one of the first British warships to have a production radar set, and the rest of the *Counties* were also early recipients. By the late 1930s these ships were outclassed by later foreign 8in (203mm) cruisers, and *London* was completely rebuilt between 1939 and 1941 with a tower bridge, two funnels, improved AA armament and redistributed armour. She was intended to be the prototype for further reconstructions, but was not a success. The extra weight caused serious problems with her longitudinal strength. Although *London* was refitted in 1946 she was

	KENT in 1939	LONDON as built	LONDON in 1945	NORFOLK as built
Displacement:				
standard tons (tonnes)	10,570 (10,740)	9,850 (10,010)	11,015 (11,190)	9,925 (10,080)
full load tons (tonnes)	14,450 (14,680)	14,000 (14,220)	?	13,450 (13,670)
Dimensions:				
length (pp)	590ft (180·2m)	595ft (181·7m)	595ft (181·7m)	590ft (180·2m)
(oa)	630ft (192·4m)	633ft (193·3m)	633ft (193·3m)	630ft (192·4m)
beam	68·5ft (20·9m)	66ft (20·2m)	66ft (20·2m)	66ft (20·2m)
draught	21·25ft (6·5m)	21·5ft (6·6m)	?	21·5ft (6·6m)
Armament:				
8in (203mm)	8	8	8	8
4in (102mm)	8	8	8	8
2pdr (40mm)	8	—	16	—
40mm	—	—	4	—
20mm	—	—	20	—
0·5in (12·7mm)	8	8	—	8
torpedo tubes				
21in (533mm)	8	8	8	8
aircraft	1	—	3	—
Armour:				
side (belt)	1–5·5in (25–140mm)	1–5·5in (25–140mm)	?	1in (25mm)
deck (lower)	1·4–1·5in (35–38mm)	1·4–1·5in (35–38mm)	?	1·4–1·5in (35–38mm)
magazine	2·5in (64mm)	1–2·5in (25–64mm)	?	2·5in (64mm)
main turrets	1·5–2in (38–52mm)	1·5–2in (38–52mm)	1·5–2in (38–52mm)	1·5–2in (38–52mm)
barbettes	1in (25mm)	1in (25mm)	1in (25mm)	1in (25mm)
Machinery:				
boilers (type)	Admiralty 3-drum			
(number)	8			
engines (type)	Parsons or Brown-Curtis geared turbines			
shafts	4			
Total SHP:				
designed	80,000	80,000	80,000	80,000
Fuel capacity:				
oil tons (tonnes)	3,400 (3,450)	3,210 (3,260)	?	3,210 (3,260)
Performance:				
designed speed	31·5kts	32·25kts	?	32·25kts
range	12,370 miles (10,400nm) @ 14kts	12,370 miles (10,400nm) @ 14kts	?	12,370 miles (10,400nm) @ 14kts
Crew	685	700	789	700

Class:	KENT class	LONDON class	NORFOLK class
Where built:	various yards	various yards	Portsmouth Dockyard and Fairfield, Govan
Authorised:	1924–1925	1925–1926	1926–1927
Laid down:	1924	1926	1927
Launched:	1926–1927	1927–1928	1928–1929
Completed:	1928	1929	1930
Fate:	*Cornwall* sunk 5 Apr 1942; *Canberra* sunk 9 Aug 1942; *Berwick, Kent, Suffolk*, scrapped 1948; *Australia* scrapped 1955; *Cumberland* scrapped 1959	*London* rebuilt 1939–1941, scrapped 1950; remainder scrapped 1954–1955	*Dorsetshire* sunk 5 Apr 1942; *Norfolk* scrapped 1950

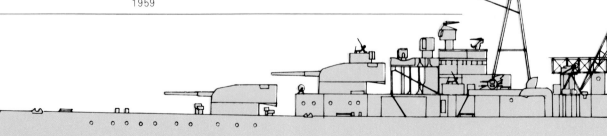

Above: The Australian Kent *class cruiser HMAS* Canberra *at speed soon after completion. Note the seaworthy hull and distinctive silhouette*

the first of the class to be scrapped. *Sussex* was partially rebuilt after bomb damage, and surviving *Counties* received extra light AA guns and improved radar during World War II. In 1947 *Devonshire* had all except A turret removed during conversion to a training ship, and extra accommodation was added aft. *Cumberland* was disarmed in 1949 and converted into a gunnery trials ship. *Cornwall* and *Dorsetshire* were overwhelmed by Japanese carrier aircraft in the Indian Ocean, and *Canberra* was torpedoed by Japanese destroyers off Savo Island.

Above: Canberra *after being torpedoed by Japanese ships on 8 August 1942. Two US* Gridley/ Benham *class destroyers are standing by*

County *Type* Kent *class* Berwick *in 1942. Note radar before bridge*

Exeter

CRUISER

CLASS: *York* class (2 ships) *York · Exeter*

Service career EXETER

1931-1933 2nd Cruiser Squadron.
1933 (Oct–Aug 1939) America and West Indies Squadron.
1939 (25 Aug) Sailed for South America.
1939 (13 Dec) Battle of the River Plate: severely damaged by *Graf Spee.*
1939 (Dec–Jan 1940) Emergency repairs at Falkland Islands.
1940 (Jan–Feb) Returned to UK.
1940 (Feb–Mar 1941) Refit and modernisation at Devonport: 4in (102mm) mounts doubled; tripod masts fitted; bridge enlarged; radar fitted; 8in (203mm) gun elevation increased from 50° to 70°.

1941 (Mar) To Home Fleet then sailed to Singapore.
1941 (Dec–Feb 1942) In Indian Ocean and East Indies.
1942 (26 Feb) Battle of Java Sea: damaged.
1942 (27–28 Feb) Temporary repairs at Surabaya.
1942 (1 Mar) Scuttled after receiving serious damage from Japanese heavy cruisers *Nachi, Haguro, Ashigara* and *Myoko.*

Although the *County* type took full advantage of the Washington Treaty limits, the British Admiralty remained convinced that a larger number of smaller cruisers was a better answer to British needs. The minimum number of guns necessary for firing accurate salvos before radar ranging was six, and this determined the size of the *Yorks.* They were specifically intended for convoy escort, and the armour thickness was reduced over the machinery on the assumption

Above: Severely damaged by the fire of four Japanese heavy cruisers in the battle of Java Sea, Exeter *is seen shortly before she sank, on 1 March 1942*

Above, right: The York *class cruiser* Exeter, *on convoy duty in the Bangka Strait, Java Sea, early in 1942, fires on attacking Japanese aircraft*

Exeter *in December 1939, carrying a Walrus amphibian. Note low bridge, unraked masts and funnels, V shaped fixed catapult abaft second funnel, and single 4in (102mm) guns*

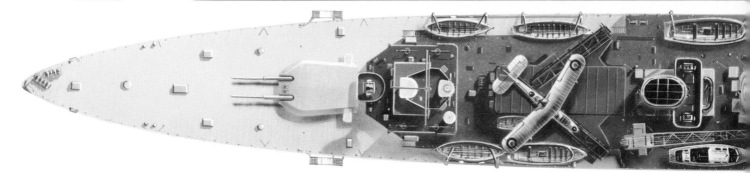

that most actions would take place on oblique rather than broadside bearings. *York* had a tall bridge, incorporating an aircraft hangar. *Exeter* had a lower bridge, vertical masts and funnels, a catapult amidships and a slightly wider beam to improve stability. *York* was sunk by an explosive motor boat in shallow water at Suda Bay, Crete, and was abandoned when the island was lost. *Exeter* was overwhelmed by four Japanese 8in (203mm) cruisers.

Displacement:	York	Exeter
standard tons (tonnes)	8,250 (8,380)	8,390 (8,520)
full load tons (tonnes)	?	?
Dimensions:		
length (pp)	540ft (164·9m)	540ft (164·9m)
(oa)	575ft (175·6m)	575ft (175·6m)
beam	57ft (17·4m)	58ft (17·7m)
draught	20·25ft (6·2m)	20·25ft (6·2m)
Armament:	**Exeter as built**	**Exeter in 1941**
guns		
8in (203mm)	6	6
4in (102mm)	4	8
2pdr (40mm)	—	16
0·5in (12·7mm)	—	2
torpedo tubes		
21in (533mm)	6	6
aircraft	2	2
Armour:		
side (belt)	2–3in (51–76mm)	
deck	2in (51mm)	
main turrets	1·5–2in (38–51mm)	
Machinery:		
boilers (type)	Admiralty 3-drum	
(number)		
engines (type)	Parsons single reduction geared turbines	
shafts	4	
Total SHP:		
designed	80,000	
Fuel capacity:		
oil tons (tonnes)	1,900 (1,930)	
Performance:		
designed speed	32kts	
range	10,000 miles (8,400nm) @ 14kts	
Crew:	630	

Ship:	**YORK**	**EXETER**
Where built:	Palmers, Jarrow	Devonport Dockyard
Authorised:	1926	1927
Laid down:	1927	1 Aug 1928
Launched:	17 July 1928	18 July 1929
Completed:	1930	21 July 1931
Fate:	Total loss 26 March 1941; abandoned 22 May 1941	Scuttled 1 March 1942. Three ships of the same class were cancelled

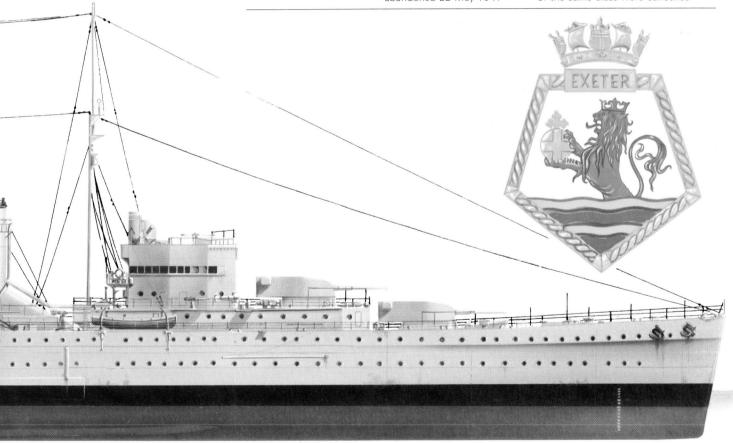

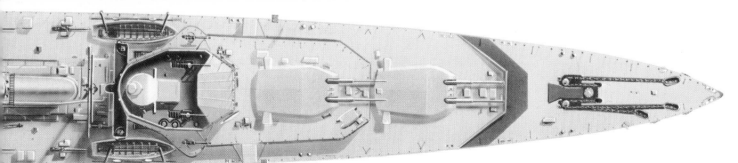

Town Class

CRUISER
CLASS: *Bristol* class (5 ships)
*Bristol · Glasgow · Gloucester ·
Liverpool · Newcastle*

CRUISER
CLASS: *Weymouth* class (4 ships)
*Weymouth · Dartmouth · Falmouth
Yarmouth*

CRUISER
CLASS: *Chatham* class (6 ships)
Britain 3 ships *Chatham · Dublin ·
Southampton ·* Australia 3 ships
Brisbane · Melbourne · Sydney

CRUISER
CLASS: *Birmingham* class (4 ships)
Britain 3 ships *Birmingham ·
Lowestoft · Nottingham*
Australia 1 ship *Adelaide*

These ships were originally classed as Second Class Cruisers, and filled the gap between the British battle-cruisers and the scouts and their derivatives. They were built for worldwide service, and were intended to counter the proliferating classes of German light cruisers. The *Bristols* displaced 1,500 tons (1,520 tonnes) more than the preceding unprotected *Boadiceas* and the contemporary *Blanches*, and the extra tonnage was used to provide an armoured deck and to increase the armament. This was originally intended to consist entirely of 4in (102mm) guns, but it was decided to fit a single 6in (152mm) fore and aft. The 4in (102mm) guns were disposed in single mounts on either side amidships. *Bristol* was experimentally fitted with Brown-Curtis twin-shaft turbines, but other members of the class had four shafts and Parsons turbines. The *Weymouth* and *Chatham* classes both had ships with two or four shafts, but the *Birminghams* standardised on the more efficient two-shaft arrangement. All *Town* type cruisers had four raked funnels. The centre pair were considerably thicker than the first and fourth funnels. The *Bristols* were felt to be underarmed for their size, so the *Weymouths* had a uniform armament of 6in (152mm) guns. They also had a longer fo'c's'le to improve their seaworthiness, and the broadside submerged 18in (457mm) torpedo tubes were replaced by the new 21in (533mm) tubes. The *Edinburgh* experiments showed that armoured decks did not in themselves provide adequate protection against high-explosive shells, and so the *Chathams* were fitted with an armour belt. They also had clipper-ram bows to make them drier forward. *Melbourne* and *Sydney* were built in Britain, but *Brisbane* was constructed in Australia. The *Birminghams* were very similar, but had an extra 6in (152mm) gun. *Adelaide* was built in Australia, and her completion was badly delayed by World War I. All the *Towns* except *Adelaide* saw considerable service during World War I. Apart from the first two classes' propensity to roll, they were excellent ships, and could survive considerable damage. Both *Falmouth* and *Nottingham* were mined. *Adelaide* survived to serve in World War II, but was already totally obsolete when she was completed.

Right: Weymouth *class* Town *type light cruiser* Dartmouth, *as built.*
Note the all-6in (152mm) gun main armament with the midships and stern guns mounted on the upper deck

Town *Type* Chatham *class in 1918. Note searchlight tower aft*

Displacement:	Bristol as built	Weymouth as built	Chatham as built	Birmingham as built
normal tons (tonnes)	4,800 (4,880)	5,250 (5,330)	5,400 (5,490)	5,440 (5,530)
full load tons (tonnes)	?	?	?	?
Dimensions:				
length (pp)	430ft (131·3m)	430ft (131·3m)	430ft (131·3m)	430ft (131·3m)
(oa)	453ft (138·3m)	453ft (138·3m)	458ft (139·8m)	457ft (139·5m)
beam	47ft (14·4m)	48·5ft (14·8m)	48·75ft (14·9m)	49·75ft (15·2m)
draught	15·5ft (4·7m)	15·5ft (4·7m)	16ft (4·9m)	16ft (4·9m)
Armament:				
guns				
6in (152mm)	2	8	8	9
4in (102mm)	10	—	—	—
3pdr (47mm)	4	4	4	4
torpedo tubes				
18in (457mm)	2	—	—	—
21in (533mm)	—	2	2	2
Armour:				
side (belt)	—	—	3in (76mm)	3in (76mm)
(ends)	—	—	2–2·5in (51–64mm)	2–2·5in (51–64mm)
deck	0·75–2in (19–51mm)	0·75–2in (19–51mm)	0·4–1·5in (10–38mm)	0·4–1·5in (10–38mm)
gunshields	3in (76mm)	3in (76mm)	3in (76mm)	3in (76mm)
ammunition tubes	3in (76mm)	3in (76mm)	3in (76mm)	3in (76mm)
Machinery:				
boilers (type)	Yarrow	Yarrow	Yarrow	Yarrow
(number)	12	12	12	12
engines (type)	Brown-Curtis turbines	Parsons turbines	Parsons turbines	Parsons turbines
shafts	2	2	4	2
Total SHP:				
designed	22,000	22,000	22,000	22,000
trial	28,711	23,380	26,247	28,858
Fuel capacity:				
coal normal tons (tonnes)	?	750 (760)	750 (760)	750 (760)
max tons (tonnes)	?	1,290 (1,310)	1,060 (1,080)	1,120 (1,140)
oil tons (tonnes)	?	260 (265)	260 (265)	260 (265)
Performance:				
designed speed	25kts	25kts	25kts	24·75kts
trial speed	27·01kts	25·95kts	26·12kts	25·53kts
range	6,030 miles (5,070nm) @ 16kts	6,660 miles (5,600nm) @ 10kts	?	4,920 miles (4,140nm) @ 16kts
Crew:	?	540	560	580

Class:	BRISTOL class	WEYMOUTH class	CHATHAM class	BIRMINGHAM class
Where built:	various yards	various yards	various British yards and Cockatoo Dockyard	various British yards and Cockatoo Dockyard
Authorised:	?	?	?	?
Laid down:	1909	1909	**RN** 1911 **RAN** 1911–13	**RN** 1912 **RAN** 1915
Launched:	1909–1910	1910–1911	**RN** 1911–12 **RAN** 1912–15	**RN** 1913 **RAN** 1916
Completed:	1910–1911	1911–1912	**RN** 1912–13 **RAN** 1913–16	**RN** 1914 **RAN** 1922
Fate:	Scrapped 1921–1927	*Falmouth* sunk 19 Aug 1916; remainder scrapped 1928–1930	**RN** scrapped 1926–1928 (**RAN** scrapped 1929–1936)	(**RN** *Nottingham* sunk 19 Aug 1916; remainder scrapped 1931) (**RAN** scrapped 1949)

Dido Class

CRUISER

CLASS: Dido class (16 ships)
Group 1 (11 ships) including Dido ·
Scylla · Group 2 (5 ships) including
Diadem (later Babur) · Spartan

The primary function of the Didos was fleet anti-aircraft defence, but they were also intended to act as normal light cruisers. They were therefore fitted with the twin 5·25in (133mm) mount, with its relatively slow traverse and elevation, rather than the 4·5in (114mm) or 4in (102mm) which were better in the anti-aircraft role but lacked weight of fire in surface actions. The Didos were based on the previous Arethusa class cruisers, armed with six 6in (152mm) and four 4in (102mm) guns, and the first group mounted a third superfiring 5·25in (133mm) turret forward to maintain the ten barrel armament. Shortage of 5·25in (133mm) turrets resulted in several of the first group being completed without one turret, and Scylla and Charybdis were fitted with four twin 4·5in (114mm). The second group had the third forward turret replaced by a quadruple 2pdr (40mm) mount. This enabled the bridge to be lowered and the masts and funnels had no rake. They had complete radar control for their armament. Naiad and Hermione were torpedoed by German U-boats and Bonaventure by an Italian submarine. Charybdis was torpedoed by German torpedo boats and Spartan was the first ship sunk by a German glider bomb. Scylla was mined in June 1944 and never completely repaired.

Displacement:	Group 1 as built	Group 2 as built
standard tons (tonnes)	5,450 (5,540)	5,770 (5,860)
full load tons (tonnes)	6,700 (6,810)	6,970 (7,080)
Dimensions:		
length (pp)	485ft (148m)	485ft (148m)
(wl)	506ft (154·5m)	506ft (154·5m)
(oa)	512ft (156·3m)	512ft (156·3m)
beam	50·5ft (15·4m)	50·5ft (15·4m)
draught (max)	17ft (5·2m)	17·25ft (5·3m)
Armament:		
guns		
5·25in (133mm)	10	8
2pdr (40mm)	8	12
20mm	—	12
0·5in (12·7mm)	8	—
torpedo tubes		
21in (533mm)	6	6
Armour:		
side (belt)	3in (76mm)	
deck (upper)	1in (25mm)	
(lower)	1in (25mm)	
main turrets	1–1·5in (25–38mm)	
barbettes	0·5–0·75in (13–19mm)	
Machinery:		
boilers (type)	Admiralty 3-drum	
(number)	4	
engines (type)	Parsons single reduction geared turbines	
shafts	4	
Total SHP:		
designed	64,000	
Performance:		
designed speed	32·25kts	
range	3,480 miles (2,925nm) @ 20kts	
Fuel capacity:		
oil tons (tonnes)	1,100 (1,118)	
Crew:	480	508

Class:	DIDO class (Group 1)	DIDO class (Group 2)
Where built:	various yards	various yards
Ordered:	1936–1939	1939
Laid down:	1932–1939	1939–1940
Launched:	1939–1941	1942
Completed:	1940–1942	1943–1944
Fate:	Naiad sunk 11 March 1942; Bonaventure sunk 31 March 1941; Charybdis sunk 23 Oct 1943; Hermione sunk 16 June 1942; remainder scrapped 1950–1959	Spartan sunk 29 Jan 1944; Diadem transferred to Pakistan 1956, renamed Babur, still in service; remainder scrapped 1959–1968

Above: The Dido *class light cruiser* Cleopatra, *designed primarily for anti-aircraft defence, under air attack during fleet exercises in 1950*

Right: Dido *class (group 1) cruiser* Phoebe *emerging from the smoke screen at the Second Battle of Sirte in 1941, being shelled by an Italian battleship and heavy cruisers*

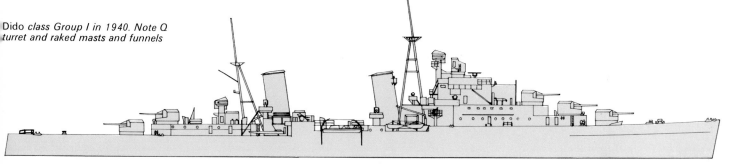

Dido *class Group I in 1940. Note Q turret and raked masts and funnels*

Town Type I-III

CRUISER
CLASS: Town Type I
Southampton Class (5 ships)
Newcastle · Southampton · Sheffield · Glasgow · Birmingham

CRUISER
CLASS: Type II (3 ships)
Manchester · Liverpool · Gloucester

CRUISER
CLASS: Type III *Edinburgh* Class
(2 ships) *Edinburgh · Belfast*

The *Yorks* were too expensive to build in quantity, and the next classes – the *Leanders*, and the improved *Amphions* which had unit machinery – mounted eight 6in (152mm) guns in four twin turrets. These were followed by the small, cheap but highly successful *Arethusas*, which had only three twin 6in (152mm) turrets. However, when the Japanese built the *Mogami* class, it was decided to build a British equivalent. The design was based on the *Amphions* but had triple turrets, armour capable of resisting 6in (152mm) shells at normal battle ranges, and a catapult and hangars for five aircraft. In order to achieve a reasonable sea speed the armour thickness was reduced slightly from the initial proposals, and the masts and funnels were raked to keep smoke and fumes away from the enlarged bridge. The result was a powerful and well balanced design, with a heavy main armament, a well arranged anti-aircraft battery and extensive armour protection. The *Towns* were capable of taking on most Washington Treaty 8in (203mm) cruisers, and the intention was that the greater rate of fire of their 6in (152mm) guns would enable the *Towns* to smother their more powerfully armed opponents at all except extreme ranges. The centre gun in the *Towns'* triple 6in (152mm) turrets was set back to avoid interference between the shells in flight. The second group differed from the first mainly by having an extra high-angle director to improve the anti-aircraft fire control. Wartime experience, particularly in the Mediterranean, was to show that the number of HA directors (and hence the number of targets that could be engaged simultaneously with controlled fire) was much more important than the number of anti-aircraft guns. The *Towns* also had rounded fronts to their bridges to save weight. A powerful body of opinion both inside and outside the Admiralty considered, mistakenly, that the *Town* Types I and II were inferior to the Japanese *Mogamis* and American *Brooklyns* because they carried fewer 6in (152mm) guns. Wartime experience was to prove once again that so long as the disparity in armament was not too great, other factors such as fire control and protection were more significant than sheer numbers of guns. Nevertheless a modified and enlarged design was prepared to carry sixteen 6in (152mm) guns in four quadruple turrets. The hull was lengthened and broadened to carry this larger armament, the aft turrets were carried one deck higher, and two more twin 4in (102mm) mounts were worked in. The catapult was moved in front of the fore funnel, leaving a large and unsightly gap between the funnels and the bridge. Problems in developing the quadruple turrets meant that *Edinburgh* and *Belfast* were eventually completed with triple rather than quadruple turrets. To enable a large force of modern cruisers to be built, a slightly smaller simplified version of the Type IIs was produced as the *Colony* class. Eleven were built (the last three with only three turrets). Three, the Indian *Mysore* (ex-*Nigeria*), the Peruvian *Captain Quinones* (ex-*Almirante Grau*, ex-*Newfoundland*) and the Peruvian *Colonel Bolognesi* (ex-*Ceylon*), are still in service. Two *Swiftsures* were completed to the original improved design, and a further three, the *Tigers*, were eventually commissioned between 1959–1961 with automatic twin 6in (152mm) and 3in (76mm) turrets. The *Towns* were considerably modified during the war. X turret was removed from all the survivors except *Belfast*, radar was fitted and the anti-aircraft armament was improved. *Belfast* was mined and broke her back on 21 November 1939, and was rebuilt with bulges (which increased her beam to 69ft

(21m) and a 5in (127mm) armour belt. The entire class saw considerable active service. *Southampton* was bombed by German aircraft in the Mediterranean, and later scuttled. *Manchester* was torpedoed by Italian MAS boats off Cape Bon. *Gloucester* was bombed by German and Italian aircraft near Crete, and *Edinburgh* was torpedoed by a German submarine and again by German destroyers and later scuttled whilst escorting an Arctic convoy. *Belfast*, now preserved in the Pool of London, took part in the sinking of the German battlecruiser *Scharnhorst* at the Battle of North Cape on 26 December 1943, and later participated in the Korean War.

Town class (Type II) Manchester *after war-time alterations. Note Walrus amphibian and recessed centre 6in (152mm) guns*

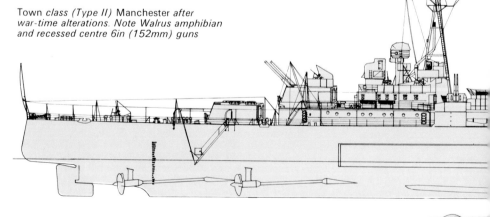

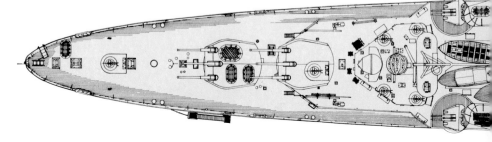

Above: A Town class cruiser of the Mediterranean Fleet fires a 21-gun salute to the Royal Yacht Britannia, en route to Malta in 1954

Left: Belfast being towed from Portsmouth to the Pool of London where she became a museum ship. Note caps on the funnels and the absence of much light equipment

Below: The Town class (First Group) cruiser Glasgow bombards the Normandy landing beaches; Baltimore class cruiser USS Quincy in background

Displacement	Type I as built	Type II as built	Type III as built
standard tons (tonnes)	9,100 (9,246)	9,394 (9,544)	10,550 (10,719)
full load tons (tonnes)	11,470 (11,654)	11,930 (12,121)	13,175 (13,386)
Dimensions			
length (pp)	558ft (170·4m)	558ft (170·4m)	579ft (176·5m)
(wl)	584ft (178·3m)	584ft (178·3m)	606ft (184·7m)
(oa)	591·5ft (180·6m)	591·5ft (180·6m)	613ft (187m)
beam	61·75ft (18·9m)	62·25ft (19m)	66ft (21m)
draught	17ft (5·2m)	17.5ft (5·3m)	19ft (5·8m)
Armament			
guns			
6in (152mm)	12	12	12
4in (102mm)	8	8	12
2pdr (40mm)	8	8	16
0·5in (12·7mm)	8	8	8
torpedo tubes			
21in (533mm)	6	6	6
aircraft	3	3	3
Armour			
side (belt)	3–4in (76–102mm)	3–4in (76–102mm)	4·5in (114mm)
deck	2in (51mm)	2in (51mm)	2in (51mm)
main turrets	1–2in (25–51mm)	1–2in (25–51mm)	1–2·5in (25–63mm)
Machinery			
Boilers (type)	Admiralty 3-drum		
(number)	4		
Engines (type)	Parsons single reduction geared turbines		
Shafts	4		
Total SHP			
designed	75,000	82,500	80,000
Performance			
designed speed	32kts	32·5kts	32kts
range	8,330 miles (7,000nm) @ 16kts	8,330 miles (7,000nm) @ 16kts	11,840 miles (10,000nm) @ 16kts
Fuel capacity			
oil tons (tonnes)	1,970 (2,000)	1,970 (2,000)	2,400 (2,440)
Crew	700	700	850

Class	Southampton class Type I	Type II	Edinburgh class Type III
Where built:	Vickers-Armstrong Tyne and Barrow, Clydebank, Devonport dockyard, Scotts Greenock	Fairfield, Govan, Hawthorn Leslie Tyne, Devonport dockyard	Harland & Wolff Belfast, Swan Hunter Wallsend
Ordered:	1933–1934	1934–1935	1935–1936
Laid down:	1934–1935	1936	1936
Launched:	1936	1937	1938
Completed	1937	1938–1939	1939
Fate:	**Newcastle** scrapped 1959	**Manchester** sunk 13 Aug 1942	
	Southampton sunk 11 Jan 1941		**Edinburgh** sunk 2 May 1942
	Sheffield scrapped 1967	**Liverpool** scrapped 1958	**Belfast** preserved as museum
	Glasgow scrapped 1958	**Gloucester** sunk 22 May 1941	
	Birmingham scrapped 1960		

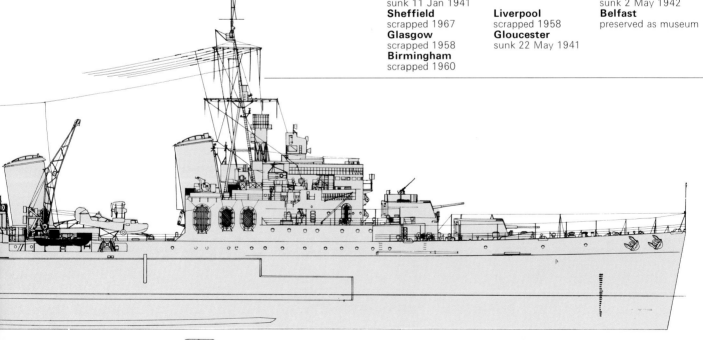

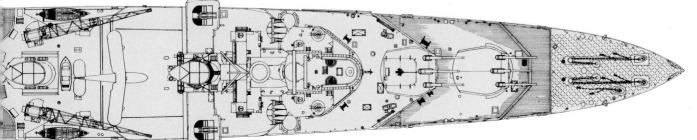

Abdiel Class

FAST MINELAYER

CLASS: *Abdiel* class (6 ships)
1st group *Abdiel · Latona · Manxman · Welshman ·*
2nd group *Apollo · Ariadne*

The British cruiser-minelayer *Adventure*, 6,470 tons (6,574t), completed in 1927, was too large and too slow for offensive minelaying. Therefore the *Abdiels*, which were intended to operate alone in enemy waters, were given a relatively small silhouette, a high sustained speed and an adequate armament against both air and surface attack. The first group's short range was rectified in the second group, which also had a better anti-aircraft armament.

Although designed to achieve 39·75kts in light conditions, their most important asset was their ability to maintain 35—36kts for long periods in reasonable conditions. Intended solely for offensive minelaying, the high speed and spacious minedeck made them invaluable as fast transports. They are most famous for their supply-running activities in the Mediterranean, particularly to Malta. *Welshman* was torpedoed by *U-617* on this duty, and *Latona* was sunk after air attack damage without laying a single mine. However, the other members of the class all laid several important fields.

Abdiel was sunk by a magnetic mine in Taranto harbour. Postwar, the survivors were mostly used as flagships of various kinds. *Manxman* was converted into a minesweeper support ship in 1960—1963, and again to a Mechanical Engineering Officers' training ship in 1969. She was discarded following a bad fire in 1970.

Displacement:	Manxman as designed	Apollo as designed
standard tons (tonnes)	2,650 (2,692)	2,650 (2,692)
full load tons (tonnes)	4,000 (4,064)	4,100 (4,166)
Dimensions:		
length (pp)	400·5ft (122·3m)	400·5ft (122·3m)
(oa)	418ft (127·6m)	418ft (127·6m)
beam	40ft (12·2m)	40ft (12·2m)
draught (max)	15·25ft (4·65m)	16·1ft (4·9m)
Armament:		
guns		
4in (102mm)	6	4
quadruple pom-pom (40mm)	1	—
40mm	—	4
20mm	—	12
quadruple 0·5in (12·7mm)	2	—
mine capacity	156	156
Machinery:		
boilers (type)	Admiralty 3-drum	
(number)	4	
engines (type)	Parsons geared turbines	
shafts	4	
Total SHP:		
designed	72,000	
Performance:		
designed speed (sustained)	36kts	
trial speed	35·59kts	35·3kts
range	4,490 miles (3,900nm)	4,606 miles (4,000nm) @ 15kts
Fuel capacity:		
oil tons (tonnes)	690 (701)	800 (813)
Crew:	236	257

Class:	1st group	2nd group
Ordered	1938	1941
Laid down:	1939	1941
Launched:	1940	1943
Completed:	1941	1943—1944
Fate:	*Latona* sunk 24 Oct 1941; *Welshman* sunk 1 Feb 1943; *Abdiel* sunk 9 Sept 1943; *Manxman* discarded Jan 1971	*Apollo* scrapped Nov 1962; *Ariadne* scrapped Feb 1965

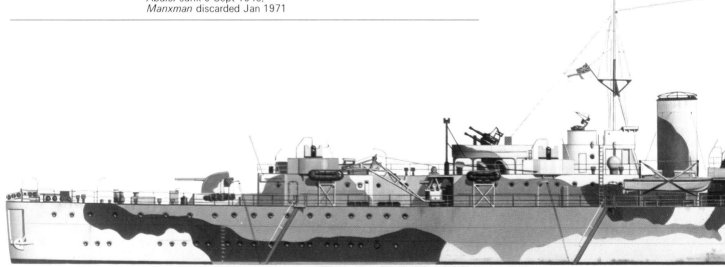

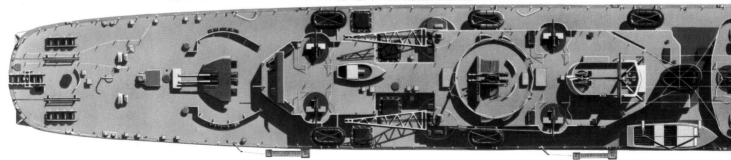

Above: HMS Abdiel, name-ship of a class of six fast minelayers completed in 1941–44. These ships were equally valuable as high-speed (36-knot) transports

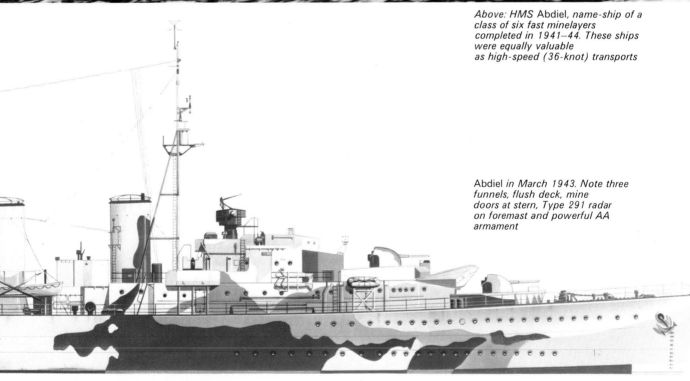

Abdiel in March 1943. Note three funnels, flush deck, mine doors at stern, Type 291 radar on foremast and powerful AA armament

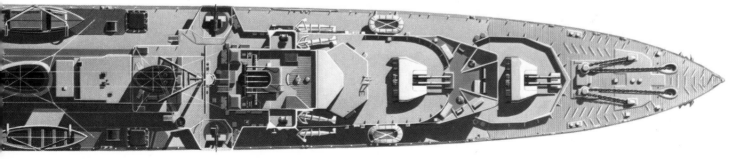

H Class
DESTROYERS
CLASS: *H* class (15 ships)
Hardy (leader) · *Hostile* · *Hunter* ·
Hereward · *Hero* · *Hotspur* ·
Hyperion · *Hasty* · *Havock* plus
following purchased from Brazilian
Navy in Sept 1939: *Harvester*
(ex- *Handy* · ex-*Jurua*) · *Havant*
(ex-*Javary*) · *Havelock* (ex-*Jutahy*) ·
Hesperus (ex-*Hearty* · ex-*Juruena*) ·
Highlander (ex-*Jaguaribe*) ·
Hurricane (ex-*Japarua*)

Continuing the alphabetical series of post-1930
British destroyers the *G* and *H* classes were very
slightly smaller than their predecessors of the
E and *F* classes. Although their oil fuel stowage
was slightly less their armament was similar,
continuing the superimposed B and X gun
arrangement first introduced in the *V*s and *W*s.
The standard number of one leader and eight
ships were ordered under the 1934 programme,
but this number was increased when six similar
ships building for Brazil were purchased by the
Admiralty on 4 September 1939. The whole
class had a hard war, 10 of the 15 being sunk.
The first naval VC of the war was won in *Hardy* by
Captain Warburton-Lee at the 1st Battle of
Narvik. This was a sound, sensible, sea-worthy
class, and was followed by the *I* class before
the much larger (1,760 ton/1,788 tonne)
J class was begun in 1937. The latter ships,
with a single funnel and six 4·7in (119mm)
guns set the design trend for all the later wartime
classes culminating in the even larger *Battle* class,
designed for operations in the Pacific.

Displacement:	H class	Hardy	ex-Brazilian ships
tons (tonnes)	1,340 (1,361)	1,505 (1,529)	1,400 (1,422)
length (pp)	312ft (95·1m)	326ft (99·4m)	
(wl)	320ft (97·5m)	?	
(oa)	323ft (98·4m)	337ft (102·7m)	
beam	32·5ft (9·9m)	34ft (10·4m)	
draught	8·7ft (2·65m)	8·75ft (2·7m)	
Armament:	**H class**	**Hardy**	
guns			
4·7in (119mm)	4	5	
0·5in (12·7mm)	8	8	
torpedo tubes			
21in (533mm)	8	8	
Machinery:			
boilers (type)	Admiralty 3-drum		
(number)	3	—	
engines (type)	Parsons geared turbines		
shafts	2		
Total SHP:	34,000		
Fuel capacity:			
oil tons (tonnes)	455 (457)		
Performance:			
speed	36kts		
Crew:	145	175	

Class:	H class
Where built:	Denny, Vickers Armstrong (Tyne), Scotts, Swan Hunter
Approved:	1934
Laid down:	1935 (Brazilian ships 1938)
Launched:	1936 (Brazilian ships 1939)
Commissioned:	1936–1937 (Brazilian ships 1940)
Fate:	*Hardy* sunk 10 Apr 1940; *Hasty* sunk 15 June 1942;
	Havock sunk 6 Apr 1942; *Hereward* sunk 29 May 1941;
	Hero transferred to RCN as *Chaudière* 1943, paid off 19 Mar 1946;
	Hostile sunk 23 Aug 1940;
	Hotspur transferred to Dominican Republic, paid off as *Duarte* 1972;
	Hunter sunk 10 Apr 1940; *Hyperion* sunk 22 Dec 1940.
	Ex-Brazilian ships: *Harvester* lost 11 Mar 1943;
	Havant lost 1 June 1940; *Hurricane* lost 24 Dec 1943;
	Havelock and *Hesperus* scrapped in 1946 and *Highlander* in 1947

Above: The H *class destroyer*
HMS *Hesperus. Building for Brazil*
as Juruena, *she was taken over by*
the RN (as Hearty) *in 1939*
and served throughout WWII

Hesperus *in early 1943 in Western*
Approaches camouflage. Note Hedgehog
in A position, DCT in Y position and
extra depth charges in place of the aft
TT mount or 4in (102mm) AA gun

River Class
DESTROYER
CLASS: *River* class (36 ships)
Palmer type (9 ships) · Laird type
(9 ships) · Hawthorn Leslie type
(6 ships) · Yarrow type (6 ships) ·
Thornycroft type (4 ships) · White
type (2 ships)

The first British destroyers were the various types
of '27-knotters', built between 1892 and 1895.
They were succeeded by the 60 '30-knotters',
built between 1895 and 1902. With a normal
displacement of between 280–440 tons (285–
445 tonnes), they were lightly built, and were
incapable of operating in heavy weather. They
were also not very reliable. After *Cobra* broke up
in bad weather in September 1901, their structural strength was investigated. Although it was
found to be adequate, the British Admiralty
decided to build stronger, more reliable and more
seaworthy destroyers, with a separate bridge
and raised fo'c's'le in place of the fore-gun
bandstand and turtle-deck fo'c's'le of previous
classes. These *Rivers'* maximum speed in smooth
water was about four knots less, but under service conditions they made only about one knot
less than the '30-knotters'. Eleven firms sub-

Displacement:		
normal tons (tonnes)	540–590 (550–600)	
full load tons (tonnes)	?–?	
Dimensions:		
length (pp)	220–230ft (67·2–70·2m)	
(oa)	?–? (?–?)	
beam	23·5–23·75ft (7·2–7·3m)	
draught	9·25–10ft (2·8–3·1m)	
Armament	**as built**	**in 1914**
guns		
12pdr (76mm)	1	4
6pdr (57mm)	5	—
torpedo tubes		
18in (457mm)	2	2
Machinery:		
boilers (type)	Reed, Yarrow, Thornycroft-Schulz or White-Forster	
(number)	4	
engines (type)	vertical triple expansion or Parsons turbines	
shafts	2	
Total HP:		
designed	7,000–7,500	
trial	6,957–8,024	
Fuel capacity:		
coal tons (tonnes)	120–138 (122–140)	
Performance:		
designed speed	25–26kts	
trial speed	25·27–26·23kts	
range	1,900–2,140 miles	
	(1,600–1,800nm) @ 11kts	
Crew:	70 (approx)	

Daring Class
DESTROYER
CLASS: *Daring* class (11 ships)
8 British including *Daring · Duchess ·
Diana ·* 3 Australian *Vampire ·
Vendetta · Voyager*

The *Darings* were a progressive development of
the two-turreted *Battle* class, and were the ideal
British late World War II destroyer. Higher steam
conditions and double reduction gearing enabled the unit arrangement to be used for the
machinery, and the Mk 6 automatic radar
controlled 4·5in (114mm) turret was adopted.
With use in the Pacific in mind, they had good
habitability and relatively long range in addition
to a powerful torpedo and anti-aircraft armament.
They were welded throughout to reduce weight
and the fore-funnel was inside the lattice mast
to save deck-space.
  Designed and laid down in a hurry in wartime,
the class was completed at a leisurely pace.
Duchess was transferred to the RAN to replace
Voyager, cut in two by the aircraft-carrier
Melbourne. Guided-missile developments have
made all-gun armed destroyers obsolete, but
although *Decoy* was temporarily fitted with a
quadruple Seacat SAM launcher in 1959, none
of the class was fitted with it permanently. The
electrical systems proved troublesome, and the
RN ships were disposed of. *Diana* and *Decoy*
were sold to Peru, renamed *Palacios* and *Ferre,*
and were fitted with eight Exocet SSM apiece
during comprehensive refits at Cammell Laird,
Birkenhead. They have since been fitted with a
helicopter platform aft. The RAN ships have been
rebuilt and are fitted with new funnels and radar.
and electronics to allow them to operate
effectively into the early 1980s. *Duchess* has
not been so extensively refitted. X turret and
the Squid launcher have been removed and a
large deckhouse erected aft. She is now used
for training. A number of discarded RN *Darings*
have been used as targets for underwater
attack and SSM tests.

Displacement:		
standard tons (tonnes)	2,800 (2,850)	
full load tons (tonnes)	3,600 (3,660)	
Dimensions:		
length (pp)	366ft (117·7m)	
(wl)	375ft (114·3m)	
(oa)	390ft (119·1m)	
beam	43ft (13·1m)	
draught (max)	17ft (5·2m)	
Armament:	**as built**	**Peruvian Navy 1974**
guns		
4·5in (114mm)	6	6
40mm	6	2
missiles		
MM-38 Exocet SSM	—	8
torpedo tubes		
21in (533mm)	10	—
A/S weapons		
Squid 3-barrel mortar	1	1
Machinery:		
boilers (type)	Babcock & Wilcox or Foster Wheeler	
(number)	2	
engines (type)	Parsons double reduction geared turbines	
shafts	2	
Total SHP:		
designed	54,000	
Fuel capacity:		
oil tons (tonnes)	580 (589·3)	
Performance:		
designed speed	34·75kts	
full load speed	31·5kts	
range	4,400 miles (3,700nm) @ 20kts	
Crew:	278–308	

Class:	DARING class (RN)	DARING class (RAN)
Ordered:	1944	—
Laid down:	1945–1948	1949–1952
Launched:	1949–1952	1952–1956
Completed:	1952–1954	1958–1959
Cancelled:	8 ships 1945	1 ship 1954
Fate:	4 stricken: *Duchess* sold to RAN 1971, converted to training ship 1973; *Diana* and *Decoy* sold to Peru 1969, renamed *Palacios* and *Ferre; Diamond* converted to training ship	*Voyager* sunk 10 February 1964

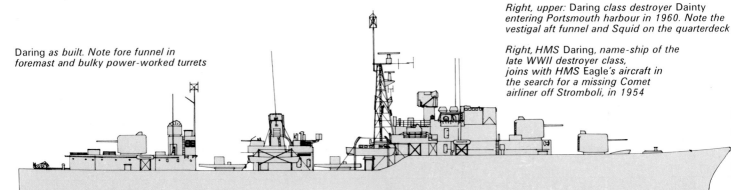

*Daring as built. Note fore funnel in
foremast and bulky power-worked turrets*

Right, upper: Daring *class destroyer* Dainty
*entering Portsmouth harbour in 1960. Note the
vestigal aft funnel and Squid on the quarterdeck*

Right, HMS Daring, *name-ship of the
late WWII destroyer class,
joins with HMS* Eagle's *aircraft in
the search for a missing Comet
airliner off Stromboli, in 1954*

mitted designs to the same basic specification, and six were accepted. Each differed from the others, particularly in hull design and the arrangement of the funnels. The Laird, Hawthorn Leslie, White and Thornycroft vessels had two funnels of varying heights, but the Palmer and Yarrow *Rivers* had four. *Rother* was built on speculation by Palmer and offered to the Royal Navy in September 1903. She was purchased in 1904. They were the last reciprocating-engined British destroyers, but *Eden* (built by Hawthorn Leslie) had turbines, as did *Stour* and *Test*. The latter two were built by Lairds on speculation in 1905 and purchased in December 1909 to replace *Gala* and *Blackwater*. The *Rivers'* small size and limited range confined them to coastal work in the Mediterranean and southern North Sea during World War I. However, they set the pattern for the later, larger British destroyers, with raised fo'c's'les, reliable machinery and seaworthy and durable hulls.

Class:	**RIVER class (later E class)**
Where built:	various yards
Authorised:	1901–1903
Built:	1902–1905
Reclassified:	September 1913
Fate:	*Gala* lost 27 Apr 1908;
	Blackwater lost 6 Apr 1909;
	6 sunk 1915–1917;
	remainder deleted 1919–1920

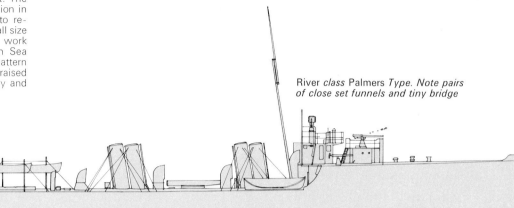

River *class* Palmers *Type. Note pairs of close set funnels and tiny bridge*

Tribal Class

DESTROYER

CLASS: *Tribal* class (27 ships)
Britain 16 ships including *Cossack* ·
Ashanti · Australia 3 ships *Arunta* ·
Bataan · *Warramunga* · Canada
8 ships including *Athabaskan* · *Haida*

K Class

DESTROYER

CLASS: K class (8 ships) including
Kelly · *Kipling*

By the mid 1930s the big 'super-destroyers'
built by other powers were worrying the
Admiralty, and so it was decided to build a
class of large destroyers with increased gunpower. The result was the *Tribal* class. This was
basically an enlargement of the previous classes
with only one quadruple torpedo tube mounting
and with twin 4·7in (120mm) substituted for
the single mounts. There were originally to
have been five twin 4·7in (120mm) but stability
considerations reduced this to four. The
greatest deficiency was in anti-aircraft fire. The 4·7in
(120mm) lacked the necessary elevation, and
the quadruple 2pdr (40mm) and particularly
the multiple 0·5in (12·7mm) were not very
good weapons. Wartime modifications included
substituting a twin 4in (102mm) for X mount,
and the addition of 20mm guns and radar. These
large and impressive ships were used inten-
sively at the start of the war, serving with distinc-
tion in Mediterranean and northern European
waters and they suffered accordingly. The
Canadian and Australian *Improved Tribals* were
completed with these modifications, and the
survivors were rebuilt in the 1950s as anti-
aircraft and anti-submarine escorts. The *Tribals*
were rather large, complex and expensive, and
the succeeding J class employed an improved
method of construction and struck a better
balance between gunpower and torpedo armament. The K class were virtually identical to the
Js, and their hull formed the basis for the series
of 'war emergency' class destroyers which
differed mainly by having four single instead of
three twin mounts. The elimination of one
boiler enabled a single funnel to be fitted,
saving deck space and improving the guns'
sky-arcs. The L and M classes were basically
similar, except that they were slightly larger
and had a more complex enclosed twin-gun
mounting. This was much heavier than the
previous twin mount, and the Ls and Ms only
had one quadruple torpedo tube mount to
maintain stability. The N class were virtually
repeat Ks. Like the *Tribals*, the Ks saw strenuous
war service, and had an equivalent loss rate.
They served in virtually all theatres.

	RN Tribal class as built	K class as built
Displacement:		
standard tons (tonnes)	1,960 (1,990)	1,760 (1,790)
full load tons (tonnes)	2,520 (2,560)	2,330 (2,370)
Dimensions:		
length (pp)	355·5ft (108·5m)	339·5ft (103·7m)
(oa)	377ft (115·1m)	356·5ft (108·9m)
beam	36·5ft (11·1m)	35·75ft (10·9m)
draught	13ft (4m)	13·5ft (4·1m)
Armament:		
guns		
4·7in (120mm)	8	6
2pdr (40mm)	4	4
0·5in (12·7mm)	8	8
torpedo tubes		
21in (533mm)	4	10
Machinery:		
boilers (type)	Admiralty 3-drum	Admiralty 3-drum
(number)	3	2
engines (type)	Parsons geared turbines	Parsons geared turbines
shafts	2	2
Total SHP:		
designed	44,000	40,000
trial (max)	46,006	41,518
Fuel capacity:		
oil tons (tonnes)	524 (532)	484 (492)
Performance:		
designed speed	36kts	36kts
trial speed (max)	37·46kts	35·51kts
range	6,780 miles (5,700nm) @ 15kts	6,540 miles (5,500nm) @ 15kts
Crew:	190	183

Class:	TRIBAL class			K class
	RN	**RAN**	**RCN**	
Where built:	various yards	Cockatoo, Sydney	V-A, Tyne and Halifax shipyard	various yards
Authorised:	1935–1936	1939	1939–1942	1937
Laid down:	1936	1939–1942	1940–1943	1937–1938
Launched:	1937	1940–1944	1941–1946	1938–1939
Completed:	1938–1939	1942–1945	1942–1948	1939–1940
Fate:	12 sunk 1940–1942; 4 scrapped 1948–1949	4 cancelled; remainder scrapped 1962–1968	*Athabaskan* (1) sunk 29 Apr 1944; *Haida* preserved as museum 1964; remainder scrapped 1964–1970	6 sunk 1940–1942; *Kelvin* and *Kimberley* scrapped 1949

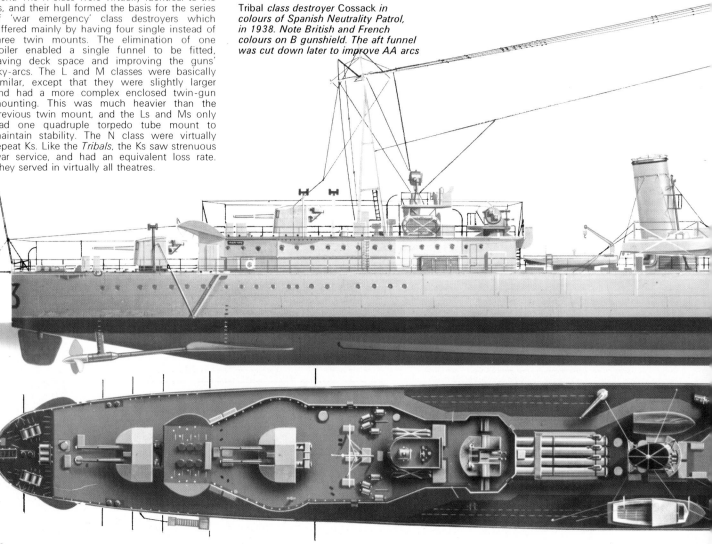

Tribal *class destroyer* Cossack *in
colours of Spanish Neutrality Patrol,
in 1938. Note British and French
colours on B gunshield. The aft funnel
was cut down later to improve AA arcs*

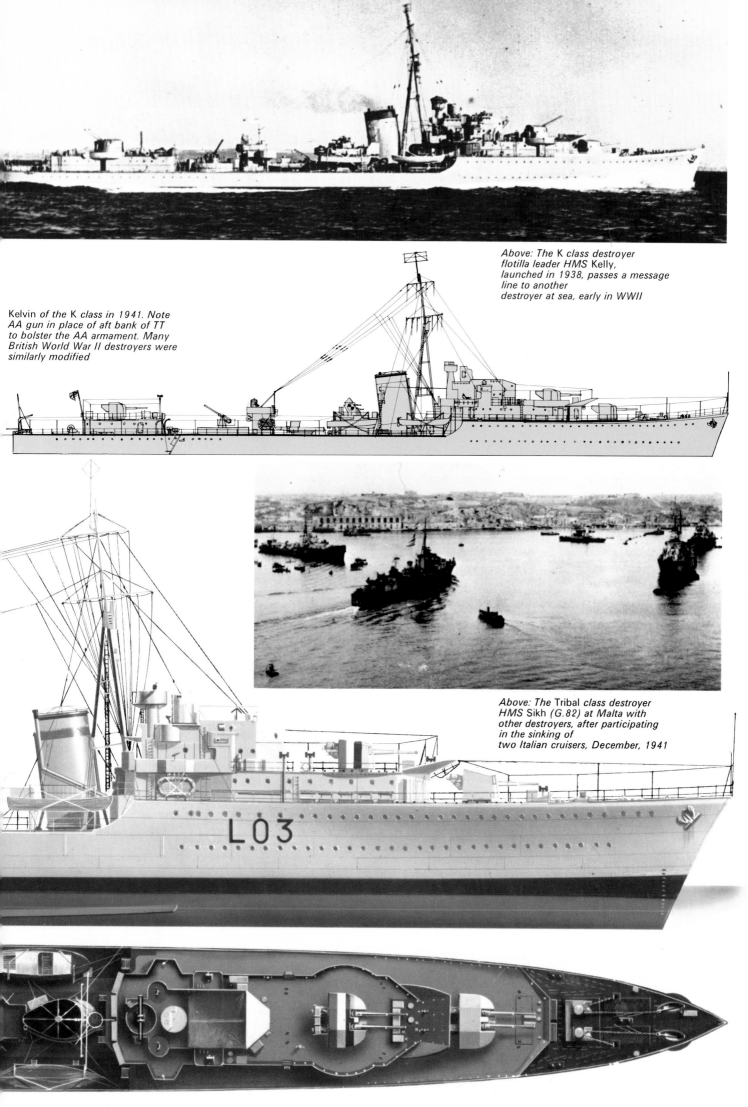

Above: The K class destroyer
flotilla leader HMS Kelly,
launched in 1938, passes a message
line to another
destroyer at sea, early in WWII

Kelvin of the K class in 1941. Note
AA gun in place of aft bank of TT
to bolster the AA armament. Many
British World War II destroyers were
similarly modified

Above: The Tribal class destroyer
HMS Sikh (G.82) at Malta with
other destroyers, after participating
in the sinking of
two Italian cruisers, December, 1941

L03

C Class
DESTROYER

CLASS: *C* class (32 ships)
CA group (8 ships) including
Cavalier · Caprice
CH group (8 ships) including
Charity · Chivalrous
CO group (8 ships) including
Cossack · Contest
CR group (8 ships) including
Crispin · Cromwell

Displacement:	CA group as built	Cavalier in 1973
standard tons (tonnes)	1,710 (1,737)	2,106 (2,140)
full load tons (tonnes)	2,530 (2,570)	2,749 (2,793)
Dimensions:		
length (pp)	339·3ft (103·5m)	339·5ft (103·5m)
(wl)	350ft (106·7m)	350ft (106·7m)
(oa)	362·75ft (110·6m)	362·75ft (110·6m)
beam	35·75ft (10·9m)	35·75ft (10·9m)
draught (max)	14·25ft (5·2m)	17ft (5·2m)
Armament:		
guns		
4·5in (114mm)	4	3
40mm	2	4
20mm	6	—
missiles		
Seacat SAM		
quadruple-launcher	—	1
torpedo tubes		
21in (533mm)	8	—
A/S weapons		
Squid triple-barrel mortar	—	2
Machinery:		
boilers (type)	Admiralty 3-drum	
(number)	2	
engines (type)	Parsons single reduction geared turbines	
shafts	2	
Total SHP:		
designed	40,000	
Fuel capacity:		
oil tons (tonnes)	615(625)	
Performance:		
designed speed	36kts	
range	4,675 miles (3,930nm) @ 20kts	
Crew:	186	

Class:	CA group	CH group	CO group	CR group
Where built:	various yards	various yards	various yards	various yards
Authorised:	?	?	?	?
Built:	1943–1944	1944–1945	1944–1945	1944–1945
Fate:	*Cavalier* to be preserved as a museum; *Caprice* paid off 1974; remainder scrapped 1967–1973	Two to Pakistan 1954–1958; *Shah Jehan* (ex-*Charity*) still in service; remainder scrapped 1961–1969	Scrapped 1956–1964	Two to Pakistan 1958 (*Alamgir*, ex-*Creole*, and *Jahangir*, ex-*Crispin*), still in service; four to Norway 1945–1946; two to Canada 1945; scrapped 1961–1969

Above: HMS Chequers, *a C class (CH group) destroyer. The CH group had an improved director and remote power control for their main armament*

Right: An early postwar shot of Consort, *a C class CO group destroyer. These differed from the CAs by having the Mk VI DCT and remote power control for the 4·5in (114mm) guns and no for'd TT*

Although the J class were to an excellent design, they were too complicated to mass-produce in an emergency, and a simplified and slightly smaller version was adopted with single 4·7in (120mm) guns for the O and P classes. The succeeding Q, R, S, T, U, V, W and Z classes reverted to the J sized hull. They differed in detail, and the Z class adopted the 4·5in (114mm) gun. The CA class were similar to the Zs. The CH class differed in having an improved director and remote power control for the 4·5in (114mm) guns, and the CO and CR classes were repeat CHs. The CAs were the last survivors in the Royal Navy because they spent a considerable period in reserve. The Cs were really too small to mount an adequate anti-aircraft armament and modern radar, and subsequent British destroyers were considerably larger.

C class, CA Group, destroyer Cavalier, *in 1972, after decommissioning. Note Seacat launcher and magazine in place of TT and deck house in place of X 4·5in (114mm) mount*

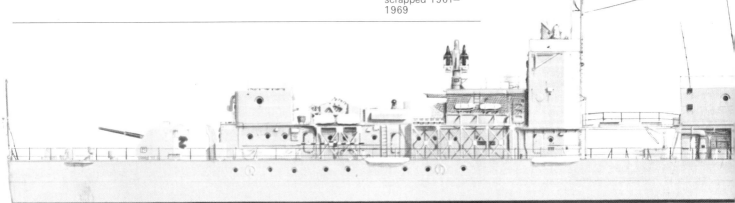

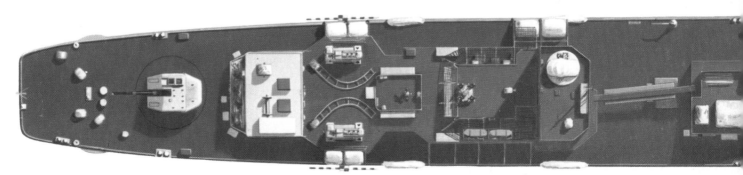

County Class

GUIDED-MISSILE DESTROYER

CLASS: *County* class (8 ships)
Group 1 (4 ships) including
Hampshire (D-08) · *Kent* (D-12)
Group 2 (4 ships) including *Antrim*
(D-18) · *Fife* (D-20)

Sheffield Class

GUIDED-MISSILE DESTROYER

CLASS: *Sheffield* class (12 ships)
Britain 10+ ships including *Sheffield*
(D-80) · *Birmingham* (D-86) ·
Argentina 2 ships *Hercules* (D-01) ·
Santissima Trinidad (D-02)

The *Counties* were intended primarily for AA defence of carrier task forces, and were designed round the Sea Slug SAM. Development of this medium range beam riding missile started in 1949, and a number of designs, including one for a 17,000 ton (17,270 tonne) cruiser, were prepared to carry it. However, a smaller cheaper ship was eventually selected, with two twin 4·5in (114mm) gun turrets forward to provide surface and shore bombardment capability. The *Counties* have a hangar and landing deck for a Wessex hunter-killer A/S helicopter, and mount a Sea Cat SAM quadruple launcher either side of the superstructure aft for close range AA defence. They are fully air-conditioned for defence against nuclear fall-out, and were the first major warships to have COSAG machinery. This enables them to get underway almost immediately, as well as providing rapid acceleration. The first four

Above, upper: The Sheffield *class guided missile destroyer HMS* Birmingham, *launched 1973, mounts a Sea Dart twin launcher and carries a Lynx WG 13 helicopter*

Above: The County *class guided missile destroyer HMS* Kent *mounts Sea Slug and Sea Cat SAM launchers and carries a Wessex Mk 3 ASW helicopter*

Counties were fitted with Sea Slug Mk I SAMs They have the Type 965 single aerial air search radar on the mainmast, which is mounted further aft on *Kent* (D-12) and *London* (D-16) than on *Devonshire* (D-02) and *Hampshire* (D-08). The last four *Counties* have Sea Slug Mk 2 SAMs which have a limited SSM capability. They have the Type 965M double aerial on the mainmast. Because of Britain's economic situation and the decline of her carrier and seaborne assault forces, the first four *Countys* have not been given a mid-life refit, and are being discarded. However, *Norfolk* (D-21) was fitted with Exocet SSM launchers in place of B turret in 1974 to allow her to operate alone against major surface warships, and the other three ships in the second group are being similarly refitted. The *Counties* were to have been followed by the *Type 82* guided missile destroyers. These three funnel 5,650 ton (5,740 tonne) standard displacement ships were designed round the smaller, more capable Sea Dart SAM, with a single 4·5in (114mm) Mk 8 mount and an Ikara ASM launcher forward. Their immense cost and the cancellation of the aircraft carrier *CVA-01* meant that only one *Type 82*, *Bristol* (D-23) was completed. The *Sheffield* class were designed as cheaper, smaller and less sophisticated versions of *Bristol* (D-23), but are still complex and highly automated vessels. They have COGOG in place of *Bristol* (D-23)'s COSAG machinery, which has proved unreliable in service, and they have a hangar and flight deck aft for a Lynx A/S helicopter instead of *Bristol* (D-23)'s Ikara ASM. The Sea Dart SAM has a limited SSM capability, and the single launcher is fitted forward between the 4·5in (114mm) Mk 8 gun mount and the bridge. *Sheffield* (D-80) had her fire-damaged stern section replaced by one from the Argentinian *Hercules* (D-01) to ensure delivery on time, and she was temporarily fitted with unsightly exhausts on the funnel to overcome problems with the gas turbine efflux. These have been overcome, and subsequent ships have a modified funnel.

Displacement:	County class		Sheffield class
standard tons (tonnes)	5,440 (5,530)		3,150 (3,200)
full load tons (tonnes)	6,200 (6,300)		4,100 (4,166)
Dimensions:			
length (wl)	505ft (153·9m)		392ft (119·5m)
(oa)	520·5ft (158·7m)		410ft (125m)
beam	54ft (16·5m)		46ft (14m)
draught	20ft (6·1m)		14ft (4·3m)
Armament:	**Group 1 as built**	**Group 2 in 1977**	
guns			
4·5in (114mm)	4	2	1
20mm	2	2	2
missiles			
Sea Slug Mk 1 SAM			
twin-launcher	1	—	—
Sea Slug Mk 2 SAM			
twin-launcher	—	1	—
Sea Dart SAM			
twin-launcher	—	—	1
Sea Cat SAM			
quadruple-launcher	2	2	—
MM-38 Exocet SSM	—	4	—
torpedo tubes			
12·7in (324mm)	—	—	6
aircraft	1 helicopter	1 helicopter	1 helicopter
Machinery:			
boilers (type)	Babcock & Wilcox		—
(number)	2		—
engines (type)	AE1 geared steam turbines and G6 gas turbines		Rolls-Royce Olympus and Rolls-Royce Tyne gas turbines
shafts	2		2
Total SHP:			
designed	60,000		(Olympus) 50,000 (Tyne) 8,000
Fuel capacity:			
oil tons (tonnes)	600 (610)		? (?)
Performance:			
designed speed	30kts		30kts
range	4,160 miles (3,500nm) @ 28kts		5,350 miles (4,500nm) @ 18kts
Crew:	471		299

Class:	COUNTY class		SHEFFIELD class
	Group 1	**Group 2**	
Where built:	various yards	various yards	various yards in Britain and Argentina
Authorised:	1955–1956	1961–1965	1968 to date
Laid down:	1959–1960	1962–1966	1970 to date
Launched:	1960–1961	1964–1967	1971 to date
Completed:	1962–1963	1966–1971	1975 to date
Converted:	—	1974–1977	—
Fate:	*Hampshire* paid off Apr 1976; remainder in service	in service	in service and under construction

A Class
SUBMARINE
CLASS: *A class* (13 boats) *A1–A13*

E Class
SUBMARINE
CLASS: *E class* (57 boats)
Britain 55 boats *E1–E27 · E29–E56*
Australia 2 boats *AE1 · AE2*

Although the Royal Navy built no submarines prior to 1902, the British Admiralty kept a close eye on developments abroad, and particularly in France and America. The aftermath of the 1898 Fashoda incident made it politically impossible to obtain the first successful French submarine designs, but in 1900 negotiations were entered into to acquire the Holland design that had just been successfully tested by the USN. In 1902 the British Admiralty entered into an exclusive agreement with the firm of Vickers to build RN submarines for the Royal Navy till 1906, later extended to 1912. The first, *Holland 1-5*, were similar to the American *A* class. It was obvious that these were difficult to control both on the surface and submerged, and an enlarged and modified version was immediately ordered. *A1* was a great improvement, but her hull form was not particularly efficient, and the later boats of this class were given an improved hull form which gave increased speed at economical power. Although more controllable than *Holland 1-5*, they were prone to dive without warning — although she was subsequently raised, all *A8*'s crew were drowned when she did this. The use of petrol engines meant that there were several explosions, from build-ups of vapour in the enclosed hull. *A-13* was specially ordered with a Hornsby-Acroyd heavy oil engine and was the first British submarine with heavy oil machinery. Launched in 1905, tests delayed her completion until 1908. By that date the class was obsolete and was used for training or experiments. They were followed by the larger *B* and *C* classes, both of which had a surface displacement of 280 tons (284 tonnes). Although they had the same armament as the *A* class, these larger boats had two sets of hydroplanes to improve controllability and more powerful machinery giving a better performance. They retained the single screw arrangement and had petrol engines, but had improved habitability and an increased range. Ten *B* class and 37 *C* class were built. Both

Above, upper: Submarine E-2 *returns from a patrol in the Sea of Marmora, 1915. The* E *class boats' diesel/electric propulsion gave 15 knots surfaced, 10 knots submerged.*

Above: The A *class submarine A-11, launched in 1905, mounted two 18in torpedo tubes and carried a crew of 14. Three boats of this class were lost before WWI*

classes were obsolete in 1914, and five *B* class were converted to surface patrol boats in Italy in 1917. These boats were still only suitable for local service, and *D1* (ordered before *C20-37*) which had a surface displacement of 550 tons (559 tonnes) was fitted with twin screw Vickers diesel machinery to give a longer range. She also had much greater reserve buoyancy and an armament of three 18in (457mm) torpedo tubes and a 12pdr (76mm) gun. Seven more *D* class were built, but they were still not large enough for long range work. The *E* class were an enlarged version of the *D*s with an increased torpedo armament. Although trainable tubes mounted in the superstructure or Drzwiecki frames were proposed, they were actually fitted with two fixed broadside tubes amidships. Although they had a tendency to dive at high speeds on the surface, they were otherwise an excellent design. Like all early British submarines they could submerge rapidly, they had an adequate armament and range, and their solid injection diesel engines, though less sophisticated than German submarine diesels, were extremely reliable for that time. They were to have been succeeded by the double-hulled *G* class, which had a surface displacement of 700 tons (711 tonnes), but these took longer to build; so in November 1914 twenty more *E* class were ordered to build up the British submarine forces as rapidly as possible. The subsequent *L* class of 890 tons (904 tonnes) surface displacement were developed from the *E*s. The *E* class had a distinguished record in World War One, particularly in the North Sea, the Baltic and the Dardanelles.

Displacement:	A1	A5	E1	E7/E24
surface tons (tonnes)	165 (168)	180 (183)	660 (671)	662 (673)
submerged tons (tonnes)	180 (183)	207 (210)	810 (823)	835 (848)
Dimensions:				
length (oa)	100ft (30·5m)	94ft (28·7m)	176ft (53·7m)	181ft (55·2m)
beam	11·5ft (3·5m)	13ft (4m)	22·5ft (6·9m)	22·5ft (6·9m)
depth	10ft (3·1m)	10ft (3·1m)	12ft (3·7m)	12·5ft (3·8m)
Armament:				
guns				
12pdr (76mm)	—	—	1	1/1
torpedo tubes				
18in (457mm)	2	2	4	5/3
mine capacity	—	—	—	—/20
Machinery:				
engines (type)	petrol	petrol	petrol	Vickers Diesel
(number)	1	1	1	2
electric motor (type)	?	?	?	?
shafts	1	1	1	2
Total BHP:	500	550	550	1,600
Total SHP:	150	150	150	840
Fuel capacity:				
petrol tons (tonnes)	?	?	?	—
oil tons (tonnes)	—	—	—	45 (46)
Performance:				
surface speed	11kts	11·5kts	15kts	
submerged speed	7kts	7kts	10kts	
range (surface)	310 miles (270nm) @ 10kts		3,090 miles (2,600nm) @ 10kts	
(submerged)	?	?	118 miles (99nm) @ 3kts)	
designed diving depth	100ft (30m)	100ft (30m)	200ft (60m)	
Crew:	11	14	30	

Class:	A class	E class
Where built:	Vickers, Barrow	various yards
Authorised:	1902	1910–1914
Built:	1902–1905	1913–1917
Fate:	*A1* sunk Aug 1911; *A3* sunk 17 May 1912; *A7* lost 16 Jan 1914; remainder paid off 1920	*E28* cancelled 20 Apr 1915; 25 lost 1914–1918; *E13* interned in Denmark 3 Sept 1915; deleted 1921; remainder paid off 1921–1922

S Class

SUBMARINE

CLASS: S class (64 boats) first group (4 boats) including *Swordfish* · *Sturgeon* · second group (8 boats) including *Sealion* · *Sunfish* third group (50 boats) including *Seraph* · *Springer*

T Class

SUBMARINE

CLASS: T class (53 boats) first group (15 boats) including *Thetis* · *Taku* · second group (7 boats) including *Tempest* · *Trusty* · third group (31 boats) including *Tally-Ho* · *Tiptoe*

U Class

SUBMARINE

CLASS: U class (49 boats) first group (15 boats) including *Undine* · *Upholder* · second group (38 boats) including *Unbroken* · *Varangian*

Like the *County* type cruisers, the first British interwar submarines were designed for operations in the Pacific, and were large boats with a long range. The single cruiser submarine, *X-1*, had a surface displacement of 2,425 tons (2,634 tonnes), an armament of two twin 5·2in (132mm) mounts and six 21 in (533mm) torpedo tubes, and a surface range of 14,750 miles (12,400nm). Her experimental diesels were very unreliable and she was scrapped in 1936 after only ten years service. The nineteen *O*, *P* and *R* class boats built between 1925 and 1931 were more conventional submarines. They had a surface displacement of between 1,311 and 1,475 tons (1,332–1,499 tonnes) and an armament of 4in (102mm) gun and eight 21in (533mm) torpedo tubes. The prototype, *Oberon*, had a surface range of over 20,000 miles (16,800nm), though this was reduced in

subsequent boats. Except for oil leaks from the external fuel tanks they were an excellent design for Pacific warfare. Unfortunately, shortages of submarines meant that they had to be used in the Mediterranean in 1940. They were too large and unmanoeuvrable for those confined waters, and 11 out of 15 employed there were lost that year. Three *Thames* class fleet submarines were built in the early 1930s. The second two could make 22·5kts on the surface but this was no longer fast enough to keep up with the fleet, and no more were built. Eight very successful *Porpoise* class mine-laying submarines were built during the 1930s. Three more were cancelled after the development of a mine capable of being launched from a torpedo tube made the specialist minelaying submarine obsolete. Meanwhile a new medium sized patrol submarine, the *S* class, was being built. The British Admiralty was

Left: S class boats like HMS Scorcher *(Third group), with considerable design variations, were the only class to remain in production throughout WWII*

Above: HMS Tally-Ho, T *class (Third group) in 1954, soon after becoming the first of her class to make an Atlantic crossing submerged, on snort*

attempting to obtain an international limit on submarine surface displacement of 600 tons (610 tonnes), and the *S* class were designed with this in mind. They were intended for use in North European or Mediterranean waters, and were highly manoeuvrable with a very fast diving

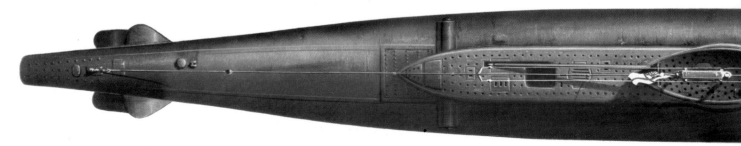

speed. To counter improved A/S techniques, a heavy torpedo armament was fitted to allow large salvos to be fired to ensure hits at long range. The first group had a 3in (76mm) gun in a raised disappearing mounting before the conning tower, whilst the second group had the gun on a fixed mount on the casing. They proved to be very successful in action, and the design was put back into production during the war. Some of these were partially welded and the last boats were completely welded. Some were modernised and had the gun removed and the conning tower streamlined postwar. The T class was designed as a new long-range patrol submarine to replace the O, P and R boats. The size was kept down to allow as many as possible to be built within the tonnage allowed for submarines by the London Treaty, but like the S class they were fitted with a very powerful torpedo armament. As with the S boats, all the fuel was carried internally, and detail improvements were made as the war progressed. Later boats were partially or wholly welded, and those specifically intended for the Pacific had extra fuel tanks fitted. After the war, some of the riveted boats were modernised and streamlined, but eight of the welded boats were lengthened and completely rebuilt, almost doubling the underwater speed. The 1,120 ton (1,138 tonne) surface displacement A class was developed from the Ts near the end of World War Two for service in the Pacific. These all-welded boats had a longer range and higher surface speed. The U class were originally developed as unarmed training boats to replace the World War One H class, but were given torpedo tubes to allow them to be used operationally. Small and handy, they could be built quickly and proved very useful in the shallow waters of the North Sea and the Mediterranean. They were replaced in production by the partially welded V class. By the end of World War Two most had reverted to the training role. The S, T and U classes were neither spectacular nor technologically advanced designs, but they were all fast diving, manoeuvrable, well-armed and reliable boats, whose operational performance compared very favourably with foreign contemporaries.

		S class (third group) as built	T class (third group) as built	Tiptoe in 1956	U class (first group) as built
Displacement:					
surface tons (tonnes)		814 (827)	1,325 (1,346)	1,505 (1,529)	630 (640)
submerged tons (tonnes)		990 (1,006)	1,571 (1,596)	1,700 (1,727)	735 (747)
Dimensions:					
length (pp)		201ft (61·4m)	245·5ft (75m)	265·5ft (81m)	171·75ft (52·4m)
(oa)		217ft (66·3m)	273·5ft (83·5m)	293·5ft (87·6m)	192·25ft (58·7m)
beam		23·5ft (7·2m)	26·5ft (8·1m)	26·5ft (8·1m)	16ft (4·9m)
draught		13·3ft (4·1m)	16·3ft (5m)	14·8ft (4·5m)	14·5ft (4·4m)
Armament:					
guns					
4in (102mm)		1	1	—	—
3in (76mm)	or	1	—	—	1
20mm		1	1	—	—
0·303in (7·7mm)		3	3	—	3
torpedo tubes					
21in (533mm)		7	11	6	4 or 6
Machinery:					
diesels (type)		Admiralty	Admiralty or Vickers	Admiralty	Admiralty or Davey Paxman
(number)		2	2	2	2
electric motors (type)		Laurence Scott or General Electric or Metrovick	Laurence Scott	?	General Electric
shafts		2	2	2	2
Total BHP:		1,900	2,500	2,500	618
Total SHP:		1,300	1,450	2,900	825
Performance:					
surface speed		14·75kts	15·25kts	15·2kts	11·75kts
submerged speed		9kts	8·75kts	15kts	9kts
range surface		7,130 miles (6,000nm) @ 10kts	9,510 miles (8,000nm) @ 10kts	? miles ? ?	4,820 miles (4,050nm) @ 10kts
submerged		?	?	?	?
designed diving depth		250ft (76m)	300ft (90m) riveted 350ft (107m) welded	350ft (107m)	200ft (60m)
Fuel capacity:					
oil tons (tonnes)		48 (49)	132 (134)	250 (254)	41 (42)
Crew:		48	61	65	33

Class	S class	T class	U class
Where built:	various yards	various yards	various yards
Built:			
first group:	1931–1933	1937–1942	1937–1940
second group:	1933–1938	1940–1942	1940–1943
third group:	1941–1945	1942–1946	—
Fate – sunk:	19	18	22
scrapped:	39	32	29
transferred:	12	8	10
cancelled:	4	6	—

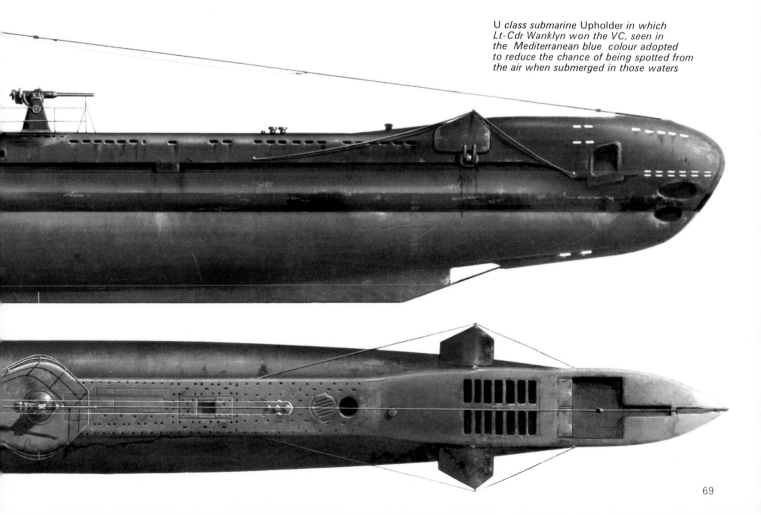

U class submarine Upholder in which Lt-Cdr Wanklyn won the VC, seen in the Mediterranean blue colour adopted to reduce the chance of being spotted from the air when submerged in those waters

O Class

SUBMARINE

CLASS: *Oberon* class (27 boats):
13 RN including *Oberon* (S-09) ·
Onyx (S-21) · 6 RAN including
Oxley (S-57) · *Ovens* (S-70) ·
3 Brazilian Navy including *Humaitá*
(S-20) · *Riachuelo* (S-22) ·
3 RCN including *Ojibwa* (ex-*Onyx*
SS-72) · *Okanagan* (SS-74) ·
2 Chilean Navy *O'Brien* (S-22) ·
Hyatt (S-23)

P Class

SUBMARINE

CLASS: *Porpoise* class (8 boats)
including *Porpoise* (S-01) · *Rorqual*
(S-02)

After 1945 Britain ran trials with a number of ex-German submarines including the Type XVIIB *Meteorite* (ex *U-1407*) which was powered by a hydrogen-peroxide fuelled Walter turbine. Two British hydrogen-peroxide fuelled experimental submarines, *Explorer* (S-30) and *Excalibur* (S-40) ran trials between 1956 and 1965, but this fuel was too dangerous for normal use, and the first British postwar operational submarines, the *Porpoise* class, combined the best features of conventional British and German wartime designs. They have a semi-streamlined hull, and are extremely quiet, with an excellent range and habitability and a deep designed diving depth. Some of the class have been discarded before the planned date to allow more money and men to be allocated to the nuclear submarine programme. The *Oberons* are virtually repeat *Porpoises* with improved equipment and a glass-fibre superstructure fore and aft of the conning tower in all except *Orpheus*, which uses light alloy aluminium. A number of these excellent submarines have been supplied to other navies, but problems with the electric cables have delayed the Chilean and last two Australian ships. *Oberon* has been modified to carry equipment to train crews for the nuclear submarines.

Although nuclear submarines are superior to conventional boats in most respects, the nuclear boats are many times more expensive, and only major powers can afford them.

Displacement:	
standard tons (tonnes)	1,610 (1,636)
surface tons (tonnes)	2,030 (2,062)
submerged tons (tonnes)	2,410 (2,449)
Dimensions:	
length (pp)	241ft (73·5m)
(oa)	295·2ft (90m)
beam	26·5ft (8·1m)
draught	18ft (5·5m)
Armament:	
torpedo tubes	
21in (533mm)	8
Machinery:	
diesels (type)	Ad Standard Range-1
(number)	2
electric motors (type)	
shafts	2
Total BHP:	3,680
Total SHP:	6,000
Fuel capacity:	
oil tons (tonnes)	?
Performance:	
surface speed	12kts
submerged speed	17kts
range (surface)	?
(submerged)	?
Crew:	71 (*Porpoise*) 68 (*Oberon*)

Class:	**PORPOISE class**	**OBERON class**
Where built:	Vickers, Barrow; Cammell Laird, Birkenhead; Scotts, Greenock	Vickers, Barrow; Cammell Laird, Birkenhead; Scotts, Greenock; Chatham Dockyard
Laid down:	1953–1955	1957–1973
Built:	1953–1961	1957 onward
Fate:	*Grampus* (S-04) paid off 1976; *Rorqual* (S-02) stationary training ship; remainder in service	RCN *Ojibwa* (SS-172) originally laid down as RN *Onyx*, renamed before launch; in service or under construction

Above, upper: HMS Orpheus, a 1,610-ton patrol submarine of the Oberon class, entered service in 1960

Above, middle: A Porpoise class submarine on the surface. These efficient boats are extremely quiet, and thus harder to detect, when submerged

Above, lower: Porpoise class submarine Finwhale entering Douglas harbour Isle of Man. The deck fittings are retractable to improve streamlining submerged. Note the bow sonar dome

Dreadnought

NUCLEAR ATTACK SUBMARINE
CLASS: *Dreadnought* class (1 boat)
Dreadnought (S-101)

Britain had been studying the possibilities for nuclear powered submarines from 1946, and in 1954 a naval section was set up at the atomic research station, Harwell. This co-operated with the Admiralty, Vickers-Armstrong, Rolls-Royce and Foster Wheeler to design a land based prototype submarine reactor, which was built at Dounreay from spring 1958. The original one was based on the American Westinghouse S5W, and it first went critical in early 1965.

To enable the British nuclear submarine programme to get underway quickly, a complete S5W reactor was bought from America and used to power *Dreadnought*, whose midsection and stern were designed by the American General Dynamics Corporation and were closely based on the USS *Skipjack* (SSN-585). The bow section, which contains the Type 2001 sonar, was designed in Britain and is much blunter than the *Skipjack*'s. Unlike later American nuclear attack submarines, the British boats have their foreplanes on the bows rather than on the fin.

Because *Dreadnought* is much deeper diving than previous British submarines, the hull was very carefully checked for cracks, and much time was spent repairing them in the first years she was in commission. *Dreadnought* also underwent a major overhaul from May 1968 to September 1970, when the reactor core was renewed. The first entirely British nuclear submarine, *Valiant* (S-102), was ordered in August 1960 and completed in July 1966. She is 19ft (5·8m) longer than *Dreadnought* but is otherwise very similar. Four more *Valiants* and three of the improved *Swiftsures* have been built, and three more are under construction.

Above: The nuclear attack submarine Dreadnought, *built 1959–63, is powered by an American Westinghouse S5W nuclear reactor and geared steam turbines*

Displacement:
standard tons (tonnes)	3,000 (3,050)
surface tons (tonnes)	3,500 (3,560)
submerged tons (tonnes)	4,000 (4,060)

Dimensions:
length (oa)	265·8ft (81·1m)
beam	32·2ft (9·75m)
draught	26ft (7·8m)

Armament:
torpedo tubes	
21in (533mm) bow	6

Machinery:
nuclear reactor (type)	S5W
(number)	1
engines (type)	Westinghouse geared steam turbines
shafts	1

Total SHP: ?

Performance:
surface speed	15kts approx
submerged speed	25kts approx
range	over 100,000 miles

Crew: 88

Ship:	DREADNOUGHT (S-101)
Where built:	Vickers, Barrow
Authorised:	1956
Laid down:	12 June 1959
Launched:	21 Oct 1960
Completed:	17 Apr 1963

Resolution Class

NUCLEAR BALLISTIC MISSILE SUBMARINE
CLASS: *Resolution* class (4 boats)
Resolution (S-22) · *Renown* (S-26) ·
Repulse (S-23) · *Revenge* (S-27)

In the late 1950s it had been planned that the Royal Air Force would provide the British strategic deterrent in the 1960s and 1970s using 'V' bombers armed with Skybolt, a stand-off missile then under development in the USA. However, at the Nassau Conference in 1962 President Kennedy told Britain that America was unilaterally abandoning the Skybolt project because of development difficulties. It was decided at that conference that Britain should build her own nuclear ballistic missile submarines. The Polaris SLBMs would be provided by the United States, but Britain would fit her own warheads.

Four submarines were commenced, and when *Resolution* was laid down in February 1964 it was announced that a fifth Polaris submarine was to be ordered. This would ensure that one would always be available on patrol, but this boat was cancelled in 1965 as part of the Labour government's cost cutting defence review.

A good deal of technical assistance was obtained from the Americans, and the *Resolutions* are very similar to the American *Lafayette* class Polaris submarines. The *Resolutions'* actual design is based on that of the *Valiant* (S-102) with a missile compartment worked in between the control centre and the reactor room. *Resolution's* Polaris A-3 missiles have a range of 2,500 miles (2,102nm) and are each fitted with three American 200 kiloton MRV warheads in British designed re-entry vehicles. Various proposals to replace the now obsolescent Polaris with Poseidon have been abandoned as a result of financial and political considerations. However, development is continuing on the existing delivery system and warheads to ensure their viability into the 1980s. Improved nuclear ballistic missile submarines are unlikely to be built owing to their immense cost.

Above: The nuclear ballistic missile submarine Resolution, *exhausting air from her tanks before diving. She carries sixteen Polaris missiles*

Displacement:
surface tons (tonnes)	7,500 (7,620)
submerged tons (tonnes)	8,400 (8,530)

Dimensions:
length (pp)	360ft (109·7m)
(oa)	425ft (129·5m)
beam	33ft (10·1m)
draught	30ft (9·1m)

Armament:
missiles	
Polaris A-3 SLBM	16
torpedo tubes	
21in (533mm) bow	6

Machinery:
nuclear reactor (type)	Rolls-Royce pressurized water-cooled NR-2
(number)	1
engines (type)	English Electric turbine
shafts	1

Total SHP:

Performance:
surface speed	20kts
submerged speed	25kts
range	?

Crew: 143

Ship:	RESOLUTION (S-22)	RENOWN (S-26)	REPULSE (S-23)	REVENGE (S-27)
Where built:	Vickers, Barrow	Cammell Laird, Birkenhead	Vickers, Barrow	Cammell Laird, Birkenhead
Ordered:	8 May 1963	8 May 1963	8 May 1963	8 May 1963
Laid down:	26 Feb 1964	25 June 1964	12 Mar 1965	19 May 1965
Launched:	15 Sept 1966	25 Feb 1967	4 Nov 1967	15 Mar 1968
Completed:	2 Oct 1967	15 Nov 1969	28 Sept 1969	4 Dec 1969

Flower Class

CORVETTE
CLASS: *Flower* class, original and revised types (135 ships built in UK) (79 ships built in Canada)
modified type (10 ships built in UK) (42 ships built in Canada)

Loch Class

FRIGATE
CLASS: *Loch* class (36 ships)

It was not until 1928 that new design of sloop followed those of the World War I *Flower* class. These were the larger *Black Swan* class, the smaller *Guillemots* and the minesweeping sloops of the *Halcyon* class. By 1938 it was clear that war was in the offing — Vice-Admiral A. B Cunningham, then DCNS, proposed the *Hunt* class destroyers in the summer of that year and in April 1939 the Admiralty and Smith's Dock were collaborating in the design of a new corvette which eventually became the *Flower* class. This was not considered adequate for work in the mid-Atlantic although many went far to prove that statement wrong. Smith's Dock once again provided a design, this time for a 'Twin Screw Corvette', soon to be known as the *River* class frigate. Just as the Smith's Dock-designed single-screwed *Castle* class was the ultimate in RN corvette design, so was the *Loch* class in frigate design. The fact that though this last was a wartime design built under wartime conditions, the last of the class was still in service in 1977 is a great tribute to both designers and builders. Sixty *Flower* class ships had been ordered before September 1939, a stop-gap before the first of the *Hunt* class were completed. Another 50 orders were out before the end of the year, vital decisions which were of great importance as the need for escort vessels grew daily. Not only in this sphere were the *Flowers* to show their worth — in 1940 32 of them were fitted with minesweeping gear. Other alterations took place to fit the *Flowers* for deep-water operations. An improved hull-form, a longer fo'c's'le deck and different bridge form were built in to both those in refit and under construction. All these changes were

Above: A total of 246 Flower class corvettes like HMS Thyme, seen here, were built in the UK and Canada for service in WWII as A/S escorts

Above, right: HMS Loch Killin; Loch class frigates mounted one 4in gun and two Squid A/S mortars. The Bay *class, otherwise similar, had four 4in guns and a Hedgehog mortar*

built into the modified *Flowers* and it is of interest that the approved complement of that class was 109 compared with the 29 considered adequate in 1939. Further improvements were, however, essential and from these was evolved the *Castle* class design. These excellent ships, of which 44 were eventually completed, displaced the *Flower* class on the building slips. A similar progression can be seen from the original *River* class frigates, designed with two 4in (102mm) guns and a Hedgehog, to the *Loch* class. These carried a single 4in (102mm) but were given two Squid mortars in B position, a notable advance for A/S work. The *Bay* class, sisters to the *Lochs* in all but armament, were a conversion for the Pacific war where the submarine threat gave way to the air problem. Out went the Squids to be replaced by a Hedgehog and in came two twin 4in (102mm) mountings. Only seven were completed in the five months before the war ended, 12 more in 1945–1949 and one was cancelled.

	Flower class (original type)
Displacement:	
standard tons (tonnes)	950 (965)
full load tons (tonnes)	1,160 (1,179)
Dimensions:	
length (pp)	190ft (57·9m)
(oa)	205·1ft (62·5m)
beam	33·1ft (10·1m)
draught	13·4ft (4·1m)
Armament:	
guns	
4in (102mm)	1
2pdr (40mm)	—
20mm	—
0·5in (12·7mm)	4
A/S weapons	
Squid	
Hedgehog	none originally, but fitted in many after June 1941
depth charges	25 to 50 (2 rails, 2 DCT)
Machinery:	
boilers (type)	cylindrical single-ended
(number)	2
engines	4 cylinder triple expansion
shafts	1
Total IHP:	2,750
Fuel capacity:	
oil tons (tonnes)	230 (234)
Performance:	
speed	16kts
range	3,450 miles (2,996nm) @ 12kt 2,630 miles (2,284nm) @ 16kt
Crew:	23 as designed, 85 later

Hunt Type I-IV

ESCORT DESTROYER
CLASS: *Hunt* class Type I (20 ships) including *Atherstone · Mendip* (later Chinese *Lin Fu* · later British *Mendip* · later Egyptian *Ibrahim el Awal* · later Israeli *Haifa*)

ESCORT DESTROYER
CLASS: *Hunt* class Type II (36 ships) including *Avon Vale · Chiddingfold* (later Indian *Ganga*)

ESCORT DESTROYER
CLASS: *Hunt* class Type III (28 ships) including *Airedale · Eggesford* (later German *Brommy*)

ESCORT DESTROYER
CLASS: *Hunt* class Type IV (2 ships) *Brecon · Brissenden*

Up to the late 1930s, British destroyers had each been designed to be capable of performing the entire range of destroyer duties. However, by 1938 numbers were more important than quality, and in December 1938 the Director of Naval Construction was instructed to prepare a new design. This underwent many alterations before the first pair was laid down by Cammell Laird on 8 June 1939 (to conform with treaty requirements). This design was not as satisfactory as the independent Thornycroft design of the Type IV *Hunts*, which was begun in October 1938. Bedevilled by Admiralty attitudes,

	MENDIP in 1942	CHIDDING-FOLD as built	AVON VALE as built	BRECON as built
Displacement:				
standard tons (tonnes)	907 (922)	1,050 (1,067)	1,087 (1,104)	1,175 (1,194)
full load tons	?	?	?	?
Dimensions:				
length (pp)	264·25ft (80·7m)	264·25ft (80·7m)	264·25ft (80·7m)	276ft (84·3m)
(oa)	280ft (85·5m)	282·5ft (86·3m)	282·5ft (86·3m)	296ft (90·4m)
beam	29ft (8·9m)	31·5ft (9·6m)	31·5ft (9·6m)	33·25ft (10·2m)
draught	7·75ft (2·4m)	7·75ft (2·4m)	7·75ft (2·4m)	9ft (2·7m)
Armament:				
guns				
4in (102mm)	4	6	4	6
2pdr (40mm)	4	4	4	4
40mm	—	—	—	2
20mm	2	2	2–6	8
torpedo tubes				
21in (533mm)	—	—	2	3
Machinery:				
boilers (type)	Admiralty 3-drum			
(number)	2			
engines (type)	Parsons single-reduction geared turbines			
shafts	2			
Total SHP:				
designed	19,000			
Fuel capacity:				
oil tons (tonnes)	280 (284)	280 (284)	280 (284)	?
Performance:				
designed speed	26kts	25kts	25kts	25kts
range	2,380 miles (2,000nm) @ 12kts	2,380 miles (2,000nm) @ 12kts	2,380 miles (2,000nm) @ 12kts	?
Crew:	146	168	168	170

the two ships of this class were not commissioned until 1942–43. The Admiralty *Hunt* Type I had inadequate stability to carry its intended armament. Only *Atherstone* was completed with

three twin 4in (102mm) turrets and torpedo tubes. The Type II's beam was increased to enable them to carry three twin 4in (102mm) whilst the Type IIIs surrendered the third turret

Flower class (revised and modified types)	Loch class
1,015 (1,031)	1,430 (1,453)
—	(Derby Haven and Woodbridge Haven 1,652/1,678, Loch Fada 2,450/2,459)
193ft (58·8m)	286ft (87·2m)
208·4ft (63·5m)	307ft (93·6m)
33·1ft (10·1m)	38·5ft (11·7m)
15·6ft (4·8m)	14·7ft (4·5m)
1	1
— (1 in some modified)	4
2 to 6 (8 in some modified)	6
—	—
—	2
1	—
70 (rev) 100 (mod) (2 rails, 2 DCT in revised type) (2 rails, 4 DCT in modified type)	15 (1 rail, 1 DCT)
as in original type	Admiralty 3-drum
as in original type	2
as in original type	4 cylinder triple expansion
as in original type	2
2,750 in revised type 2,850 in modified type	5,500
230 (234) in revised type 300 (305) in modified type	730 (741)
16kts	20kts
revised type as original type	9,500 miles (8,250nm) @ 12kts
7,400 miles (6,426nm) @ 10kts in modified type	7,000 miles (6,079nm) @ 15kts
96 in revised type, 109 in modified type	124–140

Class:	FLOWER class (original and revised)	FLOWER class (modified)	LOCH class
Where built:	various yards	various yards	various yards
Authorised:	1939–1941	1940–1941 (rev) 1941–1942 (mod)	1943
Laid down:	1939–1941	1940–1941 (rev) 1942–1943 (mod)	Feb 1943–Apr 1946
Launched:	1940–1942	1940–1942 (rev) 1942–1943 (mod)	1943–1946
Completed:	May 1940–Nov 1942	as original (rev), Aug 1943–July 1944 (mod)	Dec 1943–July 1946
Fate:	10 transferred to France; 4 to Greece; 1 to Netherlands 8 to Norway; 1 to Yugoslavia; 3 to Ireland; 1 to Denmark 1 to China; 1 to South Africa; 10 to USA; 4 building in UK for France taken over by RN; 10 were built in Canada for RN but nine stayed with RCN; the list of transfers is formidable, with continued changes of ownership; of those not transferred to other countries 25 were lost, 26 scrapped, 4 became weather ships and 40 were sold to commercial firms; Of the RCN ships 9 were lost in action	Of the 10 RN ships completed, 2 were transferred to RNZN, 4 to RCN and 4 to RIN; of the 42 Canadian-built ships 1 was lost in action	Of the 36 completed 25 were as RN escorts, of which 3 were transferred to Canada, 3 were turned over to S Africa while building, 2 were completed as despatch vessels, 4 as surveying ships and 2 as coastal forces depot ships; Of the RN total 6 were eventually transferred to RNZN, 1 to Malaysia, 1 survey ship to Portugal, 1 depot ship to Iran; the remainder were sold or scrapped by 1970

Left: RHN Pindos *(ex HMS* Bolebroke*) a Hunt Type III escort destroyer seen here from the* Captain *class frigate HMS* Bentinck *in the Mediterranean*

Class:	HUNT class			
	Type I	Type II	Type III	Type IV
Where built:	various yards	various yards	various yards	Thornycroft, Woolston
Authorised:	?	?	?	?
Built:	1939–1941	1940–1942	1941–1943	1942–1943
Fate:	4 sunk 1941–1944; 4 transferred 1948–1954; remainder scrapped 1956–1959	5 sunk 1942–1943; 1 total loss 1942; 15 transferred 1941–1958; remainder scrapped 1957–1968	6 sunk 1942–1944; 2 total loss 1943–1944; 11 transferred 1942–1958; remainder scrapped 1946–1958	Brecon scrapped 1962; Brissenden scrapped 1965

Hunt *class Type I. Note bridge, absence of TT, and 2pdr (40mm) in X position*

Leander Class

FRIGATES
CLASS: *Leander* class
(UK 16 original and 10 broad-beamed ships)
(Australia 2 basically original ships)
(Chile 2 broad-beamed ships)
(India 6 modified broad-beamed ships)
(Netherlands 6 modified original ships)
(New Zealand 1 broad-beamed and 1 original ship)

Amazon Class

FRIGATES
CLASS: *Amazon* class *(Type 21)*
(8 ships)

Postwar building of frigates by the Royal Navy began in 1952 after a considerable programme of conversions of the wartime construction destroyers. Forty-eight of these had been built — of the survivors 33 became Type 15 (full conversion) and seven of the T class, Type 16 (limited conversions). In this period designs had been prepared of the Type 12 (general-purpose *Whitby* class, six ships), Type 14 (*Blackwood* class, 2nd Rate, 12 ships), Type 41 (*Leopard* class, A/A frigates, 4 ships) and Type 61 (*Salisbury* class, air direction frigates, four ships). The first of the Type 14 and Type 61 were laid down in 1952 and the total of 26 ships was completed between 1955 and 1960. The 1954–55 programme allowed for the first of nine ships of a modified Type 12, the *Rothesay* class, all of which were completed in 1960–61, being followed in 1961–64 by the seven Type

Above, upper: HMS Antelope *(F-170) of the Amazon class. Note the boxy superstructure amidships with large funnel, and helicopter hangar and flight deck aft. The Sea Cat SAM launcher is on top of the hangar*

Above: HMS Leander, *name-ship of a class of 26 frigates, conducting trials with Ikara, which has replaced her 4·5in (114mm) turret*

81 ships, the *Tribal* class. These were a new departure in having combined steam and gas-turbine propulsion, although with only one screw and a speed of 28kts. A certain specialisa-

tion was evident here: the *Tribals* were intended primarily for Persian Gulf service, although when the last was completed in 1964 there would be only three more years of that requirement. On 10 April 1959 the first *Leander* was laid down. Although the *Rothesays* were converted to carry a helicopter, the new class was the first British frigate designed to do so. With improved radar and variable depth sonar, this was the most numerous single class to be built for the Royal Navy for many years. In the 1964–65 programme the first of the 'broad-beamed' variety was allowed for. These, the last 10 of the class, were 2ft (0·6m) broader to improve stability. Rearmament programmes were begun in 1971 when the first Ikara conversion (*Leander*) was put in hand. Seven more were to follow. The conversion involved the replacement of the 4·5in (114mm) turret by the A/S launcher, and a similar loss took place in the Exocet conversion, the first (of 18) of which, *Cleopatra*, was completed in November 1975. It is of interest that the Chilean *Leanders* have also received Exocet, but not at the expense of the turret. Before the first of the 'broad-beamed' type was laid down discussion was afoot in the Admiralty about the *Leanders*' successors and before she commissioned Vosper-Thornycroft received a contract for a new design frigate to be prepared in collaboration with Yarrow. This produced the *Amazon* class (Type 21), the first being laid down in November 1969. The variations from the *Leander* design are as interesting as their hull-form and outline are attractive. The propulsion became all gas-turbine, a system to be used in the succeeding Type 42 destroyers and Type 22 frigates. Again only one helicopter is carried and the main gun armament is reduced to one 4·5in (114mm) weapon although this is in addition to four Exocet launchers and Sea Cat. The complement has been reduced by 70–80 men while the speed and range have improved. Only eight *Amazons* are planned, their successors being the Type 22 (*Broadsword* class) with two helicopters, no main gun, Exocet, Sea Wolf and an increased complement.

Displacement:	Leander class (RN) (original)	Leander class (RN) (broad-beamed)	Amazon class
standard tons (tonnes)	2,450 (2,489)	2,500 (2,540)	2,750 (2,794)
full load tons (tonnes)	2,860 (2,906)	2,962 (3,009)	3,150 (3,202)
Dimensions:			
length (wl)	360ft (109·7m)		360ft (109·7m)
(oa)	372ft (113·4m)		384ft (117m)
beam	41ft (12·5m)	43ft (13·1m)	41·8ft (12·7m)
draught	18ft (5·5m)		14·5ft (4·4m)
Armament:			
guns			
4·5in (114mm)	2 in unconverted ships		1
40mm	2 in some (conversions)		—
20mm	2 (unconverted ships)		2
missiles			
Exocet	to be fitted in 8 original ships and all broad-beamed ships		4
Sea Cat	single in unconverted originals twin in Ikara conversions triple in Exocet conversions		1 quad (to be replaced by Sea Wolf in later ships when available)
A/S helicopter	1 Wasp with A/S torpedoes		1 Lynx with A/S torpedoes
A/S Ikara	8 conversions of original ships		—
A/S torpedo tubes	2 triple in Exocet conversions		2 triple to be fitted
Limbo	1 in non-Exocet ships		—
Machinery:			
boilers (type)	—		—
(number)	2		—
main machinery	DR geared turbines		Rolls Royce Olympus and Tyne gas turbines
shafts	2		2 of each
Total SHP:	30,000		56,000 (Olympus), 8,500 (Tyne)
Fuel capacity:			
oil tons (tonnes)	460 (467)		—
kerosene tons (tonnes)	—		?
Performance:			
speed	30kts		32kts (18kts on Tynes)
range	4,500 miles (3,908nm) @ 12kts		3,500 miles (3,039nm) @ 18kts, 1,200 miles (1,042nm) @ 30kts
Crew:	251 (original), 260 (broad-beamed)		177

Class:	LEANDER class	AMAZON class
Where built:	various yards	various yards
Approved:	1958–1967	1967
Laid down:	10 Apr 1959–Nov 1969	6 Nov 1969–30 Oct 1974
Launched:	28 June 1961–10 Sept 1971	26 Apr 1971–20 Nov 1975
Commissioned:	27 Mar 1963–10 Feb 1973	11 May 1974–1978 (?)
Fate:	In service	In service

MTB

MOTOR TORPEDO BOAT
CLASS: *Vosper 70'* (10 boats)
Nos 31–40

MOTOR TORPEDO BOAT
CLASS: *Vosper 73'* (16 boats)
Nos 380–395

MOTOR TORPEDO BOAT
CLASS: *Fairmile D Type* (200 boats)
Nos 601–800

Although large numbers of Thornycroft coastal motor boats (CMBs) were used by the Royal Navy during World War I, shortage of money and the absence of a tactical requirement for torpedo boats prevented further developments until the mid-1930s. In 1935 prototypes were ordered from the British Power Boat Company, but although they formed the basis of the British motor gun boats (MGBs) and American PT boats, most British motor torpedo boats (MTBs) were built to Vosper designs. The size and armament were increased during the war, and later boats had radar, but they all had a similar hard chine hull. The *Fairmile D* was a larger boat with the combined armament of an MTB and MGB. There was no suitable British engine, and until Italy entered the war the Italian Isotta-Fraschini was used. Eventually the Packard was fitted as standard after problems with the final drive had been cured. These petrol engines made the British boats more vulnerable than the German diesel-engined craft.

A standard hull form was used for most of the war to enable them to fit existing landing trolleys. Motor Gun Boats (MGBs) were originally modified from Motor Anti/Submarine Boats (MA/SBs), and were fitted with a heavy gun armament to counter *S-Boats*. They did not carry torpedo tubes.

Vosper 70' MTB. Note hard chine hull, torpedo tube and machine gun turret

	Nos 31-40 as built	Nos 380-395 as built	Nos 601-800 in 1945
Displacement:			
light tons (tonnes)	39·75 (40·4)	44·5 (45·2)	105 (106·7)
full load tons (tonnes)	47 (47·8)	46·7 (47·4)	?
Dimensions:			
length (wl)	?	?	110ft (33·6m)
(oa)	70ft (21·4m)	73ft (22·3m)	115ft (35·1m)
beam	14·75ft (4·5m)	19·5ft (6m)	21·25ft (6·5m)
draught (max)	5ft (1·5m)	5·6ft (1·7m)	5ft (1·5m)
Armament:			
guns			
6pdr (57mm)	—	—	2
20mm	—	2	2
0·5in (12·7mm)	2	—	4
0·303in (7·7mm)	4	4	4
torpedo tubes			
18in (457mm)	—	4	4
21in (533mm)	2	—	—
Machinery:			
petrol engines (type)	Isotta-Fraschini (Hall-Scott in Nos 35–40)	Packard	Packard
(number)	3	3	4
shafts	3	3	4
Total SHP:			
designed	3,600	4,050	5,000
Fuel capacity:			
petrol gallons (litres)	2,750 (10,000)	2,500 (9,091)	5,000 (18,182) (+3,180 (11,564) in deck tanks (max))
Performance:			
designed speed	40kts (25kts in Nos 35–40)	39·5kts	29kts
range	?	?	1,380 miles (1,200nm) @ 10kts
Crew:	12	13	30

	VOSPER 70ft Nos 31-40	VOSPER 73ft Nos 380-395	FAIRMILE D Type
Class:			
Where built:	Vosper, Portsmouth	Vosper, Portsmouth	various yards
Authorised:	1938	1944	1942
Built:	1949–1940	1944	1942–1944
Fate:	4 sunk 1940; Nos *31, 32, 34* renamed *CT 22, CT 24, CT 23* 1943 as target tugs; deleted 1945	Nos *381* and *383* target boats 1946; deleted 1945 onwards	38 sunk 1942–1945; ? transferred; deleted 1945 onwards

---

Winchester SRN-6

SRN-6 HOVERCRAFT
CLASS: *Winchester* class (20 craft)
Britain (1 craft) · Iran (8 craft) ·
Egypt (3 craft) · Saudi Arabia (8 craft)

Displacement:
light tons (tonnes) 6·33 (6·44)
full load tons (tonnes) 10 (10·2)
Dimensions:
length (oa) 48·4ft (14·7m)
beam 25·3ft (7·7m)
height 15·9ft (4·8m)
Armament:
can carry machine guns and troops
Machinery:
gas turbine (type) Gnome
(number) 1
auxiliary diesel (type) Peters
propellers 1
Total SHP:
designed 1,050
Fuel capacity:
oil tons (tonnes) ?
Performance:
designed speed 58kts
range 225 miles (190nm)@?kts
Crew: varies with role

	WINCHESTER class
Class:	
Where built:	BHC Britain
Built (for navies):	1967 onward
Fate:	in service

The SRN-6 delivered to the Royal Navy trials unit in 1967 was designed by Saunders-Roe, and is a commercial passenger craft, although it has been modified with hardpoints to carry weapons and equipment. It is a larger version of the SRN-5, six of which were licence-built by Bell in America, three for the US Navy and three for the US Army. Designated the SK-5 Patrol Air-cushion Vehicle (AACV) they were armed with two 0·5in (12·7mm) and two 0·3in (7·62mm) machine-guns and grenade launchers for their deployment in South Vietnam from 1968. Britain has also built a 50 ton (50·8 tonne) military hovercraft, the BH-7 *Wellington*, one of which was supplied to the Royal Navy in 1970, and six to Iran. They have a full load displacement of 50 tons (51 tonnes) and a speed of 60kts. These hovercraft can be used for a variety of roles, including minesweeping, troop-transport, and as patrol vessels, but they are complex and expensive and their only widespread use so far has been in the Middle East, where they are well suited to areas of desert and shallow water. The only country so far to develop the concept further is the United States, which has built the Bell SES-100B 100 ton (102 tonne) craft, and is constructing the 3,000 ton (3,050 tonne) LSES vessel. This will be an anti-submarine vessel, armed with guns, missiles and helicopters, but it will also be able to operate V/STOL aircraft. Her size will enable her to carry sufficient fuel for a reasonable range, and to operate in rough seas, thereby overcoming two restrictions on the employment of smaller hovercraft such as the 200 ton (203 tonne) British SRN-4, one of which was chartered in 1976 by the Royal Navy for minesweeping trials. The USSR also has a number of naval hovercraft, mostly the *Gus* class 27 ton (27·4 tonne) craft, although they also operate a number of 220 ton (224 tonne) vessels of the *Aist* class and other types are under evaluation.

Below: The Winchester *class SRN-6 hovercraft, a specially modified commercial craft delivered to the Royal Naval Trials Unit in 1967, runs trials in Borneo*

FRANCE

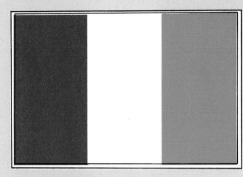

OVER the centuries the navy of France suffered frequent reversals in its fortunes but had, overall, maintained imaginative and forward-looking policies. However, the rapid technical advances brought about by the Industrial Revolution precipitated a major argument over the doctrine to be adopted. Not helped by the rapid procession of thirty-one Ministers of Marine in the thirty years following 1871, this difference resolved itself into a clash between those supporting the traditional 'big ship' policy and the 'jeune école' who were advocates of torpedo attack by small craft on enemy harbours coupled with a trade war. The latter view rejected the need for command of the sea and in 1886 battleship construction was temporarily suspended. Not only did the 'jeune école' theories influence the shape of the fleet; they also advocated the withdrawal of support from foreign possessions and the merchant marine in wartime.

The variations in policy that took place at the close of the 19th and beginning of the 20th centuries were unhealthy for morale and inhibited the build-up of a balanced fleet. The extraordinary activities of Pelletan as Minister of Marine between 1902–05 were directed as much against the Entente Cordiale as they were at the efficiency of the fleet he was supposed to serve. The effects of his attitudes rippled on through the years to 1914, resulting in delays to more realistic building programmes because of the lack of capacity in French industry.

In fact the Entente Cordiale saw the end of the theories of the 'jeune école'. The enemy across the Channel had been replaced by one beyond the effective range of torpedo craft and the early submarines – Germany. Under this new alignment France began to concentrate more on the problems of the Mediterranean where the Triple Alliance had united Italy with Germany and Austria.

Thus when World War I finally broke out the bulk of the French fleet was in the Mediterranean. This was a navy in which only one dreadnought was in commission with three others to follow in the next three months, an apt commentary on the inability of French industry to match the demands made upon it. In a similar period the Royal Navy commissioned thirty-one dreadnoughts.

During the next four years the main task of the French Navy was ensuring safe lines of communication, although before the entry of Italy into the war on the Allied side in May 1915, an inconclusive action was fought against the Austro-Hungarian fleet in the Adriatic and one battleship was lost at the Dardanelles with others badly damaged. Although the French submarine branch had been early in its inception the dangers from these craft were not appreciated and a number of ships from battleships downwards were lost to submarine attack.

In the years after 1918 a disgruntled and somewhat apathetic navy failed to make much advance until, under the guidance of Georges Leygues and with Mussolini's Italy growing in strength, a firm building programme was agreed in 1932. This plan for six battleships, six new cruisers and a number of destroyers was never completed but by 1939 the French Navy had not only a powerful fleet in commission but had regained its sense of purpose. Under Admiral Darlan they were vigorously employed in the early months but the Armistice with Germany of June 1940 changed matters dramatically. The sad engagement at Oran, designed to prevent that part of the French fleet from falling into German hands, resulted in the loss of 1,300 French lives. At Alexandria the French ships were interned and, when the Germans occupied Toulon in November 1942 seventy-seven ships were scuttled including three battleships, seven cruisers, and thirty-two destroyers.

From June 1940 to the end of the war a growing number of Free French ships operated with the Allies and, although this record was tarnished by the vindictive attitude to the flag officers who remained behind, it was the basis for the new French Navy. Today the Marine Nationale is directed with imagination and, but for the problems of political intervention and conscription, could take a senior place in Western Europe.

The French cruiser SS Gloire *in
1943 in zebra camouflage after a refit in the USA*

Bearn
AIRCRAFT-CARRIER
CLASS: *Normandie* class (1 ship)
Bearn

Service career BEARN
1914 (Aug) Work suspended.
1923 (Aug–May 1927) Converted into carrier: experimental work, then in French Fleet.
1939–1940 Aircraft transporter, USA to France.
1940 (June–July 1943) At Fort de France, Martinique.
Late 1943 Converted to aircraft transport at New Orleans: rearmed and flight deck shortened.
1945–1947 Aircraft transport in French Indo-China.
1948–1966 Hulk: training ship then submarine depot ship.
1966 (Nov) Deleted.
1967 Scrapped.

In order to increase the number of guns without increasing the size of hull, the *Normandie* class was to have had its twelve 13·4in (340mm) guns mounted in British designed quadruple turrets. These were basically two twin mounts side-by-side on a single barbette. Because turbines were so uneconomical at cruising speeds, they were to have had reciprocating engines on two shafts. However, *Bearn*, which was intended to form a squadron with the three turbine-powered *Bretagnes*, was to have had only turbine machinery. Work on the *Normandies* was suspended during World War I in order to concentrate on smaller vessels, and their guns were used by the French Army. After the war work was not resumed because they were already obsolete. However, *Bearn* was selected for conversion to a carrier, and was given *Normandie*'s machinery, which was nearly complete. She was very slow, and did not compare very favourably with foreign conversions, but she was the only French carrier until 1946. Two other carriers, *Joffre* and *Painlevé*, were laid down just before World War II, but were dismantled during the war. They were also not a particularly good design, having a very small flight deck for their size.

Above: Bearn *in 1929, two years after completion. Converted from a battleship, she was the French Navy's only inter-war aircraft carrier*

Displacement:	Bearn battleship as designed		Bearn carrier as built
standard tons (tonnes)	—		21,795 (22,146)
normal tons (tonnes)	24,833 (25,230)		
full load tons (tonnes)	?		27,950 (28,400)
Dimensions:			
length (wl)	573·1ft (175m)		573·1ft (175m)
(oa)	577·7ft (176·4m)		598ft (182·6m)
beam (hull)	88·4ft (27m)		88·75ft (27·1m)
(ext)			115·3ft (35·2m)
draught	28·5ft (8·7m)		30·5 (9·3m)
Armament:	as designed	in 1939	in 1943
guns			
13·4in (340mm) 45cal	12	—	—
6·1in (155mm)	—	8	—
5·5in (138mm)	24	—	—
5in (127mm)	—	—	4
75mm	—	6	—
40mm	—	—	24
37mm	—	8	—
20mm	—	—	26
torpedo tubes			
17·7in (450mm)	6	—	—
21·7in (550mm)	—	4	—
aircraft	—	40	
Armour:	as designed		as built
side (belt)	6·3–11·8in (160–300mm)		3·1in (80mm)
(ends)	5·1–7·1in (130–180mm)		
deck (flight)			1in (25mm)
(upper)	2in (50mm)		
(main)			1in (25mm)
(lower)	2–2·75in (50–70mm)		2·4in (60mm)
main turrets	9·8–13·4in (250–340mm)		—
barbettes	11·2in (284mm)		—
casemates	6·3–7·1in (160–180mm)		—
Machinery:			
boilers (type)	Niclausse		du Temple–Normand
(number)	21		12
engines (type)	Parsons turbines		reciprocating (2) turbines (2)
shafts	4		4
Total HP:			
designed	32,000		36,200
Fuel capacity:			
coal normal tons (tonnes)	900 (914)		—
max tons (tonnes)	2,700 (2,743)		
oil tons (tonnes)	300 (305)		2,160 (2,195)
Performance:			
designed speed	21kts		21·5kts
range	7,730 miles (6,500nm) @ 12kts		8,325 miles (7,000nm) @ 10kts

Ship:	NORMAN-DIE	LANGUE-DOC	FLANDRE	GASCOGNE	BEARN
Where built:	A et C de Loire, St Nazaire	Forges et Chantiers, Bordeaux	Brest Dockyard	Lorient Dockyard	La Seyne
Authorised:	1912	1912	1912	1912	1912
Laid down:	18 Apr 1913	18 Apr 1913	1 Oct 1913	1 Oct 1913	Jan 1914
Launched:	19 Oct 1914	1 May 1915	20 Oct 1914	20 Sept 1914	Apr 1920
Started conversion:	—				Aug 1923
Completed:	—				May 1927
Fate:	Scrapped incomplete 1924–1925	Scrapped incomplete 1924–1925	Scrapped incomplete 1924–1925	Scrapped incomplete 1924–1925	Scrapped 1967

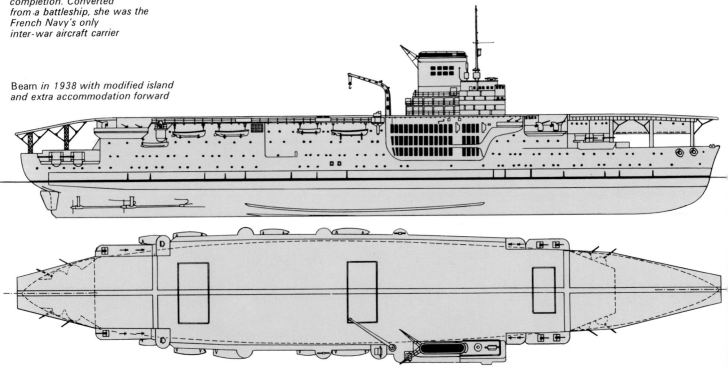

Bearn *in 1938 with modified island and extra accommodation forward*

Clemenceau
AIRCRAFT-CARRIER
CLASS: *Clemenceau* class (2 ships)
Clemenceau (R-98) · *Foch* (R-99)

After World War II *Bearn* was totally obsolete, and the French naval air arm was reformed round the escort carrier *Dixmude* (ex-*Biter*, ex-*Rio Parana*). Transferred in 1945, she was used operationally in French Indo-China, but was later reduced to an aircraft transport and then a barracks. She was returned to the USA in 1965 and sunk as a target. *Dixmude* was supplemented by *Arromanches* (R-95, ex-*Colossus*). This ex-British light fleet carrier was similar to the *Colossus* and *Majestic* class light fleet carriers transferred or sold to Argentina, Australia, Brazil, Canada, India and the Netherlands. She was originally lent for five years from August 1946, but was purchased by France after a refit in 1951. She was rebuilt with a 4° angle deck and mirror landing sight in 1957–1959 to operate modern anti-submarine aircraft, and was not discarded until the early 1970s. To fill the gap before the French built their own aircraft-carriers, two American light carriers, *Belleau Wood* (renamed *Bois Belleau*) and *Langley* (renamed *Lafayette*) were transferred in 1951. They were returned to the USA in 1960 and 1963 respectively, as the new *Clemenceaus* became ready for service. The latter are the first aircraft-carriers designed and built as such to

be completed in France. The first French postwar design, prepared in 1947, was for a 16,000 ton (16,260 tonne) light carrier, but this project was abandoned, and the *Clemenceaus* are much larger ships. They are similar in size to the American *Essex* class, which they resemble in many respects, but they have a stern similar to the later British carriers. They were designed to

Above: Clemenceau, completed 1961, was France's first purpose-built aircraft carrier and, with Foch, constitutes a carrier attack force second only to the USA

carry a powerful gun anti-aircraft armament which, unusually, they still retain. They were originally to have been armed with 12 twin 57mm guns. This was altered to 12 single 3·9in (100mm) guns in 1956, and was fixed at eight 3·9in (100mm) guns in 1958. They were completed with an armoured 8° angled flight deck, a mirror landing sight designed in France, two lifts and two steam catapults. They have one hangar deck. The funnel is blended in with the island superstructure, as in American carriers. They are fitted with the DRB1 10 three-dimensional radar and SENIT tactical data system, which is based on US equipment. They also have an SQS-505 sonar. The *Clemenceaus* are too small to operate large modern carrier aircraft, and too much may have been attempted on too limited a displacement. *Clemenceau* was fitted with bulges after trials and *Foch* received hers during construction. Nevertheless, they give France a more powerful carrier attack force than any country except the USA. A 30,000 ton (30,480 tonne) carrier was projected in the 1958 estimates, but was cancelled because of financial economies. A nuclear-powered helicopter carrier (PA-75) is at present projected. This is comparable in all but machinery with the British *Invincible* (CAH-1), and will have an uninterrupted flight deck and hangar capable of operating either ten to fifteen large or 25 small helicopters, or a mix of helicopters and V/STOL aircraft.

Displacement:

standard tons (tonnes)	22,000 (22,350)
normal tons (tonnes)	27,307 (27,744)
full load tons (tonnes)	32,780 (33,300)

Dimensions:

length (pp)	780·8ft (238m)
(oa)	869·4ft (265m)
beam (hull)	104·1ft (31·7m)
(ext)	168ft (51·2m)
draught	25·3ft (7·7m)

Armament:

guns	
3·9in (100mm)	8
aircraft	40

Armour: flight deck, island and hull

Machinery:

boilers (type)	?
(number)	6
engines (type)	Parsons geared turbines
shafts	2

Total SHP:

designed	126,000

Fuel capacity:

oil tons (tonnes)	3,720 (3,780)

Performance:

designed speed	32kts
range	7,500 miles (6,300nm) @ 18kts

Crew (including aircrew): approx 2,150

Ship:	**CLEMENCEAU (R-98)**	**FOCH (R-99)**
Where built:	Brest Dockyard	Penhoët, St Nazaire
Authorised:	1953	1955
Laid down:	Nov 1955	Feb 1957
Launched:	21 Dec 1957	28 July 1960
Completed:	22 Nov 1961	15 July 1963
Fate:	In service	In service

Service career CLEMENCEAU (R-98)
Beam when launched 98·1ft (30m). Rebuilt after trials with bulges. In service.

Clemenceau in 1977. Note lift abaft island. Detail shows hangar amidships

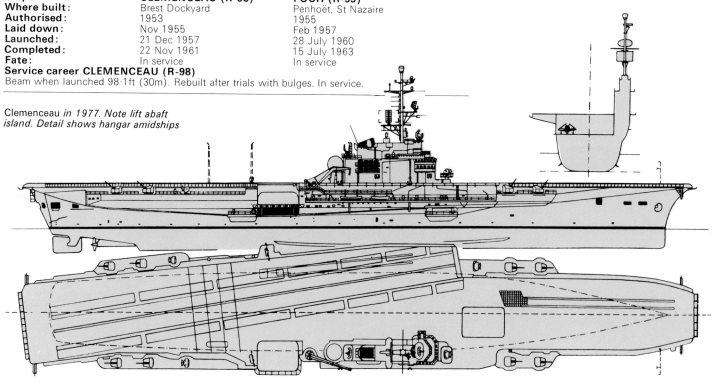

Courbet

BATTLESHIP
CLASS: *Courbet* class (4 ships)
Jean Bart · Courbet · Paris · France

Service career COURBET
1914–1915 Flagship Mediterranean Fleet.
1914 (16 Aug) Sank Austrian cruiser *Zenta*.
1916–1918 In 1st Squadron.
1921–1922 Refit.
1926–1929 Reconstructed.
1931–1939 Gunnery training ship.
1939 Harbour training.
1940 (June) Coast defence at Cherbourg, escaped to Britain.
1940 (3 July) Interned at Portsmouth. Transferred to Free French. Used as AA battery and training ship.
1944 (10 June) Scuttled as part of 'Mulberry' harbour. Broken up after World War II.

The French Navy stagnated in the first decade of the twentieth century, and although some good ships were produced, they took so long to design and build that they were outclassed before they were completed. The pre-dreadnought *Dantons*, though they compared very favourably with the last foreign pre-dreadnoughts, were laid down after *Dreadnought* herself had been completed, and because six *Dantons* were built there were no slips available to build dreadnoughts. By the time the first French dreadnoughts, the *Courbets*, were in service, Britain, Germany and the USA were producing super-dreadnoughts. The *Courbets'* dimensions were limited by the size of the available drydocks, and two turrets were superimposed to save length. Even so the short fo'c's'le made them very wet in rough weather, and the two wing turrets were poorly placed. A good feature was that they were built with fire control, but the secondary armament was badly disposed. The forward guns were too near the bow, and all of them were too close together, causing mutual interference and enabling one enemy shell to destroy several guns. Their protection was reasonable, and like the *Dantons* they used turbines. Their appearance was distinctive, with a piled-up superstructure and two funnels forward of the pole foremast. The third funnel was further aft because the wing turrets' magazines and shell-handling rooms separated the boiler rooms. *France* foundered after hitting a rock in Quiberon Bay, but the remainder had their forefunnels altered and the pole foremast replaced by a tripod mast forward of the funnels between 1921 and 1924. They were again rebuilt in 1928–1929, when new boilers and anti-aircraft guns were fitted. They were all used as training ships after 1931. *Océan* (ex-*Jean Bart*) was demilitarised in 1938, and was scuttled at Toulon on 27 November 1942. The wreck was salved in 1944 after use as a target, and was scrapped. *Paris* escaped to Britain in June 1940 and was interned. She was later handed over to the Polish Navy as a barracks, and was returned to France in 1945. The three *Bretagne* class battleships were very similar to the *Courbets* and differed mainly by having 13·4in (340mm) guns with a single centreline turret in place of the wing turrets. They also had a single forefunnel from the start, with a pole mast ahead of it.

Courbet as built.

Displacement	as built	in 1930
standard tons (tonnes)	—	22,189 (22,544)
normal tons (tonnes)	23,100 (23,470)	
full load tons (tonnes)	26,000 (26,416)	25,850 (26,264)
Dimensions:		
length (pp)	520ft (158·5m)	
(wl)	541ft (164·9m)	
(oa)	551ft (168m)	
beam	91·5ft (27·9m)	
draught	29·5ft (9m)	
Armament:		
guns		
12in (305mm) 45cal	12	12
5·5in (138mm) 55cal	22	22
3in (75mm)	—	4
3pdr (47mm)	4	—
torpedo tubes		
18in (456mm)	4	
Armour:		
side (belt)	7–10·6in (180–270mm)	
(ends)	7in (180mm)	
deck (fo'c's'le)	1·2in (30mm)	
(upper)	2in (50mm)	
(main)	2·75in (70mm)	
main turrets	3·9–11·4in (100–290mm)	
barbettes	11in (280mm)	
casemates	7in (180mm)	
Machinery:		
boilers (type)	Belleville	
(number)	24 (16 large, 8 small)	
engines (type)	Parsons turbines	
shafts	4	
Total SHP:		
designed	28,000	
trials	?	
Fuel capacity:		
coal, normal tons (tonnes)	906 (920)	
coal, maximum tons (tonnes)	2,700 (2,743)	
oil tons (tonnes)	310 (315)	
Performance:		
designed speed	21kts	
trial speed	20·81kts	
range	9,900 miles (8,400nm) @ 10kts	
Crew:	1,108	1,069

Ship:	JEAN BART	COURBET	PARIS	FRANCE
Where built:	Brest Dockyard	Lorient Dockyard	Forge et Chantiers, La Seyne	Penhoët, St Nazaire
Authorised:	1910	1910	1910	1910
Laid down:	15 Nov 1910	1 Sept 1910	10 Nov 1911	30 Nov 1911
Launched:	22 Sept 1911	23 Sept 1911	7 Nov 1912	28 Sept 1912
Completed:	5 Jun 1913	19 Nov 1913	Aug 1914	Aug 1914
Fate:	renamed *Océan* in 1937; scrapped 1945	expended as breakwater, 10 June 1944	scrapped 1956	total loss 26 Aug 1922

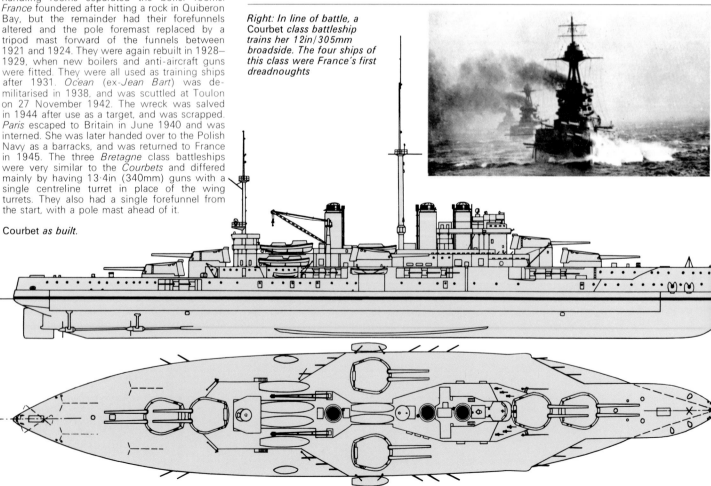

Right: In line of battle, a Courbet *class battleship trains her 12in/305mm broadside. The four ships of this class were France's first dreadnoughts*

Dunkerque

FAST BATTLESHIP
CLASS: *Dunkerque* class (2 ships)
Dunkerque · Strasbourg

Service career DUNKERQUE
1938–1939 Home waters.
1939 (Oct–April 1940) Joint anti-raider patrols with British in Atlantic and convoy escort.
1940 (April) To Mediterranean.
1940 (3 July) Battle of Mers-el-Kebir hit by four 15in (381mm) shells.
1940 (July) Badly damaged by British air attack.
1940 (July–Feb 1942) Repairs at Mers-el-Kebir.
1942 (Feb) To Toulon.
1942 (Feb–Nov) Repairs at Toulon.
1942 (27 Nov) All military equipment destroyed and ship badly damaged in dry dock.
1943 (to Aug 1945) Salvage operations.
1945 (Aug) Undocked to clear dry dock; not returned to service.
1958 Hulk sold for scrap.

Dunkerque, the end product of a series of designs dating from 1926, was designed to catch and destroy 8in (203mm) cruisers and the German *Deutschlands*. She was accordingly armoured against 11in (280mm) shells at normal battle ranges.

The main armament was a new 13in (330mm) gun mounted in two quadruple turrets, an arrangement which gave the greatest number of guns on the smallest displacement. Each turret was virtually two twin turrets mounted side-by-side on the same barbette, and these were based on those that were to have been fitted on the cancelled *Normandies* of 1913. A disadvantage of quadruple turrets (demonstrated at Mers-el-Kebir) was that one hit could halve the main armament. The two turrets were both mounted forward, in imitation of HMS *Nelson*. This reduced the length of the armour belt, but the turrets had to be well separated to avoid a single hit eliminating both simultaneously. As in other ships with all the heavy guns mounted forward, blast prevented firing on bearings much abaft of the beam.

The 5·1in (130mm) guns were mounted in three quadruple and two twin turrets. The quadruple turrets were intended to be dual-purpose, the first time the secondary armament of a major warship had been used in this way. Unfortunately the mechanisms were very fragile and they were too unwieldy for accurate anti-aircraft fire. Another innovation on the *Dunkerques* was the introduction of a hangar.

The armour belt was sloped, as in HMS *Hood*, and although the vertical and horizontal armour was weak the ship stood up to 15in (381mm) shell hits better than might have been expected. The underwater protection was very good. Altogether, despite some problems caused by trying to put new ideas into service too quickly, the ships were well balanced units, easily capable of fulfilling their designed tasks.

Displacement:		
standard tons (tonnes)	26,500 (26,924)	
normal tons (tonnes)	30,750 (31,242)	
full load tons (tonnes)	35,500 (36,068)	
Dimensions:		
length (pp)	686ft (209·1m)	
(oa)	703·7ft (214·5m)	
beam	102·4ft (31·2m)	
draught	28·9ft (8·8m)	
Armament:		
guns		
13in (330mm) 52cal	8	
5·1in (130mm) 45cal	16	
37mm	8	
13·2mm	32	
aircraft	4	
Armour:		
side (belt)	5·75–9·75in (145–245mm)	
deck (upper)	5·5in (138mm)	
(lower)	2in (51mm)	
main turrets	10–13in (254–330mm)	
barbettes	13·5in (345mm)	
secondary turrets	3·2–3·5in (80–90mm)	
barbettes	4·7in (120mm)	
Machinery:		
boilers (type)	Indret small tube	
(number)	6	
engines (type)	Parsons single reduction geared turbines	
shafts	4	
Total SHP:		
designed	112,500	
trials	114,000	
Fuel capacity:		
oil tons (tonnes)	6,500 (6,600)	
Performance:		
designed speed	29·5kts	
trial speed	30·57kts	
range	8,900 miles (7,500nm) @ 15kts	
Crew:	1,381	

Ship:	DUNKERQUE	STRASBOURG
Where built:	Brest Dockyard	Penhoët, St Nazaire
Authorised:	1931	1934
Laid down:	26 Dec 1932	25 Nov 1934
Launched:	2 Oct 1935	12 Dec 1936
Completed:	1 May 1937	Dec 1938
Fate:	severely damaged 27 Nov 1942; hulk scrapped 1958	scuttled 27 Nov 1942

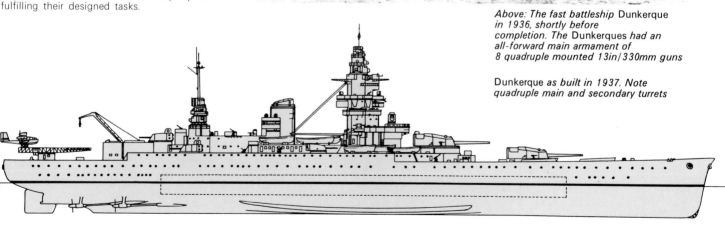

Above: The fast battleship Dunkerque in 1936, shortly before completion. The Dunkerques had an all-forward main armament of 8 quadruple mounted 13in/330mm guns

Dunkerque as built in 1937. Note quadruple main and secondary turrets

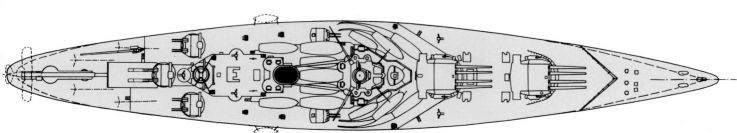

Richelieu

BATTLESHIP

CLASS: *Richelieu* class (2 ships)
Richelieu · Jean Bart

Displacement:	Richelieu as built	Jean Bart in 1952
standard tons (tonnes)	38,500 (39,116)	42,800 (43,485)
full load tons (tonnes)	47,500 (48,260)	49,850 (50,648)
Dimensions:		
length (pp)	792·9ft (242·1m)	792·9ft (242·1m)
(oa)	812·2ft (248m)	812·2ft (248m)
beam	108ft (33m)	116·3ft (35·5m)
draught	35ft (10·7m)	32·4ft (9·9m)
Armament:		
15in (380mm) 45cal	8	8
6in (152mm) 55cal	9	9
3·9in (100mm)	12	24
57mm	—	28
37mm	16	—
20mm	—	40
13·2mm	28	—
Armour:		
side (belt)	8·9–15·7in (225–400mm)	
deck (main)	5·1–6·6in (130–170mm)	
(middle)	1·6–1·9in (40–50mm)	
main turrets	6·6–16·9in (170–430mm)	
barbettes	15·9in (405mm)	
secondary turrets	5·1in (130mm)	
Machinery:		
boilers (type)	Indret	
(number)	6	
engines (type)	Parsons single reduction geared turbines	
shafts	4	
Total SHP:		
designed	150,000	150,000
trial	155,000	176,030
Fuel capacity:		
oil tons (tonnes)	6,790 (6,900)	
Performance:		
designed speed	30kts	30kts
trial speed	32kts	32·1kts
range	10,110 miles (8,500nm) @ 14kts	
Crew:	1,670	2,143

Ship:	RICHELIEU	JEAN BART	CLEMENCEAU
Where built:	Brest Dockyard	Penhoët St Nazaire	Brest Dockyard
Authorised:	1935	1935	1935
Laid down:	22 Oct 1935	12 Dec 1936	17 Jan 1939
Launched:	17 Jan 1939	6 March 1940	—
Completed:	July 1940–Aug 1943	June 1940–1952	—
Fate:	Scrapped 1968	Scrapped 1969	Incomplete hull sunk 27 Aug 1944, salvaged and scrapped 1948–1951

Service career RICHELIEU

1940 (18 June) To Dakar.
1940 (8 July) Hit by torpedo in stern from aircraft from British aircraft-carrier *Hermes*.
1940 (July–Aug) Repaired and partially completed.
1940 (23–25 Sept) Repulsed Free French and British attack: hit by one 15in (381mm) shell little damage.
1943 (Jan) to USA.
1943 (Feb–Aug) Rebuilt and finally completed radar and new anti-aircraft battery fitted.
1943 (Nov–March 1944) Attached to British Home Fleet.
1944 (Feb) Patrols off Norway.
1944 (14 March–25 Aug) Attached to British Pacific Fleet: operations in East Indies.
1944 (25 July) Bombarded Sabang.
1944 (25 Aug–Sept) Returned to France.
1944 (Oct–Jan 1945) Refitted at Gibraltar.
1945 (27 Feb–Oct) Attached to British Pacific Fleet.
1945 (4 Apr) Bombarded Sabang.
1945 (Oct–Dec) Operations in French Indo China.
1945 (Dec–March 1946) Returned to France.
1956 In reserve.
1965 Paid off for sale.
1968 Scrapped.

By the mid-1930s it was obvious that France would have to build some true battleships when the 'battleship building holiday' came to an end in 1935 if she was to retain her position even as a second rank naval power. Although the *Dunkerques* were excellent ships, capable of defeating anything yet built by Germany or Italy, they would be outclassed by the new fast battleships that other countries would inevitably lay down. The French therefore designed an enlarged version of the *Dunkerques*, with battleship armament and protection. The *Richelieus*' 15in (380mm) guns were disposed in quadruple turrets as in *Dunkerque*, and they were also fitted with an internal sloping belt. However, the *Dunkerques*' mixed quadruple and twin-turreted secondary armament was abandoned in favour of five triple 6in (152mm) turrets mounted amidships and aft. The centre 6in (152mm) turret aft was mounted above the

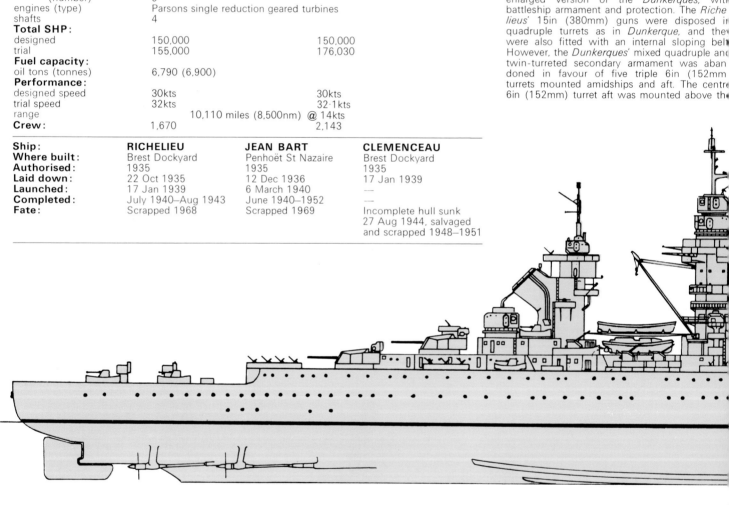

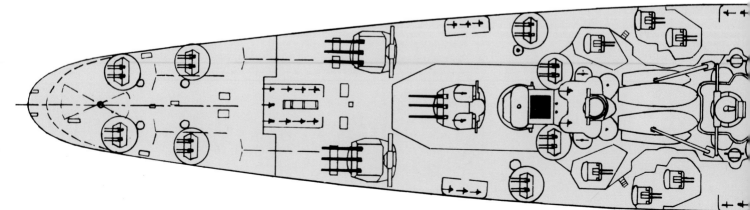

hangar, as in *Dunkerque*, and there were to be two catapults on the quarterdeck right aft. The *Richelieus* were originally to have had a similar profile to the *Dunkerques*, but their funnel was angled back before completion to avoid smoke blowing over the bridge, and it was surmounted by a considerable superstructure, creating an unmistakable silhouette. These ships were powerful and well armed vessels, but as with the *Dunkerques* weight was wasted by not adopting a completely DP secondary armament. They were built in drydocks, and as was the case with *Dunkerque* the dock at Brest was too short to accommodate the entire hull, and so *Richelieu's* and *Clemenceau's* bow section was built separately. *Richelieu* was virtually complete when France fell, and did not differ much from the original design when she was completed in the United States, except that two of the beam 6in (152mm) turrets were not fitted and her light anti-aircraft armament was greatly strengthened. *Jean Bart*, which was only just beginning to fit out when France fell, escaped in a very incomplete condition with only one main turret. When finally completed in 1952 she differed considerably from *Richelieu*. She had a completely different light anti-aircraft armament, the funnel and aft superstructure were dissimilar, and she was fitted with bulges to counteract the extra topweight. She had been very badly damaged at Casablanca on 8 November 1942 by torpedoes from US carrier aircraft and eight 16in (406mm) shell hits from the American battleship *Massachusetts*, which set her on fire. She was not repaired and completed until after the war. Neither ship ever mounted the forward 6in (152mm) turrets, and only *Richelieu* was fitted with their barbettes. *Jean Bart's* career after 1952 was similar to *Richelieu's*. The third ship, *Clemenceau*, was to have been completed with a modified secondary armament, with two superfiring triple 6in (152mm) turrets aft as well as the beam turrets amidships. She was also to have had an anti-aircraft armament of six twin 3·9in (100mm) mounts and 20 37mm guns in twin and quadruple mountings. Her construction was suspended from September to December 1939, and her incomplete hull was captured by the Germans and sunk by US bombers. The class might well have been a match for the Italian *Littorio* class battleships, and were certainly better designed than the German *Bismarcks*. However, the two quadruple turrets forward resulted in an unwieldy design, with an immense blind arc astern, as well as demanding considerable space forward to ensure adequate separation of the turrets. This was

recognised in what was to have been the fourth member of the class, *Gascogne*. Her design was modified to mount one quadruple turret fore and aft, with the superstructure moved forward and a considerably longer quarterdeck. Two superfiring 6in (152mm) turrets were to be fitted forward, and one aft. Unlike her three half sisters, *Gascogne* was to have had a hangar with a lift under the quarterdeck aft. This design was still clumsy, with half the armament tied up in each main turret, and two further battleships authorised in April 1940 were to have abandoned quadruple

Above, upper: Richelieu *with the British Pacific Fleet in 1945*

Above: Richelieu *in 1953. Her silhouette is unmistakable*

turrets in favour of more 15in (380mm) or 16in (406mm) guns mounted in triple turrets in a larger hull. None of these last three ships was laid down, although material had been assembled for *Gascogne* before September 1939.

Richelieu *in 1950. Note extra AA guns*

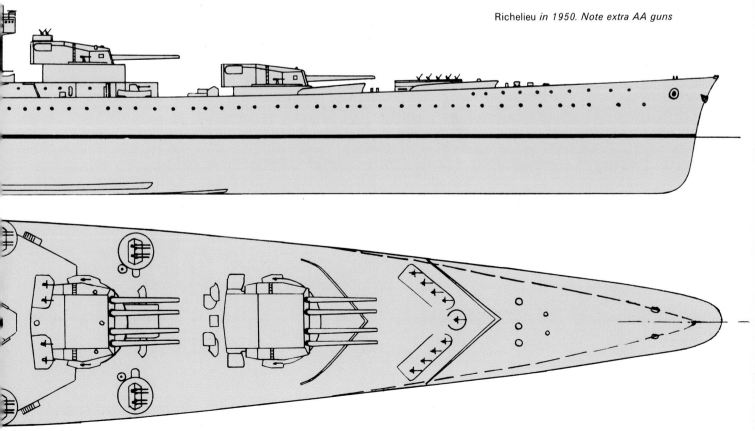

Gloire
ARMOURED CRUISER
CLASS: *Gloire* class (5 ships)
*Gloire · Marseillaise · Sully · Condé
Admiral Aube*
Service career GLOIRE
1914–1915 2nd Armoured Cruiser division, 2nd
light squadron in the Channel.
1916–1918 Patrols in South Atlantic.
1918–1919 Convoy escort in North Atlantic.
1920 In Atlantic squadron.
1922 Discarded.

In the closing years of the 19th century the
French Navy had concentrated on building up a
navy of armoured cruisers and torpedo boats in
accordance with the theories of the 'Jeune
Ecole' whose chief theoretician was Admiral
Aube.

A combination of long distance raiding by the
armoured cruisers and devastating strikes in
coastal waters by massed torpedo boats was
intended to wear down the naval and mercantile
strength of France's chief prospective enemy, at
that time Great Britain. Like the later German
pocket battleships, the cruisers were intended
to be more powerful than any faster warship,
and faster than anything which could sink them.
Beginning with the famous *Dupuy de Lôme* the
French built a series of large and supremely ugly
cruisers with this aim in view, the last of which
was completed in 1910. The *Gloires* were in
the middle of this development, and like their
predecessors and successors suffered from the
fact that the French could not build ships at the
rate that their British rivals could achieve. The
result was that these large, but comparatively
lightly armed and armoured vessels were all
virtually obsolete by the time they were commissioned. They would have fared badly against
their British contemporaries, and they were of
little use in the war that actually broke out
against Germany, being employed on patrol
duties, and seeing virtually no action.

When these 5 ships first appeared they were
considered to fall into two classes, the last two
to be launched having a slightly different
arrangement of deck armour from the others,
but otherwise being virtually identical. The
odd arrangement of grouped funnels was caused
by having two separate sets of boilers at either end
of the engine rooms, and was common to
virtually all French armoured and protected
cruisers. The most outstanding exception was
Chateaurenault which was deliberately designed
with a straight stem and four equally spaced
funnels to look like a transatlantic liner.

Displacement:		
normal tons (tonnes)	?	(?)
full load tons (tonnes)	10,400	(10,570)
Dimensions:		
length (pp)	458·5ft (140m)	
(oa)	? (?m)	
beam	66·2ft (20·2m)	
draught	25·2ft (7·7m)	
Armament:		
guns		
7·6in (194mm)	2	
6·4in (165mm)	8	
3·9in (100mm)	6	
3pdr (47mm)	18	
torpedo tubes		
17·7in (450mm)	5	
Armour:		
side (belt)	4·1–6·7in (106–170mm)	
deck	0·8–1·75in (20–45mm)	
main turrets	7·8in (200mm)	
secondary turrets	4·7in (120mm)	
barbettes	3·9in (100mm)	
Machinery		
Boilers (type)	Niclausse	
(number)	?	
Engines (type)	Vertical triple expansion	
Shafts	3	
Total IHP		
designed	20,500	
Performance:		
designed speed	21·4kts	
range	14,270 miles (12,090nm) @ 10kts	
Fuel capacity:		
coal tons (tonnes) normal	970 (985)	
max	1,590 (1,615)	
Crew:	612	

Gloire class:	MAR-SEILLAISE	GLOIRE	SULLY	CONDE	ADMIRAL AUBE
Where built:	Brest dockyard	Lorient dockyard	La Seyne p. 117	Lorient dockyard	Penhöet St. Nazaire
Authorised:	?	?	?	?	?
Laid down:	Jan 1900	Sept 1899	?	March 1901	Aug 1900
Launched:	14 July 1900	12 June 1900	1900	March 1902	May 1902
Completed:	1903	1904	1903	1904	1904
Fate	Discarded 1929	Discarded 1922	Total loss Feb 1905	Total loss 1945	Discarded 1922

*Below: The armoured cruiser Gloire
in 1908. Large, but comparatively
lightly armed and armoured,
the Gloires were inferior
to their British contemporaries*

Suffren
CRUISERS
CLASS: *Suffren* class (4 ships)
Suffren · Colbert · Foch · Dupleix

While the designs for new French battleships of the *Dunkerque* class were in preparation, the Italian Navy of Mussolini's era was growing in size, particularly in fast cruisers with side armour varying between 3in and 5in (75mm and 125mm). France's sea communications with her North African colonies were thus under threat and she continued a cruiser-building programme which had begun in 1922 with the almost unarmoured 6·1in (155mm) gun ships of the *Duguay-Trouin* class. Single ship classes were interspersed with the *Tourville* class of two 11,000 ton (11,176 tonne) ships with 8in (203mm) guns but which were also virtually unarmoured. In the *Suffrens* some speed was sacrificed for a minimal patch of armour over the machinery spaces, an advance towards the more heavily armoured ships of the *Algérie* and *La Galissonnière* classes which followed close after them. In fact each *Suffren* varied — the weight of armour in *Suffren* herself was 950 tons (965 tonnes) whilst the last of the class, *Dupleix*, carried 1,500 tons (1,524). Changes were made to the armament during the war, although with three ships being scuttled this was of little effect. *Suffren's* aircraft and catapult were landed, together with six torpedo tubes, in 1943, eight 40mm and twenty 20mm guns replacing them. By 1945 her displacement at full load was 14,400 tons (14,630 tonnes) and she remained in approximately this state until paid off to become an accommodation hulk.

Below: Suffren, *name-ship of a class of 4 cruisers entering service in 1930–32, soon after completion*

Displacement:		
normal tons (tonnes)	11,290 (11,471)	
full load tons (tonnes)	12,780 (12,984)	
Dimensions:	**Suffren**	**remainder**
length (pp)	607ft (185·1m)	607ft (185·1m)
(oa)	643ft (196m)	637ft (194·2m)
beam	65·7ft (20·3m)	63·5ft (19·4m)
draught	24·5ft (7·5m)	24·5ft (7·5m)
Armament:		
guns		
8in (203mm)	8	8
3·5in (90mm)	—	8
2·9in (75mm)	8 (and *Colbert*)	—
37mm	8	6
0·52in (13·2mm)	16	16
torpedo tubes		
21·7in (550mm)	12	—
aircraft	2	3
Armour:	2·1–2·4in (54–60mm) over engine and boiler rooms	
Machinery:		
boilers (type)	Guyot du Temple	
(number)	8 main, 1 auxiliary	
engines (type)	Rateau Chantier de Bretagne geared turbines	
shafts	3	
Total SHP:	90,000 (105,700 max on trials in *Colbert*)	
Fuel capacity:		
oil tons (tonnes)	1,800 (1,829)	
Performance:		
speed	31kts (33·1kts max on trials in *Colbert*)	
range	5,000 miles (4,342nm) @ 15kts	
Crew (peace/war):	602/773	

Ship:	**SUFFREN**	**COLBERT**	**FOCH**	**DUPLEIX**
Where built:	A & C Bretagne	A & C Bretagne	A & C Bretagne	A & C Bretagne
Authorised:	1925	1926	1927	1928
Laid down:	May 1926	June 1927	June 1928	Oct 1929
Launched:	3 May 1927	20 Apr 1928	24 Apr 1929	9 Oct 1930
Commissioned:	1930	1931	1931	1932
Fate:	Paid off 27 Dec 1962	Scuttled Toulon 27 Nov 1942	Scuttled Toulon 27 Nov 1942	Scuttled Toulon 27 Nov 1942

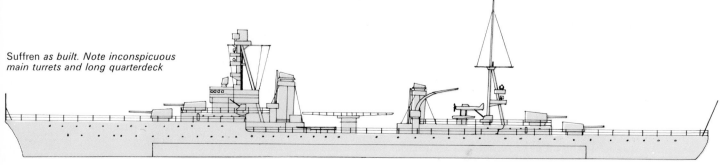

Suffren *as built. Note inconspicuous main turrets and long quarterdeck*

La Galissonnière Class

LIGHT CRUISER

CLASS: *La Galissonnière* class (6 ships) *La Galissonnière · Jean de Vienne · Marseillaise · Gloire · Montcalm · Georges Leygues*

The first French inter-war light cruisers were the three *Duguay-Trouins*, built between 1922 and 1926. They were fast and reliable ships, armed with eight 6·1in (155mm) guns in four twin mounts, but they were virtually unarmoured. These were followed by the minelaying cruiser *Pluton* (later *La Tour d'Auvergne*) and the training cruiser *Jeanne d'Arc*. The minelaying cruiser *Emile Bertin* was a greatly improved version of *Pluton*, with a much heavier armament of three triple 6in (152mm) turrets. She was lightly armoured and constructed, but reached a speed of 39·8kts on trials. The *La Galissonnières* were developed from *Emile Bertin*, but lacked her minelaying capacity. They had a much stronger hull, and were adequately protected. These excellent ships were fast (all made over 35kts on trials), well armed and very seaworthy, but all took over four years to build compared to the one to two years of their British counterparts. *La Galissonnière*, *Jean de Vienne* and *Marseillaise* were scuttled at Toulon, and although two were salved by Italy, none was returned to service. The other three were refitted in America in 1943 when radar and an improved AA armament were fitted and the catapult and hangar removed. Three improved ships were projected in 1937–1938, but only *De Grasse* was laid down. She was completed postwar with a completely different superstructure and armament as an AA cruiser.

Displacement:		
standard tons (tonnes)	7,600 (7,720)	
full load tons (tonnes)	9,120 (9,270)	
length (pp)	548ft (167·3m)	
(oa)	586·2ft (179m)	
beam	57·3ft (17·5m)	
draught	17·4ft (5·3m)	
Armament:	**as built**	**in 1950**
6in (152mm)	9	9
3·5in (90mm)	8	8
40mm	—	24
20mm	—	16
13·2mm	8	—
torpedo tubes		
21·7in (550mm)	4	4
aircraft	2	—
Armour:		
side (belt)	3–4·7in (75–120mm)	
deck	2in (50mm)	
main turrets	3–5·1in (75–130mm)	
Machinery:		
boilers (type)	Indret	
(number)	4	
engines (type)	Rateau-Bretagne or Parsons geared turbines	
shafts	2	
Total SHP:		
designed	81,000	
trial (max)	?	
Fuel capacity:		
oil tons (tonnes)	1,870 (1,900)	
Performance:		
designed speed	31kts	
trial speed (max)	35·7kts	
range	6,470 miles (5,440nm) @ 15kts	
Fuel capacity:		
oil tons (tonnes)	1,870 (1,900)	
Crew:	540	

Ship:	LA GALISSONNIERE	JEAN DE VIENNE	MARSEILLAISE	GLOIRE	MONTCALM	GEORGES LEYGUES
Where built:	Brest Dockyard	Lorient Dockyard	FC de La Loire	FC de La Gironde	FC de La Mediterranée	Penhoët, St Nazaire
Authorised:	1931	1931	1932	1931	1932	1932
Laid down:	27 Oct 1931	Dec 1931	1933	1933	1933	1933
Launched:	17 Nov 1933	31 May 1935	17 July 1935	28 Sept 1935	26 Oct 1935	24 March 1936
Completed:	31 Dec 1935	15 April 1937	25 Oct 1937	4 Dec 1937	4 Dec 1937	4 Dec 1937
Fate:	Scuttled 27 Nov 1942; salved by Italy; renamed *FR-12*; sunk 18 Aug 1944	Scuttled 27 Nov 1942; salved by Italy; renamed *FR-11*; sunk 24 Nov 1943	Scuttled 27 Nov 1942	Deleted circa 1960	Deleted circa 1960; barrack ship at Toulon; scrapped circa 1970	Deleted circa 1960

Above: The light cruiser La Galissonnière, *name-ship of a class of six fast, well-armed, handy warships*

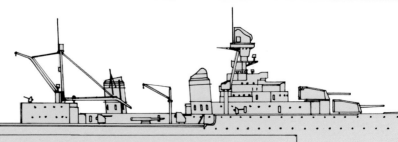

La Galissonnière as built, with catapult on aft turret. Note long quarterdeck

Bisson Class
DESTROYER
CLASS: *Bisson* class (6 ships)
including *Bisson · Mangini*

The French were among the first builders of torpedo boats and torpedo boat destroyers, but as with other aspects of French naval design, destroyer development lagged several years behind that of other major naval powers in the early years of this century. Up to 1910, the largest French destroyers were the *Spahi* class which had a normal displacement of 520–540 tons (530–550 tonnes). In that year the first of 12 *Bouclier* class destroyers were laid down. These had a normal displacement of about 790 tons (800 tonnes). They were all built in private yards, and each builder produced his own detailed design to the same general specification. Except for *Casque*, which had three funnels, they were all four-funnelled vessels with a short fo'c's'le and a long quarterdeck. The *Bisson* class were slightly enlarged versions of the *Boucliers*, with the same armament and the same basic layout. The four dockyard-built ships were almost identical, but *Mangini* and *Magon* differed slightly. They all had their funnels in two pairs, and the dockyard-built ships had taller funnels than the other two. *Mangini* was completed at Marseilles, being floated down river on a specially built barge, and *Commandant Lucas* could be distinguished by her tripod mast. They were all too lightly built, and had their hulls strengthened and their bridges enlarged during World War I, when the armament was also increased. All except *Magon* spent the entire war in the Mediterranean, *Magon* being transferred to the Dunkirk flotilla in late 1916. *Bisson* sank the Austrian submarine *U-3* by gunfire on 13 August 1915, and *Renaudin* was sunk by the Austrian submarine *U-6*.

Displacement:		
normal tons (tonnes)	850–880 (864–894)	
full load tons	?	
Dimensions:	**Bisson**	
length (pp)	256·1ft (78·1m)	
(oa)	272·6ft (83·1m)	
beam	28·2ft (8·6m)	
draught	10·2ft (3·1m)	
Armament:	**as built**	**in 1918**
guns		
3·9in (100mm)	2	2
65mm	4	4
75 or 45mm	—	1
8·8mm	—	2
torpedo tubes		
17·7in (450mm)	4	4
Machinery:		
boilers (type)	Du Temple–Guyot	
(number)	4	
engines (type)	Breguet, Parsons, Zoelly or Rateau turbines	
shafts	2	
Total SHP:		
designed	15,000	
Fuel capacity:		
oil tons (tonnes)	160 (163)	
Performance:		
designed speed	30kts	
trial speed	30·02–32·02kts	
range	1,600–1,665 miles (1,350–1,400nm) @ 14kts	
Crew:	80–83	

Above: Bisson *in 1912. Six destroyers of the* Bisson *class, were built between 1911–14*

Class:	**BISSON class**
Where built:	Toulon Dockyard
	Rochefort Dockyard
	Schneider, Chalon
	AC de Bretagne, Nantes
Authorised:	?
Built:	1911–1914
Fate:	*Renaudin* sunk 17 March 1916; remainder stricken 1926–1934

L'Adroit Class
DESTROYER
CLASS: *L'Adroit* class (14 ships)
including *L'Adroit · Bordelais*

The first French destroyers (*Torpilleurs d'Escadre*) to be designed and built after World War I were the 12 *Bourrasque* class, armed with four 5·1in (130mm) and one 3in (75mm) gun, and two triple 21·7in (550mm) torpedo tube mounts. They had a standard displacement of 1,319 tons (1,340 tonnes), and were built between 1923 and 1928. These were smaller, slower versions of the *Chacal* class 'Contre-Torpilleurs', but were considerable improvements on the French World War I destroyers. The *Adroits* were slightly enlarged *Bourrasques*. They were three funnel designs, with 5·1in (130mm) guns in superimposed single mounts fore and aft. The triple mounted torpedo tubes were fitted between the funnels and the aft deckhouse, separated by the 3in (75mm) 'bandstand' mounting. They had a tripod foremast. At the start of World War II both the *Bourrasques* and *Adroits* had X gun removed, and most were fitted with light anti-aircraft guns. From 1943 the ships under Allied control were gradually fitted with radar and asdic, and given a modern anti-aircraft armament. The aft torpedo tubes were removed from most ships to make way for this. *Railleuse* suffered an internal explosion at Casablanca. *Adroit* and *Foudroyant* were sunk off Dunkirk. *Boulonnais*, *Brestois*, *Fougueux* and *Frondeur* were destroyed at Casablanca. *Palme*, *Mars* and *Bordelais* were scuttled at Toulon. *Palme* was salved in 1943 and *Mars* in 1944.

Class:	**L'ADROIT class**
Where built:	various yards
Authorised:	1924–1927
Laid down:	1925–1927
Launched:	1926–1929
Completed:	1928–1931
Fate:	*Railleuse* blew up 27 March 1940; *Adroit* sunk 21 May 1940; *Foudroyant* sunk 1 June 1940; *Boulonnais*, *Brestois*, *Fougueux*, *Frondeur* sunk 8 Nov 1942; *Palme*, *Mars*, *Bordelais* scuttled 27 Nov 1942; remainder scrapped 1949–1951

Above: L'Adroit *in 1929.*

Displacement:		
standard tons (tonnes)	1,378 (1,400)	
normal tons (tonnes)	1,500 (1,520)	
full load tons (tonnes)	1,800–2,100 (1,830–2,130)	
Dimensions:		
length (pp)	330·9ft (101m)	
(oa)	351ft (107·2m)	
beam	32·1ft (9·8m)	
draught (normal)	13·1ft (4m)	
Armament:	**as built**	**in 1950**
guns		
5·1in (130mm) 40cal	4	3
3in (75mm)	1	—
40mm	—	1
20mm	—	8–10
torpedo tubes		
21·7in (550mm)	6	3
Machinery:		
boilers (type)	small tube	
(number)	3	
engines (type)	Parsons, Rateau-Bretagne or Zoelly single reduction geared turbines	
shafts	2	
Total SHP:		
designed	33,000–34,000	
Fuel capacity:		
oil tons (tonnes)	340 (345)	
Performance:		
designed speed	33kts	
range	1,780 miles (1,500nm) @ 15kts	
	as built	**in 1950**
Crew:	138	167

Fantasque Class

LARGE DESTROYER
CLASS: *Fantasque* class (6 ships)
including *Fantasque · Terrible*

In 1922–1923 the French laid down the *Chacal* class, the first of the *'Contre Torpilleurs'*. These were large, fast, heavily armed destroyers, but were totally unprotected. They were ideally suited for short-range operations in the Mediterranean and southern North Sea, and had a standard displacement of 2,126 tons (2,160 tonnes), a speed of 35·5kts and an armament of five 5·1in (130mm) and two 3in (75mm) guns, with two triple 21·7in (550mm) torpedo tube mounts. These three-funnelled ships were developed into the slightly larger and faster four funnelled *Guepard*, *Aigle* and *Vauquelin* classes, armed with 5·5in (138mm) guns and built under the 1926–1929 construction programmes. They were an effective counter to the Italian *Mirabelle*, *Leone* and *Navigatori* class scouts (later re-classified as destroyers) that were built between 1914 and 1930. The *Fantasques* were improved versions of the *Vauquelins*, with two instead of four funnels to reduce the silhouette and make it less instantly recognisable at long range, and with an improved bridge. All except *Terrible* also adopted a new type of boiler, then running trials on the *Aigle* class *Milan* and *Epervier*. Like most of the *'Contre Torpilleurs'*, the *Fantasque* class easily exceeded their designed horsepower and speed. Unlike most foreign ships except the British *Abdiel* class fast minelayers, they could also maintain these extremely high speeds for long periods, enabling them to conduct high speed sweeps off the German and Italian coasts in the hours of darkness. The anti-aircraft armament varied somewhat between the members of the class. Two 5·5in (138mm) guns were mounted forward, one on the forward end of the aft deckhouse, and two aft. A triple 21·7in (550mm) torpedo tube mount was fitted on either side between the funnels, and the third was fitted between the aft funnel and deckhouse. Removable mine-laying rails could be fitted on the quarterdeck. The entire class saw considerable service in the first year of the war. *L'Audacieux* was badly damaged at Dakar, and later sank whilst under repair at Bizerta. *L'Indomptable* was scuttled at Toulon. The four survivors were refitted in America in 1943–1944 with modern US anti-aircraft guns and anti-submarine equipment,

Displacement:		
standard tons (tonnes)	2,569 (2,610)	
normal tons (tonnes)	2,610–2,801 (2,651–2,846)	
full load tons (tonnes)	3,180–3,380 (3,231–3,434)	
Dimensions:		
length (pp)	411·4ft (125·4m)	
(oa)	435ft (132·6m)	
beam	40·7ft (12·4m)	
draught	15·4–16·4ft (4·7–5m)	
Armament:	**as built**	**Fantasque in 1943**
guns		
5·5in (138mm) 50cal	5	5
40mm	—	8
37mm	2	—
20mm	—	10
13·2mm	4	—
torpedo tubes		
21·7in (550mm)	9	6
mines	40	40
Machinery:		
boilers (type)	Penhoët, Gunot, Yarrow, or Babcock	
(number)	4	
engines (type)	Parsons or Rateau single reduction geared turbines	
shafts	2	
Total SHP:		
designed	74,000–81,400	
trials	86,443–93,802	
Fuel capacity:		
oil tons (tonnes)	580 (589)	
Performance:		
designed speed	37kts	
trial speed	40–43kts	
range	4,280 miles (3,600nm) @ 17kts	
Crew:	210	

Class:	**FANTASQUE class**
Where built:	Lorient Dockyard
	La Seyne
	AC de la Loire, Blainville
	AC de France, Dunkirk
Authorised:	1930
Built:	1931–1936
Fate:	*Indomptable* scuttled 27 Nov 1942
	Audacieux total loss 7 May 1943
	remainder stricken 1954–1964

and were also fitted with radar, after which they were reclassified as light cruisers. They then served in the Mediterranean and the Pacific. After the end of World War II they were employed in French Indo-China. Their greatest defect was the total lack of protection. Italy had already abandoned the large destroyer and was building the lightly protected *Condottiere* class light cruisers. British World War II experience was to show that light cruisers, with their better protection, fire control and more sea-worthy hulls, were superior to similarly armed destroyers. However, the French, though they built some fast light cruisers, and considered several schemes for armouring the *Fantasques*, continued to build *'Contre Torpilleurs'*. These were the *Mogador* class, which carried their 5·5in (138mm) guns in four twin turrets. These turrets were complex and gave constant trouble and only two were built with this armament. The other four were intended to have a modified armament, but were never laid down.

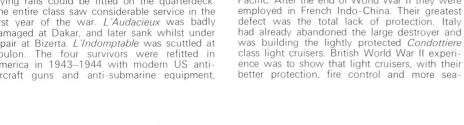

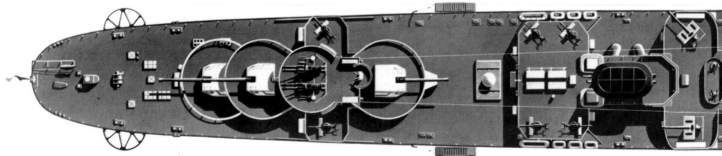

Above: Le Fantasque, *name-ship of a class of six destroyers built in 1931–36. The rounded bridge front was intended to reduce wind resistance*

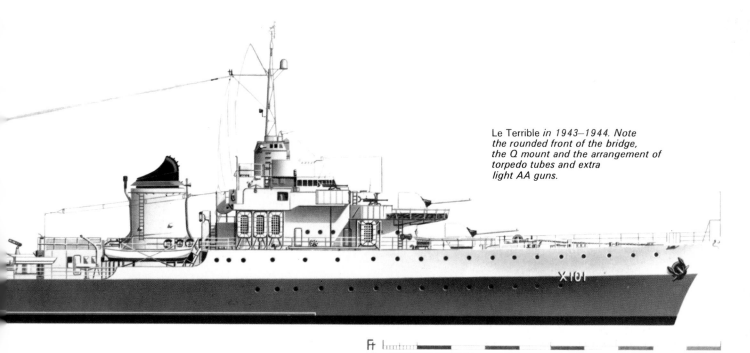

Le Terrible *in 1943–1944. Note the rounded front of the bridge, the Q mount and the arrangement of torpedo tubes and extra light AA guns.*

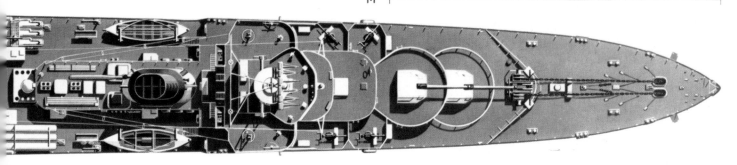

Surcouf Class

DESTROYER

CLASS: *Surcouf* class (18 ships) including *Surcouf* (D-621) · *La Galissonnière* (D-638)

The *Surcoufs* are the largest class of French destroyer ever built, and they have undergone a number of modifications. The first 12 *Surcoufs* were completed as anti-aircraft destroyers (Type T47). *Surcouf* (D-621), *Cassard* (D-623) and *Chevalier Paul* (D-626) were converted into flotilla leaders, with the forward super-firing twin 57mm mount replaced by an enlarged lower bridge. *Kersaint* (D-622), *Bouvet* (D-624), *Dupetit Thouars* (D-625) and *Du Chayla* were later converted into guided-missile destroyers. Their 5in (127mm) and aft 57mm mounts were removed, and an enlarged bridge and aft deckhouse fitted. A single Tartar Mk 13 SAM launcher was mounted on the latter. *Maille Brézé* (D-627), *Vauquelin* (D-628), *D'Estrées* (D-629), *Casabianca* (D-6 1) and *Guépratte* (D-632) were modified between 1966 and 1971 as anti-submarine destroyers. They are armed with two 3·9in (100mm), one forward and one aft, and two 20mm guns, one Malafon ASM launcher, one 14·8in (375mm) six-barrel A/S rocket-launcher and six A/S torpedo tubes. They are also fitted with variable depth sonar. Five *Surcoufs* were completed as radar picket destroyers (Type T-53) with more comprehensive radar and command facilities. *Duperré* (D-633) was used as an experimental ship between 1967 and 1971, aiding the development of the new generation of French escorts. She was converted into a command ship from 1972–1974. She carries a single 3·9in (100mm) gun, four MM-38 Exocet SSMs, between the funnels, and a helicopter pad and hangar aft, as well as light A/S torpedo launchers and variable depth sonar. *La Galissonnière* (D-638) (Type T56) was completed as an anti-submarine escort, and has a helicopter hangar aft that opens up to become the landing pad.

Displacement:			
standard tons (tonnes)	2,750 (2,800)		
full load tons (tonnes)	3,740 (3,800)		
Dimensions:	**Surcouf as built**		**La Galissonnière as built**
length (pp)	?		?
(oa)	421·3ft (128·4m)		435·7ft (132·8m)
beam	41·7ft (12·7m)		41·7ft (12·7m)
draught	17·7ft (5·4m)		17·7ft (5·4m)

Armament:	**Surcouf as built**	**La Galissonnière in 1977**	**Kersaint in 1977**
5in (127mm)	6	—	—
3·9in (100mm)	—	2	—
57mm	6	—	6
20mm	6	—	—
missiles			
Tartar Mk 13 SAM single launcher	—	—	1
A/S weapons			
Malafon ASM launcher	—	1	—
14·8in (375mm) 6-barrel rocket-launcher	—	—	1
torpedo tubes			
21·7in (550mm)	12	6	6
aircraft	—	1 helicopter	—

Machinery:	
boilers (type)	Indret
(number)	4
engines (type)	Parsons geared turbines
shafts	2
Total SHP:	
designed	63,000
Fuel capacity:	
oil tons (tonnes)	800 (810)
Performance:	
designed speed	32kts
range	5,000 miles (4,200nm) @ 18kts
Crew:	293 270 277

Class:	SURCOUF class
Where built:	various yards
Authorised:	1947–1956
Laid down:	1951–1958
Launched:	1953–1960
Completed:	1955–1962
Fate:	*Surcouf* (D-621) sunk 6 June 1971; remainder in service or deleted

D621

Above: Surcouf, completed as an anti-aircraft destroyer, in 1957. Converted to a flotilla leader, this name-ship of a class of 18 was lost in June 1971

Surcouf class T 47 DLG conversion with single Tartar launcher aft

Suffren Class
GUIDED-MISSILE DESTROYER

CLASS: *Suffren* class (2 ships)
Suffren (D-602) · *Duquesne* D-603)

The *Suffrens* (F-60 Type) are the first of a new generation of French warships, and are also the first French purpose-built guided-missile destroyers. They mount two single 3·9in (100mm) guns in the bows, the Malafon ASM launcher is immediately abaft the prominent mack, and the Masurca SAM launcher is on the quarter-deck, with variable depth sonar at the stern. There are four Exocets in place of one 100mm gun in *Duquesne*. These ships are easily recognisable by their enormous glass fibre dome on the top of the bridge, which carry DRB1 23 three-dimensional radar. The Dutch *Tromp* class guided-missile destroyers, which also have a large dome on the bridge, have a much bulkier silhouette. The *Suffrens* are excellent seaboats, and make an interesting comparison with the British *County* class guided-missile destroyers. The latter have two close-range Sea Cat SAM launchers and a helicopter pad and hangar, whereas the French ships have two tracking radars for their single SAM system, A/S torpedo tubes, a long-range ASM launcher and variable depth sonar. The British adopted COSAG machinery, whilst the French, who were the first major Western power to adopt an operational SSM, stuck to steam turbines until gas turbine power had been proved by other countries. The *Suffrens* will soon be fitted with MM-38 Exocet SSMs. The subsequent *Tourville* class (F-67 Type) combine the best features from this design with that of the smaller anti-submarine *Aconit* (D-609) (C-65 Type). They are turbine powered, and carry MM-38 Exocet SSMs and a helicopter pad and hangar in place of the Masurca SAM. The *Tourvilles* have themselves been replaced by the *Aconit*-sized *Georges Leygues* class (C-70 Type) powered by gas turbines and diesels. The Malafon ASMs on the *Suffrens* provide long distance A/S defence, and mean that a helicopter, with its associated pad and hangar need not be carried. The use of a Mack has also increased the available deck space for other weapons systems. A comprehensive selection of radar and ECM aerials are carried on the fore part and top of the Mack. Although they carry a smaller crew for their size than earlier vessels, later French ships are more automated and need an even smaller crew. Personnel costs are of major importance to modern navies, and so every effort is made to make ships and their associated weapons systems as automated as possible.

Right: Suffren, *seen here launching a Masurca SAM, and her sister-ship* Duquesne, *completed in 1967–70, were France's first purpose-built guided missile destroyers*

Displacement:		
standard tons (tonnes)	5,090 (5,170)	
full load tons (tonnes)	6,090 (6,190)	
Dimensions:		
length (oa)	517·1ft (157·6m)	
beam	50·9ft (15·5m)	
draught	20ft (6·1m)	
Armament:	**as built**	**in 1977**
guns		
3·9in (100mm)	2	2
missiles		
Masurca SAM twin launcher	1	1
MM38 Exocet SSM	—	4
A/S weapons		
Malafon rocket-launcher	1	1
torpedo tubes		
21in (533mm)	4	4
Machinery:		
boilers (type)	?	
(number)	4	
engines (type)	Rateau double reduction geared turbines	
shafts	2	
Total SHP:		
designed	72,500	
Fuel capacity:		
oil tons (tonnes)	?	
Performance:		
designed speed	34kts	
range	5,100 miles (4,290nm) @ 18kts	

Ship:	**SUFFREN (D-602)**	**DUQUESNE (D-603)**
Where built:	Lorient Dockyard	Brest Dockyard
Authorised:	1960	1960
Laid down:	Dec 1962	Nov 1964
Launched:	15 May 1965	12 Feb 1966
Completed:	July 1967	April 1970
Fate:	In service	In service

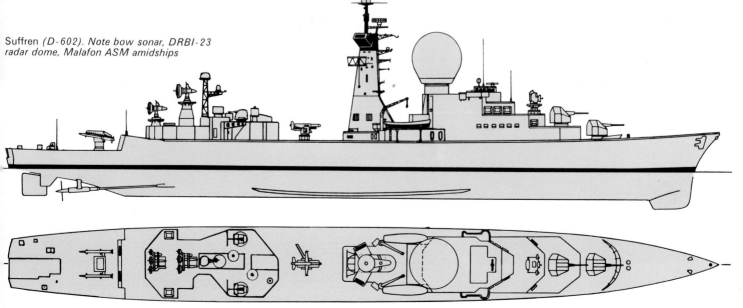

Suffren *(D-602). Note bow sonar, DRBI-23 radar dome, Malafon ASM amidships*

Saphir Class

MINELAYING SUBMARINE

CLASS: *Saphir* class (6 boats)
including *Rubis · Saphir*

Requin Class

SUBMARINE

CLASS: *Requin* class (9 boats)
including *Narval · Requin*

The French built up a formidable submarine force in the interwar period. Apart from the one-off *Surcouf*, these boats were divided into three types, the first class submarines intended for overseas patrols, the second class submarines for short-range defensive patrols and the mine-laying submarines. The *Requin* class were the first interwar first class submarines. They were quite heavily armed for their size, with four bow and two stern tubes, and two pairs of revolving tubes in the superstructure fore and aft of the conning tower. Revolving tubes were fitted on most French interwar submarines, and were intended for use against merchant ships. Unfortunately, the *Requins* had a relatively short range, and were superseded by the 29 *Redoutable* class, which had a surface displacement of 1,570 tons (1,600 tonnes) and a range of 11,890 miles (10,000nm) at 10kts on the surface. Five improved *Roland Morillots* were laid down between 1937 and 1940, but all were destroyed incomplete on their slips. The *Requins* were all modernised between 1935–1937. *Morse* was mined off Sfax and *Narval* was also mined off Tunisia. *Souffleur* was sunk by the British submarine *Parthian*, and *Caiman* was scuttled at Toulon. *Requin, Dauphin, Phoque* and *Espadon* were captured at Bizerta, and incorporated in the Italian Navy. *Phoque* was sunk off Sicily. *Marsouin* was taken over by the Free French. The *Saphir* class minelaying submarines were a rather better design. They carried their mines in 16 vertical tubes in the ballast tanks on either side fore and aft of the conning tower. This arrangement, called the Normand-Fenaux system, was based on the British system used on the E-class minelaying submarines during World War I. They had two 21·7in (550mm) bow tubes, and a triple tube revolving mounting on the superstructure aft with one 21·7in (550mm) tube flanked by two 15·7in (400mm) tubes. The 15·7in (400mm) torpedo had a short range and was intended specifically for use against merchant vessels, but it was not a success. Except for a period between November 1936 and May 1939 the class was based in the Mediterranean. All

Displacement:	Requin class	Saphir class
surface tons (tonnes)	974 (990)	762 (774)
submerged tons (tonnes)	1,441 (1,464)	923 (938)
Dimensions:		
length (pp)	?	?
(oa)	256·3ft (78·3m)	216·2ft (66m)
beam	22·4ft (6·8m)	23·3ft (7·1m)
draught	16·7ft (5·1m)	13·5ft (4·1m)
Armament:		
guns		
3·9in (100mm)	1	—
3in (75mm)	—	1
13·2mm	2	1
torpedo tubes		
21·7in (550mm)	10	3
15·7in (400mm)	—	2
mine capacity	—	32
Machinery:		
diesels (type)	Sulzer or Schneider	Vickers-Normand
(number)	2	2
electric motors (type)	Schneider	Schneider
Total BHP:	2,900	1,300
Total SHP:	1,800	1,000
Performance:		
surface speed	16kts	12kts
submerged speed	9kts	9kts
range surface	6,720 miles (5,650nm) @ 10kts	8,320 miles (7,000nm) @ 7·5kts
submerged	125 miles (105nm) @ 5kts	95 miles (80nm) @ 4kts
designed diving depth	263ft (80m)	263ft (80m)
Fuel capacity:		
oil tons (tonnes)	166 (169)	?
Crew:	51	42

Class:	REQUIN class	SAPHIR class
Where built:	Cherbourg Dockyard, Brest Dockyard, Toulon Dockyard	Toulon Dockyard
Authorised:	1922–1923	1925–1929
Laid down:	1923–1925	1928–1935
Launched:	1924–1927	1930–1937
Completed:	1926–1927	
Fate:	*Morse* sunk 10 June 1940; *Narval* sunk 15 Dec 1940; *Souffleur* sunk 29 June 1941; *Caiman* scuttled 27 Nov 1942, salved 1943, sunk 11 Mar 1944; *Requin, Dauphin, Phoque* and *Espadon* captured 8 Dec 1942, renamed *FR113, FR115, FR111, FR114*; *Requin* and *Dauphin* scrapped 1944; *Phoque* sunk 28 March 1943; *Espadon* scuttled 13 Sept 1943; *Marsouin* scrapped 1946	*Diamant* scuttled 27 Nov 1942, salved 1943, sunk 1944; *Saphir, Turquoise, Nautilus* captured 8 Dec 1942; *Saphir* scuttled 15 Sept 1943; *Turquoise* scuttled 6 May 1943; *Nautilus* sunk 31 Jan 1943, salved and scrapped 1947; *Perle* sunk 8 July 1944; *Rubis* deleted 1950, scuttled as a/s target 1957

carried out a number of mining sorties before the French surrender. *Diamant* was scuttled in Toulon, and *Saphir, Turquoise* and *Nautilus* were captured at Bizerta. *Perle* and *Rubis* joined the Free French. *Perle* was sunk in error by Allied aircraft, but *Rubis*, which made 22 minelaying sorties, survived the war.

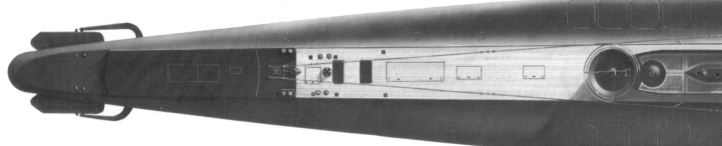

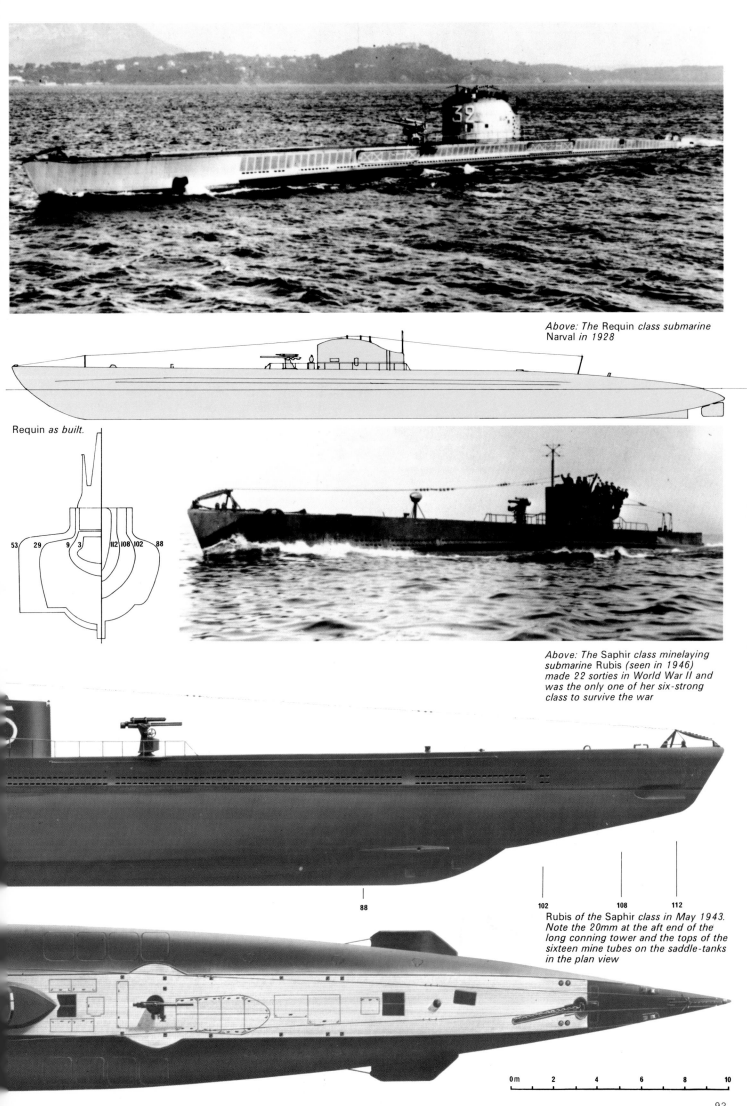

Above: The Requin *class submarine*
Narval *in 1928*

Requin *as built.*

53   29   9 3   112 108 102   88

Above: The Saphir *class minelaying
submarine* Rubis *(seen in 1946)
made 22 sorties in World War II and
was the only one of her six-strong
class to survive the war*

88

102   108   112

Rubis *of the* Saphir *class in May 1943.
Note the 20mm at the aft end of the
long conning tower and the tops of the
sixteen mine tubes on the saddle-tanks
in the plan view*

0 m   2   4   6   8   10

Surcouf Class

CRUISER SUBMARINE

CLASS: *Surcouf* class (1 boat)
Surcouf

During World War I the Germans developed the concept of the 'U-cruiser', the large long-range submarine armed with heavy guns intended for the destruction of merchant ships steaming independently well out in the oceans. After the end of the war both the Americans and Japanese built several vessels of the type. However, up to 1939 the two biggest submarines were the sole experimental cruiser submarines built by Britain (the *X.1*, the only interwar vessel in the Royal Navy scrapped before 1939) and by France (the *Surcouf*). The latter carried the heaviest guns ever put into a submarine apart from the British M class (guns which were the same model as those carried in French naval treaty cruisers), a Besson seaplane and a motor boat to carry a boarding party. The last was removed after a time. The small torpedoes were light short-range weapons intended for use against merchant ships, but this ingenious idea did not, apparently, work very well. The 8in (203mm) guns had a full fire-control system, and should have been able to eliminate a convoy escort of armed merchant cruisers, sloops, or other lightly armed ships from a range at which they would be unable to reply. The *Surcouf* seems a somewhat dubious investment, however, with her high cost, large size and big crew. At the time when she was built France was unlikely to have to fight Britain, against whom the submarine might have been useful. As it was, she was rather a white elephant in the early part of World War II. Her chance came when she was sent out to the Pacific, where she might have scored successes against the Japanese merchant fleet. She was accidentally rammed and sunk by a merchant ship on her way there, however. She had already proved somewhat unlucky,

Displacement:	
standard tons (tonnes)	2,835 (2,880)
surface tons (tonnes)	3,252 (3,304)
submerged tons (tonnes)	4,304 (4,373)
Dimensions:	
length (pp)	?
(oa)	361ft (110m)
beam	29·5ft (9m)
draught	23·25ft (7·3m)
Armament:	
guns	
8in (203mm)	2
37mm	2
13·2mm	4
torpedo tubes	
21·7in (550mm)	8
15·7in (400mm)	4
aircraft	1
Machinery:	
diesels (type)	Sulzer
(number)	2
electric motors (type)	?
shafts	2
Total BHP:	7,600
Total SHP:	3,400
Fuel capacity:	
oil tons (tonnes)	?
Performance:	
surface speed	18·5kts
submerged speed	10kts
range surface	12,000 miles (10,000nm) @ 10kt
submerged	83 miles (70nm) @ 4·5kts
Crew:	118

Ship:	**SURCOUF**
Where built:	Cherbourg Dockyard
Authorised:	1926
Laid down:	Dec 1927
Launched:	18 Oct 1929
Completed:	May 1934

Above: The cruiser submarine Surcouf *mounted two 8in/203mm guns with a full fire control system. She was the largest submarine afloat in 1939*

being caught refitting at Brest when the Germans invaded in 1940. She did succeed in escaping to Britain only to be seized in an unpleasant scuffle by her hosts. Later in Free French hands she was hit by one of the first anti-submarine rockets ever fired. Unfortunately this came from a 'friendly' aircraft! She was the last submarine to be armed with heavy guns.

Le Redoubtable

NUCLEAR BALLISTIC MISSILE SUBMARINE

CLASS: *Le Redoutable* class
(5 ships) *Le Redoutable* (S-611) ·
Le Terrible (S-612) · *Le Foudroyant*
(S-610) · *L' Indomptable* (S-613) ·
Le Tonnant (S-614)

Like Britain, France decided to build nuclear ballistic missile submarines to ensure a viable nuclear deterrent, but unlike the British Polaris submarines, the French 'Force de dissuasion' was developed completely independently of the United States. This resulted in a much greater effort spread over a longer timescale (the French are only now able to start their nuclear attack submarine building programme), and in heavier missiles than Polaris carrying a smaller warhead over a shorter range. The MSBS-M1 SLBM fitted in the first two boats has a range of 1,300 miles (1,000nm). *Le Foudroyant* carries

Above: Le Redoutable, *France's first nuclear ballistic missile submarine, entered service in 1971. She carries 16 MSBS-M1 SLBMs (range 1,300 miles)*

Displacement:	
surface tons (tonnes)	7,500 (7,620)
submerged tons (tonnes)	9,000 (9,140)
Dimensions:	
length (oa)	419·9ft (128m)
beam	34·8ft (10·6m)
draught	32·8ft (10m)
Armament:	
missiles	
MSBS SLBM	16
torpedo tubes	
21·7in (550mm)	4
Machinery:	
nuclear reactor (type)	pressurised water-cooled
(number)	1
turbo-alternators (type)	?
(number)	2
electric motor (type)	?
(number)	1
auxiliary motor (type)	diesel
(number)	1
shafts	1
Total SHP:	
designed	15,000
Fuel capacity:	
oil fuel (auxiliary)	?
Performance:	
surface speed	20kts
submerged speed	25kts
range (nuclear reactor)	?
(auxiliary)	5,000 miles (4,200nm)
diving depth	over 656ft (200m)
Crew:	135

Above: Le Redoutable *(S-611) being launched from its covered building slip at Cherbourg Dockyard on 29 March 1967. The modified teardrop hull and casing for the missiles can be clearly seen.*

Ship:	LE RE-DOUTABLE (S-611)	LE TERRIBLE (S-612)	LE FOU-DROYANT (S-610)	L'INDOMPT-ABLE (S-613)	LE TONNANT (S-614)
Where built:	Cherbourg Dockyard	Cherbourg Dockyard	Cherbourg Dockyard	Cherbourg Dockyard	Cherbourg Dockyard
Authorised:	?	?	?	4 Dec 1967	Feb 1972
Laid down:	30 March 1964	24 June 1967	12 Dec 1969	4 Dec 1971	Oct 1974
Launched:	29 March 1967	12 Dec 1969	4 Dec 1971	17 Aug 1974	1976
Completed:	July 1969	1971	May 1973	Dec 1975	—
Fate:	In service	In service	In service	In service	Completing

the improved M2 SLBM, which is also being retrofitted in *Le Redoutable*, and the M-20 SLBM can be fitted in *L'Indomptable*. This has a thermonuclear reinforced warhead and has a range of about 1,500 nautical miles. An enlarged version, the M4 SLBM, with a MIRV warhead, will be tested in 1978–1979 in the experimental

diesel-electric submarine *Gymnote* (S-655). which has been used to develop the *Le Redoutables* and their missiles. It was built between 1963 and 1966, and has two SLBM launching tubes and laboratories. The *Le Redoutables* resemble the American nuclear ballistic missile submarines, with two rows of

eight vertical SLBM launching tubes abaft the fin, which carries the forward hydroplanes. Possibly reflecting doubts about the reliability of their nuclear reactor, the *Le Redoutables* have turbo-electric propulsion with an auxiliary diesel that can be cut in to provide power and propulsion in the event of a reactor failure.

D'Estienne d'Orves Class

FRIGATE

CLASS: *D'Estienne d'Orves* class (14 ships) including *D'Estienne d'Orves* (F-781) · *Amyot d'Inville* (F-782)

The French built 18 *Le Corse* (Type E-50) and *Le Normand* (Type E-52) class seagoing fast escorts between 1951 and 1960. They had a speed of 28kts, a standard displacement of about 1,290 tons (1,310 tonnes) and an armament of three twin 57mm mounts and A/S weapons. They were steam-turbine powered and had a reasonable range. An enlarged class, the *Commandant Rivières* (Type-E-52), which are diesel powered with a speed of 25kts and armed with three single 3·9in (100mm) guns and A/S weapons, were built between 1957 and 1965. They can carry two landing craft and an 80-man commando unit for operations in French possessions abroad. They are being refitted with four MM-38 Exocet SSMs in place of B mount. The *D'Estienne d'Orves* are smaller, more specialised vessels with a very limited anti-aircraft armament, and are mainly intended for anti-submarine operations in coastal waters, though they can also be used for service overseas. The single 3·9in (100mm) gun is mounted forward, immediately ahead of the large bridge, and the 14·8in (375mm) A/S rocket-launcher is mounted on the deckhouse aft. Those vessels used overseas can mount an MM-38 Exocet SSM on either side of the funnel to confer some independent offensive capability, but this design is mainly dependent on other vessels or aircraft for protection against a serious threat from surface warships or aircraft. However, these relatively cheap and unsophisticated vessels can be built in greater numbers than the much larger missile- and helicopter-armed *Georges Leygues* class (Type C-70). The overseas units can also carry an 18-man landing unit. The similarly sized but improved Type A-70 has been postponed indefinitely by financial economies.

Above: Drogou *(F-783) of the* D'Estienne d'Orves *class. Note the different arrangement of radar and ECM aerials at the top of the mast compared with* Détroyat *(F-784) below left*

Displacement:	
standard tons (tonnes)	950 (970)
full load tons (tonnes)	1,170 (1,190)
Dimensions:	
length (pp)	249·3ft (76m)
(oa)	262·5ft (80m)
beam	33·8ft (10·3m)
draught	9·8ft (3m)
Armament:	
guns	
3·9in (100mm)	1
20mm	2
missiles	
MM38 Exocet SSM	2
A/S weapons	
14·8in (375mm) rocket-launcher	1
torpedo tubes	
21in (533mm)	4
Machinery:	
diesels (type)	SEMT—Pielstick
(number)	2
shafts	2
Total BHP:	
designed	11,000
Fuel capacity:	
oil (tons)	?
Performance:	
designed speed	24kts
range	4,500 miles (3,780nm) @ 15kts
Crew:	64

Class:	**D'ESTIENNE D'ORVES class (A-69 type)**
Where built:	Lorient Dockyard
Laid down:	Sept 1972 onward
Launched:	June 1973 onward
Completed:	Nov 1975 onward
Fate:	In service or under construction; two transferred to South Africa

Above: Détroyat *(F-784) of the* D'Estienne d'Orves *class. Note the 3·9in (100mm) gun forward and the 14·8in (375mm) A/S rocket launcher on the aft deckhouse. She is intended for service in home waters and so does not carry the Exocet SSM launchers amidships. The lack of freeboard forward shows that they are intended for relatively enclosed waters*

Right: The frigate D'Estienne d'Orves, *completed 1975, fires an MM-38 Exocet SSM. Fourteen ships of this class are now in service or building*

D'Estienne d'Orves *class as fitted with Exocet for overseas patrol*

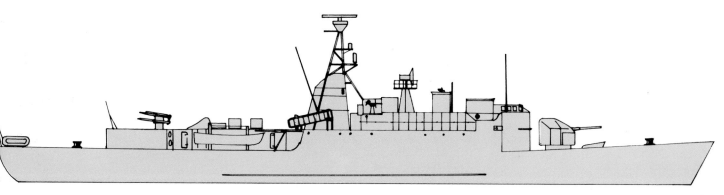

GERMANY

IN the ten years before the start of the present century Admiral von Tirpitz set about the rebuilding of what was then a disparate group of coast-defence ships into a major navy. Firstly as Chief of Staff from 1892–94 and later from his recall in 1897 his theoretical approach to the role and requirements of this fleet underwent significant changes. In his Service memorandum No 9 he originally enunciated a doctrine of sea-warfare based on the achievement of command of the sea, a function requiring a thirty per cent preponderance over the opposition's forces. While these were the navies of France and Russia there was a chance of fulfilment but, when Great Britain became a possible opponent as German overseas ambitions increased, this policy underwent a fundamental change. The 'risk policy', by which a fleet of such proportions should be built in Germany to deter any military operations by the opposition, became the hub of a continuing series of Navy Laws.

This was in direct opposition to the sound appreciation in his Service memorandum and meant that, should an incalculable psychological error be made, the German Navy would inevitably be landed in a position of inferiority. The aim was simply one of deterrence which, in the event of failure, was to be followed by 'Der Tag', the cataclysmic meeting of the two battlefleets of Germany and Britain in a Wagnerian battle for supremacy. This emotional approach ignored two fundamental facts – the Royal Navy was immeasurably stronger than the German one and, because of its superior geographical position, would be able to effect a long range blockade without becoming embroiled in a fleet action. When this did occur at Jutland the result, despite heavy British losses, was to confine the German fleet to its bases for the rest of the war with the exception of one or two inglorious sorties.

The strategic and material volte-face made by Tirpitz in 1897 meant that the German fleet was built around a core of battleships destined to engage in battle in the North Sea. The steadily rising construction costs of this programme meant that Germany was mortgaging her resources in pursuit of what should have been recognised as a fantasy of

ambition. The result in World War I was that 'Der Tag' never came and morale deteriorated as it always must do in a fleet confined to its buoys. The ultimate degradation came at Scapa Flow with the scuttling of the High Seas Fleet after its surrender.

Post-war thought in the German Navy accepted a proportion of the lessons of this earlier period but, with not only wishful thinking but also a desire to transfer the blame for failure onto the politicians, prepared a new approach – the descent on an enemy's merchant shipping. A fleet was built which was to concentrate on a world-wide disruption of hostile lines of communication without any consideration of what was again far beyond Germany's grasp, control of the seas. The battleships, pocket-battleships, cruisers and submarines were aimed at diverse attacks on sea-lanes – after the Munich period primarily those of Great Britain. This approach ignored the need to oppose the British command of the seas and resulted in the slow but inevitable destruction of their ships when deployed abroad while those remaining ships in home waters were woefully inadequate to contest such command. Had the command integrated the activities of their surface ships and submarines there would have been a greater chance of breaking what became almost tenuous links between Europe and North America. The chance was lost and Germany defeated.

In the post World War II period the division of Germany has placed the navy of East Germany under Warsaw Pact orders whilst that of the West is a part of NATO strategy. The original constraints of Treaty requirements added to a very natural unease about their Eastern frontier have resulted in a West German navy which is largely designed for Baltic operations – some destroyers, an increasing number of missile-armed frigates, small submarines, fast-attack craft.

The Bismarck *class battleship* Tirpitz *in Norwegian
waters with a* Narvik *type destroyer in the background*

König

BATTLESHIP

CLASS: *König* class (4 ships)
Grosser Kurfürst · König · Markgraf · Kronprinz

Service career KÖNIG

1914 (Aug–Nov 1918) 3rd Battle Squadron, High Seas Fleet.
1914 (Aug–May 1916) Sorties in North Sea.
1915 Six 3·4in (88mm) guns removed.
1916 (31 May) Battle of Jutland: ten heavy shell hits.
1916 (June–21 July) Repaired at Kiel Dockyard.
1916 (Aug–Nov) Three sorties in North Sea.
1916 Two 3·4in (88mm) anti-aircraft guns added.
1917 (Oct) Supported shore operations in Baltic.
1917 (17 Oct) Action with Russian battleship *Slava*.
1918 (23 Apr) Sortie in North Sea.
1918 (6 Dec) Interned at Scapa Flow.
1919 (21 June) Scuttled at Scapa Flow.

The five *Kaisers* were a great improvement over the *Helgolands*. Turbines were used for the first time in a German battleship, and superfiring was adopted for the aft turrets, allowing the broadside to be increased from six to ten 12in (305mm) guns. To achieve the required characteristics on a hull of 24,380 tons (24,770 tonnes) normal displacement, the flush deck had to be abandoned. These ships were exact contemporaries of the first British 13·5in (343mm) gunned battleships, the *Orions*. Whereas the British opted for a heavier gun with moderate protection, the Germans retained their lighter 12in (305mm) gun and used the weight saved to improve the protection and subdivision. However, wartime experience showed that the lighter German shell was unable to penetrate even relatively thin British armour, whereas the heavier British shells penetrated the German battleships' main belt armour at Jutland. The German ships' wide beam meant that the *Kaisers*, like all German heavy ships of this period, had excellent underwater protection. In this Germany benefited from starting late in producing a navy. Unlike the British, who had built a number of drydocks and whose designs were restricted by their dimensions, Germany concentrated on building a number of very large

Displacement:

normal tons (tonnes)	25,390 (25,796)
full load tons (tonnes)	28,148 (28,598)

Dimensions:

length (pp)	573·2ft (174·7m)
(oa)	576·4ft (175·7m)
beam	96·8ft (29·5m)
draught	27·2ft (8·3m)

Armament:

guns	as built	in 1918
12in (305mm) 50cal	10	10
5·9in (150mm) 45cal	14	14
3·4in (88mm)	8	4
torpedo tubes		
19·7in (500mm)	5	5

Armour:

side (belt)	7·9–13·8in (200–350mm)
(ends)	5·9in (150mm)
deck (superstructure)	1·2in (30mm)
(battery)	1·2in (30mm)
(armour deck)	1·2–3·9in (30–100mm)
main turrets	3·2–11·8in (80–300mm)
barbettes	11·8in (300mm)
casemates	7·9in (200mm)

Machinery:

boilers (type)	Naval
(number)	15 (12 coal and 3 oil)
engines (type)	Parsons turbines
shafts	3

Total SHP:

designed	31,000
trials	43,300

Fuel capacity:

coal, normal tons (tonnes)	980 (1,000)
max tons (tonnes)	3,540 (3,600)
oil tons (tonnes)	690 (700)

Performance:

designed speed	21kts
trial speed	22·5kts
range	10,000 miles (8,400nm) @ 10kts
Crew:	1,150

Ship:	GROSSER KURFÜRST	KÖNIG	MARKGRAF	KRONPRINZ
Where built:	Vulcan, Hamburg	Wilhelmshaven Dockyard	Weser, Bremen	Germania, Kiel
Authorised:	1911	1911	1911	1912
Laid down:	Oct 1911	Oct 1911	Nov 1911	May 1912
Launched:	5 May 1913	1 March 1913	4 June 1913	21 Feb 1914
Completed:	30 July 1914	10 Aug 1914	1 Oct 1914	8 Nov 1914
Fate:	Scuttled 21 June 1919; raised and scrapped 1936	Scuttled 21 June 1919; salvaged 1962 onward	Scuttled 21 June 1919; salvaged 1962 onward	Renamed *Kronprinz Wilhelm* 1 Jan 1918; scuttled 21 June 1919; salvaged 1962 onward

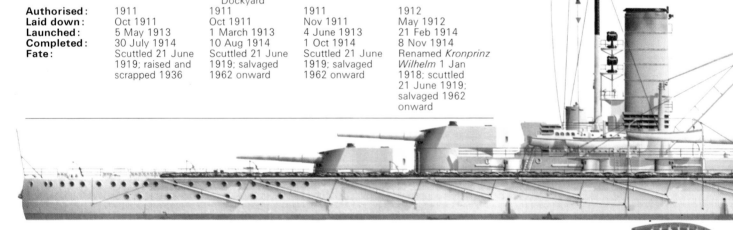

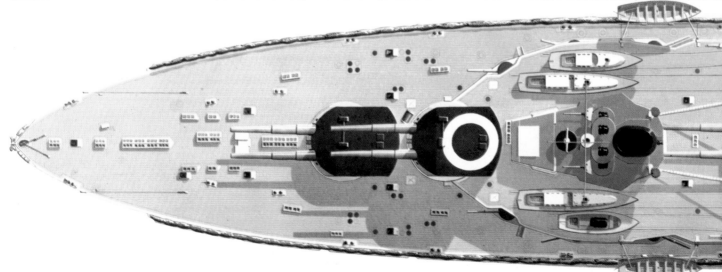

oating docks, and were able to build much wider ships. Even so. they had to enlarge several drydocks, and widen the Kiel Canal, an operation that was not complete until the summer f 1914. The *Kaisers'* main armament was not as well arranged as the *Orions',* with two wing urrets in echelon amidships. Although these were capable of firing on either beam, this ended to strain the hull. However, unlike Q turret on the *Orions*, these wing turrets were mounted at fo'c's'le deck level. *Prinzregent Luitpold* was originally designed to have a diesel engine on the centre shaft. Early direct drive turbines used large quantities of fuel even at cruising power, and this was one of several attempts to solve this problem, which was eventually overcome by the use of geared turbines and closer tolerances. Whereas other countries planned to conduct trials with mixed diesel and turbine power in small ships, Germany was the only one to plan a trial installation in a battleship. It proved impossible to build a diesel of the required power, and *Prinzregent Luitpold* was completed with only two shafts. She was slower than the other ships in the class. The *Kōnigs* were an improved version of the *Kaisers.* On a slightly longer hull the *Kōnigs* were able to mount all the main turrets on the centre line, with a superfiring pair fore and aft and a single turret at fo'c's'le deck level between the funnels. It was originally intended to fit a diesel on the centre shaft as in *Prinzregent Luitpold,* but after the failure of that plan the class was completed with a three-shaft turbine installation. Like the *Kaisers* the centre guns' magazine divided the boilers and machinery. The 5·9in (150mm) secondary armament was concentrated in the centre part of the ship, where it would be least affected by bad weather, and bow and stern embrasures for 3·4in (88mm) guns were omitted. These were the first German battleships to be built with anti-aircraft guns. Although laid down at the same time as the British *King George V* class, they were completed at the same time as the later *Iron Dukes.* Compared with the latter, the *Kōnigs* had a thicker armour belt and a wider hull with much better subdivision. The use of a lighter main armament (even though the centre turret was carried one deck higher) and of small-tube boilers allowed this to be achieved on a smaller displacement. However, the continued retention of 12in (305mm) guns entailed the same lack of armour penetration shown by the *Kaisers'* armament. The secondary armament was considerably better positioned than *Iron Duke's,* which was vulnerable to weather damage. Whereas the British used coincidence rangefinders, the Germans adopted the stereoscopic variety. Both types had their advantages; although the stereoscopic type was initially more accurate its performance was more likely to degrade in action. The state of training of the crew was more important than the differences between the types of rangefinder. *Grosser Kurfürst, Markgraf* and *Kronprinz* (later *Kronprinz Wilhelm*) had similar careers to *Kōnig.* All except *Kronprinz* were damaged at Jutland. *Kronprinz* and *Grosser Kurfürst* were both torpedoed by the British submarine *J1* on 5 November 1916, but were repaired. *Grosser Kurfürst* was again damaged by a mine in October 1917.

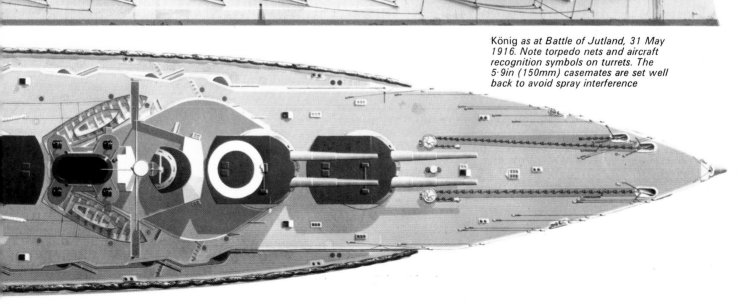

Kōnig as at Battle of Jutland, 31 May 1916. Note torpedo nets and aircraft recognition symbols on turrets. The 5·9in (150mm) casemates are set well back to avoid spray interference

Nassau

BATTLESHIP
CLASS: *Nassau* class (4 ships)
Nassau · Westfalen · Rheinland · Posen

Service career NASSAU
1910–1918 1st Battle Squadron, High Seas Fleet.
1914 (Aug–May 1916) Sorties with High Seas Fleet.
1915 Two stern 3·4in (88mm) guns removed.
1916 (31 May) Battle of Jutland: hit by two medium shells, and collided with British destroyer *Spitfire* during night action.
1916 (June–10 July) Repaired.
1916 (Aug–April 1918) Three sorties in North Sea with High Seas Fleet.
1916–1917 Remaining 3·4in (88mm) guns removed; four 3·4in (88mm) anti-aircraft guns mounted.
1919 (5 Nov) Stricken.
1920 (7 April) Transferred to Japan and sold for scrap.
1924 Scrapped.

Not until the *Braunschweig* class, built between 1901 and 1906, did the Germans produce a first-class battleship comparable with those built abroad. These were followed by a slightly improved version, the *Deutschlands*, built between 1903 and 1908. When the British battleship *Dreadnought* appeared, the German designers were not yet ready to build a comparable vessel. Their first all-big-gun ships, the *Nassaus*, were not laid down until nine months after *Dreadnought* had been completed, and were simply enlarged *Deutschlands*. They used a slightly more powerful version of the *Deutschlands'* reciprocating machinery, and this prevented turrets being mounted in the centre of the ship as in the turbine-powered *Dreadnought*. The *Nassaus* therefore adopted the very wasteful arrangement of four wing turrets, and they retained the *Deutschland*'s 11in (280mm) gun. The Germans preferred to use a small shell with a high muzzle-velocity. The weight saved by not using a larger calibre gun was utilised to improve the protection. In this respect the *Nassaus* were superior to their British contemporaries, though as with most ships with wing turrets, these were very close to the side of the ships. The layout of the wing turrets' magazines was very cramped. Unlike the British, the Germans retained a heavy calibre secondary armament, because they considered, wrongly as it turned out, that most battles in the North Sea would take place at ranges where the secondary

Displacement:	Nassau as built	
normal tons (tonnes)	18,900 (19,200)	
full load tons (tonnes)	20,210 (20,530)	
Dimensions:		
length (wl)	477·7ft (145·6m)	
(oa)	479·3ft (146·1m)	
beam	88·3ft (26·9m)	
draught	27·9ft (8·5m)	
Armament:	**as built**	**in 1918**
guns		
11in (280mm) 45cal	12	12
5·9in (150mm) 45cal	12	12
3·4in (88mm)	16	4
torpedo tubes		
17·7in (450mm)	6	6
Armour:		
side (belt)	3·9–11·5in (100–300mm)	
armour deck	2·2–3·9in (55–100mm)	
main turrets	3·5–11in (90–280mm)	
barbettes	11in (280mm)	
casemates	6·3in (160mm)	
Machinery:		
boilers (type)	Naval	
(number)	12	
engines (type)	vertical triple expansion	
shafts	3	
Total IHP:		
designed	22,000	
trials	26,244	
Fuel capacity:		
coal, normal tons (tonnes)	940 (950)	
max tons (tonnes)	2,950 (3,000)	
Performance:		
designed speed	19·5kts	
trial speed	20kts	
range	9,400 miles (7,900nm) @ 10kts	
Crew:	963	

Ship:	NASSAU	WESTFALEN	RHEINLAND	POSEN
Where built:	Wilhelmshaven Dockyard	Weser, Bremen	Vulcan, Stettin	Germania, Kiel
Authorised:	1907	1907	1907	1907
Laid down:	22 July 1907	12 Aug 1907	1 June 1907	11 June 1907
Launched:	7 March 1908	1 July 1908	26 Sept 1908	12 Dec 1908
Completed:	Oct 1909	Nov 1909	April 1910	May 1910
Fate:	Scrapped 1924	Scrapped 1924	Scrapped 1922	Scrapped 1921

Right: SMS Rheinland. *Mounting the main armament partly in wing turrets, to give extra machinery space, limited the* Nassau *class to an eight-gun broadside*

Below: The battleship SMS Nassau, *name-ship of a class of four, Germany's first all-big-gun ship (twelve 11in/280mm), completed in 1909–1910*

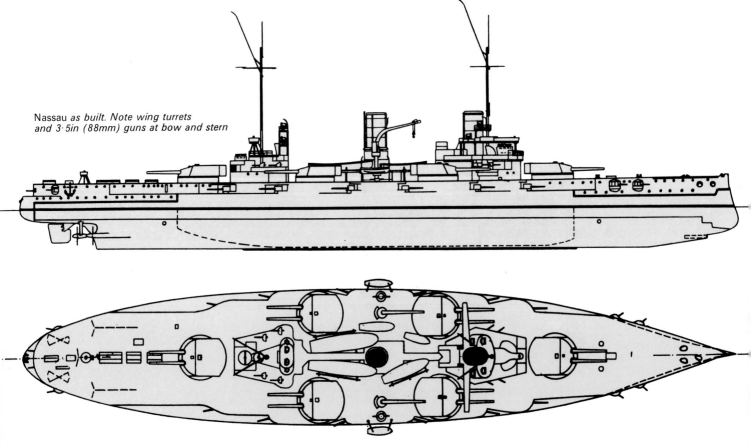

Nassau *as built. Note wing turrets and 3·5in (88mm) guns at bow and stern*

mament could play a significant part. These guns also doubled as a defence against destroyers which the Germans, again unlike the British, considered to be primarily the responsibility of the battleships rather than the escorting destroyers. The 5·9in (150mm) guns were well placed, but the 3·4in (88mm) guns at the bow and stern were very poorly positioned. The wide beam and heavy turrets near the ships' sides meant a large metacentric height. This ought to have given a steady gun platform on the North Sea, but unfortunately an oversight resulted in their period of roll coinciding with that of an average North Sea swell. This was discovered in the initial sea trials, and the class were hastily fitted with bilge keels in an attempt to eliminate this undesirable feature. In any case, they would have been very poor gun platforms in the longer Atlantic swells. The next German battleships, the four Helgolands, were enlarged and improved Nassaus, with twelve 12in (305mm) guns on a larger hull. The boilers were grouped together, allowing the wing turrets to be moved further inboard, but the same wasteful turret arrangement was adopted, and because German manufacturers could not build turbines in the required time, reciprocating engines were retained. Westfalen, Rheinland and Posen had similar careers to Nassau, and the first two were slightly damaged at the battle of Jutland (31 May 1916). Westfalen was hit by a torpedo from the British submarine E-23, on 19 August 1916 and was under repair until October 1916. Rheinland damaged her hull after running aground off the Finnish coast on 11 April 1918. She was towed to Kiel but was not repaired.

Seydlitz

BATTLE-CRUISER
CLASS: *Seydlitz* class (1 ship)
Seydlitz

Service career SEYDLITZ
1914 (to Nov 1918) Scouting Group, High Seas Fleet.
1914 (28 Aug) Sortie in North Sea.
1914 (3 Nov) Bombardment of Yarmouth.
1914 (16 Dec) Bombardment of Hartlepool.
1915 (24 Jan) Battle of Dogger Bank: hit by

two heavy shells, D and E turrets burned out.
1915 (Jan–Apr) Repaired.
1915 (Aug) Operations in Baltic.
1915 (16 Aug) Fired on British submarine *E-9*.
1916 (25 Apr) Mine hit near torpedo flat: 1,400 tons of water in hull.
1916 (27 Apr–28 May) Repaired.
1916 (31 May) Battle of Jutland: hit by 21 heavy and 2 medium shells and one torpedo; 5,300 tons of water in hull; 98 men killed.
1916 (1 June) Grounded on Horns Reef; salvaged.
1916 (3 June–16 Sept) Repaired.
1916 (Nov–Apr 1918) Two sorties in North Sea.
1918 (24 Nov) Interned at Scapa Flow.
1919 (21 June) Scuttled.
1928 (2 Nov) Raised.
1930 Scrapped at Rosyth.

Misleading British leaks convinced the Germans that the *Invincible* class battle-cruisers were to be armed with 9·2in (234mm) guns, and so the Germans' reply, *Blücher*, was an armoured cruiser with 8·2in (210mm) guns and reciprocating engines. She was completely outclassed by the British battle-cruisers, and was overtaken and sunk by them at the Battle of Dogger Bank on 24 January 1915. The next German fast armoured ship, *Von der Tann*, was a much better design. Unlike the British battle-cruisers, which concentrated on speed and armament to the detriment of protection, *Von der Tann* was a well balanced ship, with adequate protection. Her 11in (280mm) guns were arranged in a similar fashion to the *Invincible*'s 12in (305mm), but she had 8·5ft (2·6m) greater beam, a 3·5in (89mm) main armour belt and much better underwater protection. However, she had a lower freeboard than the *Invincibles*, and the wing turrets were also one deck lower. She was the first large German warship to use turbines. Unlike other large German warships, the battle-cruisers all used a four-shaft arrangement. The next two battle-cruisers, *Goeben* and *Moltke*, were enlarged *Von der Tanns*, with an extra superfiring turret aft. Their protection was improved, and was little inferior to the contemporary *Kaiser* class battleships. They retained *Von der Tann*'s low fo'c's'le, but proved capable of absorbing a good deal of damage without sinking. *Goeben*, which was trapped in the Mediterranean in August 1914 and technically transferred to Turkey as *Yavuz Sultan Selim*,

Displacement:		
normal tons (tonnes)	24,610 (25,000)	
full load tons (tonnes)	28,550 (29,000)	

Dimensions:		
length (pp)	?	
(oa)	652·2ft (200m)	
beam	93·5ft (28·5m)	
draught	27ft (8·24m)	

Armament:	as built	in 1918
guns		
11in (280mm) 50cal	10	10
5·9in (150mm) 45cal	12	12
3·4in (88mm)	14	2
torpedo tubes		
19·7in (500mm)	4	4

Armour:		
side (belt)	5·9–11·8in (150–300mm)	
(ends)	3·9in (100mm)	
deck (upper)	1·2–3·1in (30–80mm)	
(armour)	1·2–3·1in (30–80mm)	
main turrets	2·8–9·8in (70–250mm)	
barbettes	3·9–7·9in (100–200mm)	
casemates	5·9in (150mm)	

Machinery:		
boilers (type)	Naval	
(number)	27	
engines (type)	Naval turbines	
shafts	4	

Total SHP:		
designed	67,000	
trials	89,738	

Fuel capacity:		
coal, normal tons (tonnes)	980 (1,000)	
maximum tons (tonnes)	3,540 (3,600)	

Performance:		
designed speed	26·5kts	
trial speed	29·12kts	
range	4,200 (3,530nm) @ 14kts	
Crew:	1,068	

Ship:	SEYDLITZ
Where built:	Blohm und Voss, Hamburg
Authorised:	1909
Laid down:	4 Feb 1911
Launched:	30 March 1912
Completed:	22 May 1913
Fate:	Scuttled 21 June 1919; raised 1928; scrapped 1930

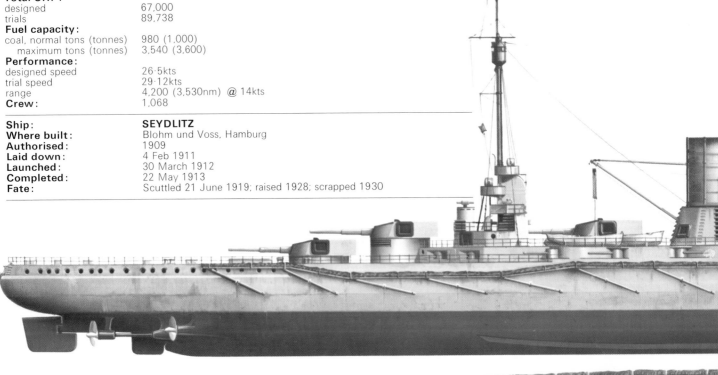

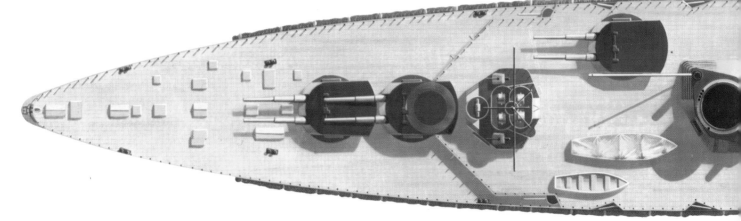

was very seriously damaged by mines and bombs in 1914 and January 1918. However, she survived to become the last World War I capital ship to remain in service and was not finally scrapped until 1971. *Seydlitz* was a modified version of the *Moltkes*, with the same armament and thickness of armour, but with a longer and narrower hull to improve the speed. Her fo'c's'le and wing guns were raised by one deck to improve the seaworthiness, and this extra freeboard undoubtedly saved her after extensive damage at Jutland. Completed a year later than the first two British *Lion* class battle-cruisers, she had a much lighter armament, with ten 11in (280mm) against eight 13·5in (343mm) guns. The *Lions*' guns were all on the centreline, whilst *Seydlitz* had two wing turrets, which had the same drawbacks as those fitted in the *Kaisers*. Moreover, only one of the *Lions*' turrets was below fo'c's'le deck level, whereas all but one of *Seydlitz*'s were. The two types were similar in size, but *Seydlitz*, with small-tube boilers and a lighter armament, had a 2in (50mm) thicker main belt and much better internal subdivision. However, this was offset by the much greater penetrating power of the larger British shell, and the British boilers and machinery, though larger and heavier, were also more reliable. The main difference in performance lay not so much in the designs as such, as in the cordite and shell used. When her aft barbettes were pierced, *Seydlitz*'s two aft turrets simply burned out. In similar circumstances, *Lion*'s Q turret was only just prevented from exploding, and *Queen Mary* was probably lost through a cordite explosion. Until late 1916, British armour-piercing shells also did not perform as well as they ought, but after this

date the *Lions* were probably more than a match for *Seydlitz*. Although *Seydlitz*'s underwater protection amidships was good, like all contemporary German armoured ships she was vulnerable to damage fore and aft, and was seriously disabled by the mine exploding by her forward torpedo flat in April 1916. The next German battle-cruisers, the three *Derfflingers*, were greatly improved. They had four twin centreline 12in (305mm) turrets, with a flush decked hull of greater beam than *Seydlitz*'s. They had a thicker main belt and even better subdivision. Whereas *Seydlitz*'s heavier armour was eventually outweighed by the *Lion*'s heavier armament, the *Derfflingers* were at least the equal of the British *Tiger* (herself a beamier

Lion with better arranged armament and protection). The *Derfflingers* could absorb a great deal of damage, and *Lützow*, sunk after Jutland, might have been saved by more efficient damage control. *Derfflinger* and *Lützow* were poorly constructed, and required considerable modification before entering service. *Hindenburg* was delayed by the priority given to U-boats, and was not completed until May 1917. For the same reason none of the enlarged *Mackensen* class, armed with 13·8in (350mm) guns was completed. An improved single-funnelled version with 15in (380mm) guns, the *Erzatz Yorcks*, was projected but not laid down. All the German battle-cruisers except *Goeben* and *Lützow* were scuttled at Scapa Flow.

Above, upper: Seydlitz *after the Battle of Jutland, May 1916*

Above: The battle-cruiser Seydlitz *was lighter armed than the British* Lions. *Her high fo'c's'le stood her in good stead after Jutland*

Seydlitz *as at Battle of Jutland, 31 May 1916. Note bow shield carried by all German major warships, high fo'c's'le, wing turrets amidships and the low torpedo tube under the forefoot*

Baden

BATTLESHIP
CLASS: *Bayern* class (2 ships)
Bayern · Baden

Service career BADEN
1917 (March–Nov 1918) Fleet flagship, High Seas Fleet.
1918 (23 Apr) Sortie in North Sea.
1918 (14 Dec) Interned at Scapa Flow (substitute for incomplete *Mackensen*).
1919 (21 June) Scuttled at Scapa Flow but beached and salved.
1920–1921 Comparative trials with British ships.
1921 Gunnery target.
1921 (6 Aug) Sunk as target off Portsmouth.

When the Germans learned that the British planned to use a 15in (380mm) gun in the *Queen Elizabeth* class battleships, they abandoned the 13·8in (350mm) gun for their next design, and substituted a 15in (380mm) gun instead. The *Bayern*s used a slightly enlarged version of the *König*'s hull, with similar protection, but only four turrets in two superfiring pairs fore and aft, and with the boilers and machinery grouped together. Unlike the *König*s, which had a pole foremast, the *Bayern*s had a tripod to carry the heavy fire-control. *Baden* differed from *Bayern* by having a slightly larger bridge, and *Sachsen* was intended to have a MAN diesel on the centre shaft and differed considerably from the first two. Because the German battle-cruisers were well armoured, they did not require fast battleship support as much as the British, and the *Bayern*s more closely resembled the British *Revenge* than *Queen Elizabeth* class battleships. Detailed comparative trials were conducted after the war by the British between *Baden* and *Revenge*, which had a similar armament, speed and protection. *Baden* had better subdivision and underwater protection, conferred by her greater beam, but in most other respects the British ship proved superior. Whereas the British 15in (380mm) was an excellent gun, the German 15in (380mm) was a disappointment, firing a lighter shell than the British gun and lacking the accuracy of earlier German weapons. Because the Germans considered long-range actions unlikely given normal North Sea conditions, the main armament only had 16° elevation. Much to British surprise, German armour proved inferior to its British equivalent, and was easily penetrable by the improved British heavy shells. The standard German battleship three-shaft arrangement and small-tube boilers gave lighter machinery, but it was less reliable, and the overall standard of construction of *Baden* was inferior to that of *Revenge*. Although the British ship had a large metacentric height, *Baden*'s was even larger, making her a steady gun platform in confined waters but not in the open Atlantic. *Baden*'s freeboard was lower than

Displacement:
normal tons (tonnes)	28,000 (28,500)
full load tons (tonnes)	31,691 (32,200)

Dimensions:
length (wl)	588·6ft (179·4m)
(oa)	598·4ft (182·4m)
beam	99·1ft (30·2m)
draught	27·9ft (8·5m)

Armament:
guns	
15in (380mm) 45cal	8
5·9in (150mm) 45cal	16
3·4in (88mm)	8
torpedo tubes	
23·6in (600mm)	5

Armour:
side (belt)	6·7–13·8in (170–350mm)
(ends)	1·2–3·9in (30–100mm)
deck (superstructure)	1·6in (40mm)
(battery)	1·2in (30mm)
(armour)	1·2–4·7in (30–120mm)
main turrets	4·7–13·8in (120–350mm)
barbettes	13·8in (350mm)
casemates	9·8in (250mm)

Machinery:
boilers (type)	Naval
(number)	14 (11 coal and 3 oil)
engines (type)	Schichau turbines
shafts	3

Total SHP:
designed	52,000

Fuel capacity:
coal, normal tons (tonnes)	890 (900)
max tons (tonnes)	3,350 (3,400)
oil, normal tons (tonnes)	197 (200)
max tons (tonnes)	610 (620)

Performance:
designed speed	22·25kts
range	9,000 miles (7,570nm) @ 10kts

Crew: 1,171

Above: SMS Baden; *the* Baden*s were distinguished from other World War I German battleships in having tripod foremasts to carry the fire-control*

Ship:	**BAYERN**	**BADEN**	**SACHSEN**	**WÜRTTEMBERG**
Where built:	Howaldtswerke, Kiel	Schichau, Danzig	Germania, Kiel	Vulcan, Hamburg
Authorised:	1912	1912	1913	1914
Laid down:	20 Sept 1913	29 Sept 1913	1914	1 Jan 1915
Launched:	18 Feb 1915	30 Oct 1915	21 Nov 1916	20 June 1917
Completed:	18 March 1916	19 Oct 1916	—	—
Fate:	Scuttled 21 June 1919; scrapped 1934–1935	Sunk 21 August 1921 as a target	Work stopped Nov 1918; scrapped incomplete 1920–1921	Work stopped 1917; scrapped incomplete 1920–1921

Revenge's making her less seaworthy, though this was not very significant for operations in the southern North Sea. Like most German ships, the ends were not very well protected, and the bow torpedo flat was a point of weakness. *Bayern* joined the High Seas Fleet just after Jutland, and took part in operations in the North Sea and Baltic, where she was mined and damaged on 12 October 1917. She was surrendered in November 1918 and scuttled at Scapa Flow. The wreck was later raised and scrapped. Work on *Sachsen* and *Württemberg* was slowed after 1915, when U-boats were given first priority. *Württemberg* was eventually suspended, but work on *Sachsen* continued on a stand-by basis until the armistice.

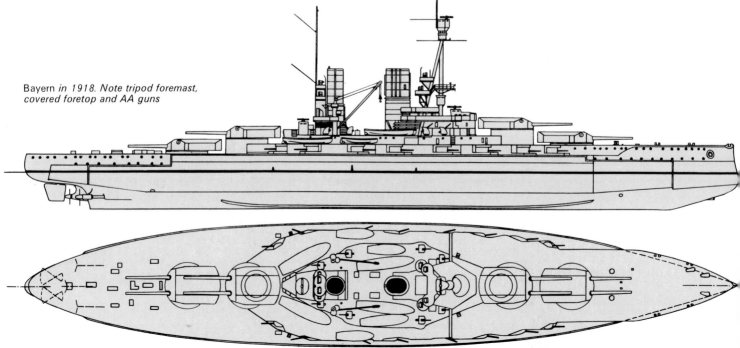

Bayern in 1918. Note tripod foremast, covered foretop and AA guns

Scharnhorst

ARMOURED CRUISER
CLASS: *Scharnhorst* class (2 ships)
Scharnhorst · Gneisenau

Service career SCHARNHORST
1909 To Far East station.
1909-1914 Flagship, Cruiser Squadron, Far East Station.
1914 (June) Sailed from Tsingtao to South-West Pacific.
1914 (July–6 Aug) At Ponape.
1914 (6 Aug–26 Oct) Cruiser Squadron sailed from Ponape to Juan Fernandez Island via Pagan Island, Christmas Island, Tahiti and Easter Island.
1914 (1 Nov) Battle of Coronel: light damage, overwhelmed British armoured cruiser *Good Hope.*
1914 (8 Dec) Battle of Falklands: sunk with *Gneisenau* by British battle-cruisers *Inflexible* and *Invincible*; no survivors.

Most German armoured cruisers were either in reserve or used as training ships by 1914. They were mostly not very good designs, being badly laid out and poorly protected, with large, vulnerable silhouettes. *Roon* and *Yorck*, built between 1902 and 1906 with an armament of four 8·2in (210mm) and ten 5·9in (150mm) guns and a normal displacement of 9,200 tons (9,350 tonnes), were particularly unsuccessful. *Yorck* was mined and sunk in November 1914, but *Roon* was disarmed in 1916 and used as an accommodation ship. The next class, the somewhat larger *Scharnhorsts*, were much more successful. Like all German armoured cruisers except *Blücher*, they had a short two-level centre citadel. The upper guns were single-mounted 8·2in (210mm) guns, with single 5·9in (150mm) guns beneath. As with all ships carrying guns near the waterline, the 5·9in (150mm) were of little use in heavy weather. The remaining four 8·2in (210mm) guns were carried in two twin turrets fore and aft. Unlike *Roon* and *Yorck*, the centre citadel guns were well separated, and were unlikely to be disabled by a single lucky hit. Eight 3·4in (88mm) guns were mounted in casemates at the extreme bow and stern an arrangement abandoned by all other countries except France. The remainder were distributed around the superstructure. The *Scharnhorsts* were well sub-divided, and could absorb a considerable amount of battle damage. Like all large German warships prior to 1918, they were fitted with a bow torpedo tube at the foot of the stem. The exaggerated 'swan's-neck' bow fixed to previous German armoured cruisers was reduced to a gentle curve on these ships. They were clearly superior to the French *Waldeck Rousseaus* and the American *Washingtons* and were the equal of the Italian *Pisas* and the larger British *Duke of Edinburghs*. However, they were outclassed by the British *Warriors* and

Displacement:	
normal tons (tonnes)	11,433 (11,616)
full load tons (tonnes)	12,780 (12,985)
Dimensions:	
length (wl)	470·9ft (143·8m)
(oa)	473·6ft (144·6m)
beam	70·7ft (21·6m)
draught	27·5ft (8·4m)
Armament:	
guns	
8·2in (210mm) 40cal	8
5·9in (150mm) 40cal	6
3·5in (88mm)	20
torpedo tubes	
17·7in (450mm)	4
Armour:	
side (belt)	5·9in (150mm)
(ends)	3·1in (80mm)
deck	1·4–2·4in (35–60mm)
main turrets	1·2–6·7in (30–170mm)
barbettes	5·9in (150mm)
casemates	5·9in (150mm)
Machinery:	
boilers (type)	Marine Schulz Thornycroft
(number)	18
engines (type)	vertical triple expansion
shafts	3
Total IHP:	
designed	28,000
trial	28,783
Fuel capacity:	
coal normal tons (tonnes)	790 (800)
max tons (tonnes)	1,970 (2,000)
Performance:	
designed speed	22·5kts
trial speed	23·5kts
range	6,090 miles (5,120nm) @ 12kts
Crew:	764

Above: Scharnhorst was the flagship of Vice Admiral Graf von Spee's Far Eastern Squadron, which sank two British armoured cruisers at Coronel, 1 November 1914

Ship	SCHARNHORST	GNEISENAU
Where built:	Blohm und Voss, Hamburg	Weser, Bremen
Authorised:	1904	1903
Laid down:	1905	1904
Launched:	23 March 1906	14 June 1906
Completed:	24 Oct 1907	6 March 1908
Fate:	Sunk 8 Dec 1914	Sunk 8 Dec 1914

Minotaurs, with their heavier and better arranged armament. As was conclusively demonstrated at the Battle of the Falklands, the British *Invincible* class battle-cruisers, completed at the same time as the *Scharnhorsts*, were immeasurably superior. They were able, with their higher speed and 12in (305mm) guns, to pick their own range and destroy the *Scharnhorsts* without the latter being able to make any effective reply. *Blücher* was an enlarged version of the *Scharnhorsts*, and was comparable to the British *Minotaurs*, Japanese *Kuramas* and Russian *Rurik*, but was also outclassed by the British *Invincibles*. *Blücher* mounted twelve 8·2in (210mm) guns in six twin turrets arranged in a similar fashion to the *Nassaus*, with eight 5·9in (150mm) guns in casemates below. She had a normal displacement of 15,260 tons (15,500 tonnes) and was powered by reciprocating

engines. On 32,000 IHP she made 24·5kts. She was sunk at the Battle of Dogger Bank on 24 January 1915 by the British battle-cruisers. The *Scharnhorsts* were both fitted with fire-control in 1912, but the reason for the ease of their victory over the older and weaker British armoured cruisers at the Battle of Coronel, 1 November 1914, was the length of time the crews had served abroad and the high state of training achieved by these two cruisers on the China Station. *Gneisenau* had a similar career to *Scharnhorst* and was also sunk by British battle-cruisers *Invincible* and *Inflexible* at the Battle of the Falklands.

Below: The armoured cruiser SMS Scharnhorst, completed 1907. The single mounted 5·9/150mm guns were little use in heavy weather

Bismarck

BATTLESHIP
CLASS: *Bismarck* class (2 ships)
Bismarck · Tirpitz

Service career BISMARCK
1941 (April–May) Working-up in the Baltic.
1941 (18 May) Sailed on Operation 'Rheinü-bung' with *Prinz Eugen*.
1941 (21–22 May) In Grinstedt fjord, Norway.
1941 (23 May) Shadowed by HMS *Suffolk* and *Norfolk*.
1941 (24 May) Battle of Denmark Strait: sank HMS *Hood* and slightly damaged HMS *Prince of Wales*, but hit 3 times by *Prince of Wales*. *Prinz Eugen* separated. *Bismarck* hit by torpedo from aircraft from HMS *Victorious*. Little damage. Lost shadowers.
1941 (26 May) British regained contact. Torpedo attack by HMS *Ark Royal*'s aircraft. Torpedo hit jammed rudders.
1941 (26–27 May) Night attack by British destroyers. No damage.
1941 (27 May) Overwhelmed by HMS *King George V* and *Rodney*. Scuttled by crew. Finally sunk by torpedoes from HMS *Dorsetshire*.

The enforced cessation of design and experimental work at the end of World War I affected all Germany's World War II designs. Not only had Germany's naval architects been unable properly to evaluate the lessons of World War I concerning warship design, but they also lacked the continuity of design experience essential for the creation of new designs. In addition they were unable to compare, evaluate and test to destruction vessels designed by countries other than their own, as the Allies were able to do in the early 1920s.

Thus German naval architects started out in the late 1920s at a considerable disadvantage to those of the other major powers. When they came to design the *Gneisenaus* they were able to take a short cut by utilising the World War I *Mackensen* design, but there was no suitably sized World War I design with the requisite speed for a modern battleship. Moreover, whereas the *Gneisenaus'* equivalents abroad were either smaller (the French *Dunkerques*) or were themselves built in World War I, the new battleship was intended to be superior to any foreign contemporary, most of which were based on a decade of research and development that the Germans did not possess. In addition, they did not have the time to catch up. Theoretical studies had been started for a battleship in 1933, and on 18 June 1935, the Anglo-German naval agreement gave Germany enough surplus battleship tonnage to build three 35,000 ton (35,560t) standard displacement battleships. Contracts to build two were allocated by the beginning of 1936. In this emergency the German naval architects used the World War I *Baden* design as the basis of the new ships. It was necessary to enlarge the design to cope with the 6 knot increase in speed and the enormous increase in the anti-aircraft armament, as well as to provide improved anti-torpedo protection. This last was helped by the need to keep the draught as small as possible because of the shallowness of the waters round the German coast. As with the Japanese *Yamatos*, the result was to increase the beam, allowing an excellent anti-torpedo system to be worked in.

Although the result was an undeniably powerful ship, *Bismarck* was not as powerful as she might have been. Lack of research into protection systems meant that whereas her foreign contemporaries mounted their main armour deck at or near the top of the armour belt, protecting the communications systems, *Bismarck*'s was near the bottom. Her communications systems were left virtually unprotected, which contributed to her speedy and easy final destruction. Also the same lack of protection to the rudders that ensured *Bismarck*'s inability to escape had shown itself in German ships at Jutland, 25 years previously. Lack of research into dual-purpose secondary armaments meant that *Bismarck* had a separate secondary and heavy anti-aircraft battery, making her unnecessarily large for her armament. Lack of research also meant that German armour was not up to British or American standards. Her armoured conning tower, protected theoretically against battleship shells, was knocked out by a British 8in (203mm) shell early in the final action. Like most German World War II heavy units, *Bismarck* was a poor seaboat for her size. Finally, too, many German shells were duds. Only one of those that hit HMS *Prince of Wales* exploded properly.

Bismarck's design did have its good points however. The fire control in general, and that of the anti-aircraft armament in particular, was very good. Moreover, she was fitted with gunnery radar. She was extremely difficult to sink (although this was much less important than the ease with which she could be put out of action). Not until the crew had fired scuttling charges and HMS *Dorsetshire* had fired torpedoes at her did she finally sink.

Tirpitz was very similar to *Bismarck*, differing mainly by having a longer range and different derricks and main mast. She was badly damaged by British midget submarines (X-craft) on 22 September 1943 and never properly repaired. She survived several bombing attacks, and was finally sunk near Tromso by 5·5 ton (5·6t) bombs.

Right: Bismarck *class battleship* Tirpitz *firing at Spitzbergen in 1943. The hull armour can be clearly seen. The hemispheres amidships and on the aft superstructure are the AA fire control*

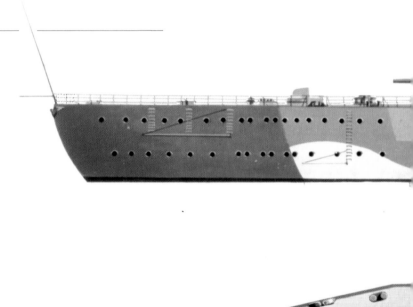

Displacement:		
standard tons (tonnes)	41,676 (42,344)	
normal tons (tonnes)	45,226 (45,951)	
full load tons (tonnes)	50,153 (50,996)	
Dimensions:		
length (wl)	792·3ft (241·5m)	
(oa)	823·5ft (251m)	
beam	118·1ft (36m)	
draught	29·6ft (9m)	
Armament:	**Bismarck**	**Tirpitz**
guns	**as built**	**in 1944**
15in (380mm) 47cal	8	8
5·9in (150mm) 55cal	12	12
4·1in (105mm) 65cal	16	16
37mm	16	16
20mm	12	58
torpedo tubes		
21in (533mm)	—	24
aircraft	6	6
Armour:		
side (belt)	5·7–12·75in (145–323mm)	
deck (upper)	2in (50mm)	
(main)	1·2in (30mm)	
(armour)	3·2–4·7in (80–120mm)	
main turrets	5·1–14·1in (130–360mm)	
barbettes	8·7in (220mm)	
secondary turrets	0·75in–3·9in (20–100mm)	
Machinery:		
boilers (type)	Wagner	
(number)	12	
engines (type)	Blohm und Voss single reduction geared turbines	
shafts	3	
Total SHP:		
designed	138,000	138,000
trials	150,170	163,000
Fuel capacity:		
oil tons	7,344 (7,461)	
Performance:		
designed speed	29kts	29kts
trial speed	30·1kts	30·8kts
range	11,038 miles (9,280nm) @ 16kts	
Crew:	2,092	2,500

Ship:	**BISMARCK**	**TIRPITZ**
Where built:	Blohm und Voss, Hamburg	Wilhelmshaven Dockyard
Ordered:	1935	1936
Laid down:	1 July 1936	26 Oct 1936
Launched:	14 Feb 1939	1 April 1939
Completed:	24 Aug 1940	25 Feb 1941
Fate:	Sunk 27 May 1941	Sunk 12 Nov 1944 and broken up 1948–1957

Above: Bismarck *on trials. Note the absence of fire control positions on the forebridge, on the top on the tower mast, and on the superstructure aft, and the boat hoisted out amidships*

Bismarck *just prior to her final sortie. Fire control and gunnery radar have been fitted. The camouflage was painted out in May 1941 and replaced by an all-grey scheme*

Above: Gneisenau *seen from* Scharnhorst *on
8 June 1940, firing at the British
aircraft carrier HMS* Glorious. *The
prominent hemispheres are the AA fire
control positions*

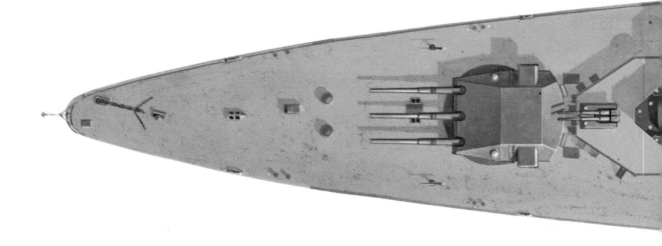

Scharnhorst *in February 1942 at the time of the 'Channel Dash'. Note the extra 20mm AA, the gunnery radar tower on the foretop and the Arado 196 seaplane*

Above: Bismarck *leaving Blohm und Voss shipyard, Hamburg, on trials in 1940. She has not yet been fitted with fire control. A group of sailors and dockyard workers can be seen on deck*

Above: The World War I Baden class *battleship* Bayern *leaving Wilhelmshaven. The circles on the turrets are for aircraft recognition. This design formed the basis for the much larger and faster* Bismarck.

Above: Gneisenau *in 1940 after refitting with 'Atlantic' bow and funnel cap. She can easily be distinguished from Scharnhorst by having her mainmast immediately abaft of her funnel*

Right: Scharnhorst *in 1940 after being rebuilt similarly to* Gneisenau. *Note position of mainmast and the prominent armour belt amidships. She has just recovered her seaboat*

Scharnhorst

BATTLE-CRUISER

CLASS: *Scharnhorst* class (2 ships)
Gneisenau · Scharnhorst

Service career SCHARNHORST

1939 (21–27 Nov) Sortie with *Gneisenau* in North Sea.

1939 (23 Nov) Sank HMS *Rawalpindi*.

1940 (Apr–June) Norwegian campaign: operations with *Gneisenau*.

1940 (9 Apr) Exchanged shots with battle-cruiser HMS *Renown* in bad weather off Norway.

1940 (8 June) Sank aircraft-carrier HMS *Glorious* and destroyers HMS *Acasta* and *Ardent;* hit by one torpedo aft from *Ardent;* turret and part of machinery out of action; 2,500 tons of water in hull.

1940 (13 June) Hit by dud bomb from HMS *Ark Royal*'s aircraft.

1940 (June–Nov) Repairs at Kiel.

1941 (22 Jan–23 March) Sortie in Atlantic with *Gneisenau:* sank 22 ships and encountered convoys protected by battleships HMS *Ramillies* (8 Feb 1941), HMS *Malaya* (7 March 1941) and HMS *Rodney* (15 March 1941), which they did not engage.

1941 (23 Mar–11 Feb 1942) At Brest.

1941 (24 July) Hit by five bombs.

1942 (11–13 Feb) 'Channel Dash' with *Gneisenau* and *Prinz Eugen*.

1942 (12 Feb) Attacked by British aircraft and light forces; hit two mines and badly damaged.

1942 (15 Feb–Oct) Repaired at Kiel.

1943 (March) To Norway.

1943 (6–9 Sept) Spitzbergen raid with *Tirpitz*.

1943 (22–26 Dec) Sortie against Russia convoy JW 55B.

1943 (26 Dec) Battle of North Cape: sunk by battleship HMS *Duke of York*, cruisers HMS *Norfolk, Sheffield, Belfast* and *Jamaica*, destroyers HMS *Savage, Saumarez* and *Scorpion* and Norwegian *Stord;* damaged HMS *Norfolk* but hit by at least thirteen 14in (356mm) shells and 11 torpedoes; 36 crew saved.

In 1932 the French laid down the fast battleship *Dunkerque*, and this made the *Deutschland* type 'Panzerschiff' obsolete. Despite the fact that this would break the provisions of the Versailles Treaty, the Germans had already prepared plans for a ship of about 19,000 tons (19,300 tonnes) standard displacement with three triple 11in (280mm) turrets in 1928, and by 1932 had designed a ship with *Panzerschiff* armour, eight 12in (305mm) guns in four twin turrets, three triple 5·9in (150mm) turrets and four 3·4in (88mm) anti-aircraft guns. 160,000 SHP would give a speed of 34kts. This was too weakly armoured, and the design that was evolved into the *Scharnhorsts* was for a ship officially of 26,000 tons (26,410 tonnes) standard displacement, with moderate armour, three twin 15in (380mm) turrets, high speed and a reasonable range. Unfortunately, because of the limited scale of design work since 1918, no

Displacement:		
normal tons (tonnes)	34,840 (35,400)	
full load tons (tonnes)	38,900 (39,520)	
Dimensions	**as built**	**in Sept 1939**
length (pp)	?	
(oa)	753·9ft (229·8m)	770·7ft (234·9m)
beam	98·4ft (30m)	98·4ft (30m)
draught	26·9ft (8·2m)	26·9ft (8·2m)
Armament:	**as built**	**in 1943**
guns		
11in (280mm) 54·5cal	9	9
5·9in (150mm) 55cal	12	12
4·1in (105mm)	14	14
37mm	16	16
20mm	8	22
torpedo tubes		
21in (533mm)	6	6
aircraft	4	4
Armour:		
side (belt)	6·7–9·8in (170–250mm)	
(ends)	1·2in (30mm)	
deck (upper)	2in (50mm)	
(armour)	0·8–2in (20–50mm)	
main turrets	5·9–14·2in (150–360mm)	
barbettes	7·9–13·8in (200–350mm)	
secondary turrets	2–5·5in (50–140mm)	
Machinery:		
boilers (type)	Wagner	
(number)	12	
engines (type)	Brown, Boveri single reduction geared turbines	
shafts	3	
Total SHP:		
designed	165,000	
Fuel capacity:		
oil, normal tons (tonnes)	2,760 (2,800)	
maximum tons (tonnes)	6,200 (6,300)	
Performance:		
designed speed	32kts	
range	10,000 miles (8,400nm) @ 17kts	
Crew:	1,840	

Ship:	GNEISENAU	SCHARNHORST
Where built:	Deutschewerke, Kiel	Wilhelmshaven Dockyard
Authorised:	1934	1934
Laid down:	March 1935	16 May 1935
Launched:	8 Dec 1936	3 Oct 1936
Completed:	21 May 1938	7 Jan 1939
Rebuilt:	1939	July–Sept 1939
Fate:	27 Feb 1942 bow destroyed; 27 March 1945 scuttled; 1947–1951 scrapped.	Sunk 26 Dec 1943

heavy gun turret design was available, and since these take longer to prepare and build than a ship, no twin 15in (380mm) turrets would be ready until 1938–1939, despite being based on a World War I design. However, four triple 11in (280mm) turrets had already been ordered and were under construction for the projected fourth and fifth *Deutschlands*, so two more of these were ordered and they were incorporated in the *Scharnhorsts*' design as an interim measure. It was intended to replace them with the 15in (380mm) turrets at a later date. Because of the design team's lack of recent experience with large high-speed warships, the hull was based on that of the World War I battle-cruiser *Mackensen*. Originally it was intended to mount all the secondary armament in twin turrets, but the use of machinery of nearly twice the *Mackensen*'s power, even though it was of modern high-pressure design, meant that there was insufficient room for the centre turrets' shell hoists. Therefore use was made of four single 5·9in (150mm) guns originally ordered for the fourth and fifth *Deutschlands*, despite their inferior protection. The best feature of the *Scharnhorsts*' design was the adequate provision of directors for the heavy anti-aircraft armament, but even so, better use could have been made of the weight by having a dual-purpose secondary armament. Lack of design staff prevented this. The *Scharnhorsts* used new lightweight high-pressure machinery. This was notoriously unreliable, having been pressed into service before being adequately tested. The use of turbines rather than diesels to secure high speed also meant a reduction in range. A feature retained from the *Mackensen* was the low freeboard forward, and even after the lengthened 'Atlantic' bow was fitted the fo'c's'le was still very wet. This handicapped the ships in rough seas, including during the engagement with *Renown* and in the Battle of North Cape. Despite the mixed origins of the design, the *Scharnhorsts* were powerful ships, but would have been much improved if it had been possible to fit the 15in (380mm) guns, as the 11in (280mm) gun was incapable of dealing with even an old capital ship. They made effective raiders, though troubled by engine failure and restricted range, but the German Admiralty were wise to insist that they did not engage even an old capital ship, for their armour, and particularly their horizontal protection, was totally inadequate against heavy calibre shells. *Gneisenau* could be distinguished from *Scharnhorst* after 1939 by a heavy pole mast at the rear of the funnel. Her career up to February 1942 was similar to *Scharnhorst*'s. She was badly damaged by a bomb which wrecked the forepart, and it was planned to fit a longer, more seaworthy bow and 15in (380mm) guns, but this was abandoned, and she was eventually scuttled without being refitted.

Arms of the German military reformer, Scharnhorst, carried by the battle-cruiser

Arms of the German Napoleonic war general, Gneisenau, carried by the battle-cruiser

Admiral Graf Spee

ARMOURED CRUISER
CLASS: *Deutschland* class (3 ships)
*Deutschland · Admiral Scheer ·
Admiral Graf Spee*

Service career ADMIRAL GRAF SPEE
1936–1938 Fleet flagship.
1936–1939 Cruises in Spanish waters during Spanish Civil War.
1937 (May) Attended British Coronation review at Spithead.
1938 Refit: tower bridge modified, radar fitted.
1939 (21 Aug–13 Dec) In Atlantic and Indian Ocean.
1939 (Sept–Dec) Sank nine ships, 50,089 GRT.
1939 (13 Dec) Battle of River Plate: severely damaged cruiser HMS *Exeter* and damaged cruiser HMS *Ajax;* received 20 shell hits, fire control destroyed and fo'c's'le holed; took refuge in Montevideo.
1939 (17 Dec) Scuttled off Montevideo.
1942 Wreck blown up.

The Versailles Treaty limited Germany to armoured ships of not more than 10,000 tons (10,160 tonnes) standard displacement and a maximum gun calibre of 11in (280mm). This was the size and armament of the pre-dreadnoughts Germany had been permitted to retain for training, and the intention was to restrict Germany to ships of the same type as the Swedish *Sverige* class coast defence battleships. However, the Germans were inspired by the success achieved in the first months of World War I by surface raiders, and they considered that more powerful ships with a long range should be able to do even better. After producing several alternative designs, they constructed a ship that whilst not exceeding the treaty limits too blatantly was also a useful modern fighting unit. The *Deutschlands* were designed round their diesel engines. Although these were not in themselves much lighter than steam turbines, they needed fewer men to run

Continued on page 116▶

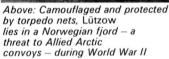

*Above: Camouflaged and protected
by torpedo nets, Lützow
lies in a Norwegian fjord — a
threat to Allied Arctic
convoys — during World War II*

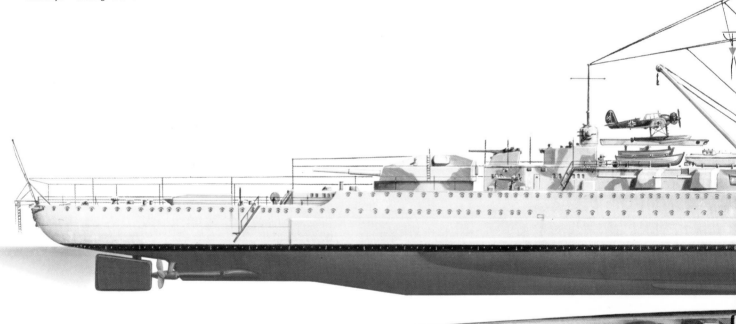

Above: Led by her sister-ship
Lützow (ex-Deutschland,
renamed 1939); the Deutschland
class armoured cruiser
Admiral Graf Spee in 1939

Admiral Graf Spee in December 1939,
with an Arado 196 seaplane on the
catapult. Note the armoured tower
bridge and the triple TT mounts on
the quarterdeck

►Admiral Graf Spee

them, occupied less space and were much more economical on fuel, giving a longer range for a smaller ship. They also produced less smoke, which could (and should) have enabled *Graf Spee* to avoid the British cruiser squadron off the River Plate, because their smoke was sighted 15 minutes before they saw *Graf Spee*. However, the use of diesels did reduce the maximum speed. The need to save weight was paramount, and the hull was welded and a great deal of light alloy was used. The main armament was mounted in two triple turrets, which saved weight but meant that only one target could be engaged with any accuracy — as was shown when *Graf Spee* was forced to fire at *Exeter* and the light cruisers simultaneously at the Battle of the River Plate. The 5·9in (150mm) guns were grouped around the funnel in single mounts, with only splinter shield protection. Two quadruple 21in (533mm) torpedo tubes were mounted on the quarterdeck and were mainly intended to sink merchant ships rapidly, and a catapult and spotter aircraft were carried. All three ships differed. *Deutschland* and *Scheer* had a smaller hull with thinner armour, and were initially fitted with 3·4in (88mm) anti-aircraft guns, whereas *Graf Spee* had a thicker main belt, a beamier hull and had 4·1in (105mm) guns (fitted in the other two in autumn 1939) from the start. *Scheer* and *Graf Spee* had a tower bridge, whereas *Deutschland* had a pole foremast. The two former also had active roll-damping. All three had a sloped main belt with an overlapping armoured torpedo bulkhead behind. They were really no more than slow, long ranged armoured cruisers, a fact recognised by the Germans in February 1940 when *Lützow* and *Scheer* were reclassified as heavy cruisers. They would have been more effective ships if they had been fitted with a lighter main armament in place of the 11in (280mm) and 5·9in (150mm) guns, and the weight saved used to increase the speed and protection. However, they would not have had the same propaganda effect. Because they lacked the speed to choose to fight at long range, they were very vulnerable to 8in (203mm) cruisers, whose shells could easily pierce their armour. The French fast battleship *Dunkerque* confirmed the type's obsolescence and although three more *Deutschlands* were projected, they were never laid down. However, the guns of two of them were constructed and used in the two *Scharnhorsts*. Both *Deutschland* and *Scheer* made raiding cruises, and both were later fitted with slightly lengthened bows in an attempt to remedy the type's wetness forward. *Deutschland*, renamed *Lützow* to avoid a propaganda success for the Allies if she were sunk, was twice badly damaged by torpedoes, once by the British submarine *Spearfish* on 11 April 1940, and once by a British aircraft on 13 July 1941. She saw action off Norway and in the Baltic. *Scheer* also saw action off Norway and in the Baltic.

Below: Severely damaged in the Battle of the River Plate, Graf Spee *is scuttled off Montevideo*

	Deutschland as built	Admiral Graf Spee as built	Admiral Scheer in 1945
Displacement:			
standard tons (tonnes)	11,700 (11,890)	12,100 (12,290)	
normal tons (tonnes)	?	13,880 (14,100)	
full load tons (tonnes)	15,900 (16,150)	16,200 (16,460)	
Dimensions:			
length (pp)	596·1ft (181·7m)	596·1ft (181·7m)	596·1ft (181·7m)
(oa)	610·2ft (186m)	610·2ft (186m)	616·5ft (187·9m)
beam	67·6ft (20·6m)	69·9ft (21·3m)	69·9ft (21·3m)
draught	19ft (5·8m)	19ft (5·8m)	19ft (5·8m)
Armament:			
11in (280mm) 54·5cal	6	6	6
5·9in (150mm) 55cal	8	8	8
4·1in (105mm)	—	6	6
3·4in (88mm)	4	—	—
40mm	—	—	6
37mm	8	8	8
20mm	—	10	24
torpedo tubes			
19·7in (500mm)	6	—	—
21in (533mm)	—	8	8
aircraft	—	2	2
Armour:			
side (belt)	2·4in (60mm)	3·1in (80mm)	
(torpedo bulkhead)	1·8in (45mm)	1·6in (40mm)	
armour deck	1·6in (40mm)	1·8in (45mm)	
main turrets	3·3–5·5in (85–140mm)	3·3–5·5in (85–140mm)	
barbettes	3·9in (100mm)	3·9in (100mm)	
secondary armament	0·4in (10mm)	0·4in (10mm)	
Machinery:			
diesels (type)	MAN	MAN	
(number)	8	8	
shafts	2	2	
Total BHP:			
designed	56,000	56,000	
trials	48,390	?	
Fuel capacity:			
oil tons (tonnes)	2,784 (2,830)	2,523 (2,564)	
Performance:			
designed speed	26kts	26kts	
trial speed	28kts	28·5kts	
range	10,000 miles (8,400nm) @ 19kts	9,000 miles (7,570nm) @ 19kts	
Crew:	1,150	1,150	

Ship:	**DEUTSCHLAND**	**ADMIRAL GRAF SPEE**	**ADMIRAL SCHEER**
Where built:	Deutschewerke, Kiel	Wilhelmshaven Dockyard	Wilhelmshaven Dockyard
Authorised:	1928	1932	1931
Laid down:	5 Feb 1929	1 Oct 1932	25 June 1931
Launched:	19 May 1931	30 June 1934	1 April 1933
Completed:	1 April 1933	6 Jan 1936	12 Nov 1934
Fate:	15 Nov 1939 renamed *Lützow*; Feb 1940 reclassified as heavy cruiser; 16 Apr 1945 sunk in shallow water; 4 May 1945 destroyed by crew; Sept 1947 salvaged; 1948–1949 scrapped	17 Dec 1939 scuttled; 1942 onwards wreck scrapped	Feb 1940 reclassified as heavy cruiser; Feb–Sept 1940 refit: bow altered and bridge modified, funnel cap added; 9 April 1945 sunk; 1946–1947 wreck scrapped

Prinz Eugen

HEAVY CRUISER

CLASS: *Hipper* class (3 ships)
Admiral Hipper · Blücher · Prinz Eugen

Service career PRINZ EUGEN

1939 (Aug–Dec) Negotiations to be sold to Russia.
1940 (1–2 July) Hit by two bombs.
1941 (23 Apr) Damaged by mine.
1941 (18 May) Sailed with *Bismarck.*
1941 (23 May) Shadowed by British cruisers *Suffolk* and *Norfolk*: *Prinz Eugen* moved ahead of *Bismarck.*
1941 (24 May) Battle of Denmark Strait: scored first hit on British battle-cruiser *Hood*; broke away from *Bismarck* after action.
1941 (1 June–11 Feb 1942) At Brest.
1942 (11–13 Feb) Channel dash with *Scharnhorst* and *Gneisenau*: damaged British destroyer *Worcester.*
1942 (21–23 Feb) To Norway.
1942 (23 Feb) Hit by torpedo aft from British submarine *Trident*: Stern badly damaged.
1942 (Feb–Mar) Emergency repairs to stern in Norway.
1942 (May–Oct) Permanent repairs at Kiel: new stern fitted.
1943 (May–May 1944) In fleet training squadron.
1944 (June–April 1945) Supported land operations in Baltic.
1944 (14 Oct) Rammed *Leipzig.*
1945 (Apr) To Copenhagen.
1945 (9 May) Surrendered at Copenhagen.
1945 (13 Dec) Transferred to USA.
1946 (Jan) To USA.
1946 (17 June) Target in Bikini A-bomb test.
1947 (22 Dec) Sank at Kwajalein atoll.

Up to 1935, the Versailles Treaty restricted German construction of heavy ships, but in that year the Anglo-German Naval Treaty gave Germany permission to build up to 35 per cent of the tonnage of the Royal Navy. This meant Germany could construct up to five Washington Treaty cruisers. These were laid down as the *Hippers*, but Germany was more concerned with building powerful ships than keeping to international treaty limitations, and they considerably

Continued on page 118/119▶

Below: Prinz Eugen. Although the silhouette is very similar to the Bismarck class battleship, they can easily be distinguished by their smaller turrets, smaller superstructure, catapult and much narrower beam

Displacement		
standard tons (tonnes)	14,475 (14,707)	
normal tons (tonnes)	16,230 (16,490)	
full load tons (tonnes)	18,400 (18,694)	
Dimensions:	**Admiral Hipper**	**Prinz Eugen**
length (wl)	641·1ft (195·4m)	654·5ft (199·5m)
(oa)	677·2ft (206·4m)	690·3ft (210·4m)
beam	69·9ft (21·3m)	71·8ft (21·9m)
draught	25·9ft (7·9m)	25·9ft (7·9m)
Armament:	**Prinz Eugen as built**	**Prinz Eugen in 1945**
guns		
8in (203mm)	8	8
4·1in (105mm)	12	12
40mm	—	18
37mm	12	—
20mm	8	28
torpedo tubes		
21in (533mm)	12	12
aircraft	3	3
Armour:		
side (belt)	2·75–3·1in (70–80mm)	
deck (upper)	0·5–1·2in (12–30mm)	
(armour)	0·8–2in (20–50mm)	
main turrets	2·75–4·1in (70–105mm)	
Machinery:		
boilers (type)	Wagner	
(number)	12	
engines (type)	Brown, Boveri single reduction geared turbines	
shafts	3	
Total SHP:		
designed	132,000	
trials	132,000	
Fuel capacity:		
oil tons (tonnes)	4,250 (4,320)	
Performance:		
designed speed	32kts	
trial speed	33·4kts	
range	6,540 miles (5,500nm) @ 18kts	
Crew:	1,600	

Ship:	ADMIRAL HIPPER	BLÜCHER	PRINZ EUGEN	SEYDLITZ	LÜTZOW
Where built:	Blohm und Voss, Hamburg	Deutschewerke, Kiel	Germania, Kiel	Weser, Bremen	Weser, Bremen
Authorised:	1935	1935	1936	?	?
Laid down:	1935	1936	1936	?	?
Launched:	6 Feb 1937	8 June 1937	22 Aug 1938	19 Jan 1939	1 July 1939
Completed:	1938	1939	1 Aug 1940		
Fate:	Scuttled 3 April 1945	Sunk 19 April 1940	Sunk 22 Dec 1947	1942 conversion started to aircraft carrier; conversion abandoned; scuttled 10 April 1945; salved, hulk to Russia	1940 sold (incomplete) to Russia: renamed *Tallin*, then *Petropavlovsk*; scrapped (incomplete) circa 1950

►Prinz Eugen

exceeded the 10,000 tons (10,160 tonnes) limit. The initial designs had been prepared in 1934, when planning also started on the *Bismarcks*, and they were specifically intended to defeat the French heavy cruisers and prevent French troops and supplies sailing from North Africa to France. The first two ships, *Hipper* and *Blücher*, were completed with the straight stem and uncapped funnel typical of German pre-World War II designs. *Blücher* was sunk before modification, but *Hipper* was later modified to have a lengthened bow and capped funnel, as well as two more anti-aircraft directors. *Prinz Eugen* had a longer hull, and was completed with four anti-aircraft directors, a capped funnel and a raked bow. They all had bulged hulls. All three had a powerful torpedo armament, and were fitted with passive bow sonar. They were designed after most countries had stopped building 8in (203mm) cruisers, and were superior in many respects to earlier designs. They were undoubtedly better than the early French Washington Treaty cruisers, but would have been in difficulties against the smaller but better armoured French *Algérie,* and they were definitely inferior to the similarly sized but slightly later American *Baltimore* class, which carried a heavier armament and thicker armour, as well as more aircraft. One particularly disappointing feature of the design was a relatively short range which, coupled with unreliable machinery, proved a great handicap in their use

as commerce raiders despite the extensive system of oilers that the Germans built up in the Atlantic. Apart from this they were well fitted to operate on their own, with a powerful main battery (*Prinz Eugen* obtained hits on the British battle-cruiser *Hood* before *Bismarck*) and a very well controlled anti-aircraft armament. After the signing of the Russo-German pact in 1939, it was proposed to barter the last three *Hippers* (which had not yet been completed) to Russia in exchange for raw materials. In the event, only the one furthest from completion, *Lützow,* was transferred. *Prinz Eugen* was completed as designed and it was proposed to convert *Seydlitz* into an aircraft-carrier. Germany had already launched *Graf Zeppelin*, of 23,200 tons (23,570 tonnes) standard displacement, and laid down a sister ship, but the vital importance of integral airpower at sea was not appreciated, and their construction continued only spasmodically. When the. loss of the *Bismarck* showed how necessary sea-borne airpower was, work on *Graf Zeppelin* restarted and *Seydlitz* began her conversion. However, the Allies now had too great a superiority at sea and neither was completed. *Admiral Hipper* took part in operations off Norway and in the Atlantic. She was in the Baltic from 1944. She was damaged in an air raid and later scuttled. *Blücher* was sunk in Oslo Fjord by Norwegian coast defences. Neither *Lützow* nor *Seydlitz* (which was raised and salved by the Russians) was completed, and both were later scrapped.

Prinz Eugen in 1941–1942 colour scheme with Arado 196 seaplane and air recognition swastika on fo'c's'le. Note extra light AA guns fitted for the Channel Dash in February 1942

Right: The surrendered Prinz Eugen *passes through the Gatun Locks, Panama Canal, on 15 March 1946, en route to the atomic bomb tests at Bikini Atoll*

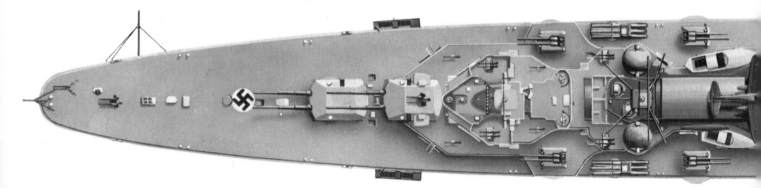

Emden

LIGHT CRUISER

CLASS: *Dresden* class (2 ships)
Emden · Dresden

Service career EMDEN
1908 (May–July 1909) In home waters.
1909 (Aug–April 1910) Refit.
1910 (Apr–Sept) To Cruiser Squadron, Far East Station, based at Tsingtao.
1914 (2 Aug–9 Nov) Commerce-raiding cruise in Pacific and Indian Ocean: sank 16 ships of 70,825 gross register tons.
1914 (12–14 Aug) Rendezvoused with Cruiser Squadron at Pagan Island; *Emden* detached.
1914 (22 Sept) Fired 130 shells at Madras.
1914 (29 Oct) Sank Russian cruiser *Zemchug* and French destroyer *Mousquet* in Penang harbour.

Displacement:		
normal tons (tonnes)	3,650 (3,710)	
full load tons (tonnes)	4,150 (4,220)	
Dimensions:		
length (pp)	364·5ft (111·1m)	
(wl)	387·8ft (118·2m)	
(oa)	389·8ft (118·8m)	
beam	44ft (13·4m)	
draught (max)	16·1ft (4·9m)	
Armament:		
guns		
4·1in (105mm)	10	
8mm	4	
torpedo tubes		
17·7in (450mm)	2	
Armour:		
side (belt)	3·1–3·9in (80–100mm)	
deck	0·4–1in (10–25mm)	
gun shields	0·8–2in (20–50mm)	
Machinery:	**Emden**	**Dresden**
boilers (type)	Schulz-Thornycroft	Schulz-Thornycroft
(number)	12	12
engines (type)	vertical triple expansion	Parsons turbines
shafts	2	2
Total IHP:		
designed	13,500	—
trials	16,171	—
Total SHP:		
designed	—	15,000
trials	—	?
Fuel capacity:		
coal, normal tons (tonnes)	400 (410)	
max tons (tonnes)	900 (910)	
Performance:		
designed speed	24kts	25kts
trial speed	25·1kts	?
range	4,470 miles (3,760nm) @12kts	?
Crew:	361	

Ship:	EMDEN
Where Built:	Danzig Dockyard
Authorised:	?
Laid down:	6 April 1906
Launched:	26 May 1908
Completed:	10 July 1909
Fate:	Total loss 9 Nov 1914; wreck scrapped 1950

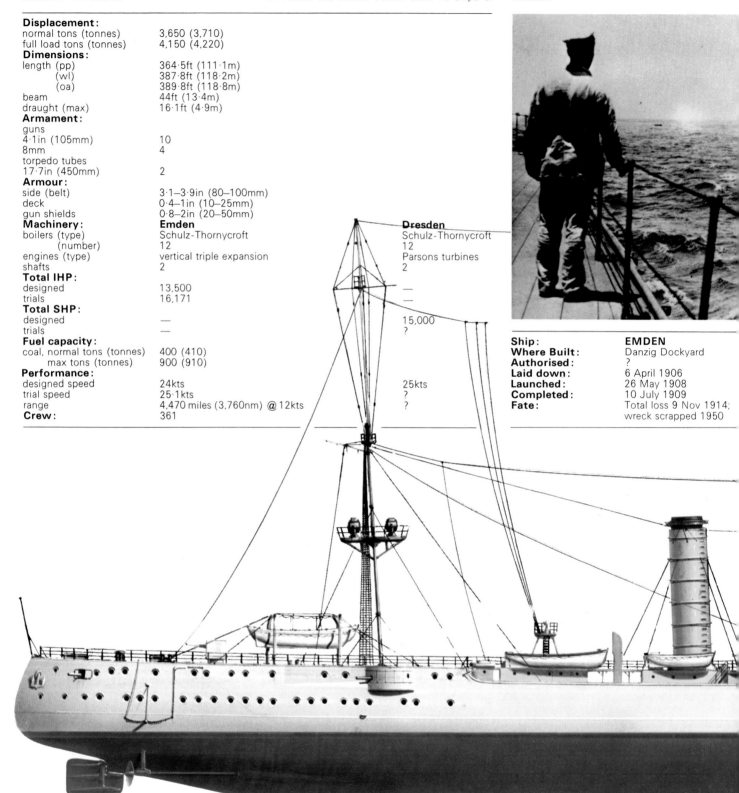

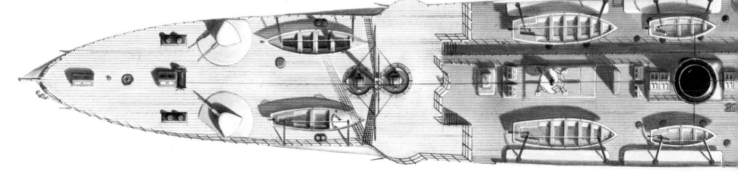

1914 (9 Nov) Destroyed radio station at Cocos Islands; caught and destroyed by Australian cruiser *Sydney*; beached as total loss.
1950 Wreck scrapped.

The *Dresdens* were an excellent design, as were most of the German light cruisers built after 1900. Their best feature was the 4·1in (105mm) gun. As with the later 5·9in (150mm), this fired a heavy shell for its size, with a good range and penetrating power. They were also well protected for their size, and had good 'ship' qualities. *Dresden* and *Stettin* of the preceding class were trial ships for turbines, which were adopted as standard by subsequent classes. They were not ideal commerce raiders, being relatively short ranged and having only a small crew, but *Emden* successfully disrupted the Indian Ocean trade for a considerable time. *Dresden* was also on the China Station in 1914. She was attached to the main squadron, and after the Battle of the Falklands escaped to Juan Fernandez Island, where she was found by the British cruisers *Kent* and *Glasgow*. After an exchange of shots, she scuttled herself.

Left: The light cruiser SMS Emden lies wrecked on North Keeling, Cocos Islands

DRESDEN
Blohm und Voss, Hamburg
?
Oct 1906
5 Oct 1907
1909
Scuttled 3 March 1915

Coat of arms of the German port, Emden

Emden in pre-1914 Far East Squadron colour scheme. Note 4·1in (105mm) guns mounted side by side fore and aft, and in casemates amidships. When sunk she was painted grey overall

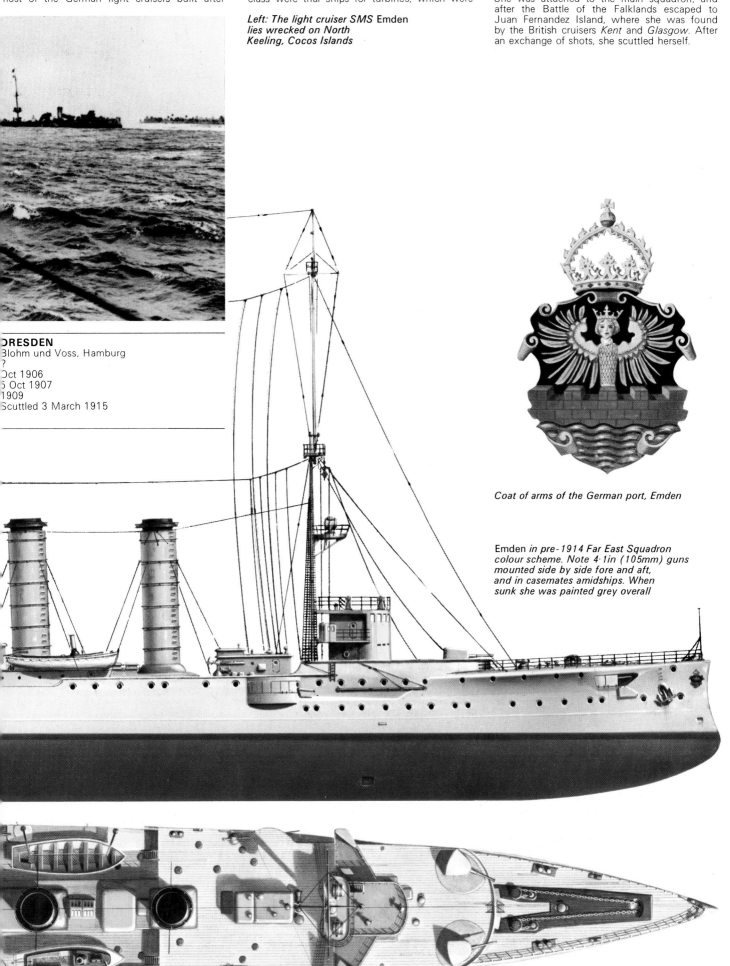

Bremse
MINELAYING CRUISER
CLASS: *Bremse* class (2 ships)
Bremse · Brummer

In World War I both sides made extensive use of mine warfare. Both Britain and Germany used converted warships and merchantmen for this purpose. However, most warships could only carry a limited number of mines, and most merchant vessels were too slow (*Königin Luise*, a converted liner and the first German warship sunk in World War I, was lost for this reason). Germany had built two cruiser mine-layers before the war, the 1,970 ton (2,000 tonne) normal displacement *Nautilus* and the 2,200 ton (2,230 tonne) normal displacement *Albatross*, but although these could carry 200 mines, they were weakly armed and could make only 20kts. They were employed mainly in the Baltic during World War I. The Germans there-fore laid down two large cruiser minelayers, *Bremse* and *Brummer*, which were well armed and adequately protected, with a high speed and large mine capacity. They had three raked funnels and could lower their mainmasts, and were deliberately designed to resemble the British *Arethusa* and *Cleopatra* class light cruisers. Their most famous action was the destruction of a British Scandinavian iron ore convoy and its escorting destroyers *Mary Rose* and *Strongbow* off Norway on 17 October 1917. Both ships were interned at Scapa Flow in 1918, and were scuttled with the rest of the High Seas Fleet. *Brummer* sank in deep water, but *Bremse* was beached in a sinking condition and was later salved and scrapped. They inspired several postwar imitations, including the rather larger British *Adventure*, which had mixed steam and diesel machinery.

Displacement:		
normal tons (tonnes)	4,400 (4,470)	
full load tons (tonnes)	?	
Dimensions:		
length (pp)	?	
(oa)	460·5ft (140·6m)	
beam	44ft (13·4m)	
draught	19·5ft (6m)	
Armament:		
guns		
5·9in (150mm)	4	
3·4in (88mm)	2	
torpedo tubes		
19·7in (500mm)	2	
mine capacity	400	
Armour:		
side (belt)	1·5in (38mm)	
deck	0·6in (16mm)	
Machinery:		
boilers (type)	Schulz-Thornycroft	
(number)	?	
engines (type)	? turbines	
shafts	2	
Total SHP:		
designed	47,000	
Fuel capacity:		
coal tons (tonnes)	?	
oil tons (tonnes)	?	
Performance:		
designed speed	28kts	
range	?	
Crew:	309	

Above: The Bremse *class minelaying cruiser SMS Brummer.*
The two Bremses *were deliberately designed to resemble the British* Arethusas *and* Cleopatras

Ship:	**BREMSE**	**BRUMMER**
Where built:	Vulcan, Stettin	Vulcan, Stettin
Authorised:	?	?
Laid down:	1915	1915
Launched:	11 March 1916	11 Dec 1915
Completed:	1916	1916
Fate:	Scuttled 21 June 1919; salved and scrapped 1929	Scuttled 21 June 1919

Köln
LIGHT CRUISER
CLASS: *Königsberg* class (3 ships)
Königsberg · Karlsruhe · Köln

After 1918 all Germany's modern cruisers were either scuttled or surrendered. The enforced cessation of design work meant that the first postwar ship, *Emden*, was based on the *Dresdens* (the last wartime design). She was coalfired, with eight single-mounted 5·9in (150mm) guns arranged to give a six-gun broadside. The *Königsbergs* were improved oil-fired versions, with three triple 5·9in (150mm) turrets. They had diesel engines for cruising, to extend the range and enable them to be used as raiders, but they were never used as such. They were better arranged than *Emden*, but too much was attempted on too limited a displacement, and the ten year old basic hull design was un-suitable for modern armaments. The two aft turrets had to be staggered to fit the magazines and shell rooms in the shallow quarterdeck, and the forward turret was very near the bow. They were not particularly seaworthy, despite attempts to save weight, and *Karlsruhe* was rebuilt with bulges in 1939. *Königsberg* was the first warship sunk by dive-bombers. She was caught in Bergen by British land-based carrier aircraft. *Karlsruhe* was torpedoed by the British submarine *Truant* off Denmark, and was scuttled by torpedoes from the German torpedo boat, *Greif*.

Displacement:	as built	Karlsruhe in 1940
standard tons (tonnes)	6,650 (6,756)	6,730 (6,838)
full load tons (tonnes)	8,130 (8,260)	8,350 (8,484)
Dimensions:		
length (wl)	553·5ft (169m)	553·5ft (169m)
(oa)	569·9ft (174m)	569·9ft (174m)
beam	49·9ft (15·2m)	54·4ft (16·6m)
draught	21·4ft (6·5m)	21·2ft (6·5m)
Armament:	**Köln as built**	**Köln in 1943**
guns		
5·9in (150mm) 60cal	9	9
3·5in (88mm)	4	6
37mm	—	8
20mm	—	4
torpedo tubes		
19·7in (500mm)	12	6
aircraft	2	
Armour:		
side (belt)	2–2·8in (50–70mm)	
deck	0·8–1·6in (20–40mm)	
main turrets	0·8–1·2in (20–30mm)	
barbettes	1·2in (30mm)	
Machinery:		
boilers (type)	Marine	
(number)	6	
engines (type)	Germania, Schichau or Blohm und Voss single reduction geared turbines	
(number)	2	
diesels (type)	MAN	
(number)	2	
shafts	2	
Total SHP:	68,200	
Total BHP:	1,800	
Fuel capacity:		
oil tons (tonnes)	1,165 (1,184)	
Performance:		
designed speed	32kts	
range	6,780 miles (5,700nm) @ 19kts	
Crew:	820	

Above: The Königsberg *class light cruiser* Köln, *completed 1930. These ships were not handy, and the WWI hull design was unsuited to modern armaments Note Heinkel He 51 B-2 seaplane on catapult and offset X and Y turrets*

Ship	**KÖNIGSBERG**	**KARLSRUHE**	**KÖLN**
Where built:	Wilhelmshaven Dockyard	Deutsche Werke, Kiel	Wilhelmshaven Dockyard
Authorised:	1924	1925	1925
Laid down:	1925	1926	1926
Launched:	26 March 1927	20 Aug 1927	23 May 1928
Completed:	17 Apr 1929	6 Nov 1929	1 Jan 1930
Rebuilt:	—	1938–1940	—
Fate:	Sunk 10 Apr 1940, salved 1943, finally sunk 22 Sept 1944	Scuttled Apr 10 1940	Sunk 30 Apr 1945, wreck scrapped 1946

Von Roeder Class

DESTROYER
CLASS: *Von Roeder* class (6 ships)
Z17 (later *Diether von Roeder*) · Z18
(later *Hans Lüdemann* · Z19 (later
Hermann Küne) · Z20 (later *Karl
Galster*) · Z21 (later *Wilhelm
Heidkamp* · Z22 (later *Anton
Schmitt*)

Z31 Class

DESTROYER
CLASS: *Z31* class (7 ships) Z31 ·
Z32 · Z33 · Z34 · Z37 · Z38 · Z39

The first German interwar destroyers were the Type 1934 Z1-Z16. Z9-Z16 differed slightly from Z1-Z8, and had a different make of boiler. They were very large destroyers, with a standard displacement of between 2,232 and 2,270 tons (2,268 and 2,306 tonnes), though to evade treaty limitations they were said to displace only 1,782 tons (1,811 tonnes). They were intended to make up in quality for lack of numbers. They were developed from the World War I *V-116*, and were conventional two-funnelled destroyers with a superfiring pair of single 5in (127mm) guns fore and aft, with a fifth single mount at the forward end of the aft superstructure. The aft funnel separated two quadruple 21in (533mm) torpedo tube mounts, and the break of the fo'c's'le was just abaft the fore funnel. To achieve high speeds with the smallest and lightest possible machinery a new type of high-pressure boiler was employed. This was also used in subsequent German warships, but unfortunately it was put into service before it had been fully developed, and it was extremely unreliable. As a result, German destroyers of this period were very prone to breakdowns, and few could achieve their designed speeds. Z1-Z16 were also very wet forward, and were poor seaboats. Their best feature was their powerful AA armament. The *Von Roeders* were very similar, except that Z20-Z22 were fitted with a clipper bow in an attempt to improve the seaworthiness. This increased the overall length to 409·4ft (125m) and was adopted in subsequent classes. All the *Von Roeders* except Z20 were destroyed during the First and Second Battles of Narvik. These actions clearly demonstrated that the large and expensive German vessels were no better than the considerably smaller British destroyers. Later in the war Z20 had her third 5in (127mm) gun removed to enable her AA armament to be greatly strengthened. The next class of German destroyers, Z23-Z30 (Type 1936A), were somewhat larger, and had their main armament increased to five 5·9in (150mm) guns. These were arranged in three single mounts aft and a twin turret forward. At first this turret was not available, and a single gun was fitted instead. When the twin turret was finally fitted it was found that its weight of nearly 100 tons (about 102 tonnes) so far forward drastically reduced seaworthiness. Z26 was fitted as a flotilla leader and had two single guns fore and aft. The *Z31* class were very similar. *Z31* was also completed before the twin turret was available, and was fitted with the turret in 1942, but this was replaced by a single 4·1in (105mm) gun after bomb damage in 1945. Z32 was driven ashore off the Ile de Batz by the Canadian destroyers *Haida* and *Huron*, and *Z37* was sunk in a British air attack whilst in dry dock at Bordeaux. Surviving ships were fitted with a greatly strengthened AA armament in the latter part of the war. As was shown in the action in the Bay of Biscay with the British cruisers *Glasgow* and *Enterprise* on 28 December 1943, these ships lacked the necessary seaworthiness and fire control to fight such a heavy armament. The next class, the Type 1936B Z35-Z36 and Z43-Z45, reverted to five 5in (127mm) guns to improve seaworthiness and to provide sufficient stability for radar and extra AA guns to be mounted.

Displacement:	Z17 as built	Z37 as built
standard tons (tonnes)	2,373 (2,411)	2,562 (2,603)
normal tons (tonnes)	2,762 (2,806)	?
full load tons (tonnes)	3,415 (3,470)	3,540 (3,597)
Dimensions:		
length (wl)	393ft (120m)	399·2ft (121·9m)
(oa)	404·5ft (123·5m)	415·9ft (127m)
beam	38·6ft (11·8m)	39·3ft (12m)
draught	14·7ft (4·5m)	15·1ft (4·6m)
Armament:		
guns		
5·9in (150mm)	—	5
5in (127mm)	5	—
37mm	4	4
20mm	6	5
torpedo tubes		
21in (533mm)	8	8
mine capacity	60	—
Machinery:		
boilers (type)	Wagner	Wagner
(number)	6	6
engines (type)	Wagner	Wagner
shafts	2	2
Total SHP:		
designed	70,000	70,000
Fuel capacity:		
oil tons (tonnes)	750 (760)	810 (825)
Performance:		
designed speed	38·3kts	38·2kts'
range	5,770 miles (4,850nm) @ 19kts	7,020 miles (5,900nm) @ 19kts
Crew:	313	321

Class:	VON ROEDER class	Z31 class
Where built:	Weser, Bremen	Weser, Bremen and Germaniawerft, Kiel
Authorised:	1936	?
Laid down:	1936	1940
Launched:	1937–1938	1941–1942
Completed:	1938–1939	1942–1943
Fate:	Z21 and Z22 sunk 10 Apr 1940; Z17, Z18 and Z19 scuttled 13 Apr 1940; Z20 to USSR 1946, renamed *Protschny*, scrapped circa 1960	Z32 total loss 9 June 1944; Z37 scuttled 24 Aug 1944; Z31 to Britain 1945, to France 1946, renamed *Marceau*, scrapped 1956; Z33 to Russia 1946, renamed *Provorny*, scrapped 1960; Z34 to USA 1945, scuttled 26 March 1946; Z38 to Britain 1945, renamed *Nonsuch*, scrapped 1949; Z39 to USA 1945, renamed *DD-939*, to France 1951, cannibalised, scrapped 1962

Above: The Z31 *class destroyer*
Z38 *mounted five 5·9in/150mm
guns and eight 21in/533mm TTs.
She was taken over by
the RN as HMS* Nonsuch *in 1945*

Z38 *in 1945 with AA guns in Q position.
Note twin 5·9in (150mm) turret forward*

T150 Class

DESTROYER
CLASS: *T150* class · ex-*V150* class
(12 ships) *V150* + *T151–T161*
(ex-*V151–V161*)

B109 Class

DESTROYER
CLASS: *B109* class (4 ships)
B109-B112

The Germans placed great emphasis on the use
of destroyers in night actions, and produced
small designs to reduce the chances of detection.
Seaworthiness was of secondary importance.
The *T150* class were typical German World War I
destroyers. Their primary weapon was the
torpedo, and the three tubes were mounted
singly on the centreline: one was located in a
well before the bridge, one between the funnels
and one aft. The class, which took part in most
of the major World War I actions, were originally
V150-V161, the prefix being the initial letter of
the builder's name. *V161* was experimentally
fitted with turbines. *V150* was sunk in collision
with *V157*.

By 1918 they were obsolete, but were retained as the Allies did not allow Germany to
keep her modern vessels. After the High Seas
Fleet was scuttled, *T159-T161* were handed to
the Allies as part of the required reparations.
When the remainder were replaced by newer
torpedo boats, *T156-T158* became submarine
tenders, *Edouard Jungmann* became a gunnery
school ship and *Komet* a control ship for radio
controlled target vessels. *T152* and *T157* were
sunk by air attack. Although no large destroyers
had been built for Germany, Vulcan and Blohm
und Voss supplied drawings, parts, and machinery for the excellent Russian *Noviks*. At the out-
break of war in 1914 these parts were left on
their hands and the two firms suggested to the
German Navy that they should incorporate them
in some destroyers to the same basic design for
Germany. The German Admiralty, conscious of
the large size of British and Russian destroyers,
immediately agreed. The first to be completed
were *B97-B98* and *V99-V100*. *B109-B112*
differed from the former in the layout of the
armament. They carried twice as many torpedo
tubes as the *T150* class. Their 3·4in (88mm) guns
were replaced by 4·1in (105mm) guns in early
1916 after *Novik* had demonstrated the superiority of its 4in (102mm) weapons on *B99*. They
fought at Jutland, and in other North Sea,
Channel and Baltic actions. They were scuttled
with the rest of the High Seas Fleet at Scapa
Flow.

Above: The T150 *class destroyer*
T151 (V151 *until 1917).*
These small ships mounted three
17·7in/450mm TTs and were
designed for night actions

Right: The B109 *class destroyer*
B112, *completed 1915. The*
four 1,374-ton ships of this class,
mounting four 4·1in guns and
six 19·7in TTs, fought at Jutland

B110 of the B 109 class with 3·4in (88mm)
guns and black colour scheme in 1915.
Note the torpedo tubes in well before
bridge and the fixed angle between
the aft TT

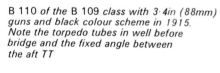

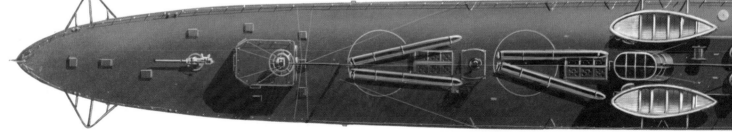

	T150 class as built	T150 class in 1939	B109 class as built	
Displacement:				
normal tons (tonnes)	558 (567)	660 (671)	1,374 (1,396)	
full load tons (tonnes)	670 (681)	800 (813)	1,843 (1,872)	
Dimensions:				
length (pp)	238·2ft (72·6m)	238·2ft (72·6m)	?	
(oa)	242·8ft (74m)	242·8ft (74m)	321·6ft (98m)	
beam	25·6ft (7·8m)	25·6ft (7·8m)	31·2ft (9·5m)	
draught	10·2ft (3·1m)	10·5ft (3·2m)	12·6ft (3·83m)	
Armament:			**B109 class in 1915**	**B109 class in 1916**
guns				
4·1in (105mm) 45cal	—	—	—	4
3·4in (88mm) 45cal	2	1	4	—
20mm	—	1	—	—
torpedo tubes				
17·7in (450mm)	3	—	—	—
19·7in (500mm)	—	—	6	6
mine capacity	—	—	24	24
Machinery:	**T150-T160**	**T161**	**B109 class**	
boilers (type)	Schulz-Thornycroft	Schulz-Thornycroft	Schulz-Thornycroft	
(number)	4	4	4	
engines (type)	vertical triple expansion	turbines	turbines	
shafts	2	2	2	
Total IHP:				
designed	10,900			
Total SHP:				
designed		14,800	40,000	
trials		?	40,700	
Fuel capacity				
coal tons (tonnes)	160 (163)	—	?	
oil tons (tonnes)	—	181 (184)	—	
Performance:				
designed speed	30kts	33kts	36kts	
trial speed	?	?	37·4kts	
range	3,500 miles (2,940nm) @ 17kts		3,120 miles (2,620nm) @ 20kts	
Crew:	83	87	114	

Class:	T150 class (ex-V150 class)	B109 class
Where built:	Vulcan, Stettin	Blohm und Voss, Hamburg
Ordered:	1907–1908	Oct 1914–Jan 1915
Laid down:	1907–1908	1915
Launched:	1907–1908	1915
Completed:	1908	1915
Fate:	*V150* sunk 18 May 1915; remainder renumbered on 24 Sept 1917; *T159-T161* surrendered to UK 20 Aug 1920, scrapped 1922; *T154* stricken 8 Dec 1928; *T152* stricken 31 March 1931; *T157* sunk 22 Oct 1943; *T155* sunk 22 April 1945; *T156* scuttled 3 May 1945; *T151* renamed *Komet* 1931, surrendered to USA and scrapped in 1949; *T153* renamed *Edouard Jungmann* 1938, surrendered to USA in 1945 and scrapped in 1949; *T158* surrendered in 1945 to USSR, renamed *Prosorlivi*, and scrapped circa 1955	All interned at Scapa Flow 22 Nov 1918. All scuttled at Scapa Flow 21 June 1919; raised and scrapped 1925–1926

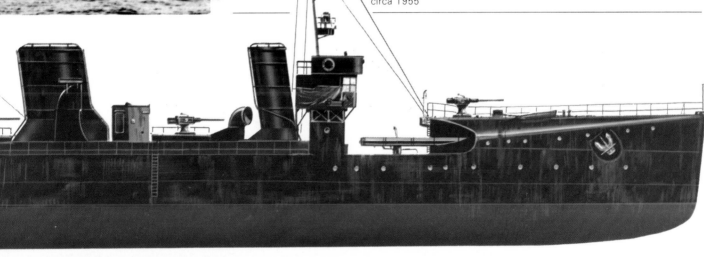

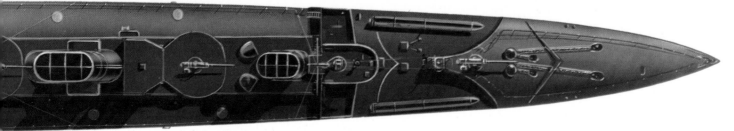

Hamburg Class

DESTROYER

CLASS: *Hamburg* class (4 ships)
Hamburg (D-181) · *Schleswig-Holstein* (D-182) · *Bayern* (D-183) · *Hessen* (D-184)

Unlike the interwar German Navy, which had at least had some continuity with its predecessor, the Federal German Navy was forced to rebuild virtually from scratch. The first requirement was for light craft, but larger vessels were soon required. The first major units were the *Köln* class frigates, but after the Federal Navy had been permitted to exceed the 3,000 ton (3,048t) limit that had been imposed on it after World War II, and had laid down the 4,880 ton (4,958t) armed training vessel *Deutschland*, the way was open to build the *Hamburg* class destroyers.

They have the piled-up appearance typical of all modern German warships, with a relatively low freeboard and the guns mounted near the ends of the ship. The *Hamburgs* are designed for the Baltic, where seaworthiness is less important than a powerful AA armament, high speed and manoeuvrability. They can carry mines, a useful weapon in the shallow Baltic, but do not operate helicopters because all the likely operational areas can be covered by land-based aircraft. The greatest weakness in the original design was the lack of a weapon capable of dealing with a major surface warship, so the class is in process of being fitted with four Exocet SSMs in place of X mounting.

Below: Hamburg, *completed in 1964,
is the name-ship of a
class of four destroyers. Note
the piled-up appearance
typical of modern German warships*

Displacement:		
standard tons (tonnes)	3,340 (3,393)	
full load tons (tonnes)	4,330 (4,399)	
Dimensions:		
length (pp)	419·9ft (128m)	
(oa)	439·6ft (134m)	
beam	44ft (13·4m)	
draught (max)	17·1ft (5·2m)	
Armament:	**as built**	**in 1977**
guns		
3·9in (100mm)	4	3
40mm	8	8
missiles		
MM38 Exocet SSM	—	4
A/S weapons		
Bofors TT-2 rocket-launcher	2	2
torpedo tubes		
21in (533mm)	5	—
12in (305mm)	—	2
Machinery:		
boilers (type)	Wahodag	
(number)	4	
engines (type)	Wahodag double reduction geared turbines	
shafts	2	
Total SHP:		
designed	68,000	
Fuel capacity:		
oil tons (tonnes)	674 (684·8)	
Performance:		
designed speed	35kts	
range	920 miles (773nm) @ 35kts	
Crew:	282	

Ship:	HAMBURG	SCHLESWIG-HOLSTEIN	BAYERN	HESSEN
	(D-181)	(D-182)	(D-183)	(D-184)
Where built:	Stülcken, Hamburg	Stülcken, Hamburg	Stülcken, Hamburg	Stülcken, Hamburg
Laid down:	1959	1959	1961	1962
Launched:	26 Mar 1960	20 Aug 1960	14 Aug 1962	4 May 1963
Completed:	23 Mar 1964	12 Oct 1964	6 July 1965	31 Oct 1968
Modernised:	1975–1976	1976–1977	1977–	1975–1976
Fate:	In service	In service	In service	In service

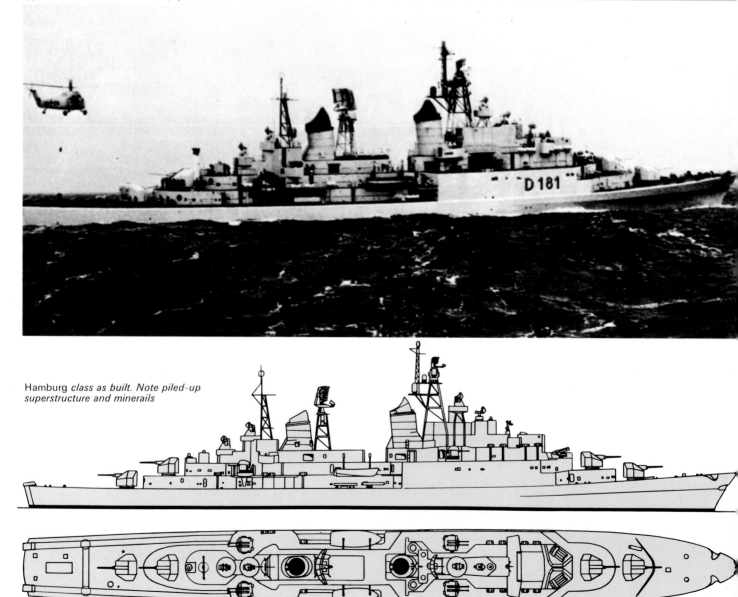

Hamburg *class as built. Note piled-up
superstructure and minerails*

U9 Class

SUBMARINE
CLASS: *U-9* class (4 boats)

U96 Class

SUBMARINE
CLASS: *U-96* class (3 boats)

UCII Class

SUBMARINE
CLASS: *UC II* type (18 boats)
UC-16 to *UC-33*

While the Russian second order for submarines was in hand at Kiel, the German Navy started their submarine programme. *U-1* to *U-8* were driven by heavy oil engines, which emitted a column of exhaust and sparks but were basically safer than petrol engines. After *U-1* all the remainder of these early boats had stern tubes, a relief for an unsuccessful CO wishing to fire on a retiring turn. The heavy oil engines continued in the *U-9* class, which also perpetuated the twin-screw, double-hulled design of their predecessors. Twin tubes in bow and stern were also continued and this miniscule armament by later standards enabled *U-9* under Otto Weddigen to sink the three British armoured cruisers *Hogue*, *Cressy* and *Aboukir* on 22 September 1914. This attack did convince some people of the efficacy of the submarine as a fighting weapon, although one of the more difficult groups to persuade was the German Naval Staff. Battleships were still considered the key, but sufficient appreciation of such actions as well as success against merchant ships brought the submarine requirements to the fore. Despite this it was not until 1917 that the *U-96* class was built, the forerunners of World War II designs. With six torpedo tubes and a gun they were formidable opponents. The contemporary *UCII* class was much smaller but amongst the early custom-built minelayers. Their capacity was much less than that of the Russian *Krab* and their mines were housed in vertical shafts instead of horizontal tubes.

Displacement:	U-9 class	U-96 class	UC II type
surface tons (tonnes)	493 (501)	838 (851)	400/434 (406/441)
submerged tons (tonnes)	611 (621)	1,000 (1,016)	480/511 (488/519)
Dimensions:			
length	188ft (57·3m)	235·5ft (71·8m)	162–173ft (49·4–52·3m)
beam	19·7ft (6m)	20·6ft (6·3m)	17ft (5·2m)
draught	11·5ft (3·5m)	12·7ft (3·9m)	12ft (3·7m)
Armament:			
guns			
3·4in (88mm)	—	—	1
torpedo tubes			
18in (457mm)	4	—	—
19·7in (500mm)	—	6	3
mines	—	—	18
Machinery:			
main engines (type)	heavy oil	diesel	diesel
main motors (type)	electric	electric	electric
shafts	2	2	2
Total SHP:	1,000	2,400	500–600
Total BHP:	1,150	1,200	460–620
Fuel capacity:			
heavy oil tons (tonnes)	?	—	—
diesel oil tons (tonnes)	—	?	?
Performance:			
surface speed	14kts	16·8kts	?
submerged speed	9kts	8·6kts	?
range	?	?	?
diving depth	?	?	?
Crew:	29	38	28

Class:	U-9 class	U-96 class	UC II type
Approved:	1909	1916	1915
Where built:	Danzig	Germaniawerft, Kiel	Blohm und Voss; A. G. Vulcan; A. G. Weser
Commissioned:	1910	1917	1916–1917
Fate:	*U-9* scrapped 1919; *U-10* mined (?); *U-11* mined; *U-12* sunk by ramming	*U-96* scrapped 1920; *U-97* sank on way to England to surrender 1918; *U-98* scrapped 1920	majority sunk

Above: U-96, one of a class of 3 boats built in 1917

U151 Class

SUBMARINE
CLASS: *U-151* class (8 boats)
Deutschland (later *U-155*)
Oldenburg (later *U-151*) · *Bremen* ·
U-152 · *U-153* · *U-154* · *U-156*
U-157

In 1915, with the first effects of the British blockade being felt, Germany decided to build three merchant submarines to carry supplies from the still neutral USA, and for propaganda purposes. They were bigger than any undersea craft built previously, and were designed by Germaniawerft. They were of double-hull form. Though *Deutschland* made the headlines on her first voyage to the United States her practical effect was small, and it was soon decided to convert her and her sisters into long-range raiders, or 'U-cruisers'. *Bremen* was lost, most probably by mining, before this could be done. Another five submarines were ordered to the modified design, and more effective variants were later developed. These went some way to reducing the lack of manoeuvrability and difficulties of steering that hampered the *U-151* class. These later designs greatly influenced foreign designers after the end of World War I, particularly the Americans and Japanese. The *U-151* class were obsolete by 1918, but were important as the first really long-range submarines. An interesting feature of the class was that the diesels used in the first boats were originally intended to drive the auxiliaries of capital ships.

Right: U-151, built as the merchant submarine Oldenburg in 1916–17, was converted to a U-cruiser. The U-151s were the first long range submarines

Displacement:	Deutschland as built		U-152 as built
surface tons (tonnes)	1,575 (1,600)		1,512 (1,536)
submerged tons (tonnes)	1,860 (1,900)		1,875 (1,905)
Dimensions:			
length (wl)	186·7ft (57m)		
(oa)	212·9ft (65m)		
beam	29·1ft (8·9m)		
draught	17·4ft (5·3m)		

Armament:	Deutschland as built	U-152 as built	in 1918
guns			
5·9in (150mm)	—	—	2
4·1in (105mm)	—	2	—
3·4in (88mm)	—	—	2
torpedo tubes			
19·7in (500mm)	—	2	2
Machinery:			
diesels (type)	Germania		
(number)	2		
electric motors (type)	?		
shafts	2		
Total BHP:	800	800	
Total SHP:	750	800	
Fuel capacity:			
oil tons (tonnes)	323 (328)		
Performance:			
surface speed	12·4kts		
submerged speed	5·2kts		
range (surface)	29,730 miles (25,000nm) @ 5·5kts		
(submerged)	77 miles (65nm) @ 3kts		
Crew:	56 (plus 20 prize crew)		

Class:	DEUTSCHLAND class
Where built:	Germaniawerft, Wilhelmshaven
Ordered:	1915–1916
Laid down:	1915–1917
Launched:	1916–1917
Completed:	1916–1917
Fate:	*Bremen*, *U-154* and *U-156* lost 1917–1918; remainder scrapped

Type VII
SUBMARINE
CLASS: *Type VII* (730 boats)

Type IXB
SUBMARINE
CLASS: *Type IX* (180 boats)

Type XIV
SUBMARINE
CLASS: *Type XIV* (10 boats)

These 920 boats bore the brunt of Germany's submarine offensive during World War II. After initial tests with Finnish-built submarines completed in 1930–1933 and after the possession of submarines had been unilaterally legalised by Great Britain in the 1935 Anglo-German Naval Agreement, Germany had gone ahead with a submarine building programme. Germany had claimed parity with the British Commonwealth, averring she would not build more than 45 per cent of that amount unless she considered the situation 'made it necessary'. Sir Samuel Hoare, then Foreign Secretary, noted that 'The Naval Staff, believing at the time that we had mastered the submarine danger, did not object to this concession.' This complacency led to Britain's near-defeat as the result of the German building programme begun in 1935. The *Types IA, IIA, IIB, IIC* and *IID* were no more than training boats compared with the *Type VIIA* boats and their successors, the first of which were laid down in 1936 on a design which must have been started some years before. These were magnificent submarines of their generation. With a speed of 17kts on the surface and great manoeuvrability from their twin rudders they were ideal for surface wolf-pack attacks. They were the equal of any contemporary boats, dived with an

Continued on page 130 ▶

Below: The Type IXB U-124, *an enlarged version of the* Type VIIs. *180 Type IXs were commissioned in 1938–44; 142 were lost in World War II*

Displacement:	Type VIIC	Type IXB	Type XIV
surfaced tons (tonnes)	769 (781)	1,051 (1,068)	1,688 (1,715)
submerged tons (tonnes)	871 (885)	1,178 (1,197)	1,932 (1,963)
Dimensions:			
length	220·3ft (67·1m)	251ft (76·5m)	220·3ft (67·1m)
beam	20·3ft (6·2m)	22ft (6·7m)	30·7ft (9·4m)
draught	15·7ft (4·8m)	15·5ft (4·7m)	21·3ft (6·5m)
Armament:			
guns			
4·1in (105mm)	—	1	—
3·5in (88mm)	1	—	—
37mm	1	1	2
20mm	1 (increased to 3)	2	1
torpedo tubes			
21in (533mm)	5	6	—
mines	14 in place of torpedoes	32+6 torpedoes	—
Machinery:			
main engines (type)	diesel	diesel	diesel
	2	6	?
main motors (type)	electric	electric	electric
shafts	2	2	2
Total SHP:	2,800	2,400	2,800
Total BHP:	750	1,000	750
Fuel capacity:			
oil tons (tonnes)	?	?	?
Performance:			
surface speed	17kts	18·3kts	14·5kts
submerged speed	8kts	7kts	6·3kts
range (surfaced)	6,500 miles (5,645nm) @ 12kts	8,700 miles (7,555nm) @ 12kts	9,300 miles (8,075nm) @ 12kts
(dived)	18 hours @ 4kts	20 hours @ 4kts	14 hours @ 4kts
diving depth	?	?	?
Crew:	44	57	53

Class:	Type VII	Type IX	Type XIV
Where built:	AG Weser, Germaniawerft; Blohm and Voss, Flenderwerft; Nord Seewerke, Flensburg; Howaldtswerke, Danzig; Schichau, Stülcken; Wilhelmshaven, Stettin; Vulcan Stettin, Rostock	AG Weser, Bremerhaven; Deutschewerft	Deutsche Werke, Kiel
Approved:	1935	1937	1941
Launched:	June 1936 (*U-27*)– Nov 1944 (*U-1308*)	May 1938 (*U-37*)– Feb 1944 (*U-1238*)	1942–1943
Commissioned:	1936–1945	1938–1944	1942–1943
Fate:	559 sunk by various causes; 63 scuttled; 103 surrendered	142 sunk by various causes; 10 scuttled; 28 surrendered	9 sunk by air attack; 1 by ships

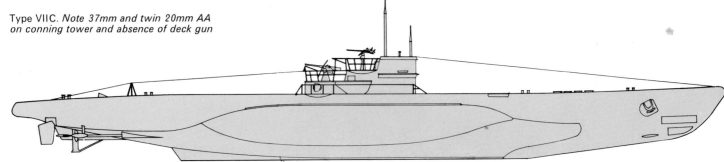

Type VIIC. *Note 37mm and twin 20mm AA on conning tower and absence of deck gun*

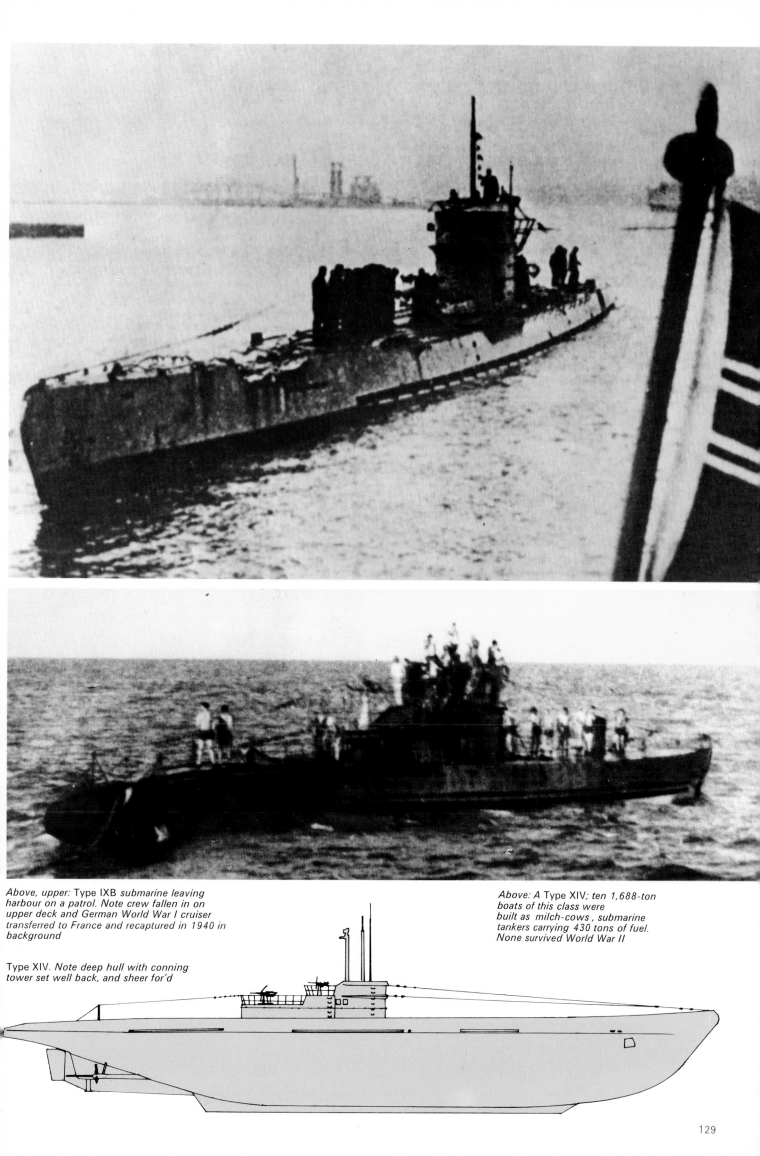

Above, upper: Type IXB *submarine leaving harbour on a patrol. Note crew fallen in on upper deck and German World War I cruiser transferred to France and recaptured in 1940 in background*

Above: A Type XIV; *ten 1,688-ton boats of this class were built as* milch-cows, *submarine tankers carrying 430 tons of fuel. None survived World War II*

Type XIV. *Note deep hull with conning tower set well back, and sheer for'd*

▶*Type IXB*

endurance of some 18 hours at 4kts. Weakness lay mainly in the stowage of high-pressure air bottles in the casing, where they could fracture under attack, and in the discomfort of the central gangway in all living spaces. The *Types VIIA, B* and *C* were generally similar attack boats. The *Type VIIC* (1941–1942) had a stronger pressure hull, the *VIID* was lengthened by 32ft (10m) to accommodate five mine shafts each carrying three mines, while the *VIIF* was of similar length to the *VIID* to carry 25 reload torpedoes to replenish other boats at sea. The *Type IXA, B, C,* and *C40* were enlarged editions of the *Type VII* but the *IXD*(1) and (2) were 36ft (11m) longer and had two slow-running diesels in the *IXD*(2) in place of their predecessors' six. This rearrangement gave a surface range of 23,700 miles (20,580nm) at 12kts. Some of the *IXD* boats were used for importing vital stores from Japan but many were employed

as submarine tankers and a large number were lost in that task. Ten of the *Type XIV* were built as submarine tankers, often known as 'milch-cows'. None survived the war — most were sunk because German codes were broken. They did, however, carry 430 tons (437 tonnes) of fuel each as well as four reload torpedoes and contributed signally to the success of operations as the U-boats descended on the 'woefully unprepared' eastern seaboard of the USA in early 1942. The 'Friendly Cow' must have been a welcome sight in the 'Happy Days' — on 22–23 April 1942 14 submarines were refuelled in an area 500 miles (800km) from Bermuda, thus allowing the Germans to operate 18 boats between Cape Sable and Key West in May. But these milch-cows were particularly vulnerable, and with what must have been a lengthy diving time, nine fell victim to aircraft attack and only one was destroyed by surface ships.

U107

U108

U47

U130

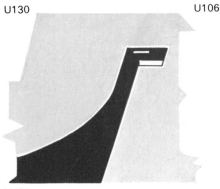

U106

U552

U564

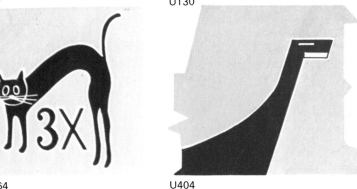

U404

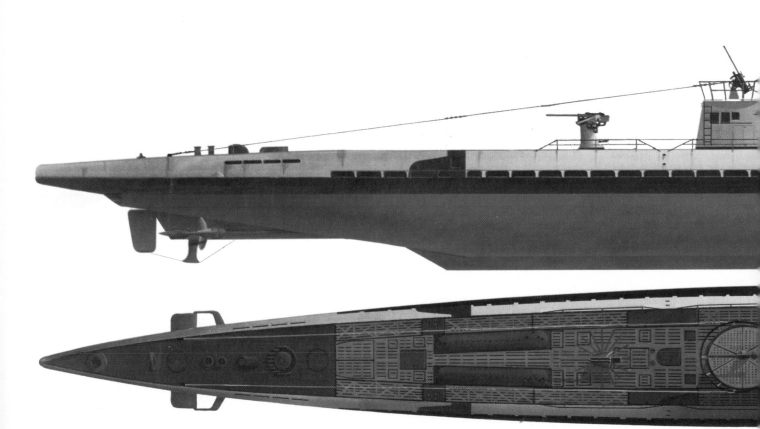

Above: The Type VIIC U-565. *Capable of 17 knots surfaced and highly manoeuvrable, the* Type VII *boats were ideal for wolf-pack operations*

Type IXB *submarine U-107, which sank a record tonnage, seen in 1941 colours. Note the 4·1in (105mm) gun before the conning tower, and the 20mm and 37mm AA guns on top and abaft of it*

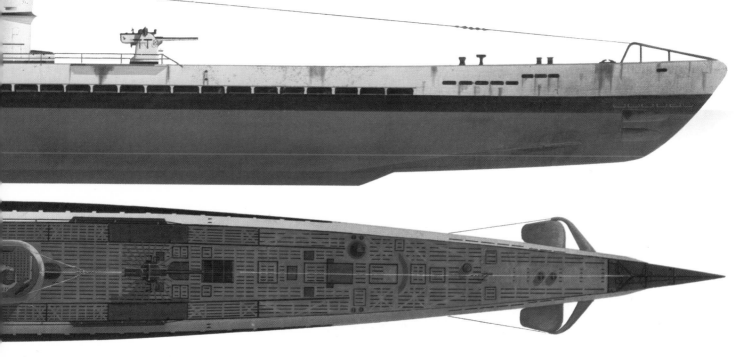

Type XXI

SUBMARINE
CLASS: TYPE XXI (134 plus boats) Germany 129 boats and Russia 5 plus boats *U-2501 to U-3000*

Type XXIII

SUBMARINE
CLASS: TYPE XXIII (58 boats) *U-2321* to *U-2500 · U-4001* to *U-4500 · U-4701* to *U-5000*

To combat increasing U-boat losses from mid-1943, Germany turned to true submarine designs. The Walter boats, powered by hydrogen peroxide, were too unreliable for service use, though a number were built. The other alternative, successfully adopted in the Type XXI ocean-going and Type XXIII coastal submarine, was to streamline the outer casing and increase vastly the battery power of diesel-electric boats. New hull forms were adopted, giving better performance submerged than on the surface, and the boats could use the schnorkel to travel at high speed at periscope depth on diesel power.

Although both designs were intended for extensive fabrication, and large numbers were built, very few carried out operational patrols. Their true significance lay postwar, when they formed the basis of all diesel-electric submarine developments. The Russian *Whisky* and French *Narval* classes were both basically improved Type XXIs, and Russia built a number of Type XXIs until her own postwar designs were ready.

Right: U-3035, a Type XXI boat with a streamlined outer casing and increased battery power, giving a maximum 15·5 knots surfaced and 16 knots submerged. Note twin 20mm turrets at either end of conning tower, and virtual absence of projections on hull

	Type XXI	Type XXIII
Displacement:		
surface tons (tonnes)	1,621 (1,647)	232 (236)
submerged tons (tonnes)	1,819 (1,848)	256 (260)
Dimensions:		
length (oa)	252·6ft (77m)	112·2ft (34·2m)
beam	21·7ft (6·6m)	9·8ft (3m)
draught	20·3ft (6·2m)	12·3ft (3·75m)
Armament:		
guns		
20mm or 30mm	4	—
torpedo tubes		
21in (533mm)	6	2
Machinery		
diesels (type)	MAN	MAN
(number)	2	1
electric motors (type)	main silent	main silent
shafts	2	1
Total BHP:	4,000	580
Total SHP:		
main	5,000	600
silent	226	35
Fuel capacity:		
oil tons (tonnes)	250 (254)	18 (18·3)
Performance:		
surface speed	15·5kts	9·75kts
submerged speed (main)	16kts	12·5kts
(silent)	5kts	2kts
range surface	11,150 miles (9,375nm) @ 12kts	1,350 miles (1,135nm) @ 9·75kts
(submerged)	285 miles (240nm) @ 6kts	175 miles (147nm) @ 4kts
Crew:	57	14

Class:	TYPE XXI	TYPE XXIII
Where built or assembled:	Blohm und Voss, Hamburg; Weser, Bremen; Schichau, Danzig	Deutschewerft, Hamburg; Toulon; Genoa; Monfalcone; Nicolaiev; Linz; and Germaniawerft, Kiel.
Built:	1944–1945	1944–1945
Number completed:	131 (plus 5+ by USSR)	58
Fate:	120 sunk or scuttled; 11 surrendered	38 sunk or scuttled; 20 surrendered

Köln Class

FRIGATE
CLASS: *Köln* class (6 ships) including *Köln* (F-220) · *Augsburg* (F-222)

Köln (F-220) was the first escort to be built in Germany after World War II, and entered service in April 1961. Designed mainly for use in the Baltic, the *Köln* class, like most modern Baltic warships, concentrate on speed and a powerful anti-aircraft armament rather than range and seaworthiness. In common with the *Hamburg* class destroyers, they have a low flush-deck hull and a piled-up superstructure. The French-designed automatic 3·9in (100mm) guns are arranged in two single mounts, one at either end of the ship. There is a twin 40mm mount in B and X position, and a single 40mm gun on either side of the superstructure aft. The two Bofors A/S rocket-launchers are mounted side-by-side between the forward 40mm mount and the open bridge. There are prominent air intakes for the gas turbines on either side of the bridge and the large, lipped funnel makes the class easy to identify. The CODAG machinery consists of two diesels and one gas turbine coupled to each shaft, with controllable pitch propellers. The radar is Dutch, but the ships have German hull-mounted sonar. The class was refitted and modernised from 1967. They still lack a medium- or close-range anti-aircraft missile, and it was intended to build a developed version displacing 3,200 tons (3,250 tonnes) standard, armed with two 3in (76mm) guns and a single Tartar SAM. This was the Type 121 Frigate 70 design, but it has now been discarded in favour of building 12 Type 122 frigates, based on the Dutch *Kortenaer* design. Slightly larger than the Type 121, these will have Harpoon SSMs and Sea Sparrow SAMs, as well as guns and A/S weapons and two helicopters.

Displacement:	
standard tons (tonnes)	2,100 (2,130)
full load tons (tonnes)	2,550 (2,590)
Dimensions:	
length (pp)	343·75ft (105m)
(oa)	360·9ft (110m)
beam	36·1ft (11m)
draught	11·2ft (3·4m)
Armament:	
guns	
3·9in (100mm)	2
40mm	6
A/S weapons	
Bofors 4-barrel rocket-launcher	2
torpedo tubes	
21in (533mm)	4
mine capacity	80
Machinery:	
gas turbines (type)	Brown-Boveri
(number)	2
diesels (type)	MAN
(number)	4
shafts	?
Total BHP:	
gas turbine	24,000
diesel	12,000
total designed	36,000
Fuel capacity:	
oil tons (tonnes)	333 (338)
Performance:	
designed speed (max)	32kts
(diesel only)	23kts
range	920 miles (770nm) @ 32kts
Crew:	200

Class:	KÖLN class
Where built:	Stülcken, Hamburg
Ordered:	March 1957
Built:	1957–1964
Fate:	In service

Left: Köln, which entered service in 1961–64, was the first escort built in Germany since World War II

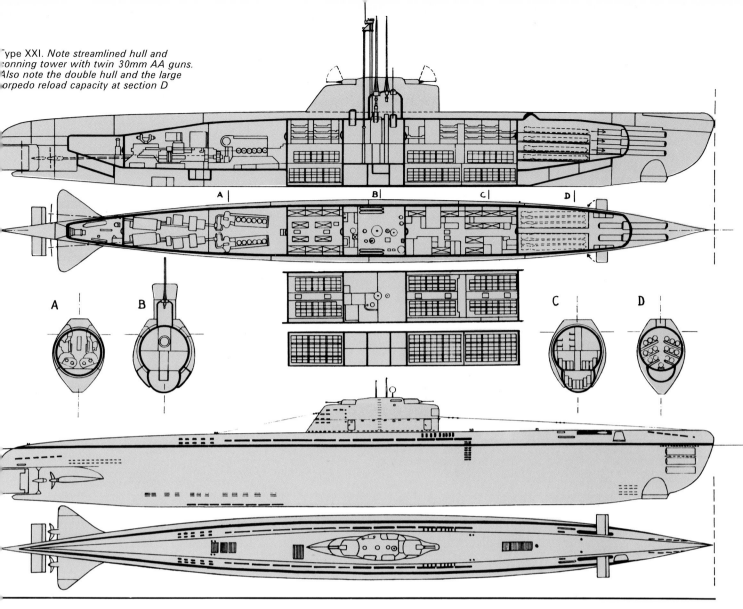

Type XXI. *Note streamlined hull and conning tower with twin 30mm AA guns. Also note the double hull and the large torpedo reload capacity at section D*

Type 143

GUIDED-MISSILE PATROL BOAT
CLASS: *Type 143* class (10 ships)
P-6111–P-6120

Lürssen, the designers of the World War II *Schnellboote,* built a number of modified versions for the German Navy and for export after the war. These were eventually developed into the Type 141 and Type 142 torpedo boats, built between 1957 and 1963. Meanwhile Lürssen had developed a general-purpose hull that could be fitted with a variety of engines and armaments depending on the requirements of the purchasing navy. For political reasons this was transferred to France, where it was lengthened and modified and became *La Combattante.* A scaled-up version of this type was chosen to

form the basis of a missile-armed patrol boat for the Federal German Navy, which became the Type 143. These boats are intended to operate in the Baltic, so have a high speed and are fitted with an OTO Melara 3in (76mm) Compact mount fore and aft to ensure adequate anti-aircraft protection. They have AG15 automatic data link with their shore base (which can fire and control their MM-38 Exocet SSMs) and they have Dutch tracking radar. The Type 143s also carry two torpedo tubes firing Seal wire-guided torpedoes with a range of about 22,000 yards (20,000m). The French variant of this design (known as the *Combattante III* type) is being built for Greece, and Spain and Turkey have similar Lürssen-designed boats. The Israeli *Reshef* class (also building for South Africa) is also very similar. The types and mix of guns and missiles, and the power required, vary from country to country. Twenty of the smaller *Combattante II* type, the Type 148, have been built for Germany between 1972 and 1975. They also have AG15 and Exocet SSMs.

Displacement:	
light tons (tonnes)	295 (300)
full load tons (tonnes)	378 (384)
Dimensions:	
length (pp)	178·5ft (54·4m)
(oa)	188·6ft (57·5m)
beam	24·9ft (7·6m)
draught	9·2ft (2·8m)
Armament:	
guns	
3in (76mm) 62cal	2
missiles	
MM38 Exocet SSM	4
torpedo tubes	
21in (533mm)	2
Machinery:	
diesels (type)	MTU
(number)	4
shafts	4
Total BHP:	
designed	16,000
Fuel capacity:	
oil tons (tonnes)	116 (118)
Performance:	
designed speed	38kts
range	1,600 miles (1,340nm) @ 30kts
Crew:	40

Class: Type 143	
Where built:	Lürssen, Vegesack and Kröger, Rendsburg
Authorised:	1972
Laid down:	1972–1975
Launched:	1973–1976
Completed:	1974–1977
Fate:	In service

Left: A Type 143 *guided missile patrol boat. 10 of these, mounting four MM38 Exocet SSMs and two 21in/533mm TTs, were completed in 1974–1977*

Schnellboote
MOTOR TORPEDO BOAT
CLASS: included *S1* (1 boat) ·
S18–25 (8 boats) · *S38–53* ·
S62–S99 · *S101* · *S135* · *S137*
(89 boats) · *S186* · *S195–S218*
(24 boats)

These excellent craft, known by the Allies as E-boats, were of round-bilge rather than hard-chine design to give them good seaworthiness. They were developed by Lürssen, who had had considerable experience of building high-speed pleasure craft. The first S-boat, *S-1*, had highly inflammable petrol engines, but the safer diesel was introduced in *S-6*. *S7-13* were the first to use the definitive knuckled hull form, and *S18-25* introduced the Daimler-Benz diesel. Later boats had a raised fo'c's'le over the torpedo tubes, with reloads carried aft. Armament was increased throughout the war. The last classes carried aircraft type 30mm cannon, and an armoured wheelhouse was introduced on the *S100* type. Extensively used in the North Sea, the S-boats were more than a match for the earlier British boats. However, although they sank a number of Allied vessels, they were not as effective as the British boats, possibly due to less aggressive leadership. Some more boats to the same general designs were built for various navies postwar, and later Lürssen boats relied heavily on experience with these craft. They were complemented by the slower but more seaworthy general-purpose *Raumboote* (R-boat).

S 80 series S boat (E boat), in camouflage used by the 1st flotilla in the Baltic. Note TT in fo'c's'le, torpedo reload rails amidships and depth charge rails aft

	S1 type as built	S18 type as built	S38 type in late war	S186 type as built
Displacement:				
light tons (tonnes)	39·75 (40)	92·5 (94)	92·5 (94)	92·5 (94)
full load tons (tonnes)	51·5 (52)	104·5 (106)	104·5 (106)	105·5 (107)
Dimensions:				
length (oa)	88·5ft (27m)	113·5ft (34·7m)	114·5ft (35m)	114·75ft (35·1m)
beam	13·75ft (4·2m)	16·75ft (5·1m)	16·75ft (5·1m)	16·75ft (5·1m)
draught	3·5ft (1·1m)	4·75ft (1·4m)	5ft (1·5m)	4·75ft (1·4m)
Armament:				
guns				
37 or 40mm	—	—	1	
30mm				2
20mm	1	2	3	—
torpedo tubes				
19·7in (500mm)	2	—	—	—
21in (533mm)	—	2	2	2
Machinery:				
petrol (type)	Daimler Benz			
diesel (type)	—	Daimler Benz	Daimler Benz	Daimler Benz
shafts	3	3	3	3
Total BHP:				
designed	3,300	6,600	6,600	7,500
Performance:				
designed speed	34kts	38·5kts	39kts	41kts
range	582 miles (489nm) @ 22kts	700 miles (588nm) @ 35kts	700 miles (588nm) @ 35kts	700 miles (588nm) @ 35kts
Fuel capacity:				
petrol tons (tonnes)	10 (10·2)	—	—	—
oil tons (tonnes)	—	16·5 (16·8)	16·75 (17)	16·75 (17)
Crew:	18	21	21	21

Class:	S1 type	S18 type	S38 type	S186 type
Where built:	Lürssen, Vegesack	Lürssen, Vegesack	Lürssen, Vegesack and Schlichting, Travemunde	Lürssen, Vegesack
Built:	1929–1930	1938–1939	1942–1943	1944–1945
Fate:	Originally *UZ(S)-16*, renamed *W1* 31 March 1931, renamed *S1* 16 March 1932	Sunk scrapped or surrendered 1939–1945	4 transferred to Spain 1943; May 1945 survivors surrendered; 2 transferred Norway	1 transferred to Spain 1943; May 1945 survivors surrendered; 2 returned to Germany 1957 from UK

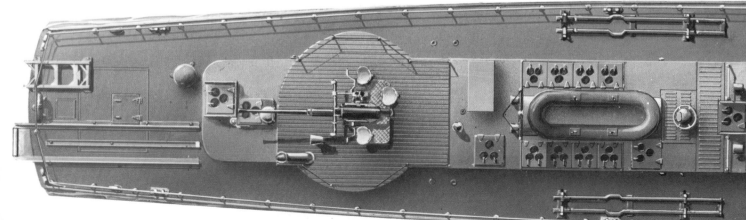

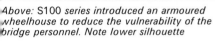

Above: S100 series introduced an armoured wheelhouse to reduce the vulnerability of the bridge personnel. Note lower silhouette

Right: A 105-ton motor torpedo boat (called Schnellboote, fast boat, by the German Navy; E-boat, enemy boat by the Allies) of the S-100 series

Above: Plan view of armoured wheelhouse. Note how it covers TTs

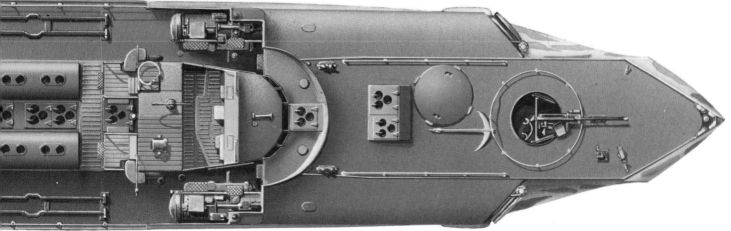

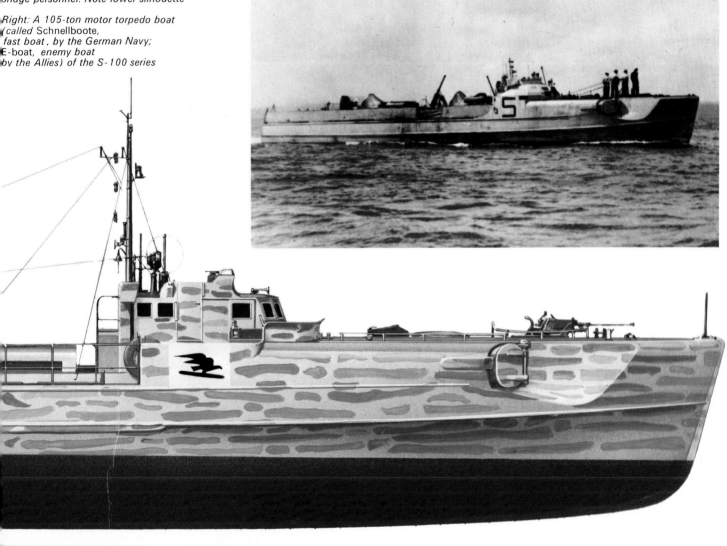

Kilkis
BATTLESHIP
CLASS: *Mississippi* class (2 ships)
Kilkis (ex-*Mississippi* BB-23)
Lemnos (ex-*Idaho* BB-24)

Service career KILKIS
1908 (Sept–Jan 1909) Refit: cage mainmast added.
1910 (Nov–Jan 1911) Goodwill voyage to England and France.
1911 Refit: bridge modified and cage foremast fitted.
1912 (June) Carried troops to Cuba.
1912 (1 Aug–Jan 1914) In reserve.
1914 (6 Jan–3 July) Aircraft depot ship.
1914 (4 Apr–June) Vera Cruz incident.
1914 (25 Apr) First operational flight by a shipborne aircraft.

1914 (21 July) Sold to Greece, renamed *Kilkis*.
1914 (Aug–1930) Flagship of Greek Navy. Boilers retubed.
1932 Relegated to minor duties.
1935–1941 Anti-aircraft training ship.
1941 (23 Apr) Sunk by German aircraft in Piraeus harbour.

The *Mississippi* class were imposed by Congress on the US Navy in a vain attempt to combat the rising size and cost of first-class battleships. Although they carried a very similar armament to the preceding *Connecticuts*, they were inferior in every respect, and were hopelessly outclassed by HMS *Dreadnought* (which was completed before them). They were therefore sold as soon as possible, and the money used to buy a new dreadnought of the *New Mexico* class. The excessive multiplication of secondary calibres was unnecessary, and wasted valuable space and weight. *Lemnos* was sunk at the same time as *Kilkis*.

Displacement:
standard tons (tonnes)	12,517 (12,717)
normal tons (tonnes)	12,945 (13,152)
full load tons (tonnes)	14,465 (14,696)

Dimensions:
length (wl)	375ft (114·5m)
(oa)	382ft (116·4m)
beam	77ft (23·4m)
draught	24·8ft (7·6m)

Armament:
guns	
12in (305mm) 45cal	4
8in (203mm) 45cal	8
7in (178mm) 45cal	8
3in (76mm)	12
3pdr (47mm)	4
1pdr (37mm)	4
0·3in (7·6mm)	8
torpedo tubes	
21in (533mm)	2

Armour:
side (belt)	7–9in (178–229mm)
deck	3in (76mm)
main turrets	8–12in (203–305mm)
barbettes	10in (254mm)
secondary turrets	6–6·5in (152–165mm)
casemates	7in (178mm)

Machinery:
boilers (type)	Babcock & Wilcox
(number)	8
engines (type)	triple expansion
shafts	2

Total IHP:
designed	10,000
trial (max)	13,607

Fuel capacity:
coal normal tons (tonnes)	600 (610)
max tons (tonnes)	1,750 (1,778)

Performance:
designed speed	17kts
trial speed (max)	17·11kts
range	8,230 miles (6,920nm) @ 10kts
Crew:	745

Ship:	KILKIS (ex-MISSISSIPPI BB-23)	LEMNOS (ex-IDAHO BB-24)
Where built:	Cramp, Philadelphia	Cramp, Philadelphia
Authorised:	1903	1903
Laid down:	12 May 1904	12 May 1904
Launched:	30 Sept 1905	9 Dec 1905
Completed:	1 Feb 1908	March 1908
Transferred and renamed:	21 July 1914	30 July 1914
Fate:	Sunk 23 Apr 1941	Sunk 23 Apr 1941

State of Mississippi flag

State of Mississippi seal

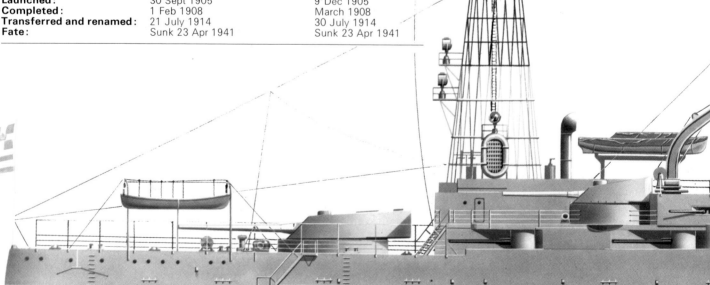

Above: The pre-dreadnought Kilkis,
originally the USS Mississippi.
She was purchased by the
Greek government, with
Lemnos (ex-USS Idaho), in 1914

Right: Sunk by Italian Stuka divebombers
on 23 April 1941, Kilkis
lies on the bottom in
Salamis harbour. Lemnos
was sunk in the same attack

Kilkis (ex-Mississippi BB-23) in 1941.
Note large cagemasts, small hull and
multiple calibre secondary armament.
Her lighter guns had been removed
some years earlier

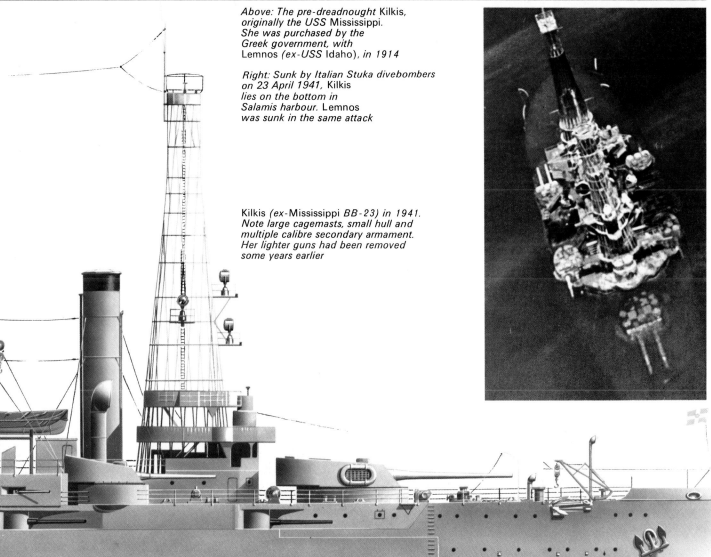

Koningin Regentes

BATTLESHIP
CLASS: *Koningin Regentes* class
(3 ships) *Koningin Regentes · De
Ruyter · Hertog Hendrik* (later
Vliereede, later *Ariadne*)

Service career KONINGIN REGENTES
1902-1920 Served in Dutch East Indies
Squadron.
circa 1920 Discarded.

Unlike the other small north European navies,
the Dutch coast defence battleships were not
intended for home defence. This was left to
torpedo craft, and the coast defence ships, including the *Koningin Regentes* class, were all
employed in the Dutch East Indies. Although
classed as battleships they were really small,
slow, but well armed armoured cruisers. Because they were employed overseas they had a
high freeboard, and were very seaworthy. The
Dutch had a flourishing shipbuilding industry
and built all their own large warships, although
they obtained their guns and some of the
armour from Germany. The *Koningin Regentes*
class mounted one 9·4in (240mm) fore and aft,
with two single 5·9in (150mm) on each broadside. Two improved vessels, *Tromp* and *Jacob
van Heemskerck*, were completed in 1908, and
an enlarged version, *Zeven Provincien*, with two
funnels and two single 11in (280mm) guns was
completed in 1910. *De Ruyter* was discarded at
the same time as *Koningin Regentes*. *Hertog
Hendrik* was converted into a training ship in
1926. Her aft 9·4in (240mm) turret was
removed, and she later carried two seaplanes. In
1941 she was converted into a floating anti-
aircraft battery, and she was hulked after World
War II.

Above: The coastal defence battleship
Koningin Regentes, *name-ship
of a class of three*

Below: Koningin Regentes *at Sabang in the
Dutch East Indies in 1916. Note frames of
targets slung either side of the bows, bow
torpedo tube, and range finders on bridges
fore and aft*

Displacement:

standard tons (tonnes)	4,560 (4,724)
normal tons (tonnes)	5,000 (5,080)
full load tons (tonnes)	5,150 (5,232)

Dimensions:

length (pp)	?
(oa)	316·9ft (96·8m)
beam	49·8ft (15·2m)
draught (max)	19ft (5·8m)

Armament:	Koningin Regentes as built	Ariadne in 1945
guns		
9·4in (240mm) 40cal	2	—
5·9in (150mm) 40cal	4	—
4·1in (105mm)	—	6
13pdr (76mm)	8	—
1pdr (37mm)	2	—
37mm	—	4
20mm	—	16
torpedo tubes		
18in (457mm)	3	—

Armour:

side (belt)	6in (152mm)
(ends)	4in (102mm)
deck (middle)	4·7in (120mm)
(main)	2in (51mm)
main turrets	4in (102mm)
barbettes	4—9·7in (102—245mm)

Machinery:

boilers (type)	Yarrow
(number)	6
engines (type)	vertical triple expansion
shafts	2

Total IHP:

designed	6,300

Fuel capacity:

coal normal tons (tonnes)	680 (690)
maximum tons (tonnes)	830 (840)

Performance:

designed speed	16 kts
range	4,100 miles (3,450nm) @ 9·25kts

Crew: 347 (home waters) 375 (East Indies)

Ship:	KONINGIN REGENTES	DE RUYTER	HERTOG HENDRIK
Where built:	Amsterdam Shipyard	Amsterdam Shipyard	Amsterdam Shipyard
Authorised:	?	?	?
Laid down:	1899	?	?
Launched:	1900	1900	1902
Completed:	1902	1904	1903
Fate:	scrapped circa 1920	scrapped circa 1920	renamed *Vliereede* 1939; captured by Germany 14 May 1940; sunk 22 June 1940; salved 1941; renamed *Ariadne*; returned 1945; renamed *Rotterdam*; scrapped circa 1950

Tromp Class

LIGHT CRUISER

CLASS: *Tromp* class (2 ships)
Tromp · Jacob van Heemskerck

When the first Japanese *Special Type* destroyers appeared in the late 1920s, they completely outclassed the *Evertsen* class destroyers serving in the Dutch East Indies fleet. Partially to counter this threat, the Dutch proposed in 1931 to build two heavily armed 2,500 ton (2,540 tonne) standard displacement flotilla leaders. The *Tromp* design was evolved from this project, but it was greatly enlarged to enable adequate protection to be fitted. The *Tromps* were light cruisers rather than destroyers, and possessed the seaworthiness and fire-control to make full use of their heavy armament. They were intended for the Dutch East Indies, and carried a seaplane forward of the aft 5·9in (150mm) mounting. *Tromp* was completed as designed, and in some ways resembled the much larger *De Ruyter*, but *Heemskerck* was still incomplete when the Germans invaded Holland. She was towed to Britain and completed at Portsmouth Dockyard. She was fitted with a similar armament to the British *Carlisles,* and had radar and a tripod mainmast. *Tromp* received radar later in the war, and both ships had their AA armament considerably increased by 1945. They proved to be very useful ships, and saw extensive service in most theatres of action. As designed, their armament was very similar to the larger German destroyers, but because more attention and displacement was given to 'ship' qualities, they were much more effective vessels.

Below: The light cruiser Tromp, *seen here, and her sister-ship*
Jacob van Heemskerck, *saw extensive action in World War II and were in service until the 1950s. Note searchlight on foretop, 'goalpost' mainmast, 5·9in (150mm) twin turrets and TTs at break of fo'c's'le, which is, unusually, situated amidships on this class*

	Tromp as built	Jacob van Heemskerck in 1945
Displacement:		
standard tons (tonnes)	3,787 (3,848)	4,150 (4,216)
full load tons (tonnes)	4,215 (4,282)	4,860 (4,938)
Dimensions:		
length (pp)	426·5ft (130·2m)	
(oa)	433ft (132·2m)	
beam	40·75ft (12·4m)	
draught	15ft (4·6m)	
Armament:		
guns		
5·9in (150mm)	6	
4in (102mm)	—	10
40mm	8	8
20mm	—	8
12·7mm	4	—
torpedo tubes		
21in (533mm)	6	—
aircraft	1	—
Armour:		
side (belt)	0·6in (16mm)	
(internal belt)	0·75–1·25in (19–32mm)	
deck (main)	1in (25mm)	
(lower)	0·6–1in (16–25mm)	
main turrets	0·6in (16mm)	
Machinery:		
boilers (type)	Yarrow	
(number)	4	
engines (type)	Parsons geared turbines	
shafts	2	
Total SHP:		
designed	56,000	
Fuel capacity:		
oil tons (tonnes)	860 (870)	
Performance:		
designed speed	33·5kts	
range	?	
Crew:	309	

Ship:	TROMP	JACOB VAN HEEMSKERCK
Where built:	Netherlands Shipyard, Amsterdam	Netherlands Shipyard, Amsterdam
Authorised:	1935	1935
Laid down:	17 Jan 1936	31 Oct 1938
Launched:	24 May 1937	16 Sept 1939
Completed:	18 Aug 1938	1941
Fate:	Deleted circa 1958	Towed incomplete to Britain May 1940; completed at Portsmouth Dockyard; deleted circa 1958

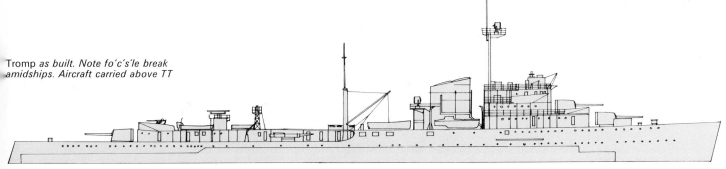

Tromp *as built. Note fo'c's'le break amidships. Aircraft carried above TT*

De Ruyter

LIGHT CRUISER
CLASS: *De Ruyter* class (1 ship)
De Ruyter

Service career DE RUYTER
1937 (Jan–Mar) To Dutch East Indies.
1937 (May) Joined East Indies Squadron.
1937 (Oct–Feb 1942) Flagship East Indies Squadron.
1940 (Jan–Feb) Refit and repairs to turbines at Surabaya.
1941 (Dec–Feb 1942) Patrols and convoy escort.
1942 (27 Feb) Allied flagship at Battle of the Java Sea.
1942 (27 Feb) Hit by Japanese torpedo and sank in two hours.

De Ruyter was originally intended to displace only 5,250 tons, with an armament of six 5·9in (150mm) guns in three twin turrets, one forward and two aft. It was recognised that this was too small for the needs of the East Indies, so the design was enlarged to increase the speed and allow a catapult to be worked in. At the same time the opportunity was taken to add a single superfiring 5·9in (150mm) gun forward. It would not have been possible to fit a twin turret without enlarging the ship still further. This gave *De Ruyter* the same broadside as *Java* and *Sumatra*, two slightly larger Dutch cruisers laid down in 1916.

De Ruyter was specifically intended for service in the Dutch East Indies, and habitability was excellent. There was a tower bridge reminiscent of the German *Panzerschiff*, and smoke deflectors on the funnel gave her an ungainly appearance. Weight was saved by having no torpedoes or heavy anti-aircraft armament, but the 40mm anti-aircraft guns were fitted with very advanced power mountings with excellent fire control.

She was hit by one 24in (610mm) Type 93 torpedo fired by the Japanese cruiser *Haguro*, and sank two hours later. Over 200 of the crew were killed.

Displacement:	
standard tons (tonnes)	6,442 (6,545)
full load tons (tonnes)	7,548 (7,669)
Dimensions:	
length (wl)	552·2ft (168·3m)
(oa)	561ft (171m)
beam	51·5ft (15·7m)
draught	16·4ft (5m)
Armament:	
guns	
5·9in (150mm) 50cal	7
40mm	10
0·5in (12·7mm)	8
Armour:	
side (belt)	1·2–2in (30–50mm)
deck	1·2in (30mm)
main turrets	1·2in (30mm)
barbettes	1·2in (30mm)
Machinery:	
boilers (type)	Yarrow
(number)	6
engines (type)	Parsons single reduction geared turbines
shafts	2
Total SHP:	
designed	66,000
Fuel capacity:	
oil tons (tonnes)	1,300 (1,320)
Performance:	
designed speed	32kts
range	8,100 miles (6,800nm) @ 12kts
Crew:	435

Ship:	**DE RUYTER**
Where built:	Wilton-Fijenoord, Schiedam
Ordered:	1 Aug 1932
Laid down:	1 Sept 1933
Launched:	11 May 1935
Completed:	3 Oct 1936
Fate:	Sunk 28 Feb 1942

Above: The light cruiser De Ruyter, *soon after completion in 1936. She was torpedoed and sunk by the Japanese cruiser* Haguro *in the Java Sea, in February 1942*

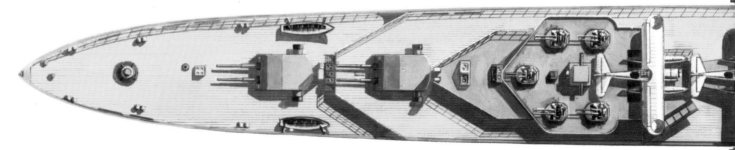

Above: De Ruyter *had a main armament
of seven 5·9in/150mm guns
and carried two aircraft. Her
tower bridge was much like
that of a German* Panzerschiff

De Ruyter *as completed. Note the single
5·9in (150mm) gun in B position,
the two Fokker CW-1 seaplanes on the
catapult amidships and the very powerful
light armament*

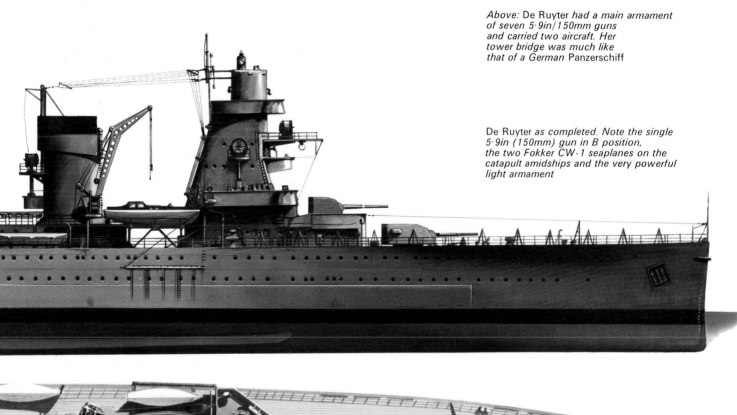

De Zeven Provincien Class
LIGHT CRUISER

CLASS: *De Zeven Provincien* class (2 ships) *De Ruyter* (C-801) (ex-*De Zeven Provincien* · later *Almirante Grau*) · *De Zeven Provincien* (C-802) (ex-*De Ruyter* · ex-*Eendracht* · ex-*Kijkduin*)

These cruisers were originally designed for the Dutch East Indies fleet. They were intended to replace *Java* and *Sumatra*, and were enlarged *De Ruyters*. The main armament, which was ordered from Sweden, was originally intended to be four twin 5·9in (150mm) turrets, but this was altered before they were laid down to two twin and two triple turrets. They were captured on their slips in 1940, and work continued throughout World War II. *De Ruyter* was launched with the German 'Atlantic' bow. Work restarted in 1947 to a different design. The 5·9in (150mm) turrets had been used in the Swedish *Gota Lejons,* and the Dutch ships mounted four twin 6in (152mm) turrets instead. Unit machinery was fitted, with twin funnels and one less shaft, and the anti-aircraft armament was improved. To save space the forward funnel is blended into the bridge and fore lattice mast. *De Zeven Provincien* had her aft turrets removed and a Terrier SAM twin-launcher fitted in 1962–1964. This was removed before she was transferred to Peru.

Above: The light cruiser De Zeven Provincien *after conversion to a guided missile cruiser. The twin Terrier launcher has been removed since her sale to Peru*

	Original design in 1939	De Ruyter in 1953	De Zeven Provincien in 1976
Displacement:			
standard tons (tonnes)	9,325 (9,474)	9,529 (9,681)	
full load tons (tonnes)	10,795 (10,968)	11,850 (12,040)	
Dimensions:			
length (pp)	598ft (182·6m)	590·5ft (180m)	590·5ft (180m)
(oa)	613·5ft (187·3m)	614·5ft (187·6m)	609ft (186m)
beam	56·5ft (17·3m)	56·7ft (17·3m)	56·7ft (17·3m)
draught	18·5ft (5·6m)	22ft (6·7m)	22ft (6·7m)
Armament:			
guns			
6in (152mm)	—	8	4
5·9in (150mm)	10	—	—
57mm	—	8	6
40mm	14	8	4
12·7mm	8	—	—
missiles			
Terrier SAM twin-launcher	—	—	1
torpedo tubes			
21in (533mm)	6	—	—
aircraft	2	—	—
Armour:			
side (belt)	4in (102mm)		
(ends)	3in (76mm)		
deck (main)	0·75–1in (20–25mm)		
(lower)	0·75–1in (20–25mm)		
main turrets	2–4in (51–102mm)		
barbettes	?		
Machinery:			
boilers (type)	Yarrow	Yarrow	
(number)	6	4	
engines (type)	Parsons geared turbines	Parsons geared turbines	
shafts	3	2	
Total SHP:			
designed	78,000	85,000	
Fuel capacity:			
oil tons (tonnes)	1,750 (1,780)	?	
Performance:			
designed speed	32kts	32kts	
range	?	?	
Crew:	700	920	940

Ship:	DE RUYTER (C-801)	DE ZEVEN PROVINCIEN (C-802)
Where built:	Wilton Fijenoord, Schiedam	Rotterdam Dry Dock Co
Authorised:	1938	1938
Laid down:	5 Sept 1939	19 May 1939
Launched:	24 Dec 1944	22 Aug 1950
Completed:	18 Nov 1953	17 Dec 1953
Fate:	Launched as *De Zeven Provincien;* renamed 1947; sold to Peru March 1973; renamed *Almirante Grau*	Renamed *De Ruyter* 1944; renamed 1947; sold to Peru 1976; renamed ?

Tromp Class

GUIDED-MISSILE DESTROYER

CLASS: *Tromp* class (2 ships) *Tromp* (F-801) · *De Ruyter* (ex-*Heemskercke*, F-806)

These ships are the equivalent of the Canadian *Iroquois*, the French *Georges Leygues*, the British *Sheffield* and Italian *Audace* classes. They are to be fitted with eight Harpoon SSMs between the bridge and funnels, and are amongst the best ships of their type. The 4·7in (120mm) twin mountings come from scrapped *Holland* class destroyers, but have been thoroughly modernised. The short-range Sea Sparrow BPDMS mounting is fitted in B position. Behind it is a massive bridge, surmounted by a Dutch 3-D radar in a large glass-fibre dome. The uptakes are splayed out in a similar way to the Canadian *Iroquois* class to keep the exhaust clear of the radars. The Standard Tartar Mk 13 SAM launcher is aft, just forward of the hangar and flight deck for a Lynx A/S helicopter. Triple Mk 32 torpedo tubes are mounted either side of the aft superstructure. The *Tromps* have COGOG machinery, the Olympus' providing full speed and the Tynes' cruising. They have controllable-pitch propellers. Twelve *Kortenaer* class frigates have been ordered. These are smaller versions of the *Tromps*, without the Standard Mk 13 SAM launcher, and having a 3in (76mm) OTO Melara Compact and a twin 35mm mount, temporarily replaced by a second 76mm mount. They also have a conventional funnel and a much smaller bridge without the 3-D radar. All these ships are intended for the European theatre, and are well balanced vessels capable of dealing with air, surface and underwater threats. The *Tromps* replace the *De*

Displacement:	
standard tons (tonnes)	4,300 (4,369)
full load tons (tonnes)	5,400 (5,486)
Dimensions:	
length (pp)	425·75ft (130m)
(oa)	453·9ft (138·6m)
beam	48·5ft (14·8m)
draught	15·1ft (4·6m)
Armament:	**as built**
guns	
4·7in (120mm)	2
missiles	
Standard Tartar Mk 13 SAM single-launcher	1
Sea Sparrow BPDMS SAM octuple-launcher	1
Harpoon quadruple-launcher	2
torpedo tubes	
12·7in (324mm) Mk 32	6
aircraft	1 helicopter
Machinery:	
gas turbines (type)	Rolls-Royce Olympus and Rolls Royce Tyne
(number)	2
shafts	2
Total SHP:	
maximum	54,000
cruising	8,200
Fuel capacity:	
oil tons (tonnes)	?
Performance:	
maximum speed	30kts
cruising speed	18kts
range	5,950 miles (5,000nm) @ 18kts
Crew:	301

Zeven Provincien class light cruisers, and these highly effective vessels save considerably in manpower.

Above: Tromp *at speed. Note the gun turret, Sea Sparrow launcher forward and Tartar launcher and helicopter pad aft. The 3-D radar dome has given these ships the nickname of 'Kojak'.*

Ship:	TROMP (F-801)
Where built:	De Schelde, Flush
Authorised:	1967
Laid down:	4 Sept 1971
Launched:	4 June 1973
Completed:	3 Oct 1975
Fate:	In service

Dolfijn Class

SUBMARINE
CLASS: *Dolfijn* class (4 boats)
Dolfijn · Zeehond · Potvis · Tonijn

These four submarines were originally ordered together. *Potvis* and *Tonijn* were then delayed for several years and their equipment differed somewhat from the first two when they finally entered service. However, all four submarines have since been refitted to a virtually identical standard. The outstanding feature of this class is that instead of having the usual single pressure hull of a normal submarine, they have three separate though interconnected pressure hulls in a 'treble bubble' arrangement. The uppermost and largest contains the crew and most of the equipment, whilst below it and alongside each other are two smaller hulls, each containing machinery and stores. The advantage of this odd layout is that it gives increased strength and compactness. However, the lower two hulls

Displacement:
standard tons (tonnes)	1,140 (1,160)
surface tons (tonnes)	1,494 (1,518)
submerged tons (tonnes)	1,826 (1,855)

Dimensions
length (pp)	?
(oa)	260·4ft (79·5m)
beam	25·8ft (7·9m)
draught	15·7ft (4·8m)

Armament:
torpedo tubes 21in (533mm)	8

Machinery:
diesels (type)	MAN
(number)	2
electric motors (type)	?
shafts	2

Total HP:
surfaced	3,100
submerged	4,200

Fuel capacity:
oil tons (tonnes)	?

Performance:
surface speed	14·5kts
submerged speed	17kts
Crew:	64

are extremely cramped, making machinery maintenance and replacement very difficult. This, combined with the increased complexity and therefore increased manufacturing cost, would appear to have stopped the Dutch from developing the design further. Their latest submarines have reverted to the conventional single pressure hull arrangement. However, the triple hull arrangement has allowed a designed

Above: The Dolfijn *class submarine* Potvis. *These boats, completed 1960–66, have three pressure hulls, housing crew and armament, batteries and diesels respectively*

diving depth of 980ft (300m). The streamlined hull gives an excellent performance submerged and they are very quiet boats.

Ship:	**DOLFIJN**	**ZEEHOND**	**POTVIS**	**TONIJN**
Where built:	Rotterdam Dry Dock	Rotterdam Dry Dock	Wilton – Fijenoord	Wilton – Fijenoord
Authorised:	?	?	?	?
Laid down:	Dec 1954	Dec 1954	17 Sept 1962	28 Nov 1962
Launched:	20 May 1959	20 Feb 1960	1 Jan 1965	14 June 1965
Completed:	Dec 1960	March 1961	Nov 1965	Feb 1966
Fate:	In service	In service	In service	In service

Right: The guided missile destroyers De Ruyter, *seen here with* HMS Ark Royal, *and* Tromp, *in service since 1975, are among the best warships of their type*

DE RUYTER (F-806)
De Schelde, Flushing
1967
22 Dec 1971
9 March 1974
3 June 1976
In service

ITALY

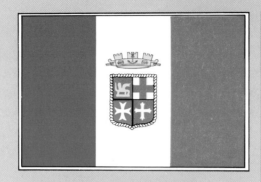

ONE of the longest traditions of seaborne military power is marked out in the names of many of the ships in today's Italian Navy. But it was not until Garibaldi's campaigns led to a unified Italy in 1861 that the conjunction of the individual states' fleets once again formed a navy with responsibilities around the whole Italian coast. In this troubled period war was to come again in 1866 when the Prussians and Italians attacked Austria. The battle off Lissa on 20 July was the first meeting of ironclads and the Austrian Tegetthof's tactics of ramming, a move which sank one ship, and discouraged the remainder, was to affect a whole generation of naval thought quite profoundly

Within ten years of Lissa, Whitehead produced his mobile torpedo, a fact rapidly appreciated by one of the great Italian designers, Benedetto Brin. In over twenty years both as constructor and at times, Minister of Marine, Brin produced a series of ingenious designs which took account and recognised the potential of this new underwater danger in their watertight subdivisions.

Having aligned herself with Germany and Austria in the Triple Alliance of 1882 Italy began to move her navy forward to new bases at Taranto and Maddalena in Sicily. France was alarmed and reacted by applying economic pressure which, in the mid 1890s caused Italy to seek a rapprochement with the French. In the Grab for Africa, Italy had annexed Eritrea and parts of Somaliland — overseas requirements for a fleet became important. This was further demonstrated in the Turkish War of 1911–12 in which the Italian Navy under Admiral Cattolica played a notable part and, at its conclusion, found itself responsible for communications with the newly-ceded colonies of Libya, Rhodes and the Dodecanese.

In 1913 Italian and Austrian naval leaders met to co-ordinate plans for war. By now the Italians had six dreadnoughts, the Austrians four — a notable force to influence the balance in the Central and Eastern Mediterranean. But when war did come in the next year Italy did not step in with her long-term allies, waiting until May 1915 to join forces with the Western countries. The naval events in the Mediterranean were not of major importance but the activities of small fast torpedo-armed craft off the Austrian coast

demonstrated the Italian ability to conduct such operations with a considerable degree of success.

With the rise of Mussolini came the Imperialist postures and the cries of 'Mare Nostrum'. To impose his imperial will on his neighbours Little Caesar needed a navy and the abilities of the Italian shipyards to produce fast, beautiful ships were seen again. The fleet grew in all types but the ultimate result was not what Mussolini had hoped for. During World War II fleet actions were invariably either inconclusive or to the Italian disadvantage. It was once again in the smaller craft and in single ship operations that the particular bravery and capacity of individuals was evident. But this could not win a war and in September 1943 the Italian fleet lay under the guns of the fortress of Malta.

In the years after 1945 the problems of Italy were those well-known in the pre-Fascist days — economic stress and a divided country. Membership of NATO brought some stability to the armed forces and, after a period when the main fleet was bolstered by ex-American ships, the products of her own shipyards began to be seen in increasing numbers. Not only did the Italians build their own hulls but, in a manner similar to France, provided their own sensors, engines and weapons. Today the result is an integration of resources which is as impressive as it is efficient, resulting in steadily increasing export orders for all forms of naval armament. The Italian Navy itself is well-balanced for its present purposes. Emphasis has been placed on the use of helicopters and missiles with home-designed submarines and minewarfare ships now coming off the slips. Whereas reliance was placed on home bases for support a new programme of fleet supply ships will provide greater range. The Legge Navale of 1975 will, if not interfered with, give the Italians a strong well-balanced fleet by the early 1980s.

The Alpino class frigate Carabiniere (F581) *and* Centauro *class frigate* Castore (F553) *in the Tyrrhenian Sea in 1977*

145

Caio Duilio

BATTLESHIP
CLASS: *Andrea Doria* class (2 ships)
Caio Duilio · Andrea Doria

Service career CAIO DUILIO
1915–1918 1st Division, Battle Squadron, Italian Fleet, based at Taranto.
1925 (8 Apr) Explosion in centre turret.
1926 (Apr 1928) Rebuilt.
1937 (1 Apr–15 July 1940) Reconstructed: hull lengthened; centre turret removed; new machinery and shafting fitted; main guns bored out; new secondary and anti-aircraft battery fitted; horizontal armour and underwater protection improved; new superstructure fitted.
1940 (Aug–Oct) Patrols in eastern Mediterranean.
1940 (12 Nov) Hit by one torpedo from aircraft from British carrier *Illustrious* in Taranto harbour: severely damaged.
1940–1941 Repaired.
1941 (Dec–Feb 1942) Escorted Italian convoys and patrols against British convoys.
1942 (March–Sept 1943) Non-operational.
1943 (9–11 Sept) To Malta.
1943 (11 Sept) Surrendered with rest of Italian Battle Squadron.
1944 (June) Transferred back to Italy.
1945 (–Sept 1946) Training ship.
1956 (Sept) Deleted.
1957–1958 Scrapped.

Dante Alighieri, Italy's first dreadnought, was also the world's first battleship to have triple turrets. These British designed mountings were adopted to allow the maximum broadside on the minimum length of hull, and like most Italian heavy units, *Dante Alighieri* sacrificed protection and freeboard for speed and heavy armament. On a normal displacement of 19,552 tons (19,865 tonnes) she could achieve 22·75kts, but her belt armour had a maximum thickness of only 9·8in (250mm). Her 12in (305mm) guns were mounted in four triple centreline turrets. One turret was mounted on the fo'c'sle, and the other three were a deck lower. The two centre turrets separated the two pairs of funnels, and *Dante Alighieri* had minimal superstructure. Eight of the 4·7in (120mm) secondary armament guns were well positioned in pairs of twin turrets fore and aft, but the remainder were mounted in casemates set very low in the hull, where they were unworkable in any sea. In common with the similar but larger Russian

Displacement:	in 1915	in 1940
standard tons (tonnes)	—	26,018 (26,434)
normal tons (tonnes)	22,632 (22,994)	—
full load tons (tonnes)	24,326 (24,715)	28,928 (29,391)
Dimensions:		
length (pp)	556ft (170m)	556·6ft (170m)
(oa)	576·4ft (176m)	612·1ft (186·9m)
beam	91·7ft (28m)	91·8ft (28m)
draught	29·1ft (8·9m)	28ft (8·6m)
Armament:		
guns		
12·6in (320mm) 44cal	—	10
12in (305mm) 46 cal	13	—
6in (152mm) 45cal	16	—
5·3in (135mm) 45cal	—	12
3·5in (90mm)	—	10
3in (76mm)	19	—
37mm	—	8
20mm	—	12
torpedo tubes		
17·7in (450mm)	3	—
Armour:		
side (belt)	9·8in (250mm)	9·8in (250mm)
deck	1·6in (40mm)	5·4in (138mm)
main turret	9·4in (240mm)	11in (280mm)
barbettes	9·4in (240mm)	11in (280mm)
battery	6in (152mm)	
secondary turrets	—	4·7in (120mm)
Machinery:		
boilers (type)	Yarrow	Yarrow
(number)	20	8
engines (type)	Parsons geared turbines	Parsons geared turbines
shafts	4	2
Total SHP:		
designed	32,000	75,000
Performance:		
designed speed	22kts	27kts
range	5,710 miles (4,800nm) @ 10kts	4,250 miles (3,573nm) @ 12kts
Fuel capacity:		
coal normal tons (tonnes)	606 (616)	—
max tons (tonnes)	1,488 (1,512)	—
oil tons (tonnes)	886 (901)	2,250 (2,286)
Crew:	1,233	1,485

Ship:	**CAIO DUILIO**	**ANDREA DORIA**
Where built:	Castellammare Naval Yard	La Spezia Naval Yard
Authorised:	1911	1911
Laid down:	24 Dec 1912	24 March 1912
Launched:	24 Apr 1913	30 March 1913
Completed:	10 May 1915	13 March 1916
Rebuilt:	1 Apr 1937–15 July 1940	8 Apr 1937–26 Oct 1940
Fate:	Deleted Sept 1956; scrapped 1957–1958	Deleted Nov 1956; scrapped 1957–1958

Ganguts, *Dante Alighieri* reflected the ideas of General Cuniberti. The need for a larger armament and improved end-on fire resulted in the three *Conte di Cavour* class battleships, built between 1910 and 1915. They had a normal displacement of 22,800 tons (23,160 tonnes)

Vittorio Veneto

BATTLESHIP
CLASS: *Littorio* class (3 ships):
Group 1 *Vittorio Veneto · Littorio*
Group 2 *Roma*

Service career VITTORIO VENETO
1940 (Aug–Oct) Patrols in central Mediterranean.
1941 (28 March) Battle of Cape Matapan: hit by torpedo from aircraft from British aircraft-carrier *Formidable* and damaged.
1941 (Apr–Aug) Repaired.
1941 (Sept–Dec) Patrols and convoy escort in central Mediterranean.
1941 (14 Dec) Torpedoed by British submarine *Urge*.
1941 (Dec–March 1942) Repaired.
1943 (5 June) Damaged by bombs.
1943 (9–11 Sept) To Malta.
1943 (11 Sept) Surrendered with Italian Battle Squadron; transferred to Lake Amaro, Suez.
1943-1944 Possibility of serving with Allied Pacific fleet: not carried out.
1946 Returned to Italy; allocated to UK as reparations.
1948-1950 Scrapped.

With France intransigent over ratification of the London Naval Agreement and with news of the French intention to build battleships of the *Dunkerque* class, Italy moved swiftly to implement the battleship designs first drawn up in

Continued on page 148 ▶

Right: The Littorio *class battleship* Vittorio Veneto. *Note the height of the aft main turret*

Displacement:	Group 1	Group 2
standard tons (tonnes)	41,377 (42,043)	41,650 (42,320)
full load tons (tonnes)	45,752 (46,489)	46,215 (46,959)
Dimensions:		
length (pp)	733·8ft (224m)	733·8ft (224m)
(oa)	778·7ft (237·8m)	786·3ft (240m)
beam	107·8ft (32·9m)	107·8ft (32·9m)
draught	31·4ft (9·6m)	31·6ft (9·7m)
Armament:		
guns		
15in (381mm) 50cal	9	
6in (152mm) 55cal	12	
4·7in (120mm) 40cal	4	
3·5in (90mm)	12	
37mm	20	
20mm	32	
aircraft	3	
Armour:		
side (belt)	3·9–13·75in (100–350mm)	
(ends)	2·4–5·1in (60–130mm)	
deck (main)	1·4–1·8in (36–45mm)	
(armour)	3·9–8·1in (100–204mm)	
main turrets	3·9–13·75in (100–350mm)	
barbettes	13·75in (350mm)	
secondary turrets	1·3–5·9in (35–150mm)	
Machinery:		
boilers (type)	Yarrow	
(number)	8	
engines (type)	Belluzzo single reduction geared turbines	
shafts	4	
Total SHP:		
designed	130,000	
trial (Group 1)	134,616–139,561	
Fuel capacity:		
oil tons (tonnes)	4,000 (4,064)	
Performance:		
designed speed	30kts	
trial speed (Group 1)	31·42–31·29kts	
range	4,580 miles (3,850nm) @ 16kts	
Crew:	1,861	1,960

and an armament of thirteen 12in (305mm) guns. These were carried in a triple turret with a superfiring twin-gun turret fore and aft, and a third triple turret amidships. This arrangement avoided excessive topweight, and gave two extra guns on most fore and aft bearings, and one more gun on the broadside. The *Cavours* had the same thickness of armour as *Dante Alighieri*, but had a much longer fo'c's'le, and carried their 4·7m (120mm) secondary armament one deck higher. Whereas *Dante Alighieri* had two pairs of funnels with pole masts between them, the *Cavours* had two large funnels and tripod masts separated by the mid-ships turret. The *Dorias* had a similar hull and main armament to the *Cavours*, but their secondary armament was increased to 6in (152mm) calibre to cope with larger destroyers, and the centre turret and the aft 6in (152mm) guns were carried one deck lower to preserve stability. Like the *Cavours*, the *Dorias* had two large funnels, but the fore tripod was placed in front of rather than behind the fore funnel. Despite the help given by British firms, who did much of the detail design and built most of the turrets, guns, armour and machinery, these ships took longer to build than most foreign con-temporaries. As a result they were outclassed on completion by the better armed and protected foreign super-dreadnoughts. They had one more heavy gun than the Austrian *Viribus Unitis* class which were their most likely opponents, but in view of the Italian dreadnoughts' weak armour it was perhaps as well that they saw no action in World War I. A class of very fast but poorly protected 15in (381mm) battleships, the *Carraciolos*, were laid down in 1914–1915 but were cancelled during the war. By the 1930s, the Italians needed to counter the new French *Dunkerques*, and drastically rebuilt the two surviving *Cavours* and the *Dorias*. The *Cavours* were converted between 1933 and 1937 and had new longer bow and stern sections with two instead of four screws and new machinery to increase the speed by six knots. The centre turret was removed to make way for the machinery and the guns were bored out to match those of the *Dunkerques*. A new second-ary armament and superstructure were fitted, but although the horizontal protection was slightly increased the thin side armour could not be strengthened. A new Pugiliese underwater protection system was also fitted. The *Dorias* underwent a similar conversion, but benefiting from lessons learned with the *Cavours*, they had a rearranged and strengthened secondary and anti-aircraft armament. They were virtually new ships, but although they were now much

more effective than the old French battleships, they were inferior to the *Dunkerques* and were totally outclassed in all but speed by the reconstructed British *Queen Elizabeths*. As was shown at Taranto, the underwater protection was inadequate, and the vertical and horizontal protection was very thin.

Above, upper: Caio Duilio *on a courtesy visit to Malta in 1949*

Above: Caio Duilio, *after rebuilding in 1937–40. She bears little resemblance to the original dreadnought of 1915*

▶Vittorio Veneto

1928. The first pair, *Vittorio Veneto* and *Littorio*, were laid down in October 1934 at Trieste and Genoa. When they started trials in December 1939 they were seen to be fine, handsome ships whose original designed tonnage of 35,000 (35,560 tonnes) had grown by over 10,000 tons (10,160 tonnes) to a deep load displacement of nearly 46,000 tons (46,736 tonnes). They were originally intended to carry midget submarines, but fortunately these were omitted from the final design. Apart from the unsuccessful Pugliese underwater protection, they were well armoured. *Littorio* was put out of action for many months when she was hit by three torpedoes during the Fleet Air Arm attack on Taranto on 11 November 1940. The main armament of nine 15in (381mm) guns was disposed in three turrets in A, B and X positions, leaving a long cut-away quarterdeck on which a catapult was mounted aft. The secondary armament consisted of four triple 6in (152mm) turrets while the HA battery of 12 single 3·5in (90mm) guns was heavily supplemented by twenty 37mm and up to thirty-two 20mm guns, a concentration capable of putting up a 'Volcano of fire' as it was described by one participant in the Taranto raid. The histories of the four ships of the class were in no case happy ones. *Vittorio Veneto* had several unsuccessful brushes with the British Mediterranean Fleet, was torpedoed from the air and by a submarine and hit by bombs in La Spezia. She was finally surrendered at Malta on 11 September 1943 as was her sister *Littorio* who had been renamed *Italia* three months previously. The latter also had a short, eventful but unsuccessful career. After post-Taranto repairs she was hit by bombs, a torpedo and, once more, bombs. As a final blow she was hit by a German glider-bomb while on passage to surrender in Malta. *Roma* was sunk en route for Malta in September 1943. In all but underwater protection these powerful vessels were the equal of any foreign contemporaries, and but for problems with spares and equipment would have been incorporated in the British Pacific fleet. However, this proved not to be possible and the ships were laid up until they were scrapped in the late 1940s.

Ship:	VITTORIO VENETO	LITTORIO	IMPERO	ROMA
Where built:	CRDA, Trieste	Ansaldo, Genoa	Ansaldo, Genoa	CRDA, Trieste
Authorised:	1934	1934	1938	1938
Laid down:	28 Oct 1934	28 Oct 1934	14 May 1938	18 Sept 1938
Launched:	25 July 1937	22 Aug 1937	15 Nov 1939	9 June 1940
Completed:	28 Apr 1940	6 May 1940	—	14 June 1942
Fate:	Scrapped 1948–1950	Scrapped 1948–1950	Used as target by Germans; sunk by USAF 20 Feb 1945; salved and scrapped incomplete 1947–1950	Sunk 9 Sept 1943

Above, upper: Littorio *in wartime camouflage. Name-ship of a class of three completed in 1940–42, she mounted a main armament of nine 15in/381mm guns*

Above: The Littorio *class battleship* Vittorio Veneto.

Vittorio Veneto *in 1943. Note light AA*

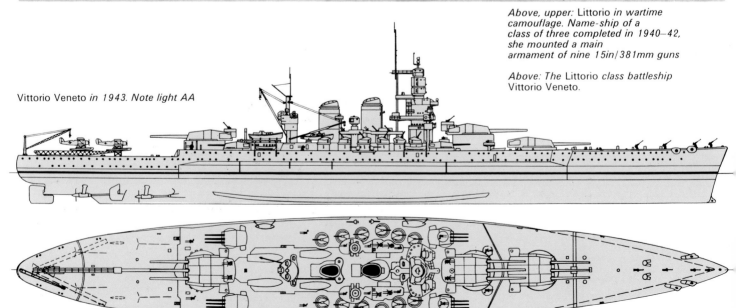

Condottieri Class

LIGHT CRUISER

CLASS: *Condottieri* type (12 ships)
Group 1 (4 ships) *Alberto di Giussano · Giovanni delle Bande Nere · Alberico da Barbiano · Bartolomeo Colleoni*
Group 2 (2 ships) *Armando Diaz · Luigi Cadorna*
Group 3 (2 ships) *Raimondo Montecuccoli · Muzio Attendolo*
Group 4 (2 ships) *Emanuele Filiberto Duca d'Aosta · Eugenio di Savoia*
Group 5 (2 ships) *Luigi di Savoia Duca degli Abruzzi · Giuseppe Garibaldi*

Displacement:	Giussano as built	Garibaldi as built
standard tons (tonnes)	5,191 (5,274)	9,195 (9,342)
normal tons (tonnes)	6,571 (6,676)	9,959 (10,118)
full load tons (tonnes)	6,954 (7,065)	11,262 (11,442)
Dimensions:		
length (pp)	524ft (160m)	562·6ft (171·8m)
(oa)	554·4ft (169·3m)	612·4ft (187m)
beam	50·8ft (15·5m)	61·9ft (18·9m)
draught	17·4ft (5·3m)	22·3ft (6·8m)
Armament:		
guns		
6in (152mm)	8	10
3·9in (100mm)	6	8
13·2mm	8	8
torpedo tubes		
21in (533mm)	4	6
aircraft	2	4
Armour:		
side (belt)	1in (24mm)	5·1in (130mm)
deck	0·8–1·6in (20–40mm)	1·6in (40mm)
main turrets	0·9in (23mm)	5·3in (135mm)
Machinery:		
boilers (type)	Yarrow	Yarrow
(number)	6	8
engines (type)	Beluzzo geared turbines	Parsons geared turbines
shafts	2	2
Total SHP:		
designed	95,000	100,000
trial (max)	123,479	104,030
Fuel capacity:		
oil tons (tonnes)	1,130 (1,150)	?
Performance:		
designed speed	37kts	34kts
trial speed (max)	42·05kts	37·78kts
range	4,520 miles (3,800nm) @ 18kts	?
Crew:	507	640

Above, upper: The Condottieri *(Group 4)* Emanuele Filiberto Duca d'Aosta *was completed in 1935. She ended service in 1957 as the Russian* Kerch *(ex-Z.15, ex-Stalingrad)*

Above: The Condottieri *class (Group 1) light cruiser* Giovanni delle Bande Nere. *She was sunk by HM submarine* Urge *on 1 April 1942*

Class:	CONDOTTIERI type				
	Group 1	**Group 2**	**Group 3**	**Group 4**	**Group 5**
Where built:	Ansaldo and Castellammare	CRDA and OTO	CRDA and Ansaldo	OTO and Ansaldo	OTO and CRDA
Authorised:	?	?	?	?	?
Laid down:	1928	1930	1931–1933	1932–1933	1933
Launched:	1930	1931–1932	1934	1934–1935	1936
Completed:	1931–1932	1933	1935	1935–1936	1937
Fate:	*Colleoni* sunk 19 July 1940; *Barbiano* and *Giussano* sunk 13 Dec 1941; *Bande Nere* sunk 1 Apr 1942	*Diaz* sunk 25 Feb 1941; *Cadorna* deleted May 1951	*Attendolo* sunk 4 Dec 1942; *Montecuccoli* deleted June 1964	*d'Aosta* to Russia in 1949 as *Z15*, renamed *Stalingrad*, renamed *Kerch*, deleted 1957; *Savoia* to Greece 1951, renamed *Elli* deleted 1964	*Abruzzi* deleted Apr 1961; *Garibaldi* deleted Jan 1972

The *Condottieris* represented Italian interwar light cruiser development, and each group was a class in itself. The first group was designed to cope with the 'super-destroyers' that France was building at that time and protection was sacrificed to speed. In fact, despite the high trial speeds (obtained when the ships were very lightly loaded and not fully complete), their service speed proved no better than those of their foreign contemporaries. This was how *Colleoni* was caught and sunk by the theoretically much slower Australian cruiser *Sydney*. The similar second group had altered lines to give more stability, a little more protection and a slightly revised anti-aircraft armament. The *Montecuccolis* had much better protection, a revised arrangement of main armament and a new type of tower bridge. The *Aostas* repeated the pattern of improving protection and stability and had unit machinery, but carried less ammunition. The last two ships were larger, better armed and better balanced than any of their predecessors. They had a new type of 6in (152mm) gun and their protection approached that of their foreign contemporaries. *Garibaldi* was extensively rebuilt between 1957–1962. Her original armament was removed and her funnels trunked. She was fitted with two twin 5·3in (135mm) mounts forward, a twin Terrier SAM launcher in X position, and tubes for four Polaris ICBMs in Y position. Although she never carried the missiles, she was the only surface ship to be fitted for this weapon.

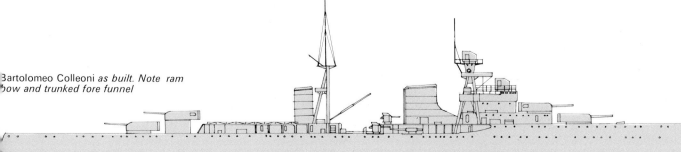

Bartolomeo Colleoni as built. Note ram bow and trunked fore funnel

Zara
HEAVY CRUISER
CLASS: *Zara* class (4 ships) *Zara ·*
Fiume · Gorizia · Pola

Displacement:
standard tons (tonnes)	11,870 (12,060)
normal tons (tonnes)	13,580 (13,797)
full load tons (tonnes)	14,530 (14,762)

Dimensions:
length (pp)	589·2ft (179·6m)
length (oa)	599·4ft (182·7m)
beam	66·6ft (20·6m)
draught (standard)	19·4ft (5·9m)
(max)	23·6ft (7·2m)

Armament:

	as built	in 1940
guns		
8in (203mm) 53cal	8	8
3·9in (100mm) 47cal	16	12
40mm	4	—
37mm	—	8
13·2mm	—	8
aircraft	2	2

Armour:
side (belt)	3·9–5·9in (100–150mm)
deck	2·75in (70mm)
main turrets	4·7–5·5in (120–140mm)
barbettes	5·5–5·9in (140–150mm)

Machinery:
boilers (type)	Thornycroft 3-drum
(number)	8
engines (type)	Parsons single reduction geared turbines
shafts	2

Total SHP:
designed	95,000
trials	118,000

Fuel capacity:
oil tons (tonnes)	2,116 (2,150)

Performance:
designed speed	32kts
trial speed (without armament)	34·2kts
range	5,360 miles (4,500nm) @ 16kts

Crew: 830

Zara: transverse section (see profile below)

Ship:	ZARA	FIUME	GORIZIA	POLA
Where built:	OTO, La Spezia	Stabilimento Technico, Trieste	OTO, Leghorn	OTO, Leghorn
Ordered:	27 Sept 1928	15 Sept 1928	16 Oct 1929	1930
Laid down:	4 July 1929	29 April 1929	17 March 1930	17 March 1931
Launched:	27 Apr 1930	27 Apr 1930	28 Dec 1930	5 Dec 1931
Completed:	20 Oct 1931	23 Nov 1931	23 Dec 1931	21 Dec 1931
Fate:	Sunk 29 March 1941	Sunk 28 March 1941	Scuttled 8 Sept 1943; salvaged by Germans; sunk 26 June 1944	Sunk 29 March 1941

Above: The heavy cruiser Zara in 1938. With emphasis on armour protection rather than range or speed, the Zaras were well suited to the Mediterranean

Zara as painted at Matapan, 28 March 1941. Note the air recognition stripes and catapult on the fo'c's'le and RO 43 seaplane. Her motto, Tenacemente, is painted on Y turret

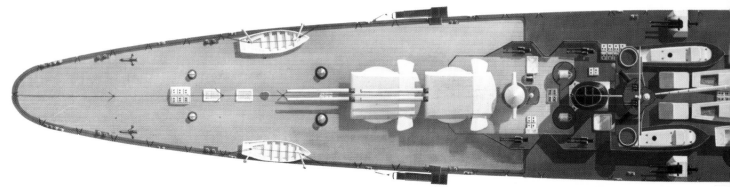

Service career ZARA

1931 onwards 1st Cruiser Division (Flagship Sept 1933–Nov 1938 and Jan 1940–March 1941).
1940 (June) Patrols from Taranto.
1940 (9 July) Action off Calabria: fired nine salvoes.
1940 (Aug–Nov) Patrols.
1941 (27–29 Mar) Battle of Cape Matapan.
1941 (28 Mar) Hit at 3,000 yards (2,745m) by 15in (380mm) shells from British battleships *Valiant, Barham* and *Warspite;* Fighting power destroyed.
1941 (29 Mar) Scuttled by crew; finished off by

three torpedoes from British destroyer *Jervis.*

The first Italian 'Washington Treaty' cruisers, the *Trentos,* were fast but lightly armoured and constructed. To achieve a high fairweather speed a large part of the displacement was taken up by the machinery, leaving only enough for a short 2.95in (75mm) belt and 1.97in (50mm) armoured deck, even though they exceeded the 10,000 ton (10,160t) limit. With no modern heavy units, Italy urgently required some well armoured ships to have a credible fleet. The result was the *Zaras,* which sacrificed a measure of range and speed in order to be better armoured than any foreign contemporary. Even so, the Italians found it difficult to fulfil their requirements without too obviously exceeding 10,000 tons. It had originally been intended to fit 7.87in (200mm) of armour in a flush-decked ship, but *Zara* had only 5.91in (150mm) of armour and was fitted with a long quarterdeck to save weight. Helped by the evasion of the Washington Treaty, however, the result was an excellent design well suited to Mediterranean conditions, where long range is not of prime importance.

One oddity was the fitting of the catapult on

the foc's'le, as in the *Trentos,* with the two sea-planes stowed in a hangar below. This exposed the catapult to weather and blast damage, but did keep the size of the ship down because room did not have to be found for it amidships. It also simplified the superstructure, and enabled a well sited (and for that date extremely large) anti-aircraft armament to be mounted.

Italian 8in (203mm) cruisers were not equipped with flashless ammunition, but this did not affect the result of the Battle of Cape Matapan. *Zara* and *Fiume* were caught with their turrets trained fore and aft, and poor Italian lookout and British use of radar meant that the Italian cruisers were smothered with pointblank fire from the British battleships before they could fire a shot. It is to the credit of her design that *Zara* proved so difficult to sink.

Fiume was also sunk in the same engagement. *Pola,* which was stopped on 28 March 1941 by a torpedo hit in her machinery space from a British carrier aircraft, was finally sunk by a British destroyer's torpedo. *Gorizia* was scuttled at La Spezia, salvaged by the Germans, then sunk again at La Spezia by Italian and British human torpedoes.

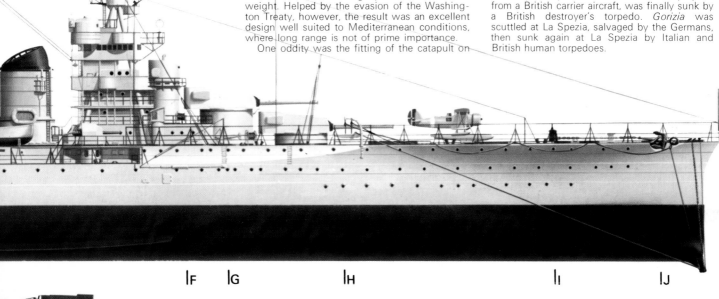

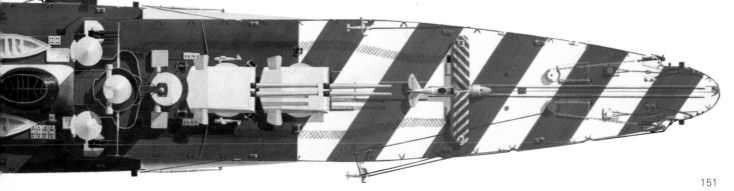

ITALIAN NAVY

Caio Duilio Class
ESCORT CRUISER
CLASS: *Caio Duilio* class (2 ships) *Andrea Doria* (C-553) · *Caio Duilio* (C-554)

Vittorio Veneto
HELICOPTER CRUISER
CLASS: *Vittorio Veneto* class (1 ship) *Vittorio Veneto* (C-550)

The *Caio Duilios* are the first of the modern escort cruisers, which can operate and maintain a number of A/S helicopters. They were evolved from the *Impavido* class destroyers, but are larger and beamier ships. They have a flush deck, and were designed round the ability to carry Terrier SAMs and four Agusta-Bell 204B A/S helicopters. The Terrier SAM twin-launcher is carried forward, and the 3in (76mm) AA single mounts are arranged around the slab-sided superstructure in lozenge fashion. They have unit machinery separated by living spaces, and the hangar is arranged around and abaft of the second funnel. The 98·5ft by 52·5ft (30m by 16m) flight deck is right aft, and is canti-levered out at the stern to ensure the maximum possible area for operating helicopters. *Andrea Doria* (C-553) was used for Harrier V/STOL aircraft handling trials in 1969 but she is too small to carry them operationally. They have SQS-23 hull-mounted sonar and two triple Mk 32 A/S torpedo tube mounts, one either side of the hangar. Although the *Caio Duilios* are very useful ships, they are really too small to fulfil their designed role. Despite being stabilised (like almost all modern warships) a larger hull is necessary to operate helicopters safely in rough weather, and the hangar and flight deck are extremely cramped. They also lack any weapons capable of countering a major surface threat. However, they are intended to operate under friendly air cover and as part of a task force, and *Caio Duilio* (C-554) will be fitted with Standard SAMs which have a limited SSM capability. Two designs were proposed for improved *Caio Duilios*. The first was for a large ship capable of being used for amphibious assault as well as for A/S work. In some ways she would

Above, upper: Vittorio Veneto *carries nine helicopters aft and can fire ASROC ASMs and terrier SAMs from the twin launcher forward*

Above: Caio Duilio *was completed in 1964. She carries a Sikorsky S-58 on the flight deck rather than the normal Agusta-Bell 204B*

have resembled the French *Jeanne d'Arc* (ex-*La Résolue*). She was originally to have been named *Italia*, though this was later changed to *Trieste*. This project was cancelled in 1968. The other project was for a larger *Caio Duilio*. This became *Vittorio Veneto* (C-550), and her design was considerably modified to take advantage of operational experience with the previous two ships. Like the *Caio Duilios*, she has a twin-launcher forward, but this can fire ASROC ASMs as well as Terrier SAMs, thereby providing the ship with a self-contained long-range A/S system. She also has her 3in (76mm) AA guns arranged in lozenge fashion round the superstructure, but has macks instead of funnels. In order to carry more than twice the *Caio Duilios*' number of helicopters, she has a raised quarterdeck over a hangar, which is served by two lifts. The flight deck measures 131ft by 60·6ft (40m by 18·5m), and the facilities for handling helicopters are much less cramped than on her predecessors. She is a very effective vessel, ideally suited for Mediterranean A/S warfare. Like the *Caio Duilios*, she lacks a powerful surface weapon, but she, like them, is designed to operate as part of a task force. She is the largest warship in the Italian Navy, and is used as the flagship. Several proposals have been made to build a larger version of *Vittorio Veneto* (C-550), but so far none of them have come to fruition, although a through-deck design of 10,000–12,000 tons is being developed by CNR for laying down possibly in 1980

Displacement:	Vittorio Veneto	Caio Duilio
standard tons (tonnes)	7,500 (7,620)	5,000 (5,080)
full load tons (tonnes)	8,850 (8,990)	6,500 (6,600)
Dimensions:		
length (oa)	589·2ft (179·6m)	489·8ft (149·3m)
beam	63·6ft (19·4m)	56·4ft (17·2m)
draught	19·7ft (6m)	16·4ft (5m)
Armament:		
guns		
3in (76mm) 62cal	8	8
missiles		
Astor (Terrier/ASROC) SAM/ASM launcher	1	—
Terrier SAM twin launcher	—	1
A/S weapons		
torpedo tubes		
12·7in (324mm)	6	6
aircraft	9 helicopters	4 helicopters
Machinery:		
boilers (type)	Foster-Wheeler	Foster-Wheeler
(number)	4	4
engines (type)	Tosi double reduction geared turbines	Tosi double reduction geared turbines
shafts	2	2
Total SHP:		
designed	73,000	69,000
Fuel capacity:		
oil tons (tonnes)	1,200 (1,220)	1,100 (1,120)
Performance:		
designed speed	32kts	31kts
range	6,000 miles (5,040nm) @ 20kts	6,000 miles (5,040nm) @ 20kts
Crew:	560	485

Ship:	VITTORIO VENETO (C-550)	ANDREA DORIA (C-553)	CAIO DUILIO (C-554)
Where built:	Castellammare Dockyard	Tirreno, Riva Trigoso	Castellammare Dockyard
Authorised:	1959	?	?
Laid down:	10 June 1965	11 May 1958	16 May 1958
Launched:	5 Feb 1967	27 Feb 1963	22 Dec 1962
Completed:	12 July 1969	23 Feb 1964	30 Nov 1964
Fate:	In service	In service; renamed before completion	In service

Audace Class

DESTROYER

CLASS: Audace class (2 ships)
Audace class, Italy, one ship ·
Audace ex-Intrepido ex-Japanese
Kawakaze · later German TA 20 ·
Urakaze class, Japan, one ship
Urakaze

Most Italian destroyers up to 1918 were designed in Britain, even though they were built in Italy. Audace was unique in that she was built in Britain for Japan, and purchased by Italy when she was almost complete. She was one of several warships of that period built in Britain and Germany to be designed to use turbines and diesels in an attempt to bypass the turbine's poor cruising performance. Urakaze and Kawakaze were inspired by the British Hardy, which had been designed for turbines and diesels, and were to have been fitted with Göttinger hydraulic couplings which were not delivered because of the war. With no couplings, the diesels were not fitted either. The two ships were designed as sisters, but Audace's armament was altered before completion.

Audace was reclassified as a torpedo boat on 1 September 1929, and became the control ship for the radio-controlled target ship San Marco from 1937 to 1940. She was given an extensive anti-aircraft armament in 1942 and, non-operational, was captured by the Germans at Venice on 12 September 1943. Repaired and renamed TA 20, she was sunk by the British escort destroyers Avon Vale and Wheatland.

Urakaze was used by the Japanese to develop their destroyer designs. She was sunk in an air attack at Yokosuka.

Below: Audace leaving Venice on 10 November 1918 with King Victor Emmanuel III on the fo'c's'le. The Royal standard is flying from the mainmast. Note the gap between bridge and fore funnel. The Japanese Urakaze was very similar apart from the armament

Displacement:

standard tons (tonnes)	816 (829)
full load tons (tonnes)	995 (1,011)

Dimensions

length (pp)	275·3ft (83·9m)
(oa)	285·1ft (86·9m)
beam	27·6ft (8·4m)
draught (mean)	8·2ft (2·5m)

Armament:

	Urakaze as built	Audace as built	Audace in 1942	Audace in 1944
guns				
4·7 (120mm) 40cal	1	—		
4in (102mm) 35cal	—	7	7	2
3in (76mm)	4	—		
40mm	—	2		
20mm	—	—	20	8
6·5mm	—	2		
torpedo tubes				
21in (533mm)	4	—	—	—
17·7in (450mm)	—	4	—	—

Machinery:

boilers (type)	Yarrow
(number)	3
engines (type)	Brown Curtis turbines
shafts	2

Total SHP:

designed	22,000

Fuel capacity:

oil tons (tonnes)	?

Performance:

designed speed	30kts
trial speed (light)	34·5kts
range	2,590 miles (2,180nm) @ 15kts

	as designed	**in 1942**
Crew:	118	120

Ship:	**URAKAZE**	**AUDACE**
Where built:	Yarrow, Scotstoun	Yarrow, Scotstoun
Ordered:	1913	1913
Laid down:	1913	1 Oct 1913
Launched:	1915	27 Nov 1915
Completed:	14 Sept 1915	23 Dec 1916
Fate:	Training ship 1 July 1936; renamed Hai Kan No 18; stricken 1939; hulk sunk 18 July 1945.	Originally Kawakaze; transfer to Italy agreed 3 July 1916; purchased 5 July 1916 and renamed Intrepido; renamed Audace 25 Sept 1916; seized by Germans 12 Sept 1943 and renamed TA 20; sunk 1 Nov 1944.

Audace in 1917. Note gap between break of fo'c's'le and fore funnel

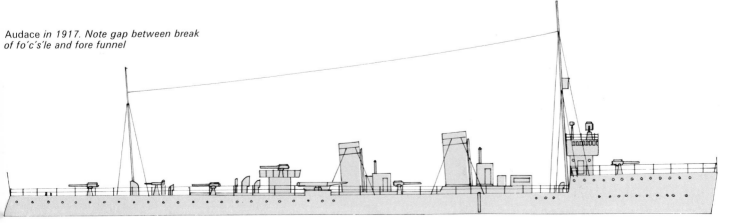

Audace Class
DESTROYER
CLASS: *Audace* class (2 ships)
Audace (D-551) · *Ardito* (D-550)

Displacement:	
standard tons (tonnes)	3,600 (3,660)
full load tons (tonnes)	4,400 (4,470)
Dimensions:	
length (oa)	448·2ft (136·6m)
beam	47·2ft (14·4m)
draught (average)	15·1ft (4·6m)
Armament:	
guns	
5in (127mm) 54cal	2
3in (76mm) 62cal	4
missiles	
Tartar SM-1 SAM single launcher	1
A/S weapons	
torpedo tubes	
21in (533mm)	4
12·7in (324mm)	6
aircraft	2 helicopters
Machinery:	
boilers (type)	Foster-Wheeler
(number)	4
engines (type)	geared turbines
shafts	2
Total SHP:	
designed	73,000
Performance:	
designed speed	33kts
range	?
Fuel capacity:	
oil tons (tonnes)	?
Crew:	380

Above: The destroyer Audace, *completed in 1972, has the capacity to operate two Agusta-Bell 204B or one Sikorsky SH-3D Sea King ASW helicopters*

The *Impetuoso* class, the first postwar destroyers to be designed and built in Italy, were ordered in 1950, and were strongly influenced by American designs. Flushdecked and twin-funnelled, they were armed with American guns and fitted with American radar and sonar. However, they were closely tailored to Mediterranean requirements. In addition to four 5in (127mm) guns mounted in twin turrets fore and aft, they had a powerful anti-aircraft (16×40mm) and anti-submarine (Menon triple barrel mortar and ASW torpedo) armament and a high speed.

The next class, the *Impavidos* ordered in 1957 and 1959, were enlarged and improved versions with the aft 5in mount replaced by a single Mk 13 Tartar SAM launcher capable of launching Tartar or Standard missiles. There is magazine space for 40 missiles. The 40mm guns were replaced by the Italian Brescia 3in (76mm) gun. They have no hangar, but operate a single Agusta Bell 204B ASW helicopter from the stern. In the late 1960s, replacement of the *Impetuosos'* aft twin 5in mount with a single Tartar SAM launcher was considered but not carried out.

The *Audace* class is a further enlargement and development of the *Impavidos*. On a slightly larger hull, the American twin 5in mount is replaced by two single superimposed OTO Melara guns. The AA armament amidships is the 3in (76mm) OTO Melara Compact mount, and a hangar has been provided aft for one Sikorsky SH-3D Sea King ASW helicopter. The Mk 13 missile-launcher is mounted above the hangar, and has a magazine capacity of 40 missiles. The ships have a comprehensive fit of US radar and the Dutch full mounted sonar.

Ship:	AUDACE (D-551)	ARDITO (D-550)
Where built:	Tirreno, Riva Trigoso	Castellammare Dockyard
Ordered:	Apr 1966	Apr 1966
Laid down:	27 Apr 1968	19 July 1968
Launched:	2 Oct 1971	27 Nov 1971
Completed:	16 Nov 1972	5 Dec 1972

Medusa Class
SUBMARINE
CLASS: *Medusa* class (8 boats)
including *Medusa* · *Velella*

The Italians built a number of submarines prior to 1914, the most successful of which were the Fiat-Laurenti boats designed by Colonel Cesare Laurenti. Like the French Laubeuf type, the Fiat-Laurenti submarines had double hulls, but unlike the Laubeufs the inner pressure hull was not circular. The biggest class of Fiat-Laurenti submarines built prior to World War I was the *Medusas*. Their two torpedo tubes were mounted side-by-side beneath the forefoot. Submarines were built to this design for Russia, and also under licence in Britain, and a slightly larger boat was built in America. The first Russian boat, *Sviotoy Georgi*, was seized by the Italian navy in 1915 and renamed *Argonauta*, but another was built to replace it and delivered in 1917. *Argonauta* was later fitted with a 3in (76mm) gun. The British *S* class were built by Scotts, Greenock between 1913 and 1915. The British found they were inferior to their own designs and since they were dissimilar from other British submarines they were transferred to Italy in September 1915, as were the Laubeuf-designed *W* class in August 1916. The American-built *Thrasher* (later *S-4*) (SS-26) was a slightly enlarged version and was not very successful. During World War I the *Medusas* were based in the northern Adriatic. *Jalea* was mined off Trieste, and *Medusa* was torpedoed by the German submarine *UB-15*. In December 1917 *Argo* started a conversion into an assault submarine. It was intended to use her to force the entrance of the Austrian fleet base at Pola. An improved version, the *24 F* class, were built from 1915. Like *Argonauta*, these were fitted with a 3in (76mm) gun.

Displacement:		
surface tons (tonnes)	300 (306)	
submerged tons (tonnes)	345 (350)	
Dimensions:		
length (oa)	147·9ft (45·2m)	
beam	13·8ft (4·2m)	
draught	9·8ft (3m)	
Armament:		
torpedo tubes		
17·7in (450mm)	2	
Machinery:	**Velella**	**remainder**
diesels (type)	MAN	Fiat
(number)	1	2
electric motors (type)	Siemens	Savigliano
shafts	2	2
Total BHP:	650	
Total SHP:	300	
Fuel capacity:		
oil tons (tonnes)	?	
Performance:		
surface speed	12·5kts	
submerged speed	8kts	
range (surface)	1,430 miles (1,200nm) @ 8kts	
(submerged)	64 miles (54nm) @ 6kts	
designed diving depth	130ft (40m)	
Crew:	22	

Class:	MEDUSA class
Where built:	various yards
Authorised:	?
Built:	1910–1912
Fate:	*Jalea* sunk 17 Aug 1915; *Medusa* sunk 10 June 1915; remainder paid off 26 Sept 1918

Right: Medusa *class submarine* Medusa *just after being launched from the FIAT-San Giorgio shipyard at La Spezia on 30 July 1911*

EnricoTotiClass

SUBMARINE

CLASS: *Enrico Toti* class (4 boats)
Enrico Toti (S-506) · *Attilio Bagnolini* (S-505) · *Enrico Dandolo* (S-513) · *Lazzaro Mocenigo* (S-514)

The postwar Italian Navy's first submarines were three World War II boats, two *Flutto* and one *Acciaio* class, that were eventually rebuilt with streamlined bows and conning towers, and given new equipment. Five modernised *Gato* and *Balao* class submarines were transferred from America, but the first to be built in Italy after World War II were the *Enrico Toti* class. As requirements changed, their design was recast several times, but was finalised before construction began as a coastal hunter-killer submarine. Intended for the shallow and confined waters of the central Mediterranean and Adriatic, their restricted surface range is no handicap, and enables the size to be kept down. They are small and highly manoeuvrable, with a teardrop hull and single screw, and they have diesel-electric drive. The active sonar is mounted in a dome on top of the bow, and the passive sonar is contained in the stem. The four torpedo tubes are also mounted in the bow. They have been succeeded in production by the much larger *Nazario Sauro* class, the first of which was launched on 9 October 1976. To maintain the size of Italy's submarine force, two more modernised *Balaos* and two *Tang* class submarines have been transferred from America between 1972 and 1974.

Above: Lazzaro Mocenigo, *a coastal hunter-killer submarine, has four 21in/533mm torpedo tubes. The dome on the boat's bow houses the active sonar gear*

Enrico Toti as built. Note single screw, streamlined hull and fin and sonar dome

Displacement:

standard tons (tonnes)	460 (467)
surface tons (tonnes)	524 (532)
submerged tons (tonnes)	582 (591)

Dimensions:

length (pp)	?
(oa)	151·5ft (46·2m)
beam	15·4ft (4·7m)
draught	13·1ft (4m)

Armament:

torpedo tubes 21in (533mm)	4

Machinery:

diesels (type)	Fiat
(number)	4
electric motor (type)	?
shafts	1

Total BHP: ?
Total SHP: 2,200

Fuel capacity:

oil tons (tonnes)	?

Performance:

surface speed	14kts
submerged speed	15kts
range (surface)	3,000 miles (2,500nm) @ 5kts
(submerged)	?
designed diving depth	?

Crew: 26

Ship:	ENRICO TOTI (S-506)	ATTILIO BAGNOLINI (S-505)	ENRICO DANDOLO (S-513)	LAZZARO MOCENIGO (S-514)
Where built:	CRDA Monfalcone	CRDA, Monfalcone	CRDA, Monfalcone	CRDA, Monfalcone
Authorised:	?	?	?	?
Laid down:	15 Apr 1965	15 Apr 1965	10 March 1967	12 June 1967
Launched:	12 March 1967	26 Aug 1967	16 Dec 1967	20 Apr 1968
Completed:	22 Jan 1968	16 June 1968	25 Sept 1968	11 Jan 1969
Fate:	In service	In service	In service	In service

Carlo Bergamini Class

FRIGATE

CLASS: *Carlo Bergamini* class (4 ships) *Luigi Rizzo* (F-596) · *Carlo Margottini* (F-595) · *Carlo Bergamini* (F-593) · *Virgilio Fasan* (F-594)

Originally rated as fast corvettes, the *Carlo Bergamini* class are much larger developments of the *Albatros* class corvettes built under the American 'Offshore' Mutual Defence Assitance Programme. *Carlo Bergamini* herself was to have been built at Taranto Naval Yard, but the order was transferred to CRDA's San Marco yard at Trieste. After launching she was transferred to CRDA's Monfalcone yard, also at Trieste, for completion. They are flush decked anti-submarine frigates, and were originally armed with three 3in (76mm) guns, two of which were mounted forward and one aft. The Menon automatic loading A/S mortar was mounted just forward of the bridge, and there was a small helicopter landing pad abaft the funnel with a tiny telescopic hangar from which an Agusta-Bell 47 helicopter was operated. This had virtually no offensive capabilities, and so the entire class were rebuilt to take the Agusta-Bell 204B helicopter. This can carry a dipping sonar and two Mk 44 lightweight torpedoes. The aft 3in (76mm) mount was removed and the landing pad extended over it, and the telescopic hangar was enlarged. The design was developed first into the mixed gas turbine- and diesel-powered *Alpino* class, built 1963–1968, and then into the *Lupo* class, armed with Otomat SSMs, which is building for Italy, Peru and Venezuela.

Below: The Carlo Bergamini *class frigate* Carlo Margottini, *one of a class of four completed 1961–62. Note the Menon A/S mortar mounted just forward of the bridge*

Displacement:		
standard tons (tonnes)	1,410 (1,430)	
full load tons (tonnes)	? 1,650 (? 1,680)	
Dimensions-		
length (pp)	283·3ft (86·5m)	
(oa)	311·7ft (95m)	
beam	37·1ft (11·4m)	
draught	10·2ft (3·1m)	
Armament:	**as built**	**as rebuilt**
guns		
3in (76mm)	3	2
A/S weapons		
Menon single-barrel mortar	1	1
torpedo tubes		
12·7in (324mm) Mk 32	6	6
aircraft	1 helicopter	1 helicopter
Machinery:		
diesels (type)	Fiat or Tosi	
(number)	4	
shafts	2	
Total BHP		
designed	15,000	
Fuel capacity:		
oil tons (tonnes)	?	
Performance:		
designed speed	24·5kts	
range	4,350 miles (3,600nm) @ 18kts	
Crew:	158	

Ship:	LUIGI RIZZO (F-596)	CARLO MARGOTTINI (F-595)	CARLO BERGAMINI (F-593)	VIRGILIO FASAN (F-594)
Where built:	Castellammare Dockyard	Castellammare Dockyard	CRDA Trieste	Castellammare Dockyard
Authorised:	?	?	?	?
Laid down:	26 May 1957	26 May 1957	19 May 1959	6 March 1960
Launched:	6 March 1960	12 June 1960	16 June 1960	9 Oct 1960
Completed:	15 Dec 1961	5 May 1962	23 June 1962	10 Oct 1962
Rebuilt:	1971	1968	1970	1969
Fate:	In service	In service	In service	In service

Spica Class

TORPEDO BOAT

CLASS: *Spica* class (32 ships)
Group 1 (2 ships) *Spica* (later
Romulus) · *Astore* (later *Remus*) ·
Group 2 (6 ships) including *Castore* ·
Cassiopea · Group 3 (8 ships)
including *Sirio* · *Sagittario* ·
Group 4 (16 ships) including *Clio* ·
Calliope

The naval treaties of the interwar years allowed torpedo boats to be built in unrestricted numbers, provided they were under 600 tons (610 tonnes) standard displacement. The Italians, like the French, Germans and Japanese, built numbers of this type of vessel, although none of them stuck to the displacement restriction. The *Spica* class, the first to be built, were originally designed in 1932. They were basically small destroyers with a good armament for their size but with a short range. This, however, made them useful ships for the Mediterranean. They saw considerable service during World War II, several being sunk in gallant actions with superior British forces. Though not really intended for anti-submarine work they played their part in sinking at least five Allied submarines. The few surviving after the war were converted to anti-submarine vessels in the early 1950s. They retained only one of their 3·9in (100mm) guns, but were fitted with a powerful A/S armament, and they were reclassified as fast corvettes.

Right: Spica, name-ship of a class of 32 torpedo boats built in 1933–38, was sold to Sweden in 1940

	Group 1 as built	Group 4 as built
Displacement:		
standard tons (tonnes)	630 (640)	679 (690)
full load tons (tonnes)	901 (915)	1,050 (1,067)
Dimensions:		
length (pp)	255·5ft (78m)	258·7ft (79m)
(oa)	263·1ft (80·4m)	266·7ft (81·4m)
beam	26·9ft (8·2m)	25·9ft (7·9m)
draught	9·2ft (2·8m)	10·1ft (3·1m)
Armament:		
guns		
3·9in (100mm)	3	3
40mm	4	—
13·2mm	4	8
torpedo tubes		
17·7in (450mm)	4	4
mine capacity	20	20
Machinery:		
boilers (type)	Yarrow	
(number)	2	
engines (type)	Tosi geared turbines	
shafts	2	
Total SHP:		
designed	19,000	
Fuel capacity:		
oil tons (tonnes)	?	?
Performance:		
designed speed	34kts	
range	2,055 miles (1,728nm) @ 16kts	2,270 miles (1,910nm) @ 15kts
Crew:	99	116

Class:	**SPICA class**
Where built:	various yards
Authorised:	?
Built:	1933–1938
Fate:	*Spica* and *Astore* to Sweden 1940, renamed *Romulus* and *Remus*; 23 sunk 1940–1944; remainder rebuilt 1950–1953, deleted 1958–1964

Sparviero Class

GUIDED-MISSILE HYDROFOIL

CLASS: *Sparviero* class (1 ship)
Sparviero (P-420)

Displacement:	
standard tons (tonnes)	?
full load tons (tonnes)	62·5 (63·5)
Dimensions:	
length (foils down)	75·3ft (23m)
(foils up)	80·7ft (24·6m)
beam (foils down)	22·9ft (7m)
(foils up)	39·7ft (12·1m)
draught	
(foils down, hull-borne)	14·4ft (4·4m)
foil-borne	4·3ft (1·3m)
Armament:	
guns	
3in (76mm) 62cal	1
missiles	
Otomat SSM	2
Machinery:	
diesel (type)	?
(number)	1
retractable propeller	1
gas turbines (type)	Rolls-Royce Proteus
(number)	1
water jet pumps	2
Total BHP:	4,500
Total SHP:	?
Fuel capacity:	
oil tons (tonnes)	?
Performance:	
designed speed	50kts
range	400 miles (336nm) @ 45kts
Crew:	10

Ship:	**SPARVIERO (P-420)**
Where built:	Alinavi, La Spezia
Authorised:	?
Laid down:	April 1971
Launched:	March 1973
Completed:	15 July 1974
Fate:	In service; nine more planned

In the early 1960s the Americans built three experimental hydrofoil patrol boats. These were tested for several years then between 1966 and 1968 two competitive patrol hydrofoils were built. *Flagstaff* (PGH-1), built by Grumman, was a conventional surface piercing hydrofoil with two struts forward and one aft. *Tucumcari* (PGH-2), based on the previous *High Point* (PCH-1), adopted her fully submerged foil system. This uses one strut forward and two aft. It is inherently unstable, and when foil-borne relies on a small computer and a wave height sensing system to keep the foils submerged and hull clear of the water. The foils can be retracted for cruising. *Tucumcari* (PGH-2) displaced 58 tons (59 tonnes) light, and was armed at one time with one 40mm and two twin 0·5in (12·7mm) machine-guns and one 81mm mortar. Powered by one Rolls-Royce Proteus gas turbine with water-jets when foil-borne, and a General Motors diesel for cruising, she had a foil-borne speed of over 40kts. She was discarded in 1973, but in her five years of trials operated successfully in Sea State 6, despite being designed for Sea State 4. *Sparviero*

Above: The guided missile hydrofoil Sparviero, completed 1974, carries two Otomat Mk 1 SSMs and was intended as the basis for a NATO hydrofoil class

(P-420) is an improved version of *Tucumcari*, with a slightly larger hull and greatly improved armament. She was designed and built by Alinavi, a consortium of Boeing, the Italian government and the Italian commercial hydrofoil builder Carlo Rodriguez. She was intended as the basis for a NATO hydrofoil class, but like most western patrol hydrofoils, only the prototype has so far been built. A further nine of this class and four similar to the US *Pegasus* are planned in the 1975 *Legge Navale*. She is well suited for short-range operations in the Mediterranean, and has successfully fired Otomat Mk 1 SSM, which have an effective range of over 37 miles (31mm).

JAPAN

DESPITE a scattering of maritime operations over the years it was not until the 19th century that the Imperial Japanese Navy was founded. With a British naval mission in the country it was not surprising that the majority of the fleet was built in British yards. Twenty-two years after its formation the Japanese Navy was engaged in the successful war against China, then much weakened internally and by external aggression. The centre of the struggle was Korea and it was here and in the Yellow Sea that Japan fought the naval war. In the years immediately after the end of hostilities in 1895 there was a press of foreign interest in the North-West Pacific — Russia, Germany, France, Britain and USA all moved in and Japan's alarm reached a peak after the Russian annexation of Manchuria following the Boxer rebellion of 1899–1900.

In a matter of a few years Japan was one of the five leading naval powers in the world so far as order-of-battle was concerned. The fluency of their strategic thought had been shown in the Chinese war — it was soon to be put to the test again. In 1902 the Anglo-Japanese Treaty was agreed and almost simultaneously Russia failed to honour an agreement with China to leave Manchuria, began to make threatening noises over Korea and strengthened her fleet in the Pacific. She was clearly spoiling for the war which came in 1904. Once more the Japanese concentrated on a single area, the Yellow Sea, and put new theories of torpedo-attack into practice. Within six months and with the army's help, the majority of the Russian fleet was sunk or interned in the Chinese ports to which it had fled. In October 1904 the Russian Baltic Fleet was despatched to the Far East to redress the balance only to be demolished by Togo at the Battle of Tsushima in May 1905. Four months later peace was concluded.

Five years later in 1910 Japan ordered its last foreign built battle-cruiser and, with only two years to the foundation of the Chinese Republic, was supreme in the North-West Pacific, a position bolstered by a renewal of her Treaty with Great Britain in 1911. The war of 1914 gave her further excuse for expansion. She occupied Tsingtao and the German Pacific Islands — in 1915 she was pressing hard upon China. By 1918 she had formulated a six-year programme of four battleships, three cruisers, twenty-one destroyers and forty-eight submarines, a plan drastically curtailed by the 1921 Washington Naval Treaty. In 1930 the London Treaty re-imposed rationing on naval building programmes, a move much reviled by the military caste in Japan. The murder of the Prime Minister stimulated a violent nationalist reaction in 1931 and within three years her quitting of the League of Nations and renunciation of the naval treaties led, on the naval side, to a rapidly expanding building programme.

Not only were the aims of the military rulers greatly inflated; so also were the sizes of some of their ships. Bigger guns were put in bigger battleships, large aircraft carriers were designed, huge submarines laid down. Although some of the senior admirals were opposed to war with America the motion of the machine was not to be stayed. In December 1941 the brilliantly planned attack on Pearl Harbor led to six months of triumph. In June 1942 the intervention of the American carriers at the Battle of Midway turned the scales. Four Japanese carriers sunk with a high proportion of the best aircrew was a deadly blow. Perhaps even more deadly was the effect of the American submarine operations in Japanese home waters, a contingency that had not been anticipated in Tokyo. Anticipated or not, this campaign sank some five million tons of shipping. This success highlighted the fiasco of the Japanese submarines. A complete failure to appreciate the true aims and nature of submarine warfare had led to the construction of vast and vulnerable craft designed to work with the fleet or for specialised operations.

Today many of the lessons of 1941–45 have been applied to the build-up of the Japanese Maritime Self-Defence Force, an efficient and steadily expanding fleet.

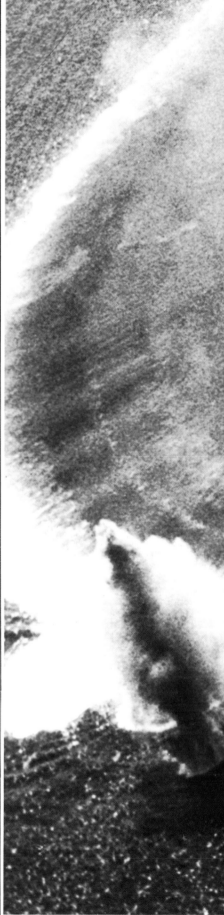

The Ashigara class cruiser Nachi *under bombardment, Manila Bay, 1944*

Akagi

AIRCRAFT-CARRIER
CLASS: *Amagi* class (1 ship) *Akagi*

Service career AKAGI

1919 Ordered as battle-cruiser.
1922 (5 Feb) Work suspended.
1922 (Nov–March 1927) Completed as aircraft-carrier.
1930 Forward 7·9in (200mm) turrets raised one deck.
1936 (Apr–Aug 1938) Rebuilt: hull bulged, two bow flight decks and bow 7·9in (200mm) turrets removed. Main flight deck lengthened, existing two lifts enlarged and third lift added, fixed island fitted on port side, machinery removed, funnels modified and 4·7in (120mm) replaced by 5in (127mm) anti-aircraft guns.
1939–1942 Flagship of Carrier Division 1.
1941 (7 Dec) Pearl Harbor attack.
1942 (Jan–March) Raids in South-West Pacific.
1942 (Apr) Raid in Indian Ocean.
1942 (4–6 June) Battle of Midway.
1942 (5 June) Hit by two bombs from US carrier aircraft: severely damaged and set on fire.
1942 (6 June) Sunk by torpedoes from Japanese destroyers.

The *Amagi* class battlecruisers were laid down as part of the 8-8 plan, which was intended to provide Japan with eight modern battleships and eight modern battle-cruisers in answer to the USA's large building programme of 1916. The *Amagis* were intended to counter the *Lexingtons*, and were the battle-cruiser version of the *Tosa* class battleships. These were improved *Nagatos* with a flush decked hull with torpedo bulges, an extra 16in (406mm) turret, a sloped main belt and a single funnel. The *Amagis* developed 40,000 SHP more, giving an extra 4kts on a 60ft (18m) longer hull. They had two funnels, and carried their third turret one deck higher. The armour thicknesses were slightly reduced. However, the entire programme was cancelled under the terms of the Washington Treaty. Japan was allowed to convert two *Amagis* into aircraft-carriers to balance with the British and Americans, but although *Amagi* began her conversion, she was damaged beyond repair by the Tokyo earthquake of 1 September 1923, and had to be scrapped. The *Tosa* class battleship *Kaga* was therefore reprieved and converted in her stead. As first converted *Akagi* had a main flight deck 624ft (190·2m) long, with two lifts from the hangars. She was completed without an island, but was soon given a small navigating bridge to starboard. There was a very clumsy arrangement of funnel uptakes on the starboard side amidships. The forefunnel exhausted at an angle downwards, but the aft funnel was vertical and frequently exhausted smoke and fumes over the main flight deck. The 7·9in (200mm) guns were arranged in two twin turrets on the lower hangar flight deck forward, and in individual casemates

Displacement:	battle-cruiser design	aircraft-carrier as built in 1927	as rebuilt in 1938
standard tons (tonnes)	40,000 (40,640)	26,900 (27,330)	36,500 (37,080)
normal tons (tonnes)	41,217 (41,878)		
full load tons (tonnes)	47,000 (47,750)	33,693 (34,232)	42,541 (43,221)
Dimensions:			
length (pp)	770ft (234·7m)	763ft (232·6m)	771ft (235m)
(wl)	820ft (230m)	817ft (249m)	821·5ft (250·3m)
(oa)	826·75ft (251·8m)	855·3ft (260m)	855·3ft (260·6m)
beam (wl)	101ft (30·8m)	95ft (29m)	102·75ft (31·3m)
(flight deck)	—	100ft (30·5m)	100ft (30·5m)
draught	31ft (9·5m)	26·5ft (8·1m)	28·5ft (8·6m)
Armament:			
guns			
16in (406mm) 50cal	10	—	—
7·9in (200mm) 50cal	—	10	6
5·5in (140mm)	—	—	12
4·7in (120mm)	4	12	—
25mm	—	—	28
torpedo tubes			
24in (610mm)	8	—	—
aircraft	—	60	91
Armour:			
side (belt)	10in (254mm)		
deck (main)	0·8–4in (20–102mm)		
main turrets	9–11in (229–280mm)		
barbettes	9–11in (229–280mm)		
Machinery:			
boilers (type)	Kanpon	Kanpon	Kanpon
(number) (coal)	8	8	—
(coal and oil)	11	11	—
(oil)	—	—	19
engines (type)	Gijutsu Honbu turbines	Gijutsu Honbu turbines	Kanpon geared turbines
shafts	4	4	4
Total SHP:			
designed	131,200	131,200	133,000
Fuel capacity:			
coal max tons (tonnes)	2,000 (2,030)	2,100 (2,130)	—
oil max tons (tonnes)	4,000 (4,060)	3,900 (3,960)	5,770 (5,860)
Performance:			
designed speed	30kts	31kts	31kts
range	?	9,510 miles (8,000nm) @ 14kts	9,750 miles (8,200nm) @ 16kts
Crew:	1,600	?	1,340

Ship:	AKAGI	AMAGI	ATAGO	TAKAO
Where built:	Kure Dockyard	Yokosuka Dockyard	Kawasaki Dockyard	Mitsubishi, Nagasaki
Authorised:	1918	1918	1918	1918
Laid down:	6 Dec 1920	16 Dec 1920	22 Nov 1921	19 Dec 1921
Cancelled:	—	—	5 Feb 1922	5 Feb 1922
Started conversions:	Nov 1923	1923	—	—
Launched:	22 Apr 1925	—	—	—
Completed:	3 March 1927	—	—	—
Fate:	Scuttled 6 June 1942	Hull destroyed on slip 1 Sept 1923; wreck scrapped incomplete 1923–1924	Scrapped incomplete	Scrapped incomplete

in the hull at the stern. She had two lifts, and her flight deck sloped up from the stern to a point just aft of the funnels to aid landing aircraft. *Kaga* was converted in a somewhat similar fashion, but had two long horizontal funnels one on each side just below the flight deck exhausting near the stern. Both were rebuilt in the late 1930s. *Akagi* had her main flight deck

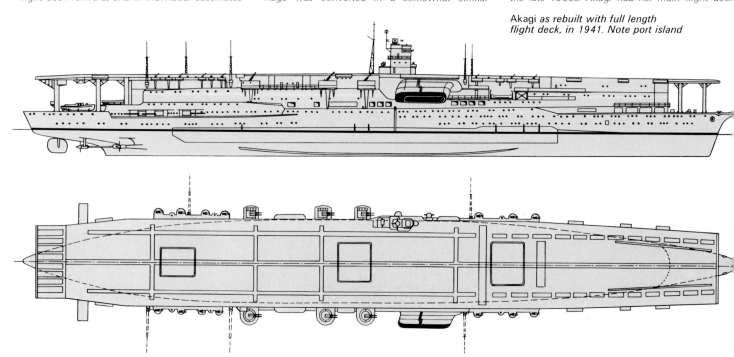

Akagi as rebuilt with full length flight deck, in 1941. Note port island

engthened to 817·75ft (249·2m), the lower light decks being removed, the space being lated in and converted into a hangar for an xtra 31 aircraft. A third lift was added forward. he second funnel was removed and the remaining one was enlarged. As with *Hiryu*, *Akagi* was itted with an island on the port side. It was ntended that *Kaga* (which was given a starboard island) and *Akagi*, and *Soryu* and *Hiryu*, should operate as pairs, with their aircraft naking circuits on opposite sides of each

ship so that they would not interfere with each other. Unfortunately the idea was a failure, and was not repeated. As battle-cruisers, the *Amagi* class would have easily outfought the *Lexingtons*, being superior in everything but speed, but as first converted *Akagi* was not so successful. They made much less use of the available displacement, and it was not until the late 1930s rebuild that *Akagi* became almost the equal of the *Lexingtons* as an aircraft carrier. *Kaga* was sunk at the Battle of Midway 1942.

Below, upper: Akagi *at sea in mid-1941; in December 1941 she participated in the attack on Pearl Harbor. She was sunk in the Battle of Midway, on 6 June 1942*

Below: Akagi, *seen here in 1939, was based on the hull of an* Amagi *class battlecruiser. She was able to operate 91 aircraft after rebuilding 1936–38*

Yamato
BATTLESHIP
CLASS: *Yamato* class (3 ships)
Yamato · Musashi · Shinano
(converted to aircraft carrier)

Service career YAMATO
1942 (12 Feb) Became flagship of Combined Fleet.
1942 (4–6 June) Battle of Midway.
1942 (Aug–May 1943) Based at Truk.
1943 (May–July) To Japan and refit at Kure.
1943 (July–Dec) Based at Truk.
1943 (24 Dec) Torpedoed by US submarine *Skate*.
1943 (Dec–April 1944) To Japan: repairs and refit at Kure.
1944 (May) To Singapore.
1944 (June) Battle of Philippine Sea, then to Japan.
1944 (July–Oct) At Singapore.
1944 (24–26 Oct) Battle of Leyte Gulf, fired at US escort carriers.
1944 (23 Nov–April 1945) Based in Japan.
1945 (6–7 Apr) Sortie to Okinawa.
1945 (7 Apr) Sunk by US air attack.

The *Yamato* class were the largest and most powerful battleships ever built, and the only ones this century to carry guns larger than 16in (406mm) calibre. Under the terms of the Washington and London Treaties, Japan was limited to fewer capital ships than either Britain or the United States. She refused to extend the Treaties on 31 December 1936, but her limited production facilities made it difficult to build sufficient battleships and aircraft-carriers simultaneously. Fatally, this was what was attempted, overstraining Japan's building capacity and resulting in severe delays to both the carrier and the battleships, and so neither were available in sufficient strength when they were most needed. The size of the projected large battle ships, which became the *Yamato* class, was determined by the largest size of battleship the Japanese considered the Americans would build. They thought, wrongly, that the US Navy would insist on ships being able to use the Panama Canal so that they could transfer rapidly from the Atlantic to the Pacific and vice-versa, and when the first plans were drawn up for the *Yamato*

(all data, except gun armament, are for YAMATO as built)

Displacement:

standard tons (tonnes)	64,000 (65,020)
final tons (tonnes)	69,500 (70,605)
full load tons (tonnes)	72,809 (73,970)

Dimensions:

length	(pp)	800·5ft (244m)
	(wl)	839·9ft (256m)
	(oa)	862·9ft (263m)
beam	(wl)	121·1ft (36·9m)
	(ext)	127·6ft (38·9m)
draught (mean)		38·4ft (11·7m)

Armament:

guns	in 1941	in 1945
18·1in (460mm) 45cal	9	9
6·1in (155mm) 55cal	12	6
5in (127mm) 40cal	12	24
25mm	24	146
13mm	4	—
aircraft	6	6

Armour:

side (belt)	3·9–16·1in (100–410mm)
deck	7·9–9in (200–230mm)
main turrets	7·5–25·5in (190–650mm)
barbettes	15–22in (380–560mm)
secondary turrets	1in (25mm)

Machinery:

boilers (type)	Kanpon
(numbers)	12
engines (type)	Kanpon geared turbines
shafts	4

Total SHP:

designed	150,000
trials	153,000

Fuel capacity:

oil tons (tonnes)	6,300 (6,400)

Performance:

designed speed	27kts
trial speed	27·46kts
range	7,200 miles (6,054nm) @ 16kts

Crew: 2,200

Ship:	YAMATO	MUSASHI	SHINANO	No 111
Where built:	Kure Dockyard	Mitsubishi, Nagasaki	Yokosuka Dockyard	Kure Dockyard
Ordered:	1937	1937	1939	1939
Laid down:	4 Nov 1937	29 March 1938	4 May 1940	7 Nov 1940
Launched:	8 Aug 1940	11 Nov 1941	8 Oct 1944	—
Completed:	16 Dec 1941	5 Aug 1942	19 Nov 1944	—
Fate:	Sunk 7 April 1945	Sunk 24 Oct 1944	Completed as aircraft-carrier 29 Nov 1944	Cancelled Sept 1942

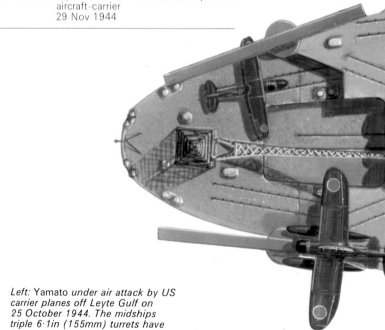

Left: Yamato *under air attack by US carrier planes off Leyte Gulf on 25 October 1944. The midships triple 6·1in (155mm) turrets have been replaced by more AA guns*

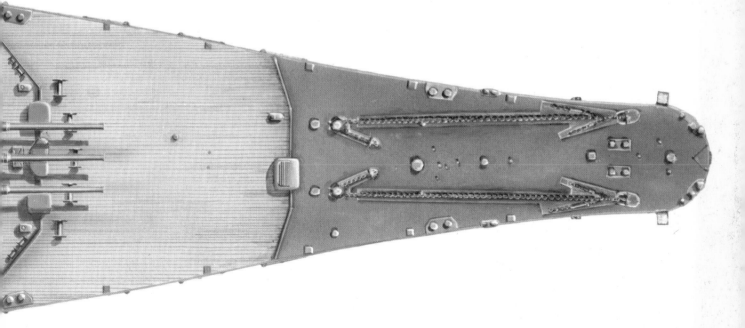

Yamato *in final condition in 1945.
Note the powerful AA armament and
the aircraft arrangements aft. She
is carrying Mitsubishi F1M2 'Pete'
and Aichi E13A1 'Jake' seaplanes*

Above: Kongo *class battleship* Hiei *as demilitarized at a fleet review in the 1930s.* A and Y turrets have been removed. The aircraft carrier Kaga lies astern

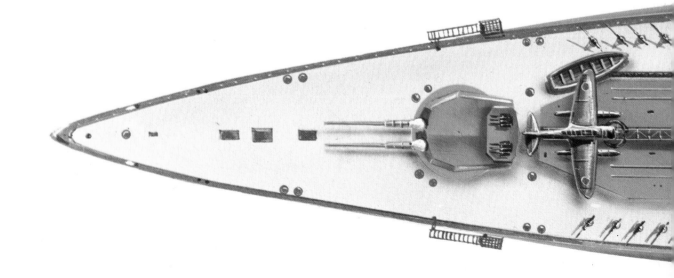

Above: Four Japanese battleships in the 1930s. From top to bottom they are the Ise class Hyuga *and* Ise, *the* Kongo *class* Kirishima *and the* Nagato *class* Nagato. *Behind lies a* Tenryu *class light cruiser*

Kongo *in 1944. Note bulges amidships, pagoda foremast with radar at the foretop, additional AA guns and Aichi E13A1 'Jake' seaplane on the catapult*

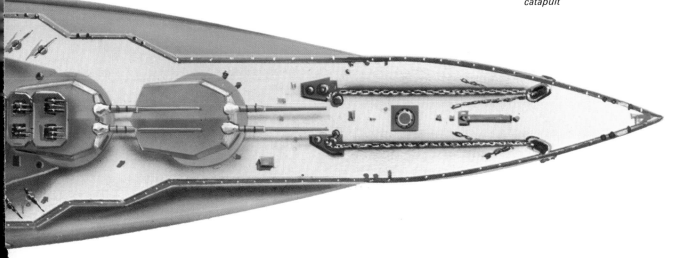

class in March 1935 the Japanese considered that the Americans would be limited to a battleship of 63,000 tons (64,000 tonnes) standard displacement, with an armament of ten 16in (406mm) guns and a speed of not more than 23kts. The first Japanese plans were for a ship of 69,500 tons (70,610 tonnes) standard displacement, with a speed of 31kts. This was too big even for the Japanese, and the size was reduced by limiting the speed to 27kts. Twenty-three different designs were drawn up before the final one was accepted in March 1937. At one stage it was intended to fit diesel engines to give greater range on less fuel. Designs were prepared with diesels as main engines or as cruising engines with steam turbines for the main machinery. However, the diesels fitted in other Japanese warships proved extremely unreliable, and they were abandoned in the final design. The hull form was unusual. If *Yamato*'s draught

had been comparable with contemporary foreign battleships, she would not have been able to use most Japanese fleet anchorages, and the use of a relatively shallow draught meant that the *Yamatos* had an immense beam. The large bulbous bow reduced resistance by over 8 per cent at full speed. To reduce weight the main armour belt, inclined at 20° to the vertical, was incorporated as an integral part of the hull. The armour was intended to resist 18·1in (460mm) shells, and the armour deck rested on top of the armour belt. This 'armoured raft' was relatively short, and the ends of the ship were very vulnerable. The underwater protection was also comparatively poor for a ship of this size. Weight was also saved by welding parts of the hull, but surprisingly *Yamato* had both low and high angle rather than weight-saving dual-purpose medium calibre guns. The triple 6·1in (155mm) guns, taken from the *Mogami* class

light cruisers, were a weak point in the design, since the armour on these turrets was not thickened when they were fitted on the battleships. The blast from the main armament was such that the light AA guns and boats were originally fitted with light armoured shields, and a hangar was provided for the aircraft in the stern. On her final sortie, *Yamato* only had fuel for a one-way trip. She was overwhelmed in two hours. *Musashi* was almost identical to *Yamato* and they normally operated together. She was sunk by US carrier-borne aircraft.

Shinano was completed as an aircraft-carrier, but was sunk by the American submarine *Archerfish* before even running trials. *No 111* was cancelled when less than 30 per cent complete, and the material was re-used to build aircraft-carriers.

Right: Yamato *running trials in original condition in 1941. Note the piled-up superstructure, undulating deck line, and 6·1in (155mm) turret amidships. The Y-shaped spreader carries radio aerials*

The Imperial Standard of Japan

The ensign of the Imperial Japanese Navy

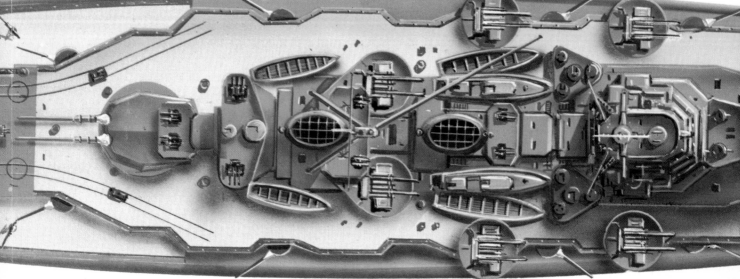

Kongo

FAST BATTLESHIP

CLASS: *Kongo* class (4 ships)
Kongo · Hiei · Haruna · Kirishima

Service career KONGO

1913 (16 Aug) Turned over to IJN: Classed as battle-cruiser.
1913 (28 Aug–5 Nov) Delivery voyage from Plymouth to Yokosuka.
1914 (Aug–Sept) Escort duty in Central Pacific.
1917 Director Control Tower fitted.
1920 Forefunnel raised.
1921 Fitted to carry seaplanes.
1924 Fire control improved and main armament elevation increased.
1927 'Pagoda' bridge mast fitted.
1928 Improved funnel cap fitted on second funnel.
1929 (Sept– March 1931) First major reconstruction: deck, magazine and turret armour and underwater protection strengthened; 14in (356mm) guns elevation increased to 43°; boilers replaced and forefunnel removed; fitted to carry three seaplanes; reclassified as battleship.
1933 Catapult fitted between X and Y turrets.
1936 (Jan–Jan 1937) Second major reconstruction: stern lengthened by 25ft (7·6m); new machinery fitted and speed raised by 4kts; fuel capacity increased and two 6in (152mm) guns and torpedo tubes removed.
1941 Vertical protection and barbettes of main turrets strengthened.
1941 (Dec–March 1942) Escorted Malaya invasion force and covered Japanese landings in Indonesia.
1942 (March–Apr) Raid in Indian Ocean.
1942 (4–6 June) Battle of Midway.
1942 (Oct–Jan 1943) Operations in Solomon Islands.
1942 (13 Oct) Bombarded Henderson Field on Guadalcanal.
1943–1944 Refits in Japan: anti-aircraft armament strengthened; Type 21 and Type 22 radar fitted; six 6in (152mm) guns removed.
1944 (19–22 June) Battle of Philippine Sea.
1944 (July) Refit in Japan: anti-aircraft armament increased; Type 13 radar fitted.
1944 (24–25 Oct) Battle of Leyte Gulf.
1944 (29 Oct) Fired at US escort carriers.
1944 (21 Nov) Hit and sunk by one torpedo from American submarine *Sealion*.

Kongo was the largest and last Japanese capital ship to be built abroad. Although the two previous classes had been built in Japan, *Kongo* was so much larger and faster that it was decided to have the first member of the class built abroad as a pattern. The other three were built in Japanese yards, although many of their parts were made in Britain and shipped out. *Kongo* was based on the British *Lion* class battlecruisers, but incorporated many improvements to meet Japanese requirements. A new British 14in (356mm) gun was fitted to match American developments, and the third main turret was moved from between the funnels to a position aft of the superstructure, though it was still awkwardly placed between the boilers and the engine rooms. *Kongo* herself served as a model for the British *Tiger*. Like most British-designed battle-cruisers, *Kongo* suffered from very weak armour protection, which was theoretically penetrable by heavy shells at most ranges. Even so, she was still a formidable vessel against lighter units, and carried a heavy armament at high speed. In both 1916 and 1917 the British, who were overstretched in both the North Sea and the Mediterranean, tried to borrow or buy the *Kongos*. However, the Japanese were unwilling to part with four of their six modern heavy units, so this came to nothing. Throughout the interwar period the *Kongos* underwent a continuous series of minor improvements, and they were completely rebuilt twice. The Washington Treaty deprived Japan of the 8-8 programme capital ships, and the IJN was very short of battleships. The *Kongos*' first reconstruction was intended to bring them into line as far as possible with the *Nagato* class, and after reconstruction they were reclassified as battleships. More detailed improvements followed, but the growth of the new Japanese fast carrier force created a need for high speed escorts. Therefore, the *Kongos* underwent a second reconstruction, after which they were again reclassified as fast battleships. However, they

Displacement:	Kongo in 1912	Kongo in 1931	Kongo in 1937	
standard tons (tonnes)	26,330 (26,750)	29,330 (29,800)	32,156 (32,670)	
trial tons (tonnes)	27,900 (28,340)	31,780 (32,290)	36,610 (37,190)	
Dimensions:				
length (pp)	629ft (191·7m)	629ft (191·7m)	654ft (199·3m)	
(wl)	695ft (211·8m)	695ft (211·8m)	720·5ft (218·6m)	
(oa)	705ft (214·6m)	705ft (214·6m)	723·5ft (222m)	
beam	92ft (28m)	95·25ft (29m)	95·25ft (29m)	
draught (trial)	27·5ft (8·4m)	28·5ft (8·7m)	31·8ft (9·7m)	
Armament:	**in 1912**	**in 1931**	**in 1937**	**in 1944**
guns				
14in (356mm) 40cal	8	8	8	8
6in (152mm) 50cal	16	16	14	8
5in (127mm)	—	—	8	—
80mm	—	7	—	—
25mm	—	—	20	118
torpedo tubes				
21in (533mm)	8	4	—	—
aircraft	—	3	3	3
Armour:	**in 1912**	**in 1931**	**in 1937**	
side (belt)	6–8in (152–203mm)	6–8in (152–203mm)	6–8in (152–203mm)	
(ends)	3in (76mm)	3in (76mm)	3in (76mm)	
deck (upper)	1·5in (38mm)	1·5in (38mm)	1·5in (38mm)	
(lower)	0·75in (19mm)	0·75–4·75in (19–120mm)	0·75–4·75in (19–120mm)	
main turrets	3–9in (76–229mm)	6–9in (152–229mm)	6–9in (152–229mm)	
barbettes	10in (254mm)	11in (280mm)	11in (280mm)	
casemates	6in (152mm)	6in (152mm)	6in (152mm)	
Machinery:				
boilers (type)	Yarrow	Kanpon RO	Kanpon RO	
(number) (coal+oil)	36	6	—	
(oil)	—	4	8	
engines (type)	Parsons turbines	Parsons turbines	Parsons geared turbines	
Total SHP:				
designed	64,000	64,000	136,000	
Fuel capacity:				
coal tons (tonnes)	4,200 (4,270)	2,661 (2,704)	—	
oil tons (tonnes)	1,000 (1,020)	3,292 (3,345)	6,330 (6,430)	
Performance:				
designed speed	27·5kts	25·9kts	30kts	
range	9,520 miles (8,000nm) @ 14kts	11,300 miles (9,500nm) @ 14kts	11,660 miles (9,800nm) @ 18kts	
Crew:	1,221	1,118	1,437	

Ship:	KONGO	HIEI	HARUNA	KIRISHIMA
Where built:	Vickers, Barrow	Yokosuka Dockyard	Kawasaki, Kobe	Mitsubishi, Nagasaki
Ordered:	1910	1910	1911	1911
Laid down:	17 Jan 1911	4 Nov 1911	16 March 1912	17 March 1912
Launched:	18 May 1912	21 Nov 1912	14 Dec 1913	1 Dec 1913
Completed:	16 Aug 1913	4 Aug 1914	19 April 1915	19 April 1915
First conversion (reclassified as battleship):	Sept 1929– March 1931	Sept 1929– Dec 1932	July 1926– July 1928	March 1927– March 1930
Second conversion (reclassified as fast battleship):	Jan 1936– Jan 1937	Nov 1936– Jan 1940	Aug 1933– Sept 1934	June 1935– June 1936
Fate:	Sunk 21 Nov 1944	Scuttled 13 Nov 1942	Sunk 19 March 1945; wreck broken up 1945–1946	Sunk 15 Nov 1942

Above: Kongo *class battleship* Kirishima *in Sukumo Bay in 1937. She has completed her second reconstruction as a fast battleship. Note the Nakajima E8N 'Dave' seaplane on catapult*

classified as fast battleships. However, they were still very vulnerable to air, surface and underwater attack, but the effect of the treaty limitations had left Japan with little option but to improve these ships as far as possible. Most of the wartime improvements were aimed at strengthening the anti-aircraft armament. *Hiei* was not reconstructed as a battleship like the other three, but was converted into a demilitarised training ship under the terms of the Washington Treaty. Her second reconstruction brought her up to the same standard as her sisters. *Hiei*'s, *Haruna*'s and *Kirishima*'s wartime service was similar to *Kongo*'s. *Hiei* was damaged by US cruisers, destroyers and aircraft near Guadalcanal, and was finally scuttled. *Kirishima* was overwhelmed by the American battleship *Washington* after seriously damaging *South Dakota*. *Haruna* was sunk in shallow water by US carrier-borne aircraft.

Hosho

AIRCRAFT-CARRIER
CLASS: *Hosho* class (1 ship) *Hosho*

Service career HOSHO
1922 Experimental duties.
1923 Modified and bridge removed.
1924–1933 Experimental duties
1933 Refit: funnels modified.
1935–1939 Training ship.

1940–1941 Part of 1st fleet: operations off Chin[a] coast.
1941 (Dec–June 1942 Operations in Sou[th] China Sea.
1942 (June) Battle of Midway.
1942 (July–July 1945) Training ship.
1945 (19 March) Damaged in US air attack [on] Kure.
1945 (Aug) Surrendered.
1945–1946 Repatriation transport for Japanes[e] troops in China.

Displacement:

normal tons (tonnes)	7,470 (7,590)
full load tons (tonnes)	?

Dimensions:

length (pp)	510·2ft (155·5m)
(wl)	541·3ft (165·0m)
(oa)	552·2ft (168·3m)
beam (wl)	59·1ft (18·0m)
(ext)	74·5ft (22·7m)
draught	20·3ft (6·2m)

Armament:

	as built	in 1944
guns		
5·5in (140mm) 50cal	4	—
3in (76mm) 40cal	2	—
25mm	—	30
aircraft	21	21

Machinery:

boilers (type)	Kanpon
(number)	8
engines (type)	Kanpon geared turbines
shafts	2

Total SHP:

designed	30,000

Fuel capacity:

oil tons (tonnes)	550 (559)

Performance:

designed speed	25kts
range	8,680 miles (7,300nm) @ 12kts

Crew: 550

Ship:	**HOSHO**
Where built:	Asano, Tsurumi
Ordered:	1918
Laid down:	16 Dec 1919
Launched:	13 Nov 1921
Completed:	27 Dec 1922
Fate:	Scrapped 1947

Japan was one of the first countries to use sea[-] borne aircraft in action, at Tsingtao in 1914, an[d] although she was laid down after the Britis[h] carrier *Hermes*, *Hosho* was the first purpos[e] built carrier to be completed. Her hull, unlike tha[t] of *Hermes*, was based on that of an oil tanke[r]. When first built she had a small bridge to sta[r]board, with three movable funnels just abaft [of] it. She was also initially fitted with a primitiv[e] deck landing aid. The bridge was too small an[d] interfered with flying operations, so it was re[-] moved, and the funnels were later replaced wi[th] fixed ones to mitigate the smoke and fumes. Sh[e] was fitted with two lifts.

Hosho was very small, and after performin[g] the initial experiments from which Japan's ma[in] carrier force was to be developed, she wa[s] relegated to training pilots in carrier landing[s]. She was only briefly employed on active servic[e] since she was almost totally unprotected. Sh[e] soon returned to the training role, and after th[e] Japanese surrender was used as a troo[p] transport.

A considerably larger variant, *Shokaku*, wa[s] authorised in 1922, but was cancelled to enabl[e] *Kaga* and *Akagi* to be converted under the term[s] of the Washington Treaty.

Below: Hosho *soon after completion.*
The bridge and the three
moveable funnels were removed in
1933, when downward-facing
funnels were fitted

Hosho *after rebuilding. Note flush*
flight deck and three funnels

Soryu

AIRCRAFT-CARRIER
CLASS: *Soryu* class (2 ships)
Soryu · Hiryu

Displacement:	Soryu	Hiryu
standard tons (tonnes)	15,900 (16,160)	17,300 (17,580)
full load tons (tonnes)	18,800 (19,100)	20,250 (20,575)
Dimensions:		
length (pp)	677·5ft (206·5m)	677·5ft (206·5m)
(wl)	728·3ft (222m)	731·3ft (223m)
(oa)	746·2ft (227·5m)	746ft (227·3m)
beam (hull)	70ft (21·3m)	73·25ft (22·3m)
(ext)	85·3ft (26m)	88·5ft (27m)
draught	25ft (7·5m)	25·3ft (7·7m)
Armament:		
guns		
5in (127mm) 40cal	12	12
25mm	28	31
aircraft	71	73
Machinery:		
boilers (type)	Kanpon	
(number)	8	
engines (type)	Kanpon single reduction geared turbines	
shafts	4	
Total SHP:		
designed	152,000	153,000
Fuel capacity:		
oil tons (tonnes)	3,400 (3,454)	3,700 (3,760)
Performance:		
designed speed	34·5kts	34·33kts
range	7,680 miles (6,460nm) @ 18kts	7,670 miles (6,450nm) @ 18kts
Crew:	1,101	1,100

Ship:	SORYU	HIRYU
Where built:	Kure Dockyard	Yokosuka Dockyard
Authorised:	1934	1936
Laid down:	20 Nov 1934	8 July 1936
Launched:	23 Dec 1935	16 Nov 1937
Completed:	29 Dec 1937	5 July 1939
Fate:	Sunk 4 June 1942	Sunk 5 June 1942

Service career SORYU
1939 (to June 1942) 2nd Carrier Division.
1941 (7 Dec) Attack on Pearl Harbor.
1941 (21 Dec) Covered attack on Wake Island.
1942 (1 Jan–9 March) Covered landings in Dutch East Indies.
1942 (19 Feb) Air strike on Darwin.
1942 (March–Apr) Sortie in Indian Ocean.
1942 (June) Attack on Midway.
1942 (4 June) Battle of Midway: hit by three bombs and set on fire; exploded and sank.

In the interwar years the Japanese, like the Americans, considered their converted capital ships to be too large to be effective fighting vessels, tying up too great a percentage of their naval air arm in two ships. In any case, to build similar sized ships would be to use up far too much of the limited carrier tonnage permitted by the Washington Treaty. However, that treaty did not count carriers of less than 10,000 tons (10,160 tonnes) standard displacement towards the carrier tonnage total, and so Japan's next carrier, *Ryujo*, was originally designed to displace only 8,000 tons (8,130 tonnes) standard. When it was realised that this would result in her carrying too few aircraft to be an effective unit, an extra hangar deck was added to the design, raising the standard displacement to 10,600 tons (10,770 tonnes). As built she lacked stability (too much had been attempted on too small a hull), and she was fitted with larger bulges and a ballast keel, and all possible topweight was removed. Following damage on trials, her fo'c's'le was raised one deck in 1936. By the time the designs for *Soryu* were being prepared, it was already clear that *Ryujo* was far too small, and *Soryu* was made half as large again. Experience with *Kaga* and *Akagi* showed that a fixed island was essential, and this was fitted on the starboard side just ahead of the funnel uptakes, which exhausted at an angle downwards below flight deck level. As with all Japanese carriers of this period, the flight deck and upper hangar decks were not

Continued on page 172 ▶

Below: Hiryu *burning after attack by US carrier borne aircraft at Midway. Note the damage forward and the lift blown onto the forward end of the island by an explosion*

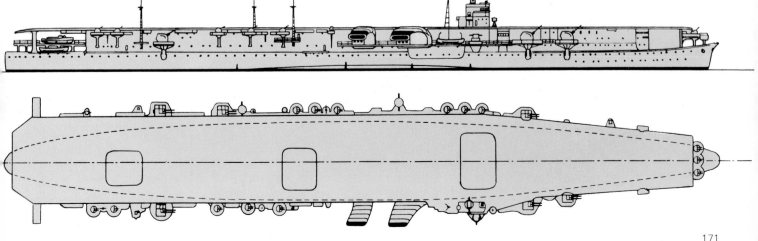

Soryu as built. Note low fo'c's'le, funnel downtakes, and three lifts

▶*Soryu*

strength decks, but were built on the hull as superstructure. The design had many good qualities. There were two hangars served by two large lifts, and she could operate a large number of aircraft for her size. The flight deck stretched virtually the length of the hull, and for the period the anti-aircraft armament was good, though it was controlled by only two directors. She also had a high speed. However, although at first glance she compared favourably with her larger American counterparts *Yorktown* and *Enterprise*, in practice the American ships were considerably superior. The Japanese designers had concentrated on carrying and operating the maximum number of aircraft combined with a sizeable gun armament, on the minimum tonnage, to evade as far as possible the treaty carrier tonnage limitations. The Americans, on the other hand, produced a balanced design that was far more seaworthy, and that had almost twice the bunker capacity, conferring a much greater radius of action. Whereas *Hornet* differed in only minor respects from *Yorktown*, *Hiryu*, *Soryu*'s half sister, was built to a considerably modified plan. To improve *Hiryu*'s stability, 1,400 tons (1,420 tonnes) of ballast were added, and the fo'c'sle

was raised by one deck to make her more seaworthy. She benefited by being completed after Japan had refused to extend the naval limitation treaties, but she would have been a much more effective ship if she had been designed to take full advantage of the improvements that were incorporated in her piecemeal. As with *Akagi*, the worst feature of the design was the positioning of the island on the port side. Because the uptakes were on the starboard side, both ships suffered from turbulence over the flight deck induced by the interaction of the disturbed airflow over the island and the hot funnel gases. Because the increasing size of carrier planes meant increased take-off runs, the island was placed further aft than normal to improve control, but this restricted the landing run. The next two ships, *Shokaku* and *Zuikaku*, remedied most of *Hiryu*'s defects. Unrestricted by treaties, they had a standard displacement of 25,675 tons (26,087 tonnes), and although they could carry only 11 more aircraft, they had a more seaworthy hull and a considerably improved radius of action. Their protection was also improved, although like all Japanese carriers until *Taiho* they did not have an armoured flight deck. They carried a very powerful anti-aircraft armament, although the four directors were not ideally

arranged, and the island was positioned one-third back on the starboard side, thereby eliminating the problems found with *Hiryu*. *Hiryu*'s design was resurrected when carriers were urgently required after Midway. The *Unryu* class closely followed *Hiryu*'s design, except that the bridge was repositioned to starboard and radar and more light anti-aircraft guns were fitted. This design was chosen because it could be produced more quickly than the later, larger carriers, but even so only three of the six laid down between August 1942 and July 1943 were completed by the end of the war. All the Japanese carriers completed before *Taiho* were either sunk or put out of action for long periods as the result of bombs penetrating the hangars through the unarmoured flight deck, and this was the reason for the loss of both *Soryu* and *Hiryu* at the Battle of Midway. *Hiryu* had a similar career to *Soryu*, but did not succumb immediately to the bomb damage as did her half-sister. She was scuttled the following day by torpedoes from the Japanese destroyers *Kazegumo* and *Yugumo*.

Below: Hiryu *runs trials in 1939. Positioning the island on the port side, with the uptakes to starboard, created turbulence over the flight deck*

Taiho
AIRCRAFT-CARRIER
CLASS: *Taiho* class (1 ship) *Taiho*

At the same time as the Japanese Navy was evading the Washington Treaty limitations on carrier tonnage by understating the size of their ships, they were also designing a number of fleet auxiliaries that could easily be converted into carriers if the necessity arose. These were the submarine depot ships *Tsurugizaki* (later *Shoho*), *Takasaki* (later *Zuiho*), *Taigei* (later *Ryuho*), and the seaplane carriers *Chitose* and *Chiyoda*, all of which were converted into aircraft-carriers between 1940 and 1943. In addition, a number of liners were converted into carriers, including *Nitta Maru* (later *Chuyo*), *Argentina Maru* (later *Kaiyo*) and *Scharnhorst* (later *Shinyo*). Although, like the British *Argus* and Italian *Roma*, these were intended as fleet rather than escort carriers, they were all small and underpowered. However, two liners, *Kashiwara Maru* and *Idzumo Maru*, had been designed (like the fleet auxiliaries) so that they could easily be converted into aircraft-carriers. Aviation fuel tanks were fitted from the start and space left for lifts. They were laid down in 1939 and requisitioned in October 1940 when they were about 50 per cent complete. They were finished as the aircraft-carriers *Hiyo* and *Junyo*, with two hangars, lifts and arrester wires. They were also fitted with a funnel on the large island, angled out at 26° to the vertical. This was the first time the funnel had been fitted on the island on a Japanese carrier, and it proved much more successful than those of previous designs, whose funnels vented below flight deck level. This feature was adopted by *Taiho*, which in other respects was a modified version of the *Shokaku* class. By the time *Taiho* was designed, the value of the armoured flight deck fitted to British *Illustrious* class carriers had already been demonstrated in the Mediterranean, and so *Taiho* was fitted with an armoured flight deck: she was the first Japanese carrier to have one. To offset the extra topweight, she was one deck lower than the *Shokakus*, and could operate fewer planes. She was fitted with the new 3·9in (100mm) anti-aircraft gun, and was also the

first Japanese carrier to have a fully enclosed bow, making her more seaworthy than previous Japanese designs. Her construction was not pressed forward with any urgency, despite the catastrophic Japanese carrier losses. However, the Japanese losses in trained naval aircrew were equally heavy and even more disastrous, because, unlike Britain and America, Japan lacked the facilities to train new naval aircrew in sufficient numbers. Thus when *Taiho* was ready for action, Japan no longer possessed sufficient trained aircrew to man her. However, she was lost not because of lack of aircrew, but because of poor detail design of the fuel pipes

and damage control system and because the ship was not yet fully worked up. With a properly trained crew it is unlikely that she would have exploded and sunk after only one torpedo hit. Two slightly modified *Taihos* were ordered under the 1942 programme, but were cancelled in favour of five slightly larger *Taihos* with a greatly increased anti-aircraft armament. These five were later cancelled in favour of simpler ships, however.

Below: Taiho; *by 1941, the* Illustrious *class had demonstrated the value of an armoured flight deck.*

Displacement:	
standard tons (tonnes)	29,300 (29,770)
full load tons (tonnes)	37,270 (37,870)
Dimensions:	
length (pp)	780·75ft (238m)
(wl)	830ft (253m)
(oa)	855ft (260·6m)
beam (hull)	90·75ft (27·7m)
(ext)	98·5ft (30m)
draught	31·5ft (9·6m)
Armament:	
guns	
3·9in (100mm) 65cal	12
25mm	51
aircraft	74
Machinery:	
boilers (type)	Kanpon
(number)	8
engines (type)	single reduction geared turbines
shafts	4
Total SHP:	
designed	160,000
Fuel capacity:	
oil tons (tonnes)	5,700 (5,790)
Performance:	
designed speed	33kts
range	10,000 miles (8,400nm) @ 18kts
Crew:	1,751

Ship:	**TAIHO**
Where built:	Kawasaki, Kobe
Authorised:	1939
Laid down:	10 July 1941
Launched:	7 Apr 1943
Completed:	7 March 1944
Fate:	Sunk 19 June 1944

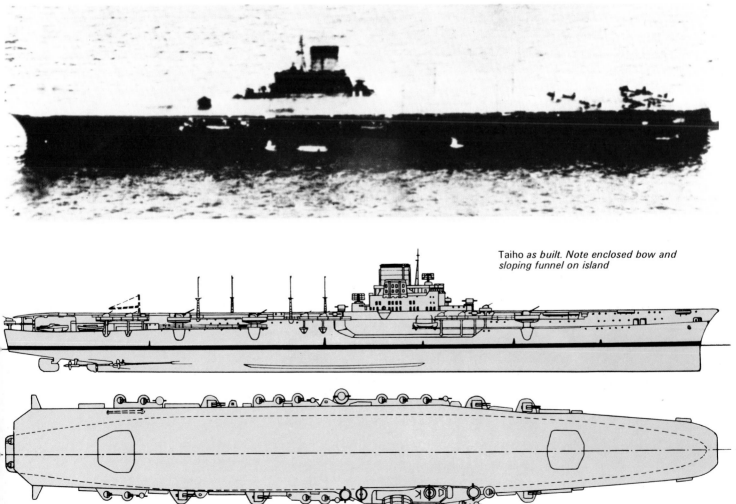

Taiho as built. Note enclosed bow and sloping funnel on island

Mikasa

BATTLESHIP
CLASS: *Mikasa* class (1 ship)
Mikasa

Service career MIKASA

1904 (Feb) Flagship Japanese combined fleet.
1904 (Feb–Jan 1905) Blockade of Port Arthur.
1904 (10 Aug) Battle of Yellow Sea: damaged.
1905 (27 May) Battle of Tsushima: damaged.
1905 (12 Sept) Suffered magazine explosion in Sasebo harbour and sank.
1906–1907 Salvaged.
1907–1908 Reconstructed: new main armament, and fighting top removed.
1914–1918 Coast defence duties.
1921 (Sept) Reclassified as 1st class coast defence ship.
1921 Covered Japanese force in Siberia.
1922 Disarmed.
1923 Stricken: preserved as national monument.
1944–1945 Badly damaged.
1960 Reinstated as national memorial.

Mikasa was the last of four very similar battleships built in British yards for Japan at the turn of the century. Under the 1896 programme, *Shikishima* (built by Thames Iron Works, London), *Asahi* (built by John Brown, Clydebank), *Hatsuse* (built by Armstrong Whitworth, Elswick) and *Mikasa* (built by Vickers, Barrow) were all built to the same basic specification. They had a normal displacement of about 15,000 tons (15,240t), a main armour belt of 9in (229mm) thickness, a speed of 18kts and an armament of four 12in (305mm) and fourteen 6in (152mm) guns. They were based on the British battleship *Majestic*, and in appearance were typical British battleships, with their virtues of high freeboard, good stability, and a clean unclutterd design with sensibly arranged armour. Each of the half-sisters differed (*Shikishima* having three funnels, the others two) because each yard did its own detail design. *Mikasa* benefited by being the last to be laid down. She had the new Krupp cemented armour, and her 6in (152mm) guns were in a battery rather than individual casemates, giving much improved protection. As with all Japanese warships from the mid-1880s to 1910, she was armed with Elswick guns.

Mikasa was the last Japanese battleship to be completed before the Russo–Japanese War, and was Admiral Togo's flagship. At the Battle of the Yellow Sea she had one 12in (305mm) gun completely destroyed, and was seriously damaged at Tsushima. Because she was at the

head of the Japanese line, she received most of the Russian fire. By 1905 she and her half-sisters were already obsolescent. The next two battleships, *Kashima* and *Katori*, already completing in British yards, were fitted with a mixed armament of 12in (305mm), 10in (254mm) and 6in (152mm) guns, and Japanese designers were already moving as a result of war experience to all-big-gun ships, though not necessarily with

all of the same calibre. The last surviving battleship of her period, she is now preserved in a drydock.

Below: An autographed picture of Admiral Heihachiro Togo, victor of Tsushima in 1905, with his flagship Mikasa, *now preserved as a national memorial.*

Displacement:		
normal tons (tonnes)	15,140 (15,382)	
full load tons (tonnes)	15,179 (15,423)	
Dimensions:		
length (pp)	400ft (121·9m)	
(wl)	415ft (126·5m)	
(oa)	432ft (131·7m)	
beam	76·2ft (23·2m)	
draught (max)	27·2ft (8·3m)	
Armament:	**as built**	**in 1908**
guns		
12in (305mm) 40cal	4	—
12in (305mm) 45cal	—	4
6in (152mm) 40cal	14	14
12pdr (76mm)	20	20
3pdr (47mm)	8	8
torpedo tubes		
18in (457mm) submerged	4	4
Armour:		
side (belt)	6–9in (152–229mm)	
(ends)	4in (102mm)	
deck	2–3in (51–76mm)	
main turrets	8–10in (203–254mm)	
barbettes	10–14in (254–356mm)	
battery	2–6in (51–152mm)	
Machinery:		
boilers (type)	Belleville	
(number)	25	
engines (type)	vertical triple expansion	
shafts	2	
Total SHP:		
designed	15,000	
trial	16,400	
Fuel capacity:		
coal normal tons (tonnes)	700 (711)	
max tons (tonnes)	1,521 (1,545)	
Performance:		
designed speed	18kts	
trial speed	18·6kts	
range	5,300 miles (4,450nm) @ 10kts	
Crew:	830	

Ship:	**MIKASA**
Where built:	Vickers, Barrow
Authorised:	1896
Laid down:	24 Jan 1899
Launched:	8 Nov 1900
Completed:	1 March 1902
Fate:	Preserved as national memorial 1923

Above: The 15,140-ton battleship Mikasa, *built in Britain by Vickers, Barrow, soon after completion in 1902. A British cruiser lies alongside in the dock*

Hyuga
BATTLESHIP
CLASS: *Ise* class (2 ships) *Ise · Hyuga*

Service career HYUGA
1918 1st Squadron.
1930–1931 Refit: pagoda mast fitted, two 5·5in (140mm) and four 3in (76mm) guns removed, eight 5in (127mm) guns added.
1935 (Aug–March 1937) total rebuild: new stern fitted, machinery replaced, hull bulged; 40mm and 13mm AA guns added, elevation of 14in (356mm) guns increased by 18° to 43°, two 5·5in (140mm) guns removed, main armour deck strengthened and a catapult fitted.
1940 40mm and 13mm guns replaced by 25mm.
1941–1942 2nd Battleship Squadron, 1st Fleet.
1942 (4–6 June) Battle of Midway.
1943 (July–Nov) Second rebuild: X and Y turrets removed and replaced by two-storey hangar with flight deck and a lift, all 5·5in (140mm) guns removed, eight 5in (127mm) and 37 25mm guns added.
1944 (June) 51 25mm guns added.
1944 (Sept) 180 5in (127mm) rockets fitted on flight deck.
1944 (20–27 Oct) Battle of Leyte Gulf: hit by one bomb, slight damage.
1945 (19 and 28 March) Attacked by US aircraft: damaged.
1945 (24 July) Sunk in shallow water in Kure by US aircraft.
1946 Wreck scrapped.

Japan's first dreadnoughts, *Kawachi* and *Settsu*, built between 1909 and 1912, were succeeded on the stocks by *Fuso* and *Yamashiro*. These were battleship versions of *Kongo*, and with a 3in (76mm) thicker armour belt and two extra 14in (356mm) turrets made 23kts on 40,000shp. The use of twin turrets made them much longer than their American triple-turreted contemporaries, but twin turrets have a higher rate of fire and are more reliable, and the long narrow hull made it easier to achieve the higher speeds required by the Japanese. The arrangement of the centre turrets was unique. The third turret was at fo'c's'le level between the funnels, and the fourth turret, abaft the second funnel, was mounted one deck higher. Two more ships of this class were projected, but the design was recast before they were laid down, and these became the *Hyuga* class. The centre turrets were better arranged in a superfiring pair abaft the second funnel, and they were the first Japanese ships to adopt the British 5·5in (140mm) gun. Both the *Fusos* and *Hyugas* were modernised interwar, receiving pagoda bridge masts, new machinery and lengthened sterns. After four carriers were lost at the Battle of

	as built	after first reconstruction in 1936	after second reconstruction in 1943
Displacement:			
standard tons (tonnes)	—	36,000 (36,575)	35,200 (35,760)
normal tons (tonnes)	29,980 (30,460)	—	—
full load tons (tonnes)	31,260 (31,760)	39,700 (40,340)	38,700 (39,310)
Dimensions:			
length (pp)	640ft (195m)	665ft (202·7m)	642ft (195·7m)
(wl)	675ft (205·7m)	700ft (213·3m)	700ft (213·3m)
(oa)	683ft (208·1m)	708ft (215·8m)	720·5ft (219·6m)
beam	94ft (28·6m)	111ft (33·8m)	111ft (33·8m)
draught	27ft (8·8m)	30ft (9·2m)	29·5ft (9m)
Armament:	**as built**	**in 1940**	**in 1943**
guns			
14in (356mm) 45cal	12	12	8
5·5in (140mm) 50cal	20	16	—
5in (127mm) 40cal	—	8	16
3in (76mm)	4	—	—
25mm	—	20	57
torpedo tubes			
21in (533mm)	6	—	—
aircraft	—	3	22
Armour:			
side (belt)	12in (305mm)		12in (305mm)
(ends)	3in (76mm)		3in (76mm)
deck (main)	2in (51mm)		2in (51mm)
(lower)	1·25in (32mm)		1·25–4·7in (32–120mm)
main turrets	8–12in (203–305mm)		8–12in (203–305mm)
barbettes	12in (305mm)		12in (305mm)
casemates	6in (152mm)		6in (152mm)
Machinery:			
boilers (type)	Kanpon coal and oil		Kanpon oil
(number)	24		8
engines (type)	Parsons or Curtis turbines		Kanpon geared turbines
shafts	4		4
Total SHP:			
designed	45,000		80,000
Fuel capacity:			
coal max tons (tonnes)	4,534 (4,607)	—	—
oil tons (tonnes)	1,389 (1,411)	5,229 (5,313)	4,182 (4,249)
Performance:			
designed speed	23kts	25–33kts	
range	11,510 miles (9,680nm) @ 14kts	9,360 miles (7,870nm) @ 16kts	11,240 miles (9,449nm) @ 16kts
Crew:	1,360	1,376	1,463

Ship:	ISE	HYUGA
Where built:	Kawasaki, Kobe	Mitsubishi, Nagasaki
Authorised:	1912	1912
Laid down:	10 May 1915	6 May 1915
Launched:	12 Nov 1916	27 Jan 1917
Completed:	15 Dec 1917	30 Apr 1918
1st rebuild:	Aug 1935–March 1937	Oct 1934–Sept 1936
2nd rebuild:	March 1943–Oct 1943	July 1943–Nov 1943
Fate:	Sunk 28 July 1945	Sunk 24 July 1945

Midway *Hyuga* and *Ise* were converted to carry bomber reconnaissance seaplanes. The flight deck that replaced X and Y turrets was not intended for landing-on, but was designed for handling the seaplanes. Neither was used operationally in this role, and by late 1944 the flight decks were used to mount extra anti-aircraft guns. *Ise* had a similar career to *Hyuga*, and was sunk in shallow water at Kure by American carrier-borne aircraft.

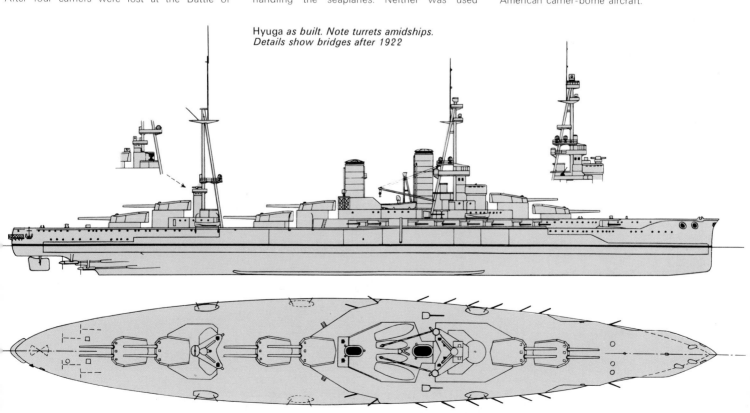

Hyuga *as built. Note turrets amidships. Details show bridges after 1922*

Nagato

BATTLESHIP
CLASS: *Nagato* class (2 ships)
Nagato · Mutsu

Above: Nagato *under air attack whilst returning at speed from Leyte Gulf in October 1944*

Above: Nagato, *seen here, and* Mutsu, *mounting 16in/406mm guns, were when built the most powerful battleships in the world*

Displacement:	as built:	as rebuilt in 1936
standard tons (tonnes)	32,720 (33,245)	38,000 (38,600)
normal tons (tonnes)	33,800 (34,340)	—
full load tons (tonnes)	38,500 (39,115)	42,785 (43,470)
Dimensions:		
length (pp)	660·75ft (201·2m)	660·75ft (201·2m)
(wl)	700·5ft (213·4m)	725·33ft (221·m)
(oa)	708ft (215·8m)	738ft (225m)
beam	95ft (29m)	113·5ft (346m)
draught	29·75ft (9m)	31ft (9·5m)
Armament:		
guns		
16in (406mm) 45cal	8	8
5·5in (140mm) 50cal	20	18
5in (127mm)	—	8
3in (76mm)	4	—
25mm	—	20
torpedo tubes		
21in (533mm)	8	—
aircraft	—	3
Armour:		
side (belt)	3–11·8in (75–300mm)	3–11·8in (75–300mm)
(ends)	3·9–7·9in (100–200mm)	3·9–7·9in (100–200mm)
deck (fo'c's'le)	1in (25mm)	2·5in (63mm)
(main)	1·7in (44mm)	1·7–2·7in (44–69mm)
(lower)	2–3in (50–75mm)	2–3in (50–75mm)
main turrets	14in (356mm)	14in (356mm)
barbettes	11·8in (300mm)	11·8in (300mm)
casemates	0·75–1in (19–25mm)	0·75–1in (19–25mm)
Machinery:		
boilers (type)	Kanpon	Kanpon
(number)	15 oil, 6 coal and oil	4 oil
engines (type)	Kanpon turbines	Kanpon geared turbines
shafts	4	4
Total SHP:		
designed	80,000	82,000
Performance:		
designed speed	26·75kts	25kts
range	6,540 miles (5,500nm) @ 15kts	10,300 miles (8,650nm) @ 16kts
Fuel capacity:		
coal tons (tonnes)	1,600 (1,625)	—
oil tons (tonnes)	3,400 (3,450)	5,600 (5,690)
Crew:	1,333	1,368

Ship:	**NAGATO**	**MUTSU**
Where built:	Kure Dockyard	Yokosuka Dockyard
Authorised:	1916	1917
Laid down:	28 Aug 1917	1 June 1918
Launched:	9 Nov 1919	31 May 1920
Completed:	25 Nov 1920	24 Oct 1921
Rebuilt:	April 1934–Jan 1936	Sept 1934–Sept 1936
Fate:	Sunk 29 July 1946	Blew up 8 June 1943

Service career NAGATO
1921 Forefunnel altered.
1924 Refit: forefunnel top swept back, bow altered and pagoda mast fitted.
1934 (Apr–Jan 1936) Rebuilt: machinery replaced, stern lengthened, hull bulged, forefunnel removed, pagoda mast enlarged; two 5·5in (140mm) and four 3in (76mm) guns removed; eight 5in (127mm) and 20 25mm anti-aircraft guns added; elevation of main guns increased by 13° to 43°.
1939–1941 Flagship of Combined Fleet.
1941 Barbette armour increased to 22in (500mm).
1941-1942 In Battleship Division 1, 1st Fleet.
1942 (4–6 June) Battle of Midway.
1942 (25 Dec) Hit by torpedo from US submarine *Skate* near Truk.
1944 Type 21 and Type 13 radar fitted, two 5·5in (140mm) guns removed and 78 25mm added.
1944 (20–26 Oct) Battle of Leyte Gulf: helped sink US carrier *Gambier Bay*.
1945 (Jan) Funnel and mainmast removed; used as floating anti-aircraft battery.
1945 (18 July) Damaged by US air attack.
1946 (1 and 25 July) Used as target for Bikini A-bomb tests.
1946 (29 July) Sunk.

The *Nagatos* were inspired by the British *Queen Elizabeth* class fast battleships. They were the first dreadnoughts to have 16in (406mm) guns and had a very high speed. They used a modified version of the *Hyugas'* hull, but the much larger 16in (406mm) shell, 2,185lbs (993kg) as opposed to the 14in (356mm) shell's 1,485lbs (675kg), meant that the number of guns could be reduced for the same weight of broadside. When built these were the most powerful battleships in the world, with an excellent balance between armament, protection, seaworthiness and speed. They were the first Japanese battleships to be fitted with the pagoda bridge mast, and were, like the others, reconstructed in the 1930s. *Mutsu* had a similar career to *Nagato*, but sank after a magazine exploded while the ship lay at anchor in Hashirajima Bay.

Mutsu *of the* Nagato *class in 1921.*
Note sextuple foremast and shape of bow

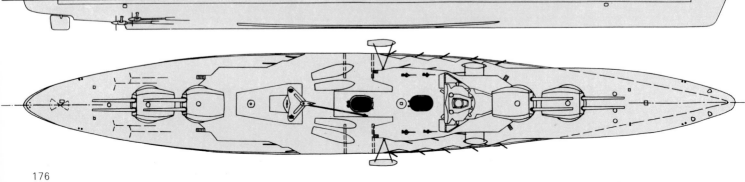

Mogami

HEAVY CRUISER
CLASS: *Mogami* class (4 ships)
*Mogami · Mikuma · Kumano ·
Suzuya*

Above: The heavy cruiser Mogami *in
1935. Trials revealed structural
weaknesses caused by extensive welding*

Service career MOGAMI

1936 (late-1937) Reconstructed due to lack of
stability and poor construction.
1939 Second reconstruction: triple 6·1in
(155mm) turrets replaced by twin 7·9in (200mm).
1939 (30 Dec) Recommissioned.
1941 (Dec–Mar 1942) Operations against
Malaya and Dutch East Indies.
1942 (28 Feb) Battle of Sunda Strait.
1942 (April) Operations in Indian Ocean.
1942 (June) Battle of Midway.
1942 (5 June) Rammed *Mikuma;* both ships
badly damaged.
1942 (6 June) Further damaged by US air
attack.
1942 (July–April 1943) Converted into seaplane
carrier: aft turrets replaced by flightdeck.
1943 (mid) To Truk.
1943 (5 Nov) Damaged by US air attack on
Truk.
1943 (Nov) Returned to Japan for repairs.
1944 (June) Battle of Philippine Sea.
1944 (Oct) Battle of Leyte Gulf.
1944 (25 Oct) Damaged by US battleships in
Surigao Strait; after further damage, sunk by
Japanese destroyer *Akebono.*

In the late 1920s Japan developed two very
successful classes of heavy cruiser, the *Myokos*
and *Takaos,* from the lightweight 7·9in (200mm)
gunned *Kakos* and *Aobas.* By paying only lip-
service to the weight limitations imposed by the
Washington Treaty, Japan had created a series
of fast, long ranged and powerfully armed heavy
cruisers, with an impressive ability to absorb
battle damage. However, by 1931 Japan had
built twelve heavy cruisers, the maximum permitted under the terms of the treaty. Determined
to overcome the inferiority with respect to the
US and Britain that this implied, Japan designed
a class of large light cruisers. These were only
light insofar as they were armed with 6·1in
(155mm) guns, which were the largest permitted for a light cruiser. They were designed
specifically so that twin 7·9in (200mm) mounts
could be substituted for the triple 6·1in (155mm)
when international regulations permitted. The
main armament was arranged in five turrets as
in the preceding heavy cruisers, with the third
rather than the second forward turret superfiring. The class carried a powerful anti-aircraft
battery, two catapults with three seaplanes, and
four triple 24in (610mm) torpedo tubes plus
reload torpedoes. They were also given the very
high speed of 37kts, though this was at the
expense of range.

However, despite the fact that they com-
fortably exceeded 10,000 tons (10,160t), too
much had been attempted on the displacement,
and serious weaknesses appeared in the hull
during the gunnery trials. Extensive use had
been made of welding to reduce weight, and
much of this proved defective in service. *Mogami*
and *Mikuma,* the first two ships to be completed,
were immediately sent to Kure dockyard to be
rebuilt, and the remaining two, *Kumano* and
Suzuya, were altered whilst still under construction. Stability, which had proved suspect,
was improved by increasing the beam with
added bulges. Opportunity was also taken to
upgrade the anti-aircraft armament. In 1939 the
6·1in (155mm) turrets were replaced by 7·9in
(200mm) twin mounts, and extra armour was
added outside the bulges, increasing the beam
still further to 66·3ft (20·2m). Some of the
surplus 6·1in (155mm) turrets were used, without increasing their armour, as secondary
armament on *Yamato* and *Musashi.*

Although the class were very effective and
powerful ships after the second reconstruction,
with an ability to shrug off a large amount of
battle damage, there is no doubt that even better
ships could have been produced if too much
had not originally been attempted on too small
a displacement, and the same ingenuity had
been used in producing a balanced design on
the original displacement. Even so, the class
had a very considerable effect on British and
American designs. Both the *Towns* and the
Brooklyns were designed after information had
been received about the *Mogamis,* and Britain
completely abandoned building the 8in (203mm)
cruiser after seeing the merits of the large light
cruiser.

Mogami was very seriously damaged in the
Battle of Midway, 5–6 June 1942, during which
Mikuma was sunk after being rammed by
Mogami, which was under repair until April
1943. She was rebuilt to resemble the *Tone*
class seaplane cruisers, themselves a modified
Mogami design. X and Y turrets were removed
and replaced by a level deck for handling seaplanes. She was sunk by US aircraft off Surigao.

Suzuya was sunk by aircraft from the US
escort carriers at Leyte Gulf.

Kumano was badly damaged at the Battle of
Leyte Gulf on 22 October 1944, her bow being
blown off. On 6 November 1944 she was
further damaged by torpedo hits from a US
submarine and was finally sunk off Luzon by air
attack.

Displacement	Mogami as built		Mogami in 1939	
Standard tons (tonnes)	?		12,400 (12,598)	
Full load tons (tonnes)	?		—	
Dimensions:				
Length (pp)	620·1ft (189m)		615·8ft (187·7m)	
(wl)	648·9ft (197·8m)		646·3ft (197m)	
(oa)	661·4ft (201·6m)		661·1ft (201·5m)	
Beam	59·1ft (18m)		66·3ft (20·2m)	
Draught	17·7ft (5·4m)		19ft (5·8m)	
Armament:	Mogami as built	Mogami in 1939	Mogami in 1943	
Guns				
7·9in (200mm) 50cal	—	10	6	
6·1in (155mm) 55cal	15	—	—	
5in (127mm) 40cal	8	8	8	
40mm	4	—	—	
25mm	—	8	30	
13mm	—	4	—	
Torpedo tubes				
24in (610mm)	12	12	—	
Aircraft	3	3	11	
Machinery:				
Boilers (type)	Kanpon			
(number)	10			
Engines (type)	single reduction geared turbines			
Shafts	4			
Total SHP:				
Designed	152,000		152,000	
Fuel capacity:				
Oil tons (tonnes)	?		?	
Performance:				
Designed speed	37kts		—	
Service speed	—		34·5kts	
Range	8,000 miles (6,726nm) @ 14kts			
Crew:	850		?	

Ship:	MOGAMI	MIKUMA	KUMANO	SUZUYA
Where built:	Kure Dockyard	Mitsubishi, Nagasaki	Kawasaki, Kobe	Yokosuka Dockyard
Authorised:	1931	1931	1931	1931
Laid down:	27 Oct 1931	24 Dec 1931	5 April 1934	11 Dec 1933
Launched:	14 March 1934	31 May 1934	15 Oct 1936	20 Nov 1934
Completed:	28 July 1935	29 Aug 1935	31 Oct 1937	31 Oct 1937
First reconstruction:	1937	1936–1937	—	—
Second reconstruction:	1939	1939	1939	1939
Fate:	Sunk 25 Oct 1944	Sunk 6 June 1942	Sunk 25 Nov 1944	Sunk 25 Oct 1944

*Mogami rebuilt as seaplane carrier in
1943. Note flight deck aft*

Kuma Class
LIGHT CRUISER
CLASS: *Kuma* class (5 ships)
Kuma · Tama · Kitakami · Kiso · Oi

The Japanese did not build any light cruisers between 1912 and 1917, and the first of the new type, the *Tatsutas*, were closely based on the British C type light cruisers. These ships were too small for the exposed Japanese waters and the next class, the *Kumas*, were half as large again, though they followed the same basic design. They were powerful ships, but the arrangement of the main armament on one level, with all but two guns on the centreline, had little to recommend it, although it was repeated in the subsequent *Nagara* and *Sendai* classes.

All except *Kiso* received a catapult between 1927 and 1935, and all were fitted with 24in (610mm) torpedo tubes in 1940. In 1941 *Kitakami* and *Oi* had their midsections sponsored out to enable five quadruple 24in (610mm) torpedo tubes to be fitted on each side.

Kitakami, after serving as a landing craft carrier with her torpedo tubes removed, was converted in February 1944 into a carrier for *Kaiten* suicide submarines whilst undergoing repairs for damage caused by a torpedo from the British submarine *Templar*. These could be dropped whilst she was underway. The aft engine room was converted into a hold and her speed was reduced. She was damaged in an air attack on 24 June 1945 but survived the war.

Kiso was sunk by air attack and the other members of the class were sunk by British and U.S. submarines. Like the British *C* and *D* classes, these ships were obsolete by World War II, and succumbed easily to modern torpedo attack.

Below: Kuma, *name-ship of a class of 5 light cruisers completed in 1920–21. She was torpedoed and sunk by the submarine HMS* Tally-Ho *on 11 January 1944*

Displacement:			
standard tons (tonnes)	5,100 (5,180)		
full load tons (tonnes)	5,830 (5,925)		
Dimensions:			
length (pp)	500·3ft (152·5m)		
(wl)	520ft (158·5m)		
(oa)	534·8ft (163·0m)		
beam	46·6ft (14·2m)		
draught	15·7ft (4·8m)		
Armament:	**as built**	**Kitakami in 1941**	**Kitakami in 1945**
guns			
5·5in (140mm) 50cal	7	4	4
13pdr (80mm) 40cal	2	—	—
25mm	—	36	·65
torpedo tubes			
21in (533mm)	8	—	—
24in (610mm)	—	40	—
mine capacity	80	—	—
Kaiten capacity	—	—	8
Armour:			
side	1·97in (50mm)		
deck	1·46in (37mm)		
Machinery:			
boilers (type)	Kanpon coal and oil fired and Kanpon oil fired		
(number)	2 and 10		
engines	Gihon geared turbines		
shafts	4		
Total SHP:			
designed	90,000	90,000	35,000
Fuel capacity:			
oil tons (tonnes)	1,500 (1,524)		
coal tons (tonnes)	300 (305)		
Performance:			
designed speed	36kts	36kts	23kts
range	9,000 miles (7,570nm) @ 10kts		
Crew:	439		

Class:	**KUMA class**
Ordered:	1917
Laid down:	1918–1919
Launched:	1919–1920
Completed:	1920–1921
Fate:	*Kuma* sunk 11 Jan 1944 by the British submarine *Tally-Ho*; *Tama* sunk 25 Oct 1944 by the US submarine *Jallao*; *Kitakami* scrapped 1947; *Kiso* sunk 13 Nov 1944 by air attack; *Oi* sunk 19 July 1944 by the US submarine *Flasher*

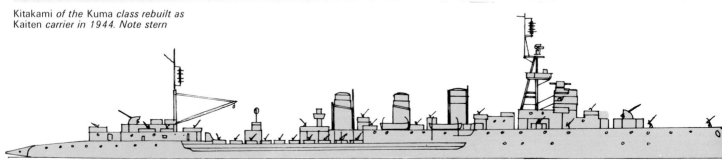

Kitakami of the Kuma *class rebuilt as* Kaiten *carrier in 1944. Note stern*

Kamikaze Class

DESTROYER

CLASS: *Kamikaze* class (9 ships)
including *Kamikaze · Harukaze*
(ex-Nos *1, 3, 5, 7, 9, 11, 13, 15, 17*)

In 1919 Japan evolved a new type of destroyer, influenced by German rather than British designs. The *Minekaze* class had a well between the bridge and the fo'c's'le to help break the force of the long Pacific swells. All the 4·7in (120mm) 45cal guns were mounted at fo'c's'le deck level to enable them to be fought in bad weather. They were the first Japanese destroyers with geared turbines.

The *Kamikazes* were an improved version, with a strengthened bridge and increased beam to maintain stability, and a new 50 calibre gun. The first five ships were originally given names in the 1920 programme. When the entire class was put in the 1921 programme they were all given numbers, and were not renamed until August 1928.

Asakaze, Matsukaze, Asanagi and *Yunagi* were sunk by American submarines, *Hatakaze* and *Oite* were sunk by air attack, and *Hayate* was sunk by Wake Island's coast defence guns. *Kamikaze* was scrapped after running aground on 7 June 1946. *Harukaze* was damaged when she surrendered, and was scrapped in 1947. Despite their extra beam, the high mounted main armament meant that these ships were not particularly stable, especially after the addition of a large number of light AA guns during World War II. The well before the bridge, though it broke up the force of large waves, also caused problems with spray. It was not adopted in the later 'Special Type' destroyers. In most respects they were not the equal of the earlier British *V* and *W* class destroyers.

Below: The Kamikaze *class destroyer* Yunagi *(ex-No. 17) in 1928.* Yunagi *was torpedoed and sunk by the US submarine* Picuda *on 25 August 1944*

Displacement:	as built	in 1945
standard tons (tonnes)	1,270 (1,290)	1,300 (1,320)
full load tons (tonnes)	1,720 (1,750)	?
Dimensions:		
length (pp)	319·9ft (97·5m)	
(wl)	326·4ft (99·5m)	
(oa)	336ft (102·4m)	
beam	31·8ft (9·7m)	
draught	9·5ft (2·9m)	
Armament:		
guns		
4·7in (120mm) 50cal	4	3
25mm	—	20
13mm	—	4
0·303in (7·7mm)	2	—
torpedo tubes		
21in (533mm)	6	6
A/S weapons		
depth-charge throwers	—	4
Machinery:		
boilers (type)	Kanpon	
(number)	4	
engines (type)	Parsons single reduction geared turbines	
shafts	2	
Total SHP:		
designed	38,500	
Fuel capacity:		
oil tons (tonnes)	350 (356)	
Performance:		
designed speed	37·25kts	—
service speed	—	35kts
range	4,000 miles (3,360nm) @ 15kts	
Crew:	148	

Class:	**KAMIKAZE class (ex-Nos 1, 3, 5, 7, 9, 11, 13, 15, 17)**
Authorised:	1921–1922
Laid down:	1921–1922
Launched:	1922–1924
Completed:	1922–1925
Named:	1928
Rearmed as escorts:	1941–1942
Fate:	*Asakaze* ex-*No 3* sunk 23 Aug 1944;
	Matsukaze ex-*No 7* sunk 9 June 1944;
	Hatakaze ex-*No 9* sunk 15 Jan 1945;
	Oite ex-*No 11* sunk 17 Feb 1944;
	Hayate ex-*No 13* sunk 11 Dec 1941;
	Asanagi ex-*No 15* sunk 22 May 1944;
	Yunagi ex-*No 17* sunk 25 Aug 1944;
	Kamikaze ex-*No 1* surrendered Aug 1945, scrapped 1946;
	Harukaze ex-*No 5* surrendered Aug 1945, scrapped 1947

Kamikaze class as built. Note torpedo tubes in well before bridge

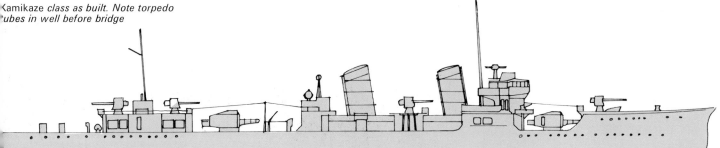

Kagero Class

DESTROYER

CLASS: *Kagero* class (18 ships) including *Kagero · Yukikaze* (later *Tan Yang*)

When the Washington Treaty limited the Japanese Navy to six-tenths the size of that of Britain and America, the Japanese attempted to ensure that their ships were individually superior to those of other countries. In 1925 they drew up specifications for what becam the *Special Type* destroyer, with three twin 5 (127mm) turrets and three triple 24in (610mm torpedo tubes with reloads. These had standard displacement of about 1,750 tor (1,780 tonnes) and speeds of between 37 38kts. They employed the same weight-savir techniques as the experimental light cruise *Yubari*. Three types were built. The 5in (127mm fitted to the *Type I* had 55° elevation, but th was increased to 75° on the *Type II*, which als had an altered bridge. The *Type III* had onl three boilers, and had shields to the torped tubes and a modified bridge. The London Nav Treaty of 1930 limited individual destroyers t a maximum standard displacement of 1,850 tor (1,880 tonnes), and imposed a total tonnag limit of 105,500 tons (107,188 tonnes) fo Japanese destroyers, of which only 16 per cer could displace over 1,500 tons (1,524 tonnes An attempt was therefore made in the *Hatsuhar* class to fit as many of the *Special Type* features as possible in a hull having a standar displacement of only 1,400 tons (1,420 tonnes However, these lacked stability, and a modifie design, the *Shiratsuyus*, were built with on less triple torpedo tube mount and a rearrange armament on a hull with a standard displace ment of 1,685 tons (1,712 tonnes). The elevatio of the 5in (127mm) guns was reduced to 55 to reduce complexity and save weight. Th storms during the 1935 and 1939 fleet exercise showed that more emphasis was needed c 'ship' qualities and less on the maximum arma ment that could be carried on the smallest hul and the 1,700 ton (1,730 tonnes) *Asashio* were designed. Actually displacing 1,961 tor (1,992 tonnes), these returned to an armamer of three twin 5in (127mm), but had eight 24i (610mm) torpedo tubes in two quadrup mounts. They had adequate stability and hu strength, but they had other problems, includin vibrating machinery and a large turning circl The *Kageros*, the first Japanese destroyers to b designed after Japan withdrew from the nava limitation treaties, were improved *Asashios*. A

Displacement:

standard tons (tonnes)	2,033 (2,065)
full load tons (tonnes)	?

Dimensions:

length (pp)	363·75ft (110·8m)
(wl)	381ft (116m)
(oa)	388·5ft (118·4m)
beam	35·5ft (10·8m)
draught	12·3ft (3·7m)

Armament:

	as built	Tan Yang in 1970
guns		
5in (127mm) 50cal	6	—
5in (127mm) 38cal	—	3
3in (76mm)	—	2
40mm	—	17
25mm	4	—
torpedo tubes		
24in (610mm)	8	—

Machinery:

boilers (type)	Kanpon
(number)	3
engines (type)	Kanpon single reduction geared turbines
shafts	2

Total SHP:

	Amatsukaze	remainder
designed	?	52,000
trial	52,150	?

Fuel capacity:

oil tons (tonnes)	400 (406)

Performance:

designed speed	?	35kts
trial speed	34·55kts	?
range	5,950 miles (5,000nm) @ 18kts	

Crew: 240

Class:	**KAGERO class**
Where built:	various yards
Authorised:	1937 and 1939
Built:	1937–1941
Fate:	*Amatsukaze* sunk 6 Apr 1945;
	Arashi sunk 7 Aug 1943;
	Hagikaze sunk 7 Aug 1943;
	Hamakaze sunk 7 Apr 1945;
	Hatsukaze sunk 2 Nov 1943;
	Hayashio sunk 24 Nov 1942;
	Isokaze scuttled 7 Apr 1945;
	Kagero sunk 8 May 1943;
	Kuroshio sunk 8 May 1943;
	Maikaze sunk 17 Feb 1944;
	Natsushio sunk 8 Feb 1942;
	Nowaki sunk 26 Oct 1944;
	Oyashio sunk 8 May 1943;
	Shiranui sunk 27 Oct 1944;
	Tanikaze sunk 9 June 1944;
	Tokitsukaze sunk 3 March 1943;
	Urakaze sunk 21 Nov 1944;
	Yukikaze surrendered August 1945,
	transferred to China 6 July 1947,
	renamed *Tan Yang* and wrecked May 1970

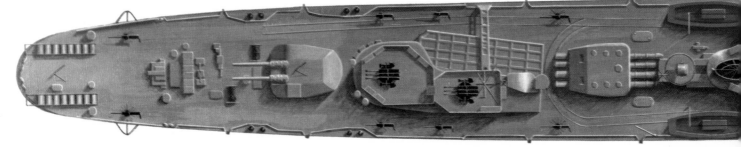

st Japan had a heavy destroyer design that lfilled her requirements. They were extremely ■ccessful, having good seaworthiness, long nge and extremely powerful armament. As ith all Japanese destroyers, the torpedo arma ■ent was particularly impressive. From 1941 ey were armed with the oxygen-fuelled Type ■ 24in (610mm) torpedo which had a powerful arhead and a range of 24,000 yards (22,000m) 48kts, and nearly 44,000 yards (40,000m) 36kts. This was three times the range of con ■ntional torpedoes, and the provision of

rapid reload facilities virtually doubled the existing armament. At the Battle of Java Sea and the various engagements in the Solomons in 1942–1943 this torpedo gave the Japanese a decisive advantage. The forward tubes' reloads were carried either side of the forefunnel, and the aft tubes on the port side of the aft deckhouse. *Amatsukaze* was fitted with experimental high temperature/high pressure boilers, but these proved a disappointment in service. *Hamakaze* was the first Japanese destroyer to have radar, and all surviving members of the class were

Above: Amatsukaze; *this* Kagero *class destroyer was fitted with experimental high temperature/high pressure boilers, which proved disappointing*

fitted with this. The anti-aircraft armament was greatly increased during the war, and some ships had X turret removed to maintain stability. The class saw extensive service throughout the Pacific, and all except *Yukikaze* were sunk during the war. Surprisingly, she survived completely undamaged, despite seeing a good deal of action. An improved version, the *Yugumo* class, was built during World War II with a slightly larger hull and 75° instead of 55° elevation for the 5in (127mm) guns. All 20 of this class built were sunk during World War II.

Yukikaze in 1945, with X turret replaced by 25mm AA guns and Type 22 radar on foremast and Type 13 on mainmast. Note 24in (610mm) TT with V shaped reloads by forefunnel and offset to port aft

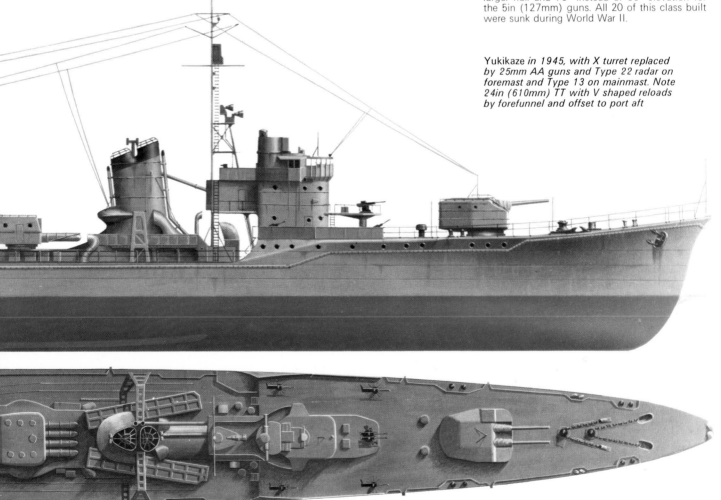

Haruna Class
HELICOPTER DESTROYER
CLASS: *Haruna* class (2 ships)
Haruna (DD-141) · *Hiei* (DD-142)

The Japanese Maritime Self Defence Force is limited to a purely defensive function, and as a result it has not been permitted to build any major warship that might be used in an offensive role. Therefore, unlike other helicopter-equipped destroyers and cruisers, the *Haruna* class have been optimised for the anti-submarine role, with a very limited anti-aircraft and surface capability. This has, however, meant that the *Harunas* carry virtually the same anti-submarine armament as the Italian *Andrea Doria* helicopter cruisers on 1,300 tons (1,320 tonnes) less standard displacement. *Haruna* carries her two 5in (127mm) Mk 42 guns in single mounts forward, with the ASROC launcher between B gun and the massive bridge. The uptakes are arranged in a mack which is surmounted by a lattice mast. The hangar, which can accommodate three HSS-2 helicopters, is an integral part of the superstructure. The flight deck stretches the entire aft third of the ship. The Mk 32 torpedo tubes are in two triple mounts one on either side of the bridge. The armament and much of the equipment is American, as with all postwar Japanese ships. Two improved *Harunas*, DD-143 and DD-144, are being built. These go far towards remedying the *Harunas*' deficiencies in anti-aircraft armament, having a BPDM Sea Sparrow SAM launcher and two twin 35mm anti-aircraft guns in addition to the *Haruna*'s armament. They are slightly larger, having a standard displacement of 5,200 tons (5,280 tonnes).

Displacement:	
standard tons (tonnes)	4,700 (4,775)
full load tons (tonnes)	?
Dimensions:	
length (oa)	502ft (153m)
beam	57·4ft (17·5m)
draught	16·7ft (5·1m)
Armament:	
guns	
5in (127mm)	2
A/S weapons	
ASROC octuple launcher	1
torpedo tubes	
12·7in (324mm) Mk 32	6
aircraft	3 helicopters
Machinery:	
boilers (type)	?
(number)	?
engines (type)	geared turbines
shafts	2
Total SHP:	
designed	70,000
Fuel capacity:	
oil tons (tonnes)	?
Performance:	
designed speed	32kts
range	7,000 miles (5,880nm) @ 20kts
Crew:	364

Above: ASROC anti-submarine missile being fired from Haruna *in 1975. Note the raised segment of the launcher between the superimposed 5in (127mm) gun and the bridge, and the box-like hangar flush with the side of the hull*

Ship:	HARUNA (DD-141)	HIEI (DD-142)
Where built:	Mitsubishi, Nagasaki	Ishikawajima, Tokyo
Authorised:	1967	1967
Laid down:	19 March 1970	8 March 1972
Launched:	1 Feb 1972	13 Aug 1973
Completed:	22 Feb 1973	27 Nov 1974
Fate:	In service	In service

Haruna (DD-141). Note ASROC before bridge and hangar and flight deck aft

I 400 Class
CRUISER SUBMARINE
CLASS: *I 400* (3 boats) *I 400–I 402*

I 201 Class
SUBMARINE
CLASS: *I 201* (3 boats) *I 201–I 203*

These two classes represent the two extremes of Japanese submarine design. After the end of World War I, the Japanese obtained the plans of the German cruiser submarines, and from them developed successive classes of large submarines, in much the same way as the Americans, that were capable of operating throughout the Pacific. From *I5* (launched in 1931) onward, several classes were fitted to carry seaplanes to enable them to reconnoitre large areas. These cruiser submarines gradually increased in size until the *I13* class, ordered in 1942, which had a range of 21,000 miles (17,700nm) with a submerged displacement of 4,762 tons (4,838 tonnes). Even these were outmatched by the *I 400*s. The Japanese had developed three different types of cruiser submarine. The Type A headquarters boats had extra telecommunications equipment to co-ordinate groups of the other two types. The Type B attack submarines were standard cruiser

Displacement:	I 400 class	I 201 class
standard tons (tonnes)	3,530 (3,586)	1,070 (1,087)
surface tons (tonnes)	5,223 (5,306)	1,291 (1,311)
submerged tons (tonnes)	6,560 (6,665)	1,450 (1,473)
Dimensions:		
length (pp)	380·5ft (116m)	249·3ft (76m)
(wl)	394ft (120·1m)	257·5ft (78·5m)
(oa)	400·25ft (122m)	259ft (79m)
beam	39·3ft (12m)	19ft (5·8m)
draught	23ft (7m)	18ft (5·4m)
Armament:		
guns		
5·5in (140mm)	1	—
25mm	10	—
torpedo tubes		
21in (533mm)	8	4
aircraft	3	—
Machinery:		
diesels (type)	MAN	MAN
(number)	4	2
electric motors (type)	?	?
shafts	2	2
Designed BHP:	7,700	2,750
Designed SHP:	2,400	5,000
Fuel capacity:		
oil tons (tonnes)	?	?
Performance:		
surface speed	18·75kts	15·75kts
submerged speed	6·5kts	19kts
range (surface)	30,000 miles (25,200nm) @ 16kts	5,800 miles (4,870nm) @ 14kts
(submerged)	60 miles (50nm) @ 3kts	135 miles (114nm) @ 3kts
Crew:	144	31

I 400 class. Note catapult for'd hangar under bridge and gun aft

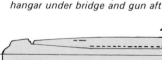
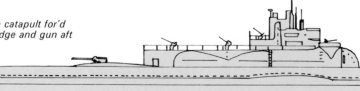

Type S

SUBMARINE

CLASS: Type S (2 boats) *No 14* (later *Armide*) · *No 15* (later *Ha 10*)

The two Type S submarines, *No 14* and *No 15*, were the first seagoing submarines ordered by the Japanese. They were considerably larger than the Holland and Vickers 'C' types and their derivatives which had provided the first submarines operated by the Japanese Navy, and they were armed with six rather than one or two 18in (457mm) torpedo tubes. The Type S were standard French Schneider-Laubeuf type submarines, designed and built in France, and were almost identical to two submarines building by Schneiders for Greece. *No 14* was requisitioned by France and renamed *Armide*, but *No 15*, completed at a time when Japan was not only providing convoy escorts in the Mediterranean but also building warships for France, joined the Japanese Navy as planned. She was fitted with a 3in (76mm) gun after the end of World War I, and was renumbered *Ha10* in 1924. A replacement for *No 14*, also numbered *No 14*, was built at Kure Dockyard between 1918 and 1920. She was slightly larger, and was designated Type S2. She was not fitted with the two external bow tubes mounted in the first pair. Renumbered *Ha9* in 1924, she was deleted in 1929. The design was progressively enlarged between 1917 and 1923 in the Types K1–K4. The latter had a surface displacement of 770 tons (782 tonnes) and an armament of four 21in (533mm) torpedo tubes and one 3in (76mm) gun.

Right: Type S *submarine* No 15 *in March 1917. The long casing and small conning tower are characteristic of the Schneider-Laubeuf boats. No 14 and the two ex-Greek boats were almost identical. Note the ventilators aft of the conning tower. These were stowed and the holes blanked off when the boat dived*

Displacement:		
standard tons (tonnes)	418 (424)	
surface tons (tonnes)	457 (464)	
submerged tons (tonnes)	665 (675)	
Dimensions:		
length (oa)	186·25ft (56·7m)	
beam	17ft (5·2m)	
draught	9·75ft (3m)	
Armament:	**as designed**	**Armide in 1916**
guns		
47mm	—	1
torpedo tubes		
18in (457mm)	6	6
Machinery:		
diesels (type)	Schneider-Carels	
(number)	2	
electric motor (type)	?	
shafts	2	
Total BHP:	2,000	
Total SHP:	850	
Fuel capacity:		
oil tons (tonnes)	32 (32·5)	
Performance:		
surface speed	17kts	
submerged speed	10kts	
range (surface)	2,440 miles (2,050nm) @ 10kts	
(submerged)	71 miles (60nm) @ 4kts	
designed diving depth	?	
Crew:	31	

Ship:	No 14 (later ARMIDE)	No 15 (later Ha 10)
Where built:	Schneider, Chalon-sur-Saône	Schneider, Chalon-sur-Saône
Authorised:	1912	1912
Laid down:	1912	Nov 1913
Launched:	July 1915	1916
Completed:	June 1916	July 1917
Fate:	Taken over by French, renamed *Armide*, stricken July 1932	1924 renamed *Ha 10*, stricken 1929

submarines, and the Type C scouting submarines carried seaplanes. The *I400*s were intended to fulfil all these roles, and in addition carried bombs and torpedoes to enable their seaplanes to attack the Panama Canal. To keep the draught of these very large submarines as shallow as possible they had a 'figure of eight' shaped hull set on its side. However, it was as well that they did not see action, because the larger Japanese submarines proved easy to destroy once located because of their lack of manoeuvrability; and because they could break many Japanese naval codes, the Americans were frequently able to give the Japanese submarines' location to their anti-submarine vessels. However, the Japanese had already found the answer, although they had not developed it as quickly as they ought. In 1937, 20 years after the British R class and several years before the Germans, they had tested a highly streamlined test submarine, *No 71*, which had a better performance submerged than surfaced. From this were developed the Type ST (*I 201* class) and Type STS (*Ha 201* class) submarines, comparable in many ways with the German Type XXI and Type XXIII. Unfortunately the Japanese obsession with large cruiser submarines meant that these types were not put into production until 1944–1945. Both types were thoroughly tested by the Americans after the war, as were the *I400*s. The Type ST (*I201* class) were the first boats of their type to see service in World War II, and their performance was in many ways superior to the German design.

Right, above: I 400 *class submarine after the Japanese surrender in 1945. Note catapult on fo'c's'le, hangar amidships with conning tower offset to port and AA guns on hangar*

Right: I 402 *of the* I 400 *class, the largest non-nuclear submarines built, with the* I 46 *class (C2 Type)* I 47 *and the* I 15 *class (B1 Type)* I 36

Class:	I 400	I 201
Ordered:	1942	1943
Laid down:	1943	1944
Launched:	1944	1944
Completed:	1944–1945	1945
Fate:	2 boats scrapped incomplete; 3 boats cancelled; *I400* sunk 1946; *I401* sunk 1946; *I402* sunk 1946	5 boats scrapped incomplete; 15 boats cancelled; *I201* sunk 1946; *I202* sunk 1946; *I203* sunk 1946

Kaiten Class

MIDGET SUBMARINE
CLASS: *Kaiten* Types 1 to 4 (over 2,000 of all types were built)

The Japanese built a number of midget submarines from 1934 onward, and fitted several submarines and seaplane carriers to transport them. The Type A had two 18in (457mm) torpedo tubes and a two-man crew. The Types B and C had a diesel generator to recharge their batteries, and a three-man crew, and the Type D *Koryu* had a diesel engine and a five-man crew. The first three types were intended for offensive operations, but the *Koryu* were built in considerable numbers in 1945 for close-range defence off Japan, Okinawa and the Philippines. A number were fitted with high explosive warheads in place of the torpedoes as

Above: A Kaiten Type 1, *basically a manned* Type 93 *torpedo, is experimentally launched from the stern of the cruiser* Kitakami, *on 26 February 1945*

Displacement:	Type 1	Type 2	Type 3	Type 4
surface tons (tonnes)	?	18·4 (18·7)	?	18·2 (18·5)
submerged tons (tonnes)	18·5 (18·8)	18·5 (18·8)	18·3 (18·6)	18 (18·3)
Dimensions:				
length (pp)	?	?	?	?
(oa)	48·5ft (14·8m)	54ft (16·5m)	54ft (16·5m)	54ft (16·5m)
beam	3·25ft (1m)	4·5ft (1·4m)	4·5ft (1·4m)	4·5ft (1·4m)
draught	3·3 (1m)	4·4 (1·3m)	?	4·4 (1·3m)
Armament:				
warhead				
TNT lbs (kg)	3,410 (1,550)	3,410 (1,550)	3,300 (1,500)	3,960 (1,800)
Machinery:				
engine (type)	Type 93 torpedo engine	No 6 hydro-hydrazine	No 6 hydro-hydrazine	No 6 hydro-hydrazine
shaft	1	1	1	1
Total SHP:				
designed	550	1,500	1,800	1,800
Fuel capacity:				
tons (tonnes)	?	?	?	?
Performance:				
designed speed	30kts	40kts	30kts	40kts
range	25,100yds (23,000m) @ 30kts	54,700yds (50,100m) @ 30kts	41,500yds (38,000m) @ 30kts	41,600yds (38,100m) @ 30kts
Crew:	1	2	2	1

Class:	KAITEN Types 1 to 4
Where built:	various yards
Authorised:	1944–1945
Built:	1944–1945
Fate:	Sunk, scrapped or discarded

suicide craft. A modified version of the Type A, the *Kairyu*, was also built as suicide craft, but both these and the *Koryu* were too large and complicated to build in quantity. The Japanese therefore modified the Type 93 24in (610mm) torpedo to carry a man as the *Kaiten* Type 1. The Type 2 and Type 3 were fitted with an unsuccessful hydrogen-peroxide motor, but whereas the Type 2 was built in some numbers the Type 3 was purely experimental. To produce a workable boat the Type 2s were fitted with torpedo motor as the Type 4, which was the final production version. The *Kaiten* were a weapon of desperation, and despite being built in quantity, they do not seem to have achieved much success.

Chikugo Class

FRIGATE
CLASS: *Chikugo* class (12 ships) including *Chikugo* (DE-215) · *Teshio* (DE-222)

The first Japanese postwar frigates were Japanese and American World War II destroyer escorts. Both steam and diesel propulsion were tried in the 1953 programme escorts, but steam power was abandoned in the subsequent *Isuzu* class, built between 1960 and 1964. These were flush-decked diesel-powered frigates of 1,490 tons (1,510 tonnes) standard displacement armed with a twin 3in (76mm) mount fore and aft. The first pair have a single Weapon Able A/S rocket-launcher in B position, with a four-barrel 12in (305mm) rocket-launcher, while the second pair have a triple-barrel Bofors 14·75in (375mm) A/S rocket-launcher and six A/S torpedo tubes. They have hull-mounted sonar, with VDS in two ships. The *Chikugo* class were developed from the *Isuzus*, but have an ASROC A/S launcher and bow and variable depth sonar. They have a much larger bridge, and the ASROC launcher is mounted just aft of the funnel. Their twin 3in (76mm) mount is forward of the bridge and the twin 40mm mount is at the stern, just forward of the variable depth sonar. The later members of the class incorporated minor improvements. A larger version, the *Yamagumo/*

Displacement:	
standard tons (tonnes)	1,470–1,500 (1,494–1,524)
full load tons (tonnes)	1,700–? (1,727–?)
Dimensions:	
length (oa)	304·6ft (93m)
beam	35·4ft (10·8m)
draught	11·5ft (3·5m)
Armament:	
guns	
3in (76mm) 50cal	2
40mm	2
A/S weapons	
ASROC octuple-launcher	1
torpedo tubes	
12·7in (324mm)	6
Machinery:	
diesels (type)	Mitsui or Mitsubishi
(number)	4
shafts	2
Total BHP:	
designed	16,000
Fuel capacity:	
oil tons (tonnes)	?
Performance:	
designed speed	25kts
range	?
Crew:	165

Ship:	CHIKUGO class
Where built:	Ishikawajima, Tokyo; Mitsui, Tamano; Hitachi, Maizuru
Authorised:	?
Laid down:	Dec 1968–1977
Launched:	Jan 1970 onward
Completed:	July 1970 onward
Fate:	In service or under construction

Minegumo class destroyers, built since 1964, have a standard displacement of 2,066 tons (2,100 tonnes) and a speed of 27kts. They have a very similar armament to the *Isuzus* and *Chikugos*, but the second group had a landing pad and hangar for DASH helicopters, which are being replaced by ASROC in 1977. The frigates are too small to carry a helicopter and balanced anti-aircraft and anti-submarine armament, but like all postwar Japanese warships they operate within range of land-based anti-submarine aircraft.

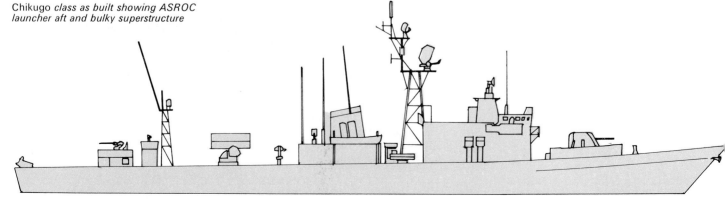

Chikugo *class as built showing ASROC launcher aft and bulky superstructure*

Matsu Class
DESTROYER ESCORT

CLASS: *Matsu* class (34 ships)
Matsu group 18 ships including
Matsu · Kaede · Kaya · Tachibana
group 16 ships including *Tachibana ·
Hatsuyume · Shii*

Japan had concentrated prewar on building powerful heavy units and large destroyers to offset American numerical superiority and had neglected anti-submarine escorts, a weakness the Americans were swift to exploit. No suitable fast general purpose escort design existed, and Japan continued building large and complicated destroyers until 1943. The *Matsu* class was intended to fill this gap, and were designed for simplicity of construction. Fitted with the unit machinery arrangement, they were capable of absorbing a large amount of damage and they carried a heavy armament (particularly of anti-aircraft guns) for their size. Most had radar. However, even these simple ships took too long to build, and the design was simplified still further, the *Tachibana* type having virtually no curved hull plates to ease production. Depth charge capacity was increased from 36 to 60 in the light of war experience, and a shorter mast was fitted. The *Matsus* were an excellent design, comparing very favourably with the British and American equivalents. Had it been possible to concentrate more on purely A/S capabilities, a slower, even simpler design could been built. However, by the time the *Matsus* appeared, American surface and air superiority was such as to necessitate a reasonably high speed and a powerful surface and AA armament. They formed the basis for Japan's first postwar frigate designs.

Below: A Matsu *class destroyer escort at speed. Note the prominent armament and the vestigial masts and funnels*

Displacement:	Matsu	Tachibana
standard tons (tonnes)	1,262 (1,282)	1,289 (1,310)
full load tons (tonnes)	?	?
Dimensions:		
length (pp)	302·3ft (92·2m)	
(wl)	321·5ft (98m)	
(oa)	328ft (100m)	
beam	30·5ft (9·3m)	
draught	10·75ft (3·3m)	
Armament:		
guns		
5in (127mm)	3	
25mm	24	
torpedo tubes		
24in (610mm)	4	
A/S weapons		
DCT	4	
Machinery:		
boilers (type)	Kanpon	
(number)	2	
engines (type)	Kanpon single reduction turbines	
shafts	2	
Total SHP:		
designed	19,000	
Fuel capacity:		
oil tons (tonnes)	395 (401)	
Performance:		
designed speed	27·75kts	
range	4,680 miles (3,935nm) @ 16kts	
Crew:	210	

Class:	MATSU group	TACHIBANA group
Where built:	various yards	various yards
Ordered:	1943	1944
Laid down:	1943–1944	1944–1945
Launched:	1944	1944–1945
Completed:	1944	1944–1945
Fate:	11 cancelled 1944; *Hinoki* sunk 7 Jan 1945; *Kuwa* sunk 3 Dec 1944; *Matsu* sunk 4 Aug 1944; *Momi* sunk 5 Jan 1945; *Momo* sunk 15 Dec 1944; *Sakura* sunk 11 July 1945; *Ume* sunk 31 Jan 1945; 11 surrendered, *Kaede* and *Sugi* incorporated in Chinese Navy as *Hen Yang* and *Hwei Yang*, *Kaya* and *Kiri* incorporated in Soviet Navy	10 cancelled March 1945; 10 scrapped or sunk incomplete; *Enoki* sunk 26 June 1945; *Nashi* sunk 28 July 1945; 14 surrendered, *Hatsuyume* incorporated in Chinese Navy as *Hsin Yang*, *Hatsuzakura* (ex-*Sutsuki*) and *Shii* incorporated in Soviet Navy

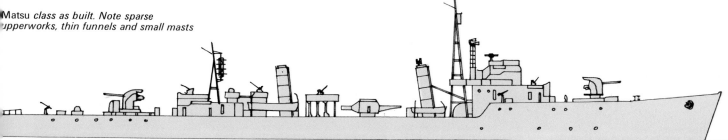

Matsu *class as built. Note sparse upperworks, thin funnels and small masts*

Nasty Class

TORPEDO BOAT

CLASS: Nasty (Tjeld) class
(42 ships)
Norway 20 ships including *Tjeld·Delfin*
Turkey 2 ships *Dogan · Marti*
USA 14 ships including *PTF 3· PTF 12*
Greece 6 ships including
Andromeda · Inionos

After the end of World War II, the Royal Norwegian Navy was re-equipped with British destroyers and escorts, and also acquired some British and German torpedo boats and submarines. Since then she has built up a force of small submarines and torpedo- and missile-armed patrol boats. These are ideally suited for warfare amongst the many fjords and islands that make up Norway's coastline. The *Nasty* class was developed from the six *Rapp* class torpedo boats built by Batservice at Mandal from 1951 to 1956. They use the much less inflammable diesel-fuelled Napier Deltic lightweight engines in place of the *Rapps'* Packard petrol motors, and their hulls are built of two layers of mahogany with a fibreglass layer sandwiched between them. This gives a strong, light and resilient hull. They can be armed either as torpedo boats, with four torpedo tubes and one 40mm and one 20mm gun, or as gunboats, with two 40mm guns but only two torpedo tubes. They can also be used for minelaying. The Federal German Navy acquired two boats of this type, but found them less well suited to Baltic conditions than the relatively beamy Lürssen designs, so they were transferred to Turkey. America classed theirs as PTF (Fast

Displacement:		
standard tons (tonnes)	69 (70)	
full load tons (tonnes)	76 (77)	
Dimensions:		
length (pp)	75ft (22·9m)	
(oa)	80·4ft (24·5m)	
beam	24·6ft (7·5m)	
draught	6·9ft (2·1m)	
Armament:	**Tjeld**	**PTF3**
guns		
40mm	2	1
20mm	—	2
0·5in (12·7mm)	—	1
3·2in (81mm) mortar	—	1
torpedo tubes		
21in (533mm)	4	—
Machinery:		
diesels (type)	Napier Deltic	
(number)	2	
shafts	2	
Total BHP:		
designed	6,200	
Fuel capacity:		
oil tons (tonnes)	?	
Performance:		
designed speed	43kts	
range	600 miles (505nm) @ 25kts	
Crew:	22	

Class:	NASTY class	
Where built:	Batservice, Mandal	
Authorised:	?	
Built:	1959–1967	
Fate:	Turkey:	*Hugin, Munin* delivered to Germany, lent to Turkey Aug 1964, later transferred and renamed *Dogan, Marti*, deleted circa 1974
	USA:	*PTF 4* deleted 1965; *PTF 8, 9, 14, 15, 16* deleted 1966; *PTF 13* deleted circa 1973
	Greece:	*Inionos* deleted 1972

Luta Class

GUIDED-MISSILE DESTROYER

CLASS: Luta class (7+ ships)
including *No 240 · No 241*

The Chinese Navy is now one of the most powerful in the Far East. Its first equipment after the People's Republic was set up in 1949 was ships captured from the Nationalists. These were a mixture of World War II Japanese, British and American designs. The seagoing vessels had mostly been transferred since 1945, and there was also a large number of river gunboats, some of which had actually been built for China. Russia soon supplied a number of World War II vessels to bolster this motley force, including four *Gordi* class destroyers and seven submarines. These were followed by four *Riga* class frigates, several *Whisky* class submarines and a number of guided-missile and patrol boats. Despite the political breach with Russia after 1956, the Chinese have built a number of modern warships to Russian designs, including *Golf, Romeo* and *Whisky* class submarines. The parts for some of these have been supplied from Russia, but others have been built entirely in Chinese yards. The Chinese have also produced modified versions of Russian designs. A number of modified *Riga* class frigates, *Kiangnans*, have been built since 1968, and the largest Chinese surface warships, the *Lutas*, are modified Russian *Kotlin* class destroyers. They have less powerful machinery than the *Kotlins*, and carry SSM launchers between and abaft the funnels in place of the *Kotlins'* torpedo tubes. These missiles are SSN-2 'Styx' SSMs, and although they are obsolescent, they are still effective against any ship not equipped with modern ECM. The *Lutas* are much more

Displacement:	
standard tons (tonnes)	3,250 (3,300)
full load tons (tonnes)	3,750 (3,810)
Dimensions:	
length (pp)	?
(oa)	450ft (137·3m)
beam	45ft (13·7m)
draught	15ft (4·6m)
Armament:	
guns	
5·1in (130mm)	4
57mm	8
25mm	8
missiles	
SSN-2 'Styx'-type SSM	
triple launcher	2
A/S weapons	
rocket-launcher	2
Machinery:	
boilers (type)	?
(number)	?
engines (type)	geared turbines
shafts	2
Total SHP:	
designed	approx 60,000
Fuel capacity:	
oil tons (tonnes)	?
Performance:	
designed speed	approx 32kts
range	approx 4,000 miles (3,400nm) @ 15kts
Crew:	approx 300

Above: A 1973 photo of the prototype Luta guided missile destroyer, No 240.
The Square Tie missile fire control radar is on the pole mast between the lattice main mast and the second funnel.

Class:	LUTA class
Where built:	Dairen (Luta) Shipyard
Built:	1968 onward
Fate:	In service and under construction

effectively armed than the original Russian *Kildins*. These were modified *Kotlins* which carried a single SSN-1 'Scrubber' SSM launcher in place of the aft 5·1in (130mm) mount.

However, the *Kildins* have since been rearmed with a much improved anti-aircraft armament and four SSN-2(mod) SSM launchers, and are now better armed than the *Lutas*.

Prominent SSM launchers distinguish Chinese Lutas *from Russian* Kotlins

Patrol Boats), and fitted them with a variety of different armaments. In Norwegian service they operate alongside the guided-missile patrol boats armed with the 'Penguin' SSM. *Nasty* herself has already been discarded. The twenty *Storm* and six *Snögg* class guided missile patrol boats (the latter being a steel hulled improved variant of the *Storms*), which are armed with the Penguin SSM, have been built from 1964 onward. The Penguin SSM is a short ranged missile, and the boats are intended to be used defensively, lying in ambush in the narrow channels and fjords along Norway's extensive coastline. The new *Hauk* class is under construction and is armed with four longer ranged versions of the Penguin SSM. Seventeen of the very similar *Jagaren* class are being built for Sweden, which has the same need for fast missile boats to defend her coastline against larger warships. Most of Norway's larger warships have been discarded, except for the five *Oslo* class frigates, which are modified versions of the American *Dealey* class escorts. The major strength of the Norwegian navy, apart from her patrol boats, is the large force of small highly manoeuvrable submarines of the German Type 207 and Type 210 class.

Right: The Nasty *class patrol boat* Skarv. *These can be armed as torpedo boats or gunboats, to operate alongside guided missile patrol boats.*

Shanghai Class

FAST ATTACK CRAFT
CLASS: *Shanghai Types I–IV*
(350+ craft)

The Chinese Navy now possesses the largest force of light craft in the world. It operates Russian and Chinese versions of a number of Russian designs, including *Osa* and *Komar* class guided-missile patrol boats and *P6* class torpedo boats. They also operate the Chinese-designed *Huchwan* class hydrofoils. However, over a third of its light craft are various types of *Shanghai* class patrol boat. These are conventional general purpose craft, similar in many ways to the larger Russian *So1* class, a modified version of which is built in China as the *Hainan* class. The *Shanghais* are mainly intended for coastal patrol work, and have a powerful armament of light weapons. The initial boats differ from the later types by not having a twin 25mm mount immediately abaft the bridge. Some have an extra twin 37mm mount, and differ mainly from one another by the outline of their bridges. *Shanghais* have been supplied to several other countries, and a number of North Vietnamese boats were sunk by American ships and aircraft. The Romanians have given their *Shanghais* an increased armament, and have also built their own modified version.

Displacement:	Shanghai I	Shanghai II–IV
standard tons (tonnes)	?	120 (122)
full load tons (tonnes)	100 (102)	155 (157)
Dimensions:		
length (pp)	?	?
(oa)	115ft (35·1m)	128ft (39m)
beam	18ft (5·5m)	18ft (5·5m)
draught	5·5ft (1·7m)	5·6ft (1·7m)
Armament:	**Shanghai I**	**Shanghai II**
guns		
57mm	1	—
37mm	2	4
25mm	—	4
torpedo tubes		
18in (457mm)	2	—
mine capacity	10	10
Machinery:		
diesels (type)	?	?
(number)	4	4
Total BHP:		
designed	4,800	4,800
Fuel capacity:		
oil tons (tonnes)	?	
Performance:		
designed speed	28kts	30kts
range	800 miles (670nm) @ 17kts	
Crew:	25	

Class:	**SHANGHAI TYPES I–II**
Where built:	various yards
Authorised:	?
Built:	1959 onward
Fate:	In service: China over 350; 1966 onward transferred to Albania 4, Congo 3, Guinea 6, North Korea 8, Pakistan 14, Sri Lanka 5, Sierra Leone 3, Tanzania (?) 12, Vietnam 8; Romania has built 18, of which 6 are to a modified A/S design

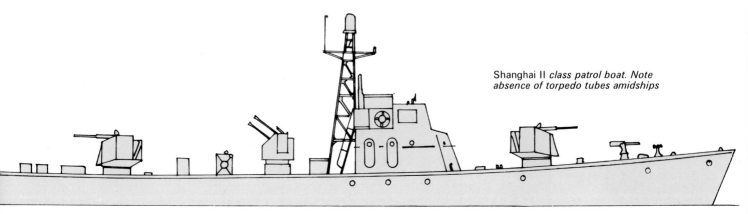

Shanghai II *class patrol boat. Note absence of torpedo tubes amidships*

SOVIET UNION

IN the mid 19th century the Russian navy was under powerful control but had suffered over the previous 150 years from a wealth of foreign talent in senior positions. Despite the ability of the senior commanders, the vast gulf between the officers and the sailors was not designed to sustain good morale. The main aim of the navy was home defence with, after 1885, a swing towards a trade war with the embodiment of armed merchant cruisers in the 'Volunteer Merchant Fleet'. A running engagement with Japan expanded into the war of 1904–05 in which, firstly, the Russian Pacific Fleet was neutralised and, secondly, the Russian Baltic Fleet was demolished at the Battle of Tsushima.

Russian naval policy had undergone a series of reversals but, after the Japanese War, sound appraisals of the country's strategic needs led to a planned deployment similar to that now obtaining in the Soviet fleet. But the bureaucratic stranglehold was felt in naval circles as everywhere else. Sound plans were frustrated by the interminable time taken to approve and build ships. As a result the Russian navy was in no position to take any major part in World War I and, as the October Revolution came to pass in 1917, the navy began to crumble away.

When there was a little stability in the new regime the requirement for a revival of the fleet came up but the destruction of many shipyards delayed any new construction programme. The main effort was directed to refitting the remnants of the Imperial navy until in 1926 the Defence Council approved the building of twelve submarines and eighteen escorts. The navy's task was defence of the home shores in conjunction with the army and under the wing of the air force. The First Five Year Plan of 1928 gave further approval for new ships and from then on new construction was pressed forward. New classes of submarines, cruisers and destroyers as well as a mass of smaller craft came off the slips. Stalin, dismayed at his inability to use the sea to reinforce the Communists during the Spanish Civil War, determined to provide a fleet of major proportions. When the German invasion brought war in June 1941 plans were in hand to build eight battleships, eight battlecruisers and a dozen extra cruisers, but none was ever completed. As a result the

USSR entered the war weak in large ships but with some sixty destroyers and 180 submarines. Despite this considerable force the only impact the Soviet Navy achieved was in amphibious operations and infantry actions by shore-based sailors. The equipment in their ships was antiquated by Western standards, their tactical ideas outmoded but, above all, their leadership was generally poor as the result of Stalin's purges in the 1930s.

Thus the fleet in the immediate post-war years was a hotch-potch of old and new ships, lend/lease ships and war booty with little technical background amongst the personnel. The efforts to improve this situation must have been herculean because by the time Admiral Gorshkov took over as C-in-C in January 1956 the first ballistic-missile submarines were fitting out, nigh on 300 petrol submarines were built or completing and some eighty major surface ships had been commissioned since 1945. Ships and submarines were being fitted with cruise missiles in the late 1950s and plans for new and improved designs were on the drawing boards. In 1962 came the world's first all gas-turbine major warship, the *Kashin*, by which time the first fourteen nuclear submarines had commissioned, outdistancing in time the first of the British programme.

It was now that Gorshkov began despatching his ships on cruises to many distant areas. New classes of ships and submarines were sighted en route to the Indian Ocean, the Pacific, the South Atlantic. The C-in-C believed that his fleet had a major role to play in his country's foreign policy and every effort was made to prepare them for their task. Today, with a huge fleet including all forms of ships and submarines including the new aircraft-carriers of the *Kiev* class and a naval air force of great strength, it has to be accepted that Admiral Gorshkov has amply fulfilled his government's expectations.

Kiev

'ANTI-SUBMARINE CRUISER' (AIRCRAFT-CARRIER)

CLASS: *Kiev* class (1 ship+2, or possibly 3, building) *Kiev · Minsk* and one, possibly two, still un-named

Although there had been considerable interest in both airships and fixed-wing aircraft in both the Imperial and Soviet Navies, all plans to build any form of aircraft-carrier failed to materialise. These varied from a cruiser (*Komintern*) conversion to seaplane carrier, through two custom-designed seaplane carriers for the Pacific, to two fixed-wing carriers in the Third Five Year plan (1938–1942). The first was abandoned and the remainder cancelled. During and after World War II a formidable naval air force was built up, consisting of some 4,000 fighters, bombers and reconnaissance planes. In the Khruschev reorganisation this was drastically cut back and its fighters removed, but at no time was there any move back to planning aircraft-carriers. In fact the arguments for and against such ships were conducted with considerable heat and vigour. The first *Kresta I* cruiser, commissioned in early 1967, carried a helicopter with a hangar and paved the way for the appearance a year later of *Moskva*, an 18,000 ton (18,288 tonne) helicopter-carrier with 18 'Hormone' helicopters embarked. She and her sister *Leningrad* may well have been planned as the forerunners of a large class but no more were completed. Their duties were clearly anti-submarine as reflected in the majority of Soviet type designations for their major ships. They did, however, have considerable potential in other directions such as intervention situations. Shortly before *Moskva* commissioned, the first Soviet V/STOL aircraft appeared at an air display near Moscow. Subsequently little else was seen of this type of aircraft and when a large hull was seen building at Nikolayev in 1971 it was no great strain on the intelligence to marry up the two. The first British Harrier had flown in 1966 and in the next five years had carried out a series of deck-landings on the ships of several navies. When *Kiev* finally emerged from the Black Sea in August 1976 something totally new was revealed. Not only was she an aircraft-carrier in all but name, although restricted to the operation of V/STOL aircraft and helicopters; she was also a very heavily armed warship. Eight surface-to-surface launchers decorated

her fo'c's'le, and missiles of other kinds dotted her upper deck. 76mm (3in) guns and Gatlings provided more conventional armament. New radars had been fitted and she carried sonar — an enormous departure from US practice where neither sonar nor guns are fitted in carriers and the only missiles are for point-defence. The somewhat tentative approach of the V/STOL pilots and general Soviet inexperience in this field, particularly when compared to the highly professional US Navy approach, may have been behind part of this design. Nevertheless *Kiev* is a very potent warship capable of operating to advantage in both war and intervention situations. She may suffer from her comparatively low freeboard but her successors will no doubt benefit from lessons learned — flat-faced

sponsons at the head of the flight deck as an example. The next generation may well be larger and it is certain that the embarkation of ordinary fixed-wing aircraft, including the many problems of catapults, arrester-wires, landing-aids and training, have been examined.

Displacement:

(estimated)		
light tons (tonnes)	40,000 (40,640)	
full load tons (tonnes)	54,000 (54,864)	

Dimensions:

length (oa)	934ft (284·8m)
beam (hull)	135ft (41·2m)
(flight deck)	170ft (51·8m)

Armament:

guns	
3in (76mm)	4
AD Gatling	4 mounts
A/S weapons	
12-barrelled A/S missiles launchers	2
SSN-12 (SSM)	8
SAN-3 (SAM)	4
SAN-4 (SAM)	2
SUWN-1 (A/S)	1
aircraft (est)	20 fixed wing V/STOL or 25 'Hormone' helicopters

Machinery:

boilers (type)	?
(number)	?
engines (type)	steam turbines
shafts	?
Total SHP:	?
Fuel capacity:	
oil tons (tonnes)	?

Performance:

speed	30+kts
range	?

Ship:	KIEV	MINSK	un-named	un-named
Where built:	Nikolayev South	Nikolayev South	Nikolayev South	Nikolayev South
Laid down:	1971	1972	1973	?
Launched:	1973	1974	1976	?
Commissioned:	1976	1977 (?)	1979 (?)	?
Fate:	in service	building	building	?

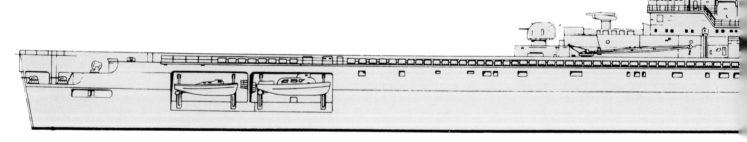

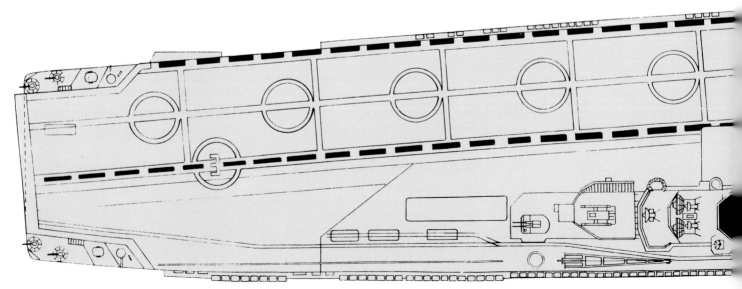

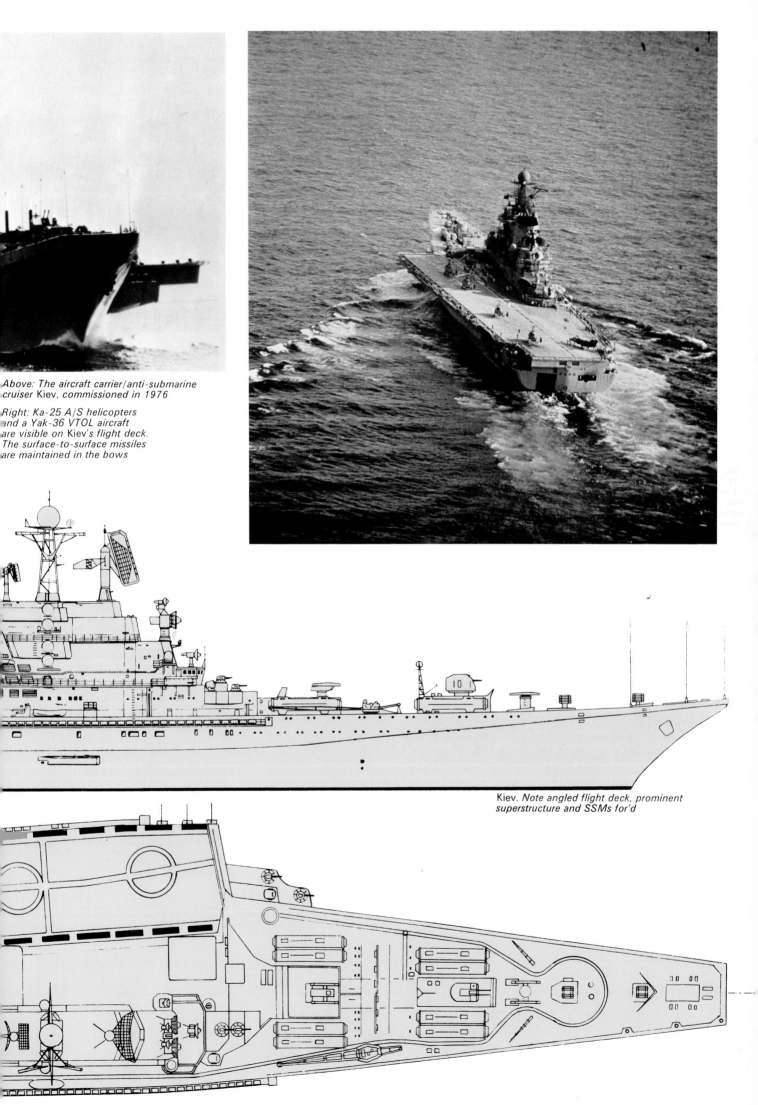

Above: The aircraft carrier/anti-submarine cruiser Kiev, commissioned in 1976

Right: Ka-25 A/S helicopters and a Yak-36 VTOL aircraft are visible on Kiev's flight deck. The surface-to-surface missiles are maintained in the bows

Kiev. *Note angled flight deck, prominent superstructure and SSMs for'd*

Kniaz Suvorov
BATTLESHIP
CLASS: *Borodino* class (5 ships)
*Borodino · Imperator Aleksandr III ·
Orel* (later *Iwami*) *· Kniaz Suvorov ·
Slava*

Service career KNIAZ SUVOROV
1904 (Sept) Flagship, 2nd Pacific Squadron.
1904 (15 Oct) Sailed from Libau in Baltic.
1905 (25 Apr) Joined by 3rd Pacific Squadron at
Camranh Bay, French Indochina.
1905 (27 May) Battle of Tsushima: sunk by
Japanese battle squadron and torpedo boats.

The *Borodinos* were slightly modified versions of
the Russian battleship *Tsarevich*, designed and
built in France between 1899 and 1903. The
use of twin turrets for the secondary armament
was an advanced feature, but they were set too
high in the hull. Combined with the typically
French tumblehome (intended to reduce topweight), this made them very unstable and
Borodino, Aleksandr III and *Kniaz Suvorov* all
capsized before sinking. The 3in (76mm) were
set too low to be used at sea, and they had high,
vulnerable silhouettes. Nevertheless, they were
powerful ships, and all put up a considerable
resistance before being disabled or captured.
Slava and *Iwami* (ex-*Orel*) both had their topweight reduced to improve stability after
Tsushima, and the latter had her twin 6in
(152mm) replaced by single 8in (203mm)
turrets. *Borodino* and *Aleksandr III* were both
sunk at the Battle of Tsushima. *Orel* surrendered
after being badly damaged at the Battle of
Tsushima. She was deleted in 1923. *Slava* was
completed too late to take part in the Battle of
Tsushima. She was very badly damaged by the
German battleships *König* and *Kronprinz* on
17 October 1917 and was sunk in shallow water
by torpedoes from the Russian destroyer
Turkmenets-Stavropolsky. Although these
ships did not have very successful careers,
they were well armed, and their 12in (305mm)
guns outranged and outshot the British armed
Japanese battleships in the opening phases of
the battle of Tsushima. Had they been better
manned and led they would have performed
much better. *Slava*, though outranged by the
German battleships, put up a stiff fight before
succumbing. The final Russian predreadnought
design, the two *Imperator Pavel* class battleships, built between 1903–1911, incorporated
several lessons learned by the Russians from
the Russo-Japanese War. Easily identifiable by
the two cage masts and the long quarterdeck,
they had their anti torpedo-boat armament
mounted high in the superstructure, and the
entire hull outside the armour belt was protected by thin armour against light guns and
splinters. Had they been completed earlier
they would have been effective vessels.

Displacement:	Kniaz Suvorov in 1904		Slava in 1906	
normal tons (tonnes)	13,516 (13,730)		13,516 (13,730)	
full load tons (tonnes)	15,275 (15,520)		14,400 (14,630)	
Dimensions:				
length (pp)	376·5ft (115m)			
(oa)	397ft (121·2m)			
beam	76ft (23·2m)			
draught	26·2ft (8m)			

Armament:	Kniaz Suvorov in 1904	Slava in 1906	Iwami in 1907
guns			
12in (305mm) 40cal	4	4	4
8in (203mm) 45cal	—	—	6
6in (152mm) 45cal	12	12	—
3in (76mm)	20	20	16
47mm	22	4	2
37mm	8	—	8
torpedo tubes			
18in (457mm)	6	2	2

Armour:	
side (belt)	6–7·5in (152–191mm)
(ends)	4–5·75in (102–146mm)
decks (upper)	1·5in (38mm)
(middle)	1·75–2·4in (44–61mm)
main turrets	10in (254mm)
barbettes	10in (254mm)
secondary turrets	3in (76mm)

Machinery:	
boilers (type)	Belleville or Niclausse
(number)	20
engines (type)	vertical triple expansion
shafts	2

Total IHP:	
designed	15,800

Fuel capacity:	
coal normal tons (tonnes)	800 (810)
max tons (tonnes)	1,580 (1,600)

Performance:	
designed speed	18kts
range	6,624 miles (5,570nm) @ 10kts

Crew:	Kniaz Suvorov in 1904	Iwami in 1907
	825	806

Ship:	Borodino	Imperator Aleksandr III	Orel	Kniaz Suvorov	Slava
Where built:	New Admiralty Yard, St Petersburg	Baltic Yard, St Petersburg	Galerny Yard, St Petersburg	Baltic Yard, St Petersburg	Baltic Yard, St Petersburg
Authorised:	?	?	?	?	?
Laid down:	26 May 1899	5 May 1899	2 June 1900	1900	2 Oct 1902
Launched:	8 Sept 1901	3 Aug 1901	19 July 1902	25 Sept 1902	29 Aug 1903
Completed:	1904	1904	Sept 1904	Sept 1904	1905
Fate:	Sunk 27 May 1905	Sunk 27 May 1905	Captured by Japan 28 May 1905; rebuilt 1906–1907; renamed *Iwami*; scrapped 1924–1925	Sunk 27 May 1905	Scuttled 17 Oct 1917; wreck scrapped 1935

Right: Slava *of the* Borodino *class just
prior to World War I. The awning aft
conceals the aft 12in (305mm) twin turret,
mounted very low on the quarter deck.
Note the absence of fire control
positions on the masts and the very
low mounted 3in (76mm) casemates
amidships. The very short fo´c´sle
with the heavy weight of the 12in
(305mm) turret mounted well forward
made them wet ships*

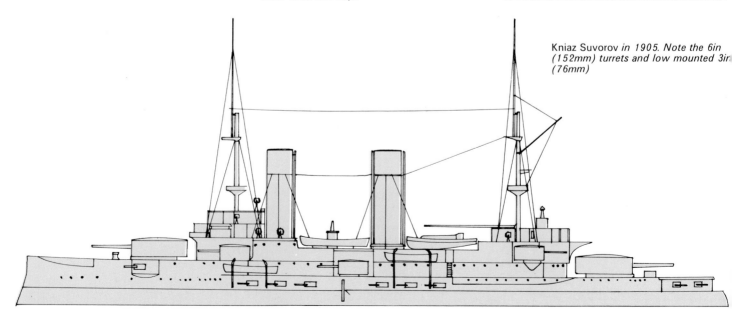

Kniaz Suvorov *in 1905. Note the 6in
(152mm) turrets and low mounted 3in
(76mm)*

Petropavlosk

BATTLESHIP
CLASS: *Gangut* class (4 ships)
Gangut renamed *Oktyabrskaya Revolutsia*. *Sevastopol* renamed *Parizhskaya Kommuna* · *Petropavlosk* renamed *Marat* · *Poltava* renamed *Mikhail Frunze*

Service career PETROPAVLOSK
1915 Covered minelaying operations.
1916–1917 Operations in Gulf of Finland.
1919 Supported Red Army operations.
1919 (30 May) Exchanged fire with British ships.
1919 (18 Aug) Torpedoed in Kronstadt harbour: sank in shallow water and salved.
1920 (28 Feb) *Petropavlosk* revolution: crew ded rising.
1923 Renamed *Marat*.
1926–1928 Refit and partial modernisation: bridge enlarged; bow altered; oil-fired boilers fitted; fore-funnel raised and upper part raked.
1937 (May) Attended British Coronation Review, Spithead.
1939 (Dec) Bombarded Finnish shore positions.
1941 (Sept) Damaged in Kronstadt harbour by German 150mm land artillery.
1941 (23 Sept) Hit by several bombs on bow: a magazine exploded and bow blown off; sank in shallow water.
1941–1944 C and D turrets used as artillery; B turret also used after repairs.
1943 Renamed *Petropavlosk*; bow not replaced.
circa 1952 Scrapped.

After Russia's catastrophic losses during the Russo-Japanese War, the Russian fleet had to be totally rebuilt. Her first dreadnoughts, the *Ganguts*, replaced the lost Baltic battleships. Before they were begun, designs were commissioned from most major warship builders, but none was adopted, partly because of Russia's insistence on an indigenous design. However, many features from these designs were incorporated in the *Ganguts*, which closely followed the Italian General Cuniberti's ideas for heavily armed fast ships with less emphasis on armour. They were similar in many respects to the smaller Italian battleship *Dante Alighieri*, with triple centreline 12in (305mm) turrets, but they had flush decks, and a different arrangement of machinery and armour. Unfortunately, their extra size was largely wasted. They were only marginally faster, carried virtually the same armament, and their armour was not as well arranged. This last was spread thinly over a large area of the hull to deal with the threat from quick-firing guns · revealed by the Russo-Japanese war, but gave little protection against longer range fire now being adopted by other navies. Curiously, the Russian 12in (305mm) 52cal gun was extremely accurate at long range. The size and weight of the machinery and armour meant that torpedo bulkheads were not fitted. In an attempt to reduce scantlings, high-tensile steel was used throughout. Unfortunately

Displacement:		
standard tons (tonnes)	25,000 (25,400)	
full load tons (tonnes)	26,170 (26,590)	
Dimensions:		
length (pp)	590·5ft (180m)	
(oa)	606·5ft (184·9m)	
beam	88·25ft (26·9m)	
draught	30·5ft (9·3m)	
Armament:	**as built**	**in 1941**
guns		
12in (305mm) 52cal	12	12
4·7in (120mm)	16	16
3pdr (47mm)	1	—
45mm	—	7
0·3in (7·62mm)	8	—
torpedo tubes		
18in (450mm)	4	4
aircraft	—	1
Armour:		
side (belt)	8·9in (255mm)	
(ends)	4·9in (125mm)	
deck	1–1·5in (25–38mm)	
main turrets	4·1–8in (105–203mm)	
barbettes	8in (203mm)	
casemates	5in (127mm)	
Machinery:		
boilers (type)	Yarrow	Yarrow
(number)	25 coal and oil	22 oil
engines (type)	Parsons single reduction geared turbines	
shafts	4	
Total SHP:		
designed	42,000	
total	61,000	
Fuel capacity:		
oil tons (tonnes)	2,050 (2,080)	
Performance:		
designed speed	23kts	
trial speed	23·4kts	
range	1,120 miles (940nm) @ 23kts	
Crew:	1,286	

Ship:	SEVASTOPOL	POLTAVA	GANGUT	PETROPAVLOSK
Where built:	Baltic Yard, St Petersburg	Admiralty Yard, St Petersburg	Admiralty Yard, St Petersburg	Baltic Yard, St Petersburg
Ordered:	1908	1908	1908	1908
Laid down:	13 July 1909	13 July 1909	13 July 1909	13 July 1909
Launched:	26 June 1911	10 July 1911	7 Oct 1911	9 Sept 1911
Completed:	17 Nov 1914	17 Dec 1914	5 Jan 1915	3 Nov 1915
Fate:	Renamed *Parizhskaya Kommuna* circa 1924; renamed *Sevastopol* 1943; scrapped 1957	Renamed *Mikhail Frunze* 1920; cannibalised for spares; hulk scrapped 1956	Renamed *Oktyabrskaya Revolutsia* 7 July 1925; scrapped 1956	Renamed *Marat* 1923; renamed *Petropavlosk* 1943; scrapped 1952

it was beyond the capacity of Russian heavy industry to produce this in sufficient quantities in the required time. Partly because of this, the *Ganguts* took longer to build than their foreign contemporaries and were outclassed before they were completed. Their detail design and construction were supervised by the British firm of John Brown, one of several foreign shipbuilders that were assisting the modernisation of the Russian shipyards at this time. Although the use of triple turrets meant that a powerful armament could be carried, the absence of superfiring caused the bow and stern turrets to be mounted near the ends of the hull, and the *Ganguts* were very wet in any sea. It also

meant lack of adequate end-on fire. The secondary armament was badly sited, and was of little use in rough weather. Because they were intended for the Baltic, they had an icebreaking bow. An improved version, the *Imperatritsa Maria* class with thicker armour, was designed by the British firm of Vickers, and built in the Black Sea, and an enlarged version, the *Borodino* class battle-cruisers, armed with 14in (356mm) guns, was laid down but not completed in the Baltic. *Poltava* (renamed *Mikhail Frunze*) was badly damaged by fire in 1922 and cannibalised for spares. *Gangut* (renamed *Oktyabrskaya Revolutsia*) and *Sevastopol* had similar careers to *Petropavlosk*.

Left: Petropavlosk of the Gangut *class as completed in 1915. Note the flush deck, vestigial upperworks, upright fore-funnel and the arrangement of main turrets*

Far left: Battleships of the Russian Baltic fleet during World War I. The nearest vessels are battleships of the Gangut *class*

Marat of the Gangut *class after rebuilding. Note the arrangement of turrets*

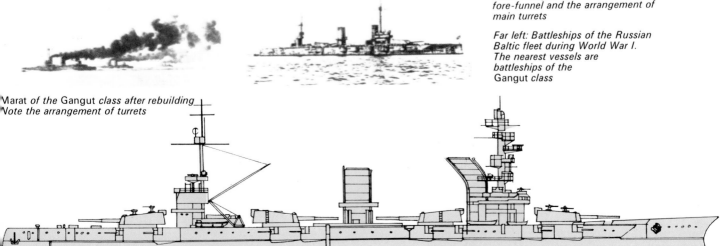

Moskva
HELICOPTER-CARRIER
CLASS: *Moskva* class (2 ships)
Moskva · Leningrad

By the mid-1960s the Soviet Navy had begun to maintain semi-permanent fleets in the North Atlantic and Mediterranean, in much the same way that the Americans have done since the end of World War II. In addition to the anti-aircraft defence provided by individual ships' normal complements of guns and missiles, some of the older SSM-armed guided-missile destroyers have been converted into specialist anti-aircraft escorts. In the same way, although every modern Soviet warship down to patrol boat size has a multiplicity of anti-submarine weapons and detectors, these are insufficient in themselves to counter the threat posed by the very sophisticated Western nuclear submarines. A requirement therefore existed for a specialist large anti-submarine vessel. The resulting single-ended *Moskva* class helicopter carriers resemble the earlier French *Jeanne d'Arc* (R-97) and the later Italian *Vittorio Veneto* (C-550), but are much larger and more sophisticated ships, equipped not only with a sizeable force of helicopters but also with a complete range of anti-submarine and anti-aircraft weapons and detectors. They are not intended to operate on their own, and therefore do not require SSMs. The hull design is unique, with the maximum width at flight deck level coming three-quarters aft. There is massive flare to the hull aft to permit a flight deck 295·3ft (90m) long and 115ft (35m) wide to be carried. This has three elevators to the hangar below, two in the flight deck itself and one inside the superstructure at the forward end of the flight deck. The *Moskvas* can operate up to 18 Kamov Ka-25 'Hormone' anti-submarine helicopters with dipping sonars and A/S torpedoes. The quarterdeck is open right aft to allow a variable depth sonar to be operated, and they also have a hull mounted sonar. The two MBU-2500 A/S rocket-launchers are mounted in the bows, and immediately behind them there is a SUWN-1 twin-launcher firing FRAS-1 and SSN-14 long-range anti-submarine missiles. Behind this there are two superimposed SAN-3 'Goblet' SAM twin launchers. The two twin 57mm guns are mounted either side of the bridge, and quintuple 21in (533mm) A/S torpedo tubes are fitted either side amidships. The large piled-up superstructure terminates abruptly in a large mack surrounded by 'Topsail' 3-dimensional radar. Despite their unconventional design, the *Moskvas* are good seaboats, able to operate helicopters in rough weather. They are very useful ships, but lack the flexibility of a through-deck design, which is better suited for operating V/STOL aircraft. They have therefore been succeeded by the much larger *Kievs*. *Moskva* was modified for a time to act as a trials ship for the Yakovlev Yak-36 'Forger' V/STOL aircraft.

Displacement:	
standard tons (tonnes)	14,500 (14,730)
full load tons (tonnes)	18,000 (18,290)
Dimensions:	
length (wl)	624·8ft (190·5m)
(pp)	644·8ft (196·6m)
beam (wl)	75·9ft (23m)
(ext)	115ft (35m)
draught	24·9ft (7·6m)
Armament:	
guns	
57mm	4
missiles	
SAN-3 SAM twin launchers	2
A/S weapons	
SUWN-1 twin launcher	1
MBU 2500A 12-barrel rocket-launcher	2
torpedo tubes	
21in (533mm)	10
aircraft	18 helicopters
Machinery:	
boilers (type)	watertube
(number)	4
engines (type)	geared turbines
shafts	2
Total SHP:	
designed	100,000
Fuel capacity:	
oil tons (tonnes)	?
Performance:	
designed speed	30kts
range	?
Crew:	approx 800

Ship:	**MOSKVA**	**LENINGRAD**
Where built:	Nikolayev South	Nikolayev South
Built:	1962–1967	1963–1968
Fate:	In service	In service

Service career MOSKVA
1967 Commissioned. Has operated in Northern Fleet, Mediterranean, Black Sea, Red Sea and Indian Ocean. Used as a trials ship for V/STOL aircraft.

Right, upper: Hormone helicopters on Moskva's flight deck. Other A/S armament includes a SUWN-1 twin launcher, two 12-barrel rocket launchers and 10 21in/533mm TTs

Right: The helicopter carrier Moskva at sea in 1969. This view clearly shows the unique flared flight deck, with its maximum width three quarters aft

Right, lower: British Nimrod A/S aircraft overflying a Moskva class helicopter cruiser. Note the wide beam aft, open stern, lift on flight deck, and entrance to another lift below the funnel

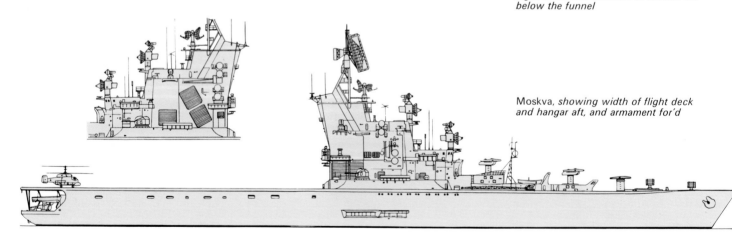

Moskva, showing width of flight deck and hangar aft, and armament for'd

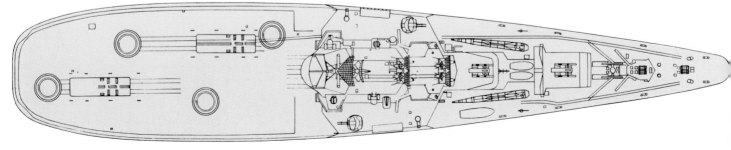

Kirov Class
CRUISER
CLASS: *Kirov* class (6 ships)
including *Kirov · Kalinin*

Sverdlov Class
CRUISER
CLASS: *Sverdlov* class (14 ships)
including *Sverdlov · Zhdanov*

After the Revolution, the Soviet Navy completed three of eight light cruisers laid down in 1913. The last of these, *Krasny Kavkaz* (ex-*Admiral Lazarev*), was completed in 1932 with a new 7·1in (180mm) gun mounted in single turrets. This gun was mounted in triple turrets in the new *Kirov* class. These were designed with the help of the Italian firm of Ansaldo, and were very similar in many respects to contemporary Italian light cruisers. They had a long fo'c's'le extending to just abaft the forward funnel, and there was a catapult between the fore and aft funnel. This was replaced in 1941 by more anti-aircraft guns. The last four ships had a slightly different rig and superstructure. *Molotov* (renamed *Slava* in 1958) had her damaged stern replaced by that of the incomplete *Chapaev* class cruiser *Frunze* in 1942–1944. *Kirov* was latterly employed as a training ship, and *Voroshilov* as an experimental vessel. Five of six improved and lengthened cruisers, the *Chapaevs*, were completed after World War II, although they were laid down in 1938–1939. These had four triple 5·9in (150mm) turrets, and had a standard displacement of 11,300 tons (11,480 tonnes). These were a more seaworthy design, and had a considerably greater range. The sixth *Chapaev* was destroyed on its slip, as were several larger cruisers and one of the two *Sovietsky Soyuz* class battleships. The other, building at Leningrad, was scrapped incomplete after the war. In the late 1940s the Russians were very short of modern heavy units, and 24 improved *Chapaevs* were projected. The *Sverdlovs* are very similar to the *Chapaevs*, but have the fo'c's'le break abaft X turret instead of abaft the fore funnel, and they also have a beamier hull, with an improved AA armament and higher powered engines. They are the last all-gun-armed cruisers to be built, and they compare unfavourably in protection and armament with the somewhat earlier American *Oregon City* class, which are of similar size. Nevertheless, they are powerful ships, with a good range and a large anti-aircraft armament. Seventeen were laid down, but only 14 completed before Krushchev stopped the programme. The later ships have a slightly differently arranged light anti-aircraft armament. *Ordzhonikedze* was transferred to Indonesia and renamed *Irian* in 1962, but she proved a white elephant and was later returned and scrapped. *Dzerzhinski* was fitted with an SAN-2 Guideline SAM twin launcher in place of X turret in 1961, and both *Admiral Senyavin* and *Zhdanov* were fitted with a SAN-4 SAM twin retractable launcher in place of X turret, an altered light anti-aircraft gun armament and improved communications facilities in 1972. Both can operate a helicopter, and *Admiral Senyavin* has had Y turret removed, X turret being replaced by a hangar. They are the Russian equivalent of the American converted *Cleveland* class light cruisers, now used as flagships.

Later Sverdlov *class. Note massive control tower and minerails aft*

	Kirov class		Sverdlov class	
Displacement:				
standard tons (tonnes)	8,800 (8,940)		15,450 (15,700)	
full load tons (tonnes)	11,500 (11,680)		18,000 (18,290)	
Dimensions:				
length (pp)	613·5ft (187m)		656·2ft (200m)	
(oa)	626·7ft (191m)		689ft (210m)	
beam	59ft (18m)		72·2ft (22m)	
draught	20ft (6·1m)		24·5ft (7·5m)	
Armament:	**Kirov as built**	**Kirov in 1970**	**Sverdlov as built**	**Zhdanov in 1972**
guns				
7·1in (180mm)	9	9	—	—
6in (152mm)	—	—	12	9
3·9in (100mm)	6	8	12	12
45mm	6	—	—	—
37mm	—	16	32	16
30mm	—	—	—	8
12·7mm	4	—	—	—
missiles				
SAN-4 SAM twin launcher	—	—	—	1
torpedo tubes				
21in (533mm)	6	—	10	—
mine capacity	90	90	150	—
aircraft	2	—	—	1 helicopter (*Senyavin* only)
Armour:	**Kirov**		**Sverdlov**	
side (belt)	3in (75mm)		3·9–4·9in (100–125mm)	
(ends)	—		1·6–2in (40–50mm)	
deck (upper)	—		1–2in (25–50mm)	
(main)	2in (50mm)		2–3in (50–75mm)	
main turrets	3·9in (100mm)		4·9in (125mm)	
Machinery:				
boilers (type)	Yarrow or Normand		?	
(number)	6		4	
engines (type)	geared turbines		geared turbines	
shafts	2		2	
Total SHP:				
designed	113,000		130,000	
Fuel capacity:				
oil tons (tonnes)	1,280 (1,300)		4,000 (4,050) (approx)	
Performance:				
designed speed	35kts		34kts	
range	3,570 miles (3,000nm) @ 18kts		10,350 miles (8,700nm) @ 18kts	
Crew:	734		1,000 (approx)	

Class:	**KIROV class**	**SVERDLOV class**
Where built:	various yards	various yards
Authorised:	?	?
Built:	1935–1944	1950–1958
Fate:	stricken circa 1958–1975	*Admiral Nakhimov* and *Irian* (ex-*Ordzhonikedze*) scrapped; remainder in service

Above: A Sverdlov *class cruiser at sea in 1974. Entering service in 1952–58, the 14 ships of this class were the last all-gun-armed cruisers built*

Kresta I and II Class

GUIDED-MISSILE CRUISER
CLASS: *Kresta I* class (4 ships)
Vice-Admiral Drozd · Admiral
Zozulya · Sevastopol · Vladivostok

GUIDED-MISSILE CRUISER
CLASS: *Kresta II* class (11 ships)
including *Admiral Isakov · Marshal
Voroshilov*

Kara Class

GUIDED-MISSILE CRUISER
CLASS: *Kara* class (5+ ships)
including *Nikolayev · Azov*

The Russian guided-missile cruisers were originally built in response to the threat posed to the Soviet Union by the large American carrier force. The four *Kynda* class were the first Russian cruisers to be designed for this purpose. Built between 1960 and 1965, with a standard displacement of 4,800 tons (4,877 tonnes), they were armed with two quadruple-launchers for SSN-3 'Shaddock' SSMs. This large cruise missile has a range of about 475 miles (400nm) and is also mounted in the early Russian cruise-missile armed submarines. The *Kyndas* have a SAN-1 'Goa' SAM twin-launcher forward and two twin 3in (76mm) mounts aft. Two tracking radars are fitted for the SSMs, enabling them to engage two targets simultaneously, but no helicopter is carried. This makes the *Kyndas* dependent on other ships or aircraft for mid-course guidance for the SSMs. The *Kresta Is* are enlarged developments of the *Kyndas*. Whereas the latter design gave priority to the SSM armament, the *Kresta Is* (and the *Kresta II* and *Kara* classes developed from them) have a very powerful anti-aircraft and anti-submarine armament. In the *Kresta Is* the SSN-3 SSMs are mounted in pairs on either side of the bridge. They are double-ended ships, with a SAN-1 'Goa' SAM twin-launcher fore and aft on deckhouse magazines. Whereas the *Kyndas* have two prominent masts and funnels, the *Kresta Is* have their SSM guidance radar on a single enormous mack amidships. Instead of the *Kyndas'* long quarterdeck, the *Kresta Is* have a very short one with a helicopter pad and hangar mounted on it. The Kamov Ka-25 'Hormone' was designed for anti-submarine work, but could also be used for mid-course guidance for the SSMs. By the late 1960s the A/S problem apparently took precedence and the *Kresta IIs* were fitted with two quadruple launchers for the long-range SSN-14 A/S weapon. The SAN-1 'Goa' SAMs were replaced by the improved longer ranged SAN-3 'Goblet' SAMs. Close-in anti-aircraft defence is provided by the 30mm mounts amidships. Bow sonar is fitted, and as with all modern Soviet warships, a powerful anti-submarine armament is fitted. The helicopter pad and hangar are raised by one deck, which makes them less likely to be damaged in rough seas, and this and the large 'Topsail' 3-dimen-

Continued on page 198 ▶

Displacement:	Kresta I class as built	Kresta II class as built	Kara class as built
standard tons (tonnes)	6,140 (6,230)	6,000 (6,090)	8,200 (8,330)
full load tons (tonnes)	7,500 (7,620)	7,500 (7,620)	10,000 (10,160)
Dimensions:			
length (oa)	510ft (155·5m)	519·9ft (158·5m)	570ft (173·8m)
beam	55ft (16·8m)	55·1ft (16·8m)	60ft (18·3m)
draught	18ft (5·5m)	19·7ft (6m)	20ft (6·2m)
Armament:			
guns			
3in (76mm)	—	—	4
57mm	4	4	4
30mm multi-barrel	—	4	4
missiles			
SSN-3 SSM twin launcher	2	—	—
SSN-14 ASW quadruple launcher	—	2	2
SAN-1 SAM twin launcher	2	—	—
SAN-3 SAM twin launcher	—	2	2
SAN-4 SAM twin launcher	—	—	2
A/S weapons			
MBU 2500A 12-barrel rocket-launcher	2	2	2
MBU 4500A 6-barrel rocket-launcher	2	2	2
torpedo tubes			
21in (533mm)	10	10	10
aircraft	1 helicopter	1 helicopter	1 helicopter
Machinery:			
boilers (type)	watertube	watertube	—
(number)	4	4	—
engines (type)	steam turbine	steam turbine	gas turbine
shafts	2	2	2
Total SHP:			
designed	100,000	100,000 approx	120,000
Fuel capacity:			
oil tons (tonnes)	?	?	?
Performance:			
designed speed	34kts	33kts	34kts
range	4,500 miles (3,780nm) @ 18kts	5,000 miles (4,200nm) @ 18kts	? ? ?
Crew:	400	500	(?) 500

Class:	KRESTA I class	KRESTA II class	KARA class
Where built:	Zhdanov, Leningrad	Zhdanov, Leningrad	Nikolayev
Built:	1964–1968	1968 onward	1971 onward
Fate:	*Vice-Admiral Drozd* refitted 1975; in service	In service and under construction	In service and under construction

Above: The Kara *class guided
missile cruiser Ochakov.
Enlarged versions of the* Kresta IIs,
*these are the first
large gas-turbine powered warships*

Admiral Oktyabrsky of the Kresta II
class. Note the raised flight deck

▶Kresta I and II Class/Kara Class

sional radar serve to distinguish the *Kresta II*s from the *Kresta I*s. The *Kara*s are enlarged gas-turbine powered versions of the *Kresta II*s. The extra size has been used to mount two retractable SAN-4 SAM twin-launchers, and the heavy anti-aircraft armament has been increased in calibre. They are the first large warships to have gas turbines, which have been in service with the Soviet Navy in the *Kashin* class destroyers for over a decade. The *Kara*s can be distinguished from the *Kresta II*s by their longer hull and the large separate funnel necessitated by the use of gas turbines. Compared with contemporary American cruisers, the Russian ships are much more heavily armed, but the long-ranged American ships have large and very seaworthy hulls, and until recently they have relied mainly on the carrier-borne aircraft for long-range surface attack. They are intended mainly as anti-submarine and anti-aircraft escorts, whereas the Russian ships have not only had to provide protection against the mo[st] sophisticated American submarines and aircra[ft] but also provide their own long-range surfac[e] attack capability. As a result the Russian ship[s] have a relatively short range, and although the[y] have a low silhouette, this is at the expense [of] freeboard and room for the crew and sophist[i-] cated electronics. As a result they may well n[ot] be able to function as efficiently in action as th[e] less cramped American vessels.

Kara *class. Note large funnel with four Gatling mounts abreast of it*

Above: Ochakov *on exercise in 1976. Although much more heavily armed than their American equivalents, the* Kara *class have a relatively short range*

Leningrad Class

DESTROYER
CLASS: *Leningrad* class (6 ships)
including *Leningrad · Minsk*

Gordi Class

DESTROYER
CLASS: *Gordi* class (Type VII)
(29 ships) including *Gordi ·*
Steregushilly

When new destroyers came to be designed in the 1930s assistance was sought, as with the *Kirov* class cruisers, from Italy. The resulting Type VII *Gordi* class bore a marked resemblance to contemporary Italian designs. Unfortunately their scantlings and hull form were more suited to Mediterranean than Arctic conditions, and they were structurally weak and poor seaboats. Russian manufacturers could not produce engines to the required tolerances, and their machinery gave constant trouble. Few could attain the designed 38kts. A modified and strengthened version, the Type VII-U was built with unit machinery, twin funnels, thicker scantlings and a more seaworthy hull. The anti-aircraft armament was increased and modern electronics equipment fitted when it was obtained from Britain and America towards the end of the war. The *Leningrad* class were even less successful. Loosely based on the French super-destroyers and designed with French assistance, too much was attempted on too small a displacement. They succumbed very quickly to battle-damage. The 5·1in (130mm) mount between the bridge and fore-funnel was badly sited, with very limited arcs of fire. The *Kiev* class, a modified version with twin 5·1in (130mm) turrets, was laid down but none was completed. The *Leningrads* were even worse seaboats than the *Gordis*. A large fast destroyer, *Tashkent*, was built for the Russians in Italy, but it was also very lightly built and had many teething troubles. The Russian destroyers saw little action during World War II, being used mostly as fast troop transports in the Black Sea, and for purely local defence purposes in Arctic and Pacific waters.

Displacement:	Gordi class	Leningrad class
standard tons (tonnes)	1,660 (1,687)	2,225 (2,260)
full load tons (tonnes)	2,039 (2,072)	2,582 (2,623)
Dimensions:		
length (pp)		
(oa)	370·25ft (112·9m)	418ft (127·5m)
beam	33·5ft (10·2m)	38·5ft (12·7m)
draught	12·25ft (3·8m)	13·25ft (4·1m)
Armament:		
guns		
5·1in (130mm)	4	5
3in (76mm)	2	2
45mm	—	2
37mm	4	
20mm	1	—
7·62mm	8	
torpedo tubes		
21in (533mm)	6	8
mine capacity	60	68
Machinery:		
boilers (type)	?	?
(number)	3	3
engines (type)	single reduction geared turbines	
shafts	2	3
Total SHP:		
designed	48,000	66,000
Fuel capacity:		
oil tons (tonnes)	540 (550)	600 (610)
Performance:		
designed speed	38kts	36kts
range	2,600 miles (2,190nm) @ 19kts	2,100 miles (1,770nm) @ 20kts
Crew:	197	250

Class:	GORDI class	LENINGRAD class
Where built:	Various yards	Various yards
Authorised:	?	?
Built:	1936–1943	1932–1940
Fate:	*Reshityelny* (i) total loss (incomplete) 7 Nov 1938; *Bdytelny* sunk 2 July 1942; *Bezpushchadny* sunk 6 Oct 1943; *Bezuprechny* sunk 26 June 1942; *Bystry* total loss 1 July 1941; *Gnevny* sunk 23 June 1941; *Gremyashchy* sunk 14 Nov 1941; *Stremitelny* sunk 20 July 1941; *Smetlivy* sunk 4 Nov 1941; *Sokrushitelny* lost 22 Nov 1942; remainder scrapped 1950s–1060s; *Reshitelny* (ii), *Retivy*, *Rezhky* and (?) *Razyashchy* transferred to China in 1955; *Gordi* sunk 14 Nov 1941	*Moskva* sunk 26 June 1941; *Kharkov* sunk 6 Oct 1943; remainder scrapped 1950s–1960s

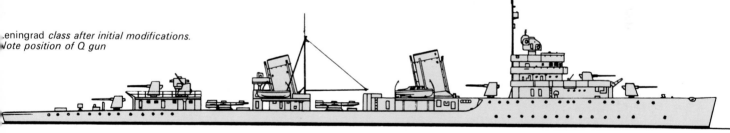

Leningrad *class after initial modifications.
Note position of Q gun*

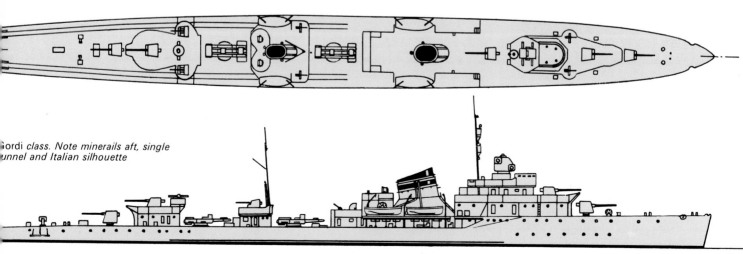

Gordi class. Note minerails aft, single funnel and Italian silhouette

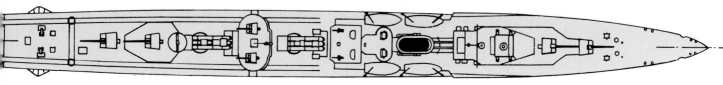

Skory Class

DESTROYER
CLASS: *Skory* class (75 ships)
including *Skory · Svobodny*

The *Otlichny* class, an improved version of the Type VII-U, was designed in 1937 as *Projekt 30*. At least 17 were laid down before Russia was invaded, but only about eight were completed after the war. One, *Georgi Dmitrov* (ex-*Ogneroi*), was transferred to Bulgaria in 1956. These had four 5·1in (130mm) guns in two twin mounts to reduce topweight and improve seaworthiness. The *Skorys* were developed from this design, with a modified hull and quintuple rather than quadruple torpedo tubes. About 85 of this successful conventional design were projected, but the last 10 or so were cancelled in favour of the improved *Tallin* and *Kotlin* classes. The *Skorys* used the same 5·1in (130mm) twin mount as the *Otlichnys*, and had an identical anti-aircraft armament as first completed. Minor differences exist in such details as the type of foremast between various members of the class. The modernised *Skorys* have improved anti-aircraft and anti-submarine weapons and more modern electronics. They can be distinguished from the unmodified ships by their two heavy latticed tripod masts surmounted by radar, with another small lattice mast aft, and by reduction to one torpedo tube mounting. The *Skorys* were built in greater numbers than any other Russian destroyers, and several have been transferred. They are now obsolete and over-age, and are being rapidly discarded. An enlarged version with a flush deck, known as the *Tallin* class, were built between 1952 and 1954. They had four 5·1in (130mm) guns in two fully stabilised twin turrets with integral directors.

Below: A Skory *class destroyer. These were built in greater numbers than any other Russian destroyers.*

Displacement:		
standard tons (tonnes)	2,600 (2,640)	
full load tons (tonnes)	3,100 (3,150)	
Dimensions:		
length (oa)	395·2ft (120·5m)	
beam	38·9ft (11·8m)	
draught	15·1ft (4·6m)	
Armament:	**as built**	**as modernised**
guns		
5·1in (130mm) 50cal	4	4
3·4in (85mm) 50cal	2	—
57mm	—	5
37mm	8	—
torpedo tubes		
21in (533mm)	10	5
A/S weapons		
DCT	4	—
MBU-2500 16-barrel rocket-launcher	—	2
mine capacity	80	80
Machinery:		
boilers (type)	?	
(number)	4	
engines (type)	geared turbines	
shafts	2	
Total SHP:		
designed	60,000	
Fuel capacity:		
oil tons (tonnes)	?	
Performance:		
designed speed	33kts	
range	3,900 miles (3,280nm) @ 13kts	
Crew:	260	

Class:	**SKORY class**
Where built:	Molotovsk, Leningrad; Nikolayev Zhdanov, Leningrad; Komsomolsk
Authorised:	?
Built:	1948–1954
Fate:	Several modernised from 1959 with improved radar and armament; 12 ships transferred 1956–1964: Egypt 6 ships including *Suez*; Indonesia 4 ships including *Diponegoro*; Poland 2 ships *Grom* (ex-*Smetlivy*) and *Wicher* (ex-*Skory*)

Unmodified Skory class. Note two TT mounts, minerails and radar on foremast

Krivak Class

GUIDED-MISSILE DESTROYER
CLASS: *Krivak* class (14+ ships)
including *Bditelny · Bodry*

The 19 *Kashin* class guided missile destroyers built between 1962 and 1966 were the world's first operational warships to be fitted with gas turbines. Displacing 3,750 tons (3,810 tonnes) standard, they are a relatively conventional double-ended anti-aircraft design, armed with two SAN-1 'Goa' SAM twin-launchers. A number of the class have been converted to allow an SSM to be mounted, and to improve the anti-submarine armament. With a 10ft (3m) hull extension, they have four SSN-2 (mod) SSMs, variable depth sonar and a helicopter pad aft. *Otvazkny* of this class was destroyed by an internal explosion in the Black Sea on 31 August 1974. The *Krivaks* take full advantage of the gas turbine's light weight and high power, and mount a very powerful multi-purpose armament on a hull with a very high beam-to-length ratio. Contrary to initial reports these ships are anti-submarine vessels, with a quadruple SSN-14 ASW missile mounting in the bow. The SAN-4 SAM retractable launchers are mounted fore and aft, and the 3in (76mm) twin turrets are mounted aft just ahead of the variable depth sonar. The two quadruple A/S torpedo tubes are fitted either side of the superstructure amidships. These ships have high speed and very heavy armament compared with Western designs, but are not able to operate a helicopter. They must have very cramped accommodation for the necessary electronics and large crew. Unlike most western vessels, their gas turbines are all the same size.

Displacement:		
standard tons (tonnes)	3,300 (3,350)	
full load tons (tonnes)	3,900 (3,960)	
Dimensions:		
length (oa)	404·8ft (123.4m)	
beam	45·9ft (14m)	
draught	16·4ft (5m)	
Armament:	first ships	later ships
guns		
3·9in (100mm)	—	2
3in (76mm)	4	—
30mm.	4	4
missiles		
SSN-14 ASW		
quadruple launcher	1	1
SAN-4 SAM twin launcher	2	2
torpedo tubes		
21in (533mm)	8	
A/S weapons		
MBU 2500A 12-barrel		
rocket-launcher	2	
Machinery:		
gas turbines (type)	?	
(number)	4	
shafts	2	
Total SHP:		
designed	70,000	
Performance:		
designed speed	33kts	
range	?	
Fuel capacity:		
oil tons (tonnes)	?	
Crew:	approx 250	

Class:	**KRIVAK class**
Where built:	Kaliningrad and Kamysh Borun, Kerch
Delivered:	1971 onward
Fate:	In service and under construction

Above: A Krivak *class guided-missile destroyer. Entering service since 1971, these gas-turbine powered ships mount a powerful A/S armament*

Krivak *class. Note SAN-4 silos abaft SSN-14 launchers, and VDS aft*

Krab
SUBMARINE
CLASS: *Krab* class (1 boat) *Krab*

Displacement:	
surface tons (tonnes)	500 (508)
submerged tons (tonnes)	740 (752)
Armament:	
torpedo tubes	
18in (457mm)	2
mines	60
Machinery:	
diesels (type)	Curtis
electric motors	—
shafts	2

Boat:	KRAB
Where built:	?
Authorised:	1908
Laid down:	1911
Launched:	1913
Commissioned:	1915
Fate:	Scuttled 1919

This somewhat undistinguished submarine is included here for only one reason — she was the first submarine minelayer. At a time when the Russian navy, which had been early in the field of interest although not of development of the submarine, was trying to decide between a number of designs there came *Krab*. In 1899 the Russians had built two 60 ton (61 tonne) boats at St Petersburg, had improved on this design, bought six of Simon Lake's boats, which had the somewhat dubious advantage of wheels for bottom-riding and, after the Japanese war, had tried Holland's designs. They then turned to Professor Bubnov's designs and, later, to Germaniawerft, Kiel. The *Forel* was the first submarine ever built in Germany and though unsuccessful, was followed by an order for the *Karp* class which was built simultaneously wit the German *U-1*. Thus by 1914 the Russian had 30 operational submarines but *Krab*, lai down in 1908, was still under constructio Although details are a little sketchy this mediun sized boat (though large for her era) was revo lutionary in having two long free-flood tube each containing 30 moored mines lying hor zontal. Laying was achieved by an endless trac driven from within the pressure-hull. In he short life she succeeded in laying sever successful fields in the Black Sea and wa eventually scuttled by the Allies in April 191 'to prevent her falling into the hands of th Bolsheviks'. This took place, in fact, durin 1935 when she was raised and scrapped.

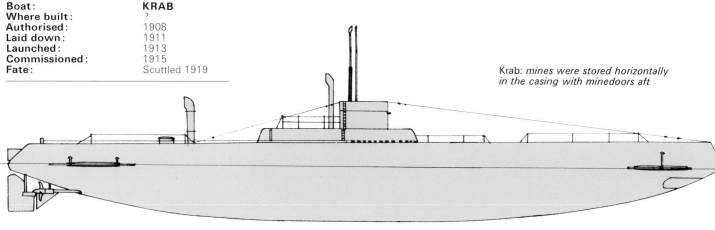

Krab: *mines were stored horizontally in the casing with minedoors aft*

SHCH Class (Chuka Class)
SUBMARINE
CLASS: *SHCH* class (88 boats)
Baltic 26 boats (8 transferred to Arctic) · Pacific 40 boats · Black Sea 16 boats · Arctic 16 boats
(1 transferred to Pacific)

This class, also known as the *Chukas*, was Soviet Russia's first wholly original submarine design. The initial Series III boats were designed in the late 1920s and were progressively developed. They were capable of a 20-day patrol, and the succeeding Series V boats (of which there were two variants) had an increased endurance as well as a strengthened conning tower and an extra gun. The first Series IIIs could only make 11kts on trials, and the Series Vs had an increased surface speed. The Series X were faster and had a better endurance, whilst the final Series X-*Bis* type had their performances further improved. As far as is known, surviving members of the early groups were updated to Series X-*Bis* standard. Early examples were named after types of fish as well as being given numbers. Units serving in the Baltic were numbered in the 300 series. In the Arctic the 400 series was used, whilst the 100 series was for the Pacific and the 200 for the Black Sea. Wartime service was unspectacular, like most of the Russian fleet. Few Axis vessels were lost to submarine attack, whilst the Russians suffered a high casualty rate. This poor performance was probably due more to inadequate equipment and training than to any inherent defect in the design of this class of submarine. *SHCH 305* was rammed and sunk in 1942 by the Finnish submarine *Vetehinen*, and *SHCH 214* was torpedoed by an Italian *MAS* boat.

Displacement:	Series III	Series X-Bis
surface tons (tonnes)	577 (586)	590 (599)
submerged tons (tonnes)	704 (715)	705 (716)
Dimensions:		
length (pp)	?	?
(oa)	187ft (57m)	192·5ft (58·7m)
beam	21ft (6·4m)	21ft (6·4m)
draught	12·5ft (3·8m)	?
Armament:		
guns		
47mm	1	2
12·7mm	—	2
torpedo tubes		
21in (533mm)	6	6
Machinery:		
diesels (type)	?	
(number)	2	
electric motors (type)	?	
shafts	2	
Total BHP:	1,370	
Total SHP:	800	
Fuel capacity:		
oil tons (tonnes)	?	
Performance:		
surface speed	13kts (designed)	14kts
submerged speed	8kts	8kts
range surface	3,866 miles (3,250nm) @ 8·3kts	
range submerged	131 miles (110nm) @ 1·75kts	
Crew:	37	

Class:	SHCH class
Where built:	Leningrad, Nicolayev, Vladivostok
Authorised:	?
Built:	1933–1948
Fate:	One sunk 1938; one wrecked 1940; 34 sunk 1941–1945; one wrecked circa 1950; remainder stricken circa 1960s

Chuka (SHCH) class showing the conning tower in 1940

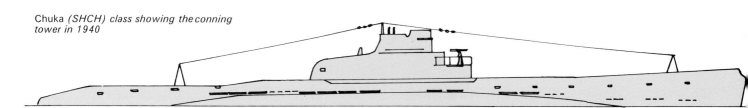

Whisky Class

SUBMARINE
CLASS: *Whisky* class (about
260 boats: USSR about 240, China
about 21)

SUBMARINE
CLASS: *Whisky Twin-Cylinder* class
(5 boats)

SUBMARINE
CLASS: *Whisky Long-Bin* class
(7 boats)

In the early 1950s the Russians built three types
of submarine, the *Quebec* class coastal boats
developed from prewar Russian designs, and
the medium range *Whisky* and the long range
Zulu classes, both of which were developed from
German designs. The *Whiskys* based on the
German Type XXIs, were formidable submarines
despite their relatively unsophisticated equipment, and the large numbers in which they were
built gave a considerable impetus to the development of a new generation of western anti-
submarine escorts, weapons and techniques. By
today's standards the *Whiskys* are noisy and
relatively easy to detect, and they are rapidly
being phased out of the Soviet Navy. Six
variants of the basic design were produced,
most of which differed mainly by the presence or
absence of a gun. The *Whisky Twin-Cylinder*
and the more efficient *Whisky Long-Bin* conversions were the first Russian cruise-missile-
armed submarines. Eighteen improved *Whiskys*,
the *Romeo* class, were built between 1958 and
1961, six being transferred to Egypt. The
Chinese have built about forty *Romeos*, and
they are still in production. The *Whisky Canvas
Bag* type were a radar picket version of the
basic *Whisky* design, and were the equivalent
of the American radar picket submarine conversions.

Right: A Whisky *class submarine,
one of a large class with
six design variants, based on the
German* Type XXIs, *which
entered service in the 1950s*

Displacement:	Whisky	Whisky Twin-Cylinder	Whisky Long-Bin
surface tons (tonnes)	1,030 (1,050)	1,100 (1,120)	1,200 (1,220)
submerged tons (tonnes)	1,180 (1,200)	1,600 (1,625)	1,800 (1,850)
Dimensions:			
length (oa)	249·3ft (76m)	249·3ft (76m)	275·6ft (84m)
beam	22ft (6·7m)	22ft (6·7m)	22ft (6·7m)
draught	15ft (4·6m)	15ft (4·6m)	15ft (4·6m)
Armament:			
missiles			
SSN-3 SAM single launcher	—	2	4
torpedo tubes			
21in (533mm)	6	6	6
Machinery:			
diesels (type)	?		
(number)	2		
electric motors (type)	?		
shafts	2		
Total BHP:	4,000		
Total SHP:	2,500		
Fuel capacity:			
oil tons (tonnes)	?		
Performance:			
surface speed	17kts		
submerged speed	15kts		
surface range	13,000 miles (11,000nm) @ 18kts		
submerged range	?		
Crew:	60		

Class:	**WHISKY class**
Where built:	various yards, USSR and China
Authorised:	?
Built:	1951–1964
Fate:	USSR: 5 converted to *Whisky Twin-Cylinder* 1958–1960; 7 converted to research submarines, renamed *Severyanka*, *Slavyanka*, circa 1972; 30 boats transferred: Albania 2 boats, Bulgaria 2 boats, Egypt 6 boats (2 from Poland), Indonesia 14 boats including *Nagapanda*, North Korea 4 boats, Poland 4 boats including *Orzel*. Over half the class have been stricken; China about 21 boats assembled from components from USSR or built in Chinese yards

Zulu V Class

BALLISTIC MISSILE
SUBMARINE
CLASS: *Zulu V* class (6 boats)
including *Lira · Orion · Vega*

The *Zulu* class are long-range versions of the
Whiskys, and like them are based on the
German Type XXI. They have a larger hull than
the *Whiskys*, with three rather than two shafts,
and have four more torpedo tubes. An improved
version, the *Foxtrot* class, was built between
1958 and 1975, with a longer hull and improved
performance. Eight *Foxtrots* were supplied to
India between 1968 and 1975. Five variants of
the basic *Zulu* design have been produced.
Four differ only in minor details. The *Zulu Vs*, on
the other hand, were converted from *Zulus*
and were fitted with a greatly enlarged fin containing two vertical launching tubes outside the
pressure hull for SSN-4 'Sark' SLBMs. These
surface-launched missiles have a nuclear warhead but have a range of only 350 miles (300nm)
which makes the *Zulu Vs* very vulnerable to
countermeasures. The SSN-4 SLBMs became
operational in 1958 and the *Zulu Vs* were the
first Russian ballistic missile submarines. They
are now obsolete and only one missile-armed
boat possibly remains in service. Two have been
reconverted to patrol submarines by removing
the missile tubes, and three are now research
vessels. The *Zulu Vs* acted as prototypes for the
Golf I and *II* diesel and the nine *Hotel* nuclear-
powered ballistic missile submarines.

*Zulu V class with two SSN-4 launching
tubes at aft end of fin*

Displacement	Zulu V	Zulu IV
surface tons (tonnes)	2,100 (2,130)	2,000 (2,030)
submerged tons (tonnes)	2,600 (2,640)	2,200 (2,240)
Dimensions:		
length (oa)	295·3ft (90m)	
beam	23·9ft (7·3m)	
draught	19ft (5·8m)	
Armament:		
missiles		
SSN-4 SSM	2	—
torpedo tubes		
21in (533mm)	6	10
Machinery:		
diesels (type)	?	
(number)	3	
electric motors (type)	?	
shafts	3	
Total BHP:	9,000	
Total SHP:	4,500	
Fuel capacity:		
oil tons (tonnes)	?	
Performance:		
surface speed	18kts	
submerged speed	15kts	
surface range	12,000 miles (10,000nm) @ 5kts	20,000 miles (16,670nm) @ 5kts
submerged range	?	?
Crew:	85	70

Class:	**ZULU V class**
Where built:	Various yards
Built Zulu IV:	1951–1955
Converted:	1955–1957
Fate:	Three converted to research submarines, renamed *Lira, Orion, Vega*; two in reserve

Echo II Class

NUCLEAR ATTACK SUBMARINE
CLASS: *Echo II* class (27 boats)

Charlie Class

NUCLEAR ATTACK SUBMARINE
CLASS: *Charlie I* class (12 boats)

	Echo II	Charlie I
Displacement:		
surface tons (tonnes)	4,800 (4,900)	4,300 (4,400)
submerged tons (tonnes)	5,600 (5,700)	5,100 (5,200)
Dimensions:		
length (oa)	390·7ft (119m)	304·8ft (94m)
beam	28·4ft (8·6m)	32·8ft (10m)
draught	25·9ft (7·9m)	24·6ft (7·5m)
Armament:		
missiles		
SSN-3 SSM	8	—
SSN-7 SSM	—	8
torpedo tubes		
21in (533mm)	6	8
15·7 (400mm)	4	1
Machinery:		
nuclear reactor (type)	?	?
(number)	1	1
engines (type)	steam turbines	steam turbines
shafts	2	1
Total SHP		
designed	22,500	24,000
Performance:		
surface speed	—	approx 20kts
submerged speed	approx 20kts	approx 30kts
range	?	approx 100
Crew:	approx 100	approx 100

Class:	ECHO II class	CHARLIE I class
Where built:	Severodvinsk and Komsomolsk	Gorki
Delivered:	1963–1967	1968 onward
Fate:	In service	In service

With the introduction in 1948 of the North American AJ Savage, the American carrier forces had an aircraft capable of carrying an atomic bomb. For the first time the American carrier forces represented a major threat to the Soviet Union. In the 1950s the Russians developed a number of cruise-missiles, one of which, the SSN-3 was intended for use in submarines. This could be launched at a long distance from the carrier task force's defences and at the time represented a credible answer to the threat posed by that task force. The first submarines to be equipped with the SSN-3 were the *Whisky Twin-Cylinder* and the *Whisky Long-Bin* conversions, but these were very crude, and the first true cruise-missile armed submarines were the five boats of the *Echo I* class, built between 1958 and 1962. Nuclear-powered, these were very similar to the *November* nuclear torpedo-armed and *Hotel* nuclear ballistic missile submarines. The *Echo I*s carried six SSN-3 'Shaddock' turbo-jet-powered SSMs in individual elevating tubes. in the casing, two ahead and four abaft the fin. These surface-launched missiles have a range of about 475 miles (400nm) and can carry either a high explosive or nuclear warhead, but require mid-course guidance. This makes both the missile and the aircraft or ship giving that guidance vulnerable to countermeasures. The *Echo I* class were soon superseded by the *Echo II*s, which differ mainly by having a slightly lengthened hull incorporating another pair of SSN-3 launchers abaft the fin. They are attached to both the Northern and the

Pacific Fleets. The *Echo I* class were all converted between 1973 and 1974. The SSN-3 launchers were removed and they are now armed solely with torpedoes. A conventionally powered class of SSN-3 cruise-missile armed submarines, the *Juliets*, was also built in the mid 1960s. The *Echos* are even noisier than the *Novembers*, because of the large holes in the casing around each missile launcher. This, combined with the need to surface to launch the missiles, makes them relatively easy to detect. The next class of nuclear cruise missile submarines largely rectified these faults. Although the *Charlies* are still noisier than foreign nuclear submarines, they are a great improvement on the *Echos*. They have much the same hull form and machinery as the *Victor I* class nuclear torpedo-armed submarines, and have a similarly high submerged speed. They are fitted with eight

tubes on the bow casing for SSN-7 SSM cruise-missiles. These have a range of about 30 miles (25nm), and so do not require mid-course guidance from another ship or aircraft, and they can be launched submerged, thus greatly decreasing the chances of detection. The *Charlie II* class is an enlarged version with improved capabilities and a similar but slightly longer cruise-missile submarine, the *Papa* class, has also been built. However, even the *Charlie II*s are not so sophisticated as the US nuclear submarines which can launch Harpoon anti-ship missiles from standard torpedo tubes. This missile is much smaller and less vulnerable than its Russian counterparts, and the US submarines may soon be fitted with submarine-launched long-range cruise-missiles which are ejected from standard torpedo tubes submerged. The Russians have as yet no equivalent to this.

Left: A Charlie I *nuclear cruise-missile submarine. These 4,300-ton boats mount eight SSN-7 SSMs and have eight 21in/533mm torpedo tubes*

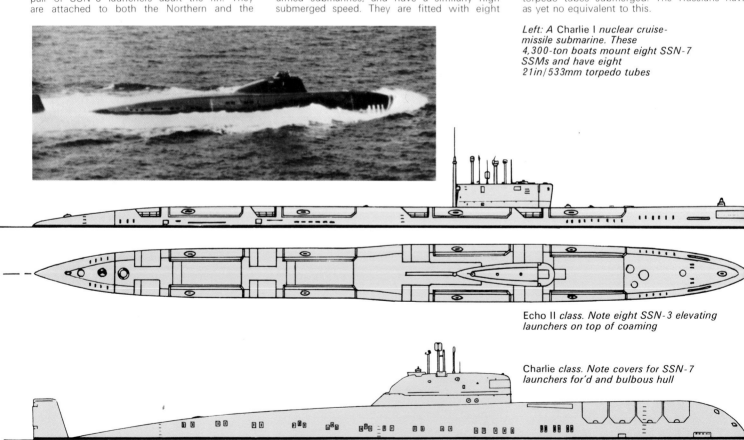

Echo II *class. Note eight SSN-3 elevating launchers on top of coaming*

Charlie *class. Note covers for SSN-7 launchers for'd and bulbous hull*

Yankee Class

NUCLEAR BALLISTIC MISSILE SUBMARINE
CLASS: *Yankee* class (34 boats)

Delta Class

NUCLEAR BALLISTIC MISSILE SUBMARINE
CLASS: *Delta I* class (10 boats)

NUCLEAR BALLISTIC MISSILE SUBMARINE
CLASS: *Delta II* class (4+ boats)

	Yankee class	Delta I class	Delta II class
Displacement:			
surface tons (tonnes)	8,000 (8,130)	9,000 (9,150)	?
submerged tons (tonnes)	9,000 (9,150)	10,000 (10,160)	? 16,000 (? 16,250)
Dimensions:			
length (oa)	426·5ft (130m)	450ft (137·2m)	500ft (152·5m)
beam	34·8ft (10·6m)	34·8ft (10·6m)	36ft (11m)
draught	32·8ft (10m)	32·8ft (10m)	34ft (10·4m)
Armament:			
missiles			
SSN-6 SLBM	16	—	—
SSN-8 SLBM	—	12	16
torpedo tubes			
21in (533mm)	8	8	8 (?)
Machinery:			
nuclear reactor (type)	?	?	?
(number)	?	?	?
engines (type)	geared turbines	geared turbines	geared turbines
shafts	2	2	2
Total SHP:			
designed	24,000	24,000	24,000
Performance:			
surface speed	?	?	?
submerged speed	approx 30kts	approx 25kts	approx 25kts
range	?	?	?
Crew:	about 120	about 120	?

Class:	YANKEE class	DELTA I class	DELTA II class
Where built:	Severodvinsk	Severodvinsk	Severodvinsk
Authorised:	?	?	?
Completed:	1967–1975	1973–1976	Circa 1975 onward
Fate:	In service	In service	In service and under construction

The *Yankee* class were the first Russian purpose-designed nuclear ballistic missile submarines to enter service, and (a decade after the Americans) they were the first Russian submarines to use hull-mounted SLBMs. The 16 missiles are arranged in two vertical rows of eight abaft the fin in a similar fashion to the American *Polaris* boats. They were initially armed with the SSN-6 'Sawfly' SLBM Mod 1, which has a single warhead and a range of 1,300 miles (1,100nm). In 1974 this was replaced by a longer range version, the Mod 2, which has a range of 1,600 miles (1,400nm) and a single warhead. In the same year an improved version, Mod 3, with the same range as Mod 2, but having three MRV warheads, was introduced, and this may replace both Mod 1 and Mod 2 missiles. As with all Russian submarines they are noisier than their Western equivalents, and correspondingly easier to detect. The relatively short range of the SSN-6, even in its later variants, means that the *Yankees* must approach the American coast before launching their missiles, but the ability to launch the SSN-6 submerged makes the *Yankees* somewhat less vulnerable than previous Russian ballistic missile submarines. Up to 1973 the

Americans had a considerable advantage in the quality of their SLBMs, but in that year the Russians introduced the SSN-8 SLBM. With a range of over 4,000 miles (3,500nm) and a CEP of only 1,300ft (400m), this not only has a larger range than the Poseidon but also outranges Trident. Initial trials were made using a *Hotel III* class nuclear ballistic missile submarine, and the missile is fitted in the *Delta I* and *II* class submarines. The *Delta I* class carries 12 missiles in two rows of six abaft the fin, and the considerably enlarged *Delta II*s carry two more rows

of two missiles. The SSN-8 Mod 1 carries a single warhead of between 1 to 2 megatons, the Mod 2 has three MRVs, and the Mod 3 has been tested with three MIRVs. A second slipway was built at the Severodvinsk shipyard in 1975 to enable the class to be built more quickly. These submarines are a great threat to the USA, because they can hit targets in the United States from launching areas in the Western Pacific or Murmansk regions, well out of reach of effective countermeasures.

Above: A Delta *class ballistic missile submarine. These 9,000-ton boats, which entered service from 1973 onwards, mount 12 to 16 SSN-8 missiles*

Yankee *class with 16 SSN-6 missile launching tubes in hull abaft fin*

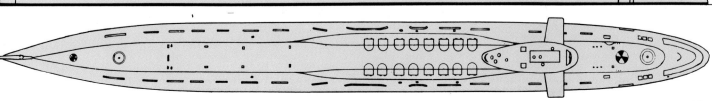

Grisha Class
CORVETTE
CLASS: *Grisha I* class (18+ ships) ·
Grisha II class (4+ ships) ·
Grisha III class

Since World War II the Russians have progressively developed designs of coastal anti-submarine vessels. The first postwar type, the *Kronstadt* class, was based on prewar submarine catcher designs. They were diesel-powered vessels of 310 tons (315 tonnes) standard displacement. The next class, the *So 1s*, introduced the MBU anti-submarine rocket. These displaced 215 tons (218 tonnes) light. The *Poti* class, built between 1961 and 1968, carried a much heavier anti-submarine armament and had mixed diesel and gas turbine machinery in a much larger hull which had a standard displacement of 550 tons (560 tonnes). They mounted two 12-barrel MBU-2500 rocket-launchers and two 16in (406mm) anti-submarine torpedo tubes as well as a twin 57mm gun turret. The *Grisha I* and *II* classes are enlarged versions of the *Potis*, with the hull again enlarged to improve seaworthiness and to enable a heavier anti-aircraft armament to be mounted. The *Grisha I* class mounts a retractable twin SAN-4 SAM launcher forward, which is replaced in the *Grisha IIs* by a second twin 57mm gun turret. In order to accommodate a balanced armament, the *Grishas* have been enlarged into something that is no longer a small expendable vessel, but a fully fledged warship capable of defending itself adequately against aircraft whilst possessing a reasonable anti-submarine armament. Examples of both the *Grisha I* and *Grisha II* are to be found in all the Russian fleets.

Displacement:			
standard tons (tonnes)	750 (760)		
full load tons (tonnes)	900 (910)		
Dimensions:			
length (oa)	246ft (75m)		
beam	32·8ft (10m)		
draught	9·2ft (2·8m)		
Armament:	Grisha I	Grisha II	Grisha III
guns			
57mm	2	4	4
30mm	—	—	1
missiles			
SAN-4 SAM twin launcher	1	—	—
A/S weapons			
MBU 2500A 12-barrel rocket-launcher	2	2	2
torpedo tubes			
21in (533mm)	4	4	4
mine capacity	?	?	?
Machinery:			
diesels (type)	?		
(number)	2		
gas turbines (type)	?		
(number)	1		
shafts	3		
Total HP:			
designed	24,000		
Fuel capacity:			
oil tons (tonnes)	?		
Performance:			
designed speed	30kts		
range	?		
Crew:	?		

Class:	GRISHA class
Where built:	?
Built:	1969 onward
Fate:	In service and under construction

Above: Grisha II *class. These small but seaworthy vessels provide an effective solution to the need for large numbers of short ranged A/S vessels for use in coastal waters*

Grisha II *class with twin 57mm mount for'd in place of SAN-4 silo*

Nanuchka Class
MISSILE PATROL BOAT
CLASS: *Nanuchka* class (14+ boats)

Osa Class
MISSILE PATROL BOAT
CLASS: *Osa* class (180+ boats)

The SSN-2 'Styx' SSM is one of several cruise-missiles developed by the Soviet Union in the mid-1950s, and is specifically intended as an anti-ship weapon for small surface vessels. It has a range of (?) 27 miles (23nm) and a high explosive warhead of about 900lbs (400kg). It is mounted on the *Komar* and *Osa I* classes. The *Komars*, which are an adaptation of the *P-6* torpedo boat design, carry two missiles on their launchers aft. Experience has shown that larger salvoes are necessary to ensure success and the *Komars* are too small to operate in anything other than moderate seas. The *Osa I* class, on the other hand, was designed specifically to take 'Styx', and has four launchers aft on a much larger hull. The *Osa II* class are fitted with four smaller and lighter launchers for the SSN-II (an improved 'Styx'), and was introduced in 1968–1969. A version of the *Osas* without missiles but possessing a torpedo armament, the *Stenka* class, has been built in considerable numbers from 1967 onward. The first success obtained by a shipborne guided missile came on 21 October 1967, when 'Styx' fired from Egyptian *Komars* sank the Israeli destroyer *Eilat*. Further successes were obtained by Indian *Osas* during the Indo-Pakistan war of December 1971. However, these successes were achieved against relatively unsophisticated targets. The Arab-Israeli war of 1973 showed that these missiles were obsolete against modern electronic countermeasures. A larger vessel with better electronics and more sophisticated missiles was needed. This was realised by the Russians in the late 1960s, and the result was the *Nanuchka* class. On a much larger hull than the *Osas* they not only carry a much more effective missile, the SSN-9 SSM, but also possess an adequate missile and gun anti-aircraft armament. The large hull also means that the *Nanuchkas* can operate in rough seas, and they have a wide hull to make them steady missile platforms. They complement the anti-submarine *Grisha I* and *II* class corvettes. The SSN-9 missiles have a range of about 180 miles (150nm) and require mid-course guidance if fired 'over-the-horizon'. They provide a very adequate mobile defence for the coasts of the Soviet Union.

Nanuchka class. Note SAN-4 silo for'd and triple SSN-9 launchers amidships

Displacement:	Osa class		Nanuchka class
standard tons (tonnes)	165 (168)		?
full load tons (tonnes)	200 (203)		850 (865)
Dimensions:			
length (oa)	128·7ft (39·3m)		196·8ft (60m)
beam	25·1ft (7·6m)		39·6ft (12m)
draught	5·9ft (1·8m)		9·9ft (3m)
	Osa	Osa	
Armament:	Type I	Type II	Nanuchka
guns			
57mm	—	—	2
30mm	4	4	—
missiles			
SSN-2 A or B SSM	4	—	—
SSN-11 SSM	—	4	—
SSN-9 SSM	—	—	6
SAN-4 SAM twin launcher	—	—	1
A/S weapons			
MBU rocket-launcher	—	—	1 or 2
Machinery:			
diesels (type)	?		?
(number)	3		4
shafts	3		2
Total BHP:			
designed	13,000		28,000
Fuel capacity:			
oil tons (tonnes)	?		?
Performance:			
designed speed	34kts		30kts
range	800 miles (670nm) @ 25kts		?
Crew:	25		70

Class:	OSA class	NANUCHKA class
Where built:	?	?
Authorised:	?	?
Built:	Type I—circa 1959–? Type II—circa 1965–?	1969 onward
Fate:	Over 100 transferred: Algeria 3 ships; Bulgaria 3 ships; China 20+ ships, Cuba 6 ships; Egypt 12+ ships; East Germany 12 ships; India 10 ships; Iraq 12 ships; Poland 12 ships; Romania 5 ships; Somalia 3 ships; Syria 8+ ships; and Yugoslavia 10 ships. At least 4 Egyptian and 2 Syrian ships sunk Oct 1973. Remainder in service	In service and under construction

Right: Osa II *dressed overall for inspection. Note the beamy hard chine hull and prominent launchers.*
The Osa I *can be distinguished by having larger, squarer launchers*

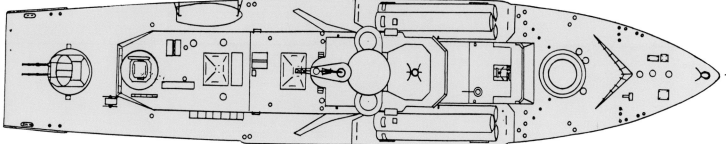

Espana

BATTLESHIP
CLASS: *Espana* class (3 ships)
Espana · Alfonso XIII · Jaime I

Above: Espana, *completed 1913, fires her broadside of eight 12in/305mm guns. The three 15,452-ton* Espanas *were the smallest dreadnought battleships ever built*

Displacement:
normal tons (tonnes)	15,452 (15,699)
full load tons (tonnes)	15,740 (15,992)

Dimensions:
length (pp)	435ft (132·6m)
(wl)	435·7ft (132·8m)
(oa)	459ft (139·9m)
beam	78·7ft (24m)
draught (max)	25·6ft (7·8m)

Armament:
guns	
12in (305mm) 50cal	8
4in (102mm) 50cal	20
3pdr (47mm)	2
0·303in (7·7mm)	2

Armour:
side (belt)	8in (203mm)
(bow)	3in (76mm)
(stern)	4in (102mm)
deck	1·5in (38mm)
main turrets	8in (203mm)
battery	3in (76mm)

Machinery:
boilers (type)	Yarrow
(number)	12
engines (type)	Parsons turbines
shafts	4

Total SHP:
designed	15,500
trials	22,260

Fuel capacity:
coal normal tons (tonnes)	900 (910)
max tons (tonnes)	1,900 (1,930)

Performance:
designed speed	19·5kts
trial speed	20·5kts
range	6,000 miles
	(5,040nm) @ 10kts

Crew: 850

Service career ESPANA

1914 (June) Extensive gunnery trials.
1914–1920 In home waters.
1920 (Oct) Escorted Spanish mission to Chile.
1921–1923 Patrols off Riff coast, Morocco.
1923 (26 Aug) Ran aground near Cape Tres Forcas on coast of Morocco; became total loss.

A British consortium of Armstrong Whitworth, Vickers and John Brown designed *Espana*, built by the shipyard at Ferrol, and provided the guns, armour, engines and a great deal of technical assistance. The actual design was done by Armstrong Whitworth to Spanish specifications which demanded a broadside fire of eight 12in

(305mm) guns with four gun end-on fire at minimum cost. This was achieved by sacrificing some speed, armour protection and radius of action. Superimposed turrets were considered, but would have meant a larger (and more expensive) hull. The smallest dreadnoughts ever built, the *Espanas* were, nevertheless, effective and well balanced ships, with as powerful a broadside as any earlier dreadnought.

Before *Espana*'s hull broke up in the autumn gales, the main armament was salvaged and was later used as coast-defence artillery.

Alfonso XIII (renamed *Espana*) was taken over by the Nationalists after declaring first for the Republic in 1936, and was sunk by a mine off Bilbao.

Jaime I's completion was delayed by the non-supply of material from Britain due to World War I. Work did not restart until 1919. She fought on the Republican side.

Ship:	ESPANA	ALFONSO XIII	JAIME I
Where built:	SECN Ferrol	SECN Ferrol	SECN Ferrol
Authorised:	7 Jan 1908	7 Jan 1908	7 Jan 1908
Laid down:	5 Feb 1909	23 Feb 1910	5 Feb 1912
Launched:	5 Feb 1912	7 May 1913	21 Sept 1914
Completed:	23 Oct 1913	16 Aug 1915	1921
Fate:	Wrecked 26 Aug 1923	Renamed *Espana* 1931; sunk 31 Apr 1937	Scrapped 1939

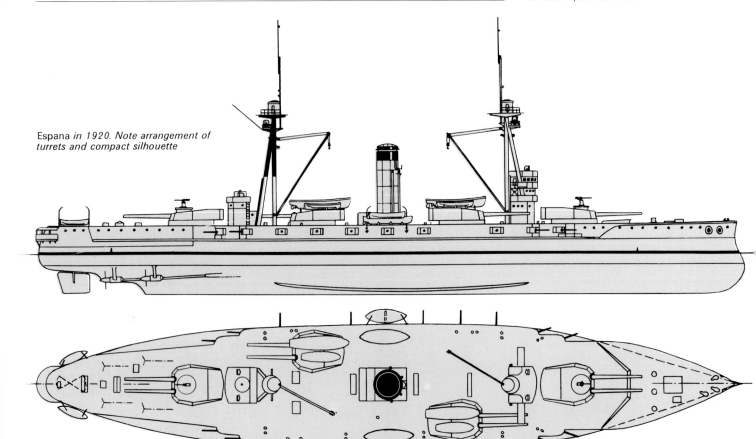

Espana *in 1920. Note arrangement of turrets and compact silhouette*

Descubierta Class

FRIGATE
CLASS: *Descubierta* class (8 ships) including *Descubierta* (F-81) · *Diana* (F-82) · *Infanta Elena* (F-83) · *Infanta Cristina* (F-84)

The Spanish Navy, which had been brought up to date in the early 1960s by the transfer of American vessels and the fitting of American weapons and electronics on to its warships, began a programme of re-equipping with new ships in the late 1960s. *Baleares* class frigates have been built since 1968 at Bazan's Ferrol yard. These are based on the US *Knox* class frigates, and have a standard displacement of 2,900 tons. For a modern small frigate design, they have adopted the *Descubierta* class a modified version of the Portuguese *Joao Coutinho* class. Three of the latter were built at the Spanish Bazan yard between 1968 and 1971, and three more by the German firm of Blohm und Voss. These have a standard displacement of 1,252 tons (1,272 tonnes) and are unsophisticated ships, with an armament of one twin 3in (76mm), a twin 40mm and a Hedgehog A/S projector. They also have a helicopter pad aft. Four of an improved version, the *Joao Robys*, have also been built at Bazan for Portugal. These have a French 3·9in (100mm) gun and improved electronics. The Spanish ships have a similar but slightly larger hull, and they are faster and more sophisticated vessels, with a much improved armament. Only the first four have so far been started, and all these have been launched. The single 3in (76mm) is mounted forward and the two 40mm in single mounts on the deckhouse aft. The Bofors A/S launcher is in 'B' position and the BPDMS Sea Sparrow launcher is fitted right aft. The funnel is split into two uptakes to avoid fume damage to the radar on the mainmast. These small and relatively cheap vessels are ideal for smaller navies which cannot afford the more sophisticated vessels adopted by the major navies. They are capable of coping with most threats short of a major surface warship or a nuclear submarine, and the lack of more elaborate equipment means that the maintenance load is reduced. The *Descubiertas* may be completed with SSMs, which will give them an anti-surface capability.

Right: Descubierta, *launched in 1975, was the first of a class of eight small, unsophisticated frigates based on the Portuguese* Joao Coutinhos

Below: A Joao Coutinho *class frigate. Note the limited armament and small amount of electronics carried by this vessel. Unlike the* Descubiertas *they have a single funnel and no mainmast*

Displacement:

standard tons (tonnes)	1,200 (1,220)
full load tons (tonnes)	1,497 (1,520)

Dimensions:

length (oa)	291·3ft (88·8m)
beam	34·4ft (10·5m)
draught	11·5ft (3·5m)

Armament:

guns	
3in (76mm) 62cal	1
40mm	2
20mm 6 barrel	1 or 2
missiles	
BPDMS octuple Sea Sparrow SAM launcher	1
A/S weapons	
14·8in (375mm) Bofors 2 barrel rocket-launcher	1
torpedo tubes	
12·7in (324mm) Mk 32	6

Machinery:

diesels (type)	MTU-Bazan
(number)	4
shafts	2

Total BHP:

designed	16,000

Fuel capacity:

oil tons (tonnes)	?

Performance:

designed speed	26kts
range	4,760 miles (4,000nm) @ ?kts

Crew: approx 100

Class:	**DESCUBIERTA class**
Where built:	Bazan, Cartagena and Bazan, Ferrol
Authorised:	1973
Laid down:	Nov 1974 onward
Launched:	July 1975 onward
Completed:	1976 onward
Fate:	*Descubierta* (F-81) complete; *Diana* (F-82) completing; *Infanta Elena* (F-83) and *Infanta Cristina* (F-84) under construction; others not yet laid down.

Sverige

COAST DEFENCE BATTLESHIP
CLASS: *Sverige* class (3 ships)
Sverige · Gustaf V · Drottning Victoria

Service career SVERIGE
1926 Refitted with heavy foremast.
1932–1933 Refit: forefunnel top raked aft; aft superstructure built up.
1938–1940 Modernisation: oil-firing boilers fitted and funnels trunked; armament modified.
1950s (early) Discarded.
c1952 Scrapped.

Sweden has a thriving armaments industry, and prior to World War I built up a sizeable fleet of small craft, backed up by a considerable number of coast defence battleships. The last and largest of these were the *Sverige* class. *Sverige* herself was cancelled in late 1911 by the new Liberal government to save money, but enough was collected by public subscription in the next few months not only to build *Sverige* but also to make a start on her two sisters. The armour plate was bought in America because Sweden lacked the facilities to manufacture it, and *Drottning Victoria* and *Gustav V* were delayed when the war prevented its delivery. They differed from *Sverige* by having an icebreaking rather than a ram bow, and had geared Westinghouse instead of direct-drive Brown-Curtis turbines. All ships had a turtle-deck fo'c'sle, and the 11in (280mm) turrets had an armoured bulkhead between the two guns. All three ships were modernised between the wars, the *Gustav V* had her funnels trunked. They were amongst the last coast defence battleships to be discarded. Allied limitations on the size of German battleships under the Versailles Treaty were based on these ships, the intention being to confine the Germany navy to similar vessels.

Below: Sverige *is seen here with trunked funnels after extensive modernization in 1938–40. The three Sveriges were in service until the 1950s*

Displacement: (all data for Sverige only)

standard tons (tonnes)	7,080 (7,190)
full load tons (tonnes)	?

Dimensions:

length (wl)	393·3ft (119·9m)
(oa)	
beam	61ft (18·6m)
draught (max)	22·3ft (6·8m)

Armament:

guns	as built	in 1940
11in (280mm) 45 cal	4	4
6in (152mm) 50cal	8	6
3in (76mm)	—	4
14pdr (76mm)	8	—
6pdr (57mm)	2	—
40mm	—	6
25mm	—	4
torpedo tubes		
18in (457mm) submerged	2	—

Armour

side (belt)	8in (203mm)
(ends)	3–6in (76–152mm)
side	1·5in (38mm)
main turrets	4–8in (102–203mm)
barbettes	6in (152mm)
secondary turrets	2·5–5in (63–127mm)

Machinery:

boilers (type)	Yarrow	Penhoët
(number)	12	4
engines (type)	Curtis turbines	
shafts	4	

Total SHP:

designed	20,000

Fuel capacity:

coal normal tons (tonnes)	350 (360)	
max tons (tonnes)	700 (710)	
oil tons (tonnes)	100 (102)	550 (560)

Performance:

	as built	in 1940
designed speed	22·5kts	?
trial speed	23kts	?
range	?	?
Crew:	450	600

Ship:	SVERIGE	DROTTNING VICTORIA	GUSTAF V
Where built:	Götaverken, Göteborg	Götaverken, Göteborg	Kockums, Malmö
Authorised:	1911	1915	1915
Laid down:	1912	1915	1915
Launched:	3 May 1915	15 Sept 1917	31 Jan 1918
Completed:	1917	1921	1921
Rebuilt:	1926, 1932–1933, 1938–1940	1927, 1934–1935	1929, 1930, 1936–1937
Fate:	Scrapped 1953	Discarded 1957	Discarded 1958

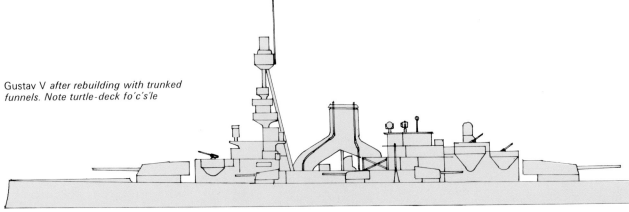

Gustav V after rebuilding with trunked funnels. Note turtle-deck fo'c'sle

Spica Class
TORPEDO BOAT
CLASS: *Spica* class (6 craft)
including *Spica* (T-121) · *Capella*
(T-123)

Like most other Baltic navies, the Swedish Navy now consists mainly of small submarines and missile- and torpedo-armed patrol boats. The shallow seas, many islands and dominance of land-based aircraft in the area put a premium on small size, speed and an effective anti-aircraft armament. The use of gas turbines gives the *Spicas* a high speed and rapid acceleration, and the bridge is sited aft in order to give the 57mm anti-aircraft gun as large a field of fire as possible. This very effective Swedish-built weapon has a rate of fire of 200 rounds per minute, with a high rate of traverse and elevation, and the Swedish Navy considers it more effective than a missile in the anti-aircraft role. It can also be used against surface targets. It is controlled by the S62 combined search and target designation radar, mounted in a fibreglass dome on the bridge. The torpedoes are wire-guided. Twelve improved *Spica II*s have been built between 1973 and 1976 with a modified hull and separate search and target designation radars. The Swedes have not adapted the *Spicas* to carry missiles, preferring to use a modified Norwegian design with 'Penguin' SSMs. However, the Danes are producing 10 modified *Spicas*, the *Willemoes* class, at the Royal Dockyard, Copenhagen. These are armed with Harpoon SSMs and wire-guided 21in (533mm) torpedoes, as well as a 3in (76mm) Oto Melara Compact gun. The bridge is much further forward on this class. The *Spicas* and their derivatives have a long and relatively narrow Lürssen-type hull, which is better suited to Baltic conditions than the beamier hull used in British designs. Four *Spicas* with MTV diesels are building for Malaysia. Over the years the Swedes have built a number of rock shelters along their coastline to act as 'hangars' for vessels up to the size of destroyers. These are capable of withstanding most weapons apart from atomic bombs, and considerably increase the survivability of the Swedish navy. Each would require a 'set-piece' attack to destroy, which would be very costly to the attacker.

Right: The Spica II *class torpedo boat* Strömstad *is typical of the craft now built for use in the restricted Baltic waters*

Displacement:	
standard tons (tonnes)	200 (203)
full load tons (tonnes)	230 (234)
Dimensions:	
length (wl)	134·5ft (41m)
(oa)	143·7ft (43·8m)
beam	23·3ft (7·1m)
draught	5·2ft (1·6m)
Armament:	
guns	
57mm	1
torpedo tubes	
21in (533mm)	6
Machinery:	
gas turbines (type)	Rolls-Royce Proteus
(number)	3
shafts	3
Total SHP:	
designed	12,750
Fuel capacity:	
oil tons (tonnes)	?
Performance:	
designed speed	40kts
range	?
Crew:	28

Class:	**SPICA class**
Where built:	?
Built:	1965–1967
Fate:	In service; followed 1973–1976 by 12 craft of *'Repeat Spica'* (T131) class; four modified versions building for Malaysia at Karlskrona

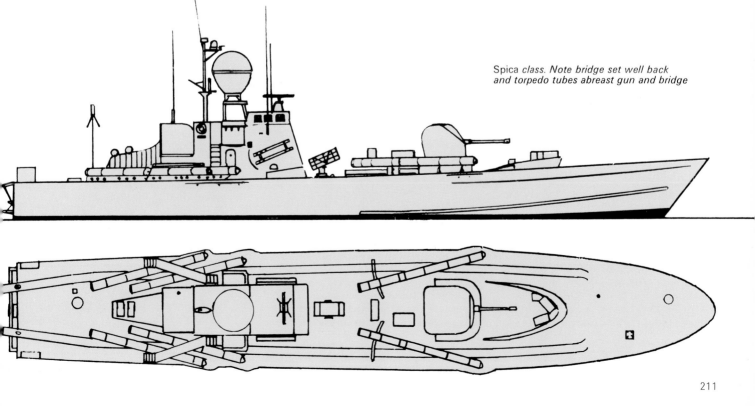

Spica *class. Note bridge set well back and torpedo tubes abreast gun and bridge*

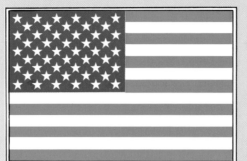

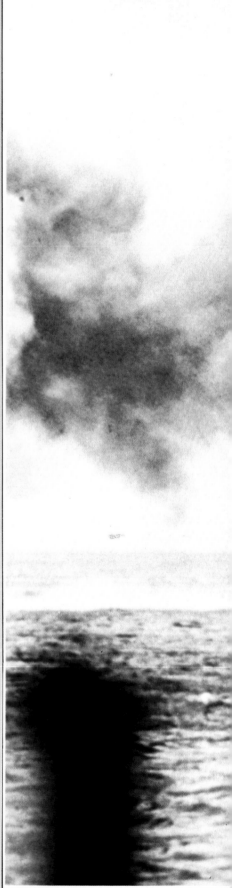

THE American Civil War saw the birth of various technical ideas on the naval side but very little in the way of tactical advance. The war was confined in the main to coastal operations and single ship actions and it was in this groove that US naval thinking remained for a number of years. With the British fleets acting as a bulwark against European expansion and American energies being concentrated on industrial expansion at home there was little need for anything more.

By the 1880s a change was at hand which was accelerated by the writings on sea power of Captain A. T. Mahan. The USA was growing at a prodigious rate into a major world power and such a nation needed protection for its maritime interests. This attitude was reflected in a growing imperialism which would have horrified the self-righteous anti-colonialists of Washington DC in the 1940s. A series of problems in the Caribbean and South America preceded the Spanish-American War of 1898, a period of hostilities which resulted in a Spanish defeat and the American acquisition of the Philippines, Guam and Puerto Rico as well as a Cuban protectorate.

At this time the Assistant Secretary of the Navy was Theodore Roosevelt, who, fortuitously, was to become President in 1901 and hold that office until 1909. Under his powerful impulse great improvements were made in the organisation and building programmes. In 1907 the sixteen battleships of the Atlantic Fleet were the most powerful concentration of capital ships in the world. As the Panama Canal was pressed towards its completion in 1914, new bases were established in its vicinity and in 1910 the US position in the Pacific was strengthened by the establishment of the Asiatic Fleet. By this time anti-German feeling in the USA was rising and Great Britain gradually turned over a large proportion of her West Atlantic duties to the USN. This coincided with a series of long-range cruises by fleets and squadrons from the USA which had now truly become a world power to be reckoned with.

After 1914 the USA had her own problems in Mexico while many Americans made the same inaccurate forecast of the United Kingdom's defeat as they were to do twenty-five years later. The importance of this attitude was that if the USA were to 'go-it-alone' a much increased navy was needed and the first provisions for this were made in the 1915 appropriations and the 1916 Naval Pact. However, Britain survived and by the time the USA entered the war in May 1917 the German surface fleet was mutinous and the main battle had become the struggle against the U-boats, including the start of convoys.

The 1918 Armistice found the USN with seventeen dreadnoughts and several building plus a flotilla of 250 destroyers building or ordered. The Washington Treaty of 1921 controlled the ultimate strength of the battle fleet and allowed the USA at least five aircraft carriers. No such limit was placed on submarines and US building programmes were tailored to treaty requirements. Without it being realised the ultimate weapons for victory in the Pacific War were being worked upon twenty years before they were to be put to the test.

The USA had been the home of the practical submarine and, although not the first country to build an aircraft-carrier, she was well in the running with USS *Langley* commissioned in March 1922. Two battlecruiser hulls, *Lexington* and *Saratoga*, were converted to carry ninety aircraft and were followed by *Ranger* and the *Yorktown* class. The USN was on the trail which was to bring the overdue eclipse of the battleship and a series of Pacific victories beginning with Midway in 1942.

The submarines of the USN were primarily designed for Pacific operations and, though hindered by inefficient torpedos in the early days of the war, were to contribute in a considerable degree to Japan's defeat with the destruction of five million tons of shipping.

Today the USN leads the world's navies in the construction of aircraft carriers and nuclear propelled submarines, part of a very large, well-balanced and well-trained fleet designed to operate worldwide.

AMERICA

The Mississippi *class USS* Idaho *(BB 42) on shore bombardment duty off Okinawa, 1945*

Lexington

AIRCRAFT-CARRIER
CLASS: *Lexington* class (2 ships)
Lexington (CV-2) · *Saratoga* (CV-3)

Service career LEXINGTON
1922 (1 July–14 Dec 1927) Converted to aircraft-carrier.
1927–1942 In Pacific.
1941 8in (203mm) guns removed, four 3in (76mm) guns added.
1941 (Dec) Ferried aircraft to Midway Island.
1941 (Dec–May 1942) Patrols in Pacific.
1942 (20 Feb) Abandoned attempt to attack Rabaul after air attack.
1942 (7–8 May) Battle of Coral Sea.
1942 (7 May) Aircraft, with those from US aircraft-carrier *Yorktown*, sank Japanese aircraft-carrier *Shoho*.
1942 (8 May) Aircraft damage Japanese aircraft-carrier *Shokaku*; hit by two torpedoes and three bombs from aircraft from Japanese carriers *Shokaku* and *Zuikaku*; explosion and fire three hours later; sunk by 5 torpedoes from US destroyer *Phelps*.

At first, the US Navy did not build any battle-cruisers, preferring to concentrate on slow, well armoured battleships. However, by the early part of World War I the need for some type of modern fast armoured ship was obvious. In August 1916 six battle-cruisers were authorised, and a number of designs were drawn up. These were all for ships with very high speed, 14in or 16in (356mm or 406mm) guns and virtually no armour. These would all have been extremely vulnerable, and were very poorly thought-out designs. The most extreme had boilers on two levels and seven funnels. After the US entered the war, Britain let the US Navy see the plans of

Continued on page 216▶

	battle-cruiser final design	aircraft-carrier as built	Saratoga in 1945
Displacement:			
standard tons (tonnes)	43,500 (44,200)	33,000 (33,540)	35,000 (35,560)
full load tons (tonnes)	49,000 (49,780)	39,000 (39,620)	39,000 (39,620)
Dimensions:			
length (wl)	850ft (259·5m)	830ft (253·4m)	830ft (253·4m)
(oa)	874ft (266·9m)	888ft (271·1m)	901·25ft (275·2m)
beam (wl)	105·5ft (32·2m)	105·5ft (32·2m)	105·5ft (32·2m)
(flight deck)	—	130ft (39·7m)	130ft (39·7m)
draught (max)	31·25ft (9·5m)	32ft (9·8m)	32ft (9·8m)
Armament:			
guns			
16in (406mm) 50cal	8	—	—
8in (203mm) 55cal	—	8	—
6in (152mm) 53cal	16	—	—
5in (127mm) 25cal	—	12	—
5in (127mm) 38cal	—	—	16
3in (76mm) 50cal	6	—	—
40mm	—	—	96
20mm	—	—	32
torpedo tubes			
21in (533mm)	8	—	—
aircraft	—	90	80
Armour:			
side (belt)	7in (178mm)	6in (152mm)	6in (152mm)
deck (main)	2·25in (57mm)	3in (76mm)	3in (76mm)
(lower)	1–3in (25–76mm)	1–3in (25–76mm)	1–3in (25–76mm)
main turrets	14in (356mm)	1·5–3in (25–76mm)	1–3in (25–76mm)
barbettes	14in (356mm)	5in (152mm)	5in (152mm)
Machinery:			
boilers (type)	Yarrow	Yarrow	White-Foster
(number)	24	16	16
engines (type)	General Electric geared turbines and General Electric electric motors		
shafts	4	4	4
Total SHP:			
designed	180,000	180,000	180,000
trial	—	210,000	210,000
Fuel capacity:			
oil tons (tonnes)	?	8,884 (9,026)	8,884 (9,026)
Performance:			
designed speed	33·25kts	33·25kts	33·25kts
trial speed	—	34·2kts	33·91kts
range	?	?	?
Crew (inc aircrew):	1,315	2,122	3,300

Boeing F4B carrier-borne fighter dive bomber circa 1930

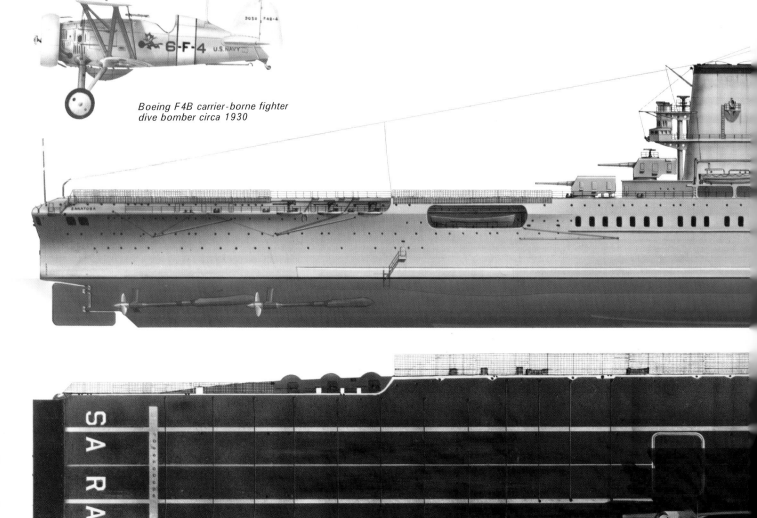

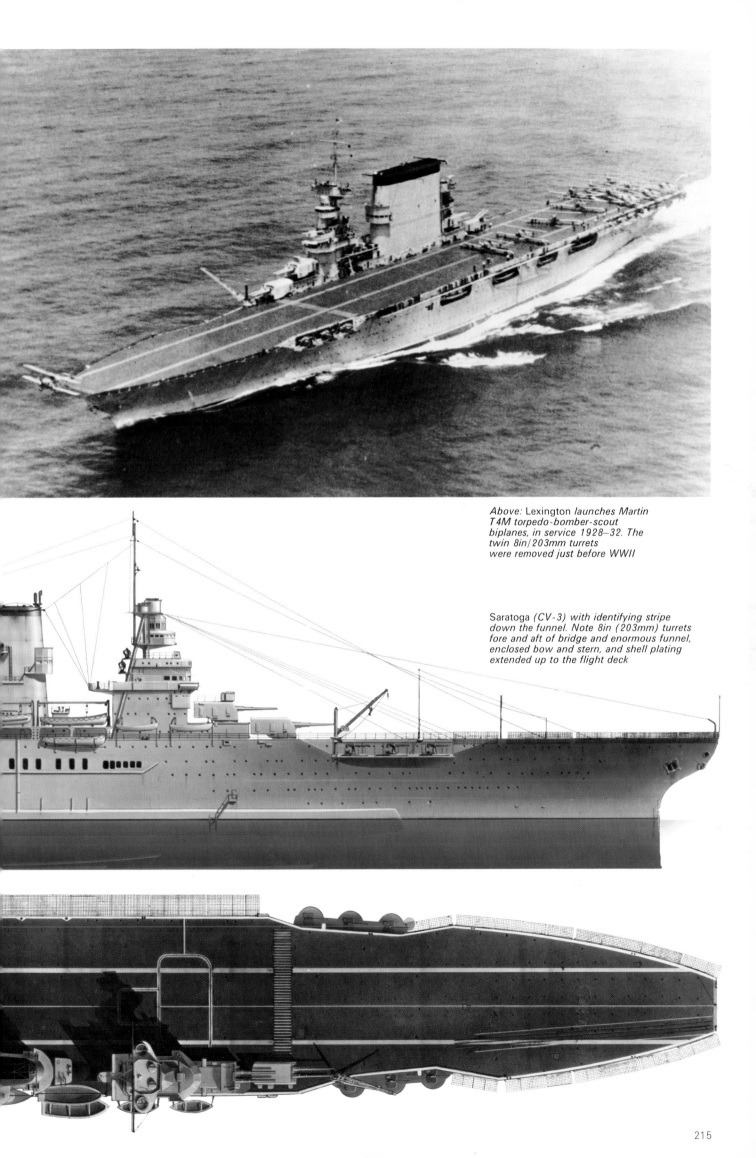

Above: Lexington *launches Martin T4M torpedo-bomber-scout biplanes, in service 1928–32. The twin 8in/203mm turrets were removed just before WWII*

Saratoga *(CV-3) with identifying stripe down the funnel. Note 8in (203mm) turrets fore and aft of bridge and enormous funnel, enclosed bow and stern, and shell plating extended up to the flight deck*

►*Lexington*

HMS *Hood*. This was a great advance on American designs, and greatly affected the latters' subsequent development. Fresh plans were prepared for a two-funnelled ship with moderate armour, and six were laid down in 1920–1921. They had virtually the same displacement as the contemporary *South Dakota* class battleship but were about 200ft (60m) longer and had twin instead of triple 16in (406mm) turrets. The *Lexingtons* were 10kts faster on three times the power, but the belt armour was only half as thick and the horizontal armour was also inferior. Both classes were cancelled under the terms of the Washington Treaty, but as with the Japanese, the Americans were allowed to convert two battle-cruisers into aircraft-carriers to equate with the British conversions. The first American carrier, *Langley* (CV-1), ex-*Jupiter* (AC-3), had been converted from a fleet collier and was small and slow. In contrast, *Lexington* and *Saratoga* were the largest and fastest carriers in the world until the

Midway class was built at the end of World War II. The two ships retained their original turbo-electric machinery, and were fitted with two hangars and a large flight-deck. Unlike other US carriers until the *Midways*, the bows were fully plated, and they had from the start a fixed bridge and island and an enormous vertical funnel. The Washington Treaty permitted carriers to be armed with guns of up to 8in (203mm) calibre, and both the Americans and the Japanese took advantage of this. The *Lexingtons* had four twin 8in (203mm) turrets arranged in superfiring pairs fore and aft of the island, and the main armour belt, though thinned, was also retained as a protection against attack from cruisers or destroyers. It was eventually realised that carriers could not protect themselves with guns and armour against surface attack, and both *Lexingtons* had their 8in (203mm) turrets removed just before the war. Because they were not designed as carriers, they did not carry as many aircraft as their size would suggest, but they were still able to carry more than any

contemporary carrier. Although their size and capacity were deplored by many American naval officers, they helped ensure the growth of US naval aviation and enabled the US Navy to conduct realistic exercises which were turned to good advantage in the Pacific war. Although as battle-cruisers they would have been too lightly armoured, they were much better value as carriers than any of the Japanese or British conversions. *Saratoga* survived the war but was badly damaged in a *kamikaze* attack on 21 February 1945. She was sunk as a target in the Bikini atom bomb tests.

Below: USS Lexington *(CV-2). Launched in 1925, the 39,000-ton (full load)* Lexington *and* Saratoga *were the largest and fastest carriers in service until 1945*

Below, lower: Burning after the Battle of the Coral Sea, Lexington *was sunk by a US destroyer's torpedoes*

Ship:	SARATOGA CV-3 (ex-CC-3)	LEXINGTON (ex-CONSTITUTION) CV-2 (ex-CC-1)	CONSTELLATION (CC-2)	RANGER (CC-4)	CONSTITUTION (CC-5)	UNITED STATES (CC-6)
Where built:	New York Shipyard	Fore River Shipyard	Newport News Shipyard	Newport News Shipyard	Philadelphia Naval Yard	Philadelphia Naval Yard
Authorised:	1916	1916	1916	1916	1917	1919
Laid down:	23 Sept 1920	8 Jan 1921	18 Aug 1920	23 June 1921	23 Sept 1920	25 Sept 1920
Work stopped:	8 Feb 1922	8 Feb 1922	7 Feb 1922	8 Feb 1922	8 Feb 1922	8 Feb 1922
Cancelled:	—	—	17 Aug 1923	17 Aug 1923	17 Aug 1923	17 Aug 1923
Ordered as aircraft-carrier:	CV-3 1 July 1922	CV-2 1 July 1922	—	—	—	—
Launched:	7 Apr 1925	3 Oct 1925	—	—	—	—
Completed:	16 Nov 1927	14 Dec 1927	—	—	—	—
Fate:	Sunk 25 July 1946	Scuttled 8 May 1942	Scrapped incomplete	Scrapped incomplete	Scrapped incomplete	Scrapped incomplete

Casablanca

ESCORT CARRIER

CLASS: *Casablanca* class (50 ships) including *Casablanca* (CVE-55, ex-ACV-55, ex-*Alazon Bay*, ex-HMS *Ameer* AVG-55) · *Gambier Bay* (CVE-73)

The shortage of any type of carrier caused the British to convert the fast escort carrier, *Audacity* from an ex-German mercantile prize in mid-1941. The Americans immediately adopted the idea, and their first conversion, *Long Island* AVG-1 (later ACV-1, later CVE-1) was finished before *Audacity*, although started later. The diesel-powered *Long Islands* and turbine-powered *Bogues* and *Prince Williams* were conversions of existing war standard merchant ship hulls, and were mostly supplied to the British. The next class, the *Casablancas*, were the first to be built as escort carriers from the keel up. The stern was modified to fit one 5in (127mm) 38cal gun with a good arc of fire, and twin-shaft reciprocating machinery was adopted for speed of production. Like the preceding classes, they had a wooden flight deck, a small fixed island, a catapult and two lifts, with a hangar for 28 aircraft. Three were originally ordered by the British navy, but all were delivered to the USN. Nicknamed 'Jeep Carriers' the escort carriers provided air-cover for convoys in the Atlantic, and formed the nucleus of submarine hunter-killer groups. *Guadalcanal* (CVE-60)'s group captured *U-505* on 4 June 1944. In the Pacific they provided support for the many island landings. At the Battle of Leyte Gulf they were attacked by the Japanese fleet, and *Gambier Bay* (CVE-73) was the only carrier apart from the British *Glorious* to be sunk solely by surface gunfire. They were followed by a lengthened and improved version, the *Commencement Bay* class, which were fitted with turbines. Surviving carriers were reclassified as CVUs in 1955.

Displacement:	
standard tons (tonnes)	7,800 (7,920)
full load tons (tonnes)	10,400 (10,510)
Dimensions:	
length (wl)	490ft (149·6m)
(oa)	512·25ft (156·4m)
beam (wl)	65·25ft (19·9m)
(flight deck)	108ft (33m)
draught (max)	22ft (6·7m)
Armament:	
guns	
5in (127mm) 38cal	1
40mm	16
20mm	24
aircraft	28
Machinery:	
boilers (type)	Babcock & Wilcox
(number)	4
engines (type)	vertical triple expansion
shafts	2
Fuel capacity:	
oil tons (tonnes)	2,113 (2,147)
Total IHP:	
designed speed	19·25kts
range	?
Crew:	860

Class:	**CASABLANCA class**
Where built:	Kaiser
Authorised:	1942
Built:	1942–1944
Reclassified:	(from ACV to CVE) 15 July 1943
Fate:	*Liscome Bay* (CV-56, ex ACV-56) sunk 24 Nov 1943; *St Lô* (ex-*Midway*, ex-*Chapin Bay* CVE-63) sunk 25 Oct 1944; *Gambier Bay* (CVE-73) sunk 25 Oct 1944. *Ommaney Bay* (CVE-79) scuttled 4 Jan 1945; *Bismarck Sea* (ex-*Alikula Bay* CVE-95) sunk 21 Feb 1945; remainder sold or scrapped 1947–1961

The escort carriers were invaluable to the Allies. They were cheap and relatively expendable, and were also extremely versatile. Because of the shortage of fleet carriers in 1942–1943, some early escort carriers were used in a fleet role in the Mediterranean during the North Africa, Sicily and Italian amphibious operations. They were soon discarded postwar because they were too small to operate the new generation of carrier aircraft.

Above: USS Casablanca *(CVE-55) early in 1945. The 50 ships took only just over a year to construct. Note the camouflage dazzle painting*

Casablanca (CVE-55) as built. Note mercantile hull and small island

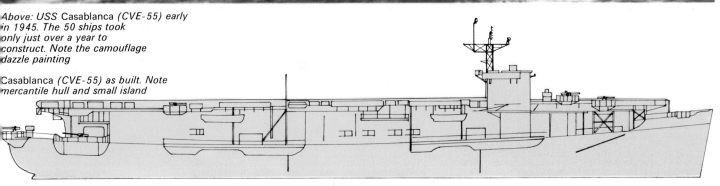

Hornet

AIRCRAFT-CARRIER

CLASS: *Yorktown* class (3 ships)
Yorktown (CV-5) · *Enterprise* (CV-6)
Hornet (CV-8)

Service career HORNET (CV-8)

1941 (Dec–Jan 1942) Hurried work-up in Atlantic.
1942 (2 Feb) Trials with B-25s, sailed for Pacific.
1942 (2–25 Apr) Doolittle raid: launched 16 B-25s off Japanese coast, a propaganda success.
1942 (4–6 June) Battle of Midway.
1942 (July–Oct) In South-West Pacific.
1942 (15 Sept–18 Oct) Only operational US carrier in Pacific.
1942 (26–27 Oct) Battle of Santa Cruz.
1942 (26 Oct) Hit by ten bombs, two aircraft and three torpedoes. US destroyers *Mustin* and *Anderson* attempted to sink her. Hit by nine torpedoes and about 400 rounds of 5in (127mm).
1942 (27 Oct) Sunk by four torpedoes fired by Japanese destroyers.

America's first purpose-built carrier, *Ranger* (CV-4), had a standard displacement of only 14,500 tons (14,730 tonnes) – well under the limit of 22,000 tons (22,350 tonnes) standard displacement set by the Washington Treaty. At that stage the US Navy considered that a large number of small carriers each operating a large number of aircraft was preferable to a few large carriers. *Ranger* normally carried 75 aircraft, almost as many as the *Lexingtons*, which had over twice the displacement. However, she sacrificed speed, seaworthiness, protection and armament to achieve this, and it was realised even before she was commissioned in 1934 that *Ranger* was far too small. Therefore the next two carriers, *Yorktown* (CV-5) and *Enterprise* (CV-6), were designed to operate virtually the same number of aircraft, but their hulls were almost half again as large. This greatly improved seaworthiness, and doubling the power increased the speed by 4 knots. The armour belt and deck were almost twice as thick, and the number of watertight compartments was greatly increased. As with the *Lexingtons* and *Ranger*, the emphasis was on aircraft and protection against surface attack. US carriers were intended mainly for Pacific operations, where the dangers from land-based aircraft were not so great as in European waters. The hangar and wooden flight deck were unarmoured, and were part of the superstructure rather than integral with the hull. There were 11 large openings in the hangar sides, covered by moveable shutters. Unlike *Ranger*, the *Yorktowns* had a conventional funnel and island. To improve the aircraft handling, they were fitted with three centreline lifts and three catapults, and the flight deck had arrester gear at each end. American carriers of this period were designed to achieve high sustained speeds astern so that aircraft could land in either direction, though this feature was never used operationally. Because most of the 135,000 tons (137,145 tonnes) that the US had been allowed for new carriers under the Washington Treaty had already been used, the next carrier, *Wasp* (CV-7), was a smaller version of the *Yorktowns*. She had a standard displacement of only 14,700 tons (15,570 tonnes). After the Treaty terminated on 31 December 1936 America was free to build as many carriers as she wished, of whatever size she required, and the Naval Expansion Act of 17 May 1938 authorised a further 40,000 tons (40,635 tonnes) for carriers. Japanese expansion in China and war scares in Europe made numbers more important than a new improved design, so the US Navy returned to the five year old *Yorktown* type for the first new carrier, which was named *Hornet* (CV-8). The most significant differences between *Hornet* and *Yorktown* were the increased width of the flight deck, more light anti-aircraft guns and a slightly greater displacement. Like her two half-sisters, *Hornet* had a very small turning circle. This was only half that of the *Lexingtons*, and proved to be vital in evading bomb and torpedo attacks. Her wartime modifications were confined to increases in her anti-aircraft armament and the fitting of an improved radar. She did not require modification to take the North American B-25 Mitchell bombers for the Doolittle raid, but because their wings did not fold they were stored on the flight deck aft. She was unable to operate her own aircraft effectively until the

Displacement:	Yorktown as built	Hornet as built
standard tons (tonnes)	19,800 (20,120)	19,900 (20,220)
full load tons (tonnes)	25,500 (25,910	29,100 (29,560)
Dimensions:		
length (wl)	761ft (232m)	761ft (232m)
(oa)	809·5ft (246·6m)	827ft (252·5m)
beam (wl)	83ft (25·3m)	83ft (25·3m)
(flight deck)	109ft (33·3m)	114ft (34·7m)
draught (max)	28ft (8·5m)	29ft (8·8m)
Armament:	**Hornet in 1941**	**Hornet in 1942**
guns		
5in (127mm) 38cal	8	8
1·1in (28mm)	16	16
20mm	—	23
0·5in (12·7mm)	16	—
aircraft	85	
Armour:		
side (belt)	4in (102mm)	
deck (main)	3in (76mm)	
(lower)	1–3in (25–76mm)	
Machinery:		
boilers (type)	Babcock and Wilcox	
(number)	9	
engines (type)	Parsons single reduction geared turbines	
shafts	4	
Total SHP:		
designed	120,000	
Fuel capacity:		
oil tons (tonnes)	6,400 (6,502)	
Performance:		
designed speed	33kts	
range	?	
Crew:	1,899	2,919

B-25s had flown off, so she was escorted on the raid by *Enterprise*. The *Yorktowns* could absorb a considerable amount of battle damage, and it is possible that *Hornet* might have been saved if she had not been in the path of the advancing Japanese fleet. *Yorktown* wa[s] damaged at the Battle of Coral Sea, but wa[s] patched up in time to take part in the Battle o[f] Midway. She was abandoned prematurely afte[r] being severely damaged by Japanese carrie[r]

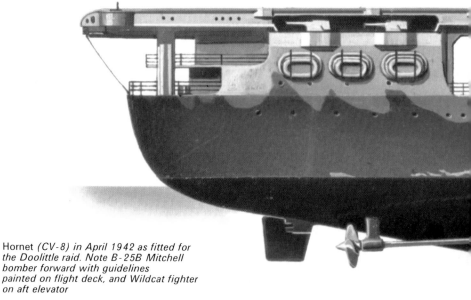

Hornet (CV-8) in April 1942 as fitted for the Doolittle raid. Note B-25B Mitchell bomber forward with guidelines painted on flight deck, and Wildcat fighter on aft elevator

Above: Hornet (CV-8) leaving Newport News
shipyard for trials in 1941. Notice complete
absence of armament. In the background
a World War I Eagle type patrol
boat

Above: Grumman Hellcat fighters and
Avenger torpedo bombers on aft flight deck
of Enterprise (CV-6) near the end of
World War II. Note Jeep parked on
flight deck

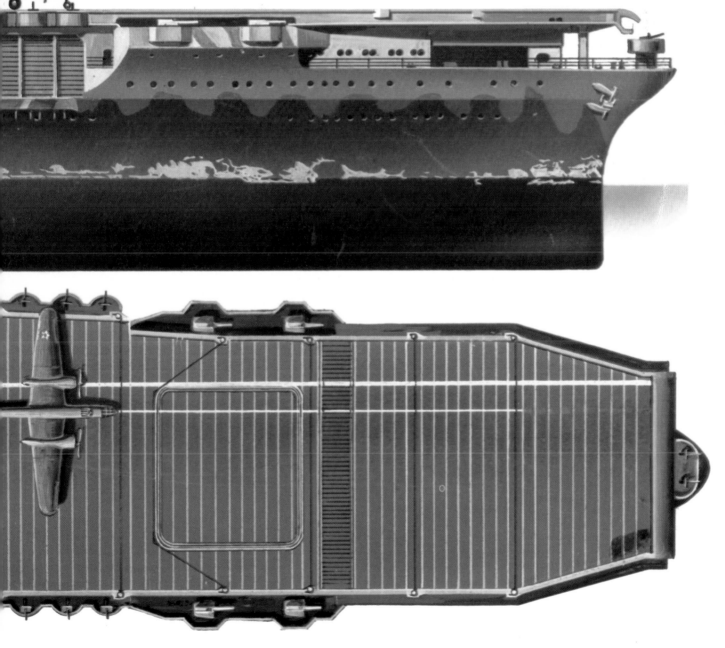

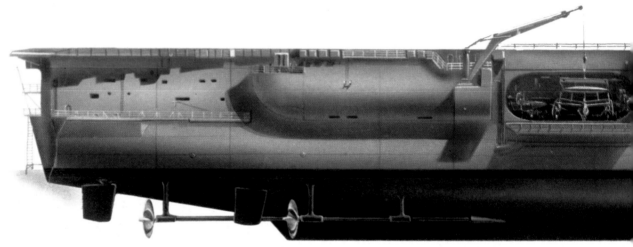

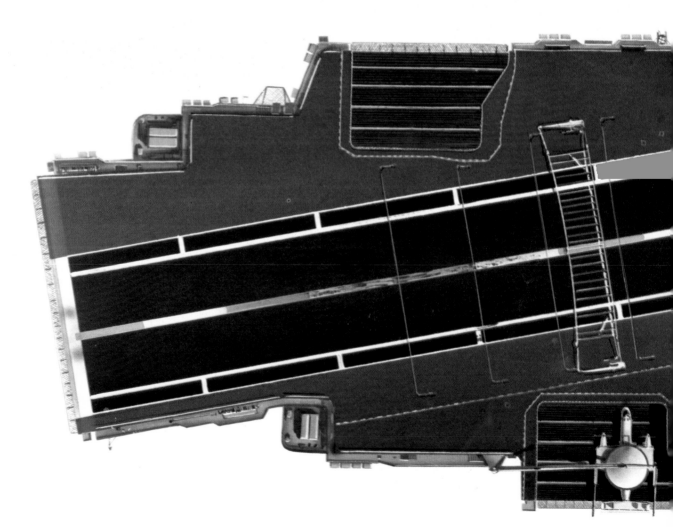

Above: Enterprise *in 1976. Note the Grumman F-14 Tomcat fighters aft, and the BPDMS Sea Sparrow launcher to port at the stern*

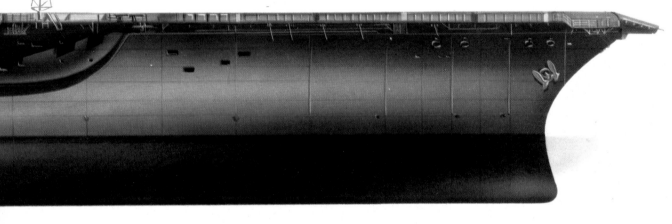

USS Enterprise *(CVN-65) in 1969. Note the enormous angled deck, the deck edge lifts, the unique island and the Vought F-8 Crusader fighter and Grumman Hawkeye early warning aircraft*

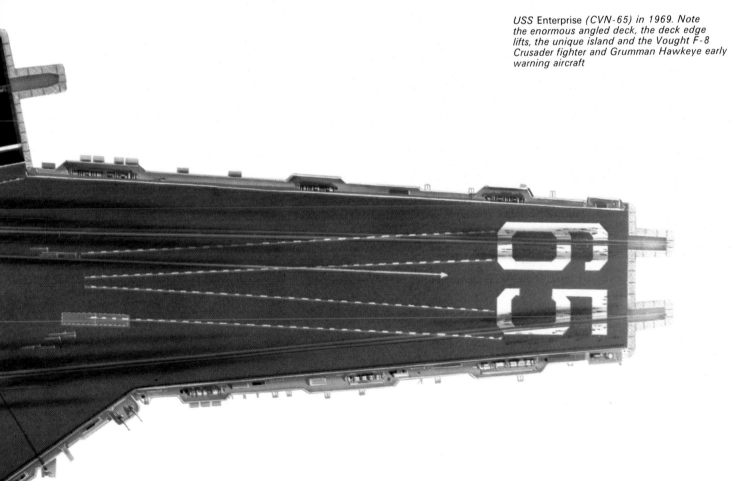

Ship:	YORKTOWN (CV-5)	ENTERPRISE (CV-6)	HORNET (CV-8)
Where built:	Newport News Shipyard	Newport News Shipyard	Newport News Shipyard
Authorised:	16 June 1933	16 June 1933	17 May 1938
Laid down:	21 May 1934	16 July 1934	25 Sept 1939
Launched:	4 Apr 1936	30 Oct 1936	14 Dec 1940
Completed:	30 Sept 1937	12 May 1938	20 Oct 1941
Fate:	Sunk 7 June 1942	Scrapped Aug 1958	Sunk 27 Oct 1942

aircraft. Salvage operations had only just resumed when she was torpedoed and sunk by the Japanese submarine *I 168*. *Enterprise* played a major role throughout the Pacific war, participating in most of the major actions.

Unfortunately, efforts to preserve her were unsuccessful. These impressive ships were the best American pre-World War II aircraft carriers, and they formed the basis of the later *Essex* class carriers.

Far left: Yorktown *(CV-5) hit by a bomb from a Japanese carrier aircraft at the Battle of Midway in June 1942. She is listing because she is turning violently to starboard*

Left: A Grumman Hellcat fighter taking off from Enterprise *(CV-6) near the end of World War II. Note quadruple 40mm mount in foreground and single 20mm along edge of flight deck*

Left: USS Enterprise (CVN-65) with
Forrestal class aircraft carrier behind.
Enterprise's small slab-sided island set well
aft easily distinguishes her from other US
aircraft carriers

Right: Enterprise at sea in the late 1960s
carrying Marine CH-53 Sea Stallion
troop carrying helicopters on deck as
well as her normal complement of
aircraft

Enterprise

AIRCRAFT-CARRIER
CLASS: *Enterprise* class (1 ship)
Enterprise (CVN-65)

Enterprise (CVN-65) was designed at a time when fierce argument was taking place in the USA over the future value of aircraft-carriers and was commissioned in the first year of the Kennedy administration whose Secretary of Defense, Robert McNamara, was by no means convinced of the cost-effectiveness of a ship which had cost $451,300,000. Her hull design was a modification of that of the *Forrestal* class but the inclusion of nuclear propulsion and other differences resulted in her being the largest warship ever built. With the cruiser *Long Beach* completing shortly before her, she was the second nuclear-powered surface warship and probably the most distinctive. Having no requirement for funnel uptakes the bridge was box-shaped with a cone top. At the lower level fixed-array radar antennae for the SPS 32 and 33 outfits are fitted to the sides and the cone is rigged with aerials for electronic counter-measures. The design of the nuclear plant was initiated in 1950, deferred from 1953 to 1954 to obtain full value from developments in sub-marine nuclear propulsion and then continued to the production stage by the Bettis Atomic Power Laboratory. On 2 December 1960, just over two months after launching, *Enterprise*'s first reactor went critical and in the next 11 months all eight, feeding 32 heat exchangers and with two reactors for each shaft, reached criticality. From her commissioning in November 1961 until her first refit and nuclear refuelling which started in November 1964 she steamed nearly 210,000 miles. With a range such as this, to be steadily and notably increased as future refuellings provide improved cores, with a higher speed than any previous carrier had achieved and with a flexibility of steam operating unknown in previous ships of her type she proved many of the points advanced by the supporters of nuclear propulsion. But with over 80 aircraft to operate and 5,500 men to be fed

Displacement:	
standard tons (tonnes)	75,700 (76,911)
full load tons (tonnes)	89,600 (91,034)
Dimensions:	
length (wl)	1,040ft (317m)
(oa)	1,102ft (335·9m)
beam	133ft (40·5m)
width (flight deck)	252ft (76·8m)
draught	35·8ft (10·8m)
Armament:	
Mk 25 BPDMS launchers with Sea-Sparrow missiles	2
aircraft	approx 84
Machinery:	
nuclear reactors (type)	pressurised water-cooled A2W by Westinghouse
(number)	8
main engines (type)	Westinghouse geared steam turbines
(number)	4
(shafts)	4
Total SHP:	
designed	280,000 approx
Performance:	
speed	35kts
range	unlimited for approx 13 years on new nuclear cores
Crew:	3,100+2,400 air personnel

Ship:	**ENTERPRISE (CVN-65)**
Where built:	Newport News
Authorised:	FY 1958
Laid down:	4 Feb 1958
Launched:	24 Sept 1960
Commissioned:	25 Nov 1961
Fate:	In service

there was the continual need for underway replenishment groups to provide fuel, munitions and food. Although the frequency of such replenishments is much less than the conventional weekly rendezvous with a tanker under intensive operating it will still cause problems for planners. The requirement for ammunition and missiles for ship-board systems is, however, minimal as *Enterprise* has no guns and, although allowance was originally made for a Terrier SAM system, her sole armament is a pair of Basic Point Defence Missile Systems installed in 1967. These launch the Sea-Sparrow missiles under either radar or visual control to a range of about 12 miles (19·3km) and the whole philosophy of carrier-defence is very different

from that of the Soviet carriers of the *Kiev* class. These, classified as 'A/S cruisers', are much smaller than *Enterprise*, carry no standard fixed-wing aircraft but are fitted with hull-mounted and variable depth sonar, surface-to-surface, surface-to-air and anti-submarine missiles as well as a strong gun armament. The deductions to be drawn from this interesting variation are discussed in the section on *Kiev* and her sisters.

Below: Another picture of Enterprise *in the Pacific in 1976, with Tomcat, Vigilante, Intruder, Corsair and Hawkeye aircraft and Sea King helicopters on the flight deck.*
The Nimitz *class carriers can be distinguished by their different islands*

Essex
AIRCRAFT-CARRIER
CLASS: *Essex* class (24 ships):
Group 1 (10 ships) including *Essex*
(CV-9 later CVA-9, CVS-9)
Group 2 (13 ships) including
Hancock (ex-*Ticonderoga*) (CV-19
later CVA-19, CV-19)
Group 3 (1 ship) *Oriskany* (CV-34
later CVA-34, CV-34)

Service career ESSEX (CV-9)
1943 (May) To Pacific.
1943 (Aug–March 1944) Operations in South-West Pacific.
1944 (March–May) Refit.
1944 (May) Operating in Pacific.
1944 (24–25 Oct) Battle of Leyte Gulf.
1944 (25 Nov) Hit by *kamikaze* on edge of flight deck off Philippines: extensive damage.
1944 (Nov–Dec) Repaired.
1944 (Dec–June 1945) Operations in Pacific.
1947 (9 Jan) In reserve.
1948 (8 Jan–2 Jan 1951) Modernised: flight deck and catapults strengthened, lifts increased in size; four twin 5in (127mm) guns removed.
1951–1953 Three tours off Korea.
1952 (Oct) Redesignated attack aircraft-carrier (CVA-9).
1955 (March–March 1956) Modernised: fitted with angled flight deck, improved arrester gear, larger island, and enclosed (Hurricane) bow.
1960 (3 Aug) Reclassified as ASW support aircraft-carrier (CVS-9).
1962 Completed FRAM II conversion: sonar fitted, combat information centre modified, gun armament reduced; ship fitted to operate ASW aircraft.
1973 Stricken.

The final design was an enlarged version of an improved *Yorktown* class carrier planned in 1939. There were two types, the second (CV-14) being 16ft (4·9m) longer than the first (CV-9). Thirty-two were planned but CV-50 to 55 were cancelled in March 1945 and *Reprisal* (CV-35) and *Iwo Jima* (CV-46) were cancelled on the slips in September 1945. The building times achieved by standardisation of equipment were remarkable, ranging from 14 months to about two years except for *Oriskany*, whose construction was halted at the end of World War II and not completed until 1950, a total of six and a half years. The distribution of the armour gave very similar lateral protection to that in British contemporaries but whereas *Illustrious* had 3in (76mm) armour on the flight deck and 2·5in (63mm) on the hangar deck the *Essex* class were unarmoured on the flight deck leaving the final defence to the 1·5in (38mm) armour of the main deck. The results of this apportionment of protection were clearly shown in two attacks on *Franklin* (CV-13). On 30 October 1944 a *kamikaze* hit her flight deck, ripped a 40ft (12·2m) hole in it, killing 56 men and destroying 33 aircraft. During the Okinawa operations on 19 March 1945 she was hit by two bombs which penetrated the flight deck. The resultant fires and explosions killed 832 men, destroyed most of her aircraft and put her out of action for the rest of the war. In all, there were 12 occasions when ships of this class were seriously damaged, all by air attack, although none was sunk. The situation would probably have been worse had not a heavy AA armament been available. The twelve 5in (127mm) guns were radar-controlled

Displacement:	Essex as built	Oriskany in 1976
standard tons (tonnes)	30,800 (31,290)	33,250 (33,780)
full load tons (tonnes)	39,800 (40,430)	44,700 (45,420)
Dimensions:		
length (pp)	820ft (250·4m)	820ft (250·4m)
(oa)	899ft (274m)	890ft (271·3m)
beam (wl)	93ft (28·4m)	106·5ft (32·5m)
(flight deck)	147·5ft (45m)	195·5ft (59·5m)
draught	28·5ft (8·7m)	31ft (9·4m)
Armament:		
guns		
5in (127mm) 38cal	12	2
40mm	68	—
20mm	52	—
aircraft	80	70
Armour:		
side (belt)	2·5–3in (60–76mm)	2·5–3in (60–76mm)
deck (flight)	—	1·5in (38mm)
(hangar)	3in (76mm)	3in (76mm)
(main)	1·5in (38mm)	1·5in (38mm)
Machinery:		
boilers (type)	Babcock & Wilcox	
(number)	8	
engines (type)	Westinghouse geared turbines	
shafts	4	
Total SHP:		
designed	150,000	
Fuel capacity:		
oil tons (tonnes)	?	6,161 (6,260)
Performance:		
designed speed	33kts	
range	18,000 miles (15,000nm) @ 12kts	
Crew (including aircrew):	3,448	3,275

Class:	ESSEX class Group 1	ESSEX class Group 2	ORISKANY (CV-34)
Where built:	various yards	various yards	New York Naval Yard
Authorised:	?	?	?
Laid down:	1941–1942	1942–1944	1 May 1944
Launched:	1942–1943	1943–1945	13 Oct 1945
Completed:	1942–1944	1944–1945	25 Sept 1950
Fate:	In reserve or scrapped from 1964	In reserve or scrapped from 1967; 8 ships cancelled 1945	In reserve

and blind-fire facilities were later included for the 40mm armament. A total of seventy 20mm Oerlikons provided a last-ditch defence in the later stages of the war. There were three large lifts to handle the ship's Air Group, which varied from the original 36 fighters, 36 reconnaissance/bombers and 18 torpedo bombers to the end-of-war total of 73 fighters, 15 bombers and 15 torpedo bombers. In the post-World War II years this class bore a great deal of the

Above: A modernized Essex *carrier, showing the angled deck. She is seen as an AS carrier. Only* Lexington *now remains in commission.*

brunt of foreign operations, four being operational at the start of the Korean War in June 1950, four completing modernisation, two paid off in reserve after World War II damage, the remainder being lined up for modernisation

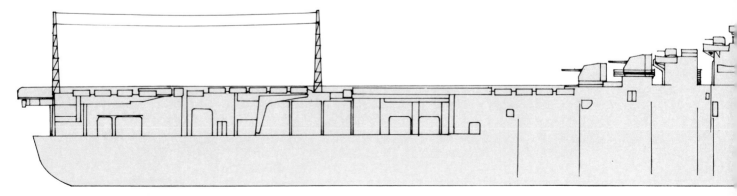

For some this meant strengthened flight decks, more deck space and larger aviation fuel stowage. Six had, in addition, steam catapults, stronger arrester gear, new lift arrangements and a 'hurricane' bow. In some cases these changes were not finished until the war was over but a new carrier advance had been fitted to *Antietam* in 1952 — the British 'angled-deck'. This was to become standard practice and was seen in the new ships of the revived US carrier programme. As these came into commission — the *Forrestals* in 1955–59, *Enterprise* in 1961 and the *Kitty Hawks* in 1961–68 — so did the operational life of the *Essex* class draw to an end. Useful to the last, some became ASW carriers and today only *Lexington* remains in commission — as a training carrier.

Right: A rebuilt Essex *class carrier in final form as an A/S carrier. Note that the lift abaft the island has been stowed vertically. Sea King helicopters can be seen on deck and overhead*

Above: USS Hornet *of the* Essex *class in 1966 after modernisation and refitting as an A/S carrier. Note rebuilt island, angled deck and starboard lift, Tracker and Tracer aircraft and Sea King helicopters*

Essex *(CV-9) as built. Note open bow and hangar sides and 5in (127mm) mounts*

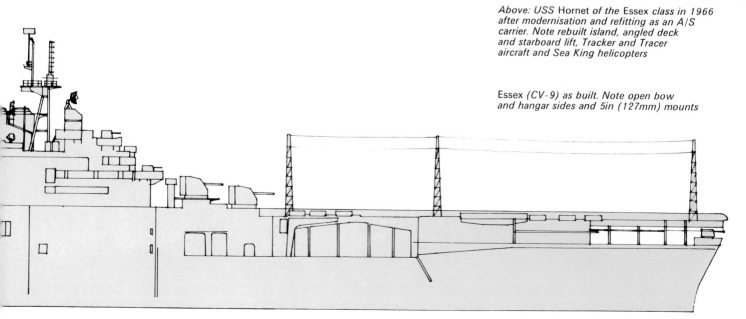

Independence

AIRCRAFT-CARRIER

CLASS: *Independence* class
(9 ships) including *Independence*
CVL-22 (ex-CV-22, ex-*Amsterdam*
CL-59) · *Dedalo* PH-01 (ex-*Cabot*
CVL-28, ex-CV-28, ex-*Wilmington*
CL-79)

Service career INDEPENDENCE
(ex-AMSTERDAM CL-59) CVL-22
(ex CV-22)

1943 (19 Jan) Commissioned.
1943 (July) Joined Pacific Fleet.
1943 (15 July) Reclassified as Light Aircraft-Carrier (CVL-22).
1943 (Sept–Nov) Operations in South-West Pacific.
1943 (20 Nov) Hit by torpedo on starboard quarter from Japanese aircraft: serious damage.
1944 (Jan–June) Permanent repairs at San Francisco: fitted with second catapult.
1944 (July–Aug) Training as Night Carrier (to provide reconnaissance at night).
1944 (Aug–Jan 1945) Operations in Pacific as Night Carrier.
1944 (24–25 Oct) Battle of Leyte Gulf.

1945 (Jan–March) Refit at Pearl Harbor.
1945 (March–Aug) Operations in Pacific as ordinary carrier.
1945 (Nov–Jan 1946) Transported returning servicemen to USA.

Above: USS Independence *(CVL-22) in
San Francisco Bay in July 1943,
when she joined the US Pacific Fleet.*
Independence *class carriers operated
some 45 planes*

1946 (July) Target vessel at Bikini atom bomb tests; then taken to Kwajalein, then to Pearl Harbor, and finally to San Francisco as test hulk.
1951 (29 Jan) Sunk as weapons test ship off California.

Although the *Essex* class aircraft-carriers were constructed extremely quickly for ships of their size, it was obvious that the US Navy would still have a shortage of fleet carriers before they came into service in any numbers. The British, who had a similar problem, produced the specially designed *Colossus, Majestic* and *Hermes* class light fleet carriers. The Americans, who were building large numbers of *Cleveland* class light cruisers, decided to convert nine incomplete hulls instead of producing a completely new design, and nine more *Clevelands* were later ordered to replace them. This was not an ideal solution. The resulting *Independence* class carriers were very cramped, maintenance facilities were extremely limited and accommodation was restricted. However, by bulging the hull to maintain stability, a reasonably large wooden flight-deck and an open hangar with the capacity to operate 45 aircraft could be fitted. There was a small island and four inclined uptakes to starboard. The flight deck was not armoured, but the original cruiser protection was retained, as was the original machinery. Unlike the early British light fleet carriers, the *Independence* class were fast enough to operate as part of the fast carrier groups. Later in the war, when numbers of *Essex* class carriers were entering service, the *Independences* were sometimes used as fast aircraft transports, when they could carry about 100 aircraft. *Princeton* ex-*Tallahassee* (CV-23) was bombed by Japanese aircraft during the Battle of Leyte Gulf, and later exploded and sank. Two *Independence* class carriers were transferred to France whilst the French were designing and building the *Clemenceaus*, and one is still in service in Spain, operating helicopters and AV-8 Matador (Harrier) V/STOL aircraft. Two somewhat similar vessels *Saipan* (CVL-48) and *Wright* (CVL-49) were based on the *Baltimore* class heavy cruisers, but with 6ft (1·9m) greater beam and without the armour belt. *Wright* (now CC-2) was converted into a command ship, and *Saipan* (renamed *Arlington*, AGMR-2) into a communications relay ship.

*Independence (CVL-22) as built. Note
cruiser hull and four funnels*

Displacement:	Independence as built	Dedalo in 1977
standard tons (tonnes)	11,000 (11,180)	13,000 (13,208)
full load tons (tonnes)	15,100 (15,340)	16,416 (16,679)
Dimensions:		
length (wl)	600ft (182·9m)	
(oa)	622·5ft (189·7m)	
beam (wl)	71·5ft (21·8m)	
(flight deck)	109·25ft (33·2m)	
draught	26ft (7·9m)	
Armament:		
guns		
5in (127mm) 38cal	4	—
40mm	26	26
20mm	40	—
aircraft	approx 45	approx 20
Armour:		
side (belt)	5in (127mm)	
(end)	1·5in (38mm)	
deck (main)	3in (76mm)	
(lower)	2in (52mm)	
Machinery:		
boilers (type)	Babcock & Wilcox	
(number)	4	
engines (type)	General Electric geared turbines	
shafts	4	
Total SHP:		
designed	100,000	
Fuel capacity:		
oil tons (tonnes)	2,419 (2,458)	1,800 (1,830)
Performance:		
designed speed	32kts	
range	11,000 miles (9,250nm) @ 15kts	7,200 miles (6,050nm) @ 15kts
Crew:	1,109	1,112

Class:	INDEPENDENCE class
Where built:	New York Shipyard
Authorised:	?
Laid down:	Aug 1941–Oct 1942
Started conversion:	?
Launched:	Aug 1942–Sept 1943
Completed:	Feb–Dec 1943
Reclassified from CV to CVL:	July 1943
Fate:	*Princeton* (ex-*Tallahassee*) CVL-23 (ex-CV-23) sunk 24 Oct 1944; *Independence* (ex-*Amsterdam* CL-59) CVL-22 (ex CV-22) sunk 29 Jan 1951; remainder scrapped except *Cabot* (ex-*Wilmington* CL-79) CVL-28 (ex CV-28) transferred to Spain 30 Aug 1967, renamed *Dedalo* (PH-01) purchased by Spain 1972

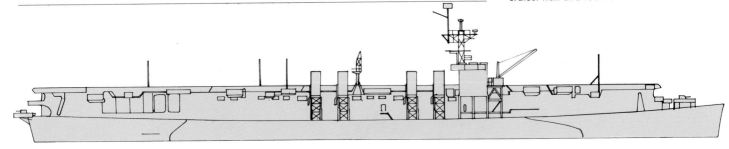

Forrestal

AIRCRAFT-CARRIER

CLASS: *Forrestal* class (4 ships)
Forrestal (CV-59, ex CVA-59) ·
Saratoga (CV-60, ex-CVA-60) ·
Ranger (CV-61, ex-CVA-61) ·
Independence (CV-62, ex CVA-62)

Service career FORRESTAL (CV-59)

1952 Initially classified as large aircraft-carrier (CVB-59).
1952 (Oct) Reclassified as attack aircraft-carrier (CVA-59).
1956-1977 Worldwide service.
1956 (Nov–Dec) In Eastern Atlantic during Suez Crisis.
1958 (July) In Eastern Atlantic during Lebanon crisis; forward 5in (127mm) guns removed.
1967 (29 July) Fire on flight deck off Vietnam: serious damage.
1967 Refit: one mast and four aft 5in (127mm) guns removed; single BPDMS Sea Sparrow SAM launcher mounted forward; NTDS fitted.
1972 Single BPDMS Sea Sparrow SAM launcher fitted aft.
1975 (30 June) Reclassified as CV-59.

United States (CVA-58), the first postwar American aircraft-carrier to be laid down, had a designed standard displacement of 65,000 tons (66,040 tonnes). She was to have had funnels flush with the flight deck and a retractable bridge to provide the maximum possible deck space for operating the large postwar carrier aircraft. However, she was cancelled almost immediately after being laid down in April 1949 because of doubts about her design and function, and because of pressure from the

Strategic Air Command. The subsequent 'Admirals' revolt' and a reassessment of the value of aircraft-carriers in the light of the Korean War resulted in the US Navy being allowed to build a fleet based on large aircraft-carriers, and *Forrestal* (CV-59) was ordered in 1952. She was the largest aircraft-carrier to be built since the Japanese *Shinano* of 1944. Her design was based on that of *United States*

Above: The 75,900-ton (full load) USS Forrestal *(CV-59) operates some 70 aircraft. Mounting four steam catapults, she can launch 32 planes in four minutes*

(CVA-58), but it was modified to take advantage of the new British angled deck. This underwent very successful trials on the American *Essex* class aircraft-carrier *Antietam* (CV-36) in 1952, and gave the necessary deck space to operate modern aircraft whilst still retaining a fixed island and funnel. *Forrestal* (CV-59) is the first American aircraft-carrier to be built with an angled deck. This is angled at 8°, and the flight deck and island are sponsored out to twice the width of the hull. The four lifts, each 52·2ft by 62ft (15·9m by 18·9m), are external to the hull, eliminating a source of weakness in previous carriers' flight decks. *Forrestal* (CV-59) is also the first American aircraft carrier to be built with steam catapults (another British invention), having two forward and two on the angled deck enabling four aircraft to be launched in very rapid succession. To improve seaworthiness the *Forrestals* have a fully enclosed hurricane bow, the first fitted to an American aircraft carrier since the *Lexingtons*. However, when first completed they were unable to maintain high speed in rough weather because the forward 5in (127mm) sponsons were liable to structural damage because of their size and position. They were therefore removed. Another weak point of the design is the positioning of the port lift at the forward end of the angled deck where it interferes with flying operations. The four improved *Forrestals* and the nuclear-powered *Enterprise* (CVN-65) and *Nimitz* class are all basically similar to the *Forrestals*, except that their islands are further aft, but they have the port lift repositioned clear of the angled deck aft. Of the improved *Forrestals*, the three *Kitty Hawks* were armed from the start with two Terrier SAM twin-launchers, and the later *John F. Kennedy* (CV-67) has three BPDMS Sea Sparrow SAM launchers. *Saratoga* (CV-60), *Ranger* (CV-61) and *Independence* (CV-62) are similar to *Forrestal*, but have higher powered engines and a higher speed. Each has slightly different dimensions.

Forrestal (CVA-59) as built. Note enclosed bow, deck edge lifts and 5in (127mm)

Displacement:	Forrestal	Saratoga
standard tons (tonnes)	59,060 (60,005)	60,000 (60,960)
full load tons (tonnes)	75,900 (77,114)	73,300 (74,473)
Dimensions:		
length (wl)	990ft (301·8m)	
(oa)	1,086ft (331m)	
beam (wl)	129·5ft (38·5m)	
(flight deck)	252ft (76·8m)	
draught	37ft (11·3m)	

Armament:	Forrestal as built	Forrestal in 1977
guns		
5in (127mm) 34cal	8	—
missiles		
BPDMS Sea Sparrow SAM octuple-launcher	—	2
aircraft	approx 100	70
Armour:	armoured flight deck	
Machinery:		
boilers (type)	Babcock & Wilcox	
(number)	8	
engines (type)	Westinghouse geared turbines	
shafts	4	
Total SHP:		
designed	260,000	287,000
Fuel capacity:		
oil tons (tonnes)	12,000 (12,190)	
Performance:		
designed speed	33kts	34kts
range	8,000 miles (6,725nm) @ 20kts	
Crew:	approx 4,900 (including aircrew)	

Ship:	FORRESTAL (CV-59)	SARATOGA (CV-60)	RANGER (CV-61)	INDEPENDENCE (CV-62)
Where built:	Newport News Shipyard	New York Naval Yard	Newport News Shipyard	New York Naval Yard
Authorised:	1952	1953	1954	1955
Laid down:	14 July 1952	16 Dec 1952	2 Aug 1954	1 July 1955
Launched:	11 Dec 1954	8 Oct 1955	29 Sept 1956	10 Aug 1957
Completed:	1 Oct 1955	14 April 1956	6 June 1958	10 Jan 1959
Fate:	In service	In service	In service	In service

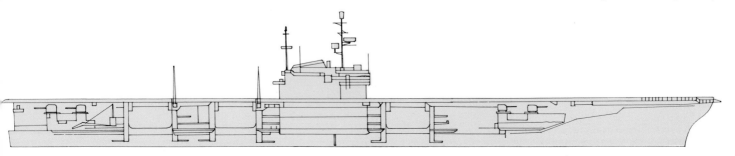

Nimitz

NUCLEAR AIRCRAFT-CARRIER
CLASS: *Nimitz* class (3 ships)
Nimitz (CVN-68) · *Dwight D. Eisenhower* (CVN-69) · *Carl Vinson* (CVN-70)

While discussion of the role of and need for aircraft-carriers continued in the USA several significant events took place. Heated exchanges in both Congress and the Pentagon throughout 1963 revolved about the question of the type of propulsion for future aircraft-carriers. CVA-67 was authorised in FY (Fiscal Year) 1963: the USN had asked that she be nuclear-powered, and two studies had been remitted by Robert McNamara, Secretary of Defense, who eventually declared in October 1963 that she should be conventionally powered. The Secretary of the Navy resigned and, admidst denunciations of McNamara by the Congressional Committee on Atomic Energy the new ship, to be called *John F. Kennedy*, was ordered on 30 April 1964 and laid down on 22 October of that year. Having won this battle McNamara then began his attack on the overall strength of the aircraft-carrier fleet. Undeterred by the circumnavigation of the world by *Enterprise* and her nuclear-powered escorts *Long Beach* and *Bainbridge* in July-October 1964 he told Congress in February 1965 of plans to reduce the carrier force with a tentative programme for a new construction ship in FY 1967. However, the effectiveness of the carrier operations off Vietnam in 1965 brought a change of heart. Without apologies McNamara told Congress in February 1966 that he had reassessed the need and was planning to ask for 15 carriers instead of the 13 he had deemed adequate a year earlier. Cost-effectiveness had been proved in action rather than on the computer. Four nuclear-powered ships were included in McNamara's new total and on 1 July 1966 funds were provided for CVAN-68, now known as *Nimitz* (CVN-68). She was then due for completion in 1971 with her sisters, CVN-69 and CVN-70, due in 1973 and 1975. The facts of the future were to be very different. Only one shipyard in the USA, the Newport News Shipbuilding and Dry Dock Co, builders of *Enterprise*, were able to take on the task and on 22 June 1968 *Nimitz* was laid down. Problems beset her construction at all points. Though she required only two reactors as opposed to the eight in *Enterprise*, delays in delivering and testing the components of the new A4W/A1G reactors caused slippage which was exacerbated by undermanning. As a result *Nimitz* was not commissioned in 1971 but on 3 May 1975, her next sister, *Dwight D. Eisenhower*, in 1977 instead of 1973, and *Carl Vinson* was not laid down until October 1975 with a tentative delivery date of 1981 instead of 1975. As a result the costs have shot up and while *Nimitz*'s price of $1·881 billion was prodigious, the next pair will be well over the $2 billion mark. Debates continue in Congress over their cost-effectiveness because although they are an excellent design, they are simply too expensive to replace older carriers on a one-for-one basis, and they tie up a large proportion of America's seaborne strike power in a very few hulls. These magnificent ships are larger than *Enterprise*, and carry more aircraft, different radar (SPS 48 in place of SPS 32/33) and three Sea Sparrow SAM systems.

Above: Nimitz *(CVN-68) with her air group on the flight deck. Note the island, very different to that of* Enterprise *(CVN-65),* with SPS-48 3-N radar on mast aft, and port aft lift

Displacement:

standard tons (tonnes)	81,600 (82,900)
full load tons (tonnes)	91,400 (92,860)

Dimensions:

length (wl)	1038·2ft (317m)
(oa)	1090·2ft (332·9m)
beam (hull)	133·8ft (40·8m)
(ext)	251·5ft (76·8m)
draught (mean)	37ft (11·3m)
(max)	42·5ft (13m)

Armament:
missiles
BPDMS Sea Sparrow SAM

octuple launcher	3
aircraft	90+

Armour: hull and flight deck are armoured

Machinery:

nuclear reactor (type)	Westinghouse A4W pressurised water-cooled
(number)	2
engines (type)	General Electric geared turbines
shafts	4

Total SHP:

designed	280,000+

Performance:

designed speed	approx. 33kts
range	800,000–1,000,000 miles (675,000–840,000nm) @ 30kts

Crew: 3,300 (ship) and 3,000 (air wing)

Ship:	NIMITZ (CVN-68)	DWIGHT D. EISENHOWER (CVN-69)	CARL VINSON (CVN-70)
Where built:	Newport News	Newport News	Newport News
Authorised:	FY 1967	FY 1971	FY 1974
Laid down:	22 June 1968	15 Aug 1970	11 Oct 1975
Launched:	13 May 1972	11 Oct 1975	—
Completed:	3 May 1975	—	—
Fate:	In service	Completing	Building

Nimitz *(CVN-68). Note island set well back, angled deck and deck edge lifts*

Above, upper: Nimitz *(CVN-68) about to replenish underway from an ammunition ship. Note the lowered starboard forward lift and the BPDMS Sea Sparrow launcher on the starboard bow*

Above: A nuclear powered task force consisting of Nimitz *(CVN-68), and the guided missile cruisers* California *(CGN-36) and* South Carolina *(CGN-37) in the Mediterranean in 1976*

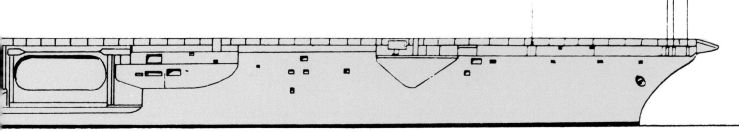

Tarawa

AMPHIBIOUS ASSAULT SHIP

CLASS: *Tarawa* class (5 ships)
Tarawa (LHA-1) · *Saipan* (LHA-2) ·
Belleau Wood (LHA-3) · *Nassau*
(LHA-4) · *Danang* (LHA-5)

The *Tarawa* class LHA combine the capabilities of the *Austin* class LPD and the *Iwo Jima* class LPH. The LPD was developed from the wartime LSD, and can carry LSMs in a floodable dock aft, with troops and their equipment forward. The LPH was evolved after the Suez operation in 1956 and the Lebanon crisis of 1958 had demonstrated the value of helicopters for landing troops. They operate 30 helicopters from a continuous full length flight deck, with a hangar and room for over 2,000 troops below. The *Tarawas* can transport a battalion group of Marines (1,800 men), and can land them with their light equipment from helicopters operating from the continuous full length flight deck. Beneath the forward part of this there is a half length hangar and troop quarters. Aft there is a floodable dock from which LCMs can land the troops' heavy equipment. The *Tarawas* have a bow thruster to help dock the LCMs. The entire class was ordered under a Total Package Procurement Contract from Litton Industries, but as with the *Spruance* class this has proved a failure. Cost overruns have been considerable, and completion of the class has been delayed by from two to four years whilst the problems are resolved.

Displacement:	
standard tons (tonnes)	?
full load tons (tonnes)	39,300 (39,930)
Dimensions:	
length (wl)	778ft (237·8m)
(oa)	820ft (242·7m)
beam	106ft (32·3m)
draught	27·5ft (8·4m)
Armament:	
guns	
5in (127mm) 54cal	3
20mm	6
missiles	
BPDMS Sea Sparrow	
SAM octuple launcher	2
aircraft	approx 26 helicopters or Harriers
Machinery:	
boilers (type)	Combustion Engineering
(number)	2
engines (type)	Westinghouse geared steam turbines
shafts	2
Total SHP:	
designed	140,000
Fuel capacity	
oil tons (tonnes)	?
Performance:	
designed speed	24kts
range	10,000 miles (8,400nm) @ 20kts
Crew:	902+1,903 troops

Ship:	TARAWA (LHA-1)	SAIPAN (LHA-2)	BELLEAU WOOD (LHA-3)	NASSAU (LHA-4)	DANANG (LHA-5)
Where built:	Ingalls Shipyard	Ingalls Shipyard	Ingalls Shipyard	Ingalls Shipyard	Ingalls Shipyard
Authorised:	1968	1969	1969	1970	1970
Laid down:	15 Nov 1971	21 July 1972	5 March 1972	13 Aug 1973	12 Nov 1976
Launched:	1 Dec 1973	18 July 1974	1976	1977	—
Completed:	29 May 1975	Jan 1976			—
Fate:	In service	In service	Completing (LHA 6–9 cancelled 1971)	Completing	Under construction

Above: The amphibious assault ship USS Tarawa *(LHA-1) on trials in 1975. Note the single-mounted 127mm anti-aircraft guns, supplementing two Sea Sparrow systems.*

Right: Carrying about 26 helicopters and equipped with a well deck for landing craft, Tarawa *can transport and land an 1,800-strong Battalion Group of Marines.*

Tarawa *(LHA-1). Note bulky superstructure, 5in (127mm) and Sea Sparrow SAM*

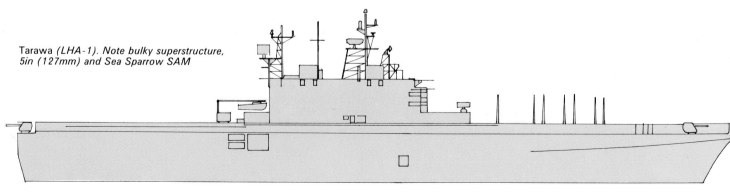

South Carolina

BATTLESHIP
CLASS: *South Carolina* class
(2 ships) *South Carolina* (BB-26) ·
Michigan (BB-27)

Service career SOUTH CAROLINA (BB-26)
1911–1916 US Atlantic Fleet.
1916 (30 Sept–3 Jan 1917) Refit.
1917 (Jan–Apr) At Cuba.
1917 (Apr–Sept 1918) Gunnery training ship.
1918 (Sept) Convoy escort.
1918 (Sept–Nov) Gunnery training ship.
1919 (Feb–July) Troop transport.
1920–1921 Midshipmen's training courses.
1923 (10 Nov) Stricken.
1924 Scrapped.

Although these were the first modern battle-ships to be designed with a single calibre main armament, they were laid down and completed well after the British *Dreadnought* because of delays in authorisation and construction. They marked a return to the steady development of American battleship designs after the *Mississippis,* but Congress was still extremely cost conscious and restricted them to the same normal displace-ment as the preceding *Connecticuts,* 16,000 tons (16,260 tonnes). Superfiring twin turrets were adopted after blast trials on a monitor, but although the *Connecticuts'* mixed secondary battery of 8in (203mm) and 7in (178mm) guns was abandoned, the weight saved was insuffi-cient to allow both a flushdecked hull and superfiring. The aft turrets were therefore mounted one deck lower, but the 3in (76mm) guns were placed at fo'c's'le deck level, where they could be worked in virtually any weather. Trials with turbines had not been completed satisfactorily when the *South Carolinas* were designed so they adopted a similar reciprocating machinery arrangement to the *Connecticuts.* Cage masts were fitted. *Michigan* had a similar career to *South Carolina.* She was stricken on 24 August 1923.

Displacement:		
normal tons (tonnes)	16,000 (16,256)	
full load tons (tonnes)	17,900 (18,186)	
Dimensions:		
length (wl)	450ft (137·4m)	
(oa)	452·75ft (138·2m)	
beam	80·25ft (24·5m)	
draught	24·5ft (7·5m)	
Armament:	**as built**	**in 1918**
guns		
12in (305mm) 45cal	8	8
3in (76mm) 50cal	22	16
1pdr (37mm)	4	4
torpedo tubes		
21in (533mm)	2	2
Armour:		
side (belt)	9–12in (229–305mm)	
deck (ends)	1·5in (38mm)	
(main)	1·5–3in (38–76mm)	
main turrets	8–12in (203–305mm)	
barbettes	10in (254mm)	
Machinery:		
boilers (type)	Babcock	
(number)	12	
engines (type)	vertical triple expansion	
shafts	2	
Total IHP:		
designed	16,500	
trial (max)	17,882	
Fuel capacity:		
coal normal tons (tonnes)	900 (914)	
max tons (tonnes)	2,380 (2,418)	
Performance:		
designed speed	18·5kts	
trial speed (max)	18·86kts	
range	5,000 miles (4,200nm) @ 10kts	
Crew	869	

Ship:	**SOUTH CAROLINA (BB-26)**	**MICHIGAN (BB-27)**
Where built:	Cramp, Philadelphia	New York Shipyard
Authorised:	3 March 1905	3 March 1905
Laid Down:	18 Dec 1906	17 Dec 1906
Launched:	11 July 1908	26 May 1908
Completed:	1 March 1910	4 Jan 1910
Fate:	Scrapped 1924	Scrapped 1924

Right: USS South Carolina *(BB-26) was the first US all big gun ship. Note the cage masts carried by all US battleships of this period*

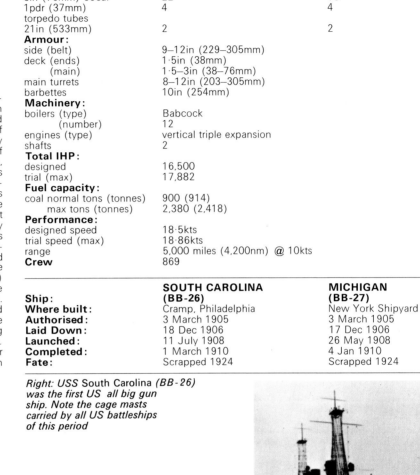

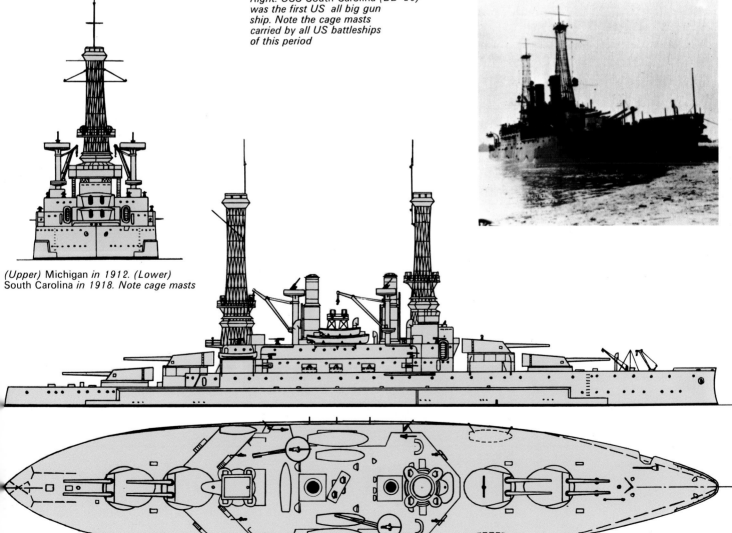

(Upper) Michigan *in 1912. (Lower)* South Carolina *in 1918. Note cage masts*

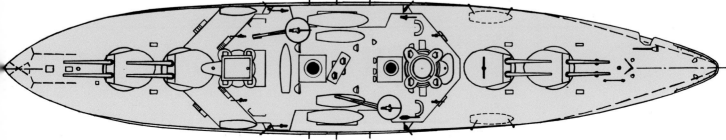

Texas
BATTLESHIP
CLASS: *New York* class (2 ships)
New York (BB-34) · *Texas* (BB-35)

Service career TEXAS (BB-35)
1917 In Battle Squadron 6 (USN).
1918 (Jan) To Grand Fleet (RN) 6th Battle Squadron.
1918 (11 Feb) Arrived at Scapa Flow.
1918 (Feb–Nov) Patrols in Atlantic and North Sea.
1918 (Dec) Returned to USA.
1919 Refit.
1920–1925 Pacific Fleet.
1925–1927 Rebuilt: oil-fired boilers fitted; one funnel removed; torpedo bulges fitted; cage masts replaced by tripods; 1in (25mm) armour added to main deck; bridge enlarged; catapult fitted to C turret.
1928–1931 Atlantic Fleet.
1931–1936 Pacific Fleet.
1936–1941 Training ship Atlantic Fleet.
1941–1943 Atlantic patrols and convoy escort.
1942 (Nov) Covered Casablanca landings.
1944 (June) Covered D-Day landings in Normandy and (Aug) southern France.
1944 (Nov) To Pacific.
1945 (Feb–Mar) Covered Iwo Jima landings.
1945 (Mar–June) Covered Okinawa landings.
1945 (27 Oct) Decommissioned.
1948 (Apr) Transferred to State of Texas as permanent memorial at San Jacinto.

The *New York* class used a slightly enlarged version of the heavy flush-decked hull introduced in the *Wyoming*, but mounted 14in (356mm) rather than 12in (305mm) guns. These 14in (356mm) turrets had been proposed for the *Florida* class, but the design had been delayed. If it had not been ready for the *New Yorks*, they would have mounted fifteen 12in (305mm) guns in triple turrets. They reverted to reciprocating engines because American engine manufacturers had found it difficult and expensive to build turbines to the tolerances used abroad and required by the US Navy. A dispute over the *Wyomings*' turbines and their price had resulted in a compromise. However, there was no improvement in manufacturing techniques so after another prolonged dispute the Bureau of Ships adopted reciprocating engines for the *New Yorks* to force the manufacturers to improve their standards and lower their prices. This drastic step worked, but it was a luxury that neither Britain nor Germany, fully engaged on a naval race, could have afforded. Apart from the engines, the major weakness of the design was the position of the secondary armament. The foremost pair of 5in (127mm) guns on either

Displacement:	as built	in 1945
standard tons (tonnes)	—	27,000 (27,430)
normal tons (tonnes)	27,000 (27,430)	29,500 (29,970)
full load tons (tonnes)	28,400 (28,850)	32,000 (32,510)
Dimensions:		
length (wl)	565ft (172·5m)	565ft (172·5m)
(oa)	573ft (175m)	573ft (175m)
beam	95·25ft (29m)	106·25ft (32·4m)
draught	28·5ft (8·7m)	31·5ft (9·6m)
Armament:		
guns		
14in (356mm) 45cal	10	10
5in (127mm) 51cal	21	6
3in (76mm)	—	10
40mm	—	42
20mm	—	36
torpedo tubes		
21in (533mm) submerged	4	
aircraft	—	3
Armour:		
side (belt)	6–12in (152–305mm)	
(ends)	6in (152mm)	
decks (main)	1·5–2·5in (38–63mm)	
(lower)	2·5–3·5in (63–89mm)	
main turrets	8–14in (203–356mm)	
barbettes	12in (305mm)	
casemates	7in (178mm)	
Machinery:		
boilers (type)	Babcock	Bureau Express
(number)	14	6
engines (type)	vertical triple expansion	
shafts	2	
Total IHP:		
designed	28,100	
trial	28,373	
Fuel capacity:		
coal tons (tonnes)	2,960 (3,010)	
oil tons (tonnes)	400 (410)	
Performance:		
designed speed	21kts	
trial speed	21·05kts	
range	10,000 miles (8,400nm) @ 10kts	
Crew:	864	1,530

Ship:	NEW YORK (BB-34)	TEXAS (BB-35)
Where Built:	New York Naval Yard	Newport News Shipyard
Authorised:	1910	1910
Laid down:	11 Sept 1911	17 Apr 1911
Launched:	30 Oct 1912	18 May 1912
Completed:	15 Apr 1914	12 Mar 1914
Fate:	'A' bomb target ship July 1946; scuttled 8 July 1948	Preserved as monument Apr 1948

side of the bow were useless in heavy weather and were removed in 1917–1918, as were the stern guns. Both ships were comprehensively modernised in the mid-1920s, when weight saved by fitting new boilers was used to improve the horizontal and underwater protection. They were the first US battleships to have radar, fitted in December 1938. In 1940–41 the 14in (356mm) guns were given 15° more elevation to increase their range. *New York* had a similar career to *Texas* and was used as a target for the Bikini atom bomb tests in July 1946.

Below: The New York *class battleship USS* Texas *(BB-35) in 1946. Since 1948 she has been preserved as a war memorial at San Jacinto, Texas*

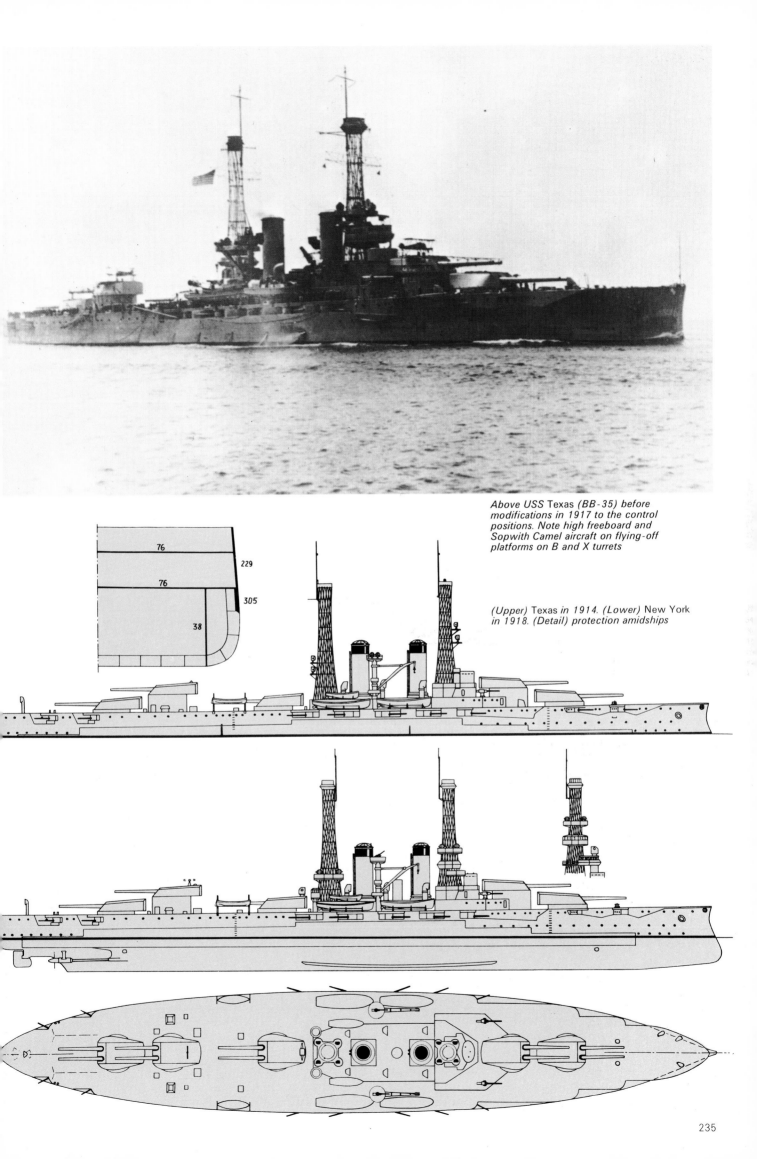

Above USS Texas (BB-35) before
modifications in 1917 to the control
positions. Note high freeboard and
Sopwith Camel aircraft on flying-off
platforms on B and X turrets

(Upper) Texas in 1914. (Lower) New York
in 1918. (Detail) protection amidships

76

76

38

229

305

Tennessee

BATTLESHIP

CLASS: *Tennessee* class (2 ships)
Tennessee (BB-43) · *California*
(BB-44)

Service career TENNESSEE (BB-43)

1921 (June–Mar 1930) In Pacific.
1922 Two 5in (127mm) removed, four 3in (76mm) added.
1928 3in (76mm) Replaced by eight 5in (127mm) 25cal; catapult fitted on quarterdeck.
1930 (Mar–May) Exercises in Atlantic.
circa 1930 Catapult fitted to X turret.
1930 (May–Oct 1934) In Pacific.
1934 (Oct–Feb 1935) In Atlantic.
1935 (Feb–Dec 1945) In Pacific.
circa 1937 Torpedo tubes removed.
1940 Two 3in (76mm) added.
1941 (7 Dec) Pearl Harbor: hit by two bombs.
1941 (20 Dec–Mar 1942) Repaired at Puget Sound Navy Yard: cage mainmast and two 5in (127mm) 51cal removed; eight 5in (127mm) 25cal, 14 20mm and 32 1·1in (28mm) guns added.
1942 (May–Aug) Patrols from Pearl Harbor.
1942 (Sept–May 1943) Rebuilt at Puget Sound Navy Yard: new superstructure, similar to *South Dakotas*, fitted with single funnel; hull widened; all 5in (127mm) 51cal, 3in (76mm) 25cal and 1·1in (28mm) removed; 16 5in (127mm) 38cal, 40 40mm and 43 20mm fitted; radar added.
1943 (Nov–Aug 1945) Operations against Tarawa, Kwajalein, Eniwetok, Kavieng, Saipan, Guam, Tinian, Palau, Leyte, Iwo Jima, Okinawa and Japan.
1944 (19 June) Hit by 6in shell off Saipan.
1944 (25 Oct) Battle of Surigao Strait: fired 69 rounds of 14in (356mm) shells.
1944 (Dec–27 Jan 1945) Refit at Puget Sound.
1945 (12 Apr) Hit by *kamikaze* aircraft, super-ficial damage.
1945 (8 Dec) In reserve.

Tennessee after complete rebuilding in 1943. Note single funnel and compact superstructure encircled by AA guns, and Kingfisher seaplane on catapult aft

Displacement	as built	in 1945
standard tons (tonnes)	—	37,000 (37,590)
normal tons (tonnes)	32,300 (32,820)	—
full load tons (tonnes)	34,000 (34,540)	40,500 (41,150)
Dimensions:		
length (pp)	600ft (183·2m)	600ft (183·2m)
(oa)	624·5ft (190·7m)	624·5ft (190·7m)
beam (ext)	92·25ft (29·7m)	114·1ft (34·8m)
draught	30·25ft (9·2m)	35ft (10·7m)
Armament:		
guns		
14in (356mm) 50cal	12	12
5in (127mm) 51cal	14	—
5in (127mm) 38cal	—	16
3in (76mm)	4	—
40mm	—	40
20mm	—	50
torpedo tubes		
21in (533mm) submerged	2	—
aircraft	—	2
Armour:		
side (belt)	14in (356mm)	
(steps)	8in (203mm)	
deck (upper armour)	3·5in (90mm)	
(lower armour)	2·5–5in (63–127mm)	
main turrets	9–18in (229–457mm)	
barbettes	13in (330mm)	
Machinery:		
boilers (type)	Babcock & Wilcox	
(number)	8	
engines (type)	Westinghouse turbines	
electric motors (type)	Westinghouse	
shafts	4	
Total SHP:		
turbines designed	28,500	
electric motors designed	27,200	
trial	30,908	
Fuel capacity:		
oil tons (tonnes)	3,328 (3,380)	
Performance:		
designed speed	21kts	
trial speed	21·01kts	
range	10,000 miles (8,400nm) @ 10kts	
Crew:	**in 1920**	**in 1945**
	1,083	2,375

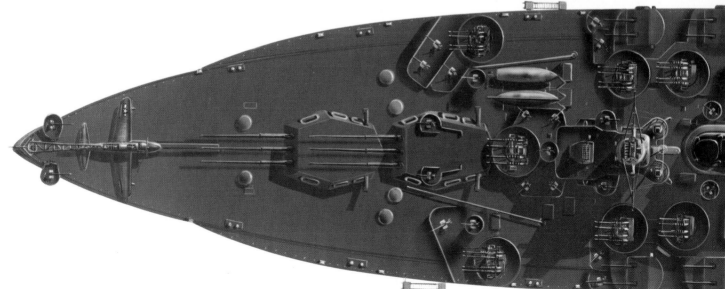

947 (14 Feb) Decommissioned.
959 (1 Mar) Stricken.
959 Scrapped.

he two ships of this class were very similar to
eir predecessors of the *New Mexico* class
ut had certain differences. The latter had hull-
ounted secondary guns but these were later
ated in; in the *Tennessees* these positions
ere removed and the secondary armament was
oncentrated on or above the fo'c's'le deck level,
e total being reduced from twenty-two to
urteen 5in (127mm) guns. Externally they
ere similar not only to the *New Mexicos* but
so to their successors of the *Maryland* class —
oth the *Tennessees* and the following three
ips benefited from lessons learned by the
ritish in actions such as Jutland. Not only was
is an advantage, but the American decisions
build a very considerable battlefleet led to the
doption of much greater standardisation than
ad previously been accepted in any navy. This
as the last class designed before the USN
ecame aware of the British *Queen Elizabeth* class
med with 15in (381mm) guns. As a result the
llowing *Colorado* class and the six uncom-
eted ships of the *South Dakota* class were de-
gned for 16in (406mm) guns. With the end of
Jorld War I only three out of the planned 10
ips, with a further six projected, were com-
leted so that it was not surprising, in an era
when the battleship remained a symbol of naval
ower, that the *Tennessee* class was retained in
ervice until 1959. During this time both were
ttached to the Pacific Fleet and were damaged
uring the Japanese attack on Pearl Harbor on
December 1941. *Tennessee* was out of action

until March 1942 and *California*, more seriously
damaged, until January 1944. By this time both
had undergone a modernisation which not only
provided a great improvement to their fighting
power and endurance but also totally changed
their appearance. The heavyweight turbine-
electric drive was continued from the *New
Mexicos*, through this class to the *Marylands*
and the later *South Dakotas*. It was not until
the *North Carolinas* were built that straight
turbine drive was adopted. The propulsion
system, main armament and hull were about all

Above: USS California *(BB-44) is
seen here before modernization,
with two funnels and lattice masts.
Badly damaged at Pearl Harbor,
she was reconstructed in 1942—44*

that remained of the *Tennessees* after their
conversion. The cost of this mammoth trans-
formation is not available but the very fact of its
happening shows the slow appreciation of the
rapidly changing forms of naval warfare in face
of the high speed aircraft and the submarine.

Ship:	**TENNESSEE (BB-43)**	**CALIFORNIA (BB-44)**
Where built:	New York Navy Yard	Mare Island Navy Yard
Authorised:	3 Mar 1915	3 Mar 1915
Laid down:	14 May 1917	25 Oct 1916
Launched:	30 Apr 1919	20 Nov 1919
Completed:	3 June 1920	8 Oct 1921
Fate:	Scrapped 1959	Scrapped 1959

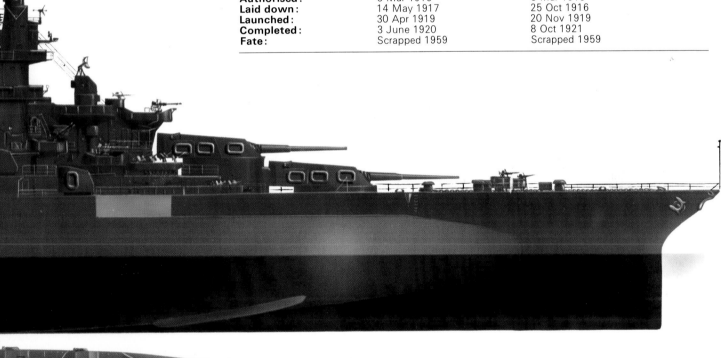

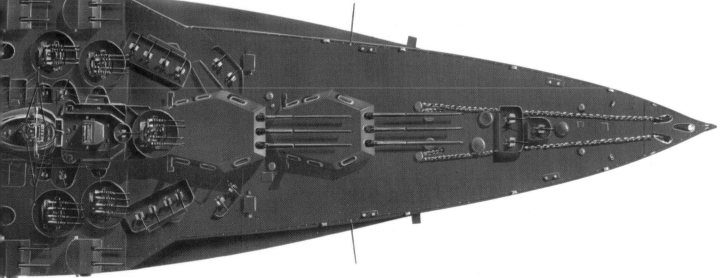

Washington

BATTLESHIP

CLASS: *North Carolina* class
(2 ships) *North Carolina* (BB-55) ·
Washington (BB-56)

Displacement:		
standard tons (tonnes)	36,600 (37,186)	
full load tons (tonnes)	44,800 (45,517)	
Dimensions:		
length (wl)	704ft (214·5m)	
(oa)	729ft (222·6m)	
beam	108ft (33m)	
draught (max)	35ft (10·7m)	
Armament:	**as built**	**in 1945**
guns		
16in (406mm) 45cal	9	9
5in (127mm) 38cal	20	20
40mm	—	60
1·1in (28mm)	16	—
20mm	—	56
0·5in (12·7mm)	12	
aircraft	3	3
Armour:		
side (belt)	?–12in (?–305mm)	
deck (upper)	1·45in (37mm)	
(main)	3·6–4·1in (92–105mm)	
main turrets	7–16in (178–406mm)	
barbettes	16in (406mm)	
Machinery:		
boilers (type)	Babcock & Wilcox	
(number)	8	
engines (type)	General Electric single reduction geared turbines	
shafts	4	
Total SHP:		
designed	121,000	
Fuel capacity:		
oil tons (tonnes)	6,583 (6,688)	
Performance:		
designed speed	28kts	
range	?	
Crew:	2,339	

Ship:	**NORTH CAROLINA (BB-55)**	**WASHINGTON (BB-56)**
Where built:	New York Navy Yard	Philadelphia Navy Yard
Authorised:	1937	1937
Laid down:	27 Oct 1937	14 June 1938
Launched:	13 June 1940	1 June 1940
Completed:	4 Apr 1941	15 May 1941
Fate:	Preserved at Cape Fear River near Wilmington, N.C. as monument Oct 1961	Scrapped 1961

Service career WASHINGTON (BB-56)

1941 Problems with machinery.
1942 (March–Aug) Attached to the British Home Fleet: escorted Russian convoys.
1942 (Aug) To USA.
1942 (Sept–Oct 1945) In the Pacific Ocean.
1942 (14–15 Nov) 2nd Battle of Guadalcanal: overwhelmed Japanese battleship *Kirishima* in seven minutes.
1943 (May–July) Refit at Pearl Harbor.
1943 (Nov–Apr 1945) Operated as escort [t]
US Fast Carrier Force: took part in the strik[e]
against various Pacific islands, the Philippine[s]
Formosa and Japan.
1944 (2 Feb) Collided with battleship *Indiana.*
1944 (Feb–May) Repaired at Puget Sound Na[val]
Yard.
1944 (19–20 June) Battle of the Philippine Se[a]
1944 (23–26 Oct) Battle of Leyte Gulf.
1945 (June–Oct) Refit at Puget Sound Na[val]
Yard.
1947 (27 June) In reserve.
1960 (1 June) Stricken.
1961 Scrapped.

Shortly before the attack on Pearl Harbor [in]
December 1941 confirmed the fears of ma[ny]
concerning the destructive capability of aircra[ft]
the two battleships of the *North Carolina* cla[ss]
were commissioned. These, *North Carolina* an[d]
Washington, had been approved in June 193[7]
but had been held back to let some other na[vies]
take the post-treaty starting gun. This attitud[e]
of self-righteousness which permeated s[o]
much pre-World War II US political thinkin[g]
ensured that the ships were not finally ordere[d]
until August 1937. Whereas the British *Kin[g]
George V* class battleships had 14in (356mm[)]
guns, the *North Carolinas* were delayed lon[g]
enough to take advantage of the failure to ratif[y]
the second London Naval Limitation treaty an[d]
were able to mount 16in (406mm) gun[s]
However, although the British ships we[re]
armoured against 16in (406mm) shell hits, th[e]
American vessels were only protected agains[t]
14in (356mm) shells. The *North Carolinas* we[re]
the slowest of the new generation of fa[st]
battleships, sacrificing speed for the immens[e]
endurance necessary for Pacific operation[s]
Some weight was saved by using welding f[or]
over a third of the hull, and rearrangement of th[e]

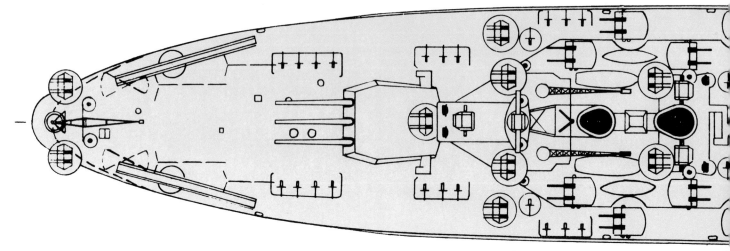

machinery spaces provided extra savings. Turbo-electric drive was abandoned in favour of geared turbines, but these proved very troublesome. North Carolina had to spend several months in dock when first completed before her turbines operated reliably, and Washington's also needed attention. They were not particularly good seaboats and had difficulty attaining their designed speed in a seaway. However, although like all London Treaty battleship designs they had a number of faults, the North Carolinas also had some good points. They had the best AA armament of any contemporary battleship, they had an excellent turning circle, and their wide beam gave them an adequate underwater protection. Their worst fault was the lightness of their armour, but in general they were a competent if uninspired design. North Carolina, like Washington, spent most of World War II in carrier escort duties. They were followed by the four South Dakotas, which were armoured against 16in (406mm) shells and carried a similar armament on a shorter, more efficient hull. As with the later American cruiser designs they only had one funnel to improve the arcs of fire of the AA guns.

Above: USS North Carolina *(BB-55), seen here in 1951, and her sister-ship* Washington *were commissioned just before the Japanese attack on Pearl Harbor*

Washington *in 1944. Note AA guns.*

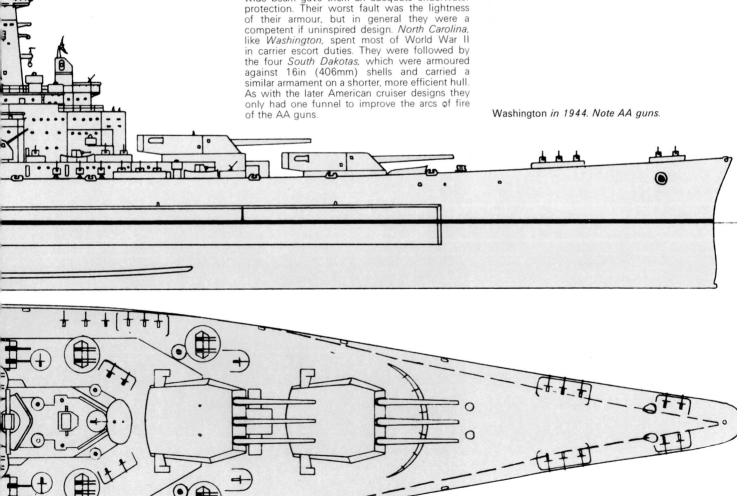

Iowa

BATTLESHIP

CLASS: *Iowa* class (4 ships)
Iowa (BB-61) · *New Jersey* (BB-62)
Missouri (BB-63) · *Wisconsin*
(BB-64)

Continuing a reactive attitude to Japanese building programmes in May 1939, Congress approved a new law to provide replacements for four elderly battleships. This was the *South Dakota* class for which design work had started in 1936 and all of which were to be completed between March and August 1942. These were shorter editions of the *North Carolina*s with a similar armament and speed but with their machinery compressed into a smaller space in the search for improved protection. A year after the *South Dakota* design had been put in hand studies were started for a 45,000 ton (45,720 tonnes) battleship on the expectation that Japan would not ratify the 1936 London Naval Treaty, thereby raising the battleship limitation of 35,000 tons (35,560 tonnes) to 45,000 tons (45,720 tonnes). A whole series of designs were considered from late 1937 until, in June 1938, the General Board accepted a 'fast battleship' design of the previous month as the basis of the new *Iowa* class. The *North Carolina*s and *South Dakota*s were too slow to keep up with the American carriers, and the *Iowa*s were primarily intended as fast carrier escorts. They were based on the *South Dakota*s' design, but were greatly lengthened to incorporate the extra machinery. A new type of triple turret had been designed to take the improved 16in (406mm) 50cal guns, giving an overall saving of nearly 850 tons (864 tonnes). They were armoured on the same scale as the *South Dakota*s, and were thus less well protected than contemporary British or Japanese battleships. It was perhaps fortunate that they never encountered the *Yamato*s. The experience of those involved in World War II during the building of this class caused concern over their protection from air-bombing but it was too late to put these lessons to use. The design of the machinery was outstandingly good and provided the highest shaft horse power (212,000) in any battleship. Careful compartmentation and very flexible interconnections gave a maximum chance of successfully overcoming action damage while the speed of 33 knots (sometimes upped to 35) gave greater possibility of avoiding such damage. The first pair was ordered in May 1938 as the General Board was still cogitating, the second pair in July 1939 and the last pair, which was never completed, in September 1940. The World War II records of the four completed were similar to most Pacific based battleships, followed by a spell in reserve before reactivation for the Korean War. All had returned to reserve by 1957 but during 1968–69 *New Jersey* was once again operational off Vietnam. Today, nearly 35 years old, they all lie in reserve. Four much larger and better armoured *Montana* class battleships, armed with twelve 16in (406mm) guns, were projected to counter the Japanese *Yamato*s. However, they were cancelled in 1943 in favour of more aircraft carriers.
These would have been the definitive US World War II battleship design, with heavier armour to allow them to survive 18·1in (460mm) shell hits. In order to keep the displacement within bounds, the Americans accepted a considerably slower speed than the *Iowa*s, but even so they would have displaced over 63,000 tons, and would not have been able to use the Panama canal. They would have had a similar AA armament to the *Iowa*s, but this would undoubtedly have been increased to cope with Japanese *kamikaze* attacks in 1945. The *Iowa*s were virtually stripped of their light AA guns postwar, and were only partially manned and

Continued on page 242▶

Right: Gun crews aboard an older USN battleship man single 5 inch (127mm) anti-aircraft guns. Iowa *had ten of the later twin 5 inch (127mm) 38 cal mounts.*

Far right: Iowa *fires her 16in/406mm guns off Korea in 1952. The* Iowas *were reactivated for fire support in Korea;* New Jersey *alone served off Vietnam*

Displacement:			
standard tons (tonnes)	44,560 (45,273)		
full load tons (tonnes)	55,710 (56,601)		
Dimensions:			
length (wl)	860ft (262·1m)		
(oa)	887·2ft (270·4m)		
beam	108·2ft (33·0m)		
draught	38ft (11·6m)		

Armament:	1943	December 1944	1957
guns			
16in (406mm) 50cal	9	9	9
5in (127mm) 38cal	20	20	20
40mm	60	76	80
20mm	60	52	—

Armour:	
side (belt)	1·6–12·1in (41–307mm)
deck (upper)	1·5in (38mm)
(main)	6in (153mm)
(splinter)	0·6in (16mm)
(lower)	0·5–0·6in (13–16mm)
main turrets	7·25–19·7in (184–495mm)
barbettes	1·5–17·3in (38–439mm)
Machinery:	
boilers (type)	Babcock & Wilcox
(number)	8
main engines (type)	GE in *Iowa* and *Missouri*, Westinghouse in *New Jersey* and *Wisconsin*
shafts (number)	4
Total SHP:	212,000
Fuel capacity:	
oil tons (tonnes)	7,251 (7,367), except *Iowa* 7,073 (7,186)
Performance:	
speed	33kts (exceeded on occasions)
range	20,727 miles (18,000nm) @ 12kts
Crew:	2,270

Ship:	IOWA (BB-61)	NEW JERSEY (BB-62)	MISSOURI (BB-63)	WISCONSIN (BB-64)
Where built:	New York Navy Yard	Philadelphia Navy Yard	New York Navy Yard	Philadelphia Navy Yard
Approved:	17 May 1938	17 May 1938	6 July 1939	6 July 1939
Laid down:	27 June 1940	16 Sep 1940	6 Jan 1941	25 Jan 1941
Launched:	27 Aug 1942	7 Dec 1942	29 Jan 1944	7 Dec 1943
Commissioned:	22 Feb 1943	23 May 1943	11 June 1944	16 Apr 1944
Fate:	in reserve	in reserve	in reserve	in reserve

▶**Iowa**

refitted for service during the Korean War. *New Jersey* was given an even more spartan refit for her service off Vietnam. Only the 16in (406mm) guns were operational and her speed was greatly reduced. Minimal electronics were added and a helicopter pad marked out on the quarterdeck. Proposals were made to refit these ships with missiles in the late 1940s and 1950s, but the expense and the superior performance of new purpose-built ships quashed this idea.

Above, right: Iowa *(BB-61) in the Pacific at the end of World War II. The long fo'c's'le with its large sheer forward makes this class easily recognisable. The aircraft handling crane can be seen aft*

Right: The Iowa *class battleship* Missouri *(BB-63). On 2 September 1945, Japanese surrender terms were signed aboard the* Mighty Mo *in Sagami Bay*

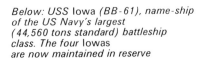

Below: USS Iowa *(BB-61), name-ship of the US Navy's largest (44,560 tons standard) battleship class. The four* Iowas *are now maintained in reserve*

Alaska

LARGE CRUISER

CLASS: *Alaska* class (2 ships)
Alaska (CB-1) · *Guam* (CB-2)

Service career ALASKA (CB-1)

1945 (Jan–Sept) Escorted Fast Carriers in Pacific.
1945 (Feb–Mar) Covered Iwo Jima landings.
1945 (Mar–May) Covered Okinawa landings.
1945 (July–Aug) Raids against Japan.
1960 (17 Feb–1 June) In reserve.
1960 (1 June) Stricken.
1961 Scrapped.

The *Alaska* class large cruisers were designed as the result of mistaken intelligence reports which claimed that Japan was developing large fast armoured surface raiders of about 17,000 tons (17,300 tonnes), mounting 12in (305mm) guns. These were false, but ironically when the Japanese learnt of the existence of the *Alaskas*, they considered building ships of the *Alaska* type themselves. The *Alaskas'* design was an improvisation. They were basically enlarged *Baltimores*, with a single funnel separated by the catapults from a large tower bridge. They had improved protection, and used the same machinery as the *Essex* class carriers. As soon as it was realised that no Japanese raiders existed, the last three *Alaskas* were cancelled, and the construction of the first three slowed to concentrate on aircraft-carriers. *Alaska* (CB-1) and *Guam* (CB-2) were completed as designed, and used as fast carrier escorts. *Hawaii* (CB-3) was suspended when 82 per cent complete, and it was planned to convert her first into a guided-missile ship, and then into a command ship similar to *Northampton* (CLC-1, later CC-1). However, it was cheaper and easier to build new ships for these roles, and *Hawaii* (CB-3) was scrapped incomplete. *Guam* (CB-2) had a similar career to *Alaska* (CB-1).

Displacement:		
standard tons (tonnes)		27,500 (27,940)
full load tons (tonnes)		34,250 (34,800)
Dimensions:		
length (wl)		791ft (241·5m)
(oa)		808·5ft (246·9m)
beam		90·75ft (27·7m)
draught (max)		32·25ft (9·8m)
Armament:		
guns		
12in (305mm) 50cal		9
5in (127mm) 38cal		12
40mm		56
20mm		34
aircraft		4
Armour:		
side (belt)		9in (229mm)
(ends)		5in (127mm)
deck (main)		3·25–4·25in (78–110mm)
(lower)		2in (51mm)
main turrets		5–12·75in (127–324mm)
barbettes		9in (229mm)
Machinery:		
boilers (type)		Babcock & Wilcox
(number)		8
engines (type)		General Electric geared turbines
shafts		4
Total SHP:		
designed		150,000
Fuel capacity:		
oil tons (tonnes)		3,710 (3,770)
Performance:		
designed speed		33kts
range		?
Crew:		2,251

Class:	ALASKA class
Where built:	New York Shipyard
Authorised:	1940
Laid down:	Dec 1941–Dec 1943
Launched:	Aug 1943–Mar 1945
Completed:	June–Sept 1944
Fate:	*Philippines* (CB-4), *Puerto Rico* (CB-5), *Samoa* (CB-6) cancelled 24 June 1943 before being laid down; *Hawaii* (CB-3) suspended 17 Feb 1947, scrapped incomplete 1960; *Alaska* (CB-1) and *Guam* (CB-2) scrapped 1961

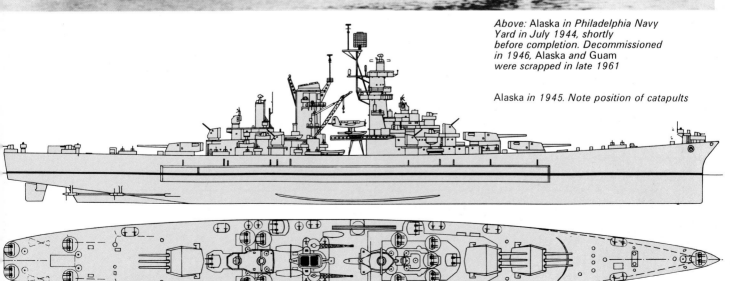

Above: Alaska *in Philadelphia Navy Yard in July 1944, shortly before completion. Decommissioned in 1946,* Alaska *and* Guam *were scrapped in late 1961*

Alaska *in 1945. Note position of catapults*

Indianapolis

HEAVY CRUISER
CLASS: *Portland* class (2 ships)
Portland (CA-33) · *Indianapolis*
(CA-35)

Service career INDIANAPOLIS (CA-35)
1933 (6 Sept–27 Oct) Carried US Secretary of the Navy on tour of US bases in Pacific.
1933 (1 Nov) Became flagship, Scouting Forces, US Fleet.
1934 (Apr–May) To Atlantic.
1934 (Nov) Returned to Pacific.
1936 (June) Refit.

1936 (18 Nov–15 Dec) Carried President Roosevelt on tour of South America.
1941 (7 Dec) Exercising off Pearl Harbor; searched for Japanese carrier force.
1942 (Jan–Mar) To South Pacific.
1942 (Mar–Apr) Refit: radar fitted, and six 20mm added.
1942 (May–Sept) In Aleutians.
1942 (7 Aug) Bombarded Kiska Island.
1942 (Sept–Oct and Dec–Jan 1943) In Aleutians.
1943 (Apr–May) Refitted as flagship, 5th Fleet: bridge rebuilt and enlarged; tripod lattice main mast and improved radar fitted; extra 40mm guns mounted; Combat Information Centre installed.
1943 (Nov–Apr 1945) Covered landings at Tarawa, Kwajalein, Saipan, Guam, Palau, Iwo Jima and Okinawa.

1944 (14 June) Hit by dud 4·7in (120mm) shell from Saipan.
1944 (19–21 June) Battle of Philippine Sea.
1944 (Oct–Jan 1945) Refit at Mare Island Navy Yard: radar updated and extra 40mm guns mounted.
1945 (31 Mar) Hit by *kamikaze* aircraft aft: bomb exploded damaging stern and propeller shafts.
1945 (May–June) Repaired at Mare Island Navy Yard: new radar fitted; anti-aircraft armament improved; starboard catapult removed.
1945 (16–26 July) Transported Hiroshima atom-bomb to Tinian.
1945 (30 July) Hit by two torpedoes from submarine *I-58*: sank in 12 minutes; 316 crew saved.

The Americans started building Washington Treaty cruisers after all the other major powers, their first, the *Pensacolas*, not being completed until 1930. They concentrated on armament rather than speed or seaworthiness. On a flush-decked hull with a standard displacement of only 9,100 tons (9,246t) they fitted ten 8in (203mm) 55cal and eight 5in (127m) 25cal guns, plus two catapults, four aircraft and six 21in (533m) torpedo tubes. They could make 32·5kts. The main armament was arranged in two triple and two twin turrets.

However, although they carried the same armament as the Japanese treaty cruisers on a much smaller displacement, they had a high centre of gravity and a low freeboard. The high centre of gravity made them steady gun platforms, but combined with the low freeboard it meant that they were not as seaworthy, nor could they absorb as much damage as other treaty cruisers. Therefore the next class, the *Northamptons*, were fitted with a raised fo'c's'le, and the main armament was reduced by one gun and rearranged in three triple turrets.

Portland and *Indianapolis* were modified versions of the *Northamptons*. The long thin waterline belt of the preceding two classes, stretching

Displacement:	Portland	Indianapolis	
standard tons (tonnes)	9,800 (9,957)	9,950 (10,110)	
full load tons (tonnes)	12,575 (12,776)	12,575 (12,776)	
Dimensions:			
length (wl)	582ft (177·7m)	584ft (178·3m)	
(oa)	610·25ft (186·3m)	610·25ft (186·3m)	
beam	66·1ft (20·2m)	66·1ft (20·2m)	
draught (max)	24·25ft (7·4m)	24·25ft (7·4m)	
Armament:	Indianapolis as built	Indianapolis in 1945	
guns			
8in (203mm) 55cal	9	9	
5in (127mm) 25cal	8	8	
3pdr (47mm)	2	—	
40mm	—	24	
20mm	—	16	
0·5in (12·7mm)	8	—	
aircraft	4	2	
Armour:			
side (belt)	3–4in (76–102mm)		
(main)	2in (51mm)		
(lower)	2in (51mm)		
main turrets	1·5–3in (38–76mm)		
barbettes	1·5–2in (38–51mm)		
Machinery:			
boilers (type)	White-Forster		
(number)	4		
engines (type)	Parsons single reduction geared turbines		
shafts	4		
Total SHP:			
designed	107,000		
Fuel capacity:			
oil tons (tonnes)	2,125 (2,160)		
Performance:			
designed speed	32·75kts		
range	?		
Crew:	952		

Ship	PORTLAND (CA-33)	INDIANAPOLIS (CA-35)
Where built:	Bethlehem, Quincy	New York Shipyard
Authorised:	13 Feb 1929	13 Feb 1929
Laid down:	17 Feb 1930	31 March 1930
Launched:	21 May 1932	7 Nov 1931
Completed:	23 Feb 1933	15 Nov 1932
Fate:	Scrapped 1959	Sunk 30 July 1945

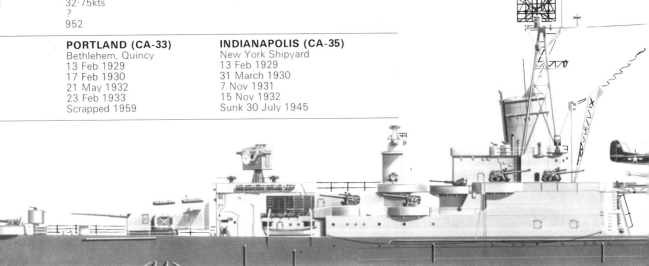

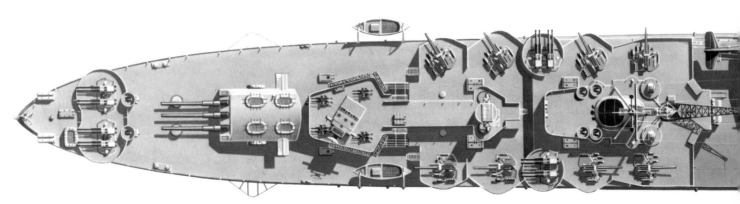

from the forward to the aft turrets, was felt to provide little protection. It would have been impossible to thicken it substantially without increasing the size of the hull, so it was shortened to cover only the machinery spaces and thickened by 1in (25mm). The deck and turret armour was also made thicker. The main external difference between the *Northamptons* and the *Portlands* was that the *Portlands'* bridge was higher and their masts lower. Whereas the preceding two classes had been fitted with torpedo tubes, which they had landed because it was felt to be unlikely that engagements would take place at ranges where torpedoes could be effective, the *Portlands* had no torpedo tubes from the start. The lack of torpedo tubes on the cruisers

was to be felt severely in the first years of the Pacific war, particularly in the Solomons.

Indianapolis spent most of her career as a flagship, and during the war she was at the front of the queue for modification. Both her antiaircraft armament and her radar and electronics equipment were constantly being updated and improved. She was used to transport the first atomic bomb from the USA to the base in Tinian whence it was dropped on Hiroshima. When she was torpedoed, her loss was not noticed for four days, despite the fact that her voyage should only have lasted a total of three. A US aircraft eventually spotted the debris and survivors, but because of the delay, only 316 of the original 800 survivors were saved. The figure of

Above: The heavy cruiser Indianapolis *(CA-35). On 30 July 1945,* Indianapolis *was torpedoed and sunk by the Japanese submarine I-58; 883 men were lost*

883 men lost was the greatest for any single ship lost by the USN.

The *Portlands* were developed into the *New Orleans* class, which had better arranged and thicker armour on a slightly shorter hull. The final treaty 8in (203mm) cruiser, the *Wichita*, was originally to have been one of the *New Orleans* class, but was given a flushdecked hull and a superstructure similar to the 6in (152mm) gunned *Brooklyn* class.

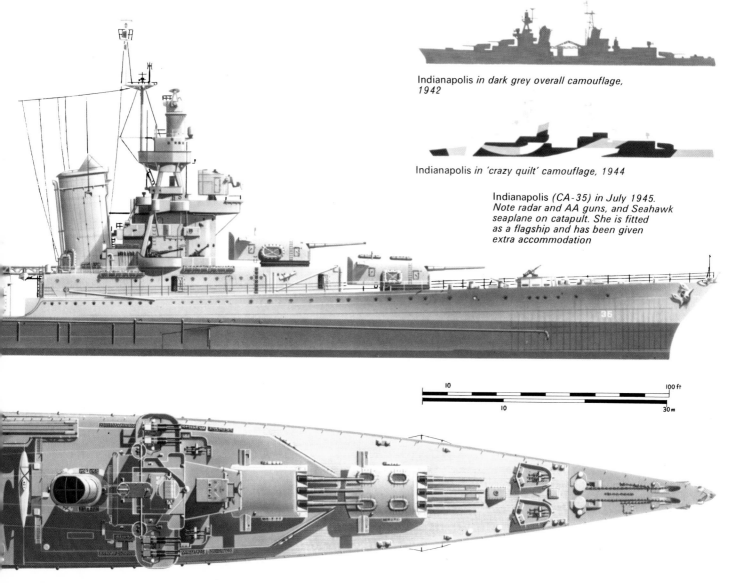

Indianapolis *in dark grey overall camouflage, 1942*

Indianapolis *in 'crazy quilt' camouflage, 1944*

Indianapolis *(CA-35) in July 1945. Note radar and AA guns, and Seahawk seaplane on catapult. She is fitted as a flagship and has been given extra accommodation*

Baltimore Class

HEAVY CRUISER

CLASS: *Baltimore* class (14 ships) including *Baltimore* (CA-68) · *Boston* (CA-69, later CAG-1) · *Chicago* (CA-136, later CG-11)

Although *Wichita* (CA-45) was originally intended to be a *New Orleans* class heavy cruiser, her design as built was an 8in (203mm) gun version of the 6in (152mm) gunned *Brooklyns*. She had a very similar flush deck hull and superstructure to the *Brooklyns*, but had three triple 8in (203mm) turrets, two forward and one aft. She had a 5in (127mm) main belt, and her 5in (127mm) guns were differently disposed, with one superfiring fore and aft and the others on either side of the superstructure. The next 8in (203mm) gunned American cruisers were the *Baltimores*. These were 8in (203mm) versions of the 6in (152mm) gunned *Cleveland* class light cruisers, but had a longer and beamier hull to enable a new mark of 8in (203mm) gun to be fitted, and they also had a considerably larger light AA armament. They could be distinguished from the *Clevelands*, apart from having only three main turrets, by having a more separated superstructure and thicker funnels. Like all American 8in (203mm) and 6in (152mm) cruisers built in the late 1930s and 1940s they had two catapults and an aircraft handling crane aft, where they were very vulnerable to weather and blast damage. However, they were very seaworthy, and were undoubtedly the best heavy cruisers in the world when they entered service. Not only did they have a powerful surface and AA armament, but they were also very well protected and subdivided, and had an adequate range for Pacific operations. Late in the war the *Cleveland* design was modified to have a single funnel and a modified superstructure to improve the AA guns' sky arcs (the *Fargo* class). A similar modification was made to the *Baltimore* design, which became the *Oregon City* class. Only three of these were completed before the end of World War II, four more were cancelled and one, *Northampton* (CA-125), was suspended. She was eventually completed in 1953 as a command ship (CLC-1, later CC-1) with an extra deck, a modified superstructure and an armament of four 5in (127mm) and eight 3in (76mm) guns. Near the end of World War II, an expanded version of the *Oregon City* design was prepared, with the hull lengthened by about 35ft (10·7m) to enable fully automatic 8in (203mm) triple turrets and their associated magazines to be fitted. Only three of these *Des Moines* class heavy cruisers were completed, the remaining nine being cancelled at the end of World War II. Although they were not built as fast as the urgently needed *Cleveland* class light cruisers, the *Baltimores* had very short building times for the size of ship. They were the largest class of heavy cruiser ever built. After the Terrier SAM had had successful trials on the trials ship *Mississippi* (ex BB-41), two *Baltimores, Boston* (CA-69, later CAG-1) and *Canberra* (ex-*Pittsburg* CA-70, later CAG-2) were converted into single-ended guided-missile cruisers between 1951 and 1956. The twin funnels were replaced with a single funnel, and the aft turret was removed and replaced by two twin Terrier SAM launchers. The superstructure was also modified. It had been intended to convert all the *Baltimores* to this standard, but the conversion was so expensive and complicated that the results achieved were that this plan was dropped. However, *Chicago* (CA-136, later CG-11) and *Columbus* (CA-74, later CG-12), together with *Albany* (CA-123, later CG-10) of the *Oregon City* class, were completely reconstructed as

double-ended guided-missile cruisers. They were converted between 1959 and 1964: the superstructure was completely removed and replaced with a new aluminium structure and two tall macks. A twin Talos SAM launcher was fitted fore and aft, and a twin Terrier SAM launcher was fitted either side of the bridge. Space was left amidships to fit Polaris ICBMs, but these were never carried, and an ASROC ASM launcher was fitted amidships instead. Originally no guns were mounted but a single 5in (127mm) gun has subsequently been fitted on each side of the aft mack to counter low-flying aircraft and fast patrol boats. All the conventionally armed *Baltimores* had their 40mm and 20mm AA guns replaced by 3in (76mm) guns, which by 1944 was the smallest calibre considered capable of destroying a hostile aircraft. Although some heavy cruisers including *St Paul* (ex-*Rochester* CA-73), which was used to help develop rocket-assisted shells, were put back into service during the Vietnam War, in which they were used for shore bombardment, all conventionally armed *Baltimores*

were deleted by 1974. *Boston* was deleted in 1973, and the remaining guided-missile armed ships are due to be discarded soon.

Above, right: USS Chicago *(CA-136) escorted by a* Fletcher *class destroyer. The* Baltimores *were the most powerful heavy cruisers in the world when they entered service*

Right: USS Baltimore *(CA-68) in 1943. The name-ship of the largest class of heavy cruisers ever built — 14 were completed — she was launched in 1942*

Displacement:	Baltimore (CA-68) as built	Boston (CAG-1) in 1973	Chicago (CG-11) in 1977
standard tons (tonnes)	13,600 (13,820)	13,600 (13,820)	13,700 (13,920)
full load tons (tonnes)	17,070 (17,340)	17,200 (17,480)	17,500 (17,780)
Dimensions:			
length (wl)	664ft (202·4m)		664ft (202·4m)
(oa)	673·5ft (205·3m)		673·5ft (205·3m)
beam	70·9ft (21·6m)		70·9ft (21·6m)
draught	26ft (7·9m)		30ft (9·1m)
Armament:			
guns			
8in (203mm) 55cal	9	6	—
5in (127mm)	12	10	2
3in (76mm)	—	8	—
40mm	48	—	—
20mm	22	—	—
Missiles:			
Terrier SAM twin-launcher	—	2	—
Tartar SAM twin-launcher	—	—	2
Talos SAM twin-launcher	—	—	2
A/S weapons			
ASROC ASM octuple-launcher	—	—	1
torpedo tubes			
12·7in (324mm) Mk 32	—	—	6
aircraft	4	1 helicopter	deck for helicopter
Armour:			
side belt	6in (152mm)		6in (152mm)
deck (main)	3in (76mm)		3in (76mm)
(lower)	2in (51mm)		2in (51mm)
main turrets	3–6in (76–152mm)		—
barbettes	6in (152mm)		—
Machinery:			
boilers (type)	Babcock & Wilcox	Babcock & Wilcox	Babcock & Wilcox
(number)	4	4	4
engines (type)	General Electric geared turbines	General Electric geared turbines	General Electric geared turbines
shafts	4	4	4
Total SHP:			
designed	120,000		
Fuel capacity:			
oil tons (tonnes)	2,620 (2,660)		2,590 (2,630)
Performance:			
designed speed	33kts		
range	?		
Crew:	1,700	1,273	1,222

Class:	**BALTIMORE class**
Where built:	Bethlehem, Quincy; New York Shipyard; and Philadelphia Navy Yard
Authorised:	?
Laid down:	1941–1943
Launched:	1942–1944
Completed:	1943–1946
Fate:	*Norfolk* (CA-137) and *Scranton* (CA-138) cancelled 12 Aug 1945; *Boston* (CA-69) and *Canberra* (CA-70) converted to single-ended guided-missile cruisers 1952–1956; *Columbus* (CA-74) and *Chicago* (CA-136) converted to double-ended guided-missile cruisers 1959–1964; all scrapped or for disposal 1971–1977; *Chicago* in commission 1977

Baltimore class as built. Note radar on mainmast, two funnels and catapult

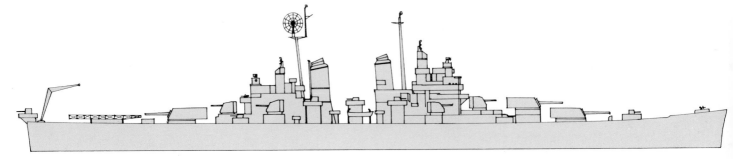

247

Long Beach

NUCLEAR GUIDED-MISSILE CRUISER

CLASS: *Long Beach* class (1 ship)
Long Beach (CGN-9) (ex-CGN-160, ex-CLGN-160)

Service career LONG BEACH (CGN-9)
1956 (15 Oct) Ordered as Guided-Missile Light Cruiser (CLGN-160).
1957 (Feb) Reclassified as Guided Missile Cruiser (CGN-160).
1961 (5 July) First surface warship to sail under nuclear power.
1962–1963 Fitted with two 5in (127mm) 38cal guns.
1965 (Aug–Feb 1966) Refit and refuelling.
1970 Radar modified, NTDS fitted.

Long Beach (CGN-9, ex CGN-160, ex CLGN-160) was the first surface warship to have nuclear propulsion, and was also the first to be armed entirely with guided-missiles. She was originally intended to be a 7,800 ton (7,920 tonne) standard displacement guided-missile frigate with a single Terrier SAM launcher. Before the design was finalised in 1956 the size had almost doubled and the armament considerably increased. As completed she had two twin Terrier SAM superimposed forward and a twin Talos SAM launcher aft. She was originally designed to carry Regulus II SSMs. This was a nuclear-armed strategic cruise missile with a range of about 1,000 miles (840nm). When this was cancelled in favour of Polaris ICBMs, it was planned to fit eight of these in tubes amidships. However, Polaris has

only been fitted in submarines, and *Long Beach* (CGN-9) was finally completed without any SSMs, and with an ASROC ASM launcher amidships. The forward superstructure is similar to that fitted on the American nuclear aircraft-carrier *Enterprise* (CVN-65). It is a large square structure with fixed 'billboard' antennae for the SPS-32 surface search and target designation and SPS-33 height finding radars. The aft superstructure is much smaller, and since the 1962–1963 refit it has been flanked by two single 5in (127mm) guns, which were fitted to counter the threat from low-flying aircraft and fast patrol boats, neither of which could be dealt with by

Above: Long Beach's armament of Talos and Standard SM 1 ER missiles is now obsolete. She will be refitted, possibly with the Aegis system of Standard SM 2s.

missiles. *Long Beach* was completed as a carrier escort, and is intended to deal with air and sub-surface threats. She relies mainly on carrier-borne aircraft or other ships for defence against surface attack, although the Talos SAM has a limited surface-to-surface capability. A smaller nuclear-powered 'frigate', later classified as a cruiser, *Bainbridge* (CGN-25, ex DLGN-25), with a standard displacement of 7,600 tons (7,720 tonnes), was built between 1959 and 1962. Apart from not having Talos SAMs, she carries a very similar armament to *Long Beach* (CGN-9) on a much smaller hull, and the next nuclear-powered escort, *Truxtun* (CGN-35, ex DLGN-35), a nuclear powered version of the *Belknap* class frigates, was very little larger. However, the next two classes, the *Californias* and *Virginias*, are once more approaching the size of *Long Beach* (CGN-9), but have a much more effective weapons fit. Both can fire Standard SSMs (which have a limited surface-to-surface capability) and ASROC ASMs, and they have A/S torpedoes and two single 5in (127mm) guns. The *Virginias* are also the first US guided-missile cruisers with hangar facilities for their helicopters. The *Virginias* are also able to fire Harpoon SSMs, and are the first American nuclear guided-missile cruisers capable of dealing adequately with air, surface and sub-surface threats. Even so, they are still not considered capable of dealing adequately with the new generation of Russian surface warships. A 15,000 ton (15,240 tonne) standard displacement cruiser, the CSGN, was proposed, with an armament of SAMs, SSMs and the new Type 71 8in (203mm) gun. This has since been abandoned on the grounds of cost, but it is possible that a similar ship will eventually be built. *Long Beach* (CGN-9), in company with *Enterprise* (CVN-65) and *Bainbridge* (CGN-25), served to show the advantages (and cost) of an all-nuclear-powered task force. *Long Beach's* weapons are now obsolete and she will shortly be refitted (possibly with Aegis), when some of the shortcomings in her surface-to-surface and close range weapons will be eliminated and her electronics updated.

Displacement:	
standard tons (tonnes)	14,200 (14,430)
full load tons (tonnes)	17,100 (17,370)
Dimensions:	
length (oa)	721·2ft (220m)
beam	73·2ft (22·3m)
draught	31ft (9·5m)
Armament	**in 1977**
guns	
5in (127mm) 38cal	2
missiles	
Talos SAM twin launcher	1
Standard ER SAM twin launcher	2
A/S weapons	
ASROC 8-tube launcher	1
torpedo tubes	
12·7in (324mm) Mk 32	6
aircraft	1 helicopter
Machinery:	
nuclear reactor (type)	CIW Westinghouse pressurised water-cooled reactor
(number)	2
engines (type)	General Electric geared turbines
shafts	2
Total SHP:	
designed	approx 80,000
Performance:	
designed speed	approx 30+kts
range	over 160,000 miles (over 130,000nm) @ 20kts
Crew:	1,160

Ship:	**LONG BEACH (CGN-9)**
Where built:	Bethlehem, Quincy
Authorised:	1956
Laid down:	2 Dec 1957
Launched:	14 July 1959
Completed:	9 Sept 1961
Fate:	In service

Above, right: The first warship to be armed entirely with guided missiles, Long Beach was refitted in 1962–3 with two single 5in (127mm) guns, seen here amidships

Right: The nuclear guided missile cruiser USS Long Beach (CGN-9) in 1963. Completed in 1961, Long Beach was the world's first nuclear-propelled surface warship

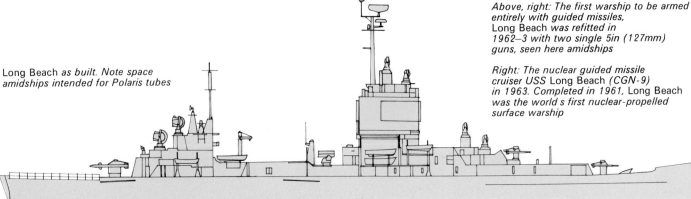

Long Beach as built. Note space amidships intended for Polaris tubes

Brooklyn Class

LIGHT CRUISER

CLASS: *Brooklyn* class (9 ships)
Group 1 (7 ships) including
Brooklyn (CL-40) (later *O'Higgins*
CL-02) · Group 2 (2 ships)
St Louis (CL-49) (later *Tamandare*
C-12) · *Helena* (CL-50)

Cleveland Class

LIGHT CRUISER

CLASS: *Cleveland* class (27 ships)
including *Cleveland* (CL-55) ·
Springfield (CL-66, later CLG-7)

The construction of the Japanese *Mogami* class cruisers caused the other major naval powers to consider the merits of large 6in (152mm) cruisers. The British built the *Towns* and the Americans the *Brooklyns*. The *Brooklyn* class were the first American 6in (152mm) gunned cruisers since the undistinguished 7,050 ton (7,160 tonne) standard displacement *Omahas*, built in the early 1920s, and were similar in size to the preceding *New Orleans* class 8in (203mm) gunned heavy cruisers. The *Brooklyns* had a similar performance, and had a slightly thinner armour belt that extended the full length of the magazines and machinery spaces. However, they had flush decks, and five triple centreline turrets. Three of these were mounted forward and two aft, and had a high rate of fire. At the stern there were two catapults, and a large hangar was fitted under the quarterdeck. On early ships of this class the secondary armament consisted of eight single 5in (127mm) guns arranged on both sides of the forward super-structure and funnels, and there was a con-siderable gap between the funnels and the aft superstructure. The last two ships mounted four twin 5in (127mm), and the aft superstruc-ture was moved nearer the funnels to improve the AA guns' sky arcs. *St Louis* (CL-49) and *Helena* (CL-50) also had a thicker armour belt than the other *Brooklyns*. They were fitted with radar just before World War II, and were powerfully armed ships. However, their effective-ness was diminished during the early part of the Pacific war by over-reliance on radar and they proved vulnerable to underwater damage. *Honolulu* (which had been damaged by a bomb at Pearl Harbor on 7 December 1941) was badly damaged by a Japanese torpedo during the fighting off Guadalcanal in 1942, as were *Boise* and *St Louis*, and *Helena* was sunk at the Battle of Kula Gulf by three torpedoes from the Japanese destroyers *Suzukaze* and *Tanikaze*. *Brooklyn*, *Honolulu* and *Savannah* were fitted with anti-torpedo bulges during wartime refits, and the remaining ships were also bulged later. *Savannah* also had her single 5in (127mm) guns replaced by twin mounts. During the war they all received greatly increased light AA armaments. After 1945 the US had so many large light cruisers that the *Brooklyns* were surplus to requirements and six were sold cheaply to the obsolete South American navies to replace their obsolete battleships. They are themselves now being replaced by modern vessels, but *General Belgrano* (C-5) has recently been refitted with Dutch radar and two quadruple Sea Cat SAM launchers. The next American light cruisers, the *Clevelands*, were very similar to *St Louis* (CL-49), but sacrificed one triple turret forward for an increased AA armament. This made very little difference to their effective-ness against surface vessels, and gave them a very powerful AA armament. They had a slightly

	Brooklyn (CL-40) as built	Tamandare (C-12) in 1977	Cleveland (CL-55) as built	Springfield (CLG-7) in 1977
Displacement:				
standard tons (tonnes)	9,700 (9,860)	10,000 (10,160)	10,000 (10,160)	10,700 (10,870)
full load tons (tonnes)	12,700 (12,900)	13,400 (13,610)	13,755 (13,975)	15,200 (15,400)
Dimensions:				
length (wl)	600ft (182·9m)	600ft (182·9m)	600ft (182·9m)	600ft (182·9m)
(oa)	608·3ft (185·4m)	608·3ft (185·4m)	610ft (185·9m)	610ft (185·9m)
beam	61·75ft (18·9m)	69ft (21m)	66·5ft (20·3m)	66·5ft (20·3m)
draught	24ft (7·3m)	24ft (7·3m)	25ft (7·6m)	27ft (8·2m)
Armament:				
guns				
6in (152mm)	15	15	12	3
5in (127mm)	8	8	12	2
40mm	—	28	8	—
20mm	—	—	10	—
0·5in (12·7mm)	8	—	—	—
aircraft	4	1 helicopter	4	1 helicopter
Armour:				
side (belt)	4in (102mm)	5in (127mm)		5in (127mm)
(ends)	1·5in (38mm)	1·5in (38mm)		1·5in (38mm)
deck (main)	3in (76mm)	3in (76mm)		3in (76mm)
(lower)	2·5in (65mm)	2·5in (65mm)		2in (51mm)
main turrets	3–5in (76–127mm)	3–5in (76–127mm)		3–5in (76–127mm)
barbettes	5in (127mm)	5in (127mm)		5in (127mm)
Machinery:				
boilers (type)	Babcock & Wilcox		Babcock & Wilcox	
(number)	8		4	
engines (type)	Parsons geared turbines		General Electric geared turbines	
shafts	4		4	
Total SHP:				
designed	100,000		100,000	
Fuel capacity:				
oil tons (tonnes)	2,245 (2,281)	2,207 (2,242)	2,415 (2,454)	2,620 (2,662)
Performance:				
designed speed	32·5kts		33kts	
range	17,840 miles (15,000nm) @ 15kts		?	
Crew:	868	980	1,200	1,680

Class:	**BROOKLYN class**	**CLEVELAND class**
Where built:	various yards	various yards
Authorised:	?	?
Laid down:	1935–1936	1940–1944
Launched:	1936–1938	1941–1945
Completed:	1938–1939	1942–1946
Fate:	*Helena* (CL-50) sunk 6 July 1943, *Savannah* (CL-42), *Honolulu* (CL-48) scrapped 1960; *Brooklyn* (CL-40), *Nashville* (CL-43) to Chile 1951, renamed *O'Higgins* (CL-02), *Capitan Prat* (CL-03); *Philadelphia* (CL-41), *St Louis* (CL-49) to Brazil 1951, renamed *Barroso* (C-11) (scrapped 1974), *Tamandare* (C-12); *Phoenix* (CL-46), *Boise* (CL-47) to Argentina 1951, renamed *Diecisiete de Octubre* (C-5) (later *Generale Belgrano*), *Nueve de Julio* (C-6)	3 cancelled; 9 converted before completion into *Independence* class aircraft-carriers; 6 converted into single-ended guided-missile cruisers 1957–1960; remainder scrapped 1959 onwards

larger beam than the *St Louis*, and a shorter main belt, and there were no openings in the hull, which was mechanically ventilated through-out. They were excellently subdivided, and despite seeing considerable action and in some cases being very badly damaged, none was sunk. The *Clevelands* were eventually built in larger numbers than any other cruiser type, and became the standard US World War II light cruiser class despite three being cancelled and nine being converted into *Independence* class aircraft-carriers. In the mid-1950s it was intended to convert 13 of them into single-ended guided-missile cruisers, but the conversions were so expensive and took so long that only six were eventually converted. CLG-3 to 5 were fitted with a twin Talos SAM aft in place of the two 6in

(152mm) turrets, whilst CLG-6 to 8 had a twin Terrier SAM. Both types had their aft super-structure completely rebuilt, and CLG-4 to 7 also had B turret removed and replaced with a twin 5in (127mm) mount and the forward bridge extended. This enabled them to be used as fleet flagships, and they have very extensive communication facilities. CLG-3 and CLG-8 have already been scrapped, and the remainder will shortly be deleted. The last ships of the *Cleveland* class were completed to a modified design and redesignated the *Fargo* class. These had a much more compact superstructure with a single large funnel to improve the AA guns sky arcs still further, and the distribution of the AA guns was also slightly altered. Only two *Fargos* were completed.

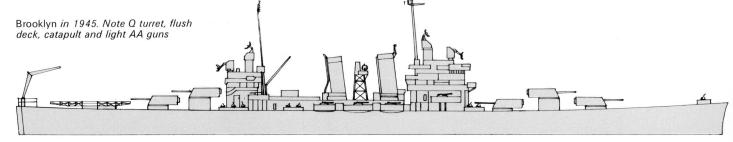

Brooklyn in 1945. Note Q turret, flush deck, catapult and light AA guns

Above: Medical and damage-control parties at work aboard USS Savannah (CL-42), struck by a German glider bomb off Salerno, Italy, on 11 September 1943

Right: The Brooklyn class light cruiser Savannah in Algiers harbour on 16 June 1943. Two Liberty ships burn in the background after an air attack

Above: USS Cleveland (CL-55), name-ship of the largest light cruiser class built — 27 were completed — in 1946. Six were converted to guided missile cruisers

Cleveland class as built. Note radar on foremast and two funnels

US NAVY

Belknap Class

GUIDED MISSILE CRUISER
CLASS: *Belknap* class (9 ships)

These are the last conventionally powered US cruisers to be built up to the present. They are anti-aircraft and anti-submarine escorts for the US carriers, and have been developed from the smaller conventionally-powered *Leahys*. These are double-ended ships with a Terrier SAM twin-launcher at bow and stern, and a separate ASROC launcher forward of the bridge. The *Belknaps* are single-ended with an ASTOR combined Standard/ASROC SAM/ASM twin-launcher in the bows, which allows a hangar to be fitted for the LAMPS Kaman SH-2D Seasprite helicopter at the aft end of the super-structure. The single 5in (127mm) mount is fitted on the quarterdeck. They are the only modern conventionally powered US cruiser with hangar facilities. Both the *Leahys* and *Belknaps* are nine-ship classes. In each case a tenth nuclear-powered half-sister has been built. The nuclear-powered *Leahy* is *Bainbridge* (CGN-25), and the nuclear-powered *Belknap* is *Truxtun* (CGN-35). Both these ships are considerably larger and much more expensive than their half-sisters. *Truxtun* (CGN-35) carries her gun forward and her missile-launcher aft. The *Belknaps* are long ranged, seaworthy ships with sophisticated electronics, but these features have been attained at the expense of weapons systems, although Harpoon is now being fitted. If the ASTOR SAM/SSM launcher were damaged, the entire anti-aircraft and anti-submarine missile capability of the ship would be put out of action. *Belknap* (CG-26) was severely damaged in collision with the US carrier *John F. Kennedy* in the Mediterranean on 22 November 1975. Her entire upperworks were removed by the carrier's overhang, and a serious fire followed. There was a possibility that she might be scrapped, but she will now be rebuilt, possibly with improved weapons systems.

Above, upper: USS Belknap, *seen before receiving severe damage in a collision with the carrier* John F. Kennedy *on 22 November 1975. She is being extensively rebuilt*

Above: The guided missile frigate USS Belknap *(DLG-26) in 1973. In July 1975, the nine* Belknaps *were reclassified as guided missile cruisers*

Displacement:

standard tons (tonnes)	6,570 (6,680)
full load tons (tonnes)	7,930 (8,060)

Dimensions:

length (pp)	?
(oa)	547ft (166·7m)
beam	54·8ft (16·7m)
draught	28·8ft (8·8m)

Armament:

guns	
5in (127mm) 54cal	1
3in (76mm)	2
missiles and A/S weapons	
Standard/ASROC SAM/AS	
twin launcher	1
torpedo tubes	
12·7in (324mm) Mk 32	6
aircraft	1 helicopter

Machinery:

boilers (type)	Babcock & Wilcox or Combustion Engineering
(number)	?
engines (type)	General Electric or De Laval geared turbines
shafts	2

Total SHP:

designed	85,000

Fuel capacity:

oil tons (tonnes)	?

Performance:

designed speed	34kts
range	approx 9,500 miles (8,000nm) @ 14kts
Crew:	418

Class:	BELKNAP class:
Where built:	Bath Iron Works, Puget Sound, Todd, San Francisco
Authorised:	1961–1962
Laid down:	1962–1963
Launched:	1963–1965
Completed:	1964–1967
Reclassified from DLG to CG:	30 June 1975
Fate:	In service. *Belknap* being rebuilt 1976–78 after collision with *John F. Kennedy* (22 Nov 1975)

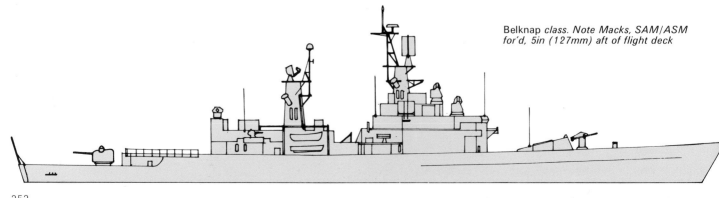

Belknap *class. Note Macks, SAM/ASM for'd, 5in (127mm) aft of flight deck*

Flush Deck Class

**DESTROYER
CLASS:** *Caldwell* class (69–74
series) (6 ships)

**DESTROYER
CLASS:** *Wickes* class (75–185
series) (110 ships)

**DESTROYER
CLASS:** *Clemson* class (186–347
series) (155 ships)

At the beginning of World War I a large building programme of destroyers was put in hand by the USA. The general design adopted was in many ways similar to the prewar *Tucker/Sampson* classes (DD-57 to 68) with the major modification of being flush-decked rather than with a break at the fo'c's'le as in the earlier vessels. The *Caldwell* class was in fact a series of experimental ships which varied considerably in their internal arrangements. The *Wickes* class was built to two general designs – those of Bethlehem and Bath Iron Works – and was much akin to the succeeding *Clemson* class although the latter had increased fuel stowage. At the end of the war only 44 had been completed but the remainder (except for the cancelled DD-200 to 205) were eventually all finished by 1922, landing the US Navy with a mass of new ships at a time when ideas on destroyer design were under close study in other navies. This meant rapid obsolescence for the flush-deckers and by 1941 only one *Caldwell* (*Manley*, APD-1)

Continued on page 254 ▶

Below: The Clemson *class flush-deck destroyer* McFarland *(DD-237), before her conversion to a seaplane tender (AVD-14) and subsequent reconversion*

	CALDWELL class	WICKES class	CLEMSON class
Displacement:			
normal tons (tonnes)	1,125 (1,143)	1,154–1,191 (1,172–1,210)	1,211–1,215 (1,230–1,234)
full load tons (tonnes)	?	?	1,308 (1,329)
Dimensions:			
length (wl)	310ft (94.5m)	310ft (94.5m)	310ft (94.5m)
(oa)	?	?	314.5ft (95.9m)
beam	30.5ft (9.3m)	30.9ft (9.4m)	30.9ft (9.4m)
draught	8ft (2.4m)	9.5ft (2.9m)	9.6ft (2.9m)
Armament:			
guns			
5in (127mm)	—	—	4 (in 231–235 in place of 4in)
4in (102mm)	4	4	4 (8 in 208, 5 in 189)
3in (76mm)	1	1	1
torpedo tubes			
21in (533mm)	12	12	12
Machinery:			
boilers (type)	Normand or Babcock & Wilcox	Yarrow, Thornycroft or White	Forster
(number)	4	4	4
engines (type)	Parsons	Westinghouse	Curtis Turbines
shafts	2	2	2
Total SHP:	20,000	26,000–27,000	27,000
Fuel capacity:			
oil tons (tonnes)	260 (264)	290 (295)	375 (381)
Performance:			
designed speed	32kts	35kts	35kts
Crew (war/peace):	122/139	122/139	122/139

	CALDWELL class	WICKES class	CLEMSON class
Class: **Where built:**	Norfolk NY; Mare Island NY; Wm Cramp & Sons; Seattle C & DD Co; Bath Iron Works	as *Caldwell* class plus: Newport News SB Co; Bethlehem (Quincy, San Francisco and Squantum); New York SB Co; Fore River SB Co; Union Iron Works; Charleston NY	
Built:	1916–1917	1917–1919	1918–1921
Fate:	(see main text)		

remained. She had been converted into the prototype fast troop transport, two had been scrapped and three transferred to the Royal Navy. With the entry of the USA into World War II in December 1941 32 of the *Wickes* class had been scrapped, 27 transferred to the Royal Navy and 20 diverted to other than escort duties. Twelve more were later converted to troop transports and by late 1945 most of the class was non-operational. The *Clemsons'* story was much the same. By the time of Pearl Harbor 64 had been scrapped, four sold, 29 converted for other tasks and 20 handed over to the Royal Navy. Eight subsequently became fast transports and by 1945 most were classified under the inglorious heading of AG (Miscellaneous Auxiliary). The history of the flush-deckers was thus a chequered one. Their existence had hampered design improvements and it was not until they were 10 to 15 years old (1932) that any new destroyers were laid down. By the time of the American entry into World War II 102 of the original 271 had been scrapped, 50 had been converted for other tasks and 50 transferred to the Royal Navy under the Anglo-US agreement of September 1940. Seventeen were lost during World War II and the remainder were scrapped within a couple of years of its end. None has survived as a memorial to these very numerous classes whose 50 sisters transferred to the Royal Navy were a vital element in sustaining Great Britain in the worst days of the Battle of the Atlantic.

HMS Campbeltown, *originally the US Four Stacker Buchanan (DD-131) as modified in March 1942 to resemble a German* Möwe *class torpedo boat for the raid on St Nazaire*

Above: The Wickes *class destroyer*
USS Schenck *(DD-159),*
launched in 1919. She was re-rated
as an auxiliary (AG-82) in 1944
and scrapped in 1947

Fletcher Class

DESTROYER
CLASS: *Fletcher* class (119 ships)

DESTROYER
CLASS: *Improved Fletcher* class
(62 ships)

Gearing Class

DESTROYER
CLASS: *Gearing* class (98 ships)

After the pause in destroyer design caused by the plethora of flush-deckers available in the years immediately after World War I the first class to be laid down was the *Farragut* class in 1932. These had superimposed guns in B and X positions and an enclosed bridge. Ten more classes were to follow, some large, some small, some with one funnel, some with two but shortly before the USA entered World War II twenty-four of the new *Fletcher* class had been laid down. They were some 30ft (9·2m) longer than their predecessors of the *Bristol* class, space which was largely occupied in providing a reasonable AA armament which was steadily improved over the years. The appearance of the *Fletchers* was radically different from their immediate predecessors in that they reverted to the flush-deck design, a silhouette that was to remain standard US Navy practice from then on. Internally the main change was the adoption of double-reduction turbines in place of the single-reduction installations of the *Bristol* and preceding classes. The second group of *Fletchers* was similar in all but a few details to the original series. The director was lower and the AA armament was increased. They were followed by the *Allen M. Sumner* class in which a *Fletcher* hull with a slightly greater beam was used but where six 5in (127mm) 38cal guns were mounted in three twin turrets. A further advance came in the *Gearing* class. Here a 14ft (4·3m) hull section was inserted into an *Allen M. Sumner* hull. 3in (76mm) guns replaced a number of 40mm

Displacement:	FLETCHER class	Improved FLETCHER class	GEARING class
standard tons (tonnes)	2,050 (2,083)	2,050 (2,083)	2,425 (2,464)
full load tons (tonnes)	2,940 (2,987)	3,040 (3,089)	3,480 (3,536)
Dimensions:			
length (wl)	369·3ft (112·6m)	369·3ft (112·6m)	383ft (116·7m)
(oa)	376–376·5ft (114·6–114·8m)	375·8–376ft (114·5–114·6m)	389·8–391ft (118·8–119·2m)
beam	39·3–40ft (12–12·2m)	39·5–39·8ft (12–12·1m)	40·8–41ft (12·4–12·5m)
draught (full load)	17·8ft (5·4m)	17·8ft (5·4m)	18·8ft (5·7m)
Armament:			
guns			
5in (127mm)	5	5	6
3in (76mm)	—	—	4–6
1·1in (28mm)	4	—	—
40mm	2–10 (later all had	6–10	4–16
20mm	4–11 6 x 40mm and 11 x 20mm or 10 x 40mm and 7 x 20mm)	4–10	11–15
torpedo tubes			
21in (533mm)	10	10	0–10
Machinery:			
boilers (type)	Babcock & Wilcox or Foster Wheeler	Babcock & Wilcox or Foster Wheeler	Babcock & Wilcox or Foster Wheeler
(number)	4	4	4
engines (type)	GE or Westinghouse DR geared turbines	GE or Westinghouse DR geared turbines	GE or Westinghouse DR geared turbines
(number)	2	2	2
shafts	2	2	2
Total SHP:	60,000	60,000	60,000
Fuel capacity:			
oil tons (tonnes)	492–525 (500–533)	492 (500)	715 (726) in 12 ships 720 (732) in 3 ships 740–745 (752–757) in the remainder
Performance:			
designed speed	37kts	37kts	34·5–35kts
range	6,000 miles (5,211nm) @ 15kts	6,000 miles (5,211nm) @ 15kts	6,000 miles (5,211nm) @ 15kts
Crew (war/peace):	273/336	319/336	336/367

Class:	FLETCHER class
Where built:	Federal SB, Kearny; Bath Iron Works; Bethlehem (Staten, San Pedro, San Francisco); Boston NY; Puget Sound NY; Charleston NY; Gulf SB Co; Seattle-Tacoma; Consolidated Steel Corp (Orange)
Built:	1942–45
Fate:	21 sunk during WWII; 32 transferred to other navies; remainder scrapped by 1975

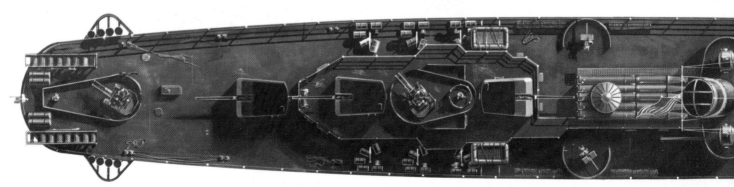

guns and, in later ships, a Hedgehog mortar was
fitted. Forty-nine were cancelled at the end of
World War II, four were scrapped before completion but the 33 still in service in the US Navy
testify to the soundness of this design.

Right: The Fletcher *class destroyer*
Nicholas *(DD-449) after FRAM-II*
conversion in 1960 with an
improved A/S armament and
VDS aft

Right, lower: A Fletcher *class destroyer in*
original condition in the Pacific during
World War II. An Essex *class carrier is in the*
near foreground. Note the dark lower hull of
the Fletcher

Improved FLETCHER class	GEARING class
as for *Fletcher*	as for *Fletcher*
plus Todd, Seattle	
1943–45	1945–51
3 sunk during WWII;	Construction stopped on
15 transferred to	57 ships; 33 in service in
other navies;	USN, 1977;
remainder scrapped	remainder scrapped
by 1975	or transferred

Fletcher *class* Charles Ausburne *(DD-570)*
later transferred to Germany as Z 6
(D-180). Note the flush deck, high
mounted TT and Q 5in (127mm) mount.
She is seen here in 1942

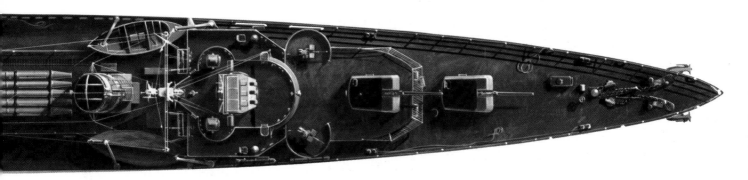

Coontz Class
DESTROYER
CLASS: *Coontz* class (10 ships)

Spruance Class
DESTROYER
CLASS: *Spruance* class (30 ships)

The *Coontz* class were the first American escorts to be designed to carry guided-missiles. They were based on the *Mitscher* class gun-armed AA and A/S escorts built between 1949 and 1954, and were the only US guided-missile destroyers built with separate masts and funnels. They were single-ended, with a 5in (127mm) and a superfiring ASROC ASM launcher forward and a twin Terrier SAM launcher aft. They were originally designed to have a second single 5in (127mm) gun in B position, but this was replaced before they were laid down by the ASROC ASM launcher. As built they had two twin 3in (76mm) guns abaft the aft funnel, but these were removed when the class was modernised between 1968 and 1975. This was intended to improve their AA capabilities, and they were fitted with Standard SAMs in place of the Terrier SAMs, NTDs and improved radar. *King* (DLG-10, later DDG-41) and *Mahan* (DLG-11, later DDG-42) were used with the aircraft-carrier *Oriskany* (CVA-34, later CV-34) as trial ships for NTDS in 1961–1962. *King* (DLG-10, later DDG-41) was later used between 1973 and 1974 for sea trials of the Phalanx 20mm CIWS gun. They have a landing pad to operate a helicopter from aft, but lack

Above, upper: USS Coontz, *then DLG-9, now DDG-40, in original condition. Note the two 3in (76mm) twin mounts amidships and ASROC launcher in B position foreward*

Above: USS Spruance, *name-ship of the first class of large American warships to be powered totally by gas turbines, giving a maximum 30+ knots*

maintenance facilities. It was originally intended for there to have been at least 20 of these ships, but the second group of nine were completed as the *Leahy* class. These have a Terrier SAM launcher fore and aft, ASROC, and four 3in (76mm) guns, and have macks. The tenth ship of this type is the similar but larger, nuclear powered *Bainbridge* (CGN-25, ex DLGN-25). The nine *Belknaps* are improved *Leahys* with a combined twin Terrier SAM/ASROC ASM launcher forward and a 5in (127mm) gun aft. The nuclear-powered *Truxun* (CGN-35, ex DLGN-35) is similar but larger. Since then the guided-missile escorts have all been nuclear-powered, but rising costs may force a return to conventionally powered ships. Whilst the US built up a considerable force of carrier-escort guided-missile destroyers, she relied on the ageing World War II destroyers to provide the bulk of her general purpose escorts. By the late 1960s these were well overdue for replacement and the *Spruance* class were intended for this purpose. They are the first large American warships to be powered totally by gas turbines, and are intended primarily for A/S work. Because weapons systems and crew cost more than the ship herself, the *Spruances* are large and extremely seaworthy ships with a relatively small number of weapons, so that a large number of ships could be built. They have excited a great deal of criticism, not least amongst officers of the US Navy, for their lack of armament. However, to a certain extent numbers were considered more important than quality, and so far as is possible all equipment is mounted in modules so that it can easily be replaced when necessary. This, and the large size of the ships, means that they can easily accommodate new weapons systems if they become available, although at great cost. In an attempt to reduce costs still further, the entire class is being built by one firm on one specially constructed production line. Unfortunately, this Total Ship Procurement Package, so far from reducing costs, has itself caused many problems and expenses.

	COONTZ class	SPRUANCE class
Displacement:		
standard tons (tonnes)	4,700 (4,775)	?
full load tons (tonnes)	5,800 (5,893)	7,300 (7,417)
Dimensions:		
length (wl)	?	529ft (161·2m)
(oa)	512·5ft (156·2m)	563·3ft (171·1m)
beam	52·5ft (15·9m)	55ft (17·6m)
draught	25ft (7·6m)	29ft (8·8m)
Armament:		
guns		
5in (127mm)	1	2
3in (76mm) 50cal	4 (removed during modernisation)	—
Phalanx 20mm system	being fitted	2 to be fitted
missiles		
Terrier/Standard ER Mk 10 Mod 0	1 twin	—
Harpoon	to be fitted	—
NATO Sea-Sparrow	—	to be fitted
A/S weapons		
helicopters	—	1 Sea King or 2 LAMPS SH-2D
ASROC	1	1
torpedo tubes	6 Mk 32	6 Mk 32
Machinery:		
boilers (type)	Foster Wheeler or Babcock & Wilcox	—
(number)	4	—
engines (type)	De Laval or Allis Chalmers	4 GE LM2500 gas turbines
shafts	2	2
Total SHP:	85,000	80,000
Performance:		
designed speed	34kts	30+kts
Crew:	377 (plus flag accommodation for 19)	296

Class Where built:	COONTZ class	SPRUANCE class
Farragut	Bethlehem, Quincy	All built or building by Litton Industries, Pascagoula, Mississippi
Luce	Bethlehem, Quincy	
Macdonough	Bethlehem, Quincy	
Coontz	Puget NY	*Spruance* *Briscoe*
King	Puget NY	*Paul F. Foster* *Stump*
Mahan	San Francisco NY	*Kinkaid* *Conolly*
Dahlgren	Philadelphia NY	*Hewitt* *Moosburger*
William V. Pratt	Philadelphia NY	*Elliott* *John Hancock*
Dewey	Bath Iron Works	*Arthur W. Radford* *Nicholson*
Preble	Bath Iron Works	*Peterson* *John Rodgers*
		Caron *Leftwich*
		David R. Ray *Cushing*
		Oldendorf *Harry W. Hill*
		John Young *O'Bannon*
		Comte de Grasse *Thorn*
		O'Brien +4 so far
		Merrill unnamed

	COONTZ class	SPRUANCE class
Approved:	FY 1956–57	1970–75
Laid down:	3 June 1957–15 Apr 1958	17 Nov 1972–1977
Launched:	18 July 1958–16 Mar 1960	10 Nov 1973–1978
Completed:	10 Dec 1960–4 Nov 1961	20 Sep 1975–1979
Fate:	In service	In service or building

Far left: USS Spruance (DD-963) on a shakedown cruise in 1976. All 30 Spruances are to be built on a special production line at Pascagoula, Mississippi

Left: Spruance (DD-963). Note the bulky superstructure, the gas turbine uptakes offset to port and starboard, and the relatively light armament

Spruance (DD-963). Detail shows 8in (203mm) lightweight gun proposed for class

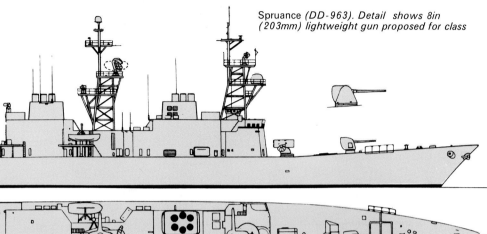

G-Class

SUBMARINE
CLASS: *G1–3* class (3 boats)
CLASS: *G4* class (1 boat)

S-Class

SUBMARINE
CLASS: *S* class (51 boats)

G1–4 were experimental submarines. *G1–3* were designed by Lake and had trainable torpedo tubes in the superstructure. *G4* was a Laurenti design. None was very successful. Five years were to pass before the S class was commissioned, nearly twice the size and carrying 21in (533mm) torpedoes. Three prototypes were built to Holland, Lake and Bureau of Construction designs. All had the same basic characteristics but the Bureau design, albeit the first provided by the US Navy, was deemed superior to that of Lake and thus the whole class was split between the Holland (*S18–41*) and Bureau (*S4–17*) designs with a follow-on programme of submarines with increased dimensions (Holland *S42–47* and Bureau *S48–51*). The advantages over previous classes were more space, more range and more reload torpedoes, and eight boats were provided with an extra stern tube. One boat, *S1*, was at one time in the early 1920s fitted with a seaplane although this plan was soon dropped. At the start of the US intervention in World War II a number of these boats carried out patrols from the Philippines but the loss of that outpost relegated them, lacking the range to cross the Pacific, to training roles. Such also was the fate of the five transferred to the Royal Navy.

S class (Navy Yard Type) as built. Note 4in (102mm) gun mounted for'd

Displacement:	G-1	G-4	S class Group 1
surface tons (tonnes)	288 (293)	360 (366)	854 (868)
submerged tons (tonnes)	540 (549)	457 (464)	1,062 (1,079)
Dimensions:			
length (wl)	?	?	211ft (64·4m)
length (oa)	134·75ft (41·1m)	157·5ft (48m)	219·25ft (66·9m)
beam	14ft (4·3m)	17·5ft (5·3m)	20·75ft (6·3m)
draught	11·75ft (3·6m)	11ft (3·4m)	16ft (4·9m)
Armament:			
guns			
4in (102mm)	—	—	1
torpedo tubes			
18in (457mm)	4	4	—
21in (533mm)	—	—	4+1 stern tube in *S48–51*
Machinery:			
engines (type)	petrol	petrol	diesel
(number)	4	2	2
electric motors (type)	?	?	various
shafts	2	2	2
Total BHP:	600	1,000	1,200
Total SHP:	520	440	1,500
Fuel capacity:			
petrol tons (tonnes)	?	?	—
oil tons (tonnes)	—	—	168 (171)
Performance:			
surface speed	13kts	14kts	14·5kts
submerged speed	10kts	9·5kts	11kts
range (surface)	?	1,680 miles	5,000 miles
	?	(1,410nm) @ 8kts	(4,200nm) @ 11kts
(submerged)	?	40 miles	?
	?	(34nm) @ 5kts	?
designed diving depth	250ft (76m)	150ft (46m)	200ft (61m)
Crew:	15	24	38

Class:	G class	S class
Where built:	various yards	various yards
Authorised:	?	?
Built:	1910–1914	1918–1924
Fate	renamed 17 Nov 1911; G-1 sunk 21 June 1921; G-2 sunk 30 July 1919; G-3 stricken 1922; G-4 stricken 1920	S-1, S-21, S-22, S-24, S-25, S-29 transferred to UK 1941–1942 as P-551 to P-556; P-551 transferred to Poland as *Jastrzab*; 11 sunk; 6 scuttled; 34 stricken 1931–1949

Gato Class

SUBMARINE

CLASS: *Gato* class (73 boats) including *Gato* (SS-212) · *Barb* (SS-220) *Wahoo* (SS-238) · *Tunny* (SS-282) · *Robalo* (SS-273) · *Scorpion* (SS-278) · *Tullibee* (SS-284)

During World War II, US submarines, normally operating at considerable distances from their bases, sank over nine-tenths of Japanese major vessels. Code-breaking played a considerable part in this, but successful American submarine design also contributed. The bulk of the later fighting was done by the 73 *Gato* class, and by the 132 *Balaos* and 31 *Tenches* that were developed from them. The main difference between the *Gatos* and the *Balaos* was the latter's stronger hull, which enabled them to dive to 400ft (120m). The *Gatos* were themselves a progressive development of the *Porpoise* class. By adopting a policy of gradual improvement, the Americans produced submarines which, although not excelling in any one aspect of their performance, were extremely reliable, had a long range and good habitability, and could carry a large number of reload torpedoes. Having already perfected four types of high speed diesel, the Americans then experimented with composite drive on the *S* class, and direct drive on the *Ts* and *Gs* before returning to the *Porpoises'* diesel-electric drive for the *Gatos*. Their high surface speed proved invaluable in achieving good firing positions for torpedoes. There were six tubes forward and four aft, and 24 reloads could be carried. This proved sufficient, but the gun armament was strengthened throughout the war. The all-welded design facilitated production, which was confined to four yards. Manitowoc yard was on Lake Michigan, and submarines built there had to be launched sideways, and then navigate over 1,000 miles down the Mississippi to the sea. Although the submarines themselves were reliable, the Mark 14 torpedo with magnetic exploder used from 1941–1943 was not, and it often failed to explode. Most of the 54 *Gatos* that survived the war were converted to *Guppy 1* standard, with no gun, with a schnorkel and a streamlined conning tower. Six were transferred abroad and seven converted to hunter-killer submarines, with more powerful batteries giving a higher underwater speed. *Tunny* was converted into a *Regulus 1* SSM launching submarine, and was altered to a transport submarine in 1964. This highly successful class and its derivatives show the soundness of the American policy of developing reliable designs of hull and engines over a long period of time, though their task was simplified by having no real requirement (unlike most other major navies) for a smaller more manoeuvrable and shorter ranged submarine. Although several smaller boats were built, they never went into mass production.

Gato class submarine *Barb (SS-220) in 1944, minus 20mm gun on forward platform*

Displacement:

standard tons (tonnes)	1,526 (1,550)
surface tons (tonnes)	1,816 (1,845)
submerged tons (tonnes)	2,424 (2,463)

Dimensions:

length (wl)	301ft (93·7m)
(oa)	311·75ft (95·2m)
beam	27·25ft (8·3m)
draught (max)	15·25ft (4·7m)

Armament:

	as built	in 1945	in 1951
guns			
5in (127mm) 25cal	—	1	—
3in (76mm) 50cal	1	—	—
40mm	—	2	—
20mm	—	2	—
torpedo tubes			
21in (533mm)	10	10	10

Machinery:

diesels (type)	Fairbanks Morse or General Motors or Hooven, Owens, Rentschler
(number)	4
electric motors (type)	General Electric or Elliot Motor or Allis-Chalmers
shafts	2
Total BHP:	5,400
Total SHP:	2,740

Fuel capacity:

oil tons (tonnes)	378–464 (384–471)

Performance:

surface speed	20·25kts
submerged speed	8·75kts
range	10,000–13,000 miles (8,400–10,930nm) @ 14kts
designed diving depth	300ft (91m)

Crew: 80–85

Class:	**GATO class**
Where built:	Electric Boat, Groton (41)
	Portsmouth Naval Yard (14)
	Mare Island Naval Yard (4)
	Manitowoc, Wisconsin (14)
Authorised:	1934
Laid down:	1940–1943
Launched:	1941–1943
Completed:	1942–1944
Fate:	*Growler* (SS-215) sunk 8 Nov 1944;
	Grunion (SS-216) sunk 30 July 1942;
	Albacore (SS-218) sunk 7 Nov 1944;
	Amberjack (SS-219) sunk 16 Feb 1943;
	Bonefish (SS-223) sunk 18 June 1945;
	Corvina (SS-226) sunk 16 Nov 1943;
	Darter (SS-227) total loss 24 Oct 1944;
	Herring (SS-233) sunk 1 June 1944;
	Trigger (SS-237) sunk 28 March 1945;
	Wahoo (SS-238) sunk 12 Oct 1943;
	Dorado (SS-248) sunk 12 Oct 1943;
	Flier (SS-250) sunk 13 Aug 1944;
	Harder (SS-257) sunk 24 Aug 1944;
	Robalo (SS-273) sunk 26 July 1944;
	Runner (SS-275) sunk June 1943;
	Scamp (SS-277) sunk Nov 1944;
	Scorpion (SS-278) sunk Feb 1944;
	Snook (SS-279) sunk April 1945;
	Tullibee (SS-284) sunk 26 March 1944
	7 converted to hunter-killer-submarines (SSK) 1951–1953;
	6 converted to radar picket submarines (SSR) 1951–1952, (lengthened) 31ft (8·3m);
	Tunny (SS-282) converted to Regulus SSM missile submarine (SS G) 1952, converted to Transport Submarine 1964;
	2 transferred to Italy 1954–1955;
	2 transferred to Greece 1957–1958;
	2 transferred to Brazil 1957;
	all scrapped 1947–1970 except
	4 immobilised and used for naval rescue training

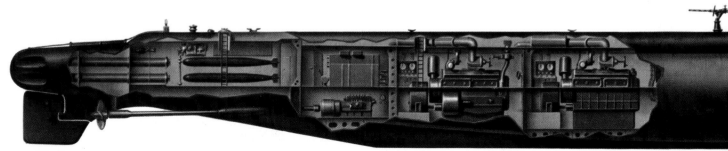

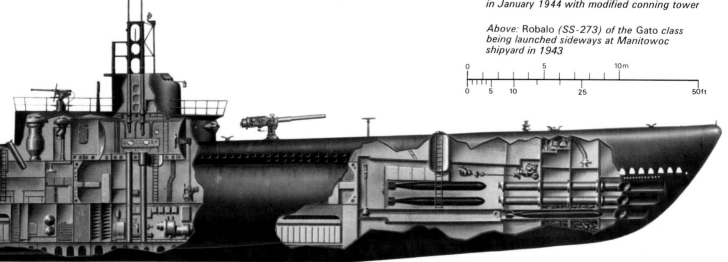

Above, upper: Barb *(SS-220) of the* Gato *class in January 1944 with modified conning tower*

Above: Robalo *(SS-273) of the* Gato *class being launched sideways at Manitowoc shipyard in 1943*

Porpoise Class

SUBMARINE

CLASS: *Porpoise* class (10 boats):
Group 1 (2 boats) *Porpoise* (SS-172)
Pike (SS-173)
Group 2 (2 boats) *Shark* (SS-174) ·
Tarpon (SS-175)
Group 3 (6 boats) including *Perch*
(SS-176) · *Pickerel* (SS-177)

The United States, like Japan, acquired German cruiser submarine designs in 1919, and used them to develop long range submarines suitable for Pacific warfare. The *Cachalot* class introduced welding, and the subsequent *Porpoise* class was the first to adopt a new range of reliable fast-running solid fuel injection diesel motors. These diesels had been sponsored by the US Navy, and were a considerable advance over foreign designs. Diesel-electric drive was used. During World War II the conning towers were modified and two 20mm anti-aircraft guns were added. Some boats were also fitted with two external bow torpedo tubes. The Winton, Fairbanks Morse and Hooven, Owens, Rentschler engines were later developed and adopted as standard by the USN for their later submarines. These became extremely reliable engines and formed the basis for the American submarine success in the Pacific during World War II. The surviving *Porpoise* class boats were not operational postwar but were assigned to the Naval Reserve. They were smaller than the

Displacement:	Group 1	Group 2	Group 3
surface tons (tonnes)	1,310 (1,331)	1,315 (1,336)	1,330–1,335 (1,351–1,356)
submerged tons (tonnes)	1,960 (1,991)	1,968 (2,000)	1,997 (2,029)
Dimensions:			
length (wl)	283ft (86·4m)	287ft (87·6m)	298ft (91m)
(oa)	301ft (91·9m)	298ft (91m)	300·5ft (91·8m)
beam	25ft (7·6m)	25ft (7·6m)	25ft (7·6m)
draught	13ft (4m)	13·75ft (4·2m)	13·75ft (4·2m)
Armament:			
guns			
4in (102mm)	—	1	1
3in (76mm)	1	—	—
0·5in (12·7mm)	2	2	2
3in (7·62mm)	2	2	4
torpedo tubes			
21in (533mm)	6	6	6
Machinery:			
diesels (type)	Winton	Winton	Winton or Fairbanks Morse, or Hooven, Owens, Rentschler (HOR)
(number)	4	4	4
electric motors (type)	Elliot	Elliot	Elliot or General Electric or Allis-Chalmers
shafts	2	2	2
Total BHP:	4,300	4,300	4,300
Total SHP:	2,085	2,085	2,336 or 2,285
Fuel capacity:			
oil tons (tonnes)	373 (379)	347 (353)	371 (377)
Performance:			
surface speed	19kts	19·5kts	19·25kts
submerged speed	8kts	8·25kts	8·75kts
range (surface)	?	?	?
(submerged)	?	?	?
designed diving depth	250ft (76m)	250ft (76m)	250ft (76m)
Crew:	55	55	55

Nautilus

NUCLEAR ATTACK SUBMARINE

CLASS: *Nautilus* class (1 boat)
Nautilus (SSN-571)

Thresher Class

NUCLEAR ATTACK SUBMARINE

CLASS: *Thresher* class (14 boats)
including *Permit* (SSN-594) ·
Thresher (SSN-593) · *Jack*
(SSN-605)

The first funds for the construction of a nuclear submarine were authorised by Congress in the FY 1952 budget and were the follow-on to research and development of a submarine reactor which had been started by the Argonne National Laboratory at the beginning of 1948 and continued by Westinghouse at the Bettis Atomic Power Laboratory. The Submarine Thermal Reactor Mark II which resulted from this work became known as S2W and was installed in the hull of *Nautilus* during two and a quarter years of construction. On 17 January 1955 she signalled 'Under way on nuclear power' giving the USN a three to four year lead on the Soviet Navy. *Nautilus* was designed with a conventional streamlined hull which nevertheless allowed her a comfortable margin over 20kts. In fact one of her earlier journeys from Key West to New London was carried out at over this speed. By August 1958 she had established sufficient confidence in her operators to be sent on the first submarine polar transit, leaving from Hawaii and finishing in Portland, England. By this time two other nuclear boats with similar hull form had been commissioned — *Seawolf* with an unsuccessful S2G liquid sodium-cooled reactor and the first of the four *Skate* class. In 1959 and 1960 these were followed by the large *Triton* and the smaller *Halibut* — the latter designed to launch cruise-missiles — as well as the first of the six *Skipjack* class. This was a design which incorporated the advantages of nuclear propulsion with an *Albacore* hull derived from the 'tear-drop'

Right: USS Nautilus *(SSN-571), the world's first nuclear submarine, made the historic signal 'Under way on nuclear power' on 17 January 1955*

Displacement:	Nautilus	Permit class
surface tons (tonnes)	3,764 (3,824)	3,750–3,800 (3,810–3,861)
submerged tons (tonnes)	4,040 (4,105)	4,300–4,470 (4,370–4,542)
Dimensions:		
length (oa)	319·4ft (97·4m)	278·5–297·4ft (84·9–90·6m)
beam	27·6ft (8·4m)	31·7ft (9·6m)
draught	22ft (6·7m)	28·4ft (8·7m)
Armament:		
torpedo tubes		
21in (533mm)	6	4
Machinery:		
nuclear reactor (type)	S2W Westinghouse pressurised water-cooled	S5W Westinghouse pressurised water-cooled
(number)	1	1
engines (type)	Westinghouse geared turbines	General Electric or De Laval geared turbines
shafts	2	1
Total SHP:		
designed	15,000	15,000
Performance:		
surface speed	20+kts	approx 20kts
submerged speed	20kts	approx 30kts
range	over 150,000 miles (over 126,000nm) @ ?kts	?
Crew:	105	103

Class: Where built:	**NAUTILUS** General Dynamics (EBC)	**PERMIT class** Mare Island Naval Yard; Portsmouth Naval Yard; Ingalls Shipyard New York Shipbuilding Corporation General Dynamics (EBC and Quincy)
Authorised:	1952	1957–1961
Laid down:	14 June 1952	1959–1961
Launched:	21 Jan 1954	1961–1966
Completed:	30 Sept 1954	1962–1967
Fate:	1972–1974 refit and modification for submarine communications research	*Thresher* (SSN-593) lost 10 Apr 1963; remainder in service

earlier US interwar submarines, but sacrificed very little in the way of armament, performance or range compared with the larger, earlier boats. The relatively small size of the engines was of considerable assistance in achieving this. Each group of the *Porpoise* class had slightly different silhouettes, but all the survivors were similarly modified during the war with extra light AA guns mounted on the conning tower.

Class:	Group 1	PORPOISE class Group 2	Group 3
Where built:	Portsmouth Naval Yard	Electric Boat Co, Groton	Electric Boat Co, Groton, Portsmouth Naval Yard, Mare Island Naval Yard
Authorised:	?	?	?
Built:	1935–1936	1935–1936	1936–1937
Fate:	Scrapped 1957	*Shark* sank Feb 1942 *Tarpon* total loss 1957	*Perch* scuttled 3 Feb 1942; *Pickerel* sunk 3 Apr 1943; *Pompano* sunk Aug–Sept 1943; remainder scrapped 1947–1958

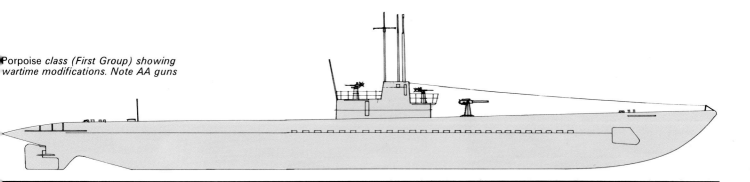

Porpoise *class (First Group) showing wartime modifications. Note AA guns*

shape which that submarine had been evaluating since 1953. Instead of '20+ knots', '30+' was listed as the speed of the new class, as it was in the later *Thresher* class. These 14 submarines, whose class name is sometimes referred to as *Permit* since the loss of *Thresher* in April 1963, were larger than the *Skipjack,* had an improved diving-depth and were the first to carry both SUBROC missiles and the BQQ-2 sonar system. To allow for bow-fitting of this sonar the number of torpedo tubes was reduced from six to four and these were fitted amidships instead of forward. The *Thresher* design was a successful advance and the following class of 37 boats of the *Sturgeon* class were very little altered as a result.

Thresher herself was lost on a deep dive in the Western Atlantic, and some wreckage was recovered after an extensive underwater search. *Nautilus* is no longer an operational submarine but has been refitted for research.

Right: The nuclear attack submarine Barb *(SSN-596) of the* Thresher *class, renamed the* Permit *class, following the loss at sea of* Thresher *(SSN-593) on 10 April 1963*

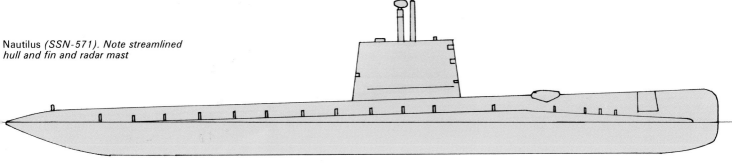

Nautilus *(SSN-571). Note streamlined hull and fin and radar mast*

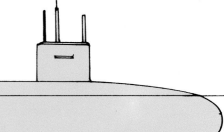

Permit *(SSN-594) showing lengthened teardrop hull and single screw*

George Washington Class

BALLISTIC MISSILE SUBMARINE
CLASS: *George Washington* class (5 boats)

Ohio Class

BALLISTIC MISSILE SUBMARINE
CLASS: *Ohio* class (5 boats approved, 2 proposed and 6 planned)

Displacement:	GEORGE WASHINGTON class	OHIO class
standard surfaced tons (tonnes)	6,019 (6,115)	16,000 (16,256)
dived tons (tonnes)	6,888 (6,998)	18,700 (18,999)
Dimensions:		
length (oa)	381·7ft (116·3m)	560ft (170·7m)
beam	33ft (10·1m)	42ft (12·8m)
draught	29ft (8·8m)	35·5ft (10·8m)
Armament:		
missile tubes	16 for Polaris A3	24 for Trident I
torpedo tubes 21in (533mm)	6	4
Machinery:		
nuclear reactors	1 pressurised water-cooled Westinghouse S5W	1 pressurised water-cooled GE S8G
main engines	2 GE geared turbines	2 GE geared turbines
shafts	1	1
Total SHP:	15,000	?
Performance:		
speed (surfaced)	20kts	?
(dived)	approx 30kts	?
range	limited only by stores	limited only by stores
Crew:	112 (double crews)	133 (double crews)

Class:	GEORGE WASHINGTON class	OHIO class
Where built:	*George Washington*, General Dynamics, Groton *Patrick Henry*, General Dynamics, Groton *Theodore Roosevelt*, Mare Island NY *Robert E. Lee*, Newport News *Abraham Lincoln*, Portsmouth NY	All possibly to be built by General Dynamics, Groton: *Ohio, Michigan* plus 11 unnamed
Approved:	Supplement to FY 1958 and 1959	FY 1974
Laid down:	1 Nov 1957–1 Nov 1958	10 Apr 1976 (*Ohio*)
Launched:	9 June 1959–18 Dec 1959	late 1977
Completed:	30 Dec 1959–11 Mar 1961	early 1979
Fate:	in service	building

In 1955 the Soviet Union began the conversion of six *Zulu* class submarines to fire ballistic missiles. The modification involved the fitting of two launching tubes in the fin, to allow the surface discharge of 300 mile (260nm) range SSN-4 'Sark' missiles. At this time the US Navy and the US Army were involved in the development of the Jupiter missile, a 60ft (18·3m) monster capable of carrying a thermo-nuclear head to a range of 1,500 miles (1,303nm). Its fuel requirements of liquid oxygen and kerosene added to the many problems in designing a 10,000 ton (10,160 tonne) nuclear submarine which it was planned would carry three of these missiles for surface launch. In retrospect it seems likely that the submarine might have suffered severe damage at this time. The production of a lighter head and the use of solid fuel brought into action an astonishing and bold plan to produce a much smaller but equally efficient weapon and a submarine capable of launching 16 of what were to be named Polaris A1 missiles. The first *Scorpion* class nuclear submarine was cut in half, a 130ft (40m) section was inserted to carry the launch tubes and on 9 June 1959 the boat was launched as *George Washington* (SSBN-598). Thirteen months later she fired the first Polaris missile in the Atlantic and a programme awe-inspiring in its drive and efficiency had reached fruition in four years. Although originally beaten to the punch by the Soviets the USA had come back fighting – *George Washington* could fire 16 missiles while dived and, at that time, the nearest Soviet equivalent was the nuclear-propelled *Hotel* class with three 'Sark' missiles in the fin for surface launch. It was seven years after *George Washington* was commissioned that the first *Yankee* class of similar capabilities became operational. In this period the US Navy commissioned the five submarines of the *Ethan Allen* class, 30ft (9·1m) longer than the five *George Washingtons* but with a similar missile armament although of longer range (Polaris A2). At the same time (1961–65) 31 SSBNs of the *Lafayette* and *Benjamin Franklin* classes had been laid down, all of which were in service by the time the first *Yankee* appeared. The first eight carried Polaris A2 (1,730 miles/1,500nm) but with the successful launch of Polaris A3 in October 1963 a range of 2,878 miles (2,500nm) was achieved, almost double that of the SSN-6 'Sawfly' which the *Yankees* were to carry. In February 1969 began the Poseidon conversion programme for the latest 31 boats to allow them to fire a missile of very similar range to the A3 but with ten instead of

three individual warheads. Eventually the plan was that by 1977 there should be 31 submarines with 2,878 mile (2,500nm) Poseidon missiles and 10 with 1,730 mile (1,500nm) Polaris A3, and this has now been achieved. While these arrangements were in hand a new programme, the Trident programme, was under way. This was to provide a much longer range missile, Trident I (4,000 miles/3,475nm) and a huge 18,700 ton (18,999 tonne) submarine to carry 24 weapons. In due course, probably in the early 1980s, it was planned to introduce the Trident II missile with a 6,000 mile (5,210nm) range for retro-fitting. While Congress havered over this plan, which would provide far more

extensive areas of invulnerability for the American submarines, the Soviet Navy again produced an ace – in 1972 the first *Delta* class with 4,200 mile (3,647nm) SSN-8 missiles appeared, and in late 1976 this range was increased to 6,450 miles (5,600nm). By now the first of the *Ohio* class had been under construction for seven months with a forecast commissioning date of early 1979. By this date, at present building rates, it would be possible for the USSR to have nearly 30 Delta and Delta II class in commission. How this will be affected by future SALT agreements it is impossible to say – all that is clear is that this is a minimum possibility.

Right: George Washington *(SSBN-598). Note the modified teardrop hull, diving planes on fin and prominent casing over the Polaris tubes. These boats perform much better submerged than on the surface*

George Washington *class with sixteen Polaris missiles in hull abaft fin*

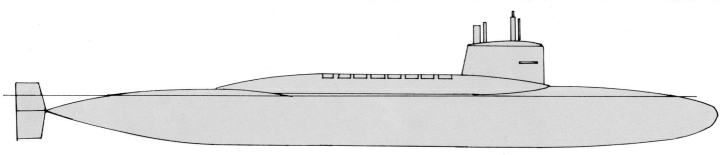

Trident class projected outline

Right: Artist's impression of Ohio class Trident submarine, showing the long missile compartment with tubes for twenty-four Trident SLBMs. These boats will be larger than most surface warships

Below: The George Washington class ballistic missile submarine Theodore Roosevelt

Below: USS Robert E. Lee (SSBN-601) when she entered service in 1960. The Washingtons mount 16 Polaris A3 missile tubes and 6 21in torpedo tubes

Knox Class
FRIGATE
CLASS: *Knox* class (46 ships) including *Knox* (FF-1052) · *Joseph Hewes* (FF-1078)

The *Knox* class frigates are second generation US postwar escorts, and are the largest class built in America since the war. The first generation postwar escorts were the *Dealey, Courtney* and *Claud Jones* classes, built between 1952 and 1960. These are conventional turbine- or diesel-powered single-screw ships, developed from World War II designs. They have a standard displacement of about 1,450 tons (1,470 tonnes). The first second-generation escorts are the *Bronstein* class, built in 1961–1963. These are much larger ships with a new hull form, capable of carrying ASROC, DASH, a twin 3in (76mm) mount and modern electronics, including a bow sonar. To save deck space they have a mack. The *Garcias,* an enlarged version built between 1962 and 1968, have a similar layout but have a flush deck and two single 5in (127mm) guns. They introduced the very high pressure boilers, which save space and weight. A version with an improved anti-aircraft armament, the *Brookes,* was built. A Tartar single-launcher replaced the aft 5in (127mm) gun, but this proved too expensive. The *Knox* class are very similar but slightly larger than the *Garcias*. Originally intended to mount the cancelled 'Sea Mauler' short-range SAM, some now have a BPDMS SAM launcher instead. In some ships the ASROC ASM launcher can fire RIM 24B Tartar SSMs, conferring a surface offensive capability. Harpoon is now being retro-fitted. The last 20 ships, built under a Total Procurement Contract by the Avondale Shipyards, Westwego, were at first known as the *Joseph Hewes* class, although they are virtually identical to the other *Knoxs*. They were mass produced from prefabricated parts, and the hulls were built upside down and rotated for launching. Like all US escorts with the new hull form, the *Knoxs* are extremely seaworthy, but the single engine and shaft makes them vulnerable to damage or breakdown. However, this reflects the US wartime experience that it is engine rather than ship production that causes bottlenecks in supply of escorts in emergencies, and it also makes the ships cheaper. Even so, they are still very sophisticated and expensive vessels, and even America has not been able to afford to replace its World War II escorts on a hull-for-hull basis. They have been superseded in production by a completely recast design, the *Oliver Hazard Perry* class. These are larger, lighter vessels, with a smaller crew and an armament of one Standard/Harpoon SAM/SSM forward and a 3in (76mm) on the superstructure amidships. They also carry two Mk 32 triple A/S torpedo tubes and a hangar and flight deck for two SH-2 LAMPS helicopters aft. This gives them a much greater anti-ship capability. They are powered by two gas turbines.

Above: A Knox *class frigate. In 1969–74, 46 of these escorts entered service, constituting the largest US warship class since WWII*

Displacement:	
standard tons (tonnes)	3,011 (3,059)
full load tons (tonnes)	3,877 (3,963)
Dimensions:	
length (pp)	?
(oa)	438ft (133·5m)
beam	46·75ft (14·25m)
draught	24·75ft (7·6m)
Armament:	
guns	
5in (127mm) 54cal	1
missiles	
BPDMS Sea Sparrow octuple-launcher	1
A/S weapons	
ASROC 8-barrel launcher	1
torpedo tubes	
12·7in (324mm) Mk 32	4
aircraft	1 helicopter
Machinery:	
boilers (type)	Babcock and Wilcox or Foster-Wheeler
(number)	2
engines (type)	Westinghouse geared turbines
shafts	1
Total SHP:	
designed	35,000
Performance:	
designed speed	27+kts
range	4,000 miles (3,360nm) @ 20kts
Crew:	245–283 when modified

Class:	**KNOX class**
Where built:	Todd, Seattle and San Pedro; Lockheed, Seattle; Avondale, Westwego
Authorised:	1964–1968
Laid down:	1965–1972
Launched:	1966–1973
Completed:	1969–1974
Fate:	In service

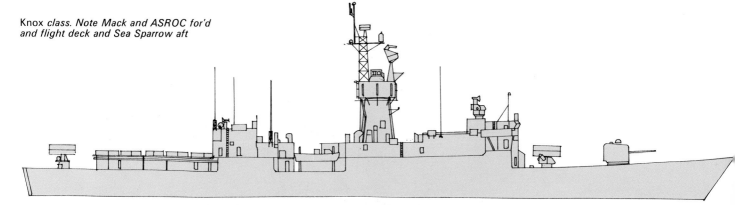

Knox class. Note Mack and ASROC for'd and flight deck and Sea Sparrow aft

PT Boat

**PT BOAT
CLASS:** Higgins Type (*PT 71* class)
(221 boats)

**PT BOAT
CLASS:** Elco Type (*PT 103* class)
(358 boats)

**PT BOAT
CLASS:** Vosper Type (*PT 368* class)
(140 boats)

The US Navy has never shown great interest in fast craft of this type in peace-time. In 1939 a series of contracts were placed with six different yards, including British Power Boats, for craft varying from 54ft (16·5m) to 80ft (24·4m). The first large batch ordered was 24 boats from Elco (*PT 21–44*) in 1940 with a similar number (*PT 45–68*) in 1941. From then on the size of contracts, except for two singletons from Huckins and Higgins, increased steadily until by 1945 over 800 boats had been ordered since 1939. The data given above is that for the three main types put into service — the armament varied as different combinations and special gear such as rockets were tried out. Although

above: The Elco type motor torpedo boat PT 337 in 1943. The PT Boat served in all major US wartime theatres

Displacement:	PT 71 class:	PT 103 class	PT 368 class
standard tons (tonnes)	46 (46·7)	45 (45·7)	43 (43·7)
Dimensions:			
length	78ft (23·8m)	80·3ft (24·5m)	70ft (21·3m)
beam	20ft (6·1m)	20·6ft (6·3m)	19ft (5·8m)
draught	6ft (1·8m)	5ft (1·5m)	4·75ft (1·4m)
Armament:			
guns			
40mm	1	—	—
20mm	2	2	?
0·5in	varied	varied	varied
torpedo tubes			
21in (533mm)	2 or 4	4	2
DCs	12in 2-tube craft	—	—
mines	or 4 racks for mines	—	—
Machinery:			
main engines	Packard 4M2500	Packard 4M2500	Packard 4M2500
shafts	3	3	3
Total SHP:	4,050	4,050	4,050
Performance:			
speed	40+kts	40+kts	40+kts
Crew:	12	14	12

Class	PT 71 class	PT 103 class	PT 368 class
Where built:	Higgins Industries, New Orleans	Elco Works, Bayonne	R. Jacob, NY; Herreshoff, Bristol, RI; Annapolis Yacht Co; Canadian Power Boats
Approved:	1941–45	1941–45	1942–44
Laid down:	1941–45	1941–45	1942–44
Launched:	1941–45	1941–45	1942–44
Completed:	1941–45	1941–45	1942–44
Fate:	Many lost on patrol, numerous boats transferred to Allies, most of remainder scrapped at end of war; some Higgins type still serve in the Argentinian and Italian Navies; Yugoslavia built several to this design in the 1950s.		

best known for their operations in the Pacific these handy, fast and useful boats were deployed to all major theatres, a number operating under Allied flags. In 1950–51 four new experimental designs were developed in *PT 809–812*. These were all of 105ft (32m) with four petrol engines and with a gun armament of two 40mm and four 20mm. By 1962 *PT 809* and *PT 812* had been deleted, the numbers of the survivors changed to *PTF 1* and *2* and 14 of a new class, the Norwegian *Nasty*, were being delivered from Mandal. Half of these had been paid off by 1975 by which date Trumpy of Annapolis had delivered six boats of a modified *Nasty* class and Sewart had built *PTF 23–26* to the 105 ton (106·7 tonne) 'Osprey' design. In 1977 these last were the sole survivors of the PTF boats while other developments based on Sewart's 'Swift' design are now in service as Patrol Boats or PCF.

Pegasus Class

**PATROL HYDROFOIL MISSILE BOAT
CLASS:** *Pegasus* class (1 ship)
Pegasus (PHM-1)

Pegasus (PHM-1) was developed from *Tucumcari* (PGH-1) and the Italian *Sparviero* (P-420), which in turn were developed from experimental hydrofoils built in the USA in the early 1960s. Hydrofoils have quick reaction times, and can operate effectively in much rougher seas than similarly armed conventional patrol boats, but are considerably more complicated and expensive. *Pegasus* was intended to form the basis of a German/Italian/American hydrofoil, and was the result of an agreement signed between those three countries in November 1972. The German boats were to have MM-38 Exocet SSMs and the Italian boats Otomat SSMs. However, they have not been built and the American programme has now been stopped with only *Pegasus* complete. *Pegasus* (PHM-1) is designed to operate in Sea State 5, and has been optimised for use in rough seas. The US has simultaneously been developing SWATH twin submerged hull boats and hovercraft. A prototype of the former, *Kaimalino*, is undergoing trials. The first American hovercraft were British SRN-5 craft. Recently the SES-100 B built by Bell has been on trials, and a 3,000 ton (3,050 tonne) SES (Surface Effect Ship) is to be built by Rohn Marine, San Diego. She will be capable of operating AV-8B Harrier V/STOL aircraft. Her main use will be in anti-submarine warfare operating LAMPS helicopters, however. Her very high speed will be a great advantage, and she will be less vulnerable to torpedo attack than a normal escort.

Right: The patrol hydrofoil missile boat Pegasus (PHM-1) runs trials on the Pacific Missile Range off Fort Hueneme, California, in October 1975

Displacement:		
standard tons (tonnes)	190 (193)	
full load tons (tonnes)	221 (225)	
Dimensions:	**foils extended**	**foils retracted**
length (oa)	131·2ft (40m)	147·5ft (45m)
beam (ext)	28·2ft (8·6m)	28·2ft (8·6m)
draught	23·2ft (7·1m)	6·2ft (1·9m)
Armament:		
guns		
3in (76m) 62cal	1	
missiles		
Harpoon SSM	4 planned, 8 fitted	
Machinery:	**foilborne**	**hullborne**
engines (type)	General Electric gas turbine	MTU (Mercedes-Benz) diesel
(number)	1	2
water jet pumps	2	2
Total SHP:	18,000	
Total BHP:	1,600	
Fuel capacity:		
oil tons (tonnes)	?	
Performance:		
designed speed	48+kts	12kts
range	?	?
Crew:	21	

Class:	PEGASUS class	Built:	1973 onward
Where built:	Boeing, Seattle	Fate:	*Pegasus* (PHM-1) in service;
Authorised:	1972–1975		*Hercules* (PHM-2) and other four deleted in Feb 1977

Glossary

AA Anti-Aircraft
Abaft Towards the stern (of)
AS Anti-Submarine
Asdic British anti-submarine sound detector. See *Sonar*
ASM Anti-Submarine Missile. See *SAM, SLBM* and *SSM*

Barbette Fixed part of armoured gun mount, including armoured ammunition hoist. See *Turret*
Belt Main armour on side of ship protecting the water line
BHP Brake Horse Power. See *IHP, SHP*
Broadside Guns that can fire on one side of the ship, or firing the guns on one side of the ship
Bulge Anti-torpedo bulge fitted to outside of major warships during and after WWI to improve the torpedo protection. Later ships had

it fitted within the hull

Casemates Positions on broadside for secondary armament protected on all sides by armour
Conning Tower Point from which ship is controlled in action. Usually armoured

Displacement Amount of water ship displaces; weight of ship. See *Full Load, Normal* and *Standard* Displacement

Flush Deck Upper deck having no breaks in level
Fo'c's'le Deck at bow or forward end of ship. Sometimes raised
Full Load Displacement Displacement usually with full load of stores, ammunition and fuel on board. See *Displacement* and *Normal* and *Standard* Displacement
F.Y. Financial Year

Hard Chine Hull of fast craft with prominent angle or knuckle rather than a smooth hull to promote high speed

IHP Indicated Horse Power. See *BHP, SHP*

Knot Nautical Mile (6,080ft) per hour. See *Nautical Mile*

Mack Combined mast and funnel (stack)
Magazine Space where ammunition is stored
Metacentric Height Distance between ship's centre of gravity and point through which ship heels at small angles. An indication of a ship's stability
MTB Motor Torpedo Boat

NM Nautical Mile (6,080ft, 1,856·5m). See *Knot*
Normal Displacement Displacement usually with ship fully equipped but with only one-third of the fuel on board. See *Displacement*

and *Full Load* and *Standard Displacement*
NTDS Naval Tactical Data System

(OA) Overall

(PP) Between perpendiculars. From Bow Load Water Line to aft end of Rudder Post

Quarterdeck Deck at stern. Sometimes raised

SAM Surface to Air Missile. See *ASM, SLBM, SSM*
Scantlings The dimensions of parts of a ship's frame which provide an idea of its overall strength
SLBM Submarine Launched Ballistic Missile. See *ASM, SAM, SSM*
SHP Shaft Horse Power. See *BHP, IHP*
Sonar American anti-submarine sound detector. Name adopted by Britain after WWII. Both active and passive (listening) sonars

are in use. See *Asdic* and *VDS*
SSM Surface to Surface Missile. See *ASM, SAM* an *SLBM*
Standard Displacement Displacement with a proportion of fuel etc fixed by Washington Treaty, 192 See *Displacement, Full Loa* and *Normal Displacement*
Superstructure Fixed part o ship above the hull

TT Torpedo Tubes
Turret Moving part of armoured gun mount. See *Barbette* and *Turret Face*
Turret Face Forward part of Turret through which guns project. See *Turret*

VDS Variable Depth Sonar, towed by a ship or helicopter. See *Sonar*
VTE Vertical Triple Expansion (reciprocating engine)

(WL) Water Line (varies with displacement)

Index

Picture Credits

The Publishers wish to thank the following photographers and organisations who have supplied photographs for this book. Photographs have been credited by page number. When more than one photograph appears on the page, references are made in the order of the columns across the page and then from top to bottom.
Some references have, for reasons of space, been abbreviated as follows:

The Conway Picture Library: CPL
The Imperial War Museum: IWM
Ministry of Defence, London: MOD
US Navy: USN

10: CPL 11: CPL/Brazilian Naval Attaché, London 13: MOD 14: IWM 15: IWM 16: IWM 17: IWM 18: IWM 19: IWM 20: IWM 21: IWM 23: IWM 24: IWM 25: MOD 26: Vickers Limited 27: IWM 28: CPL 29: IWM 30: CPL 31: IWM 33: CPL 35: IWM 36: The Science Museum, London 38: IWM 39/40: IWM 41: J. McClancy Collection 42: IWM 44: IWM 45: IWM 47: IWM 49: US National Archives 50: IWM 51: IWM 52: CPL 53: CPL/National Maritime Museum (Norman Wilkinson) 54: Associated Press/IWM 55: CPL 57: IWM 59: IWM 61: CPL 63: IWM 64: CPL 65: CPL 66: MOD 67: IWM/Popperfoto 68: CPL 70/71: MOD 72: IWM 73: CPL/IWM 74: MOD 75: British Hovercraft Corporation 76/77: US Navy/John McClancy 78: Marius Bar Phot Toulon 79: ECP Armées 80: IWM 81: Marius Bar Phot Toulon 83: IWM/Marius Bar Phot Toulon 84: Roger-Viollet 85-87: Marius Bar Phot Toulon 89: Musée de la Marine, Paris 90: Marius Bar Phot Toulon 91: ECP Armées 93: Marius Bar Phot Toulon 94: Marius Bar/ECP Armées/Associated Press 95: Marine Nationale/ECP Armées 97: J. G. Moore Collection 99: Foto Druppel 101: Nautic/Foto Druppel 103: Bundesarchiv/Foto Druppel 104: Foto Druppel 105: Bundesarchiv/Foto Druppel 107: IWM 108: IWM 109: Foto Druppel 110: IWM 111/112: Foto Druppel 114: USN 115: IWM 116: IWM 117: Foto Druppel 118/9: IWM 120/1: IWM 122-5: Foto Druppel 126: Bundesministerium der Verteidigung 127-131: Foto Druppel 132: Foto Druppel/Bundesministerium der Verteidigung 133: Bundesministerium der Verteidigung 135: Foto Druppel 137: CPL 138-140: Royal Netherlands Navy Historical Branch 141: CPL/Royal Netherlands Navy Historical Branch 145: Aldo Fracarolli 147: Italian Naval Archives/CPL 148: Italian Naval Archives/CPL 149-152: Italian Naval Archives 153: Aldo Fracarolli 154: Italian Naval Archives/Aldo Fracarolli 155: Italian Naval Archives 156: Italian Naval Attaché 157: Italian Naval Archives 159: USN 161: USN/IWM 162: USN 166/7: US Information Agency 168/9: USN 170: Fujifotos 171: USN 172: USN 173: Fujifotos 174: National Maritime Museum/Fujifotos 176: USN/CPL 177: IWM 179: CPL 181: Ships of the World/J. McClancy 182: Japanese Maritime Self Defence Force 183: USN 184: IWM 185: Fujifotos 187: Batservice Verft A/s 189-191: MOD 194/5: Novosti 195: Novosti/MOD 198: RAF 205: MOD 208: Naval Attaché, Spanish Embassy 209: Wright and Logan 210: Naval Attaché, Royal Swedish Embassy 211: Karlskrona Varvet AB 213: USN 215: USN (Miles Desomer) 216/7: USN 219: IWM 220-259: USN 261: US Naval Institute/Manitowoc Maritime Museum 263-267: USN.